American Linguistics in Transition

American Linguistics in Transition

From Post-Bloomfieldian Structuralism
to Generative Grammar

FREDERICK J. NEWMEYER

OXFORD
UNIVERSITY PRESS

Great Clarendon Street, Oxford, OX2 6DP,
United Kingdom

Oxford University Press is a department of the University of Oxford.
It furthers the University's objective of excellence in research, scholarship,
and education by publishing worldwide. Oxford is a registered trade mark of
Oxford University Press in the UK and in certain other countries

Published in the United States of America by Oxford University Press
198 Madison Avenue, New York, NY 10016, United States of America

British Library Cataloguing in Publication Data

Data available

Library of Congress Control Number: 2022930914

ISBN 978-0-19-284376-0

DOI: 10.1093/oso/9780192843760.001.0001

Printed and bound by
CPI Group (UK) Ltd, Croydon, CR0 4YY

Contents

Foreword

I am probably best known for my book *Linguistic Theory in America: The First Quarter Century of Transformational Generative Grammar (LTA)*, published in 1980, with a second edition appearing six years later (Newmeyer 1980, 1986b). While the reviews and general reaction to the book were largely positive, there were two criticisms that were raised by more than one reader. First, there was a general feeling that I treated the structural linguists who preceded transformational generative grammar (TGG) with little respect and even less understanding. Second, there were objections to the 'triumphalist' tone that pervaded the book. A number of reviewers felt that I exaggerated both the intellectual success of the theory (as measured by the number of its adherents worldwide) and its organizational success (as measured by institutional dominance). Over forty years of reflection have led me to conclude that these critics were essentially correct. This book is in part an attempt to set the record straight, as far as these two issues are concerned. But more basically, my goal here is to explore in depth the transition from post-Bloomfieldian structuralism, which dominated the American linguistics scene from the 1930s to the 1950s, to TGG, which had largely eclipsed it by around 1970.

As far as the post-Bloomfieldian structuralists are concerned, I devote the first chapter, 'The structuralist ascendancy in American linguistics', to a thorough examination of the sources of their ideas and, even more importantly, to how, for a generation or more, they managed to be so successful. I argue that several factors contributed to their success: the conviction of its leading practitioners that they were doing 'scientific linguistics', the feeling that knowledge and understanding were growing by leaps and bounds, the 'egalitarian' message that all languages could be analyzed by the same methods, the Linguistic Society of America (LSA)-sponsored summer schools that helped spread knowledge of structuralist theory, the government-sponsored work in linguistics during the Second World War, and the change in the LSA leadership around 1940.

As far as my misguided triumphalism is concerned, I devote the final chapter, 'The generativist non-dominance of the field in the 1970s and 1980s', to documenting and attempting to explain why generative grammarians, despite the high visibility of their theory and the celebrity of Noam Chomsky, were so relatively *unsuccessful* in achieving organizational power in the United States during those decades (I take it for granted that the question would not even arise in most other countries). As measured by their occupation of LSA elected offices, articles in the pages of *Language*, presentations at LSA meetings, positions at LSA Institutes, receipt of grant awards, and representation in departmental composition, generativists were quite minoritarian. Many factors combined to cause this state of affairs, including the inward-looking attitudes of many prominent generativists, the immaturity, as well as the diversity, of the field of linguistics, and Chomsky's sense of isolation from the field.

My story begins with the founding of the LSA in 1924. It was at that point, and not earlier, that one could speak of a distinct field of linguistics in the United States. My ending point—better 'points'—might seem a bit ragged. The interplay between structuralists and generativists was still ongoing in the early 1980s, so I document an interesting event from that period with respect to that interplay. However, I ignore developments internal to TGG later than the 1960s. For one thing, I have already covered these developments in *LTA*, and for another, they have little to do with the main theme of this book, namely the transition from structuralism to generativism. The most noteworthy development from this period, the 'linguistic wars' fought between interpretive semanticists and generative semanticists, will be passed over here. These wars are treated not only in *LTA*, but also in books by Randy Harris and by Geoffrey Huck and John Goldsmith (Harris 1993, second edition 2021; Huck and Goldsmith 1994).

A major gap in *LTA* was the almost complete lack of discussion of the European influence on both American structuralism and TGG, as well as the attempts of early generativists to 'internationalize' the theory. This book attempts to fill that gap. Chapter 2, 'American structuralism and European structuralism: How they saw each other', describes American-European interactions during the structuralist period and later. The Americans owed a great debt to the Europeans, a debt that they tended to downplay in the 1930s and early 1940s. At the same time, the Europeans tended to be highly critical of most post-Bloomfieldian work, given its extreme empiricist foundations. But by the late 1940s, partly as a result of the presence of a large number of European refugee scholars in the United States, a rapprochement took place between the Americans and the Europeans. This rapprochement accelerated with the advent of TGG, where the results of European theorizing played a major role from the beginning. Ironically, however, European structuralists, who had become more and more admiring of the work of their American colleagues, almost uniformly rejected TGG, a fact which I attempt to explain.

Chapter 6, 'The European reception of early transformational generative grammar', surveys how linguists in each European country greeted the advent of TGG in the 1960s and 1970s. There is no overarching generalization—the situation differed from country to country. A partial generalization, however, is that the stronger a home-grown structuralist tradition in a country, the less likely the linguists there would be to accept TGG. So the theory made few inroads in Czechoslovakia and Denmark, given the predominance of the Prague School and the Copenhagen School respectively, but did quite well in the Netherlands and Norway, where no indigenous approach was predominant. There are exceptions in both directions, however. The United Kingdom warmly greeted TGG, despite the importance of the structuralist model associated with J. R. Firth, and in any number of European countries, despite the absence of a structuralist presence, TGG fell upon deaf ears.

The central chapters of the book, both physically and thematically, are Chapter 4, 'Early transformational generative grammar: Some controversial issues' and Chapter 5, 'The diffusion of generativist ideas'. The former chapter treats a wide variety of topics related to the transition from post-Bloomfieldian structuralism to TGG, such as the key features that distinguished the latter from the former, the perennial question of whether we can speak properly of a 'Chomskyan revolution' in linguistics, and the reaction of leading structuralists to the advent of TGG. The chapter also delves into related issues, such as Chomsky's own remarks about his interactions with his teacher Zellig Harris and other structuralists, as well as the role that military funding played in the success of the early theory.

Chapter 5 is devoted to combatting the popular idea that Chomsky and his colleagues eschewed publication, preferring to disseminate their work in a murky 'underground press'. We will see that the early generativists used every means at their disposal at the time to diffuse their ideas: publishing books, journal articles, anthology chapters, and technical reports; aiding the writing of textbooks; giving conference talks; teaching at LSA Institutes; and hosting numerous visitors to MIT.

The remaining chapters focus on the last days of the structuralist ascendancy in American linguistics. Chapter 3, 'Martin Joos's *Readings in Linguistics* as the apogee of American structuralism', documents the fascinating publication history of this volume and how it came to be regarded as the 'official document' of post-Bloomfieldian structuralism. The publication date, 1957, coincided with that of Chomsky's *Syntactic Structures*, a curious coincidence which in the ensuing decades gave generativists an easy whipping boy to hold up as a symbol of how linguistics 'used to be done'. Chapter 7, 'The contested LSA presidential election of 1970', documents Dwight Bolinger's successful challenge to Martin Joos for the LSA presidency. Generativists saw Joos as the arch-representative of the linguistics of the past and hence sided with Bolinger, even though the latter was hardly one of their co-thinkers. And Chapter 8, 'Charles Hockett's attempt to resign from the LSA in 1982', covers an interesting topic, not particularly of value for his unsuccessful resignation attempt per se, but because it brought into play some stunning interactions between the prominent linguists of the day, whatever their theoretical orientation.

I wrestled for some time over whether to organize the chapters thematically or chronologically, and ended up opting for the latter. It would have been confusing for the reader, I think, to be presented too often with events that took place, say, in the 1960s before those that took place in the 1940s. Let me give one example of what I mean. Two chapters deal primarily with events in Europe, so at first thought it might seem natural to place them one immediately after the other. Instead, I have opted to present Chapter 6, 'The European reception of early transformational generative grammar', at some distance from Chapter 2, 'American structuralism and European structuralism: How they saw each other'. I felt a full understanding of how TGG was greeted in Europe in the 1960s and 1970s to be contingent upon an understanding of its development and reception in the United States in the 1950s and 1960s (which are treated in Chapters 4 and 5). Furthermore, following the suggestion of Margaret Thomas, I have constructed a timeline of some of the more important events discussed in the book, which I hope will further aid the reader to connect the dots between the chapters.

One unique feature of this book, if I may be permitted to say so, is its copious use of archival material. It incorporates letters and other documents from ten different archives in the United States and the Netherlands, and would have drawn from even more if COVID-19 had not put the kibosh on international travel. Luckily for posterity, the majority of prominent scholars in the mid-twentieth century saved their correspondence and ended up bequeathing it to libraries, generally in universities where they spent their careers. Little did they know that what they wrote to their colleagues would be used, and in some cases used against them, in a publication to appear three-quarters of a century later.

Literally dozens of colleagues deserve acknowledgement for their role in providing information and advice to me as I prepared this volume. My greatest debt is to Margaret Thomas, who reviewed the entire pre-final manuscript and passed on to me many pages of critical commentary, all of it quite useful. I also had the opportunity to discuss much of the material with colleagues around the world. The following stand out as particularly worth of mention in that regard: Stephen Anderson, Hans Basbøll, Noam Chomsky, B. Elan Dresher, Julia Falk, Camiel Hamans, Brian Joseph, John Joseph, D. Robert Ladd, Geoffrey Pullum, and Sarah Thomason. Many other colleagues are thanked in the appropriate chapters and sections. And special thanks to Julia Steer, my editor at Oxford University Press, for steering me (pun intended) in the right direction from the conception to the realization of this project.

List of Abbreviations

AHA   The Archibald Hill Archive, at the University of Texas, Austin Texas

BBA   The Bernard Bloch Archive, at Yale University, New Haven, Connecticut

CHA   The Charles Hockett Archive, at the Smithsonian Institution, Washington, D. C.

CVSC The C. H. van Schooneveld Collection in the Leiden University Library, Leiden, Netherlands

DBA   The Dwight Bolinger Archive, at Stanford University, Stanford, California

FBA   The Franz Boas Archive, at the American Philosophical Society, Philadelphia, Pennsylvania

LSAA The Linguistic Society of America Archive, at the University of Missouri, Columbia, Missouri

LSAB *Linguistic Society of America Bulletin*

MJA   The Martin Joos Archive, at the American Philosophical Society, Philadelphia, Pennsylvania

RJA   The Roman Jakobson Archive at MIT, Cambridge, Massachusetts

TSA   The Thomas Sebeok Archive at Indiana University, Bloomington, Indiana

Timeline

1924   The founding of the Linguistic Society of America (§ 1.3.1)

1925   The first issue of the journal *Language* appears (§ 1.3.1, 1.4.2)

1926   The Prague Linguistic Circle is founded § 2.2.2)

1928   The first LSA-sponsored Linguistic Institute is held (§ 2.5.3)
       The first International Congress of Linguists takes place in The Hague
       (§ 2.5.3)

1933   Publication of Leonard Bloomfield's book *Language* (§ 1.2, 1.3.3)

1940   Bernard Bloch becomes editor of *Language* (§ 1.5.5)

1941   J Milton Cowan becomes LSA Secretary-Treasurer (§ 1.5.5)
       Roman Jakobson arrives in the United States (§ 2.5.1)

1942   The LSA becomes heavily involved in supporting the war effort (§ 1.5.4)

1945   The journal *Word* is founded (§ 2.5.1)

1951   Noam Chomsky submits his MA thesis *The Morphophonemics of Modern Hebrew* (§ 4.2.2)

1955   Noam Chomsky's *The Logical Structure of Linguistic Theory* appears (§ 4.2.2, 4.5.4)

1957   Martin Joos's edited volume *Readings in Linguistics* appears (§ 3.4)
       Noam Chomsky's *Syntactic Structures* is published (§ 4.2.1)

1961   The PhD program in linguistics at MIT is founded (§ 5.2)

1965   We find the first reference to a 'Chomskyan revolution' (§ 5.1)

1970   Dwight Bolinger challenges Martin Joos for the LSA presidency and defeats him (Chapter 7)

1974   Morris Halle is the first generative grammarian to take office as LSA President (§ 9.2.1)

1977   Generative Linguistics in the Old World is founded (§ 6.2)

1982   Charles Hockett submits his resignation letter to the LSA (Chapter 8)

1

The structuralist ascendancy in American linguistics

1.1 Introduction

I did an informal survey of a few dozen of my colleagues, all faculty members in departments of linguistics in the United States, and asked them what they would identify as the most dramatic change in American linguistics in the past century. I was careful to specify both intellectual developments and sociological ones. Without an exception they pointed to the ascent of generative grammar, which originated with the publication of Noam Chomsky's *Syntactic Structures* (Chomsky 1957a) and, in their view, had swept the field by the 1970s (if not earlier). I outline in this chapter a more important change in the field, starting in the late 1920, picking up steam in the 1930s, and completed by the mid-1940s. Before this period an autonomous field of linguistics barely existed in the United States. Linguistic studies were viewed as an auxiliary discipline to studies in other fields, most prominently literature, but also to a degree anthropology and language pedagogy. By the mid 1940s linguistics had broken free of all of these other disciplines. There had developed a consensus that one could make important claims about how an individual language worked and how language in general worked without any appeal to the cultural and societal context in which language is spoken. Concretely, this meant that descriptive-analytical studies of linguistic structure and asocietal studies of language change had come to carry the day. The purpose of this chapter is to outline how and why this profound change took place.

The chapter is organized as follows. § 1.2 outlines the state of American linguistics in the mid-twentieth century, followed by § 1.3 on the early Linguistic Society of America. § 1.4 presents the changes in the field from the 1920s to the 1940s and § 1.5 attempts to explain why these changes occurred. § 1.6 is a brief summary.

American Linguistics in Transition. Frederick J. Newmeyer, Oxford University Press.
© Frederick J. Newmeyer (2022). DOI: 10.1093/oso/9780192843760.003.0001

1.2 American linguistics in the mid-twentieth century

American linguistics in the late 1940s and early 1950s was dominated by the intellectual heirs of Leonard Bloomfield and Edward Sapir.[1] As far as synchronic studies are concerned, the majority of linguists based in the United States were 'structuralists', or 'structural linguists'. Put simply, their goal was to elucidate the structural system at the heart of every language.[2] Bloomfield's classic work *Language* (Bloomfield 1933) set the tone for most mainstream American linguists in the mid-twentieth century. The book dealt with each level of grammatical structure, outlining its properties and its relationship to other levels, and at the same time serving as both a major contribution to linguistic theory and as an introductory textbook. Bloomfield himself was by the 1930s quite anti-mentalist and in touch with the logical empiricist philosophers of the Vienna Circle.[3] He contributed a monograph on linguistics to their *International Encyclopedia of the Unified Sciences*. This monograph, *Linguistic Aspects of Science* (Bloomfield 1939b), is the clearest statement in print on the intimate relationship of empiricist philosophy, behaviorist psychology, and structural linguistics. Bloomfield united all three in the following famous passage:

> If language is taken into account, then we can distinguish science from other phases of human activity by agreeing that science shall deal only with events that are accessible in their time and place to any and all observers (strict BEHAVIORISM) or only with events that are placed in coordinates of time and space (MECHANISM), or that science shall employ only such initial statements and predictions as to lead to definite handling operations (OPERATIONALISM), or only such terms that are derivable by rigid definition from a set of everyday terms concerning physical happenings (PHYSICALISM).
>
> (Bloomfield 1939b: 13)

Given such strictures, it follows that 'the only useful generalizations about language are inductive generalizations' (Bloomfield 1933: 20). That in turn led Bloomfield to be skeptical that meaning, 'the weak point in language-study' (p. 140),

---

[1] There are a great many publications that treat developments in American linguistics in the first half of the twentieth century. I particularly recommend Murray (1994: chapters 3–8); Goldsmith & Laks (2019: Chapter 6); and Anderson (2021: chapters 10–14).

[2] Many American linguists in the 1940s and 1950s preferred the self-designation 'descriptivist' to 'structuralist'. Confusingly, however, not all linguists whose goal was to describe languages saw them as integrated structural systems. Franz Boas, for example, was certainly a descriptivist, but less clearly a 'structuralist', as defined here (see § 1.3.3).

[3] Much earlier, however, his work was grounded in Wundtian (mentalist) psychology, which is reflected in his book *Introduction to the Study of Language* (Bloomfield 1914). Sources agree that his turn to behaviorism was in large part a result of discussions with his Ohio State colleague, the psychologist A. P. Weiss.

could play a central role in grammatical analysis.[4] But Bloomfield felt quite con-flicted here. While he was adamant that 'The study of language can be conducted without special assumptions only so long as we pay no attention to the meaning of what is spoken' (p. 75), he felt that 'as long as we pay no attention to meanings, we cannot decide whether two uttered forms are "the same" or "different"' (p. 77) and hence inevitably 'phonology involves the consideration of meanings' (p. 78). Nevertheless, 'linguistic study must always start from the phonetic form and not from the meaning' (p. 162).

Sapir was no less a structuralist than Bloomfield; indeed papers such as Sapir (1925a) and Sapir (1963 [1933]) probably did more to lay the foundations for struc-tural linguistics in the United States than did Bloomfield's *Language*. In the opinion of Zellig Harris, one of the leading mid-century linguists, 'Sapir's greatest contri-bution to linguistics, and the feature most characteristic of his linguistic work, was [...] the patterning of data' (Harris 1951b: 292). Unlike Bloomfield, however, Sapir was not an empiricist. One has to describe him as more 'intuitive' than Bloom-field, whereby flashes of insight led him to a brilliant analysis of some linguistic phenomenon, but without some particular philosophy of science that gave that analysis a theoretical and methodological underpinning.[5] A. L. Kroeber, one of the most distinguished anthropological linguists of the early twentieth century, wrote that 'Edward Sapir, I should say, is the only man I have known at all well, in my life, that I would unreservedly class as a genius' (Kroeber 1984: 131). Sapir's bucking the empiricist tenor of the times and his untimely death at the age of fifty-five resulted in his having less influence than Bloomfield over the next generation of linguists.

The most influential tendency within American structural linguistics at mid-century followed Bloomfield's theoretical pronouncements, though often not his actual practice. Linguists customarily included in this group are Zellig Harris, George Trager, Bernard Bloch, Martin Joos, Henry Lee Smith, Jr., and (at least at as far as his earlier work is concerned) Charles Hockett.[6] Bloomfield's view of science, which members of this group adopted enthusiastically, pointed to

---

[4] In a survey article it was written that 'The study of meaning does not have a place within descriptive linguistics, at least in its American variety [...]' (Lounsbury 1959: 191).
[5] Sapir and Bloomfield had deep respect for each other (Harris 1973: 255), but with certain reser-vations. Sapir admired Bloomfield's ability patiently to excerpt data and to file and collate slips until the pattern of the language emerged, but spoke deprecatingly of 'Bloomfield's sophomoric psychology'. Bloomfield was dazzled by Sapir's virtuosity and perhaps a bit jealous of it, but in matters outside of language referred to Sapir as a 'medicine man' (Hockett 1970: 540; Jakobson 1979: 170). Yakov Malkiel has written: 'Such young Americans as I used to meet [around 1940] referred to the unique blend of scientism and mysticism in Bloomfield's personality; perhaps they should have substituted hard moral core for mysticism. Sapir, in contrast, was remembered as a magician' (Malkiel 1980: 83).
[6] See Hymes & Fought (1981: 128); Murray (1983: 173); Hall (1987: 59); Fought (1995); and Koerner (2002a) for an (often conflicting) breakdown of American structural linguists into various categories. The views of Hockett and many others evolved over the years, making it sometimes difficult to pigeonhole particular individuals as being in particular 'camps'.

linguistic descriptions that were essentially catalogues of observables and generalizations extractible from observables by a set of mechanical procedures: 'The overall purpose of work in descriptive linguistics is to obtain a compact one-one representation of the stock of utterances in the corpus' (Harris 1951a: 366), that is, the requirement that all distinctive elements in a corpus be analyzed in the most efficient economical way. Given their subjective nature, informants' judgments were looked upon with suspicion (except perhaps for the judgment as to whether two words or utterances were 'the same' or 'different'). Analyses embodying underlying representations and derivations involving rule ordering were quite common in morphophonemic analysis (see Swadesh & Voegelin 1939; Bloomfield 1939a; Wells 1949; and, for discussion, Chapter 4, § 4.3.3.3 of this book), though they were considered distinct from phonemics and not as integral a part of the language as the latter.

For the most empiricist of the descriptivists, the idea was to arrive at a grammar of a language by performing a set of operations on a corpus of data, each successive operation being one step farther removed from the corpus. These operations, later called 'discovery procedures', aimed at the development of 'formal procedures by which one can work from scratch to the complete description of the pattern of a language' (Hockett 1952a: 27). It followed then that the levels of a grammatical description had to be arrived at in the order: first, phonemics, then morphemics, then syntax, then discourse: 'There is no circularity; no grammatical fact of any kind is used in making phonological analysis' (Hockett 1942: 20).[7] In actual practice, however, few if any linguists followed a set of (cumbersome) step-by-step procedures that were, in principle, necessary to arrive at a full grammar (for discussion, see Ryckman 1986, Chapter 2). Rather, they presented analyses which, in retrospect examination, *could have been* arrived at by means of these procedures.[8]

The order of discovery of each level of the grammar was reflected, not surprisingly, in the number of publications devoted to each level. There were many more papers on phonemics than on morphemics, and many more on morphemics than on syntax or discourse. As Robert A. Hall, Jr. explained: 'Descriptive syntactic studies have also been rather rare; but, since they normally come at the end of one's analysis, the tendency is perhaps to hold them for incorporation into a more complete description' (Hall 1951–1952: 120).

[7] By the late 1940s it was widely recognized that phonemic analysis could be simplified by appeal to (higher level) morpheme and word boundaries. The problem was that while such boundaries were at times signaled phonetically (cf. *nitrate* and *night rate*), most of the time they were not (cf. *minus* and *slyness*). There was no general consensus on how to deal with this problem.

[8] Appeals to meaning in phonemic analysis were commonplace: 'The basic assumptions that underlie phonemics, we believe, can be stated without any mention of mind and meaning; but meaning, at least, is so obviously useful as a shortcut in the investigation of phonemic structure — one might almost say, so inescapable — that any linguist who refused to employ it would be very largely wasting his time' (Bloch 1948: 5).

Three groupings existed that were less influenced by a rigid empiricist methodology than the mainstream. One was made up of Sapir's students, most of whom were based at some distance from the American East Coast and were focused more on the description of indigenous languages than on debates about procedures. Morris Swadesh, Mary Haas, Charles Voegelin, and Stanley Newman were part of this group. Morris Swadesh, perhaps the most brilliant of Sapir's students, saw 'the evidences of a struggle between realistic fact and mechanistic [i.e., Bloomfieldian — (FJN)] fetishism: particularly between the fact that meaning is an inseparable aspect of language, and the fetish that anything related to the mind must be ruled out of science' (Swadesh 1948: 254).

Others approached linguistics as a tool to aid missionary work, and included such linguists as Kenneth Pike, Eugene Nida, and William Wonderly. For these linguists practical concerns typically outweighed theoretical ones, as is illustrated by the subtitle of Pike's book *Phonemics*, namely *A Technique for Reducing Languages to Writing* (Pike 1947a). Pike and his followers had no compunction about 'mixing levels' in a grammatical analysis, that is, appealing to morphological and syntactic information to arrive at a phonemicization of a particular language.

By the 1950s, there was also a considerable presence of linguists who had been members of the Prague School or influenced by it, including Roman Jakobson, John Lotz, Thomas Sebeok, and Paul Garvin. Jakobson had arrived in the United States in 1941 as a refugee from Europe and within ten years he had built a significant American following. The Prague School linguists were rationalist in their epistemology and not loath to base formal analysis to an extent on semantic criteria.[9] They advocated constructs that were shunned by the more empiricist-minded Bloomfieldians, such as universal categories, binary distinctive features, and markedness distinctions.

Historical linguistic studies, and in particular those of Indo-European languages, were far more prominent then than they are today. To illustrate, in the 1949 volume of the journal *Language*, over half of the articles dealt with diachronic themes. The journalist H. L. Mencken even complained that *Language* devoted more space to Hittite than to American English.[10] For the most part, American-based historical linguists were practicing neogrammarians (as had been Sapir and Bloomfield themselves). In brief, the neogrammarian position is that sound change is regular and operates on distinct classes of sounds, which were later called 'phonemes' (for discussion, see Hock & Joseph 1996):

---

[9] The first three groups of linguists discussed, though not those identified with the Prague School, were often referred to as 'post-Bloomfieldians' or 'neo-Bloomfieldians'.

[10] The full Mencken quote is somewhat off-topic, but amusing enough to merit reprinting: '[T]he Linguistic Society has given a great deal more attention to Hittite and other such fossil tongues than to the American spoken by 140,000,000-odd free, idealistic and more or less human Americans, including all the philologians themselves, at least when they are in their cups or otherwise off guard' (Mencken 1948: 336).

It can only be regarded as fortunate that the later work of wise and historically well-trained linguists like Hoenigswald of Pennsylvania, showed that neogrammarian formulations were closely similar to those of twentieth century structuralists, and that the consonant pattern of Grimm's law were a firm foundation for phonemic statement, instead of a merely happy intuition.

(Hill 1966: 4–5)

Furthermore, the positivist outlook of many leading linguists was deeply compatible with neogrammarian views, as well as the idea that one could make profound generalizations about language structure and history without taking into account the culture or other societal aspects of the speakers. Some descriptivists (including both Bloomfield and Sapir) applied neogrammarian assumptions to working out the historical development and genetic classification of the indigenous languages of the Americas.

The application of the results of linguistics to language teaching had been given a great impetus by the war (see § 1.5.4). By the early 1950s, American linguists had also started to branch out into subfields that had received very little attention in earlier years, such as sociolinguistics and psycholinguistics (two terms that had been coined in the 1930s, but were only just beginning to pass into current use), as well as information theory, discourse analysis, and translation theory (for discussion, see Carroll 1953 and Hamp 1961).

1.3 The Linguistic Society of America

This section recounts the founding of the Linguistic Society of America (LSA) (§ 1.3.1), the debates that raged among its founders about the differences between linguistics and philology and their relationship to scientific endeavors (§ 1.3.2), and the leadership and composition of the early LSA (§ 1.3.3).

1.3.1 The founding of the Society

Before 1924 there was no organization and no journal in the United States that were dedicated to general linguistics. If one wished to disseminate one's ideas about language, one joined the American Oriental Society (founded in 1842), the American Philological Association (founded in 1869), the Modern Language Association (founded in 1883), or the American Anthropological Association (founded in 1902). Their journals, *Journal of the American Oriental Society*, *Transactions of the American Philological Association*, *Publications of the Modern Language Association*, and *American Anthropologist* respectively, were the main outlets for linguistic studies.[11] Robert A. Hall, Jr. noted some years later: 'But all too often, linguistics was treated as a kind of step-child, a Cinderella, in contrast to literary or philological studies. As was observed by the American Sanskritist Maurice Bloomfield in 1919 (*Transactions of the American Philological Association*, L [1919], 83), "There is pathos in that comparative philologians in America have neither independent association nor special organ of publicity." (Hall 1951–1952: 102). Leonard Bloomfield wrote: 'Thus [in the first quarter of the twentieth century] linguists met, pleasantly and profitably, but only in several disconnected groups, each of which appeared as a small and subsidiary cell within a larger society. There was no place where all linguists could meet, no reunion devoted entirely to linguistic discussion, and no journal devoted to our subject' (Bloomfield 1946: 1).

Bloomfield decided to initiate a change in this state of affairs. On January 18, 1924 he sent the following exploratory letter to Boas (see Swiggers 1994 for discussion):

Dear Professor Boas —

I should be very glad to get your response to the enclosed letter. Under our present conditions linguists do not really meet each other, except within certain accidental groups, such as the Modern Language Association and other similar bodies. Some of us feel we have far more in common with ethnologists than with students of the fine art of literature, — and hope that we can get a meeting-ground for the interest in human speech.

We want to send a similar note to Dr. Sapir; can you give me his address? With best regards,

Sincerely,

Leonard Bloomfield (FBA)

Three days later, Boas sent a favorable reply to Bloomfield's suggestion. On January 28, Bloomfield sent a slightly revised version of the enclosed letter (reproduced below from Hockett 1987c: 45), now co-signed by George Melville Bolling and Edgar H. Sturtevant, to a number of their colleagues:

Dear Sir:

To the undersigned it seems that the study of the linguistic sciences is at present greatly neglected in this country. As an indication of this condition they point to the fact that while we have historical, archaeological, and philological societies and publications in a prosperous condition, there is no important society or

---

[11] It is important, however, to call attention to the *International Journal of American Linguistics* (*IJAL*), founded by Franz Boas and Pliny Earle Goddard in 1917. *IJAL* was (and still is), 'devoted to the study of American aboriginal languages' (Boas 1917: 1). At the beginning, the mission of *IJAL* was as much to preserve indigenous texts as to analyze the grammars of indigenous languages.

publication devoted exclusively or chiefly to linguistics in any of its phases. They believe that the foundation of such a society (to have ultimately its own organ of publication) is the first step necessary to an improvement in the general condition of linguistic studies, and that an improvement in the status of linguistic science will necessarily result in the furtherance of all humanistic studies, and the promotion of the best interests of the existing historical, archaeological, and philological societies.

It is tentatively suggested that such a Society should hold biennial meetings, devoted to the discussion of linguistic problems, and related matters at such times and places as shall render it conveniently possible for the members to attend also, alternatively, the meetings of the A.P.A. or the M.L.A., to one or another of which it may be supposed to many of the members will belong.

You are respectfully invited to inform the signers whether you approve the idea in substance — indicating any changes you may think desirable. In case you disapprove the idea they would appreciate greatly a statement of the reasons that lead you to dissent.

The next step will be to circulate among those who have approved the plan in substance a preliminary draft of the call in order that it may be criticized by all before its issuance.

(Signed)
Leonard Bloomfield
George M. Bolling
E. H. Sturtevant

The three were encouraged by the response, which led them to issue 'The Call for an Organizational Meeting' on November 15, 1924. The Call repeated in essence their earlier letter and was signed by 29 scholars (all male, as it turns out[12]). The plan was to meet for the first time at the American Museum of Natural History in New York, on December 28, starting a tradition of late December meetings that would last until 1991. There were 264 Foundation Members of the LSA, 69 of whom attended that first meeting. Hermann Collitz was elected the first president, Carl Darling Buck vice-president, and Roland Grubb Kent secretary-treasurer. Bolling took office as editor of the Society's journal *Language*, which published its first issue in early 1925.

[12] Martin Joos wrote that 'for family reasons, there were no women' (Joos 1986: 9), whatever that might mean. In the 1930s the Front Matter of the *LSAB* contained the following sentence: 'All persons, whether men or women, who are in sympathy with the objects of the Society, are invited to give it their assistance in furthering its work.' The wording suggests that it was not obvious to all that women were welcome as members. There were thirty-one women Foundation Members, however. For an important study of women in the early years of the LSA, see Falk (1999).

The creation of the society was warmly welcomed by scholars in other countries. For example, Antoine Meillet, the Secretary of the Société Linguistique de Paris, enthused:[13]

> Thank you for informing me about the founding of your Linguistic Society. The names of the founders guarantee its future. Allow me nevertheless to wish you good luck and to tell you with how much affection our Society, already old, will follow the progress of your young Society, which will soon be growing. I am very aware of how you have mentioned our Society in founding your own. And I won't miss the opportunity to announce the founding at our next meeting, next Saturday. That will insure that it will appear in our *Bulletin*; and the Society will certainly send you its congratulations.
>
> (*LSAB* 1, 1925: 2)

Bloomfield was charged with the task of explaining to the academic public why a new society was needed. The following are excerpts from his article in the first issue of the first volume of *Language*:

> In our country are scholars who for a generation or more have worked in linguistics and have never met; some of them saw each other for the first time at our initial meeting on December 28th. [...] The layman — natural scientist, philologian, or man in the street — does not know that there is a science of language. [...] The layman usually has no conception of this task [of scientifically analyzing] language; he believes that languages which possess no written literature are mere 'dialects' or 'jargons', of small extent and subject to no fixed rule. Quite by contrast, linguistics finds, on the one hand, a similarity, repugnant to the common-sense view, between the languages of highly civilized people and those of savages, a similarity which disregards the use or non-use of writing. [...] Not only in the general public, but also in the academic system, linguistics is not known as a science. The notion seems to prevail that a student of language is merely a kind of crow-baited student of literature. [...] The more direct harm to science is too obvious to need exposition; one may mention the American Indian languages, which are disappearing forever, more rapidly than they can be

---

[13] In the original French: 'Merci de m'avoir appris la fondation de votre Linguistic Society. Les noms des fondateurs garantissent l'avenir de la fondation. Permettez-moi neanmoins de vous souhaiter bonne chance et de vous dire avec quelle sympathie notre Société, deja vieille, suivra le progrès de votre jeune Société, qui sera bientôt grandie. Je suis tres sensible de la façon dont vous avez bien voulu évoquer notre Société lors de la fondation. Je ne manquerai pas de signaler la fondation lors de notre prochaine séance, samedi prochain. Par là même elle sera arrivée dans notre *Bulletin*; et la Société vous enverra certainement ses félicitations.'

recorded, what with the almost total lack of funds and organization; or the case of American English, of which we know only that, both as to dialects and as to distribution of standard forms, it would present a complex and instructive picture, had we but the means and the equipment to study it.

(Bloomfield 1925c: 1–4)

One finds this statement extremely modern in more than one way. Many of the concerns raised by Bloomfield are the concerns of linguists today: public ignorance of the field of linguistics, the denigration of non-standard forms of speech, and the rapid disappearance of the indigenous languages of the Americas. Furthermore, Bloomfield stressed over and over again that linguistics is a science, just as most practitioners in the field would today. The word 'science' appears fifteen times in his four-and-one-half page article. And interestingly, he denigrated the 'philologian', who is ignorant of the 'science of language'. Bloomfield was later to write: 'I believe that in the near future — in the next few generations, let us say — linguistics will be one of the main sectors of scientific advance, and that in this sector science will win through to the understanding and control of human conduct' (from 1929; quoted in Hockett 1970: 229).

The historiographer of linguistics, Stephen O. Murray, recognized the importance of the founding of the LSA, in writing[14]:

I think [that the signers of the call] were in some sense 'revolutionaries'. They broke with most of their colleagues in according primacy to the study of speech rather than writing (literature), rejected *a priori* grammatical categories, studied unwritten languages, advanced revolutionary notions of phonemics (Sapir 1925a), and sarcastically rejected the American university methods of teaching languages (including English). Bloomfield and Sapir categorically rejected the approaches of most members of the Modern Language Association, and Bolling was at odds with leading American philologists. [...] The founders of the LSA broke with the basic assumptions of their elders more decisively, if with less proclamation of novelty, than Chomsky and his associates broke with neo-Bloomfieldian structural linguistics. (Murray 1989: 162)

Before proceeding further, then, it might prove useful to sort out the distinction between philology and linguistics as the fields were conceived at the time, as well as to what extent either could be regarded as a 'science'.

---

[14] Murray's statement was in direct response to the (unsupportable) claim by Martin Joos that 'The signers of the call were not rebels. They were continuity men. Their research, teaching, and publication continued unbroken the patterns of linguistic thinking defined [by] the neogrammarians' (Joos 1986: 9).

1.3.2 Linguistics, philology, and their relationship to science

The term 'philology' has its roots in antiquity. The applicability of the term has varied from time to time and from place to place. However, it has generally referred to two closely related endeavors. One is the study of the history and evolution of languages, particularly of those with a literary tradition. The other is the study of ancient texts themselves, from the point of view of examining their language per se, as opposed to, say, from a literary-critical point of view. The great discoveries of the Indo-European 'sound laws' in the early nineteenth century were at first described as pertaining to 'comparative philology', a term that was commonly used in the United Kingdom and continental Europe well into the twentieth century. According to Turner (2014: 146), the word 'linguistics' was coined in 1839 by John Pickering, an early student of Amerindian languages.[15] Turner also pointed out that there was no question among the early comparative philologists that their work was 'scientific': "'Only in our century," bragged Jakob Grimm (1785–1863) in 1851, has language studies matured into "a true science"' (p. 146). For quite some time, the terms 'the science of language' and 'linguistic science', both loan-translations from the German 'Sprachwissenschaft', were used more commonly than the term 'linguistics'. According to Julia Falk, these terms were 'used to distinguish systematic, analytic, inductive studies from the more speculative, even fanciful, opinions of some philologists' (Falk 2017: 3).

The first American linguist with an important international reputation was William Dwight Whitney. Falk stresses how Whitney saw linguistics as a science, comparable at least to a degree to zoology and botany:

There is no discussion in Whitney's book [Whitney 1867] of philology in general, its goals or its methods. 'Comparative philology' (or 'Indo-European philology') was 'the early growing phase of linguistic study, that of the gathering and shifting of material, the elaboration of methods, the establishment of rules, the deduction of first general results' (Whitney 1867: 241) But 'the study of Indo-European language is not the science of language' (237) because there is greater diversity among languages than is exemplified within that single family. In his later book, he restated this: 'The science of language is what its name implies, a study of all human speech' (Whitney 1875: 191). Whitney rejected the title of 'comparative philology' for 'the new science of language' — 'a title [...] now fully outgrown and antiquated [...]. [T]o call the whole science any longer 'comparative philology' is

---

[15] John Joseph informs me (p. c., 16 November 2020) that the term 'linguistics' appeared in an anonymous review from 1837 entitled 'History of Navigation in the South Seas', published in the *North American Review*. Apparently the term appeared for the first time in more-or-less its modern sense in the seventeenth century. From the *OED* in 1695: 'J. Edwards *Disc. conc. Old & New-Test.* III. i. 3 Here Linguists and Philologists may find that which is to be found no where else'.

not less inappropriate than to call the science of zoölogy 'comparative anatomy' or botanical science the 'comparison of plants' (1867: 241).

(Falk 2017: 3)

By Bloomfield's time, 'linguistics' had become more common than 'the science of language' or 'linguistic science'. The question, then, is what would be the place for philology in the new society. As indicated in the above quote, he seemed quite dismissive of 'philologians'[16] for their unscientific practice. In a joint article published a few years after the foundation of the LSA, Sturtevant and Kent explained what they saw as the difference between linguistics and philology:

> Linguists study language for itself, while philologists regard language as a means to an end; linguistics is a pure science, while philology is the corresponding applied science. But the parallel is not perfect, for the linguistic point of view may be of immediate utility, and much of the best philological work has been done without a thought beyond the establishment of a correct text or a correct interpretation.
>
> (Sturtevant & Kent 1928: 9)

A year later, Bolling attempted to clarify further the types of scholarly activity with respect to language. He identified three: 'A. The study of man's speech habits. B. The study of what his speech habits have enabled man to accomplish, that is the study of civilization as a whole. C. The establishment and interpretation of the texts of such documents as need that treatment' (Bolling 1929: 27). He stated clearly: 'To A corresponds the LINGUISTIC SOCIETY OF AMERICA' (p. 28). And a few years later still, Bloomfield in his book *Language* insisted that 'It is important to distinguish between *philology* [...] and *linguistics* [...], since the two studies have little in common'. (Bloomfield 1933: 512; emphasis in original).

One would think that, given the above statements from the leading founders of the LSA, philological studies would have played little if any role in that organization. As we see in the following sections, such was not the case.

1.3.3 The leadership and composition of the early LSA

Almost all of the founding members of the LSA were trained in philology. Of the twenty-nine who signed the Call for the founding of the Society in 1924, at least twenty-one were engaged in teaching and research on ancient and classical

---

[16] The terms 'philologian', 'philologist', and 'philologer' are essentially synonymous. Henry A. Gleason suggests that 'Bloomfieldians drew a much sharper and less permeable boundary between language and literature than did Europeans generally' because 'North American linguists had not always had the best of experiences with their literary colleagues' (Gleason 1988: 17).

languages, the historical development of languages, or the comparative linguistics formulated primarily in Europe during the nineteenth century (Falk 1999: 223). They practically had to be philologically trained: 'To be regarded as linguistically strong during the two decades from 1913 to 1933, a linguist had to know comparative linguistics—which generally meant training in Indo-European languages—whether or not he intended to pursue comparative work in one or another American Indian language family' (Voegelin & Harris 1952: 323). Bloomfield had been a student of Germanic philology, writing a 1909 University of Chicago dissertation entitled *A Semasiologic Differentiation in Germanic Secondary Ablaut*. However, his career trajectory was markedly different from that of many of his peers. First, he was from the beginning a committed neogrammarian, reinforced, I am sure, by his having studied at Leipzig with the great neogrammarians August Leskien and Karl Brugmann. His first journal article, Bloomfield (1911), hypothesized a set of sound changes from Proto-Indo-European to Sanskrit. Second, he worked on languages outside the western literary tradition (the analysis of Tagalog in Bloomfield 1917) and those with no literary tradition at all, in particular the Central Algonquin languages Menomini and Fox (Bloomfield 1924a, b, 1925a), the second-named appearing in the first volume of *Language*. Third, and most importantly, Bloomfield advocated an autonomous descriptive linguistics, that is a science of language whose basic vocabulary was entirely language-internal. His landmark article 'A Set of Postulates for the Science of Language', published in the second volume of *Language*, laid out a series of assumptions, definitions, and observations that led to a view of language that was totally self-contained. By defining 'the language of [a] speech-community' as 'the totality of utterances that can be made in a speech-community' (Bloomfield 1926: 26), he implied that the sociocultural context of language could be ignored in linguistic description.

Of the Foundation Members of the LSA, Bloomfield was not alone in advocating 'descriptivism', as the autonomous analysis of the structure of a language came to be known. The first great descriptivist was Franz Boas, generally regarded as the founder of both the fields of linguistics and anthropology in the United States. Bloomfield once described him as 'the pioneer and master in the study of American languages and the teacher, in one or another sense, of us all' (Bloomfield 1972: 265). Coming from a background in physics and geography, rather than philology, Boas produced some of the first descriptive studies of a number of Amerindian languages. His great fame was achieved for his militant, tightly argued, opposition to the idea that there is any intrinsic connection between race or level of culture and language structure (see especially Boas 1911). Boas pointed out, for example, that 'the North American negroes, a people by descent largely African [are] in culture and language, however, essentially European' (p. 4). He then called attention to 'the Magyar of Europe, who have retained their old language but have become mixed with people speaking Indo-European languages, and who have, to all intents and purposes, adopted European culture'

(p. 4). Boas also refuted the consensus of an earlier generation of students of North American indigenous languages that such languages were more 'primitive' than European languages because they contained 'alternating sounds' that defied precise transcription. He showed that such conclusions were primarily a function of the flawed perceptions of the investigators, who were unskilled in analyzing sounds that differed from those of their own languages (Boas 1889).

Boas was a descriptivist, but he was not a 'structuralist', another term that came into widespread use in the 1920s. A structuralist is a descriptivist who analyzes the grammar of a language as an integrated whole, that is, in the words of Boas's French contemporary, Antoine Meillet, where 'chaque langue forme un système où tout se tient'[17] (Meillet 1953 [1903]: 407). Boas was certainly aware that the grammars of all human languages have systematic properties:

> [E]ach dialect has its own characteristic phonetic system, in which each sound is nearly fixed, although subject to slight modifications which are due to accidents or to the effect of surrounding sounds. [...] One of the most important facts relating to the phonetics of human speech is, that every single language has a definite and limited group of sounds, and that the number of those used in any particular dialect is never excessively large.
>
> (Boas 1911:16)

Nevertheless, such knowledge played little if any role in his actual linguistic descriptions. As pointed out by Stephen Anderson, 'There is no reason to doubt his complete familiarity with "phonemic" views, but he remained at least unreceptive (if not outright hostile) to the replacement of phonetic by phonemic transcriptions as phonemic theory gradually took prominence as the cornerstone of a "scientific" approach to language' (Anderson 2021: 239). For Boas, phonetic accuracy was more important than systematic analysis, due in part to his desire to preserve and present native textual material in a fully accurate way. The task of prioritizing phonemic structure over phonetic detail was initiated in American linguistics by another Foundation Member of the LSA, Boas's student Edward Sapir.

Sapir, like Bloomfield, was trained in Germanic philology. However, as a student at Columbia University, he came under the influence of Boas, who encouraged him to work on the indigenous languages of the Americas. His book *Language* (Sapir 1921) brought him to the attention of the linguistic community. The book is replete with Boasian influence, in particular with its insistence on the independence of language, race, and culture. But it goes farther than Boas ever did in overviewing and classifying the structural possibilities of language in general. In that same decade Sapir published two important papers in *Language*, one which

---

[17] That is, where 'each language forms a system where everything is connected'.

argued that each individual language has its own unique integrated sound system (Sapir 1925a) and another which can be regarded as a manifesto for structural linguistics, as the following quote indicates:

> [L]anguage [...] develops its fundamental patterns with relatively the most complete detachment from other types of cultural patterning. [...] Linguistics would seem to have a very peculiar value [...] because the patterning of language is to a very appreciable extent self-contained and not significantly at the mercy of intercrossing patterns of a non-linguistic type.
>
> (Sapir 1929: 212–213)

Furthermore, Sapir, unlike Boas, believed that you could use comparative Indo-European methods on any language (Darnell 1990: 122). Sapir was not very active in the founding of the LSA. He couldn't be—between 1910 and 1925 he worked in Ottawa, directing the Anthropological Division of the Geological Survey of Canada. In fact, it has been written that he and Bloomfield did not meet for the first time until the organizational meeting of the LSA in December 1924 (Hall 1990b: 30). As indicated in § 1.3.1, Bloomfield had to ask Boas for Sapir's address, indicating possibly that Bloomfield did not even know that Sapir was working in Ottawa.

Edgar H. Sturtevant was one of the leading historical linguists of the twentieth century. He was trained in classical philology, but became an enthusiastic neogrammarian early in his career. More than anyone else he was responsible for confirming the hypothesis that Hittite was related to Indo-European. He had a couple dozen articles in the journal *Language* alone devoted to working out the genetic relationship between Hittite and Proto-Indo-European (he himself believed that they were sister languages, derived from 'Proto-Indo-Hittite'). Possibly more than any other LSA founding member, Sturtevant believed that the Society should be an umbrella organization, under which any student of language should be welcome. Sturtevant made it explicit how scholars in one subfield of linguistics might benefit from being exposed to results of scholars in another subfield:

> The science of language has been much retarded by the fact that linguists are, to a large extent, unacquainted with one another, and that they are sometimes ignorant of one another's work. There is little doubt, for example, that the study of the Chinese tones can contribute much to our knowledge of Greek accent, or that modern Persian verse can shed a flood of light upon ancient Greek verse; but the necessary contacts have not yet been established.
>
> (Sturtevant 1925: 128)

Furthermore, Sturtevant was very 'modern' very early on. In his book *Linguistic Change*, he asserted that 'linguistic science is [...] primarily concerned with spoken language' (Sturtevant 1917: 10) and thirty years later in an introductory text, he wrote 'We shall have to discuss writing [...], but only because writing embodies almost our only records of the speech of the past' (Sturtevant 1947: 3).

Despite all of the above, the importance that philological studies played in the research of most of the early LSA members is reflected in a passage from his 1925 article:

> There is no sharp line of division between language and literature, and the attempt to draw one would result in injury to both subjects. Grammar has frequently suffered from the imperfect philological training of its students; while the above-mentioned dependence of sound metric science upon phonetics illustrates the importance of linguistic study for the appreciation of literature. There is no doubt that American linguists will continue their connection with the several philological societies, and it is already evident that many philologists will want to join the Linguistic Society.
>
> (Sturtevant 1925: 128)

The other important founding members of the LSA were trained as philologists and, to one degree or another, continued to advocate for (if not practice) philology throughout their careers. George M. Bolling, in 1925 Bloomfield's colleague at Ohio State University, was professor of Greek Languages and Literature there. As opposed to an earlier generation of philologists, he embraced neogrammarian principles and was impressed with the results of structural linguistics (Hoenigswald 1964: 331–332). 'What Bolling liked most in Bloomfield's work was the idea of developing grammatical categories from the material itself without imposing a foreign mold' (Hoenigswald 1964: 331). However his ultimate goal was always to further the understanding of Classical Greek literature.

Hermann Collitz too extolled the results of the neogrammarians (Collitz 1926). But he felt the need to rebuke Bloomfield's egalitarian message that all speech varieties are equally worthy of study, writing that '[i]t is impossible to study any particular language without perusing at the same time specimens of the literature written in that language. The study of Greek, e.g., means the study of the Greek language and Greek authors' (Collitz 1925: 16). Carl Darling Buck, the only individual ever to be elected president of the LSA twice (in 1927 and 1937), was also a neogrammarian; indeed he has been described as the scholar 'who established study of Indo-European linguistics in the United States' (Lane 1955: 184). Lane went on to remark that 'The victory of the Junggrammatiker [neogrammarians — (FJN)] had been conceded [by the end of the nineteenth century]; the fruitfulness of their methodology was being demonstrated; and Carl Darling Buck contributed his full measure to that demonstration' (p. 187). And yet he was equally interested in purely philological questions, such as the dating of an Old Persian inscription, which he wrote up as the lead article in an early volume of *Language* (Buck 1927).

Finally, Roland G. Kent, despite of his clear understanding of the distinction be-tween linguistics and philology (see above), was primarily a practitioner of the latter, specializing in Greek and Latin literature, with an ancillary interest in Old Persian. A description of his attitude toward the study of unwritten languages seems shocking to modern ears:

> Boas and Sapir together gave the anthropological perspective that philologists did not have. What I mean by 'anthropological perspective' is a whole lot of things, including comparing across the world: you could talk about a language in Africa or Australia or Europe in the same breath. This was considered just outrageous by the Indo-Europeanists, but anthropologists were used to doing it. This was overwhelming and astounding to people like Roland Kent, who was secretary of the Linguistic Society of America for many years. He couldn't conceive of talking about a 'primitive language' and Greek in the same breath. For him they were two different things.
>
> (Mary Haas, quoted in Murray 1997: 700–701)

Of the 214 members of the LSA polled in March 13, 1926, 85 belonged to the Mod-ern Language Association, 77 belonged to the American Philological Association, 61 belonged to the American Oriental Society, 17 belonged to the American An-thropological Association, and 18 belonged to none of the four societies (*LSAB* 2, 1926: 70). As noted by Julia Falk, 'It was surely the case that many of these scholars did not see themselves as engaging in science; many were traditional philologists or specialists in contemporary languages, some were high school language teach-ers, others had no academic affiliation and were simply interested in language and languages' (Falk 2017: np).

To summarize, with the exception of Boas, Bloomfield, and Sapir, the latter two of whom would go on to be the leading lights of American structural linguistics, the founders of the LSA were as personally rooted in philology as they were in (scientific) linguistics, even though in general they did not hesitate in advocating for the latter.

1.4 The changes in the field from the 1920s to the 1940s

In the 1920s and 1930s the LSA was an organization whose leading members came to language through the study of classical literature. For the most part, they consid-ered themselves linguists, not philologists. But the work of the majority dealt with properties of classical languages with a long literary history like Latin, Greek, and Sanskrit, or with ancient languages like Hittite that had newly-discovered texts. All of that had changed by the late 1940s. The next two subsections document two aspects of this change: the composition of the LSA Executive Committee in 1936 and in 1946 (§ 1.4.1), and the steady drop in articles in *Language* that were purely philologically-oriented in the 1930s and 1940s (§ 1.4.2).

1.4.1 The LSA Executive Committee in 1936 and in 1946

Table 1.1 lists the members of the LSA Executive Committee in 1936, along with the title of one of their typical publications. Table 1.2 shows us 1946. The titles from 1936 belong to a world far removed from what we think of as linguistics. Most of the titles from 1946 have as their subject matter areas of interest that could be dealt with in linguistics books and articles today. It is also worth pointing out that the average age of the Executive Committee members in 1936 was fifty-five and the average age of the members in 1946 was forty-four. It would seem that the LSA had been captured by the young, whose number one priority was linguistic structure and analysis.

In the 1920s and 1930s the LSA and the American Philological Association usually held their winter meetings jointly. The last of these meetings (except for 1946 and 1947) was in 1937, and for the two years in the 1940s only because the successive presidents of the LSA and the APA had strong philological interests (Falk 1999: 224). Another sign that American linguistics was moving towards science and away from philology was its response to the announcement of the First

Table 1.1 Officers of the LSA in 1936 with typical publications

Title	Name	Typical publication
President	George Flom	*The Language of the Konungs Skuggsja* [a Norwegian text from the 13th century] (Flom 1923)
Vice-President	Harold H. Bender	*A Lithuanian Etymological Index* (Bender 1921)
Secretary and Treasurer	Roland G. Kent	*Language and Philology (Our Debt to Greece and Rome)* (Kent 1923)
Executive Committee member	Samuel E. Basset	*The Poetry of Homer* (Basset 1938)
Executive Committee member	Albrecht Goetze	*The Hittite Ritual of Tunnawi* (Goetze 1938)
Executive Committee member	Miles L. Hanley	*Word Index to James Joyce's Ulysses* (Hanley 1951)
Editor	George M. Bolling	*The Athetized Lines of the Iliad* (Bolling 1944)

Table 1.2   Officers of the LSA in 1946 with typical publications

Title	Name	Typical publication
President	E. Adelaide Hahn[18]	*Subjunctive and Optative: Their Origin as Futures* (Hahn 1953)
Vice-President	W. Freeman Twaddell	'On defining the phoneme' (Twaddell 1935)
Secretary and Treasurer	J Milton Cowan	'An experimental study of pause in English grammar' (Cowan 1948)
Executive Committee member	John Samuel Kenyon	*A Pronouncing Dictionary of American English* (Kenyon & Knott 1944)
Executive Committee member	George Trager	'The phonemes of Russian' (Trager 1934)
Executive Committee member	Kenneth L. Pike	*Phonemics: A Technique for Reducing Languages to Writing* (Pike 1947a)
Executive Committee member	Zellig S. Harris	*Methods in Structural Linguistics* (Harris 1951a)
Editor	Bernard Bloch	'Phonemic overlapping' (Bloch 1941)

International Congress of Linguists (ICL), held in The Hague, Netherlands in April 1928.[19] The ICL was explicitly pro-general linguistics and anti-philology from its very beginning, as is evidence by the excerpt from their letter of invitation:

> Hence it is that linguistic problems have only received scant, if any, attention, e.g., at Philological Congresses. They have never yet formed the central point of discussion at a meeting of competent students. And the want of such a discussion has become ever more strongly and generally felt.
>
> (*LSAB* 3, 1927: 276)

Five American scholars were on the ICL's Committee of Honour: Franz Boas (who was also a Vice-President of the ICL), Pliny Goddard, A. L. Kroeber, Truman

[18] 'Adelaide Hahn was the first woman to discuss a scholarly topic at an LSA meeting, the first woman to serve as LSA president, the first woman appointed to the Collitz professorship (at the 1951 Linguistic Institute at the University of California, Berkeley). She provided a link to the past and to the well-established and prestigious American Philological Association, enhancing the legitimacy of the LSA in its early years. Though her scholarship became outmoded, her constant presence, her intelligence, her impressive command of Greek and especially Latin, and her articulate outspokenness at the annual and summer meetings of the Society were models of engagement and participation for countless young linguists, both men and women, for more than forty years' (Falk 1999: 20).
[19] Yakov Malkiel remarked that 'International congresses [in American linguistics] were not organized before the First World War; [American] linguists were thus far behind orientalists and other groups of scholars (Malkiel 1979: 115).

Michelson, and Edward Sapir. All five were known for their descriptive work on Amerindian languages; not one was in any sense a philologist.[20]

1.4.2 The changing contents of the first quarter-century of *Language*

Parallel developments to those just described affected the contents of the journal *Language*, until the mid-1940s the only journal of general linguistics in the United States.[21] Looking at the pages of the journal *Language* before the late 1930s it is obvious that many or most articles were written by classically trained scholars who were also members of philological and oriental societies. By the late 1930s—and accelerating into the 1940s—there was a dramatic change. The LSA, its leadership, and the content of its journal slowly left the classics behind and began to focus on language structure and language change divorced from the classical matrix that had existed before.

Let me illustrate. In the five volumes of *Language* published in the 1920s, only about eight of the main articles could be classified as synchronic descriptive linguistics, two of them written by Sapir and two by Bloomfield. At the same time, there were no fewer than eighteen that discussed some particular linguistic feature of a text (almost always an ancient one) or a group of closely related texts. The great majority of the remaining papers dealt with historical linguistics, and the great majority of those discussed changes within the Indo-European family of languages

Things began to change a bit in the 1930s. Around the middle of that decade it became fairly common to see overtly structuralist papers, such as 'The phonemic principle' (Swadesh 1934), 'The phonemes of Russian' (Trager 1934), 'Shawnee phonemes' (Voegelin 1935), 'On defining the phoneme' (Twaddell 1935), 'Phonetic and phonemic change (Hill 1936), 'A Problem in phonological alternation' (Swadesh & Voegelin 1939), and so on. Nevertheless, these were greatly outnumbered by articles that seem more philological than linguistic. For every article that was entitled 'The phonemes of [Whatever]', there were a half dozen or more with titles like 'The subjunctive in Lazarillo de Tormes' (Keniston 1930), 'Another inscription of Xerxes' (Kent 1933), 'Studies in the diction of Layamon's Brut' (Wyld

---

[20] Unfortunately, the *LSAB* does not tell us if the five were appointed by the ICL organizers or by the LSA.

[21] There were very few such journals anywhere in the world. The *Bulletin de la Société Linguistique de Paris* dates from 1869. But *Travaux du Cercle Linguistique de Prague* did not appear until 1929, followed by *Acta Linguistica* (Copenhagen) in 1939, and the Swiss journal *Cahiers Ferdinand de Saussure* in 1941.

1934), or 'Proskynesis and adorare' (Marti 1936). Even as late as 1949, *Language* published an article entitled 'Οφρα in the Homeric poems' (Bolling 1949).[22]

By 1950 the editor Bernard Bloch was able to refer to 'The increase in the number of papers devoted to languages outside the Indo-European family [which] undoubtedly reflects the growing interest of American linguists in the description of living languages — an interest that not only proved its validity during the war years but received a new impetus from the success with which it was applied to the practical task of language teaching. This remarkable rise in the proportion of non-Indo-European studies (perhaps also the rise in the proportion of papers on English) reflects a genuine trend [...]' (*LSAB* 23, 1950: 16). The bulk of these papers were structural analyses.

1.5 Some reasons for the dramatic changes in American linguistics from the 1920s to the 1950s

This section attempts to explain why the field of linguistics in the United States was able to transform itself from a philology-oriented group of scholars to a structuralist-oriented group between the 1920s and the 1940s. They are: the sense of a distinctive field making rapid progress (§ 1.5.1); the leading linguists' commitment to the equality of all languages and their analysis (§ 1.5.2); the LSA's summer institutes (§ 1.5.3); American linguists' involvement in the war effort in World War II (§ 1.5.4); and the change of leadership in the LSA in 1940–1941 (§ 1.5.5).

1.5.1 The sense of a distinctive field making rapid progress

Sapir and Bloomfield never missed an opportunity to argue that linguistics was an autonomous field, rather than being a branch of psychology, anthropology, language studies, or anything else. And this followed directly from language structure being relatively 'insulated' from phenomena outside of language per se. For example:

> Language is probably the most self-contained, the most massively resistant of all social phenomena. It is easier to kill off than to disintegrate its individual form.
>
> (Sapir 1921: 205–206)

---

[22] Julia Falk suggests (p. c., 16 November 2020) that the editor of *Language* published Bolling's paper more as a tribute to one of the founders of the LSA than out of any commitment to elucidating some feature of Homer's poetry.

We are casting off our dependence on psychology, realizing that linguistics, like every science, must study its subject matter in and for itself, working on fundamental assumptions of its own; that only on this condition will our results be of value to related sciences (especially, in our case, to psychology).

(Bloomfield 1922: 142)

One thing that made American structuralism so distinct, and I would say so successful, was its emphasis on its own procedures, methodology, analytical techniques, and so on. This focus on methodology would be criticized by Noam Chomsky much later (see especially Chomsky 1964a), but in the 1930s and 1940s such a focus allowed American structuralists to claim that linguistics had carved out its own intellectual sphere that was unlike anything in any other field traditionally considered part of the humanities or social sciences. It must be pointed out that European structuralists certainly did not dispute the (relative) autonomy of linguistic structure. After all, Ferdinand de Saussure, posthumously recognized as the founder of structural approaches to language, stressed the 'arbitrariness of the sign' and concluded his (posthumously written) book with the slogan that 'the true and unique object of linguistics is language studied in and for itself' (Saussure 1966 [1916]: 232). Likewise Roman Jakobson noted that 'every language has a system of distinctive features and rules governing their arrangement into bundles and sequences [...]. This system is governed by autonomous phonemic laws' (Jakobson 1971e [1949]: 111). But for all that, the Europeans generally believed that the study of linguistic structure could best be understood as part of (or beholden to) the study of something broader. For Saussure, language was one of many possible or existing systems of signs. Jakobson pointed to 'a universally recognized view of language as a tool of communication', leading to 'the elemental demand to analyze all the instrumentalities of language from the standpoint of the tasks they perform [...]' (Jakobson 1971d [1963]: 523). While this is admittedly pure speculation, I suggest that part of the great appeal of American structuralism from the 1920s to the 1950s was its practitioners' single-minded focus on analysis, with little or no discussion of *why* language structure might be the way that it is.

Bloomfield's extolling the uniqueness of linguistics and its methods helped to attract a generation of bright young students who wanted to try their hand at the analysis of an unstudied language or to refine the analytic procedures. Bloomfield knew what he was doing and he was pleased that he was successful. In 1946 he wrote:

Linguistics has come more and more to resemble, in its social complexion, the type of the better established branches of science — say physics, chemistry, and biology.

(Bloomfield 1946: 2)

It is very interesting that he wrote 'social complexion', not 'results'. In other words, linguists *acted* like hard scientists were thought to act. And that in large part explained its appeal and its success. But it was more than that. In more than one respect, structural linguistics *resembled* the hard sciences. As Joseph Greenberg noted: 'It does not seem far-fetched to compare this kind of [structural] analysis with chemistry. Just as the myriad objects of the natural world could be analyzed as consisting of various combinations of a limited number of fundamental chemical elements, so the infinity of sentences of a natural language could be described as made up of combinations of a large but finite number of morphemes, and these in turn by a very restricted number of phonemes' (Greenberg 1973: 53).

While progress might be difficult to measure, the *feeling* of progress is quite easy to measure. All that one needs to do is to read what the practitioners of a field say about their perceptions about the state of the field. Commentators boasted of the 'great progress' (Hall 1951–1952: 101) and 'definitive results achieved by linguistics' (Gleason 1955a: 11). Einar Haugen, in his overview of the field, wrote that 'American linguistics is today in a more flourishing state than at any time since the founding of the Republic' (Haugen 1951: 211). The historical phonologist Harold Whitehall analogized the methods of structural linguistics 'with field physics, quantum mechanics, discrete mathematics, and Gestalt psychology' (Whitehall 1951: v), while Kenneth Pike wrote that the work of Zellig Harris and Bernard Bloch 'is an attempt to reduce language to a formal analysis of great simplicity, elegance, and mathematical rigor, and they have come astonishingly close to succeeding' (Pike 1958: 204). The great anthropologist Claude Lévi-Strauss went even further, enthusing that 'Linguists have already told us that inside our mind there are phonemes and morphemes revolving one around the other in more or less the same way as planets around the solar system' (Lévi-Strauss 1953: 349). And in his survey of the field, John B. Carroll, wrote that 'Since the publication of Bloomfield's work in 1933, theoretical discussions among linguists have largely been on matters of refinement' (Carroll 1953: 52).

No other branch of the humanities or the social sciences had anything like the phoneme. In the words of Einar Haugen:

> I think we can safely say that the dance around the phoneme was what attracted most of my generation to the Linguistic Society of America and kept us together.
> (Haugen 1980: 136)

The success of the phoneme and other products of grammatical analysis were the envy of other disciplines. At the same Wenner-Gren conference from which the above Lévi-Strauss quote is drawn, one of the topics proposed for discussion was 'the cultural equivalent of the phoneme'. As Greenberg noted, 'The promise held out by the linguistics of this period was that by the application of an analogous method to the data of non-linguistic culture, functionally relevant units of description might be isolated in terms of which the culture as a whole could be described. This seemed highly desirable because it was widely held that the cultural anthropologist had no basis in principle for choosing what to observe or for analyzing these observations once they were made' (Greenberg 1973: 54). Greenberg continued:

> A valiant attempt to develop methods for the application of structural linguistic methods to non-linguistic cultural data was that of the eminent American linguist, Kenneth Pike, in a series of stimulating volumes called, *Language in Relation to a Unified Theory of the Structure of Human Behavior* [Pike 1954]. Judged, however, by the test of application, this attempt must be judged a failure. I know of no instance in which a cultural anthropologist has been able to transpose with any real success linguistic methods into cultural materials on this model. Pike's attempt has, however, bequeathed to the language of anthropological theory the widely used terms 'emic' and 'etic'. These words are abstracted from 'phonemic' and 'phonetic' respectively, and herein lies the heart of the matter. [...] Once again, one of the characteristics of language not shared by other aspects of cultural behavior obtrudes itself. Language is basically a code by the use of which we frame messages which have a meaning in a quite definite way. The linguist's method in phonemic analysis was essentially to call a difference between sounds 'phonemic' if it had the systematic function of distinguishing messages from each other as against those differences which did not. But a religious ceremony, while in a very broad sense meaningful, does not send messages, as it were, with such precision that we can say when the message is the same or different. Or again, for all its esthetic glories, the storm in the third movement of Beethoven's pastoral symphony cannot substitute for a meteorological report.
>
> (Greenberg 1973: 54–55)

1.5.2 The leading American linguists' commitment to the equality of all languages and their analysis[23]

Recall from § 1.3.1 one of the points that Bloomfield made about why we need a linguistic society: '[L]inguistics finds [...] a similarity, repugnant to the common-sense view, between the languages of highly civilized people and those of savages [...]' (Bloomfield 1925c: 2). As was noted in § 1.3.3, such a view was shared by his contemporaries Franz Boas and Edward Sapir, the latter of whom made the same point in a well-known passage:

---

[23] Much of the material in this section appears in more detail in Joseph & Newmeyer (2012).

When it comes to linguistic form, Plato walks with the Macedonian swineherd, and Confucius with the head-hunting savage of Assam.

(Sapir 1921: 219)

Much of the work published in *Language* from the 1930s onward showed—implicitly or explicitly—that Navajo and Cherokee could be analyzed with the same methodology that one would use in analyzing English and French. Sapir was to remark that the methodology of Bloomfield's Proto-Central-Algonquian reconstruction 'is precisely the same as the methodology which is used in Indo-European linguistics' (Sapir 1949 [1931]: 75). Such an egalitarian message must have found a welcome reception among the increasingly radicalized American students in that period of time. For perhaps the first time in American history, there was a movement of students organized to combat the racism that was endemic to American society (for discussion, see Brax 1981). It has been written that 'With regard to the universalism (egalitarianism) in the methodology, no doubt the climate of opinion after World War I was favorable to the tone taken with regard to it; perhaps something of the social origins of linguists in the United States also played a part' (Hymes & Fought 1981: 59).[24] The message broadcast by the founders of descriptive linguistics in that country must have been highly encouraging to left-leaning students and might well have been a factor in their choosing linguistics as a field of study.

For all of that, the linguists in the first third of the twentieth century had few compunctions about identifying individual languages as being relatively simple or complex. For example, Franz Boas—again, one of the staunchest opponents of racism of his time—offered the opinion that 'Many primitive languages are complex' and noted that 'On the whole, the development of language seems to be such, that the nicer distinctions are eliminated, and that it begins with complex and ends with simpler forms, although it must be acknowledged that opposite tendencies are not by any means absent' (Boas 1938: 160). Sapir saw things in an analogous fashion. Some have taken the above quote as an assertion of equal complexity. But Sapir had no intention of implying by this quote that all languages are equally complex, as is evidenced by his preceding sentence:

Both simple and complex types of languages of an indefinite number of varieties may be found spoken at any desired level of cultural advance.

---

[24] Hymes and Fought do not tell us what 'social origins' they are referring to. I assume they mean to imply that a high percentage of those who entered linguistics in the 1920s and 1930s were Jewish, and many of them from left-leaning families. Morris Swadesh, for example, was an active member of the Communist Party, and, after the Second World War, could not find employment in the United States on account of it. See Hymes (1980) and, for a negative assessment of Swadesh (Hall 1975, 1980).

Bloomfield too saw languages differing in their overall complexity. Interestingly, the very last page of his book *Language* (1933) was devoted to the differential complexity of modern languages vis-à-vis their historical antecedents. He wrote that 'Even now it is clear that change in language tends toward shorter and more regularly constructed words' (Bloomfield 1933: 509), a process that he explicitly described as 'simplification'. The 'ultimate outcome [of language change] may be the state of affairs which we see in Chinese, where each word is a morpheme and every practical feature that receives expression receives it in the shape of a word or phrase.'

But by the early 1950s, a consensus had arisen among American structural linguists that all languages are equally complex. The first quote that I have found that explicitly puts forward the idea of equal complexity is from an article published in 1954 by Rulon Wells:

> Again, one can isolate the complexity of a language in phonemics, in morphophonemics, in tactics, etc.; but these isolable properties may hang together in such a way that the total complexity of a language is approximately the same for all languages.
>
> (Wells 1954: 104)

In a footnote on the same page, Wells cites a personal communication from Charles Hockett on August 2, 1952 for having suggested the idea. Just a year after the Wells article, the idea of equal complexity had found its way into the *Encyclopædia Britannica* article on 'Language' by George Trager:

> All languages of today are equally complex and equally adequate to express all the facets of the speakers' culture, and all can be expanded and modified as needed. There are no 'primitive' languages, but all languages seem to be equally old and equally developed.
>
> (Trager 1955: 698)

Not surprisingly, the idea of equal complexity was rejected by linguists whose interests were more philological than structural. Within a few years, Trager's entry would be revised by Joshua Whatmough, Professor of Comparative Philology at Harvard and founder of its Linguistics Department. In the new version the four instances of 'equally' in this passage have been removed: 'All languages of today are highly complex and are adequate to express all the facets of the speakers' culture, and all can be expanded and modified to meet changing circumstances. There are no languages which could justifiably be called primitive' (Trager & Whatmough 1966: 699). Whether Trager approved the change I do not know. Along the same lines, Gordon M. Messing, longtime professor of classics and linguistics at Cornell, asserted that 'the structuralists err in approaching a culture language [*sic*] —

say French — in precisely the same spirit in which they approach a non-culture language [sic] like Eskimo' (Messing 1951: 5).[25]

It is now standard for introductions to linguistics to assert the equal complexity of all languages. Consider examples from three popular introductory texts:

> There are no 'primitive' languages — all languages are equally complex and equally capable of expressing any idea in the universe.
>
> (Fromkin & Rodman 1983: 16)

> Contrary to popular belief, all languages have grammars that are roughly equal in complexity [...]
>
> (O'Grady, Dobrovolsky, & Aronoff 1989: 10)

> Although it is obvious that specific languages differ from each other on the surface, if we look closer we find that human languages are at a similar level of complexity and detail — there is no such thing as a primitive language.
>
> (Akmajian, Demers, Farmer, & Harnish 1997: 8)

It is only in the last decade or so that the hypothesis of equal complexity has started to be challenged (see Joseph & Newmeyer 2012).

To summarize, the message that there are no primitive languages must have been very appealing to radicalizing students in the 1930s and 1940s. However, the next step, namely the idea that all languages are equally complex, did not become current until the 1950s.

1.5.3 The LSA's summer Linguistic Institutes

Between 1928 and 1931 and then from 1936 onward, the LSA has organized a summer school at a university campus. Typically some of the major figures in linguistics would teach at them. Particularly at a time when there were very few independent linguistics department in the United States, these institutes were crucial in building up the field in America. One account of the development of American linguistics has asserted that 'probably the most important institution of all in creating "a continent-wide community" (Joos 1986: 28) was the Linguistic (LI), the "first truly great innovation" by the LSA, according to Malkiel 1979: 115)'

---

[25] The Messing paper was published in *Language*, edited at the time by the dyed-in-the-wool structuralist Bernard Bloch. Bloch's editorial notes state that the paper is 'ignorant, biased, unfair, [and the] main point is rotten'. But he published it anyway. European structuralists and historical linguists appear to have been less enamored of the equal complexity hypothesis than their American counterparts. Messing's position was endorsed by the Swedish structuralist Bertil Malmberg (see Malmberg 1964 [1959]: 185). Analogously, the Dutch comparativist Jan Gonda wrote that the comparative method was inapplicable to many non-Western languages, which share properties (like reduplication) with 'the speech of children [and] the uncultivated or less cultivated classes and groups of our own society' (Gonda 1948: 90). His position was immediately blasted by Trager as 'a counsel of despair, where it is not sheer ethnocentric racism' (Trager 1948: 209).

(Murray 1994: 139). And another has endorsed this view, stating that 'There was nothing that came close to these summer institutes when it came to developing a single consciousness of American linguistics' (Goldsmith & Laks 2019: 369).

According to Martin Joos, the 1928 LI, held at Yale and supported by a sub-vention of $2500 from the Carnegie Corporation, was intended to be more of an exchange of ideas than an ordinary summer school, though as the years progressed they took on more of the character of the latter. Before the Great Depression ended the possibility of such relatively expensive gatherings, Yale held another LI in 1929 and the locale moved to City College of New York for 1930 and 1931.

The idea of holding LIs originated with Reinhold Saleski, a sociolinguist *avant l'heure* (see Falk & Joseph 1994):

> In the spring of late 1927, Dr. R. E. Saleski, Professor of German in Bethany Col-lege, wrote to the Secretary of the Linguistic Society, suggesting the holding of a Linguistic Institute in the summer of 1928; his proposal was rather for a gathering of scholars for interchange of ideas, than for the holding of courses, though the latter was not excluded.
>
> (Falk & Joseph 1994: 139)

The first few LIs were directed by E. H. Sturtevant, with Saleski as Assistant Di-rector. The driving force behind the early institutes, as far as its program was concerned, was Sturtevant (see Falk 1998 for details) and his motivation for hold-ing them 'grew out of the same situation that had led to the formation of the Linguistic Society itself a few years before. An American teacher of linguistic sci-ence is ordinarily a member of a college or university department whose other members are primarily interested in the history and interpretation of literature. Very frequently his immediate colleagues have little understanding or sympathy for his interests [...]' (Sturtevant in *LSAB* 13, 1940: 83).[26] As noted above, he had a very broad view of the field, and from the beginning made sure that all branches of linguistics would be represented. In keeping with the times and the composition of the LSA, most of the courses had historical (and in some cases purely philological) themes, but there were also courses entitled 'Experimental Phonetics', 'Semantics', 'Some Recent Theories of Linguistic Science', 'Linguistic Anthropology', 'Methods of Studying Unrecorded Languages', and 'American English'.[27] Sturtevant was,

> however, cautious about any movement away from historical and toward non-historical linguistics even as he worked to incorporate the latter into the

[26] Stanley Newman noted that 'although a handful of language-and-literature departments wel-comed linguists, the great majority were uncompromisingly hostile' (Newman 1982: 139). Zellig Harris could not teach linguistics in his own Oriental Languages department at Pennsylvania. Rather he had to do so in Anthropology, 'under the guise of analysis of unwritten languages' (Hymes & Fought 1981: 46).

[27] And some courses were purely pedagogically oriented. For example, the third LI included a course entitled 'Linguistics in High School Latin'.

curriculum of the Institutes. Sensitive to positions taken by his more conservative peers, Sturtevant was aware of the possible danger to the Institute should it move too radically in a new direction. As he wrote to his colleague Saleski: 'we have been rather severely criticized for our excursions into non-historical linguistic science' (13 November 1930, LSAA). For himself, he said: 'personally, I am perfectly willing to admit the possibility of constructing a linguistic science that shall not be historical, but I am not convinced that such a science is yet in existence (13 November 1930, LSAA).

(Falk 1998: 174)

One of the major features of the early LIs was the furtherance of the Linguistic Atlas of the United States and Canada. The Atlas was the brainchild of Hans Kurath, Bloomfield's colleague in the late 1920s in the German Department at Ohio State, but at the same time a scholar with a keen interest in American dialectology. Kurath lobbied the LSA, other groups of potentially interested scholars, and funding organizations to take on the Atlas project. In 1929 the Executive Committee of the American Council of Learned Societies (ACLS) set up a task force to plan a dialect atlas under Kurath's chairmanship. In 1931 the ACLS authorized the spending of $60,000 for the project (Joos 1986: 44). The LSA stepped in very early on the project, making it a highlight of the 1931 LI. In December 1930 the Director of the 1931 Institute, Edgar Sturtevant, received a grant from the ACLS to provide for the traveling expenses and an honorarium for the Swiss dialectologists Jakob Jud and Paul Scheuermeier to support their teaching at that Institute. The idea was they would share their experience of preparing linguistic atlases with American linguists working on the newly launched Project for a Linguistic Atlas of the United States and Canada (*LSAB* 7, 1931: 3–5, 8; *LSAB* 8, 1931: 4–5). The following is their course description (p. 8):[28]

> **Problems in the Preparation of Linguistic Atlases. Mr. Jud and Mr. Scheuermeier.** — Critical account of the methods and goals of published atlases and those in publication. Differences between atlases and dictionaries. Preparing an atlas. Surveying an area. Classification and organization of collected material. Linguistic results. Lectures by Mr. Jud and practical exercises given by Mr. Scheuermeier, based on the questionnaire in *Sprach- und Sachatlas Italiens und der Südschweiz*, a copy of which will be made available to participants.

Among the fifteen registrants for the course were Hans Kurath (LSA President in 1942), Bernard Bloch (LSA President in 1953), Martin Joos (LSA Vice-President in 1952), H. B. Richardson (LSA Executive Committee member in 1934), and Miles

---

[28] In the original French: '**Les Problèmes de la Préparation d'un Atlas Linguistique. M. Jud et M. Scheuermeier.** — Exposé critique des méthodes et du but des atlas publiés ou en publication. Différences entre l'atlas et les dictionnaires. Les préparatifs d'un atlas. L'enquête sur les lieux. Classification et coördination des matériaux recueillis. Résultats linguistiques. Conférences par M. Jud et exercices pratiques donnés par M. Scheuermeier sur la base du questionnaire du *Sprach- und Sachatlas Italiens und der Südschweiz*, dont une copie sera remise aux participants.'

Hanley (LSA Executive Committee member in 1936) (*LSAB* 8: 12). Bloch, Hanley, and John Kepke would go on to be major figures in the project. Joos wrote: 'From August 1929 onward for a whole decade, the Linguistic Institute, the Linguistic Atlas, and the Society had practically a single history' (Joos 1986: 37).[29] Thanks to the Depression, the project had to be scaled back greatly in the 1930s; the first volume to emerge was the *Linguistic Atlas of New England* (Kurath 1939). The project remains unfinished.

All of the LIs between 1936 and 1940 were taught at the University of Michigan at Ann Arbor under the directorship of Charles C. Fries. While historically oriented courses still dominated, at these LIs there was quite a bit more variety than there had been a decade earlier. Sturtevant, Sapir, and Bloomfield taught 'Introduction to Linguistic Science' one after the other the first three years. The latter two were heavily synchronically-oriented, as can be gleaned from Bloomfield's 1938 course outline (the course itself attracted 200 students):

> The biological and social place of language. The meaning of speech-forms; semantics. Speech-sounds and phonemes. Word structure and syntax. Relationship of languages; speech families; the comparative method. Writing. The distribution of dialects. Change in language: phonetic change, creation of new forms, borrowing; the rivalry of forms. Standard languages; local dialects, jargons, slang; literary language; linguistic superstition, tabu, normative grammar. Applications of linguistics: teaching children to read; composition; the teaching of foreign languages; logical and mathematical systems. Textbooks: E. Sapir, *Language* (1921), and L. Bloomfield, *Language* (1933).
>
> (reprinted in Joos 1986: 61)

Other non-historically-oriented courses taught at the 1938 LI were 'American English', 'Anatomy and Function of the Vocal Apparatus', 'Modern English Grammar', 'English Phonetics', 'Field Methods in Linguistics' (the other course taught by Bloomfield), 'Language as a Biological (Physiological) Process', and 'Psychology of Language'. Interestingly, courses devoted to particular components of the grammar with titles like 'Phonology', 'Morphology', 'Syntax', and so on did not become the norm for another decade.

Goldsmith & Laks (2019: 369–371) write: 'That summer [LI] of 1937, in Ann Arbor, Michigan, was a transformative moment for a whole generation of linguists' and provide first-hand testimonials to that effect by several participants. That by Raven McDavid is particularly interesting:

> I went to the Linguistic Institute [in 1937]. Wayne Tyler lured me into Bloch's seminar; and Bloch discovered in me a talent for phonetics. [...] Sapir spent an hour with me on the 'M' bench, sounding me out and suggesting that I

---

[29] Though it has been suggested that 'Joos's overstatement [was] colored perhaps by his personal involvement in it' (i.e. the Atlas) (Murray 1994: 142).

study Catawba— a suggestion shortly reinforced by Swadesh. […] The Institutes of 1938, 1940, and 1941 strengthened this foundation, especially in phonetics, dialectology, and lexicography. I met most of the great people in the profession— Bloomfield, Sturtevant, Kent, Malone, Haugen, Trager, Kepke, Hockett, Harris, Voegelin, Whorf, Adelaide Hahn — as was easy when a whole Institute could fit into a large classroom. From them I learned two lessons, not in any formal curriculum. With the leaders accepting a beginner as one of themselves — before the day when linguistics was torn by ideological *Schrecklichkeit* — I could do no less for those who later came to work with me; learning first-hand about their own professional tribulations, I was prepared for what I encountered later.

(McDavid 1980: 7)

The participants at the 1938 LI provided each other a little comic relief by composing limericks, for the most part about the leading linguists of the time. I pass some of these along to provide comic relief for the current reader[30]:

L.S.A.
When meets the Linguistic Society
There's never regard for propriety
 But matters fantastic,
 As well as scholastic,
Are considered with equal sobriety. (George Bechtel)

Leonard Bloomfield
Leonard B. in a linguistic lecture
Took a crack at the proud speech-corrector
 "Just let him correct,
 But don't let it affect
Your talk or your writing, by heck, sir!"

Roland G. Kent (the LSA Secretary-Treasurer)
A bookkeeping scholar named Kent
Can tell to four-tenths of a cent
 All the back dues we owe him;
 And that's why we show him
Such courtesy — not that it's meant. (Bernard Bloch)

Bernard Bloch
There's a stalwart young man surnamed Bloch,
Who's on terms with all sounds in the stock;
 If an Injun should speak
 With a glottalized squeak

---

[30] I would like to thank Allison Burkett for uncovering these limericks and sharing them with me.

He can tell you what's ['ik] and what's ['ok].

    Edgar Sturtevant

Edgar H. is a right sturdy Fant [*sic*],

Quite free from pretensions and cant

    He's doing all right

    To prove that Hittite

Is Indo-Germanic's great aunt. (L. L. R.)

Humor aside, the Linguistic Institutes provided an arena when the latest developments in the field could be disseminated to dozens and, later, hundreds of faculty members and students from the United States and abroad. As summarized by Julia Falk:

> It would be difficult to overstate the importance of the Institutes in the history of American linguistics. The Atlas project emphasized the analysis of contemporary language, a focus on speech, and the necessity of working directly with speakers (at that time called 'informants'). These same principles applied to the study of native American languages. In both cases, new methods of collecting, recording, and analyzing data were essential, and these became a primary concern in the descriptivist tradition that dominated American work for the next quarter century.
>
>   (Falk 2014: 3)

1.5.4 American linguists' involvement in World War II

The Second World War was a humanitarian disaster in most of the world. In addition to the purely human cost of the war, academic research practically ceased in most European and Asian countries. The exception was the United States, at least as far as linguistics is concerned. The field boomed during the war and immediately afterwards. As one commentator put it, 'In the hothouse atmosphere of the wartime work, American linguistic theory was to develop far more swiftly than it had before' (Joos 1957b: 108). Robert Hall attributed the founding of the journals *Word, Studies in Linguistics, Romance Philology*, and the reestablishment of the journal *IJAL* to the 'quickened activity of linguistics during the war period' (Hall 1951–1952: 106). And with perhaps a slight touch of exaggeration, linguists found themselves 'at a time when our national existence — and possibly the existence of the human race — [depended] on the development of linguistics and its application to human problems' (McDavid 1954: 32).

    What was going on? Mortimer Graves, Executive Secretary of the ACLS in 1939, reasoned that the success that American linguists had achieved in analyzing unwritten indigenous languages could be applied to the analysis and teaching of the languages that were likely to be of strategic importance in the coming war. Many linguists concurred: 'Principles first used in recording American Indian languages have been applied to the teaching of oriental languages with unexpectedly good results' (Haas 1943: 203). With $100,000 from the Rockefeller Foundation, the ACLS organized the Intensive Language Program (ILP) in Washington, and appointed J Milton Cowan, then Secretary-Treasurer of the LSA, as director. The direct goal was language materials to support the troops. By the summer of 1943, the Intensive Language Program had conducted 56 courses, in 26 languages, at 18 universities, for about 700 students. By the end of the war, the ILP had produced materials for dozens of languages. Stanley Newman recalls:

> Linguists were soon employed in new organizations in and out of government. The Intensive Language Program, under J Milton Cowan, assigned linguists to languages in which they were to prepare courses, using native speakers as informants. Some of these projects were later incorporated into the ASTP (Army Specialized Teaching Program); hence, the method developed in these courses became known as 'the Army Method'. Civil affairs officers were trained for service in Europe and the Far East in CATS (Civil Affairs Training Schools), where the language courses were supervised by linguists.
>
> (Newman 1982: 140)

As early as 1942, the journal *Hispania* observed 'that the Director [of the ILP, J Milton Cowan] is constantly called upon for advice on language problems by practically every agency of the government which has these problems: Office of Strategic Services, Board of Economic Welfare, Department of Justice, as well as the numerous departments of the Army, Navy, and Marine Corps' (Graves & Cowan 1942: 490).

Cowen and his team were based in Washington, DC. A group that was probably more important for the future development of linguistics was headquartered at 165 Broadway in New York City. This was the Language Section of the United States War Department, which functioned as the center for the preparation of materials in several dozen languages, such as the pocket-sized Language Guides, the somewhat longer Phrase Books, the full-length basic courses, and military and other types of dictionaries. It was in operation from July 1943 through June 1945, at which point some of the linguists involved were transferred to the Foreign Service Institute (FSI) of the Department of State. Among the prominent linguists housed in this building were Madison Beeler, Paul Garvin, Robert A. Hall, Charles Hockett, Fred Householder, John Kepke, Fred Lukoff, Raven McDavid, Norman McQuown, Stanley Newman, Herbert Penzl, Allen Walker Read, Henry Lee Smith, and Morris Swadesh. Commenting on 165 Broadway and how his stay there gave him more than enough time to carry out linguistic research, Charles Hockett observed:

> I was like a war millionaire [...]. So, while many young people were [...] fighting and dying, I was living in comfort and making, not a lot of money, but a lot of intellectual progress, which people like us are inclined to consider even more important.
>
> (Hockett 1980: 103)

Graves's organizational skill in providing funding, employment, and research opportunities for the linguists of the United States was a major factor in the development of the field; indeed, he was regarded as bearing as much responsibility for the success of American linguistics as the work of Franz Boas, Edward Sapir, Leonard Bloomfield, and Benjamin Whorf (Parker 1954: 123). In Cowan's opinion, 'Mr. Graves has done more than any other one person to further the interests of our discipline during the past quarter of a century' (*LSAB* 31, 1958: 17).

As far as the FSI is concerned, it had its origin in the realization 'that the new role which the United States was destined to play in world affairs requited competence of the highest order on the part of those engaged in the conduct of foreign relations' (*FSI Catalog*, 1949, Washington, DC, p. 2). The general objective of its language and area specializations (under which linguistics was taught) was that the Foreign Service officer 'should acquire a thorough understanding of foreign peoples and should develop effective ways of communicating with them in aiding the implementation of national policy' (p. 7). Here, while enrolled in such courses as 'Public Opinion Formation in Foreign Countries', 'Economic Development of Underdeveloped Countries', and 'Oil and the Middle East', the future diplomat, career officer, or foreign administrator could also study linguistic theory under some of America's most prominent structural linguists. One should not underestimate the FSI's importance to the field; in an overview of the linguistics profession, the educational psychologist John B. Carroll noted that in order to support their language-teaching program, the School of Languages and Linguistics of the FSI became 'one of the major centers of linguistic research in the United States' (Carroll 1953: 182). Linguistics at the FSI was closed down with the arrival of the Eisenhower administration in 1953.

The passage of the National Defense Education Act in 1958 was another shot in the arm for the field of linguistics. Title IV gave a great number of linguistics graduate students financial support, while Title VI provided for language teachers' institutes, language and area centers, and language research. Actually, all four of the Title VI programs included basic linguistic research, the most sizeable being a $650,000 grant for the study of the Ural-Altaic languages spoken in the Soviet Union. There is no doubt that this level of support was intended to continue as long as linguists could convince the federal government that their findings would aid language teaching, particularly of the 'critical languages'. Albert Marckwardt emphasized this fact and commented that if structural linguists 'fail to live up to the claims they have made for their science [about its applicability to language teaching] — often too vociferously and without due modesty and caution — they may have muffed the chance for once and all. It is no exaggeration to say that the NDEA has put linguists squarely on the spot. "Put up or shut up" may be a crude phrase, but it describes the situation precisely' (Marckwardt 1959: iv). Kenneth W. Mildenberger, chief of the Language Development Section of the United States Office of Education, explained that while his office had no formal policy directed to linguistics it did have an 'attitude' about the intent and spirit of all the programs covered by the NDEA. Their 'mission' was to strengthen and extend language instruction 'to meet the needs of the national interest' (Mildenberger 1960: 161). He then repeated Marckwardt's threat to linguists to 'put up or shut up'.

1.5.5 The change of leadership in the LSA in 1940–1941

The two most important offices in the LSA, in terms of actual responsibilities, are Editor of *Language* and Secretary-Treasurer. The Editor at the time had total personal control over what appeared in the journal. The Secretary-Treasurer ran the day-to-day activities of the organization. From 1925 to 1940 the Editor was Bolling and from 1925 to 1941 the Secretary-Treasurer was Kent. Both were totally devoted to the LSA, but at the same time they were part of the older generation that focused on classical languages. Neither was a contributor to structural linguistics. In 1940 Bolling was replaced by Bernard Bloch and in 1941 Kent was replaced by J Milton Cowan. Let us have a look at these two individuals and their career trajectories.

Bernard Bloch, as noted above, was involved in the Atlas project from the beginning, several years before he received his 1935 PhD at Brown University. His dissertation, written under the direction of Hans Kurath, was entitled *The Treatment of Middle English Final and Preconsonantal R in the Present-Day Speech of New England*. At the time of his 1940 appointment, Bloch had a total of five publications, none in *Language*, all on American English phonetics, and which added up to a total of twenty-seven pages. He was only thirty-three years old at that time and an instructor (i.e., not at professor-level rank) at Brown. Nevertheless, he had made himself known to the LSA leadership, as he was selected to teach 'American Dialect Geography' and 'English Phonetics' at the 1937 LI, and the former course along with 'Phonetics and Phonemics' and the 1940 LI. Why was he chosen Editor? Years later, Yakov Malkiel suggested:

> Bloch's chief visible assets were stylistic perfectionism and sensitivity, extraordinary tidiness (acquired in the course of field work and of cartographic projection executed in the service of Hans Kurath's Linguistic Atlas of New England), and alertness to all manner of 'rumblings' in the edifice of theoretical linguistics, at that point in the process of restructuring.
>
> (Malkiel 1966: 648)

According to Martin Joos:

> George M. Bolling, Editor of *Language* from its beginning, and the other elder statesmen of the Society decided that the time was opportune for a change of editor. They wanted the youngest competent Editor that could be found, since they were sure that the office ought to change hands as infrequently as possible [...]. [A] firm consensus was soon reached, helped by a warm testimonial from Hans Kurath [...] and Bernard Bloch was elected Editor at the end of 1939. Kurath had promised to stand by him while he was learning the game, but very soon found that there was nothing substantial for him to do, so swift and sure was Bloch's grasp.
>
> (Joos 1967: 10)

The choice of Cowan for the post of Secretary-Treasurer is more puzzling. He did not receive his PhD until 1935, when, at the State University of Iowa (now called the University of Iowa), he produced a dissertation entitled *Pitch, Intensity, and Rhythmic Movements in American Dramatic Speech*. He stayed on at Iowa and became Assistant Professor of German there in 1938. Cowan attended the 1936 LI, but did not actually join the LSA until the following year. Nevertheless—and despite a skimpy publication record—he played an important role at the 1937 LI, lecturing there on 'Stroboscobic Motion Pictures of the Vocal Cords in Action' and 'Intonation in English, French, and German' (Joos 1986: 69–70). He himself later discussed his infatuation with the Society:

> I found a staff of venerable scholars and a group of bright young students [at the 1936 LI] pursuing the scientific study of language with a devotion, often with a passion, that I had never experienced before. They even listened to me when I talked (nonsense) about the psychophysiology of language or about work I had done in experimental phonetics. Better still: they invited me to come back the following year with a set of prepared lectures. By the end of the 1937 Institute I was hooked. I knew that my career was going to be linguistics and the Linguistic Society of America was the greatest organization in the world.
>
> (Cowan 1975: 28)

At some point in the mid-1930s Cowan initiated field work on the Algonquin language Fox, which was spoken on the Tama Reservation in Iowa. He recalls meeting Bloomfield at the 1938 LI and discussing his field notes on that language with him (Cowan 1975: 23). In 1940, the year of his nomination for the post of Secretary-Treasurer, he taught a regular class (on phonetics) at the LI. In other words, Cowan was hardly an unknown in 1940, but at the same time he could not have been called a leading light of the LSA.

Interestingly, it was Bloch, not Cowan, who was originally slated to be Secretary-Treasurer. The former received the following letter from Kent in early 1939:

Dear Bernard,

Now that Sturtevant has talked with you about the possibility of your being asked to take over the job which I have in the LSA, I want to write to you frankly about it. Frankly, I want to get rid of the job [...]. I know that you can be trusted [...] and that Julia [Bloch's wife — (FJN)] [...] will do the bulk of the actual work [...][31] My plan is this: At the next annual meeting, I shall be elected again to the Sec.-Treas., and accept, but at the same time present my resignation to become effective at a date, approximately March 15, when the business of the Society is at a low ebb. The Society will then receive the nomination of you for the offices, and you will be elected, to take office when my resignation becomes effective. [...]

Yours very sincerely,
Roland Kent (Kent to Bloch, March 10, 1939; BBA)

Bloch replied:

Dear Mr Kent,

Many thanks for your letter of March 10. It goes without saying, I think, that in case I should succeed you in the office of Secretary-Treasurer of the LSA I should not only be glad but very eager to get as much advice from you as you can give me concerning the job. But right now the specific proposals in your letter do not require my answer. Instead, I am still — or again — in a quandary about the whole matter. [...] What I say here is unofficial, since my appoint for next year [at Brown University] has not yet come up for final approval [...] There is, then, every chance that I will be appointed to an Assistant Professorship [...]. The terms of my appointment will be that I teach a full schedule [...] and that I shall devote all my spare time to research — that is, in this case, to editorial work on the Linguistic Atlas. [...] Ever since 1931, the Atlas has been my chief scholarly interest; and I should not like to undertake any job that would force me to skimp that. [...]

With best regards from both of us to you and Mrs Kent
Bernard Bloch (Bloch to Kent, March 12, 1939; BBA)

Kent replied on March 14, 1939 with the plea that 'I ask only that you do not decide in the negative hastily. Under the plan which I have outlined, a great deal of the work which I have been doing would remain with me, thus lightening the work of the new incumbent.'

---

[31] It was apparently taken for granted until relatively recently that an LSA officer's wife would do most of the heavy lifting. Archibald A. Hill was LSA Secretary-Treasurer between 1951 and 1968. He wrote: 'I said recently that the first requirement for a Secretary of the Society was that he have a wife like my own optima mulierum Muriela, since inevitably much of the drudgery would fall on her, which it certainly did in the nearly twenty years that I served' (Hill 1978: 36).

We do not know what went on behind the scenes for the following eight months, but somehow Bloch was now a candidate for Editor of *Language*, instead of Secretary-Treasurer: 'Dear Bernard, Sturtevant informs me that the Committee has nominated you to succeed Bolling as Editor of the publications of the Society. I know by this fact that you have consented to serve if elected' (Kent to Bloch, October 13, 1939; BBA). Bloch replied modestly that 'I sometimes doubt whether I have sufficient standing among linguists (even among younger linguists) to carry off the responsibilities of the editorship with the necessary grace and authority: it is one thing for a scholar like Bolling to reject an article, quite another thing for me to exercise the same right' (Bloch to Kent, October 14, 1939; BBA). Bloch was confirmed at the December annual meeting in Philadelphia, and by January of 1940 was deeply involved in discussing existing submissions with Bolling (Bloch to Bolling, January 4, 1940; BBA).

Cowan was nominated for Secretary-Treasurer at some point in 1940. There was by no means universal acclaim at his nomination, no doubt due to his youth and lack of experience in LSA matters. He was challenged by the well-known Indo-Europeanist George S. Lane, a challenge that left the Society deeply divided. Kent, the outgoing Secretary-Treasurer, sent to Cowan a frank, but politely worded letter:

Dear Cowan:

In all matters about the nominations for secretary-and-treasurership I have been frank with you, and I shall continue to be so. You know that I have nothing against you, and that I like your good personal and business qualities as well as your scholarly achievements. Now George S. Lane has been nominated for the Secretary-Treasurership, by the signed nomination forms which went out to the membership. There will therefore be a secret election by ballot, as the Constitution prescribes. It is only fair that you should know this. I can tell you also that in the movement for his election there has been nothing personal against you; I am without information whether any of his nominators ever met you, but am strongly of the belief that they do [*sic*] not. At any rate, their opinion is pro-Lane rather than anti-Cowan. [...] I sincerely trust that a "contested" election will not produce any rift in the Society. At the same time you will realize that members will in some cases ask me what my judgment is between you and Lane, in which event I shall have to give an answer, based on what may be called external factors, since between you two as men and scholars I can see little to make a difference.

Yours sincerely,
Roland G. Kent (Kent to Cowan, October 12, 1940; BBA)

Whatever the 'external factors' may have been, it was reported in *LSAB* 17, 1941: 31 that Cowan received 42 votes and Lane 18.

Nobody could have foreseen in 1940–1941 how Bloch and Cowan would transform the LSA. In a period of a few years, Bloch evolved from being a phonetician-cum-dialect geographer to one of the two or three leading structural linguists in the United States. Indeed, he was later called 'the truest Bloomfieldian' (Stark 1972: 387). Bloch's 'Phonemic overlapping' (Bloch 1941), *Outline of Linguistic Analysis* (Bloch & Trager 1942), 'English verb inflection (Bloch 1947a), and 'Set of postulates for phonemic analysis' (Bloch 1948) helped set the radically empiricist tone that dominated American linguistics until the mid-1950s. Immediately after the war broke out he decided to undertake the study of Japanese, partly out of personal interest and party because he knew how important knowledge of that language would be to the war effort. By 1943, the year that he moved from Brown to Yale, he was Language Director for Japanese in the Army Specialized Training Program and Civil Affairs Training Program at Yale. A series of structural analyses of Japanese followed the end of the war, including 'Studies in colloquial Japanese: II. Syntax' (Bloch 1946b), which was one of the first—as well as one of the longest—syntactic analyses within the American structuralist framework.[32]

As far as Bloch's editorship of *Language* is concerned, he established very early his total control over the journal:

> The Society elects an Editor to do a job: to publish a journal and certain other things, and to make these as good as he can. If the Society feels that the man it elected is not doing the job as well as it ought to be done, it has an effective remedy: it can elect somebody else. Beyond that, I don't think the Society can do anything whatever. Specifically, it has no right to dictate editorial policy or to interfere in any way with the Editor's execution his job.
>
> (Bloch to Kent, February 15, 1941; cited in Murray 1980: 74)

A look at the Bloch's 3×5 cards with his editorial comments (which are preserved at the LSAA) bears out the assessment that 'Bloch was in reality the only person who decided whether or not a given article or review was to appear in *Language*. He would often submit things to one member of the Editorial committee or another, or, equally often, would use someone else as a referee; but the final decision was his and his alone' (Hall 1975: 133). He would apparently accept certain submissions automatically, perhaps without having even read them: 'In passing on the contributions sent in to me for publication in the journal, my practice has been as follows. If the author of the paper is known to me as a scholar of acknowledged

---

[32] As a product of his wartime work, Bloch also coauthored two books on spoken Japanese: Bloch & Jorden (1945, 1946). According to Mary Haas, 'every Japanese who tried to teach with the book hated it' (quoted in Murray 1997: 708).

pre-eminence, or as a recognized authority in his field, I have automatically accepted the contribution, and have confined my work on it to proofreading it for
the printer' (*LSAB* 21, 1945: 13).[33]

Soon after he took office, Bloch assured the membership in a very oblique
way that he would like to see a change of direction in the contents of the
journal:

> It appears that some members of the Society regard LANGUAGE as a journal
> devoted chiefly to the ancient languages. If the distribution of articles published
> during the past few years seems to support that view, it is not through any choice
> of the Committee on Publications, but because the scholars at work in the an-
> cient languages have sent in more material than others. In order that our journal
> may more fully represent the varied interests of our membership, the Committee
> would welcome a larger number of contributions in the field of the modern lan-
> guages, especially English. Any apparent one-sidedness in LANGUAGE can only
> be corrected with the active cooperation of all our members.
>
> (*LSAB* 14, 1941: 25)

The 1940s saw a steady decline in philologically oriented articles. Bloch certainly
published articles that were not post-Bloomfieldian or neogrammarian orthodoxy (see footnote 25 for an example), but he saw to it that the most important
articles in these two closely-related approaches appeared in *Language*. Of the
34 articles reprinted in Martin Joos's post-Bloomfieldian-oriented *Readings in Linguistics: The Development of Descriptive Linguistics in America since 1925* (Joos
1957b; see Chapter 3), no less than 28 had appeared in *Language* under Bloch's
editorship. Bloch, in other words, was a major factor in the transformation of the
field of linguistics in the United States, where autonomous linguistics of the structuralist variety was predominant. Bloch himself insisted that he was unbiased and
open to all schools of linguistics:

> The papers declined in the course of these five years belong to no one 'school' of
> linguistics, represent no one approach to the goals of our science. It must be clear
> to anyone who has read the last five volumes of our journal that LANGUAGE
> has not been allowed to become the organ of any 'school' or clique. The charge,
> occasionally brought against the Committee on Publications (though never di-
> rectly), that only believers in a certain brand of psychology have any chance to
> publish in our journal, is obviously false, since the Committee cannot know, and
> does not ask, what each contributor believes in, and since one has only to read the

---

[33] See Bright (1980: 127–129) for some amusing anecdotes about Bloch's editorial style.

journal to find reflections of every kind of psychology current among productive linguists. That an editor has opinions of his own on any subject will not be held against him, so long as he does not allow them to override his judgment

(*LSAB* 21, 1945: 14)

I do not question Bloch's sincerity in the above passage. However, since by 1945 'a scholar of acknowledged pre-eminence' would most likely be one of the 'believers in a certain brand of psychology', it is not surprising that the journal took on more and more of a post-Bloomfieldian coloring in that decade.

Cowan, unlike Bloch, published very little after assuming his important LSA office. And of his few publications, none to my knowledge were enthusiastic endorsements of structural approaches to language. Cowan's role in putting post-Bloomfieldian linguistics to the fore was that of, in the words of Robert A. Hall, Jr., being an 'enabler' (quoted in Hockett 1995: 347). Cowan not only 'enabled' the field of linguistics to prosper during the Second World War by deftly seeing to it that the bulk of American linguists would be on military footing, he also made sure that it was primarily post-Bloomfieldian structuralists who would fill the most important positions in the linguistic sphere of the war effort. At the end of the war, he was named director of Cornell University's new Division of Modern Languages (later renamed the Department of Modern Languages and Linguistics), which was organized 'along the lines of applied linguistics of the ILP' (Murray 1994: 151). Virtually all of his new hires were post-Bloomfieldians, among whom were Robert A. Hall, Jr., Charles Hockett, Frederick Agard, and William Moulton. Thanks to Cowan, Cornell became the major center for structural linguistics in the United States after Yale. Cowen stepped down as Secretary-Treasurer in 1951 and received the following testimonials from Bloch and Moulton respectively:

If the Linguistic Society's national scope and influence have grown last ten years, if the Society today is vigorous and healthy, the credit for its growth and present state is largely Mr. Cowan's; and if our program of publication during this has been successful, it has been so very largely because of Mr. Cowan's enlightened support.

(*LSAB* 24, 1951: 12)

These past ten years have been critical ones in the life of our Society. Particularly during the war years, it was essential that the daily business of the Society be handled with skill, with vigor, and with foresight. In lesser hands this would have been a period of decline. The most we had any right to expect was that we should emerge unimpaired. It is an extraordinary tribute to Mr. Cowan's abilities that, far from declining or merely holding our own, we actually came out of this period stronger than ever before. We grew in numbers, in reputation, and in the scope and usefulness of our activities, both scientific and practical. For his leading part in this achievement, we express to him our heartfelt thanks.

(*LSAB* 24. 1951: 15–16)

Hockett's final tribute to Cowan emphasized his role as an enabler:

It seems to me Milt must have decided early on that, however much he might achieve in scholarly research (and he surely underestimated himself on that score), he would serve his chosen field better — and have more fun! — by pursuing a different course. In the event, his greatest strength lay in having faith in the practical relevance of linguistics, in seeing what needed to be done, in finding people who were eager and able to do it, and in smoothing the way for them. He took great pride and pleasure in the achievements of those about him, and in response to that we at Cornell (and elsewhere) were devoted to his leadership and worked very hard to be worthy of his approval. If the number of publications under his byline is small, the number of pedagogical and scientific works done under his aegis is enormous.

(Hockett 1995: 347–348)

1.6 Summary

The field of linguistics in the United States underwent a profound transformation between the 1920s and the 1940s. In the space of one generation, the predominance of philological studies gave way to structurally oriented ones. Several factors combined to drive this transformation: the sense of a distinctive field making rapid progress, the leading linguists' commitment to the equality of all languages and their analysis, the LSA's summer institutes, American linguists' involvement in the war effort in World War II, and the change of leadership in that organization in 1940–1941.

2

American structuralism and European structuralism

How they saw each other

2.1 Introduction

Aside from a fleeting reference or two, the first chapter had very little to say about the varieties of structural linguistics that were practiced in Europe between the 1920s and the 1950s.[1] But in fact, in this period a majority of the linguists in the world who identified as 'structuralist' were located in that continent. In Prague, Geneva, Copenhagen, Paris, London, and elsewhere, there were major centers of structural linguistics, each embodied with its own distinctive traits and in some cases its own academic journal. The purpose of this chapter is not to present, contrast, and evaluate the various versions of European structuralism. A number of books have appeared that do just that, and I have no desire to repeat what they have had to say (I particularly recommend Lepschy 1972). Rather, in keeping to the developments-in-America theme of this book, I focus on the reciprocal relations between American and European structuralism. That is, I examine how practitioners of the two geographical varieties of structuralism saw each other, what their mutual influences (or lack of influences) were, and how all of this changed in the time period under discussion.

The chapter is organized as follows. § 2.2 shows how indebted American linguists were to Europe in the early years of the LSA, while § 2.3 documents the Americans' increasing isolation in the following years. § 2.4 reviews European attitudes toward work carried out in the United States and § 2.5 documents the increasing American appreciation of European theorizing that began in the late 1940s. § 2.6 describes the European reaction to earliest work in generative grammar and § 2.7 the Prague School influence on American functional linguistics. § 2.8 is a brief summary.

[1] I would like to thank Stephen Anderson and Hans Basbøll for their extremely useful and detailed comments on this chapter. Julia Falk and Klaas Willems also provided valuable input.

American Linguistics in Transition. Frederick J. Newmeyer, Oxford University Press.
© Frederick J. Newmeyer (2022). DOI: 10.1093/oso/9780192843760.003.0002

2.2 The early American linguists' debt to Europe

Many American linguists in the 1920s and 1930 had European backgrounds
(§ 2.2.1), and there were particular ties to the Prague School (§ 2.2.2) and the
Geneva School and other linguists based in Switzerland (§ 2.2.3).

2.2.1 The European background of many American linguists

Until the mid-1930s or so, there was nothing particularly distinctive about American linguistics, as opposed to European linguistics. It is true that major figures in
American linguistics, such as Boas, Sapir, and Bloomfield, were strongly focused
on Amerindian languages, but then, so were many Europeans.[2] In fact, all three linguists had strong European connections: the first two named were born in Europe,
and Bloomfield had been a student there. As Table 2.1 illustrates, of the first twelve
presidents of the LSA, nine had either been born in Europe or had spent some
university time there.

Of the seven members of the LSA Executive Committee in 1936 (see Chapter 1,
§ 1.4.1), five had studied in Europe: President George Flom (Copenhagen and
Leipzig), Vice President Harold H. Bender (Berlin), Secretary and Treasurer

Table 2.1 The European background of the first LSA presidents

Year	President	Born	Studied
1925	Hermann Collitz	Germany	Germany
1926	Maurice Bloomfield	Austria-Hungary	USA
1927	Carl Darling Buck	USA	USA, Greece, Germany
1928	Franz Boas	Germany	Germany
1929	Charles H. Grandgent	USA	USA
1930	Eduard Prokosch	Austria-Hungary	Austria-Hungary
1931	Edgar H. Sturtevant	USA	USA
1932	George Melville Bolling	USA	USA
1933	Edward Sapir	Germany	USA
1934	Franklin Edgerton	USA	USA, Germany
1935	Leonard Bloomfield	USA	USA, Germany
1936	George T. Flom	USA	USA, Denmark, Germany

[2] The supposed lack of interest on the part of European linguists in American indigenous languages
has been greatly exaggerated. In 1924, the 21st International Congress of Americanists was held in two
parts, in The Hague and in Göteborg. The organizers of the first part were all Dutch, and Americans
were a fairly small part of the attendees. In fact, between the first Congress (in 1875 in Nancy) and 27th
(in 1939 in Mexico City and Lima) only three were held in the United States.

Roland G. Kent (Berlin and Munich), Executive Committee Member Samuel E. Basset (Athens), and Executive Committee Member Albrecht Goetze (Munich and Heidelberg).[3]

2.2.2 American linguists and the early Prague School

Perhaps the most influential school of European structuralists was the Prague Linguistic Circle, known more often in English as the 'Prague School'. Its founders in 1926 included the distinguished linguists Roman Jakobson, Nikolai Trubetzkoy, and Vilém Mathesius, who was its first president. The former two were pioneers in structuralist phonological studies, the latter in functionally oriented syntax. In April 1928 at the First International Congress of Linguists held in The Hague (see Chapter 1, § 1.4.1), the Prague linguists introduced a 'manifesto' outlining the tasks of phonology:

(1) To identify the characteristics of particular phonological systems, in terms of the language-particular range of significant differences; (2) To specify the types of such differences that can be found in general, and in particular to identify 'correlations', or recurrent differences that serve to characterize multiple pairs of elements (as e.g. voicing separates p from b, t from d, etc.); (3) To formulate general laws governing the relations of these correlations to one another within particular phonological systems; (4) To account for phonological change in terms of the phonological system (rather than the individual sound) that undergoes it, and especially to construe such changes as teleologically governed by considerations of the system; (5) To found phonetic studies on acoustic rather than an articulatory basis. Wording aside, this was a remarkably modern document (viewed from today's standpoint), going well beyond what American structuralists had specified in the late 1920s.

Taking into account the difficulties of inter-continental communications at the time, relations between early American structuralists and their Prague colleagues were cordial. Roman Jakobson has written:

> From the beginning there was a close connection between the Linguistic Society of America and the Prague Linguistic Circle. [...] N. S. Trubetzkoy's letters (Jakobson 1975) reveal some new data on the manifold ties between American linguists and the 'école de Prague'. At the end of 1931, Trubetzkoy, at that time immersed in the study of American Indian languages, emphasized that 'most of the American Indianists perfectly describe the sound systems, so that their outlines yield all of the essentials for the phonological characteristics of any given

---

[3] Editor of *Language* George M. Bolling completed all of his studies in the United States, but was awarded the gold cross of the Knights of the Redeemer by the Greek government in 1920 for his Homeric research (Hoenigswald 1964: 329).

language [...]'.[4] Trubetzkoy had a very high opinion of the American linguist whom he called 'my Leipzig comrade'. This was Leonard Bloomfield, who in 1913 shared a bench with Trubetzkoy and Lucien Tesnière at Leskien's and Brugmann's lectures. Bloomfield (Hockett 1970: 247) praised 'Trubetzkoy's excellent article on vowel systems' of 1929 and devoted his sagacious 1939 study on 'Menomini Morphophonemics' (Hockett 1970: 351-362) to N. S. Trubetzkoy's memory.

(Jakobson 1979: 162)

Furthermore, Robert A. Hall, Jr. notes that George Trager addressed the Yale Linguistics Club in the early 1940s on various Prague School concepts and recalls overhearing the Americans Clarence E. Parmenter, a phonetician and Manuel J. Andrade, an anthropological linguist, discuss the Prague concept of the phoneme in 1936 (Hall 1991: 160–161).

2.2.3 American linguists and the early Geneva School

I focus now on Switzerland.[5] That country is of particular interest because it was the home base of Ferdinand de Saussure, generally acknowledged as the inspiration for structuralist studies of language. His posthumous *Cours de Linguistique Générale* had been published in 1916 (Saussure 1916) and by a decade later was being heralded as a landmark work of linguistic theory, at least in Europe. Saussure's colleagues and their students had established a major school of linguistics in Geneva (henceforth the 'Geneva School') and, elsewhere in Switzerland, linguistics was thriving as well.[6] The question is to what extent Swiss linguistic research was of interest to scholars in the United States. This question is in part addressed in a noteworthy historiographical study by Julia Falk (Falk 2004), in which the author documents the lack of impact that Saussure's book had among American researchers. While it is not my intention to dispute any of Falk's findings, one might be tempted, after reading her paper, to draw the conclusion that the work of the Geneva School was either unknown to or ignored by American practitioners.

---

[4] Sapir, however, had a fairly low opinion of at least some Amerindian work carried out by Europeans (for discussion, see Andresen 1990: 237–238). He wrote, for example, that 'most of us have a shrewd suspicion that many a renowned denizen of the German universities, impressive in his balancing of imponderable phonologic nuances, would find himself sadly up a tree when confronted with the live problems of an intricate Indian language that he was forced to study by pure induction' (Sapir 1917: 79). He also had sarcastic words for *Les langues du monde* (Meillet & Cohen 1924): 'It was cruel to assign the vast field of American Indian languages to a single specialist. No one living today could even begin to get his bearings on it, let alone do justice to it' (Sapir 1925b: 375).

[5] I would like to thank Louis de Saussure and Julia Falk for their input on the material in this section.

[6] For simplicity of exposition I include the work of Saussure himself as part of the output of the 'Geneva School', even though the term was not coined (as far as I know) until after his death.

What follows is a corrective to that possible conclusion. Without wishing to exaggerate American interest, I show below that there was regular notice taken of the work of the Geneva School by American linguists in the interwar period.

A broader question also arises that is not addressed in the Falk paper: To what extent was Swiss linguistics *in general* of interest to American scholars in that time period. This question is complicated by the fact that there was not then, nor is there now, a homogenous school of linguistics in Switzerland, with uniform goals and methodologies. The linguists of Geneva did not have a great deal of contact with their co-federationists to the east. In the period under consideration, French-speaking linguists in Switzerland were best known for their grammatical and stylistic studies, while German-speaking linguists built their reputation primarily around historical linguistics and dialectology. However, I need to stress that I use the terms 'Swiss linguists' and 'Swiss linguistics' in a purely national and geographical sense, not as a reference to a particular approach to the study of language. I hope to illustrate below that there was a remarkable degree of recognition accorded to Swiss linguists by their American counterparts.

This section is organized as follows. § 2.2.3.1 reviews Falk's paper on the reception of Saussure's ideas in the United States. § 2.2.3.2 documents the references to Geneva School publications by American linguists during our time period, while § 3.2.3.3 reviews contemporary LSA recognition of the work of Swiss linguists.

2.2.3.1 Julia Falk on 'Saussure and American linguistics'

Let us begin by re-examining Falk (2004). As we have seen, the two most important American linguistic theorists in the interwar period were Edward Sapir and Leonard Bloomfield. As Falk points out, 'there is no evidence that Sapir was directly influenced by the *Cours*; he certainly never cited it in his work' (2004: 110) (but see Chapter 3, fn. 16). Nor, as far as I have been able to determine, did he cite any Geneva school linguists. Bloomfield, on the other hand, referred to the *Cours* on a number of occasions and even reviewed its second edition (though, again, there appear to be no citations to the work of other members of the Geneva School). One of Bloomfield's first references to the *Cours* was highly positive. In a review of Sapir (1921), Bloomfield (1924a: 143) remarked that the *Cours* is a book 'which gives a theoretic foundation to the newer trend of linguistic study, [...] in which restriction to historical work is [considered] unreasonable and, in the long run, methodologically impossible'. However, as Falk notes, Bloomfield's review of the *Cours* was less inclined to attribute complete originality to the ideas expressed there:

> Bloomfield [in *An Introduction to the Study of Language* = Bloomfield 1914] wrote
> of the 'social character of language' and noted that a speech utterance 'depends
> for its form entirely on the habits of the speaker, which he shares with the speech

community. These habits are in a sense arbitrary, differing for the different communities [...]' (Bloomfield 1914: 17, 81–82). It should come as no surprise, then, that when Bloomfield reviewed the second edition of Saussure's *Cours de linguistique générale* in 1924, he was to say: 'Most of what the author says has long been "in the air" and has been here and there fragmentarily expressed (Bloomfield 1924a: 318).'

(Falk 2004: 108)

Falk then points out that this 'seems to be the only review of the *Cours* published in any American journal until new editions were prepared in the second half of the twentieth century' (p. 109). She goes on: 'Bloomfield admired Saussure and on several occasions referred his readers to the *Cours*, but he did not adopt Saussurean terms. He viewed most basic Saussurean concepts as ideas that had been set forth by other, earlier scholars' (p. 111). Despite the above, in a postcard dated 15 January 1945 to J Milton Cowan, the Secretary-Treasurer of the LSA, Bloomfield wrote that '[t]here is a statement going round that de Saussure is not mentioned in my *Language* text book (which reflects his *Cours* on every page)' (Cowan 1987: 29).[7]

Finally, Falk is certainly correct when she writes that 'as in Bloomfield's own work after 1933 [the leading American linguists of the 1930s] rarely, if ever referred to Saussure or the *Cours*' (p. 112). Charles Hockett, arguably the most important American linguist between Bloomfield and Noam Chomsky, wrote to Falk that he 'didn't read the *Cours* until after [he] retired from Cornell in 1982 [...]' (quoted in Koerner 2002c: 10).

2.2.3.2 American references to the Geneva School and other Swiss-based linguistics

In this section we see that Falk's claims are in need of a bit of nuancing. The most important American-written introduction to general linguistics in the interwar years to appear after Bloomfield's *Language* (Bloomfield 1933) was Louis H. Gray's *Foundations of Language* (Gray 1939). Gray, one of the preeminent Indo-Europeanists of the period, served as LSA President in 1938. In their lengthy review of this book, Zellig S. Harris and Donald C. Swanson noted that 'Gray speaks of three aspects of language (pp. 15–18), basing himself on the langue-parole dichotomy of de Saussure and many Continental linguists' (Harris & Swanson 1940: 228). Some years earlier, in the *American Journal of Philology*, Gray had written in a review of Louis Hjelmslev's *Principes de grammaire générale* (Hjelmslev 1928) that 'Adhering in general to the principles so brilliantly enunciated by the Franco-Swiss school of de Saussure and his followers, M. Hjelmslev has not only summarized

---

[7] See (Joseph 2019) for compelling arguments that Bloomfield's remark was not intended to be interpreted ironically.

everything of importance that had previously appeared upon his theme, but has made a very appreciable advance' (Gray 1931: 77).

In fact, there were no fewer than 25 articles and reviews in *Language* between 1925 and 1940 that referred to Saussure. The majority concerned his contributions to historical linguistics, but more than a few noted the *langue-parole* distinction and other dichotomies found in the *Cours*. Saussure's synchronic work was cited in other American journals of language-related study from the period, including, as noted above, *American Journal of Philology*, and also *International Journal of American Linguistics* (Uhlenbeck 1927), *Modern Language Journal* (Bloomfield 1924a; Zipf 1938), and *Modern Philology* (Field 1927).

Other members of the Geneva School were not ignored in *Language*. For example, Henri Frei's *La grammaire des fautes* (Frei 1929) was given a highly positive review by Reinhold Eugene Saleski (Saleski 1930). Saleski informed readers that 'the Geneva School (de Saussure, Brunot, Bally, Sechehaye) is interested not in the history of language as such but in the value of language to the individual speaker and hearer and no doubt to the society concerned' (p. 91).

Charles Bally also received a mention in an article by Urban T. Holmes (Holmes 1931). Holmes was Kenan Professor of Romance Philology at the University of North Carolina and was later to become a Chevalier de la Légion d'honneur. He wrote that 'Charles Bally is not concerned with historical, only with psychological syntax, but he calls attention to a "mentalité européenne" which would account for many resemblances [between Old French and Germanic]" (p. 195).

The same issue of *Language* in which the review of Gray appeared saw a review by Holmes (Holmes 1940) of *Mélanges Bally* (Faculté des lettres de l'Université de Genève 1939). His wording suggests that the readers of *Language* had at least basic familiarity with Geneva School contributions:

> When G[eorges] Gougenheim wrote his survey of current tendencies in the field of French syntax he did not attach much importance to the Genevan school of Saussure and Bally; he emphasized rather the disciples of [Adolf] Tobler and Karl Vossler in Germany, and the work of [Ferdinand] Brunot and Lucien Foulet in France [...] The methodology of the Genevan school was made generally accessible in 1916 when Bally, Albert Sechehaye, and Riedlinger issued Saussure's *Cours de linguistique générale*. Since then, Bally's publications, including his numerous articles, and H. Frei's *Grammaire des fautes* (1929) have elaborated and crystallized the concepts and the terminology. [...] Saussure emphasizes the law of opposition: such a word as *paperasse* retains additional meanings because *papier* exists beside it [...] In opposition to von Wartburg, A. Sechehaye states that synchronic study is more basic than diachronic, though he admits that Saussure was overemphatic in insisting on the absolute separation of the two.
>
> (Holmes 1940: 237–240)

The fact that many American linguists had European backgrounds facilitated the transmission of ideas developed by European linguists to their New World counterparts. As one example, Alfred Senn, who served on the LSA Executive Committee in 1939, was born in Switzerland and early in his career taught at the University of Lithuania, where he built a reputation as the world's leading Lithuanian dialectologist.[8] Senn moved to the United States in 1930. Given his Swiss roots it is not surprising to find an article written by him in a major American journal that begins with a reference to a member of the Geneva School:

> The Swiss scholar, Charles Bally, in his book *Le langage et la vie* [*Language and Life*], second edition (Zurich: Max Niehans, 1935), makes the statement: 'La linguistique a été un art avant d'être une science' [before becoming a science, linguistics was an art]. It was a branch of practical learning studied for the purpose of acquiring efficiency in speech and writing. Up to the beginning of the nineteenth century, when the turn toward a new attitude in regard to language took place, language had never been the object of research interested only in language as such. Bally does not condemn the work of the earlier philologists, although he is outspoken in his opinion that the modern method of linguistic study constitutes a decided advance over the methods previously employed.
>
> (Senn 1937: 501)

2.2.3.3 LSA recognition of Swiss linguistics

We now turn to the significant degree of recognition accorded to Swiss linguists in the interwar period by the LSA. The highest recognition that the Society can give to a foreign scholar is that of 'Honorary Member'. As stated in the first constitution of the LSA:

> Any foreign scholar of distinction in linguistic studies, not resident in North America, may be elected an Honorary Member, by a five-sixths vote of the Society in its annual business session, provided such scholar has received the recommendation of the Executive Committee. Not more than six honorary members shall be elected at the first election, and thereafter not more than three in any one year. The total number of honorary members shall not exceed twenty-five.
>
> (*LSAB* 3, 1927: 65)

Of the six chosen at the first election, two were Swiss. One was the Indo-Europeanist Jakob Wackernagel, who was born, spent most of his career, and died in Basel. The other, Albert Debrunner, was also an Indo-Europeanist. He too was born in Basel and at the time of his election was a professor at Jena in Germany.

---

[8] In 1930 the University of Lithuania was renamed 'Vytautas Magnus University'.

However, he returned to his native country in 1935, teaching in Bern until his 1954 retirement. Both linguists were effusive in their gratitude for the honor (*LSAB* 3, 1927: 154–155):

> In your letter of January 20th you informed me that the Linguistic Society of America has named me an honorary member. Please convey to the Society my heartfelt thanks for this honor. I treasure it highly that a circle of distinguished scholars considers me worthy of such recognition and I will continue to study the rich publications of the Society as a grateful reader. Very honored colleague, I thank you once again for your kind communication concerning my appointment [...] (J. Wackernagel).[9]
>
> To my great astonishment I received from you the friendly message that I have been named an honorary member of the Linguistic Society of America. I must admit openly to you that I am rather overwhelmed to be considered an equal to people like [...] For this reason, I feel even more honored by this appointment, and my gratitude for it is even greater. I ask you to convey my feelings to your Society along with the promise that I always hold this association with the Society in high esteem and will always feel united with it in the scientific goals that we hold in common ...] (A. Debrunner)[10]

In 1936, the Indogermanische Gesellschaft, headed by Debrunner, was named an 'Associated Society' of the LSA. The only other society at the time to have received such recognition was the Société Linguistique de Paris.

The Second International Congress of Linguists (ICL) was held in Geneva from August 25 to August 29, 1931. For the LSA and its members it was an important event. The Society was represented by three delegates: George M. Bolling, Carl D. Buck, and Franklin Edgerton (LSA President in 1934). Seven other members made the time-consuming trans-Atlantic journey: Kemp Malone (LSA President in 1944), Earle Brownell Babcock, David Simon Blondheim, William Edward

---

[9] In the original German: 'In Ihrem Schreiben vom 20. Januar teilen Sie mir mit, dass die Linguistic Society of America mich zu einem Honorary Member ernannt hat. Wollen Sie der Gesellschaft meinen ergebenen Dank für diese Ehrung übermitteln. Ich schätze es sehr von einem Kreise trefflicher Gelehrten einer solchen Anerkennung gewürdigt zu werden, und werde fortfahren die lehrreichen Publikationen der Gesellschaft als ein dankbarer Leser zu studieren. Ihnen, sehr geehrter Herr Kollege, danke ich noch besonders für die freundliche Mitteilung über die Umstände meiner Ernennung [...] (J. Wackernagel)'.

[10] In the original German: 'Zu meinem grossen Erstaunen erhielt ich von Ihnen die freundliche Mitteilung, dass ich von der Linguistic Society of America zum Ehrenmitglied ernannt worden bin, und ich gestehe Ihnen offen, dass mich dabei die Gleichstellung mit Leuten wie [...] etwas bedrückt. Umsomehr fühle ich mich durch diese Ernennung hochgeehrt und umso lebhafter ist mein Dank dafür. Ich bitte Sie, diese meine Gefühle Ihrer Gesellschaft zu übermitteln zugleich mit dem Versprechen, dass ich diese Verbindung mit der Linguistic Society allzeit hochhalten und mich in den gemeinsamen wissenschaftlichen Zielen mit ihr eins fühlen werde [...] (A. Debrunner)'.

Collinson, Sanki Ichikawa, Ephraim Cross, and August Gunther. As reported in *LSAB* 7, 1931: 289:

> No attempt to appraise the achievements of the Congress can be made before the publication of its Acts; but it may be said in general that the program was most attractive. Its richness, indeed, was its only drawback; for it was of course physically impossible to hear all the papers, and it was only with regret that one missed those which it was necessary to forego. But what was one to do when, for instance, the following papers were being read at the same hour: Mlle. E[lise] Richter: Die Einheitlichkeit der Hervorhebungsabsicht und die Mannigfaltigkeit ihrer Auswirkungen; E[duard] Hermann: Die Lautgesetze; A[lfons] Nehring: Sprachwissenschaftliche Palaeontologie; Z. Blesse: Zum sprachlichen Ausdruck der abstrakten Begriffe im Lettischen; G. Piccoli: Metodo etimologico-combinatorio per l'interpretazione dei testi etruschi.

The review in *LSAB* concludes (p. 290):

> There must be added an expression of admiration for the work of the Organizing Committee [headed by Charles Bally and Albert Sechehaye, — (FJN)], thanks to which a large and complicated meeting was handled most smoothly and efficiently. One wishes also to speak with gratitude of the warm welcome and lavish hospitality that made one's sojourn in Geneva a thing of joy. Most especially to be recalled in this connection is the reception tendered to Members of the Congress by Madame Ferdinand de Saussure in her castle of Vufflens-sur-Morges.

Two of the American LSA-member attendees at the second ICL, Babcock and Collinson, were active members of the International Auxiliary Language Association, Inc. (IALA). And herein lies another American-Swiss linguistic connection (see Falk 1995 for discussion). The LSA and the IALA were founded the same year (1924) and had overlapping memberships. At the time it was considered quite a respectable occupation for professional linguists to propose and refine artificially constructed languages designed for universal use. The IALA was founded by the wealthy Americans Alice Vanderbilt Morris and her husband Dave Hennen Morris; its first president was Babcock (for a portrait of A. V. Morris, see Falk 1999: 31–92). Mrs. Morris the previous year had organized and funded the Meeting of Linguistic Research in Geneva held from March 20 to April 2, 1930, at which both Babcock and Collinson were present. Also at that IALA meeting were the Swiss Charles Bally, Albert Debrunner, Albert Sechehaye, and Otto Funke, along with other European linguists, including Otto Jespersen, who served as chair. While none of the latter, with the exception of Jespersen (see Jespersen 1928), ever, to my knowledge, joined the international auxiliary language movement, one assumes that at both Geneva meetings, there was ample opportunity for productive intellectual exchange among the linguists from the two countries.[11]

As noted in Chapter 1, § 1.5.3, Swiss linguists also played an important role in the 1931 LSA-sponsored Linguistic Institute, where Swiss dialectologists Jakob Jud and Paul Schuermeier offered a course on the preparation of linguistic atlases. Another Swiss linguist on the faculty at that Institute was Alfred Senn (see above), who gave courses entitled 'Church Slavonic' and 'Comparative Grammar of the Baltic Languages'. At the 1930 Institute he had been 'Docent in Indo-European Linguistics' (*LSAB* 6, 1930: 9) and at the 1931 Institute both he and Jud gave evening public lectures (*LSAB* 8, 1932: 15).

2.3 The American structuralists' turn away from Europe

By the early 1940s, American structural linguists had, by and large, stopped looking to Europe for intellectual inspiration. Contributing factors were the American structuralists' view of science (§ 2.3.1) and the effects of the Second World War (§ 2.3.2).

2.3.1 The American structuralists' view of science and its consequences

By the early 1940s, American structuralists had turned sour on the work of their European counterparts. As Einar Haugen put it: 'During the first quarter century of the LSA, there was a strong drift away from the European moorings' (Haugen 1979: 1). The main reason, at least at first, was the increasingly positivistic outlook of the former, leading to greater and greater divergence between the Americans and the Europeans. Never beholden to empiricist methodological constraints, the linguists of the Prague School, in particular Roman Jakobson, were developing an approach that had no reservations about hypothesizing any number of abstract constructs. They also laid the groundwork for functionalist approaches to language with the concept of 'functional sentence perspective'. To American linguists at the time all of this seemed hopelessly fuzzy. As Henry A. Gleason recalled: 'The popular wisdom [among Americans] was that some European linguists sat in their offices and dreamed up theory, often totally detached from reality of any kind' (Gleason 1988: 6). Along the same lines, Joseph Greenberg wrote:

> To a neophyte like me, American structural linguistics with its claims to rigorous scientific methodology and definitions of basic units of language without recourse

---

[11] Interestingly, Ferdinand de Saussure's brother, René de Saussure, was an important figure in the international auxiliary language movement (for discussion, see Joseph 2012, Chapter 16).

to meaning, was naturally enough, enormously impressive. In contrast, Prague linguistics seemed impressionistic and lacking in scientific rigor.

(Greenberg 1994: 22)

Not all of Prague linguistics was 'lacking in scientific rigor', by any imaginable standards. After all, acoustic phonetic research was high on their agenda. But:

Even the most patently 'scientific' (because highly technological) aspect of Jakobson's position — the appeal to data from acoustic research, which had progressed greatly by the end of the 1940s — was widely considered illicit [by Americans]. This was because of the use he made of it: in proposing a universal system of phonological description founded on properties that could be defined independent of particular languages, Jakobson threatened the position of presuppositionless, fundamentally agnostic analysis that many believed was essential to objective linguistic description.

(Anderson 2021: 138)

But there was more to the American isolationism with respect to Europe than differing views of science (and, of course, the general isolationism that characterized America at the time). American linguists felt that they *didn't need* Europe, because they had worked out the basic principles of structural linguistics on their own:

We do not know when the close-knit membership of the LSA — inhospitable to European theory — began to realize that Bloomfield had given them a wholly American and wholly explicit linguistic theory. We do, however, know that they could talk about nothing else at the half dozen Linguistic Institutes preceding World War II; and, more importantly, they could talk to Bloomfield who was present at every one of these LIs.

(Voegelin & Voegelin 1963: 20)

American structuralists were baffled by what seemed to them as an almost mystical European obsession with the *langue-parole* distinction. To the Americans, *langue* was no more than the result of the set of operations that might be performed on parole, and therefore not of special interest:

The separatism we are discussing [between US and European linguistics] dates from the spread of Saussure's influence in Europe, which was not matched in this country. For this there is a simple reason: we had our own giants, Boas, Sapir, and Bloomfield (Hockett 1952c: 86). Newer European contributions have been read with little sympathy and less understanding (p. 90) [...] The outstanding example [are debates over] the *langue* and *parole* problem. [...] The average American linguist is either unimpressed or else actively repelled [...]

(Hockett 1952c: 90)

Hockett went on: '[t]he terms "language" and "speech" can well enough be used: "speech" is behavior, "language" is habits. Perhaps, indeed, this is what Saussure meant — but if not, it is what we should mean when *we* use the terms at all' (p. 99; emphasis in original).

It is true that some European linguists attempted to minimize the differences in world view between the Americans and the Europeans at that time. For example, the Geneva School linguist Robert Godel wrote that there is 'no reason to contrast "Saussurean linguistics" with "American linguistics"' (Godel 1966: 480). I tend to agree with the following rebuke to Godel: 'Intellectual influence and a common ground there certainly is, but there has also been conscious opposition. A contemporary observer, Harold Whitehall, referred to "[...] the depressing and sometimes hysterical conflict between the "Americanist" and "Prague" schools [...]" (Whitehall 1944: 675)' (Hymes & Fought 1981: 14).

By the mid-1940s, 'It can almost be said that there was no desire to know Europeans. The Americans had been hurt in their pride by the European supremacy in certain domains. The world being split in two by the war, they took advantage of the opportunity to ignore for years the existence of European thinking and to assert their independence from Europe' (Martinet 1974: 222). Along these lines, Martinet offered the opinion:

> The Americans obstructed everything; they were very happy that there was a war that prevented the Europeans from coming and pestering them. One must say that the Europeans in America were insufferable; they arrived and they considered the Americans wretched, and the Americans were understandably not happy about that. They were very happy to be free from the Europeans, from European pressure. There were all these émigrés, in general European Jews, Germans, who had every reason to get out.
>
> (quoted from an interview in Chevalier & Encrevé 2006: 57–58)[12]

The anti-European feeling among American structuralists accelerated with Bernard Bloch taking over the editorship of *Language* in 1940. As noted in

---

[12] In the original French: 'Les Américains bloquaient tout; ils étaient contents d'avoir une guerre qui empêchait les Européens de venir leur casser les pieds. Il faut dire que les Européens en Amérique étaient insupportables; ils arrivaient, il considéraient les Américains comme de pauvers types; et les Américains n'étaient pas contents, à juste titre. Ils étaient très contents d'être libérés des Européens, de la pression européenne. Il y avait tous ces émigrés, en general des Juifs européens, allemands, qui avaient toutes sortes de raisons de s'en aller de chez eux.'

Chapter 1, § 1.5.5, Bloch's editorial practice was to favor American-style (post-Bloomfieldian) structuralism and neogrammarian historical linguistics over alternative approaches, in particular those emanating from Europe. Roman Jakobson submitted two papers to *Language* and both were rejected. In 1940, when he was in exile in Sweden, he sent Bloch an article entitled 'Les lois phoniques du langage enfantin et leur place dans la linguistique générale'. Bloch's 3×5 note card on the submission reads as follows:

> Rec. 17 Dec. 40 (via Sergius Yakobson, c/o Dr. Friedland, Woodbine, N. J.). — Not a member — Read 4 Jan 41: utter drivel! Sent to G. L. Trager same day, with letter q.v. — Trager concurs fully: balderdash; E. H. Sturtevant suggests that I return the MS with a general statement that it is not according to the taste of the American Public'. — MS back 14 Jan. — Returned 19 Jan.
>
> (LSAA)

This paper was a shorter version of what to become his celebrated book *Kindersprache, Aphasie und allgemeine Lautgesetze* (Jakobson 1941), a pioneering work that attempted to relate child language, speech disorders, and principles of phonology. And a few years later, 'Bloch had rejected an article about poetry (written by Jakobson) insisting that such poetic study was not within the science of language' (Pike 1994: 39–40).[13] In fact, no article by Jakobson appeared in *Language* until 1966, the year William O. Bright took over as editor.

Reviews of European work continued to appear in *Language*, but they were overwhelmingly negative. For example, Zellig Harris in 1941 reviewed Trubetzkoy's *Grundzüge der Phonologie* and wrote:

> The Prague School terminology [...] has two dangers: First it gives the impression that there are two objects of possible investigation, the Sprechakt (speech) and the Sprachgebilde (language structure), whereas the latter is merely the scientific arrangement of the former'.
>
> (Harris 1941: 345)

That same year George Trager reviewed Louis Hjelmslev's *La Catégorie des Cas* and wrote that he couldn't understand what a 'general category of case might be', since his operationalist methodology wouldn't allow the idea of any universal categories (Trager 1941: 172).

Even Leonard Bloomfield, who, along with other American linguists of his generation, tended to respect European scholarship, could not help making a thinly veiled barb at the European practice of forming 'schools' of thought:

---

[13] However no submission meeting this description appears on any of Bloch's 3×5 cards. Perhaps Bloch discouraged Jakobson from even sending the paper to him.

It may not be altogether wrong to say that the existence of the Linguistic Society has saved us from the blight of the odium theologicum and the postulation of 'schools'. When several American linguists find themselves sharing some interest or opinion, they do not make it into a King Charles's head, proclaiming themselves a 'school' and denouncing all persons who disagree or who merely choose to talk about something else.

(Bloomfield 1946: 3)

Hockett (1952c) agreed, claiming that no American journal could conceivably be called the 'Leonard Bloomfield Bulletin', analogously to the Swiss publication *Cahiers Ferdinand de Saussure*. I can easily imagine the outrage among European structuralists on reading these assertions by Bloomfield and Hockett. In their eyes their American colleagues were far more dogmatic and closed-minded than they were. I agree with Peter Matthews that the post-Bloomfieldians constituted 'very much a school, and one that had become inward-looking' (Matthews 1993: 18).

Negative attitudes toward European scholarship in general continued to be expressed until well into the 1950s, as the following quotations illustrate:

[...] socially biased value judgments which European scholarship has inherited from the aristocratic, theological background of mediaeval and Renaissance intellectualism.

(Hall 1946: 33–34)[14]

Thus we hear the term *scientific* applied to unprovable speculation; e.g. [...], to much of European structural studies (with their concepts of neutralization in their analyses of concepts of cases).

(Smith 1950: 5)

[This book] exhibits the usual kind of European philosophizing on the basis of insufficient evidence

(Trager 1950a: 100)

As one further sign of the changing times, as mentioned in § 2.2.1 in 1936 five of the seven LSA Executive Committee had been born in Europe and five had studied there. There were eight members of the Executive Committee in 1946. Not a single one was either born in Europe or had studied there.

---

[14] In a reply to Hall, Leo Spitzer accused Hall of wanting to set up an 'Academic FBI' (Spitzer 1946: 499).

2.3.2 The Second World War and the two-dollar bill conspiracy

Refugee scholars from Europe started arriving in the United States in the 1930s, an influx which continued after the outbreak of the war. Their arrival had short term effects, which were largely negative in terms of the relationships between American and European linguists. At first, American academics saw the Europeans as a threat to their own well-being:

> However, the strong anti-European feeling of many American linguists in the 1930s and 1940s had its main roots in often-times bitter personal experiences. Not a few young Americans saw, and frequently more than once, positions (for which they had been trained and were eminently qualified) snatched from under their noses and given to European refugees. Such a reaction, though by no means generous, was easily understandable in the days of the depression when any job at all was hard to come by, especially since American scholars, then as now, were not protected by citizenship requirements of the kind prevailing in virtually all European university systems. A frequent remark heard from [many leading American linguists] was 'We'll show those Europeans we have something they never dreamed of'.
>
> (Hall 1969: 194)

A few years later, Jakobson strongly rebuked Hall:

> Bloomfield particularly despised chauvinistic protectionists,[15] who launched quasi-ideological arguments in order to repress the competition of foreign linguistics and to gain for native American academic positions which might otherwise be 'snatched from under their noses and given to European refugees' as was so bluntly avowed by Robert A. Hall, Jr. in order to justify 'the strong anti-European feeling' of his comrades.
>
> (Jakobson 1973: 17–18)

Not all European refugee scholars were felt to be unwelcome, though many (probably most) were:

> [The] cultural divorce [between Americans and Europeans] related to World War II [...] had its human dimension. European linguists who came to the shores of America between 1935 and 1950, usually in a state of anguish and distress, in some instances received a warm welcome (I am thinking of Albert Götze and Eva

---

[15] William Moulton could 'remember all too vividly how Jakobson's teachings were roundly condemned by an influential cabal of autochthonous and lately naturalized linguists. [...] As for Bloomfield, he was incensed. Though he could be very biting on paper, this was the only time that I ever saw him truly angry in person' (Moulton to Sebeok, May 22, 1978; TSA).

Fiesel, among many peers), while in others they were exposed to a politely cool reception and in some others encountered aloofness or downright repudiation. They certainly were no longer lionized in any quarters.

(Malkiel 1979: 113)

Allan Walker Read was later to write that 'We felt that we were carrying on an American-based linguistics and were not cordial to the intrusion of certain refugee scholars. This was resented by some of them, who felt that they were superior to American scholarship. Especially difficult to deal with was Roman Jakobson, who seemed to us at that time to be overbearing and self-aggrandizing' (Read 1991: 282). And according to Thomas Sebeok:

> Jakobson's teachings [...] were roundly condemned by an influential cabal of au-tochthonous and lately-naturalized linguists — mostly a generation or two older than mine — clustering around 165 Broadway. [...] In truth, these men were mostly misguided chauvinists, afflicted with a hubris doubtless induced by pres-sures and fears of an uncertain military conflict in the backdrop. Regrettably, the behavior of this small but powerful clique — which caused Jakobson and his friends untold anguish, to say nothing of economic loss — left a sinister stain on the otherwise magnificent tapestry of achievements of American linguistics in the 1940s. Fortunately, this dark episode was transpierced by brilliant shafts of light emanating from giants like Boas and Bloomfield; their instant appreciation for Jakobson's decisive presence must be allowed to compensate for all the rest, which had better stay buried with other, similarly motivated, wartime debris.[16]
>
> (Sebeok 1977: 416)

Jakobson's arrival in New York in 1941 triggered the most despicable incident in the history of American linguistics, namely 'the two-dollar bill conspiracy'. John Kepke, a minor figure in the field, but one of the occupants of 165 Broadway, passed around some two-dollar bills to his colleagues there. (The two-dollar bill has long been considered unlucky and is rarely seen anymore.)

> The two dollars were to be a contribution towards paying the fare of Jakobson and the others back to Europe on the first cattle boat *after the war was over*. Kepke went around the office with the two-dollar-bill, but without great success. I refused to sign it, and no-one in the 'Reverse English' section was willing to do so, nor (as far as I can gather) were many others outside of Kepke's small clique. When I saw the bill, it had perhaps five or six names on it. This was in reality a minor office prank, in extremely bad taste, and not representing the attitude of the 165

---

[16] For some concrete examples on the part of Boas and Bloomfield to aid Jakobson, see § 2.5.1.

Broadway linguists as a group. [...] [H]owever, it contributed to intensified ill feeling on the part of Jakobson and his followers.

(Hall 1991: 162; emphasis in original)

One of the signers on the two-dollar-bill was Charles Hockett. He attempted to justify his signing in the following way:

> In after-hour bar sessions and evening get-togethers of our group, the resentment [against Jakobson and other émigré scholars] came to be concretized, some time early in 1943, in the form of a two-dollar bill club. Each 'member' had a two-dollar bill, on which all 'members' signed their names; the avowed 'purpose' was to pay for Jakobson's return to Europe on the first available cattle boat. I should not really have to add that all of this was intended purely for internal consumption. It was a metaphor designed as a basis for communion and mutual commiseration. Anyone in the group would have stood aghast at the notion of really delivering anyone into the clutches of the Nazis. That was so obvious to all of us that it never had to be said. I will not name 'members' of the club other than myself (most of the others are dead by now). [...] To the best of my belief, neither our 165 Broadway group nor anyone of those in or close to it was at any time in any position either to promote Jakobson's search for a decent academic appointment in this country or to stand in the way of such an appointment.
>
> (Hockett to Morris Halle, February 22, 1989; TSA)

Thomas Sebeok was cc'ed on Hockett's letter to Halle. In a reply to Hockett, after dismissing the latter's outrage at various interpretations of forty-five-year-old events in the field, Sebeok concluded his letter by writing: 'Where was your moral indignation when you, in the uniform of the U. S. Army, signed John Kepke's notorious "two-dollar bill"?' (Sebeok to Hockett, March 3, 1989; TSA). Another signatory of the two-dollar bill was Norman McQuown: 'Michael Silverstein, of the University of Chicago, in an email message (of February 28, 2004) referring to Hall's "lurid details of the $2.00-note incident," added that "Norman McQuown showed the artefact around our Monday lunch table some years back, by the way; it's the genuine article"' (Dixon 2007: 439).

2.4 European views of American linguistics

An interesting question is what European linguists thought about what was going on in the United States during the heyday of American structuralism. If we're talking about the period up to about 1950, the answer is 'probably not much, though there are conflicting views on the question'. In the 1930s and 1940s citations in European work to American structuralism were few and far between, and were mostly references in passing to Sapir and Bloomfield. Koerner (1984: xxi), for example, is aware of only three European reviews of Sapir's *Language*. Charles Bally, a leading member of the Geneva School, first published his *Linguistique générale et linguistique française* in 1932, though revised editions kept appearing until the late 1940s (see, for example, Bally 1965 [1932]). Even in the later editions, no American linguists are mentioned. Hall (1951–1952) asserted that Bloomfield was not just unknown, but also untranslated in Europe. This assertion is reinforced by the comment that 'Jakobson thinks that Trubetzkoy probably never read Bloomfield's *Language*; he did not read it himself before coming to America' (cited as a personal communication in Kilbury 1976: 126).

On the other hand, Eramian (1988) has documented at length the considerable degree to which the Prague School linguists were familiar with the work of Edward Sapir. For example, as early as 1926 Vilém Mathesius wrote approvingly of Sapir's 'Sound patterns in language' paper (Sapir 1925a), noting Sapir's 'theory about the special grouping of sounds which is individual for each language and which depends not on their phonetic similarity, but on their function in a given language' (Mathesius 1926: 39). Trubetzkoy maintained a lengthy and productive correspondence with Sapir, though most letters have unfortunately not been preserved. However, some appear in Jakobson (1975), where the deep respect that the two linguists had for each other is made evident.

By and large European linguists were dismissive of the post-Bloomfieldian zeal for attempting to construct theories of grammar where meaning was considered peripheral, if it was considered at all. Zellig Harris, in particular, was the subject of scorn. The following passage from a historiography of linguistics conveys a very typical European sentiment:

> Some American linguists on the other hand have gone much further and indulged in speculations that are divorced from reality. The analytic method of Z. S. Harris for example is a logico-mathematical construction lacking firm foundation. He deliberately restricted his research to questions of distribution, [...] thereby eliminating the meaning of words from his analysis, as B. Bloch and G. Trager had done before him. One wonders what happens, with this purely mechanical procedure, when the criterion of distribution is considered to be the only relevant one, to the expressive, stylistic, and other variants that are of prime importance in communication amongst human beings.
>
> (Leroy 1967 [1963]: 80)

But little by little 'international relations' among linguists began to change. A watershed event in European–American relations was the publication of Roman Jakobson's 'Russian conjugation' paper in 1948 (Jakobson 1971c [1948]). His debt to Bloomfield is explicit throughout the paper. For example:

In the stimulating chapter 'Morphology' of Bloomfield's *Language*, the way has been indicated: 'When forms are partially similar, there may be a question as to which one we had better take as the underlying form, and ... the structure of the language may decide this question for us, since, taking it one way, we get an unduly complicated description, and, taking it the other way, a relatively simple one' (13.9). Following Bloomfield's suggestions, we would say that 'the simple and natural description is to take as a starting-point' the non-truncated stem from which we can easily infer the truncated alternant as well as the use of each. If, on the contrary, we took the truncated stem as our basic form, we would be unable to predict the corresponding full-stem and we 'would have to show by elaborate lists' what phonemes are added.

(Jakobson 1971c [1948]: 166–167).

Jakobson's 'Russian conjugation' paper, like Bloomfield's "Menomini morpho-phonemics" (Bloomfield 1939a; see various sections of Chapter 4), presents a set of rules mapping a morphophonemic representation onto a phonemic one, although unlike in Bloomfield's, no special morphophonemic elements are posited. Jakobson derives most of the superficial complexity of the Russian conjugation system by positing a single underlying stem for each verb along with a set of rules that allow each surface stem and desinence to be derived. Jakobson's endeavor was a more modest one than Bloomfield's in two crucial respects. While Bloomfield posited rules *for the Menomini language,* Jakobson's were focused on a circum-scribed subpart of Russian. As a result, he did not state them with full generality. For example, several rules that he discusses, such as the vowel/zero alternation, substantive softening, and bare softening, occur elsewhere in Russian, yet they are stated in their verbal environments only. Furthermore, 'Russian conjugation' lacks the attention to rule ordering of 'Menomini morphophonemics'. There are instances, for example, of one rule being presented after another, even though the correct derivation demands its prior application.

The most noteworthy feature of 'Russian conjugation', from the point of view of linguistic historiography, is its 'un-Jakobsonianness'. For one thing, Jakobson seems to have had in general little interest in morphophonemics, and when he did treat such phenomena it was as a subpart of morphology. Only in his work on Gilyak (Jakobson 1971b [1957]) do we find anything resembling the rule-centered analysis presented in 'Russian conjugation'. Jakobson had little interest in rule systems in general—to him, categories and their contrasts were paramount in language. The indirect evidence points to Jakobson not considering the paper very important. While it triggered a dozen imitations from his students—one for each Slavic language—Jakobson himself gave the paper only a couple brief pub-lished references in the remaining 34 years of his career. Jakobson's own student, Michael Shapiro, felt the need to criticize the paper for ignoring the principles that he had learned from his teacher. Shapiro condemned "Russian conjugation" for valuing 'descriptive economy [as] a legitimate surrogate for explanation' (Shapiro 1974: 31).

It is worth asking why Jakobson wrote the 'Russian conjugation' paper. Halle (1988) suggests that it arose from discussions that Jakobson carried on with Bloomfield between 1944 and 1946. Jakobson was impressed with Bloomfield's *Spoken Russian* text, produced for the war effort (Lesnin, Petrova, & Bloomfield 1945), and suggested that the two collaborate on a Russian grammar. Bloomfield was constantly in contact with Jakobson for comments, suggestions, and examples. He tried hard to get Jakobson to write a descriptive grammar of Russian, perhaps in part to help establish credentials that would get him a job. While the grammar never materialized, the 'Russian conjugation' paper shows the unmistakable imprint of Bloomfield's influence. Bloomfield is the only linguist Jakobson refers to in the paper (other than himself).

Given that the paper grew out of the idea of a pedagogical grammar of Russian, it is not surprising that its goals seem more applied than theoretical. This interpretation seems to be supported by Jakobson's remarks in the conclusion. Rather than summarizing its theoretical import, he focuses entirely on the paper's relevance for pedagogy. The paper concludes: 'The rules formulated above allow the student [...] to deduce [the] whole conjugation pattern [...]. And these rules could be presented in a popular form for teaching purposes' (162–163).

By the 1950s, European knowledge of (if not approval of) American work had grown by leaps and bounds. The British phonetician-phonologist Daniel Jones in his overview of work on the nature of the phoneme (Jones 1950) showed himself to be quite knowledgeable about American contributions, while Cantineau (1952) gave a very extensive survey of American structuralist research. The encyclopedic overview of structuralism by André Martinet asserted that 'It is interesting to note that, in spite of profound theoretical divergences. there is a considerable amount of practical agreement among structuralists, [...]' (Martinet 1953: 575) and took the position that the three major structuralist schools were located in Prague, Yale, and Copenhagen. The leading British linguist in this period was J. R. Firth. His collected papers from 1934 to 1951 (Firth 1957) contain only scattered references to American work. He was critical of both Sapir's and Bloomfield's approach to meaning and of the latter's behaviorism. He saw American linguistics as developing out of the need to study indigenous languages and mentioned 'Boas, Sapir, Hoijer, and others' for their Amerindian work (p. 172). The Swedish structuralist Bertil Malmberg (1964 [1959]) discussed the internal diversity within American structuralism, and, as we will see in Chapter 3, § 3.7.4, E. M. Uhlenbeck castigated Martin Joos for not giving any space in his reader to the less positivist approaches within American linguistics. Finally, the Danish linguist Knud Togeby cited American work extensively in his *Structure immanente de la langue française* (Togeby 1965 [1951]).

Each of the European structuralist schools had its own journal or one that it published in regularly, including *Travaux du Cercle Linguistique de Prague* (1929–1939; Prague), *Acta Linguistica* (1939–present; Copenhagen—now *Acta Linguistica Hafniensia*), *Cahiers Ferdinand de Saussure* (1941–present; Geneva), *Bulletin de la Société Linguistique de Paris* (1869–present; Paris), and *Transactions of the Philological Society* (1854–present; London). It is interesting to review their pages to see how much American work was presented and how it was treated.[17] Let's begin with *Cahiers Ferdinand de Saussure*. No American work was cited before 1945. In that year the journal published an article by Thomas Sebeok on Finnish vowel assimilation (Sebeok 1945). In 1946 Thomas Godel reviewed a book of his (Sebeok 1946), noting that he was inspired by Roman Jakobson. A few years later, an article by the British linguist C. E. Bazell (Bazell 1949) cited several post-Bloomfieldian publications, including Bloch (1947b), Pittmann (1948), and Nida (1948b). American work was cited regularly in the *Cahiers* after that year.

1949 turned out to be a watershed year for European interest in American theorizing. That year the journal *Lingua* was founded by the Dutch linguists Anton Reichling and E. M. Uhlenbeck. It was almost as if the mission of *Lingua* was to acquaint Europeans with American research. The first volume had no fewer than eight articles that cited American linguists. And the second volume contained an article by Eli Fischer-Jørgensen, whose entire basis was glowing praise for Kenneth Pike's analysis of English intonation (Fischer-Jørgensen 1949). In the same issue appeared an article by the Norwegian-American linguist Einar Haugen (Haugen 1949) and one by Uhlenbeck on the structure of the Javanese morpheme that showed profound knowledge of work carried out on the other side of the Atlantic:

> In the United States, finally, morphonology has during the last ten years become the centre of the attention of those linguists who have been strongly influenced by Bloomfield. In a series of articles in the journal *Language* several linguists who for the most part seem to have been in close contact with one another, have tried, starting from Bloomfield's definition of the morpheme, to develop a theory of morpheme-analysis which was more satisfactory than what could be found about this in *Language*. On the whole they confined themselves to working out and systematizing Bloomfield's views, at the same time removing a few inconsistencies.
>
> (Uhlenbeck 1949: 246)

Aside from Bloomfield, the article cited Harris, Hockett, Bloch, Voegelin, Wells, and Nida. From the 1950s on, *Lingua* has regularly published work by American scholars, including (after 1957) articles devoted to generative grammar.

---

[17] I would very much have liked to present the material in *Travaux du Cercle Linguistique de Prague*. However, COVID-19 restrictions prevented me from leafing through its pages in my university library and I have been unable to locate online versions of the journal.

2.5 The American rediscovery of European linguistics

Beginning in the mid-1940s, American linguists began to warm up to work carried out in Europe. The presence of European refugee linguists in the United States led to more familiarity with European theorizing (§ 2.5.1) and, eventually, to a greater appreciation of this theorizing (§ 2.5.2).

2.5.1 Roman Jakobson, the École Libre des Hautes Études, and the founding of *Word*

Not all American linguists were opposed to Roman Jakobson's presence in the United States. Indeed, some went out of their way to welcome him and help him to find work. Foremost of these was Franz Boas, who wrote to Bloomfield: 'I am very much disgusted but it seems quite impossible to find any position for Roman Jakobson. [...] What annoys me the most, I heard indirectly that he had been turned down at Yale because it was feared that his method, being different from the Yale method, might be detrimental to the students. [...]' (Boas to Bloomfield, September 28, 1942; quoted in Swiggers 1991: 283). Since Boas was to die three months later, he was not there to give Jakobson further support.[18]

Both Zellig Harris and Leonard Bloomfield supported Jakobson's presence in the United States, despite their disagreements with his theoretical stance. Harris, who was teaching at the University of Pennsylvania, did his best to secure a position for Jakobson there, possibly with support from the ACLS:

Dear Dr Jakobson,

It is with great regret that I have to tell you that our plans for you here at the university have apparently come to nothing, though I think other possibilities exist. What happened was this: Drs [name illegible] and Metro both spoke with [Mortimer] Graves [of the ACLS]. Graves assured them that the ACLS would really do the best it could as soon as any university would request it for money for you. Then we tried to get a request from our university. Not only our department, but also another group interested in Slavic put through a strong joint request for you. Knowing that our university, which is one of the poorest, had a deficit, we did not request a straight appointment [...]. Now I have just learned that the university administration refused the Dean because they said that they could not take on

---

[18] A number of web pages claim that 'When the American authorities considered "repatriating" [Jakobson] to Europe, it was Franz Boas who actually saved his life.' No citations are ever given. It seems quite implausible to me that Boas, a German immigrant and a Jew, would have had any influence with the 'American authorities'. Also, Boas died the year after Jakobson's arrival in the United States. Jakobson was to honor the memory of Boas a few years later by publishing a glowing tribute to his life and work (Jakobson 1944).

anything for which they could not pay themselves. We will still try to reopen the matter, but there is a very small chance. [...] I am afraid the question now is to find anew a school which will request such courses with you. Do you have any suggestion? I am writing Boas, who wrote me recently asking if he can think of any possibility.

Regards etc. (Harris to Jakobson, August 2, 1942; RJA)[19]

A follow-up letter from Harris a few weeks letter was both more personal and more on the subject of the differences of approach between Jakobson and his American colleagues:

Dear Dr Jakobson,

I am certainly glad to have received your last letter and to have your questions, because I can imagine that the series of unjustifiable disappointments must make you wonder about the attitude or the status of scientists in America.

First, I must say that I did not know about Edgerton's letter.[20] Also that that letter cannot be responsible for some of your disappointments, certainly not the one at Pennsylvania. The Pennsylvania case, and perhaps some of the others, are ordinary examples of what faces many scientists, both refugees and Americans (though perhaps Jews more than others). The whole attitude toward scientific work is commercial and often derogatory, and appointments often depend on family connections and having the right kind of friends.

But since there is nothing we can individually do about that, it is more relevant for me to say how I understand the difference between your work and that of American linguists. You know from the Trubetzkoy review that I, and most American linguists, disagree with the philosophical approach of many European linguists (and other scientists), including that of the Prague Circle. [...] It seems that the above opinions have made some American linguists feel that much of European linguistics can be disregarded. Sapir, whom I knew well, did not feel that way, nor do I — for perhaps two reasons: First because Prague has contributed so much to modern linguistics [...] that they have demonstrated their productivity. Second, because every piece of work which is formal is of use some place or other, and most Prague work has been [...]. Especially since speaking with you I have the opinion that work like yours, precisely because it has different points of departure from ours but is still formal, and because it is so original, can give us new ideas and important suggestions. Perhaps only after you have published more in America will more Americans realize

---

[19] That same day Harris wrote to Boas imparting the same information and the same sentiment (see Swiggers 1991).
[20] There was no letter from William Franklin Edgerton in the RJA.

this. [...] And, of course, I am still looking for other possibilities instead of Pennsylvania. [...]

Cordially,
Zellig S. Harris (Harris to Jakobson, August 28, 1942; RJA)

Bloomfield went to bat for Jakobson soon after his arrival in the United States, writing to Boas: 'Of course I have been in touch with Jakobson, and I know that Edgerton and Sturtevant also have him in mind, but so far we have not found any opening' (Bloomfield to Boas, October 20, 1941; cited in Swiggers 1991: 282). A few years later Bloomfield wrote directly to Jakobson:

Dear Jakobson,

[...] Miss Petrova has spoken of you in a way that disquieted me and in fact has made it painful to write. She said that you were hard up for a job and were placing your hope in Yale. Of course, I imagine that any such report is inaccurate, but even without being told, I can see the basis. I can see it especially as I read yesterday a shocking story of how you had been treated in connection with your coming to this country. This too may have been inaccurate, but even if it is half true, it is bad enough. Therefore it is painful to have to tell you about the situation here; had I written to you even a week ago, I might have not felt it necessary to mention it. There is no possibility here of an appointment in Slavic languages. [...]

As ever,
Leonard Bloomfield (Bloomfield to Jakobson, March 28, 1944; RJA)

Jakobson was one of many European refugee scholars who entered the United States from the late 1930s to the end of the war. Some ended up in New York City, teaching at the École Libre des Hautes Études, which was founded in 1941, inaugurated on February 14, 1942 and housed by the New School for Social Research. It was a sort of a university in exile for European refugees, offering its courses in French, and supported by the Rockefeller Foundation, the Belgian and Czech governments in exile, and the Free French government. Jakobson was there from the beginning. According to Testenoire (2019), linguistics courses were offered both at its Institut de Philologie et d'Histoire Orientale and at its Institut de Sociologie. Five linguists gave courses at the École Libre: Giuliano Bonfante, teaching comparative Indo-European linguistics, Jakobson, teaching Russian and general linguistics, Wolf Leslau, teaching Semitic languages, Henri F. Muller, teaching history of the French language, and André Spiré, teaching French versification.

The École Libre was located a bit uptown from 165 Broadway, where so many post-Bloomfieldian linguists were based (see Chapter 1, § 1.5.4). At the beginning, the relations between the two groups were tense:

Between the group at 165 Broadway and that at the École, therefore, one might have hoped that good relations and profitable intellectual exchanges could have prevailed — if times had been normal. Unfortunately, however, by the early and mid 1940s, they were not normal. In many fields, including linguistics, there was hostility between American scholars, especially the younger generation, and refugees who had come to America beginning in 1933. […] In the resultant clash between '165 Broadway' and the linguists at the École, not all the members of either group were involved. It was, rather, a conflict centered on the dislike of Trager and Jakobson for each other, with theoretical disagreements between European and American structuralists in the background. […] Some 165-Broadway-ites attended Jakobson's lectures at the École, but reports differ concerning the latter's relations with the '165 Broadway' group. There was a certain amount of tale-bearing and gossip relayed by members of the secretarial staff who frequented the École, in at least two instances with harmful results in the post-war picture of American linguists that prevailed in Europe.

(Hall 1991: 161–162)[21]

With respect to the antagonism between Jakobson and Trager, Steven Anderson has offered the view:

This in part goes back to the history of the Army Language manuals for Russian [see § 2.4]. That was first assigned to Trager, who claimed expertise in Russian on the basis of what he felt he had learned as a child. He produced a set of materials that were full of inaccuracies, at least with respect to the standard language. Bloomfield sent this to Jakobson for comment, and Jakobson wrote a devastatingly negative critique of what Trager had done. Trager insisted he was right, although all the native speakers they could consult said his materials were full of mistakes. Jakobson's critique was never published, but the task of writing the Russian materials for the army was taken over by Bloomfield (with constant reference to Jakobson). Trager was not pleased.

(p. c., April 8, 2021)

Despite all of this, my feeling is that the presence of the two groups of linguists in the same city at the same time was, in the long run, positive. Even though there were personal and professional animosities, linguists from each camp came to better understand the other's orientation and motivating influences. Even Charles Hockett wrote that 'before very long I was attending Jakobson's lectures at the École

---

[21] Hall remarks in a footnote: 'According to some accounts, efforts to have Jakobson give one of the talks at the after-hours linguistic meetings at 165 Broadway were received coldly and were not acted on. Others report that he often attended these meetings and alienated other scholars' sympathies by his virulent hostility to American linguistics and by behaving like "a boor and a bore." The two accounts are not incompatible. In any case, personal antipathies were certainly involved' (p. 162).

Libre des Hautes Études, benefitting from them greatly, and coming not just to respect but to admire the man even when I disagreed with him' (Hockett to Halle,
February 22, 1989; TSA).

In any event, a year after the war ended, Jakobson secured full-time employment
in the United States, being named Thomas G. Masaryk Professor of Czechoslovak
Studies at Columbia University in New York, a position which, despite its name,
allowed him to devote most of his energies to linguistics. He moved to Harvard
University in 1949, where he remained until his death in 1982. Thanks to Jakobson and other European scholars who remained in the United States after the war,
elements of the Prague School approach to linguistics had become, while perhaps
not mainstream, at least a major pole of attraction for American students entering
linguistics in the 1940s and 1950s.

American structural linguistics continued its diversification in a European direction with the founding of the journal *Word* in 1945, which was an indirect
product of the École Libre. In 1943, several linguists connected with the École
Libre, most notably Jakobson, founded the Linguistic Circle of New York (LCNY).
Henri F. Muller, a historian of the French language, was its first president. Two
years later, the first issue of the LCNY's journal *Word* appeared, under the editorship of Pauline Taylor of New York University. The first editorial board was about
half recent arrivals from Europe, but also contained linguists born and trained
in the United States, such as the structural linguist Charles C. Fries, the Indo-
Europeanist Robert A. Fowkes, the orientalist Louis H. Gray, and the historian of
the English language Albert C. Baugh. Sapir's student Morris Swadesh edited the
second volume. From 1947 and for the next two decades the journal was edited
by the structuralist André Martinet, who had arrived from France to take a position as full professor and department chair at Columbia University in 1946.[22] In
an editorial statement in the first issue, Muller emphasized how ecumenical the
new journal would be, taking it as self-evident that the unit 'word' was a construct
that all approaches shared.[23]

Why 'Word'? Because the word, in its various aspects, is a focal point of the science of language. Linguists of diverse schools are in agreement here. Ferdinand

---

[22] Martinet remained at Columbia until 1955, at which point he returned to France. His stay at
Columbia (as well as most of the rest of his life) is documented in his fascinating quirky memoir Mar-
tinet (1993), which was the subject of a controversy within the LSA in 1994. Some members wanted the
Society to condemn Martinet for the following remark, which was deemed to be anti-Semitic: '[Jakob-
son] s'inclinait devant Troubetzkoy, car en face du prince, il était tout de même le Juif moscovite'
['Jakobson deferred to Trubetzkoy, because in the presence of the prince, he was still the Moscow Jew'].
No action was taken against Martinet, an honorary Member, by the way. It is worth pointing out that in
the same book, Martinet brags about his efforts on behalf of the Yiddish Studies program at Columbia.

[23] But it was not self-evident: 'Neo-Bloomfieldians did not deal with "words" at all. For them, "word"
was not a technical term, nor a focus for analysis. "Words" were the victims of metaphysical amateur
etymology in contrast to "morphemes," which were the object of hardboiled Professional scientific
research' (Murray 1994: 215).

de Saussure says: 'Le mot, malgré la difficulté qu'on a à le definir, est une unité qui s'impose à l'esprit, quelque chose de central dans le mecanisme de la langue'. Edward Sapir stresses 'the definitely plastic unity of the word', which is 'the existent unit of living speech, an integral whole, a miniature bit of art', and opposes it to the smaller units 'abstracted as they are from the realities of speech'. Viktor Vinogradov, the outstanding linguist of New Russia, states: 'The word, the laws of its life, its historical development, its role in the history of material culture are the basic subjects of modern linguistics'. Not only linguistics, but also sociology, anthropology, psychology, and logic deal with the word. With the title WORD we intend to emphasize the multiform natural structure of linguistic reality and the necessity for studying language in all the fullness of its various functions and relations.

(Muller 1945: 4)

From the beginning, *Word* presented a more diverse picture of linguistics than did its well established rival *Language*. Not surprisingly it featured a number of papers by linguists associated with the Prague School. But notably it published papers by American structuralists who were outside of the militantly positivist mainstream. For example, the first issue featured a paper by the missionary linguist Eugene Nida (Nida 1945) and the second volume by linguists who were more followers of Sapir than of Bloomfield (Newman 1946; Sapir & Swadesh 1946; Haas 1946). The third volume was extremely diverse, with articles by Fred Householder (Householder 1947) and Rulon Wells (Wells 1947a), two linguists who were close to the American mainstream, as well as an important paper by Kenneth Pike, in which he laid bare his differences with majority opinion over whether grammatical information was legitimate input to phonemic analysis (Pike 1947b). By the mid-1950s even the orthodox post-Bloomfieldians were publishing in *Word*, as is illustrated by the appearance there of a paper by Charles Hockett (Hockett 1954). In other words, *Word* was both a product of, and a contributor to, a growing rapprochement among the diverse schools of structural linguistics.

Even *Language* editor Bernard Bloch came to terms with Jakobson and the new journal with which he was involved.[24] Despite his earlier summary rejection of two of Jakobson's submissions, he wrote to the latter:

Dear Mr Jakobson,

I have read your article on Russian conjugation [Jakobson 1971c [1948]] with great interest and pleasure; your exposition is so clear that even my ignorance of the language did not prevent me from following it. I have, however, one regret:

---

[24] Though a number of contemporaries remember Bloch making catty remarks about *Word* in this period. One linguist recalls the following comment from Bloch after an LSA talk: 'I hope that Mr. — will thoroughly revise this paper for publication, er, perhaps in *Word*' (Gleason 1988: 17).

that you did not send the article to me for *Language*. Since it includes a detailed criticism of a paper which had appeared in *Language* [Cornyn 1948], I believe it would have been appropriate to publish this new treatment of the same subject in the same journal. The fact that it appeared in *Word* may give some readers the false impression that there is some kind of rivalry or bad feeling between the two journals; you will agree with me, I know, that we ought to do everything we can to suppress that misconception. There is plenty of room for two American periodicals devoted to linguistic science; the existence of *Word* side by side with *Language* does not mean — as a few poorly informed persons possibly suppose — that American linguistics is divided into opposite camps. [...]

Sincerely yours,
Bernard Bloch (Bloch to Jakobson, March 29, 1949; RJA)

Jakobson sent a gracious reply to Bloch, remarking: 'I am glad you liked my paper and I fully agree with the conclusion of your letter. Orally and in letters, I always emphatically fight against the false idea of two would-be linguistic factions. And I am deeply convinced that there are not.' (Jakobson to Bloch, April 18, 1949; RJA). Jakobson went on to note that the starting point of his paper was an approach developed by Bloomfield (Bloomfield 1939a, I imagine) and suggested that they get together for a personal talk.

2.5.2 Increasing American appreciation of European linguistics

By the late 1940s, the times were changing with respect to the desire of American structural linguists to understand European work. A sign of the changing attitudes is reflected by a letter that Kenneth Pike wrote to Thomas Sebeok in 1949, just before (what I believe was) his first trip to Europe. Pike told Sebeok: 'As the semester goes by I still hope as much as ever to get to Europe in the not too distant future and so I am proceeding with a note asking for information of the type you so generously offered to provide me. Which are the descriptive linguists in England, France, Netherlands, Germany, Czechoslovakia, Denmark, Hungary, Finland, and Russia whom you think I would be interested in meeting?' (Pike to Sebeok, March 16, 1949; TSA). Sebeok's reply, excerpts of which are provided below, is of great historical interest:

Denmark. The dominant figure in linguistics is Professor Louis Hjelmslev, who is also editor of *Acta Linguistica*, the journal devoted entirely to structural linguistics. There are also some excellent phoneticians, notably, a girl [*sic*], Eli Fischer-Jørgensen.

England. Professor J. R. Firth you will probably have met last summer at the Linguistic Institute, and you undoubtedly know all about Daniel Jones. You should not miss Ida Ward.

Netherlands. There are at least two first-rate linguists in Holland, namely Anton Reichling and A. W. de Groot. These two edit *Lingua* and are quite aware of American linguistics.

Czechoslovakia. You are, of course, acquainted with the publications of the Cercle Linguistique de Prague. The Cercle has broken up pretty completely since the war, but one outstanding, brilliant, young linguist remains: Joseph Vachek. Vachek is not a Communist at all, but must watch his step carefully. Give him an opportunity to speak to you in private, where no one can overhear you.

Hungary. There is only one structural linguist in Hungary: he is professor Gyula Laziczius. He is a bitter lonely old man.

Finland. We have a Visiting Professor from Finland this year at Indiana University, Professor Lauri Posti. He will introduce you to all of the Finns.

Germany. I cannot give you any further information about the present whereabouts of the people I used to know before the war.

France. Here it is best, of course, to contact everybody through the offices of the Société Linguistique de Paris.

(Sebeok to Pike, April 5, 1949; TSA)

While neither Pike nor Sebeok were in the dominant positivist wing of American structuralism, their letters manifest a new openness to an exchange of ideas between the two continents, as does the fact that Firth had been invited to teach at the 1948 Linguistic Institute.

As far as the Linguistic Institutes (see Chapter 1, § 1.5.3) are concerned, they played an important role in an American–European rapprochement:

How did the Linguistic Institute sponsored by our Society [...] influence the delicate interplay of relations between American and European linguistics? [...] [A] mechanism was created which made it possible to invite foreign linguists of high distinction, not only to visit this country in reasonable extended periods of time, but to meet, in addition to meritorious fellow scholars, and to more or less casual auditors attending public lectures, also highly select groups of qualified advanced students capable of appreciating a first-rate teaching performance. The roster of these visiting professors is impressive; it includes such names as Émile Benveniste from France, J. R. Firth from England, Louis Hjelmslev from Denmark, Jakob Jud from Switzerland, Manfred Mayrhofer from Austria. Certain disciplines, such as linguistic theory and Indo-European comparativism, seem to have been favored over others.

(Malkiel 1979: 116)

The most dramatic testimony to renewed American interest in Europe is provided by Einar Haugen's LSA Presidential Address in 1950 (published as Haugen 1951). Haugen began his address by observing that

> Linguistic science is today in every sense of the word an international science. Few disciplines can lay better claim to this term than ours, in view of its universally and specifically human subject matter, as well as its bearing on the interrelationship and communication of nations. Even within our generation a vast expansion of linguistic study has taken place when compared with the preceding one. It is characteristic that around 1930 contributions to phoneme theory were being made by men as widely scattered as Trubetzkoy in Austria and Yuen Ren Chao in China. This was already a forward step over the much narrower field of Rask and Grimm, but we have seen a still more intense effort in the last two decades.
>
> (Haugen 1951: 211)

Haugen went on to deplore that fact that 'Rarely does one see a reference in American writings on linguistic theory to the works of de Saussure, Trubetzkoy, or other European writers, although they were the thinkers who gave us the instruments with which we work' (p. 211). He attributed this fact to the increasing terminological gulf between the Americans and Europeans and went on to explain how, to a significant degree, and terminology aside, the views of the Dane Louis Hjelmslev coincided with those of American structuralists, even those in the more empiricist camp. Hjelmslev, in fact, was on the faculty at the 1952 Institute and his countrywoman Eli Fischer-Jørgensen was there as a visitor for a month (Hill 1991: 71).[25]

The same year that Haugen's address was published, Charles Hockett published a remarkably positive review (Hockett 1951) of André Martinet's book *Phonology as Functional Phonetics* (Martinet 1949). In Hockett's words: 'This booklet should be widely read; it ought to be read in this country, with a more open mind than we sometimes grant our European colleagues' (Hockett 1951: 334). In a review of another important structuralist work published in Europe, Daniel Jones's *The Phoneme: Its Nature and Use* (Jones 1950), Fred Householder made some astute comments about the differences between the various 'national' approaches to structural linguistics:

---

[25] Fischer-Jørgensen had written to the LSA on 6 December 1949: 'In Copenhagen we are very interested in American linguistics and we have often discussed American books in the Cercle Linguistique. I think that there is a certain relationship between the methods of American linguistics [...] and Hjelmslev's theories, so that a discussion of the undoubtedly existing differences would be fruitful [...]' (*LSAB* 26, 1950: 443).

Every American linguist is aware that phoneme theory and practice have been more or less independently developed in three places: the United States, England, and continental Europe. [...] The three areas, while agreeing in essentials, differ mostly in philosophical background and primary aims. The philosophical background of the British linguist is largely that empiricism and logic of terms which is most familiar to us in the works of Bertrand Russell; much more given to skepticism (in the philosophical sense) and gentlemanly moderation than either the United States or the continent. The United States background is, in the main, Deweyan pragmatism, with a strong shot of behavioristic metaphysics and a bias toward logical rigor and methodology imparted originally by Leonard Bloomfield, but carried much farther by the younger American linguists. The continental background is more complex: a strong element of idealism and grandiose system building such as we associate with Hegel is present, but also strong are the influences of Comptean positivism and Gestalt psychology. [...] The European asks 'Is it true?', the American 'Is it consistent?', the Englishman 'Will it help?' But in spite of these differences in background and purpose, the agreement on fundamentals among followers of the three schools is considerable, and Jones is in many ways closer to American theory than to continental.

(Householder 1952: 99–100).

And a year later, in his overview of the field of linguistics, John B. Carroll wrote that 'In the last year or two, there have been signs of a necessary and well-justified rapprochement, after a temporary lapse beginning in the thirties, between American and European linguistics' (Carroll 1953: 22). Furthermore, the International Congress of Linguists, held in Oslo in 1957, 'had more American members than any of the previous ones' (Mohrmann et al. 1961: 9).

Yakov Malkiel agreed that a great change in mentality was in progress in the 1950s, writing:

While the most vociferous American linguists, for twenty long years, [were committed to] the virtual exclusion of foreign heresies, the situation began to change radically around 1955. [...] [T]he younger and more resilient European intellectuals who struck root in America served as mediators between the two hemispheres and acquired a small, but rapidly growing following. [...] [T]he polarization of America vs. Europe, so far as linguistics was concerned, itself rapidly became obsolete.

(Malkiel 1979: 114)

The most vivid indicator of the cross-Atlantic rapprochement was the election of Roman Jakobson as LSA President in 1956. Hymes and Fought (1981: 175) go so far as to suggest that if a knowledgeable person were queried in the early 1950s as to who was the most prominent linguist in the United States, the answer would likely be 'Roman Jakobson'.[26]

2.6 The European reaction to early generative grammar

The era of good feeling between American and European structuralists would have continued uninterrupted for many years had it not been for an event that would turn world linguistics upside-down: the publication of Noam Chomsky's *Syntactic Structures* (Chomsky 1957a). There is not much obvious European influence in that book, given that Chomsky mainly cites American structuralists and formal philosophers. But it was his joint work with Morris Halle in phonology where Prague School influence—especially Jakobson's—became evident. Halle had been one of Jakobson's leading students. In fact, his work in generative phonology started out as a restatement of Jakobson's 1948 'Russian conjugation' paper. Chomsky and Halle's *The Sound Pattern of English* was written in 1962, but not published until six years later (Chomsky & Halle 1968). The book was dedicated to Roman Jakobson for a good reason, namely that the influence of the Prague School is evident throughout. Notions like universal phonetic and phonological elements, underlying forms, binary distinctive features, and markedness all go back to Jakobson and Trubetzkoy (for discussion, see McCawley 1977). And by the early 1960s Chomsky was asserting that the problem of the correct theory is intimately tied to the problem of child language acquisition, just as Jakobson had done in 1941.

One would think, then, that early work in generative grammar would have brought American and European linguists even closer together. Unfortunately, just the opposite happened. Many European structuralists (and their cothinkers in the United States) were appalled that Chomsky appeared to continue the post-Bloomfieldian idea that semantics is not central to grammatical theory. In particular, they found the *Syntactic Structures* advocacy of the autonomy of syntax especially troubling. The critique was led by none other than Roman Jakobson, who, true to his Prague School roots, argued that grammatical form could not be dissociated from meaning. He asserted that 'Chomsky's [...] ingenious attempt to construct a "completely non-semantic theory of grammatical structure"' was a 'magnificent argumentum a contrario' (Jakobson 1959: 144), and went on to argue that the import of Chomsky's classic sentences 'Colorless green ideas sleep furiously' and 'Golf plays John' was precisely the opposite of that intended by Chomsky. And in a situation that I find somewhat ironic, the European attack on Chomsky was continued by two Dutch linguists associated with the journal *Lingua*, Anton Reichling and E. M. Uhlenbeck, who from the start had opened that

---

[26] It is also worth mentioning that references to Saussure and Trubetzkoy increased progressively in the pages of *Language* from the 1940s to the 1970s (Joseph 2013).

journal up to American descriptivists. Reichling stressed that hermetically sealing off syntax made the process of sentence understanding intractable:

> Native speakers do not exclusively understand each other by means of their language as a closed system; the linguistic means in a natural language are always used in conjunction with data supplied by the situation [...].
>
> (Reichling 1961: 16)

Uhlenbeck's criticisms echoed those of Reichling:[27]

> Language is not a self-contained system. Its structure is founded on the assumption that it will be used not in vacuo. It functions in its setting, but as soon as a speech-utterance is observed by the linguist outside of its situational setting and as soon as the frame of reference of the speaker is taken into account, the utterance becomes for him uninterpretable, that is it becomes ambiguous.
>
> (Uhlenbeck 1963: 11–12)

André Martinet summed up the European reaction in commenting on a 1950s submission by Chomsky to the journal *Word*:[28]

> [Chomsky's submission is] a reaction against the self-imposed limitations of the Bloomfieldian approach, but one retaining all of its formalistic prejudices with a few additional ones. [...] Actually, my impression was one of utter drabness unrelieved by any glint indicating some hidden awareness of what a real language is.
>
> (André Martinet, quoted in Murray 1980: 77)

Despite Martinet's hostility, in the early 1960s *Word* published what was perhaps the most important journal article of the decade in generative syntax: Charles Fillmore's 'The position of embedding transformations in a grammar' (Fillmore 1963). Many European linguists were to adopt generative grammar in later years, which will, in fact, be the subject of Chapter 6 of this book.

---

[27] Uhlenbeck would remain a persistent critic of generative grammar. His 1963 article and four subsequent ones are collected in Uhlenbeck (1975).

[28] There is a fair degree of uncertainty about the nature of Chomsky's submission. According to Martinet: 'I was the one who, in 1957, turned down a first version of *Syntactic Structures* by a newcomer, called Noam Chomsky. [...] Weinreich read it and sent it to me with conditional approval. But I was firm in my rejection' (Martinet 1994: 30–31). According to Chomsky, however, 'it was very likely an early version of what became the rules-based part of [*Sound Pattern of English*]' (Chomsky to Stephen Anderson, p. c., May 26, 2021). Chomsky attributed its rejection to 'a feud between [Martinet] and Jakobson', the latter of whom had by then become a great advocate for Chomsky, despite their many differences.

2.7 The Prague School influence on American functional linguistics

The Prague Linguistic Circle was officially disbanded by the Stalinist regime after the war. Those in Prague who continued to do linguistic work were mainly involved in developing the idea of 'functional sentence perspective', namely that grammatical (in particular, syntactic) properties of language are a product of the communicative setting in which language is used. This work was a forerunner to modern functional linguistics, rather than to anything that generative grammarians were doing. Not just in Prague (Daneš 1964; Firbas 1965), but also in London (Halliday 1961), Paris (Martinet 1962), Amsterdam (Dik 1968), and elsewhere in Europe, functionalist studies eclipsed generative ones for several decades.

There is strong evidence pointing to the conclusion that the pioneers of American functionalism not only were familiar with the central writings of the Prague School, but found them intellectually inspiring. I will demonstrate this point by reference to the work of Dwight Bolinger, Joseph Greenberg, Wallace Chafe, and Susumu Kuno.

Bolinger had begun to refer to the work of Prague School linguists as early as 1965. A book published in that year (Bolinger 1965b) reprinted some of his early papers and contained some never published ones as well. In a new preface to one of the former (Bolinger 1965c [1952]), he remarked that when he wrote the article, he 'was not aware of the earlier work of V. Mathesius and the recent work of Jan Firbas on what Firbas calls "functional sentence perspective [...]"' (p. 279) and went on to cite a paper of Firbas's and to characterize the (rather minor) differences between their respective positions. In a new paper in that same volume (Bolinger 1965a), he expressed his debt to a 'cautious statement' (p. 167) in Daneš (1957) regarding stress-timed rhythm in English that had helped to shape his thoughts on the matter. And in his popular 1968 introductory text, *Aspects of Language*, Bolinger noted:

> A group of Czech linguists refers to this tendency of many languages to put the known first and the unknown or unexpected last as 'sentence perspective' [a footnote here cites Firbas 1964]. They point out that, in order to communicate the sentence dynamism that has been partially lost by the stiffening of word order, English must resort to other stratagems, and these are among the things that give the language its distinctive syntactic appearance.
>
> (Bolinger 1968: 119–120)

Bolinger continued to cite Prague School work until the end of his career. For example, we find in Bolinger (1986) and Bolinger (1989) some discussion of the approach to accent prominence taken in Daneš (1960).

The influence of the Prague School permeates every page of Joseph Greenberg's seminal paper 'Some universals of grammar with special reference to the order of meaningful elements' (Greenberg 1963). By Greenberg's own acknowledgement (Greenberg 1963: 104), the paper was written in response to Roman Jakobson's call for an 'implicational typology' of language universals (Jakobson 1971a [1957]). Prague School terminology is also rampant in the Greenberg paper, as is evidenced by the frequent description of one order of elements as being 'more marked' or 'less marked' than another.

In his 1970 book, Chafe notes that 'the basic role played by semantic structure in the structure of language [...] has been seriously neglected by the mainstream of linguists' (Chafe 1970: 210). To this remark he adds in a footnote:

> It has not been totally neglected, however. Some members of the 'Prague School' have given it considerable attention, beginning with Vilém Mathesius and continuing now with, especially, the work of Czech linguists such as Jan Firbas (see Firbas 1966 and numerous other publications).
>
> (Chafe 1970: 210)

Kuno bestowed upon the Prague School a signal honor—he named one of his papers 'Functional sentence perspective' (Kuno 1972), and began the acknowledgement footnote with the following remark:

> I am most grateful to Jan Firbas for discussing with me the theme-rheme (or predictable-information vs. unpredictable information) interpretation of *wa* and *ga* in Japanese. The reader will find that I have been greatly influenced in my analysis by the Prague School notion of functional sentence perspective. (Kuno 1972: 269)

We have the personal testimony of the 'second generation' of functionalists, as well, that their mentors, Chafe and Kuno, valued the work of the Prague School enough to call their attention to it:

> Wally Chafe's work in the 1960s was an important influence on my thinking, and it was Chafe who got me to reading the Prague School work [...]. I heard Chafe give lectures in the 1960s in which he referred to FSP, and spoke of it as the basis of his ideas. Pre-war names like Mathesius were often mentioned, so this wasn't merely the newer Prague School.
>
> (Paul Hopper, personal communication, January 20, 1999)

Incidentally, the person who pushed Prague School ideas on information flow the most here at Berkeley during the 70s was Wally Chafe, who of course was a major force behind the formation of the functionalist school first here and later at Santa Barbara.

(George Lakoff, *Funknet* posting, February 11, 1999)

At least by the early 1970s, Kuno was indeed talking about the Prague School. I remember reading Mathesius and Firbas on his recommendation at that time.

(Ellen Prince, *Funknet* posting, February 16, 1999)

In short, there can be no question that the American functionalist movement, as it took form in the early 1970s, was shaped to a significant degree by the conceptions of the Prague School.

2.8 Summary

This chapter has examined how American structural linguists and their European counterparts saw each other from roughly the 1920s to the 1960s. American linguistics had deep roots in Europe, though by the late 1930s, most American structuralists had turned their back on the old continent. Attitudes toward the Europeans started to warm in the late 1940s and into the 1950s. Prague School conceptions had a major influence on generative grammar (at least as far as phonology is concerned) and on the nascent functionalist movement in the United States. From the European side, there was some, but not a great deal, of interest in American theorizing until the late 1940s. A real rapprochement was underway in the 1950s, which was derailed by the appearance of generative grammar, an approach that at the time most European structuralists rejected.

3

Martin Joos's *Readings in Linguistics* as the apogee of American structuralism

3.1 Introduction

The first two chapters of this book were wide-ranging and fairly general, covering the birth and early development of American structuralism, as well as its interaction with its European counterpart. This chapter, on the other hand, is narrowly focused on one single publication: its creation, its reception, and its after-effects. In 1957 (ironically the year that Chomsky's *Syntactic Structures* was published) an anthology appeared that was seen as the crowning glory of post-Bloomfieldianism, republishing its most important articles and glowing over its perceived success. I refer to Martin Joos's *Readings in Linguistics: The Development of Descriptive Linguistics in America Since 1925*. The entire chapter will be devoted to this volume.

Joos's book is the best-known collection of papers in the history of American linguistics. It achieved celebratory status for two principal reasons: first, because it compiled in one volume some of the most noteworthy published papers by American-based linguists from the 1920s through the 1950s; second, because of the opinions expressed about how to do linguistics (and science in general) that Joos provided in the prefaces and in the paragraphs following most of the articles. The volume was taken by linguists in the middle years of the twentieth century as a valuable compendium of the thinking of the major faction within American descriptive linguistics. But today its importance mostly lies in the role it continues to play in the work of later linguists, most of whom interpret the volume's contents in a particular way and launch scathing attacks on it, based on their interpretation. Today's linguists attack Joos's introductory and summary comments sandwiched between the collected articles. While there is a literature devoted to discussing whether Joos was fairly representing the ideas of the majority of American linguists in what he wrote, the fact remains that his extreme empiricist viewpoint was taken as the mainstream view (and point of attack) by the following generations of linguists. For those reasons, it is worthwhile to devote a full chapter to the publication history of, and reaction, to Joos's reader.

The chapter is organized as follows. § 3.2 presents the background to the idea, which took root in the 1940s, of an anthology of papers central to the development

American Linguistics in Transition. Frederick J. Newmeyer, Oxford University Press.
© Frederick J. Newmeyer (2022). DOI: 10.1093/oso/9780192843760.003.0003

of linguistics in the United States. § 3.3 is devoted to the process by which Joos sought to identify the published papers deemed worthy of inclusion in the volume. § 3.4 discusses the first edition of the *Readings* and § 3.5 the subsequent editions. § 3.6 presents in graphic form a timeline of which papers were slated for inclusion at various points, while § 3.7 is devoted to the published reviews of the anthology. § 3.8 takes up some further issues relevant to Joos's reader, and § 3.9 is a brief conclusion.

3.2 Background to Joos's *Readings in Linguistics*

As early as 1946 the idea was in the air to produce a collection of readings of the most important papers in general linguistics written in the previous few decades. § 3.2.1 documents the attempt of Bernard Bloch to concretize this idea. § 3.2.2 discusses how, eight years later, the American Council of Learned Societies enlisted Martin Joos (§ 3.2.3) to put this idea into action by tapping him for the editor's role. § 3.2.4 speculates on why it was Joos, as opposed to some other leading contemporary American linguist, who was chosen for the job.

3.2.1 Bernard Bloch's idea for a collection

In his editorial rubric 'Notes' in 1946, Bernard Bloch, editor of the journal *Language,* observed that

> [s]ome of the most important articles on general linguistics and on phonemic theory published during the past twenty-five years are nearly forgotten today: they appeared in journals that are seldom read by younger workers in our field, or in early volumes of *Language* that are no longer easily accessible. Linguists will have no trouble in thinking of examples; the following are typical:
>
> Sapir, Sound patterns in language, LANG. 1.37-51 (1925).
> Bloomfield, On recent work in general linguistics, Modern Philology 25.211-30 (1927).
> Sapir, La réalité psychologique des phonèmes, Journal de Psychologie 1933.247- 65.
> Chao, The non-uniqueness of phonemic solutions of phonetic systems, Bulletin of the Institute of History and Philology (Academia Sinica) 4.363-97 (1933).
> Trubetzkoy, Anleitung zu phonologischen Beschreibungen; Brno, 1935.

Whorf, Science and linguistics [and two other articles], The Technology
Review, Vols. 42 (1940) and 43 (1941).
Twaddell, Phonemics, Monatshefte für deutschen Unterricht 34.262-8 (1942).
Bloomfield, Meaning, Monatshefte für deutschen Unterricht 35.101. (1943).

(Bloch 1946a: 267)

Bloch went on to write that the LSA had undertaken to publish a volume 'containing reprints of the most significant of these little-known articles' (p. 267). As far as
the book's contents are concerned, 'we may assume that it should reflect the main
trends of recent American linguistics' (p. 267) and it should exclude articles treat-
ing a particular language. However, he was unsure whether to limit the collection
to the writings of American linguists, whether to include articles from recent volumes of *Language*, or how to decide which articles were the most important. He
invited LSA members to send him 'suggestions on 3×5 cards with comments on
little-known items, written at the bottom of the card' (p. 267).

As it turns out, Bloch's plan was dropped for lack of response to the invitation
to nominate papers other than those on his list:

> The plan to publish a volume of reprints, announced in LANG. 22.267 (1946),
> has been temporarily abandoned. The Editor's call for help in choosing articles
> brought specific recommendations from only four members of the Linguistic So-
> ciety. In part, no doubt, this disappointingly small response is to explained by
> the fact that the deadline for suggestions had already passed before the journal
> appeared — a miscalculation on the Editor's part for which no one is to blame.
> But it may also be true that the time is not yet ripe for such a collection of arti-
> cles. Many linguists have only recently returned to their normal work from the
> exacting services, military and professional, which they formed during the war;
> they are perhaps too fully occupied with interrupted projects of their own, too
> intent upon the future progress of our science, to cooperate easily in a search of
> the past. Whatever the reason, it is clear that the proposal to issue an anthology
> was badly timed. In a year or two, when members of the Society have had leisure
> to consider the plan more carefully, can be revived and carried through. Mean-
> while, the Editor will continue welcome suggestions, not only of specific articles
> to be included in the volume, but also of the general scope and purpose that such
> a volume should have.

(Bloch 1947b: 313; see also Joos 1966a: v)

It is really not difficult to understand why there were so few responses, given Bloch's
internally contradictory message. On the one hand, he was looking for articles that
'reflect the main trends of recent American linguistics'. It is hard for me to see how
any of the eight articles listed by Bloch qualify in that respect. On the other hand,
he was seeking articles that are 'nearly forgotten today'. Such articles, by definition,
would not reflect 'main trends'.

The idea for a reader remained dormant for eight or so years until it was taken up by the American Council of Learned Societies under the editorship of Martin Joos. It is that organization and that individual to which we turn.

3.2.2 The American Council of Learned Societies

American linguistics in the 1950s would have looked very different had it not been for the ongoing support of the American Council of Learned Societies (ACLS). The ACLS is a federation of 75 scholarly organizations in the humanities and social sciences, one of which is the LSA. At the time of its founding in 1919, 13 learned societies were members and in 1955, there were 22. Its goal is 'to promote the circulation of humanistic knowledge throughout society' (from the ACLS web page). In order to carry out this goal, it is supported by income from its endowment, dues from constituent societies and affiliates, contributions from college and university associates, private and public grants, government contracts, and private gifts.

The ACLS has always been quite generous in its support of linguistics-related activities. Its Committee on Research in Native American Languages under the leadership of Franz Boas and Edward Sapir began in 1927 to 'secure an adequate record of Indian languages and dialects'.[1] The ACLS helped make possible the first LSA-sponsored Linguistic Institute at Yale in 1928 (with funds supplied by the Carnegie Corporation) with a grant of $2500 (see Chapter 1, § 1.5.3) and has supported to one degree or another most Institutes since then. The following year the Executive Committee of the ACLS set up a task force to plan a dialect atlas of the United States and Canada under the chairmanship of Hans Kurath (see also Chapter 1, § 1.5.3). And the ACLS, with the aid of the Ford Foundation, was instrumental in the setting up of the Center for Applied Linguistics in Washington, DC in 1958 (Hill 1991: 93).

Chapter 1, § 1.5.4 has already discussed the most important contribution of the ACLS to linguistics, namely, its directing, under the leadership of Mortimer Graves, American linguists' participation in the war effort. In 1949, through Graves's initiative, the wartime Intensive Language Program was replaced by the ACLS's Committee on the Language Program (renamed the Committee on Language Programs in 1958). The functions of the Committee in the 1950s were as follows:

1. To encourage research in all aspects of linguistic science; 2. To provide aids to the publication of sound linguistic research; 3. To develop and encourage instruction in linguistics for both graduate students and undergraduates; 4. To develop opportunities for integrating linguistics with the study of all other fields of human

---

[1] *ACLS Bulletin* 7 (April 1928), p. 53.

behavior; 5. To apply linguistics to the teaching of foreign languages at all levels of instruction; 6. To apply linguistics to the teaching of the native language from literacy to literature, and to the teaching of all other relevant phases of culture; 7. To develop training programs to acquaint teachers with the principles and possibilities of linguistics. 8. To develop in the public an awareness of current activities among linguistic scientists. 9. To consider and present opportunities for the employment of personnel trained in linguistics; and 10. To bring to the attention of administrators the importance of linguistics for present-day education.

(Voegelin 1954: 74)

Graves, as the ACLS liaison officer to the LSA and, between 1953 and 1957 the Executive Director of the ACLS, was directly involved in all of these activities. It is also probably relevant to our narrative that Graves, even for his time, was an inveterate cold warrior and American chauvinist. The following quotation gives a flavor of his world-view (see also Graves 1950):

Ideological World War Three has started and there is no certainty that it is well won yet. In spite of the fact that this is a war for men's minds, there exist no Joint Chiefs of Staff planning such a war, no war production authority concerning itself with material for such a war. [...] In this war for men's minds, obviously the big guns of our armament is [*sic*] competence in languages and linguistics.

(Graves 1951: 1)

Given all of the above, it is not surprising that Graves would involve the ACLS in the production of a volume of papers written by American-based linguists. His choice for editor, Martin Joos, and his reasons for that choice, are discussed in the following two sections.

3.2.3   Martin Joos

Martin Joos was an engineering-trained linguist, based at the University of Wisconsin in the 1950s. Joos described himself as 'a notorious dilettante in a number of vaguely related fields, and has been known to boast of never having published twice on the same topic or a closely similar one' (Joos 1957b: 356). His obituary seems to confirm that assertion, as well as underscoring his originality:

It is important to point out that his *Five Clocks* [= Joos 1962] is the fullest account of the various styles and registers of English; that his *Middle High German Courtly Reader* [= Joos & Whitesell 1951] contains the best directions for translations that I know; that his *English Verb* [= Joos 1964] is a pioneering work in description based on a stylistically unified and very extensive text; that his *Acoustic Phonetics* [= Joos 1948] educated a whole generation of linguists on that subject; and that his formulation of the application of simplicity to semantic interpretation, in the article "Semantic axiom number one" [= Joos 1972], is a tool which all students of meaning should use.

(Hill 1979: 666)

Joos 'was influential in bringing wartime research on the sound spectrograph to the attention of linguists (Joos 1948) and bringing linguistics to the attention of engineers (Joos 1950)' (Ladd 2020: fn. 1). During the war, he had served as a cryptanalyst for the American Signal Security Agency, leading to his receiving the highest honor attributed to a civilian by the War Department: a citation for distinguished service.[2]

Joos is generally identified as being part of the mainstream positivist wing of American linguists (see Chapter 1, § 1.2). One of his most famous dicta was that 'Text signals its own structure' (Joos 1961: 17), in other words that the structure of a language can, in principle, be extracted from an examination of texts in that language. In 1942 Joos helped George Trager found the journal *Studies in Linguistics*, which represented these 'methodological extremists' to a considerable degree, though it did give voice to other opinions. He acted as 'Associate Editor and Typist' of the journal through 1947. Joos served as Vice-President of the LSA in 1952. However, he was challenged and defeated by Dwight Bolinger for the presidency in 1970 in a bitterly contested election, a topic that will be discussed in detail in Chapter 7 of this book.

Joos has been described as 'cantankerous, opinionated, and strongly biased, though often ill- or totally un-informed' (Hall 1990a: 232). Even the author of his obituary felt the need to point out that 'Martin's personality was one which often put off those who did not fully know him' (Hill 1979: 666). According to Julia Falk, a leading historiographer of linguistics:

> Joos appears to have been rather pompous and arrogant, always sure he was right. Several of his contemporaries have told me this, and it comes through in the notes to *Readings in Linguistics*, in his error-filled *Notes on the History of the LSA* [=Joos 1986],[3] and in transcripts of his comments at the Second Texas Conference [= Hill 1962].

(Julia Falk, p. c., July 9, 2019)

---

[2] It has been written that it was Joos who cracked the Japanese secret code (see Friebert 2019). However no such claim appears either in Hill (1979) or in Joos's own account of his wartime work (Joos 1986: Chapter 5).

[3] Joos's *Notes* had quite a checkered history. While full of valuable material, including documentation of early LSA summer Institutes, its quirkiness and shameless self-promotion led to its being a hot potato. The manuscript fell onto Archibald Hill's lap in 1975 and he didn't know what to do with it. In 1979 Konrad Koerner offered to publish it as part of his Studies in the History of Linguistics series. Hill replied to him: 'I find that [Joos's manuscript] is unpublishable, so definitely so that I do not want my name associated with any part of it' (Hill to Koerner, October 31, 1979; AHA). Seven years later J Milton Cowan and Charles Hockett published it privately, distancing themselves from its contents in their preface.

Joos became increasingly eccentric as time went on. David Lightfoot recalls:

> I did meet Joos once in 1971, which was my first year at McGill, when I attended
> the annual Canadian Linguistics Association meeting in St. John's, Newfound-
> land [Joos was teaching at the University of Toronto that year — (FJN)]. He was
> a comical figure, boasting that he loved to read his own books, because he saw
> himself as a master of style. Indeed, he was reading *The Five Clocks* at that meet-
> ing. He made observations after almost all the papers, almost all referring to his
> own work that he thought relevant.
>
> (David Lightfoot, p. c., September 11, 2020)

All of the above should be kept in mind as this chapter progresses. Over the course
of his career, Joos's original contributions to the field were to be eclipsed by 'the
unique role he played as a self-appointed community builder among American
structuralists, and as something like an apologist to outsiders, boundary patroller,
and socializer of newcomers' (Margaret Thomas, p. c., July 8, 2019).

3.2.4 Why Joos was chosen as editor of the *Readings*

It is interesting to speculate on why Graves and the ACLS were to choose Martin
Joos as the editor of a volume of readings in American linguistics. Without question, Graves had a high opinion of Joos's abilities. During the war, Joos was based
in Arlington, Virginia. In 1942 he was contacted by the ACLS office on the other
side of the Potomac River, where he was also engaged in cryptanalytic work, and
got to know Graves personally (Joos 1986: 122–123). The ACLS appointed Joos as a
member of their Committee on the Language Program in 1950 and soon thereafter
charged him with the task of publication editor of a number of language learning
textbooks (Moulton 1961: 104). Ten were completed and published by the ACLS
during 1953–1956. In other words, the ACLS had confidence in Joos's competence
as an editor. As Joos himself noted:

> By 1954, when I had been a member of the Committee for several years [I] had de-
> veloped techniques for preparing such book-length pages as the present volume
> [the fourth edition of the *Readings* — (FJN)] contains, and had edited several
> books for the teaching of English as a foreign language for the ACLS, the Com-
> mittee had arrived at a new plan for the content of the needed volume of *Readings
> in Linguistics*. I was directed to circulate a list of papers for possible inclusion and
> to ask for the help of scholars in defining the scope and purpose.
>
> (Joos 1966a: v)

The Committee on the Language Program, which officially delegated Joos, was
composed as follows in 1955: The members were Joos himself (as secretary) and

Albert H. Marckwardt (chairman), Mortimer Graves (ACLS staff liaison), Norman A. McQuown, Bernard Bloch, Theodore Andersson, Archibald A. Hill, and William Moulton. The associate members were John B. Carroll, John Kepke, and Henry Lee Smith, Jr. Of these individuals, Bloch, Kepke, and Smith were very closely allied to Joos in their empiricist theoretical orientation, and Hill and Moulton fairly closely. The anthropological linguist McQuown had published a review of Harris's *Methods in Structural Linguistics* (Harris 1951a) that he described as 'epoch-making' (McQuown 1952: 495). And the psychologist Carroll had recently written that '[t]he methodology of descriptive linguistics has been developed in such a way that it is no longer an art in any sense, but simply a matter of intelligently following a number of definite operational procedures' (Carroll 1953). In other words, a solid majority of the Committee would have had no principled objection to Joos on ideological grounds.

However, several other prominent American linguists were also sufficiently well-known, competent, and aligned theoretically in the proper way to take on the editor's role for the ACLS. Why was Joos chosen? I think that the answer to this question is probably quite banal: He was the only person both willing and able to do it. Robert D. King, who had been Joos's PhD student, notes:

> I don't know for sure why Joos was chosen, but I can throw out a few observations. One, he liked that kind of assembly work and I don't think the other linguists did. I know Bloch didn't because Warren Cowgill told me that at the Institute in 1972 in Chapel Hill. Hockett? I doubt it. Win Lehmann could have done it, but he was not in the inner circle. Trager? No. (Robert D. King, p. c., July 16, 2019).

In other words, I do not think that too much should be read into the choice of Joos as editor. Perhaps alone of the leading American linguists, he could do it and he would do it.

3.3 Joos takes on the editor's role

Armed with the task of producing a book of readings of work in American linguistics, Joos swung into action. § 3.3.1 reproduces his letter soliciting the opinions of his colleagues as to what to include and § 3.3.2 summarizes their replies.

3.3.1 Joos's letter of September 12, 1955

In September 1955, Joos sent out the following letter to about a hundred American linguists, accompanied by a list of papers that he deemed possible for inclusion:[4]

---

[4] I have not edited out the numerous typos and abridgements in Joos's proposed list of publications.

University of Wisconsin, Madison, Wisconsin, 12 September 1955

Dear Colleague:

This letter goes to about a hundred American linguists whose help I need in shap-
ing a job which I have been asked to do by the Committee on the Language
Program of the American Council of Learned Societies: constructing a volume of
Readings in American Linguistics. I have already begun work on the items which
I am morally certain you will approve, but these won't take me long to finish; by
that time I hope to have received enough advice from you so that I can continue
without interruption.[5] With some good luck, I can have the book in print in time
for the Linguistic Institute of 1956. The price will not be small (between $6.00
and $8.00), but the volume will be a bargain: its contents will equal from 700 to
800 pages of the present format of Language, to be printed in between 432 and
480 two-column pages. No copies will be cloth-bound: the project can break even
only if the book is not put on library reserve but required as an individual student
purchase and not resold by the student later. For the same reason, we can't plan to
break it into two or more thinner books. The volume has to sell over 1000 copies
in 6 years (time for a replacement edition) if it is not to create a deficit.

Within these limitations it will just barely be possible to include the short and
middle-length programmatic papers of what everybody calls 'American' linguistics nowadays; indeed, we can set the upper size-limit at the generous figure of 25
pages of the Language format in our first planning: some limit has to be set at first,
and if you want me to include one of e.g. Bloch's Postulates or his Japanese Syntax,
or Harris's pair of Discourse Analysis papers, or Moulton's Stops or Spirants, or
Wells's Immediate Constituents, you must at the same time propose omitting two
or more average-length papers from the list. The tentative list I am now sending
you has at least this one virtue: it is just about the right length for the proposed
book. Therefore I expect the nominations for inclusions to be equally balanced
by nominations for omission; otherwise your advice will be very hard to make
use of.

If you are one of the authors (now or after revision of the list), it will shorten
my work significantly if you will do as many of these things as you can: (a) Send
me an offprint; it will be easier to handle than my copies of the journals. (b) Suggest omissions: there won't have to be omissions, but on rereading you may want

---

[5] Margaret Thomas makes the following interesting observation: 'I am struck, reading Joos's letter,
with how he takes *every possible opportunity* to align himself with the addressee (as in "I hope to have
received enough advice from you […]"; "[…] if you want me to include […]"; "I expect […] otherwise
your advice will be very hard to make use of"; "the way we discuss the stuff ourselves"; etc.). In Joos's
1986 *Notes,* the same rhetoric prevails; it reads like he is trying really hard to declare his own solidarity
with the group he is addressing. Do you think the group felt encroached upon by Joos? If he really was
so much a part of the intellectual commonwealth, why would he need to assert the point emphatically,
so many times over?' (p. c., 1 July 2021).

some. (c) Supply afterthoughts, which may run to a considerable postscript in some cases. (d) Supply references to later treatments of your points. (e) Correct misprints that might escape me, of course. Whatever you don't do along these lines will call for more thought on my part, and more risk of blunders: this book is intended for beginners in our science, to whom we owe more orientation than we needed when we first read these papers. (I'll supply page-cross-references within the volume).

The list is arranged by authors, the way we discuss the stuff ourselves, and the way our advanced students ought to; but if somebody works out a good mixed topical and chronological arrangement I could be prepared to adopt it. This will be the last constructional detail and need not be settled until February 1956. Other advice will be continually useful to me from now until April 1956; therefore both promptness and afterthoughts will be welcome.

Cordially yours,

Martin Joos (MJA)

Joos's cover letter was accompanied by the following list:

Readings in [American] Linguistics — Tentative list of 12 September 1955 — Revisions to be sent to Joos at the U. of W., Madison, Wisconsin

[[Journal is <u>Language</u> unless specified]]

Agard: Noun morphology in Roumanian 29.134-43.
Bloch: Japanese phonemics 26., Contrast 29.59-61.
Bloomfield: Postulates 2.153-64, Ilocano syntax 18.193-200.
Chao: Non-uniqueness … Academia Sinica Bulletin 4.363-97.
Fairbanks: Phonemic structure of Zographensis 28.360-5.
Hamp: Morphophonemics of the Keltic mutations 27.230-47.
Harris: rev. of Gray's Foundations of Language 16.216-31, rev. of Trubet-zkoy's Grundzüge der Phonologie 17. 345-9, Morpheme alternants 18.169-80, Simultaneous components 20.181-205, Yokuts structure and Newman's grammar IJAL 10.196-211, Navaho phonology and Hoijer's analysis IJAL 11.239-50, Discontinuous morpheme [*sic*] 21.121-7, From morpheme to utterance 22.161-83, rev. of Emeneau's Kota texts 21.283-9, Componential analysis of a Hebrew paradigm 24.87-91, rev. of Sapir's Selected Writings 27.288-308 [omitting 308-32].
Hartman: Segmental phonemes of Chinese 20.28-32.
Hill: Phonetic and phonemic change 12.15-22.

Hockett: System of descriptive phonology 18.3-21, rev. of Nida's
  Morphology[2] 23.273-85, Peiping phonology JAOS 67.253-67, Problems of morphemic analysis 23.321-43, Linguistic implications
  of. Bloomfield's Algonquian studies 24.117-31, Chinese morpho-
  phonemics 26, rev. of Shannon & Weaver's Mathematical theory of
  communication 26.69-93, rev. of Martinet's Phonology as functional
  phonetics 27.333-42.
Hoenigswald: Sound change and linguistic structure 22.138-43, The
  principal step in comparative grammar 26.357-64.
Jakobson & Lotz: Notes on the French phonemic pattern WORD 5.151-9.
Lounsbury: the methodological introduction to his Oneida Verb.
Martin: Korean phonemics 27.519-33.
Moulton: Juncture in German 23.212-16.
Newman: On the stress system of English WORD 2.171-87
Nida: Analysis of grammatical constituents 24.168-77.
Pike: Phonemic status of English diphthongs 23.151-9, Taxemes and
  immediate constituents 19.65-82, Coexistent phonemic systems
  25.29-50.
Pittman: Nuclear structures 24.287-92.
Sapir: Sound patterns 1.37-51.
Swadesh: The phonemic principle 10.117-29, [with Voegelin] a problem in
  phonological alternation 15.1-10, Analysis of English syllabics 23.137-
  51.
Trager: Serbo-croat accents and quantities 16.29-32, rev. of van Wijk's
  Phonologie 16.247-51, Russian declensional morphemes 29.326-38.
Trubetzkoy: Anleitungen zu phonologischen Beschreibungen (tr. Lees).
Twaddell: A note on Old High German umlaut Monatshefte für deutschen
  Unterricht 30.177-81, Prehistoric German short syllables 24.139-51.
Voegelin: A problem in morpheme alternants 23.245-54.
Wells: Automatic alternation 25.99-116, Pitch phonemes of English 21.27-
  39, rev. of Pike's Intonation of American English 23.255-73.
Whorf: Grammatical categories 21.1-11.

Of the eight papers on Bloch's 1946 list, three appeared on Joos's: Sapir's 'Sound patterns', Chao's 'Non-uniqueness', and Trubetzkoy's 'Anleitung'.

One would like to know more about the process by which Joos decided that such-and-such articles should be included and such-and-such be excluded. Unfortunately, we have nothing more to go on than what he himself wrote in his letter, supplemented by speculation. Practical considerations led him to exclude overly-long papers. And the percentage of papers devoted to phonology, morphology, and syntax seems to reflect pretty well the proportion of each in the published literature up to the mid 1950s. There were quite a few more phonological than morphological articles in Joos's list and hardly any syntactic treatments at all: an old paper of Bloomfield's and programmatic articles by Harris, Nida, and Pittman, each of which dealt with morphology as much as with syntax.

The clue to Joos's choice of material might be that he was looking for 'programmatic papers of what everybody calls "American" linguistics nowadays'. Well, what did 'everybody' call 'American linguistics' at the time? We can be pretty sure that Joos had in mind some distinctive subset of the work published in the United States before 1955. For example, the majority of the articles that appeared in *Language* dealt with historical themes, yet only one historical linguist (Hoenigswald) was on his list. Likewise, there was nothing that one might call 'anthropological linguistics', where grammatical and cultural facts about a language are treated in an integrated fashion. So, despite not saying so in his letter, Joos obviously had in mind papers on synchronic descriptive (purely) grammatical studies. It also seems quite clear that for him, not all such studies qualified equally well as 'American linguistics'. All four tendencies in descriptive linguistics referred to in Chapter 1, § 1.2 are represented, though hardly in equal number. Particularly if we count the totality of the articles mentioned, the empiricist wing of the field has an absolute majority. There are eleven publications by Harris listed and eight by Hockett. Sapir's students are fairly poorly represented (and are criticized in two publications by Harris), while the missionaries Pike and Nida have four papers. There are only two by Prague School linguists, both by founding members of that school: Trubetzkoy and a co-authored paper by Jakobson. One might assume that the Trubetzkoy piece was preserved from Bloch's list to honor one of the pioneers of modern phonology, as he was the only author on Joos's list who was not (or had not been) based in the United States. All in all, it seems clear that 'American linguistics' meant for Joos (if not for 'everybody') a particularly distinctively positivist way of doing synchronic linguistics.

3.3.2 Reactions to Joos's letter

There is no surviving record of the names of the 'about a hundred American linguists' who were sent Joos's letter. However, he does tell us that he received 'three dozen useful responses' (Joos 1958: vi). The MJA contains letters regarding the proposed volume from 42 linguists, so one can conclude that he considered that a

half dozen or so of these responses were less than 'useful'. The following is a list of
the 42 respondents:

Clarence L. Barnhart	Bernard Bloch
Dwight Bolinger	John B. Carroll
Noam Chomsky	J Milton Cowan
Francis Dinneen	Isidore Dyen
Murray Fowler	Anna Granville Hatcher
Henry Hoenigswald	Harry Hoijer
Elinor Horne	Fred Householder
Henry Kahane	Werner Leopold
Donald J. Lloyd	Floyd Lounsbury
Horace G. Lunt	Yakov Malkiel
Albert Marckwardt	William G. Moulton
Stanley Newman	Eugene Nida
D. L. Olmsted	Charles Osgood
Herbert Paper	Herbert Penzl
Kenneth Pike	Carroll Reed
Sol Saporta	Yao Shen
James Sledd	Henry Lee Smith
Otto Springer	Robert A. Stockwell
Morris Swadesh	George L. Trager
W. Freeman Twaddell	C. F. Voegelin
Joshua Whatmough	William Wonderly

It seems likely that all of the members of the 1955 LSA Executive Committee were
contacted by Joos. Three apparently did not reply: the President Zellig Harris, who
was notorious for being uncommunicative, and Executive Committee members
Eric Hamp and Rulon Wells.[6]

Most of the responses to Joos's letter were positive and encouraging. Remarks
such as 'I think your idea [is] an excellent one' (Hatcher); 'Your selections seem
sound to me on the whole' (Hoijer); 'I am wholly in favor of the projected volume' (Householder); 'You merit our congratulations and sympathies' (Saporta); 'I
think you have done a remarkable job' (Wonderly); and so on were typical. In fact,
only two replies were on the whole negative, namely those by Isidore Dyen and
George Trager, the latter of whom had 'withheld permission because of his views
on anthologies' (Trager 1958: 35):

> I wish to register a very strong objection to the title "Readings in Ameri-
> can Linguistics". I should suggest either "Readings in Contemporary American

---

[6] Other members of the LSA Executive Committee in the 1950s from whom there is no letter to
Joos in the Archive are Madison Beeler, Murray Emeneau, Charles Ferguson, Joseph Greenberg, Mary
Haas, Einar Haugen, R. M. S. Heffner, Archibald Hill, Carleton Hodge, Roman Jakobson, Hayward
Keniston, J. Alexander Kerns, George Lane, Fang-Kuei Li, Norman McQuown, Allen Walker Read,
Ralph Ward, Uriel Weinreich, William Welmers, and Joseph Yamagiwa. We know that Thomas Sebeok
received Joos's letter because it is on file in the TSA. However, he apparently did not reply to it.

Linguistics" or "Contemporary Linguistics in America: Selected Readings". Of course Trubetzkoy's work will fit neither the original title nor the others. Perhaps the title "Selected Readings in Contemporary Linguistics" is the best after all. What I object to is clear, I see no reason for us to recognize such a thing as "American linguistics" in any official way any more than I think one should recognize an "American physics" or whatnot. I can see how one might wish to collect the best produced by the linguists in a given country at any time; in view of the circumstances there is, I believe, a good reason for doing so now. At the same time there is no need to be nationalistic about it.

(Dyen to Joos, September 16, 1955; MJA)

I am rather thoroughly opposed to volumes of this kind, because, among other things, I don't believe in making students read — or rake up! — all the errors of the past. I for one would not make students buy such a volume, and very likely wouldn't put it on reserve. However, that's my personal bias, and I'm sure most of our colleagues will welcome the book.

(Trager to Joos, September 25, 1955; MJA)

Dyen was not alone in objecting to the proposed title. In particular, the bracketed 'American' was an object of concern. Bloch found the 'name "American Linguistics" [to be] both offensive and absurd'. To Kahane 'the epitheton [*sic*] American before Linguistics is as unjustifiable as would be, say, German before physics [...]'. And Malkiel, a refugee from Nazi Germany and a Romance linguist, felt that the proposed title 'could not have been less felicitous' and was 'offensive'. There were objections to the very idea of limiting the contributions to (mainly) American-based scholars. Householder would have liked to have seen some 'un-American linguistics',[7] a desire echoed by Paper, while others pointed out that Trubetzkoy had no place in a book featuring contributions by Americans (Bolinger, Chomsky, Dyen, Hoenigswald, Kahane, Moulton, Pike, Twaddell).

The remaining critical comments were quite diverse. Some respondents were concerned that some particular area of interest (generally their own) was neglected by Joos: applied linguistics (Fowler, Shen), glottochronology (Newman, Pike, Swadesh, Whatmough), psycholinguistics (Osgood), historical linguistics (Olmsted, Penzl), tone languages (Pike), semantics (Shen), linguistic geography (Sledd), acoustic phonetics (Swadesh), and communication theory (Wonderly). Still others expressed the opinion that Harris and/or Hockett were over-represented (Hatcher, Hoijer, Horne, Householder, Malkiel, Moulton, Pike, Stockwell). Several felt that Joos was being overly modest in not including any of his own work on the list

---

[7] A decade later Householder made good on his opinion by becoming coeditor of *Readings in Linguistics II*, which featured exclusively European contributions (Hamp, Householder, & Austerlitz 1966) (see § 3.5.2).

(Bolinger, Cowan, Lounsbury, Wonderly). And a few respondents took the position that the book reviews should be cut back in number or eliminated entirely (Bolinger, Hoijer, Horne, Lounsbury, Paper). The longest reply by far was from Swadesh, who wanted papers on the nineteenth century roots of American linguistics, more by Sapir and his students, and something on glottochronology. Swadesh's detailed reply accords well with the observation that 'he commented on every paper [at LSA meetings]. He had evidently set himself the task of not letting a paper go by without some sentences of criticism' (Read 1991: 280).

One is somewhat amused by the negativity expressed by some of the respondents toward particular suggestions by Joos. Bloch wrote: 'Newman: A terrible article — a complete botch' and 'Pike: The article on English diphthongs is a pitiful failure. Scrap it'. For Lunt, the Fairbanks paper 'is an egregious example of setting up a theory and then proving it with selected facts presented as serious and careful research'. And Shen had 'nothing against Mr. Bloch. However, [...] I hate like anything to tell you that every single person who speaks Japanese has given me adverse criticism on Mr. Bloch's knowledge of Japanese'. It seems safe to assume that none of the respondents would have guessed that many decades later their remarks would be published in an international journal and then in a book!

One response to Joos, namely that by Noam Chomsky, is of sufficient historical interest to merit reproduction in its entirety:

Dec. 19, 1955

Prof. Martin Joos
University of Wisconsin
Madison, Wisconsin

Dear Mr. Joos,

I'm sorry for my long delay in responding to your letter announcing the tentative contents of 'Readings in American Linguistics'. On the whole, the choice of articles seems to me very good. One omission that I hope can be remedied somehow is that of Wells' Immediate Constituents. If it cannot be added, I think it should replace some other article, perhaps Nida's Analysis of Grammatical Constituents or Wells' own Automatic Alternation, both of which seem to be less interesting than Wells IC paper.

I have a minor question about the scope of the book. If the list is to be of readings in American Linguistics, then it seems to me that Trubetzkoy's paper does not belong (nor, perhaps, does that of Jakobson and Lotz). On the other hand, if Linguistics in general is to be covered, then it seems to me that several other European articles might be included as well.

Sincerely yours,

Noam Chomsky (MJA)

Chomsky's reply is of historical interest for several reasons. First, this is, to the best of my knowledge, the oldest piece of linguistics-related correspondence from Chomsky to be published to date.[8] Second, it demonstrates clearly the high esteem in which he was held by at least one major player in post-Bloomfieldian linguistics. Even though the twenty-six year-old Chomsky had just finished his doctoral degree and had only three publications to his credit, Joos felt that he was worthy of consulting for suggestions regarding the most important papers in American linguistics in the previous three decades.[9] Joos's action accords well with the point stressed in Newmeyer (1980, 1986a) and Murray (1980) that leading figures of American linguistics at the time not only respected the young Chomsky, but also took positive steps to further his career. Third, the reply is interesting in that it captures Chomsky in what one might call a 'transitional stage'. 1955 was the year that he completed his 900-page manuscript *The Logical Structure of Linguistic Theory* (Chomsky 1955b), in which he challenged many of the basic conceptions of post-Bloomfieldian linguistics (see Chapter 4, § 4.2.2). Yet in his reply to Joos of that year, he recommended a paper for inclusion (Wells's 'Immediate Constituents'), whose underlying assumptions he rejected in that very manuscript.[10] Finally, as we will see in § 3.4.1, Joos appears to have followed Chomsky's advice. Chomsky was one of several voices that led Joos to go with his original instincts and publish the Wells paper; the four articles that Chomsky recommended dropping were indeed dropped.

One imagines that Joos was quite heartened by the set of replies that he received. Only two completely panned his idea, while many times that number expressed enthusiasm. While it is true that many of his specific choices were challenged for one reason or another, there was no consensus that the proposed anthology needed a major change of direction. Perhaps the overall positivity of the replies spurred Joos into immediate action. The last of the recommendations arrived in

---

[8] But it is not the oldest known. The RJA contains a letter from Chomsky to Jakobson from 19 February 1953 in regards to a travel grant application. In the BBA there is a letter from Chomsky to Bloch written on 13 November 1954 about a review for *Language* that the former had undertaken. I assume that when the Chomsky Archive at MIT is fully operational, still older letters will be uncovered.

[9] The LSA had about 1000 members in 1955. Assuming that the hundred or so linguists that Joos consulted were all LSA members, one can estimate that about ten percent of the membership was contacted. Nevertheless, Chomsky was still in a fairly exclusive group, since ninety percent of the membership was not contacted by Joos.

[10] Chomsky and the others, of course, were not asked for their advice on the 'best' or 'most convincing' papers that had been published, but rather on the 'programmatic papers on what everyone calls "American" linguistics nowadays'.

his mail in mid-December 1955 and the book itself was advertised as published in the *ACLS Newsletter*, vol. 8, no. 1 of April 1957.[11] By the criteria of the time (as well as by today's criteria), that was a remarkably fast turnaround time. It is to the final contents of the volume that we now turn.

3.4 The first edition of Joos's *Readings in Linguistics*

The first edition of Joos's reader appeared in 1957 under the title *Readings in Linguistics: The Development of Descriptive Linguistics in America since 1925* (Joos 1957b). § 3.4.1 presents the Table of Contents and speculates on the reasons for the divergence between the articles named in Joos's letter and those finally published. § 3.4.2 reviews what the *Readings* are most remembered for today: Joos's commentary in the Preface and after most of the articles in the volume.

3.4.1 The contents of the first edition

Below is the table of contents of the first edition, reprinted as it was in the volume, omitting the article numbers and page numbers:

1947	Rulon S. Wells: De Saussure's system of linguistics. Word 3.1-31
1925	Edward Sapir: Sound patterns in language. Lang. 1.37-51
1926	Leonard Bloomfield: A set of postulates for the science of language. Lang. 2.153-64
1934	Maurice Swadesh: The phonemic principle. Lang. 10.117-29
1934	Yuen-Ren Chao: The non-uniqueness of phonemic solutions of phonetic systems. Bulletin of the Institute of History and Philology, Academia Sinica, Vol. IV, Part 4, 363-97
1935	W. Freeman Twaddell: On defining the phoneme. Lang. Monograph No. 16
1936	Archibald A. Hill: Phonetic and phonemic change. Lang. 12.15-22
1938	W. Freeman Twaddell: A note on Old High German umlaut. MfdU 30.177-81
1939	Morris Swadesh: and Charles F. Voegelin: A problem in phonological alternation. Lang. 15.1-10
1941	Bernard Bloch: Phonemic overlapping. American Speech 16.278-84
1942	Charles F. Hockett: A system of descriptive phonology. Lang. 18.3-21

---

[11] The price announced for the volume was $6.00 for the paperback edition, as Joos had suggested in his letter. Despite Joos's dismissal of the idea of a hardbound edition, one was published at a price of $8.00.

1942   Zellig S. Harris: Morpheme alternants in linguistic analysis. Lang. 18.169-80

1944   Lawton M. Hartmann III: The segmental phonemes of the Peiping dialect. Lang. 20.28-42

1944   Zellig S. Harris: Simultaneous components in phonology. Lang. 20.181-205

1946   Henry M. Hoenigswald: Sound change and linguistic structure. Lang. 22.138-43

1946   Zellig S. Harris: From morpheme to utterance. Lang. 22.161-83

1946   Bernard Bloch: Studies in colloquial Japanese II: Syntax. Lang. 22.200-48

1947   Rulon S. Wells: Immediate constituents. Lang. 23.81-117

1947   William G. Moulton: Juncture in modern standard German. Lang. 23.212-26

1948   Werner F. Leopold: German ch. Lang. 24. 179-80

1947   Charles F. Hockett: Peiping phonology. JAOS 67.253 67

1947   Charles F. Hockett: Problems of morphemic analysis. Lang. 23. 321-43

1947   Bernard Bloch: English verb inflection. Lang. 23.399-418

1948   Eugene A. Nida: The identification of morphemes. Lang. 24.414-41

1948   Zellig S. Harris: Componential analysis of a Hebrew paradigm. Lang. 24.87-91

1948   Richard S. Pittman: Nuclear structures in linguistics. Lang. 24.287-92

1948   Charles F. Hockett: A note on 'structure'. IJAL 14.269-71

1948   Charles F. Hockett: Implications of Bloomfield's Algonquian syntax. Lang. 24.117-31

1948   W. Freeman Twaddell: The Prehistoric Germanic short syllabics. Lang. 24.139-51

1950   Henry M. Hoenigswald: The principal step in comparative grammar. Lang. 26. 357-64

1950   Robert A. Hall, Jr.: The reconstruction of Proto-Romance. Lang. 26.6-27

1950   Charles F. Hockett: Peiping morphophonemics. Lang. 26.63-85

1950   Bernard Bloch: Studies in colloquial Japanese IV: Phonemics. Lang. 26.86-125

1950   Martin Joos: Description of language design. JASA 22.701-8

1951   Einar Haugen: Directions in modern linguistics. Lang. 27.211-22

1951   Samuel E. Martin: Korean phonemics. Lang. 27.519-33

1952   Martin Joos: The medieval sibilants. Lang. 28.222-31

1953   Floyd G. Lounsbury: The method of descriptive morphology, Oneida verb morphology. Oneida Verb Morphology 11-24

1954   Charles F. Hockett: Two models of grammatical description. Word 10.
        210-31

1955   J. Donald Bowen and Robert P. Stockwell: The phonemic interpretation
        of semivowels in Spanish. Lang. 31.236-40

1956   Sol Saporta: A note on Spanish semivowels. Lang. 32.287-90

1956   Bowen and Stockwell: A further note on Spanish semivowels. Lang.
        32.290-2

1956   Stockwell, Bowen, and I. Silva-Fuenzalida: Spanish juncture and
        intonation. Lang. 32.641-65

There are major disparities between Joos's suggestions and that which finally appeared in the volume. There are 56 suggestions in the September 1955 letter, but
only 43 papers in the published volume. One assumes that space considerations
were the primary reason for this reduction. That assumption is confirmed by the
fact that two papers were included that were mentioned in Joos's cover letter as
being too long for the volume. They both were syntactically oriented: Bloch's treatment of Japanese and Wells's 'Immediate Constituents'. It is interesting that their
inclusion increased that percentage of the volume devoted to syntax a bit, perhaps
anticipating the central role that syntax would play in the immediately coming
years (e.g., Chomsky 1957a; Harris 1957).

Of the 43 articles in the published volume, 23 were on Joos's original list, with
20 (almost half) being added later. The contributions from Harris (reduced from
11 to 4) and Hockett (reduced from 8 to 7) were scaled back, as requested, and
all reviews were eliminated. And Joos allowed himself to be persuaded to reprint
two of his own articles. By any criteria, the subtitle of the *Readings* was totally
appropriate. Peter Matthews observed that the book contained twelve important
papers on morphology and syntax[12]:

> Of these all but one refer to Bloomfield at least once. *Language* is mentioned nine
> times and articles by him eight times. The other references include over a hundred
> to the authors themselves and their American contemporaries [...]. Six are to
> Sapir, two to Boas, two to Jespersen; there are none to other general works by
> European scholars, contemporary or earlier.
>
> (Matthews 1993: 19)

What is particularly interesting is which linguists from Joos's 1955 letter were
kept in and which were dropped. The first thing that one notices is that the final
content is even more theoretically narrow than Joos's original list. Let us confine
ourselves to work published after 1940, by which point American linguistics was

---

[12] Matthews, a morphologist, might also have mentioned that the 23 papers devoted to phonetics, phonology, and morphophonemics drew every bit as much from American sources as those on
morphology and syntax.

in the process of becoming factionalized, and before 1955, when Joos drafted his letter. Eleven authors of work published within that time period were named in Joos's letter but did not have articles in the *Readings*: Frederick Agard, Gordon Fairbanks, Roman Jakobson, John Lotz, Stanley Newman, Kenneth Pike, Morris Swadesh, George Trager, C. F. Voegelin, and Benjamin Whorf. Trager, as we have seen, opted out. Of the remaining ten, four were identified with the Sapirean wing of descriptive linguists (Newman, Swadesh, Voegelin, Whorf), two with the Prague School (Jakobson, Lotz), and one with missionary work (Pike).[13] A few linguists were added who were not on Joos's original list: Robert A. Hall, Einar Haugen, and Werner Leopold. Hall tended to be aligned with Joos theoretically. Leopold, whose work revolved for the most part around child language, was probably included because his one-page piece complemented the Moulton article that preceded it, by pointing to the difficulties with Moulton's procedural identification of juncture. The Haugen overview of trends in the field by a well-respected pioneer in the study of language contact and other sociolinguistic topics must have appealed to Joos (and to Graves) by its assertion that 'American linguistics is today in a more flourishing state than at any time since the founding of the Republic' (Haugen 1951: 211).

The result is that the post-1940 work that appears in the *Readings* overwhelmingly and disproportionately represents the most 'extreme' wing of American linguistics, that is, the wing that was characterized by an empiricist epistemology and an accompanying rigid methodology. Eric Hamp must have been alluding to this fact when he wrote that 'the development represented [in the *Readings*] was a highly cohesive body of doctrine whose practitioners shared a good many points of underlying outlook and a strong *esprit de corps*' (Hamp 1995b: xi).

So the question is what would lead Joos to narrow his choice of contents? I can offer an (unfortunately, speculative) answer to the question. I think that Joos was pressured by the ACLS Committee on the Language Program in general and by Mortimer Graves in particular to focus the volume to the extent possible on the empiricist wing of descriptive linguistics. As we have seen, partisans of this approach held a majority on the Committee. It does not seem implausible that they would have exerted their influence on Joos to make their views more prominent in the final version than in his original letter.[14] And as for Graves, he could hardly make a speech or write an article in the early 1950s without explicitly or implicitly extolling the 'American way of life'. No 'way of life in linguistics' was as much home-grown American as Joos's own positivistic orientation to linguistic theorizing, so no doubt he was more than willing to go along with Graves's desires.

---

[13] Though Eugene Nida was included.
[14] We know that the Committee had the final say on the contents, since the papers 'were selected by a committee of scholars' (Hamp 1961: 166).

The most noteworthy exclusion from the volume was that of Kenneth Pike. Pike was not happy about that. In a letter to Charles Hockett written in 1982, Pike attributed his exclusion from the volume to objections from certain (unnamed) individuals in the linguistics community:

> Martin Joos in his preliminary letter suggesting persons whose materials should be enclosed in his "readings" to describe "the development of descriptive linguistics in America since 1925" listed a couple of my articles. Every one was rejected from the published version — because, he told me, people in the discipline objected. Yet in that very volume you have <u>seven</u> of your articles reprinted.
>
> (Pike to Hockett, November 30, 1982; LSAA)

We do not know if the objections were ideologically, intellectually, or personally based. They could well have been a combination of the three.[15] There are, of course, fairly mundane reasons why some particular linguist might have been dropped from the printed version. Perhaps Joos took to heart Bloch's savaging of the Newman and Pike articles and Lunt's of the Fairbanks article.

In any event, the contents of the published version of Joos's *Readings* differed fairly markedly from the contents of the letter that he sent out to around a hundred linguists in September 1955.

3.4.2 Joos's editorial commentary in the first edition

As far as the organization of the volume is concerned, the Contents page was preceded by a three-page Preface (pages v–vii). Sensitive perhaps to the objections of the respondents, Joos began by acknowledging the ambiguity of the notion 'American linguistics', concluding that he would continue to use the term 'because to name any competing term would involve at least equally invidious implications' (p. v). The page went on to give a whirlwind historical sketch of American linguistics leading to its current empiricist orientation, and contained often-referred-to passages such as 'The abandonment of deduction in favor of induction has never been reversed', '[E]very language has to be explained from the inside out', and 'If the facts have been fully stated, it is perverse or childish to demand an explanation into the bargain.' Two paragraphs outlined the (very different) debts that the

---

[15] A propos of Pike's exclusion, Robert Ladd has written: 'It seems likely that Pike was marginalized in part because of his commitment to Christian missionary work (Murray 1994: 174, 189f), but comments I heard as a student suggest that he was also regarded as rather unsophisticated. His prose was inelegant and prone to occasional malapropisms' (Ladd 2020: fn. 11). George Trager, Joos's intellectual ally, might well have been one of the objecting individuals. His evaluation of Pike (1947a) was scathing, writing that he 'condemn[ed] the book as a theoretical work, and even more as a text-book – since as the latter it will lead astray many who might otherwise be valuable workers in linguistic science' (Trager 1950b: 158).

field owed to Sapir and Bloomfield and remarked that '[t]hey valued de Saussure's contribution in equal measure, but used it in ways as different as their different personalities'.[16]

Joos devoted the second page of the Preface mainly to methodology, asserting in a fairly roundabout way that what scientists do is to present the most compact and parsimonious representation of the raw data that they are able to. On the third page Joos went into what made American linguistics unique and, by implication, far superior to European linguistics. (The word 'American' on this page appears fourteen times). The following passage is typical:

> [A remark by Bloomfield] is now used to classify general theory as a science also — this gives the theoretical paper, American style, a familiar air to the American reader accustomed to reading descriptions of particular languages, wherefore both kinds of paper are read with a similarity of appreciation which, for all I know, may be unique as well as characteristic of the American scene. (p. vii)

A few paragraphs later Joos produced the following sentences, the content of which can only be described as 'astonishing':

> Altogether, then, there is ample reason why both Americans and (for example) Europeans are likely on each side to consider the other side both irresponsible and arrogant. We may request the Europeans to regard the American style as a tradition comme une autre; but the Americans can't be expected to reciprocate; they are having too much fun to be bothered, and few of them are aware that either side has a tradition. (p. vii)

As an anonymous referee has pointed out to me, 'It is paradoxical to proclaim Bloomfield and Sapir heroes of American linguistics (as Joos has just done in the Preface), and state at the same time that Europe and the US can safely ignore each other: Bloomfield and Sapir were steeped in German linguistics and German culture at large (like Boas, by the way). When such a grossly misleading declaration occurs, something more political or affective must be going on: a declaration of linguistic independence, or an affirmation of post-war nationalism.' I think that that is absolutely correct, and much in line with the remarks in §§ 3.2.3, 3.3.1, and 3.4.1 on the progressive 'Americanization' of the *Readings*.

Joos's *Readings* is perhaps best remembered for the commentary of up to several paragraphs that he inserted after most of the articles. They were quirky, at times (overly) personal, and from the point of view of someone like the present author

---

[16] If Joos believed that Sapir valued Saussure's contribution, he must have reached his conclusion from a personal communication, since it has been written that Sapir never once cited Saussure (Falk 2004: 110). However, an anonymous referee has pointed me to one citation, namely in a review of Jespersen (1925) (Sapir 1926).

for whom the volume was required reading in student days, quite entertaining. Before going into details, it is worth mentioning that 31 of the 43 articles were commented upon, but their distribution was uneven. Of the first twenty articles, nineteen had commentary, but of the final twenty, only nine. Since the articles were in chronological order,[17] Joos clearly felt more of a need to reflect on the older ones than on the newer ones. That makes sense. After all, the farther back one goes in time, the more unfamiliar theoretical assumptions, modes of analysis, and technical terminology are likely to be. The background assumptions and terminology in the articles from the seven or eight years preceding 1957 would certainly have been familiar to the average reader and therefore would not have required critical commentary or elucidation.

If the commentary had one running theme, it was the continuation and further development of the empiricist theory and methodology of the Preface. Along these lines, the one piece of commentary that is surely the most cited (and criticized) is the following, which followed Bloch's 'Phonemic overlapping' paper:

> American linguistics owes a great debt to [the stimulating new ideas that were coming out of Europe, specifically from the Cercle Linguistique de Prague]; but in the long run those ideas were not found to add up to an adequate methodology. Trubetzkoy phonology tried to explain everything from articulatory acoustics and a minimum set of phonological laws taken as essentially valid for all languages alike, flatly contradicting the American (Boas) tradition that languages could differ from each other without limit and in unpredictable ways, and offering too much of a phonological *explanation* where a sober *taxonomy* would serve as well.
>
> Children want explanations, and there is a child in each of us; descriptivism makes a virtue of not pampering that child. (p. 96)

Joos at least singled out Trubetzkoy by name. In that same commentary, he excoriated Pike without even giving him the courtesy of an overt recognition:

> It was the present article by Bloch that made clear, as it never had been before, that phonemics must be kept unmixed from all that lies on the opposite side of it from phonetics [...] the ghost of the slain dragon [of level mixing — (FJN)] continued to plague the community of linguists under such names as 'grammatical prerequisites to phonemic analysis' and has not been completely exorcized to this day" (p. 96).

---

[17] The Wells article on Saussure was published in 1947, but appeared as the first in the volume, presumably because Saussure was (chronologically) antecedent to all of the contributors.

Many, if not most, of the readers of the volume would have recognized 'Grammatical prerequisites to phonemic analysis' as the title of an article by Pike (Pike 1947b).

Despite Joos's open admiration for both Sapir and Bloomfield, he missed few opportunities to point out that they (and in particular Sapir) were not empiricist enough to satisfy current tastes. 'There was a brilliance about Edward Sapir', Joos wrote, so even though 'we normally find him right [...] we seem captious when we point out that he also said many things which are essentially uncheckable ("invulnerable") and thus not science' (p. 25). Still more negatively, Joos remarked that 'Sapir's vitalistic way of thinking welcomed this duality [between arrangements and processes — (FJN)] as an essential dualism in human nature. But these were other times, and Sapir's disciple Harris drove out the spirit [...]' (p. 115). Bloomfield is castigated as well: 'When we look back at Bloomfield's work, we are disturbed at this and that, but more than anything else Bloomfield's confusion between phonemes and morphophonemes disturbs us' (p. 92).

One feels that Joos never considered that the readers of his volume might not be Americans. I do not know how else to interpret the statement that 'The position of Saussure today is very much like that of Ibsen in the drama. Only now and then is he spoken of, and then in a ritualistic way' (p. 18). Saussure was certainly spoken of by European linguists more often than 'now and then'.[18] Later, Joos reprises his remarks in the Preface by remarking that 'these two papers [Swadesh & Voegelin's and Bloch's "Phonemic overlapping"] beautifully show the typical American way of advancing linguistic theory; by working out specific problems and then, perhaps, drawing the methodological conclusions' (p. 92).

The contributions were followed by several pages of elucidation of various technical terms used by the authors.

3.5 The later editions of the *Readings*

This section reviews the later editions of Joos's *Readings in Linguistics*: the second and third (§ 3.5.1) and the fourth (§ 3.5.2), followed by a summary section on the first four editions (§ 3.5.3). § 3.5.4 treats the 1995 combined and abridged edition.

---

[18] Joos's comments here followed the 1947 Wells piece on Saussure. Julia Falk has written that 'as in Bloomfield's own work after 1933 [the leading American linguists of the 1930s] rarely, if ever referred to Saussure or the *Cours*' (Falk 2004: 112). As noted in Chapter 2, Charles Hockett wrote to Falk that he 'didn't read the *Cours* until after [he] retired from Cornell in 1982 [...]' (quoted in Koerner 2002: 10). E. F. K. Koerner suggests (p. c., 14 December 2014) that it was Roman Jakobson who asked Wells to write his 1947 paper, a necessary task because of 'the non-reception of the *Cours* in US linguistics'.

3.5.1 The second and third editions (1958 and 1963)

The second edition of the *Readings* appeared just a year later, in 1958. Joos reported to the ACLS Committee that 'sales [of the first edition] have been gratifying large'.[19] There was no change in the articles in this edition, nor in the commentary, though a certain number of typographical errors were corrected in each. The first page of the Preface to the first edition was retained, while the second and third pages were dropped. Joos does not tell us why they were dropped, though one can imagine: the second page was no more than an introductory-level overview of empiricist methodology as applied to linguistics (and therefore out of place in the Preface) and the third, with its touting of the superiority of everything American, must have led Joos to receive a tremendous amount of negative feedback.

Despite these deletions, Joos did add a page and a quarter of text to the Preface outlining the background to the publication. This added material is quite defensive, most of it devoted to his explaining why the volume could not please everybody. So he noted and lamented the lack of papers on English phonology. To partially remedy this gap, he included at the end of the volume, the bibliography from James Sledd's review of *An Outline of English Structure* (Trager & Smith 1951).

Joos went on in the extended Preface to explain why he could not follow the advice of all of his respondents:

> From the three dozen useful responses, it appeared that about 800 pages would have satisfied the sum of the well-argued demands. The impossibility of that size of book was clear. Fortunately, however, many correspondents had foreseen that result; and, what is even more significant here, several of them had independently proposed the very same solution that ultimately forced itself upon us: to start out from the largest coherent group of papers that could be found within the list, and to associate other papers with them to the limit of useful coherence — so that each excluded paper would have (if included) yielded more distraction than benefit to the readers.
>
> (Joos 1958: vi)

It is not clear to me which groups of papers were associated with each other 'to the limit of useful coherence'. He was referring to the Moulton and Leopold papers, certainly (see § 3.4.1), and the four final papers on Spanish phonology. Beyond these, the articles included seem pretty much to be 'stand alones'.

After going into some more technical detail about the process of arriving at the final list of papers, he noted the absence of papers in linguistic anthropology, 'a departure which has been considered deplorable by anthropological reviewers of our

---

[19] Unfortunately, the ACLS is unable to provide printing and sales figures at this time. It hopes to be able to do so 'after we have hired a new archivist' (comment over the telephone).

book [...]' (p. vi)[20] Finally, he noted that the size limit forbade any articles in sub-fields such as 'perception theory, information theory, translation theory, discourse analysis, and language-teaching theory' (p. vi).

The third edition of the *Readings*, published in 1963, was identical in content to the second.

3.5.2 The fourth edition (1966)

The decision by the ACLS not to publish another edition of the *Readings* seems to have caught Joos by surprise, as did the decision of the University of Chicago Press to take it over:

> I will certainly talk about things with Richter [of the University of Chicago Press], who is a very reasonable and nice man. Actually, as I understood it, the press here [in Chicago] simply took over RIL I because ACLS felt it uneconomical to be in the publishing business. [...] In short, the intention of the CLP [Committee on Language Programs of the ACLS — (FJN)] was simply to insure that the volume was kept in print, to relieve ACLS of a role it did not covet, to handle distribution in a more effective fashion [...], but never, naturally, to be doing things that would have the effect of keeping you in the dark.
>
> (Eric Hamp to Joos, February 16, 1966; MJA)

The University of Chicago Press was at first somewhat reluctant to publish the fourth edition:

> We had deliberated for some time over the question of whether or not to re-publish this work, as ordinarily we do not like to take over publications originally issued under other imprints. The question was settled in the affirmative following our agreement to publish another collection of readings in linguistics which have been selected by Professor Hamp of our faculty with the assistance of two co-editors, from European sources. That volume is selected for publication in June under the title <u>Readings in Linguistics II</u>, which is being announced as a companion volume to yours which we now propose to issue as <u>Readings in Linguistics I</u>.
>
> (Anders Richter of the University of Chicago Press to Joos, February 10, 1966; MJA)

Chicago published both volumes simultaneously in 1966, the full title of Joos's volume now being *Readings in Linguistics I: The Development of Descriptive Linguistics in America 1925–56* (Joos 1966b). The companion volume (Hamp et al.

---

[20] Joos is presumably referring to the Voegelin and Hymes reviews (see § 3.7.2 and § 3.7.3), which appeared in 1958.

1966), was simply titled *Readings in Linguistics II*. The idea of a second volume devoted to European work had been in the air for at least a decade, as it is alluded to by Dell Hymes in a letter to Joos dated December 28, 1956. By that point in time, American linguists had begun to appreciate work being carried out in the various structuralist schools in Europe, an appreciation that continued as the decade progressed (see Chapter 2, § 2.5 and Hymes & Fought 1981: 151–154). So by 1966 Americans were 'ready' for a European-oriented anthology. In fact, five years earlier, the ACLS Committee on Language Programs asked Eric Hamp, Robert A. Hall, Jr. (soon to be replaced by Robert Austerlitz), and Fred Householder to assume responsibility for a companion volume to the *Readings*, covering areas and views ignored by Joos (Hamp 1995b: xi). This proposed volume soon morphed into a book containing exclusively European contributions. We do not know precisely why Eric Hamp was chosen as the primary editor of this volume, though two reasons come immediately to mind: first, in 1966 Hamp was the Chairman of the ACLS Committee, and hence quite aware of the ins and outs of publishing an anthology of important papers; and second, as the above quotation indicates, he was well known to the editorship of the University of Chicago Press.

Joos left the articles and commentary as they were in the first three editions. He rewrote fairly thoroughly the Preface to the fourth edition, though it did repeat earlier material about the publication history. By 1966 generative grammar was in its ascendancy and he felt the need to situate the *Readings* in the changed atmosphere of the field. He noted that 'The reissue of this volume by a second publisher [...] comes in radically altered circumstances. In 1957 a great deal was taken for granted in American linguistics which has been called into question since' (Joos 1966a: v). But now, 'most of the young men [*sic*] in the profession have turned to a new trend, what is now called generative-transformational grammar, and some of them think of it as a surely victorious competitor to our tradition' (p. vi). Joos pointed out that the tradition represented in the *Readings* is aptly called 'taxonomic linguistics,[21] which certain proponents of the new trend use as a derogatory term' (p. vi), and went on to write:

> Now when anybody holds that the existence of two kinds of linguistics — taxonomic and, for example, generative-transformational — strictly implies the inferiority or even nullity of one of them, that opinion can only be pernicious no matter which of the two is denigrated. Both extreme views will fade out in due course, especially as each side reads more of what has been published by the other. (p. vi)

---

[21] Recall from § 3.4.2 that Joos counterposed a 'taxonomic' approach to an 'explanatory' one, opting for the former. The empiricist wing of American structuralism was often described as taxonomically-oriented, since their procedures led to a taxonomic classification of grammatical elements. To repeat the words of Charles Hockett: 'Linguistics is a classificatory science' (Hockett 1942: 3).

The glossary of terms was retained in the fourth edition, but not Sledd's bibliography, which presumably would have been considered well out of date by 1966.

3.5.3 The first four editions: A summary comment

As we have seen, nothing of substance changed in the *Readings* between the first edition in 1957 and the fourth in 1966, except for the prefaces. In particular, the choice of articles remained constant, as did the accompanying commentary. Yet, as Joos himself acknowledged, the field had changed dramatically. An interesting question is why Joos would have left the much-criticized content untouched for nine years. He to some extent answered this question in the Preface to the fourth edition:

> The pressure of increasing demand has forced unchanged printing. Additions and deletions have not been called for by the market, conceivably to some extent because of inertia, but in my belief principally because of an unseen factor. Both for intrinsic and for extrinsic reasons, the development of this tradition in descriptive linguistics happened to slacken just as the time when the volume first appeared.
>
> (Joos 1966a: vi)

The 'extrinsic reasons' had to do with the rise of generative grammar, alluded to in the previous section. Joos pointed to the 'intrinsic reason [being] named in the last line of page 418, where the word *reached* was ill-advised: it should have been *touched*' (p. vi; emphasis in original). On that page, Joos had written in the last commentary to the last article:

> If [vocalizations] cannot be truly incorporated within the science as so far defined we have learned that our science has indeed reached its ultimate limit here.
>
> (Joos 1957b: 418)

I interpret these words as a concession of defeat. Joos seems to be saying that since his own approach had reached (or touched) its limits (possibly contradicting the above-cited assertion that it was not inferior to the new trend), it would be best to preserve the *Readings* and his own commentary as a testimony of how people used to do linguistics. This interpretation gains credence from a comment by Eric Hamp in the Preface to *Readings in Linguistics II*. Hamp wrote that 'It is perhaps ironical that the *Readings*, intended as a handbook on linguistic theory, has already found wide use as a textbook in the history of linguistics' (Hamp 1966: vi).

3.5.4 The abridged edition (1995)

In 1995 the University of Chicago Press issued *Readings in Linguistics I and II: Abridged Edition* (Hamp et al. 1995). The volume included 19 articles from *Readings I* (out of the original 43) and 20 articles from *Readings II* (out of the original 39). The following are those reprinted from *Readings I*:

> Edward Sapir, Sound patterns in language, 1925.
> Leonard Bloomfield, A set of postulates for the science of language, 1926.
> Morris Swadesh, The phonemic principle, 1934.
> Yuen-Ren Chao, The non-uniqueness of phonemic solutions of phonetic systems, 1934.
> Archibald A. Hill, Phonetic and phonemic change, 1936.
> W. Freeman Twaddell, A note on Old High German umlaut, 1938.
> Morris Swadesh and Charles F. Voegelin, A problem in phonological alternation, 1939.
> Bernard Bloch, Phonemic overlapping, 1941.
> Zellig S. Harris, Simultaneous components in phonology, 1944.
> Zellig S. Harris, From morpheme to utterance, 1946.
> Rulon S. Wells, Immediate constituents, 1947.
> Charles F. Hockett, Problems of morphemic analysis, 1947.
> Charles F. Hockett, Implications of Bloomfield's Algonquian studies, 1948.
> Henry M. Hoenigswald, The principal step in comparative grammar, 1950.
> Charles F. Hockett, Peiping morphophonemics, 1950.
> Bernard Bloch, Studies in colloquial Japanese IV, phonemics, 1950.
> Samuel E. Martin, Korean phonemics, 1951.
> Floyd G. Lounsbury, The method of descriptive morphology: Oneida verb morphology 1953.
> Charles F. Hockett, Two models of grammatical description, 1954.

The four-page Foreword was written by Eric Hamp, the only living member of the four editors in 1995. Hamp outlined the three aims of the combined abridged volume:

> First, since this volume is meant to be of use to the ongoing business of linguistics and is not intended as an historical archive or bibliophilic museum piece, it should be priced well within the reach of students [...]; Second, an attempt has been made to conserve something of the flavor of the original volumes. Third, in making selections the needs of students, rather than those of established scholars, have been kept foremost.
>
> (Hamp 1995a: v)

Most of Hamp's remarks are devoted to lamenting the exclusion of certain papers that had appeared in the first few editions. However, he gave no reason why some articles were included and others excluded, except to remark that 'It seems agreed that this abridgment cannot appear without a selection each from Sapir and Bloomfield drawn from *RIL I*' (p. vii). Availability seemed to play a fairly minor role in his decision, since of the nineteen included papers, fourteen had appeared in *Language* and one each in *American Speech* and *Word*, journals that most university libraries might be expected to subscribe to. On the other hand, three were included that were no doubt difficult for many to obtain: those by Chao (see § 3.6), Twaddell (a paper in a Germanics journal), and Lounsbury (an excerpt from a monograph). Hamp and his co-editors seemed to favor older (and therefore possibly harder to get) contributions: About half of oldest papers from earlier editions of the reader are included, but fewer than a quarter of the more recent ones. Interestingly, Hamp implicitly criticized Joos for not having included any papers by Pike or Trager in the earlier editions, as well as for his omission of 'actual descriptions of grammar, most especially for Native American languages' (p. vii).

Since by 1995 the tradition represented in the *Readings* had long ago ceased to be productive, it is difficult to determine whether Hamp, et al. used the perceived importance of a paper as a criterion for its inclusion. They might well have done so. In 1994 Stephen O. Murray published a history of American linguistics entitled *Theory Groups and the Study of Language in North America: A Social History* (Murray 1994). Murray's references to work in American descriptive linguistics in the period that concerns us are copious. I make the assumption that a citation in Murray to a paper from this period is an indication of its relative importance, the lack of a citation to its relative unimportance. By that criterion, the editors of the abridged edition made their selections in terms of relative importance. Twelve articles are both in the abridged edition and cited by Murray; only seven are in the abridged edition and not cited by Murray. Six articles from the first four editions that are not in the abridged edition are cited by Murray, while eighteen are not in the abridged edition and are not cited by Murray.

Hamp ended his Foreword by asserting that '[t]he comments of Joos in *RIL I* have been retained as far as the economics of reproduction would allow' (p. vii), an odd thing to write, given that none of Joos's comments at all appeared in the abridged edition.

Given that the 1995 edition was the last, it would be useful to summarize the suggestions for—and final contents of—the books of readings that were on the table between 1946 and that date. The following section is devoted to that summary.

3.6 A visual display of the progression of the book of readings

Table 3.1 illustrates graphically the progression of the proposed or actual contents of the book of readings discussed above. The first column states the name of the paper, for most in abridged form. The second column is filled in if it was mentioned

Table 3.1 A visual display of the progression of the book of readings

NAME OF PAPER	Bloch 1946a	Joos's 1955 letter	*R in L* Edns. 1–4	Abridged Edition
Agard, Noun morphology in Roumanian		■		
Bloch, Contrast		■		
Bloch, English verb inflection			■	
Bloch, Japanese phonemics		■		■
Bloch, Japanese syntax		■		■
Bloch, Phonemic overlapping		■		
Bloomfield, A set of postulates		■		■
Bloomfield, Ilocano syntax		■		■
Bloomfield, Meaning	■			
Bloomfield, On recent work general linguistics	■			
Bowen & Stockwell, Further note on Spanish semivowels			■	
Bowen & Stockwell, Semivowels in Spanish			■	
Chao, Non-uniqueness of phonemic solutions	■	■	■	■
Fairbanks, Phonemic structure of Zographensis		■		
Hall, Reconstruction of Proto-Romance			■	
Hamp, Morphophonemics ofthe Keltic mutations		■	■	
Harris, Componential analysis Hebrew		■	■	■
Harris, Discontinuous morphemes			■	
Harris, Morpheme alternants		■		
Harris, From morpheme to utterance		■	■	
Harris, Navajo phonology		■		
Harris, rev. of Emmeneau		■		
Harris, rev. of Gray		■		
Harris, rev. of Sapir		■		
Harris, rev. of Trubetzkoy		■		
Harris, Simultaneous components		■	■	
Harris, Yokuts structure			■	
Hartman, Segmental phonemes Chinese		■		
Haugen, Directions in modern linguistics			■	
Hill, Phonetic and phonemic change		■	■	
Hockett, A note on structure			■	
Hockett, Chinese morphophonemics		■		

Continued

Table 3.1 *Continued*

NAME OF PAPER	Bloch 1946a	Joos's 1955 letter	*R in L* Edns. 1–4	Abridged Edition
Hockett, Implications of Bloomfield's Algonquian studies		■	■	■
Hockett, Peiping morphophonemics			■	■
Hockett, Peiping phonology		■	■	
Hockett, Problems of morphemic analysis		■	■	■
Hockett, rev. of Martinet			■	
Hockett, rev. of Nida			■	
Hockett, rev. of Shannon and Weaver		■	■	
Hockett, System of descriptive phonology			■	
Hockett, Two models of grammatical description			■	■
Hoenigswald, Principal step in comparative grammar			■	■
Hoenigswald, Sound change and linguistic structure		■	■	■
Jakobson & Lotz, French phonemic pattern		■		■
Joos, Description of language design		■	■	■
Joos, Medieval sibilants		■	■	■
Leopold, German ch		■	■	■
Lounsbury, Method of descriptive morphology: Oneida verb morphology		■	■	
Martin, Korean phonemics		■	■	
Moulton, Juncture in German		■	■	
Newman, Stress system of English			■	
Nida, Grammatical constituents			■	
Nida, Identification of morphemes		■	■	
Pike, Coexistent phonemic systems			■	
Pike, English diphthongs		■	■	
Pike, Taxemes and immediate constituents		■	■	
Pittman, Nuclear structures		■	■	
Sapir, La réalité psychologique	■			
Sapir, Sound patterns in language	■	■	■	■
Saporta, Spanish semivowels			■	■
Stockwell, Bowen, & Silva-Fuenzalida, Spanish juncture and intonation			■	
Swadesh & Voegelin, A problem in phonological alternation		■	■	

Table 3.1 *Continued*

Swadesh, English syllabics		■		
Swadesh, Phonemic principle		■	■	
Trager, rev of van Wijk		■	■	
Trager, Russian declensional morphemes		■		
Trager, Serbo-croat accents		■		
Trubetzkoy, Anleitung	■			
Twaddell, Defining the phoneme		■	■	■
Twaddell, High German umlaut		■	■	
Twaddell, Phonemics,	■			
Twaddell, Prehistoric German short syllabics		■	■	
Wells, Automatic alternation		■	■	
Wells, De Saussure's system of linguistics		■	■	■
Wells, Immediate constituents			■	
Wells, Pitch phonemes of English		■		
Wells, rev of Pike's Intonation		■		
Whorf, Grammatical categories		■		
Whorf, Science and linguistics	■			

by Bloch (1946a). The third column identifies the papers that Joos considered for inclusion in his 1955 letter, the fourth column those that actually appeared in the first four editions of *Readings in Linguistics*, and the fifth those that appeared in the 1995 abridged edition.

As can be seen, only two papers survived the entire journey from Bloch's 1946 editorial comment to Hamp et al. 1995: Sapir's 'Sound patterns in language' and Chao's 'The non-uniqueness of phonemic solutions of phonetic systems'. I suggest that the reasons for their retention are very different. Sapir's paper, which appeared in the first volume of the journal *Language* (Sapir 1925a), was in every sense of the term 'foundational', given that it was the first clear statement of the goals and methodology of phonemic theory published in the United States and one of the first published anywhere. Even someone as 'un-Sapirean' as George Trager could write:

> The actual codifying and formulation of descriptive theory and techniques have been much more explicitly carried out by other linguists [than Bloomfield], *beginning with* Sapir's 'Sound patterns in language' [...]
>
> (Trager 1946: 462; emphasis added)

Recognition of the importance of Sapir's paper did not end with the decline of structuralism and the advent of generative grammar. The first two major books in generative phonology, Morris Halle's *The Sound Pattern of Russian* (Halle 1959) and Chomsky and Halle's *The Sound Pattern of English* (Chomsky & Halle 1968) were named in direct homage to Sapir's 'Sound patterns in language' (Morris Halle, p. c., December 7, 1978).

The 'Non-uniqueness' paper by Yuen-Ren Chao was also important, though not at the level of Sapir's. It was perhaps the first to point out a dilemma that would plague linguists in the decades to come, namely that more than one analysis is fully compatible with reigning theoretical assumptions and practical methodology. But the principal reason that it was chosen derives from the extreme difficulty that linguists at that time had in finding it. Henry Gleason has written:

> In 1934, almost as an immediate response to Bloomfield's *Language* ([Bloomfield 1933]) Chao Yuen Ren had published a paper entitled 'The nonuniqueness of phonemic solutions of phonetic systems' in the *Bulletin of the Institute of History and Philology, Academia Sinica*, a journal that was not on the regular reading lists of many North American linguists [Chao 1934]. For that matter, it was received in very few North American libraries.[22] At a later time some linguists — particularly graduate students — began to worry a little about some of the claims commonly made on behalf of linguistics — often by their teachers. Chao's paper began to attract some interest. Still, it was hard to obtain and few actually read it. I remember hearing of it — not once but repeatedly — from people who had heard about it from someone who had allegedly read it. It was said that it had been duplicated and that copies were circulating; I never saw one. (It was before the days of cheap and easy photocopying, and before the days of a highly active underground press in linguistics.) [...] Then in 1957 Joos published *Readings in Linguistics* and with this, Chao's paper became easily and generally available — bearing an imprimatur as a fundamental paper in the development of Bloomfieldianism.
>
> (Gleason 1988: 56)

Having outlined the contents of Joos's reader and the reasons for his choices, it is time to have a look at the reactions to those choices. Let us turn to the published reviews of the book.

3.7 The reviews of Joos's *Readings in Linguistics*

This section is devoted to the reviews of *Readings in Linguistics*: the 'non-reviews' in *Language* and *Word* (§ 3.7.1), followed by the published reviews: *IJAL* (§ 3.7.2),

---

[22] It was apparently the case that well into the 1960s North American libraries did not acquire the full range of European linguistic offerings, and vice-versa. For example, the Dutch linguist, E. M. Uhlenbeck complained that Chomsky (1962a) and Chomsky (1962b) were 'not accessible' (Uhlenbeck 1963: 3). But both were in books published by major American university presses.

American Anthropologist (§ 3.7.3), *Lingua* (§ 3.7.4), *Quarterly Journal of Speech* (§ 3.7.5), *Studies in Linguistics* (§ 3.7.6), *Modern Language Journal* (§ 3.7.7), and *General Linguistics* (§ 3.7.8). § 3.7.9 is a brief summary of the reviews.[23]

3.7.1 The 'non-reviews' in *Language* and *Word*

Soon after the appearance of the first edition of Joos's *Readings*, Bernard Bloch, the editor of *Language*, wrote an enthusiastic letter to Earle W. Brockman of the ACLS, which opened with the following paragraph:

> Today I got a copy of READINGS IN LINGUISTICS. It's a beautifully made book, and I am delighted to have it. It seems to me that both Martin Joos and the ACLS did a superlative job. Congratulations all around.
> (Bloch to Brockman, with a cc to Joos, May 8, 1957; BBA)

Bloch went on to promise to 'turn to and look for a reviewer — a man competent to discuss the volume but not himself represented in it'. Bloch evidently felt that it was the job of the ACLS to send out the review copies with request for reviews, since in a later letter to Brockman (May 21, 1957; BBA) he provided him with the names and addresses of twenty journals, classified by region of the world:

> Domestic (6): *American Anthropologist, International Journal of American Linguistics [IJAL], Language, Quarterly Journal of Speech, Romance Philology,* and *Word*; Western Europe (6): *Acta Linguistica* (Denmark), *Bulletin de la Société de Linguistique [de Paris], Bulletin of the School of Oriental and African Studies, Cahiers Ferdinand de Saussure, Lingua,* and *Zeitschrift für Phonetik und allgemeine Sprachwissenschaft*; Eastern Europe (7): *Acta Linguistica* (Hungary), *Biuletyn Polskiego Towarzystwa Językyoznawczego, Izvestija Akademii Nauk SSSR, Južnoslovenski filolog, Lingua Posnaniensis, Listy Filologické,* and *Voprosy jazykoznanaja*; East Asia (1): *Journal of the Linguistic Society of Japan* [= *Gengo kenkyu*].

Curiously, Bloch did not include the journals *Modern Language Journal* (founded in 1916), *Studies in Linguistics* (founded in 1942) and *General Linguistics* (founded in 1955), all three of which were to publish reviews of the *Readings*.

Despite all of Bloch's work, the *Readings* were never reviewed in *Language*. In a letter of June 6, 1957, Bloch wrote to Alfred L. Kroeber asking him for a review. Kroeber replied on July 19, declining on the following grounds: 'I don't think that I could do it justice without putting a great deal of time into reading it carefully, plus

---

[23] There was also a Short Notice of the fourth edition and its companion volume in *Foundations in Language*, vol. 4, no. 2, pp. 221–222, from 1968.

considerable other material for orientation' (BBA). Kroeber went on to tell Bloch: 'You have no idea how little I really understand of the technicalities in most of the Readings articles. [...] As a semi-outsider, I would be at a certain advantage. But being such, I could not really influence or aid the growth of linguistics; so again, my own time returns as a decisive consideration.[24] In a footnote to his letter, Kroeber suggested John Lotz as a reviewer. At that point the paper trail is lost, so we have no idea whether Bloch contacted Lotz or anybody else.

The *Readings* were also not reviewed in *Word*, the second-most important American journal of general linguistics. *Word* was the organ of the Linguistic Circle of New York, itself founded for the most part by European émigré scholars (see Chapter 2, § 2.5.1). One assumes that any review there would not have been positive, given that the journal welcomed articles that departed from post-Bloomfieldian orthodoxy.

3.7.2 The Voegelin review in *IJAL*

The review in *IJAL*, Voegelin (1958a), was quite negative. It opened with the following snarky passage:

> The general dissatisfaction expressed over the selection of papers for this book is reflected in the many alternate titles proposed for it; of these, three epitomize my own understanding of the basis for the selection: (1) The Blue Book of Linguistic Etiquette, (2) Neo-Bloomfieldian Linguistics, (3) The Development of Restatement Linguistics in America since 1925.
>
> (Voegelin 1958a: 86)

Voegelin objects to the fact that (as he sees it) 'more than half of the papers aim toward a final linguistics analysis' (p. 86), by which he seems to mean that they do no more than 'restate already analyzed linguistic systems from widely known languages, as Spanish or English or German or Japanese; or from more narrowly known languages, as Tübatulabal, where however, a preliminary analysis of the linguistic system has been stated, so that the paper in question [...] is just as much a restatement of a known linguistic system as is the paper devoted to English verbs' (p. 86). He complains that this 'final linguistic analysis' was presented 'without ever

---

[24] I find Kroeber an odd choice as a reviewer, both for the reasons he outlined (which Bloch must have been aware of) and for the fact that, contrary to the belief of every contributor to the *Readings*, he never recognized that linguistics was a field autonomous with respect to anthropology. The University of California at Berkeley had America's first department of linguistics, founded in 1901. But at Kroeber's urging it was folded into the Department of Anthropology in 1911 and not re-established until 1953, after Kroeber had retired. Still, Bloch had enormous respect for Kroeber (who had been LSA President in 1940), dedicating a number of *Language* to him in 1956.

bothering about [...] techniques for a preliminary analysis', despite the fact that the latter is a prerequisite for the former.

I confess to not fully understanding Voegelin's point here. Possibly he was objecting to presenting generalizations without sufficiently documenting the first-hand data that led to them. Or possibly he was objecting to papers that take an already published analysis and rephrase it to make it compatible with current post-Bloomfieldian descriptive presentation. If so, it is quite odd that one of the papers that he places in this negative category is his own co-authored paper with Swadesh.[25] A further curiosity is that Voegelin was one of the most enthusiastic respondents to Joos's original mailing, writing: 'Congratulations on the very imaginative editorial publication' (Voegelin to Joos, September 22, 1955; MJA). It was Voegelin who, in this letter, suggested that Joos write a paragraph of commentary on the history or particular importance of each paper.

3.7.3 The Hymes review in *American Anthropologist*

Dell Hymes, in *American Anthropologist* (Hymes 1958), began his review with words of praise:

> This is an important and useful collection which contains 43 excellent papers, mostly from *Language*, by such men as Hockett, Bloch, Harris, Twaddell, Stockwell, and Bowen. It must be read by any student of linguistics, or by any anthropologist who would understand a major school of linguistic thought. The ACLS and Martin Joos are to be congratulated for making it available.
>
> (Hymes 1958: 416)

Given Hymes's profound interest in the history of American linguistics (see Hymes & Fought 1981), that is praise indeed. The remaining page of the review, however, is quite negative, focusing on the absence of those linguists who do not adhere to what Hymes identified as 'a major school of linguistic thought', namely, the 'so-called "Yale School," whose patron saint has been Bloomfield in his behavioristic aspect' (pp. 416–417).[26] Hymes continued:

> Despite Bloomfield's great concern with descriptive linguistics in language learning, this aspect and its major American center, the University of Michigan, are unrepresented. As for the first 'Yale School', Sapir's, there is nothing of the last twenty years by Voegelin or Swadesh, nothing by Hoijer, Li, Haas, Emeneau,

---

[25] It is very rare—and arguably unethical—for a scholar to review an anthology to which he or she has contributed.

[26] By the 'Yale School', Hymes means that tendency of American descriptivism committed to an empiricist epistemology and an accompanying rigid methodology (see Chapter 1, § 1.2).

Newman, Whorf,[27] Trager, Pike. There is nothing of perhaps the greatest linguist working in America during the past decade and a half, Roman Jakobson; nor is there anything by anyone sympathetic to the Prague School (Halle, Lotz, Garvin, Sebeok, Velten). Martinet, Weinreich and the Linguistic Circle of New York are absent. Most striking of all, in view of the subtitle, the book begins with an analysis of de Saussure, a European who died 1913, but there is nothing of the man Bloomfield called 'the teacher, in one way or another, of all of us', Franz Boas. Surely all these have shaped 'the development of descriptive linguistics in America.'[28] (p. 417)

The remainder of the review is essentially a defense of Edward Sapir and his approach, citing praise for Sapir from linguists as different from each other as Louis Hjelmslev, Franz Boas, Charles Hockett, Zellig Harris, and Stanley Newman. Hymes goes on to make the remarkable observation that 'The two major developments in descriptive method at the present time, Naom [*sic*] Chomsky's "transformational grammar" and Kenneth L. Pike's "grammemic analysis" are each in its way part of the Sapir tradition' (p. 417).

3.7.4 The Uhlenbeck review in *Lingua*

The review by E. M. Uhlenbeck in *Lingua* (Uhlenbeck 1959) also starts out on a positive note, remarking on the difficulty of finding in Europe the articles by Chao, Sapir, Twaddell (on the phoneme), and Bloch (on phonemic overlapping). But the rest of his three-page review is totally negative, remarking that Joos's text 'reflects a dogmatic self-sufficiency which is difficult to harmonise with a scientific attitude of mind'[29] (p. 328). Uhlenbeck was especially offended by Joos's remarks on the differences between European and American linguistics (see § 3.4.1). He noted that American linguistics was hardly homogeneous, pointing out that Pike and other American 'dissidents' were excluded from the volume. And as he insisted:

> The viewpoints of linguists in England, Geneva and Copenhagen — not to mention other centres — are mutually too divergent (while, on the other hand, being often in accord with views that are defended by American linguists), that it does not make sense to unite them under one label. Joos binary opposition American/European indicates a lack of awareness of the situation of linguistics within and outside the U.S. (pp. 328–329)

---

[27] However, two anthologies of Whorf's work had recently been published: Whorf (1952, 1956).

[28] An anonymous referee suggests that Hymes might have compiled his own anthology (Hymes 1964b) because he found Joos's too one-sided.

[29] Uhlenbeck was to make a similar point much later in Uhlenbeck (1979).

3.7.5 The MacQueen review in *Quarterly Journal of Speech*

The one-column review in *Quarterly Journal of Speech* (MacQueen 1957) concludes that 'there is [...] a certain narrowness in the book's attack, within the limits of which, however, the treatment is excellent' (p. 324).

3.7.6 The Trager review in *Studies in Linguistics*

George Trager reviewed the *Readings* in his own journal *Studies in Linguistics* (Trager 1958), which, as will be recalled, was founded with the aid of Joos, his co-thinker. Trager had almost nothing to say about the choice of contents of the volume and everything to say about a remark that Joos made in passing about the journal in the Preface to the first edition of the *Readings*:

> A semi-journal *Studies in Linguistics*, was set up in early 1942 to facilitate circulation of work-papers; although more frequently by-passed in favor of the swifter methods, it served through that decade and is to be revived soon. Nothing could be reprinted from *SIL*, because of the definition of its purpose.
>
> (Joos 1957a: vii)

Trager was livid. He pointed out (pp. 34–35) that his 'Editorial announcement' in volume 1, number 1 (p. 1) of *SIL* (March 1942) says 'The science of linguistics in the United States has reached a point of development where it has seemed proper to inaugurate a new journal to supplement *Language* [...]' Trager went on to write that in Bulletin No. 1 (pp. 1–2) of *SIL* (also March 1942) it states that 'the undersigned [one of whom was Joos — (FJN)] [...] have agreed to [...] support [...] an informal journal to be called *Studies in Linguistics*. [...] The subject matter of *SIL* is the whole of linguistics, with emphasis (in accord with its informal nature) on theoretical problems and new techniques of analysis; it will seek to promote discussion and criticism, while avoiding mere polemics'. He continued:

> It must be a trick of memory that turned "informal" into "semi-", "the whole of linguistics" and "discussion of theory" into "work papers" [...]. [T]he fact [is] that the only papers from *SIL* suggested (casually!) for possible inclusion in the volume under review were written by the present reviewer and he withheld permission because of his views on anthologies [...]. The history of science should not be distorted, even unintentionally.
>
> (Trager 1958: 35)

Most of the rest of Trager's review was devoted to his distaste for anthologies, though he does warn 'the inexperienced reader' that Joos's 'editorial comments on the papers in the collection are highly personal in tone and content, and necessarily represent the editor's prejudices and predilections. Some readers will resent this kind of invasion of their intellectual privacy' (p. 36).

3.7.7 The Pei review in *Modern Language Journal*

Mario Pei gave a simultaneous review for *Modern Language Journal* of the fourth edition of Joos's book and the companion volume edited by Hamp, Householder, and Austerlitz (Pei 1967). Pei found the former volume 'impressive' (p. 313), but devoted the majority of his short review to gloating about Joos's defensive remarks about how the young workers in the field were turning to transformational generative grammar (see § 3.5.2). Pei, whose work lay almost entirely outside of the structuralist tradition, could not repress a smug satisfaction that his oppressors had now become the oppressed:

> At an earlier period, the structuralists, with their rigid and formalistic outlook, their intolerance of the value and achievements of the past, their scorn of the written language and its clear-cut importance in historical research, did not hesitate to venture into the field of historical linguistics and try to remold it in their own image. They now find themselves faced with a new system, a new type of thinking, and, on occasion, a spirit of intolerance that parallels their own. This is merely history repeating itself. The new tends to oust the old, as it triumphantly and arrogantly implants its banners on the conquered ramparts. (p. 314)

3.7.8 The Lightner review in *General Linguistics*

Theodore Lightner reviewed the fourth edition of the *Readings* in the journal *General Linguistics* (Lightner 1968). Lightner had received a PhD in linguistics from MIT a few years earlier, where he was a student of Morris Halle, so his perspective was naturally quite different from that of the earlier reviewers. Since nothing had changed since the first edition except for the Preface, virtually all of his comments could have been applied to any of the editions. Lightner's review was by far the longest of all of the reviews and stood out in focusing primarily on the content rather than the choice of the articles.

Lightner opened the review by remarking that he has 'no reservations concerning the importance of this anthology. Every linguist and, more important, every student of linguistics should own a copy of this book' (p. 45). Why? Primarily because 'it is not really possible to understand what is being said in linguistics today without knowing the history of the field, without knowing what events led up to the current issues that are being argued today' (p. 46). He was aware of course that Chomsky and Halle had recently critiqued a number of papers by structural linguists (Chomsky 1964c; Chomsky & Halle 1965) and promised not to repeat their arguments. As far as these arguments are concerned, Lightner dismissed the frequently-raised objection (see, for example, Voegelin & Voegelin 1963) that 'Chomsky's goal in linguistics is totally different from the goal that he is attacking; therefore, this reaction runs, it is not at all surprising that he should find these views inadequate; but it is unreasonable of him to impose his view of the goal of linguistics on others, to attack the works of others from his own personal vantage point' (p. 47). Lightner countered this objection as follows:

> For surely Bloomfield, Bloch, and Hockett — to name three of the important contributors to *RIL* criticized by Chomsky — were interested in the same thing Chomsky is interested in: an explanation of how it is possible for humans to speak. (p. 47)

Lightner devoted the remaining thirteen pages of the review to studying in fine detail a number of the analyses presented in the *Readings*, not to ridicule them, but 'to show that the problems which beset these authors in many cases remain as problems today' (p. 49). I have no way of knowing if any of the contributors to the *Readings*, most of whom were alive in 1968, ever read Lightner's review. If they had, I cannot help but feel that they would have found it both challenging and engaging.

3.7.9 The reviews: A summary

As we have seen, the published reviews of the *Readings* were generally quite negative, but not all for the same reasons. Four criticized the choice of contents, three for their narrowness and one for the types of analyses presented. One reviewer focused on Joos's arguably derogatory remarks about the journal that he edited. Only one was on the whole positive, and that because it gave the reviewer a sounding board to explore certain questions in generative phonology.

The two most trenchant reviews, those by Hymes and Uhlenbeck, zeroed in on Joos's use of the term 'American linguistics'. Since he never took the trouble to define the term, they were hardly out of line in castigating him for failing to include articles by a significant number of important linguists who carried out their work in America. Joos knew what he meant by 'what everybody calls "American" linguistics nowadays' and I am sure that Hymes (and possibly also Uhlenbeck) knew too. But many readers of the volume, particularly students, would not have known. It does little credit to Joos that he did not specify explicitly in his prefaces and commentaries that 'American linguistics' entailed, for the most part, a particularly empiricist and procedure-oriented approach to grammatical analysis.

The fact that the *Readings* went through four editions in nine years suggests that the negativity of the reviews had little if any effect on the book's sales. If Joos had taken some of the criticism in the reviews to heart, he could have changed the contents. The fact that he did not do so reinforces the point made in § 3.5.3 that he saw no problem in including papers representing only one tendency in American synchronic linguistics, even if by the fourth edition that tendency had run its course.

3.8 Further remarks on the *Readings*

This section discusses the classroom use of Joos's *Readings* (§ 3.8.1) and why the anthology continues to be of interest today (§ 3.8.2).

3.8.1 The *Readings* in the classroom

I was an MA student at a structuralist-oriented department (University of Rochester) from 1965 to 1967 and a PhD student at an generative-oriented program (University of Illinois) from 1967 to 1969. Joos's *Reader* played an important role in my education at both institutions.[30] At Rochester it was not just required reading—we were told that we needed to own our own copies. Even though most of the articles had been written twenty years earlier, we were expected to master the argumentation and take to heart many of Joos's editorial comments. At Illinois, the Chair Robert B. Lees put the volume on reserve; our preliminary exams tested us on the views of Bloch, Hockett, et al., and, of course, given the milieu, on what was wrong with them. When I arrived as an assistant professor at the University of Washington in 1969, Joos was no longer on the reading list for the PhD exam. But James Hoard, who had been a graduate student there from 1964 to 1967, notes that 'the transition from structural linguistics to generative linguistics was in full swing. Joos's reader was one item on a long list of required books and articles that served as background material for classes and seminars'.

Other colleagues report similar experiences. Stephen Anderson recalls: 'Since my very first teachers were unreconstructed American Structuralists, I was provided the Joos reader as the New Testament.' Robert D. King 'went to the University of Wisconsin in 1961 to study German literature. The first semester I took

---

[30] On 31 August 2019 I sent an email to a number of colleagues who had been students or teachers of linguistics in the 1960s, asking about their experiences (if any) with Joos's *Reader*. I would like to acknowledge and thank the eighteen individuals who replied: Stephen Anderson, Thomas Bever, Richard Demers, Ralph Fasold, Bruce Fraser, Tom Givon, Georgia Green, James Harris, James Hoard, Ray Jackendoff, Robert D. King, Jurgen Klausenburger, David Lightfoot, Barbara Partee, Paul Postal, Thomas Roeper, Michael Silverstein, and Arnold Zwicky.

phonetics from a course jointly taught by Roe-Merrill Heffner and Martin Joos. Hefner taught hard-core phonetics, Joos taught Neo-Bloomfieldian phonemics. I shifted my interest from literature to linguistics after that first semester but I stayed in the German department. Joos told me about *RIL* and I bought a copy. Hooked.'

For the generative-oriented departments, the *Reader* provided a compact way to deliver the words of the 'discredited' linguists from the previous generation. Paul Postal's 'Bad Guys Course' at MIT in the early 1960s was legendary in this respect. Thomas Bever recalls that 'we read Bloomfield's book in entirety, and then including his "Postulates", a lot of Zellig Harris, a bit of Hockett, lots of Sapir. Much of this was well known, but compactly included in Joos's massive volume, so many of us purchased it and lugged it around home and campus'. Georgia Green remembers that 'both volumes were on Eric Hamp's extensive [!] reading list for the qualifying exam at the University of Chicago in the 1960s, and several articles from volume 1 were required reading in Jim McCawley's courses in syntax and phonology, if not also morphology'.

Even undergraduates were exposed to the reader. Ray Jackendoff 'read a good deal of the Joos volume in my first and only undergraduate course in linguistics in 1964 at Swarthmore College'. And Bruce Fraser, a Cornell undergraduate in 1960, writes that he 'had a course in linguistics at Cornell in 1961, my last year, with Don Sola (Hockett was on sabbatical) and we used Joos. That was my linguistic background until I reached Halle and Chomsky the next fall. What a radical difference in the two approaches!'

The use of Joos's reader in the classroom from the 1970s onward became rarer and rarer and has been primarily confined to classes in the history of linguistics (see § 3.5.3), which have never been very common in the United States. I put it on reserve for such classes at Washington, as did Arnold Zwicky at Ohio State and then Stanford. The book, which has been out of print for many years, is rarely read in its entirety. But, as we see in the next section, certain passages from it are well remembered today.

3.8.2 On the 'staying power' of Joos's *Readings*

For a collection of papers assembled over sixty years ago and in which a majority of the content was originally published in the 1940s, Joos's *Readings* has had an incredible staying power.[31] To give an example of the assumed familiarity of the volume, consider the following. The LSA decided to publish a collection of the

---

[31] For what it's worth, Google Scholar lists 724 citations to Joos's *Readings* in their various editions. By way of comparison, the first anthology in generative grammar, Reibel & Schane (1969), has 224; the major Prague School reader, Vachek (1964), has 321; and the major Geneva School reader, Godel (1969), has 42. A JSTOR search turns up roughly comparable results: 961, 411, 321, and 185 respectively. For the latter, the reader is referred to 63 times since the year 2000. I would take all of these results with

'best' papers to appear in *Language* since its inception in 1924. Here is a paragraph from the announcement for the collection:

> The selection process that has resulted in these volumes has been long and difficult. In selecting articles we consulted a number of sources: a list of most-cited *Language* articles provided by the LSA Secretariat; the results of a survey of members conducted by the Secretariat in an effort to determine LSA members' favorite *Language* articles; the 1957 anthology edited by Martin Joos, *Readings in linguistics: the development of descriptive linguistics in America since 1925*[...], as a particularly well-known early compilation of key papers in our field; [...].
>
> (Carlson, Joseph, and Thomason 2012)

How many other anthologies from that time period could still be described as 'well-known'? But *why* is it so well-known? I would say primarily for the rabidly empiricist material in Joos's prefaces and intercalated comments. I repeat from § 3.4.2 the two most cited:

> Children want explanations, and there is a child in each of us; descriptivism makes a virtue of not pampering that child.
>
> (Joos 1957b: 96)

> [...] flatly contradicting the American (Boas) tradition that languages could differ from each other without limit and in unpredictable ways [...]
>
> (Joos 1957b: 96)

Practitioners of every current approach to linguistics have cited some of this material either as an opening wedge against opposing approaches or to express smug satisfaction that we know more about how science works now than we did in the mid-1950s. To illustrate this point, Margaret Thomas has collected numerous citations of these passages that have appeared in the literature since 1957. She writes:[32]

> Joos' claim that descriptivism avoids pandering to an appetite for explanation has been widely cited, for example by Chomsky (1962b: 153) [in paraphrase]); Hymes

---

a grain of salt, however, since many of the citations to the reader mentioned later in this section do not show up as hits.

[32] After the publication of her 2002 paper, Thomas discovered many more publications that cite Joos's 'without limit and in unpredictable ways' passage. She was gracious enough to share the following references with me: Aronoff & Padden (2011); Aurora (2017); Bach (1995); Biberauer (2008); Benítez-Burraco & Longa (2010); Berreby (1994); Bobaljik (2015); Bybee (2009); Chomsky (2007a, b; 2008; 2014b); Cinque & Rizzi (2010); Cook (2011); Cole & Hermon (2015); Croft (2000, 2003, 2017); Greenberg (1975); Halle (2011); Lehmann (2004, 2010); Lindblom (1990); Newmeyer (2005); Pullum (2017); Sampson (1979); Teeter (1963); Van Valin (2007); Wierzbicka (2012); and Yallop (1978).

& Fought (1975: 1077); Newmeyer (1980: 5); Sampson (1980: 106) [in paraphrase]; Katz (1981: 74); Moore & Carling (1982: 46); Hakuta (1986: 69); Harris (1993: 271); and Ritchie & Bhatia (1996: 5). The assertion that 'languages could differ from each other without limit and in unpredictable ways' has achieved even greater currency. It has appeared in works on the history of linguistics such those of Teeter (1964: 200); Diller (1971: 19, 27), (1978: 20, 29); Hymes & Fought (1975: 959); Newmeyer (1980: 5); Anderson (1985: 202, 280); Harris (1993: 64, 119); and in texts addressed to other audiences of linguists, students of linguistics, or laypeople, like those of Chomsky (1962a: 548; 1964: 952; 1986: 20–21); Stankiewicz (1966: 495); Wardhaugh (1970: 127); Partee (1971: 8); McCawley (1974: 268); Sampson (1975: 8; 1980: 70; 1997: 7); Rusiecki (1976: 35); Ferguson (1978: 10); Gass & Ard (1980: 443); Smith (1989: 66; 1999: 105); Borsley (1991: 1); Botha (1992: 84); Pinker (1994: 231–232); and Comrie (2001). (Thomas 2002: 357)

Let me give a few examples of how each quote has been applied. As far as the first is concerned, Chomsky took Joos's characterization as representative and remarked that for him and his co-thinkers, 'the search for explanation is a kind of infantile aberration that may affect philosophers or mystics, but not sober scientists' (Chomsky 1962b: 153). Geoffrey Sampson, despite his own empiricist leanings, could write that American descriptivists regarded explanations 'as a relic of childhood which mature scientists should have learned to put behind them' (Sampson 1980: 106) And Kenji Hakuta, citing this 'stern' passage, asserted that '[t]he prevalent attitude was to keep your head down and describe what you saw in the corpus' (Hakuta 1986: 69).

The second (Boas-related) quote had led to great numbers of linguists believing that pre-generativists in the United States believed 'that languages could differ from each other without limit and in unpredictable ways'. Stankiewicz (1966: 495) went along with this quote as correctly characterizing American descriptivism, as did I in Newmeyer (1980: 5). More recently, both functional linguists (Croft 2003: 5) and generative grammarians (Cinque & Rizzi 2010: 54) have cited this quote, generally with the view of condemning it and the backward sentiments that it embodies.

There exists an extensive literature that argues that Joos greatly exaggerated in the first quote and was dead wrong in the second (see especially Hymes & Fought 1981; Thomas 2002; and Anderson 2021: § 10.4). It is true that the positivistic outlook of many leading post-Bloomfieldians made them suspicious of broad theoretical pronouncements and led them to wish to confine themselves to observables and to formulate statements that could be derived only from observables. But well before 1957 this world view had started to break down somewhat (see Chapter 2 of this book for discussion).

There is no reason whatever to believe that Franz Boas thought 'that languages could differ from each other without limit and in unpredictable ways':

> For example, in the introduction to his *Handbook of American Indian Languages*, Boas (1911: 67) warned scholars against taking the familiar categories of European languages for granted, while at the same time he asserted the existence of linguistic commonalities. He wrote that 'the occurrence of the most fundamental grammatical concepts in all languages must be considered as proof of the unity of fundamental psychological processes'.
>
> (Thomas 2002: 362)

A fair question to raise is whether Joos even himself believed that languages could vary uncontrollably. That is certainly not the impression that one gets from his paper 'Description of language design' (Joos 1950), reprinted in *Readings*. This paper is chock-a-block with statements about universal properties of language, of which the following is only one:

> But neither this sort of thing, nor indeed any other gradation or continuity *in either form and meaning* has ever been found *in any language* on this planet. True, the sounds (and thus all the forms) occurring in the use of language are variable by continuous gradation [...] But *in the design* of the language we never find a trace of those facts!
>
> (Joos 1950: 703; emphasis in original)

The question is why Joos would explicitly advocate a position which he did not believe. We could of course simply question his mental stability and leave it at that. But Margaret Thomas relates the 'without limit and in unpredictable ways' passage to the speaking-familiarly-to-the-reader tone that pervades the commentary, in 'a context in which looseness, dramatic embellishment, and even hyperbole would be at home' (Thomas 2002: 365). Whatever drove Joos to do this:

> Regrettably, Joos's words are now passed along as a representation of pre-generative linguistics with little consciousness of the beliefs of the scholarly community which produced them, or the text out of which they were extracted. Thus many students narrowly trained in generative linguistics accept the remark that 'languages could differ from each other without limit and in unpredictable ways' as a central article of faith among early twentieth-century linguists.
>
> (Thomas 2002: 365)

Why then has Joos's *Readings* stood the test of time better than other collections? I would say that there are two principal reasons. First, because Joos's 'notorious comments', accurate or not, have continued to provide an opening wedge for generative grammarians and others for whom the idea of constructing an explanatory theory is paramount. It is always an easy way out to see only good or only evil, and for most of today's linguists, no idea could be more evil than that the desire for explanation is an infantile aberration. But also, for Americans at least, it provides a fascinating historical record of how linguistics used to be done—not so long ago that the approach documented is a mere historiographical curiosity, but also not so recently as to be no more than a quaint version of current theory.

3.9 Conclusion

Martin Joos's edited volume, *Readings in Linguistics*, is a landmark in American linguistics publishing. Very few if any anthologies of papers in the history of the field have generated as much interest. The fact that it collects the major papers of the dominant wing of American linguistics from the mid-1920s to the mid-1950s is only a part (and perhaps a small part) of its renown. As we have seen, the continued interest in Joos's *Readings* derives primarily from Joos's editorial commentary on what he regarded as the American way of doing linguistics. Linguists of all persuasions have raised these comments to a status that can only be described as 'iconic'. Indeed, Joos's commentary has endowed him with an importance to the history of linguistics that eclipses his own direct contributions to the field, which are today largely forgotten.

4

Early transformational generative grammar

Some controversial issues

4.1 Introduction

We have already seen reference made to early work in transformational generative grammar (TGG) in the preceding chapters of this book. I could not cover adequately the interactions between American and European structuralists without providing a glimpse at the latter's reception of early TGG (Chapter 2). My discussion of Martin Joos's book of readings needed to take into account the fact that that as time progressed more and more of its readers had had some generative training (Chapter 3). The present chapter focuses on the birth of TGG and on a number of issues that have arisen over the years with respect to the development of that model in the 1950s and 1960s. § 4.3 takes on the question of whether there was a 'Chomskyan revolution' and on whether the question of its existence is even worth debating. § 4.4 outlines the reaction to TGG among the established linguists of the time. In § 4.5 we examine a number of claims that Chomsky made about his 'early days', while § 4.6 discusses the tricky issues of military funding for linguistics and Chomsky's ready acceptance of this funding. But first (§ 4.2) we outline the basics of the theory as it was presented in the earliest TGG publications.

4.2 Early transformational generative grammar: A whirlwind overview

This section provides a short overview of the earliest work in TGG. It cannot substitute for more detailed accounts of the issues, such as those presented in Newmeyer (1986b: chapter 2); Harris (1993: chapter 3); Pullum (2010, 2011); and Freidin (1994, 2020). However, both for the sake of continuity and the overall exposition, it seems reasonable to provide a several-page-long sketch of the early theory.

American Linguistics in Transition. Frederick J. Newmeyer, Oxford University Press.
© Frederick J. Newmeyer (2022). DOI: 10.1093/oso/9780192843760.003.0004

4.2.1 *Syntactic Structures*

Early in 1957, Noam Chomsky's *Syntactic Structures* (Chomsky 1957a) was released by Mouton Publishers in The Hague. He has written that it was a 'slightly
revised version' of lecture notes for an undergraduate course at MIT (Chomsky
1975b: 3).[1] Later that same year, a review by Robert B. Lees appeared in the journal *Language* (Lees 1957).[2] Lees, who enjoyed a modest reputation in the field in
addition to being Chomsky's own student, left no doubt that the book, which introduced TGG, would change linguistics. It was Lees who brought up the idea
of the review with Editor Bernard Bloch, instead of being invited by Bloch to
submit one:

> As you may recall from our meeting in Philadelphia, I mentioned briefly a forth-
> coming publication by Noam Chomsky, one which I consider to be of the utmost
> importance for linguistic theory. [...] Just last week the first paper-bound copies
> were released. [...] In the confusion of the meetings were did not have the op-
> portunity to completely clarify the question of a review for Language, but I have
> nevertheless gone on to prepare a rather long article on the book [...] My review
> should be finished in a week or so [...].
>
> (Lees to Bloch, February 22, 1957; BBA)

In response to one referee's complaint that the first draft contained too many footnotes that were 'aggressive' and 'offensive', Lees sent to Bloch a cleaned up version
(Lees to Bloch, April 26, 1957; BBA). Interestingly, Bloch replied: '[...] after glanc-
ing through the rejected footnotes my first reaction in to reinsert them all in their
proper places. [...] On the whole I think that so important a review as this ought
not to pull any punches' (Bloch to Lees, May 2, 1957).

As far as Lees's review itself is concerned, I would guess that such praise for a
new approach to the study of language and such derogation of the contemporary
paradigm had never been seen before in the pages of *Language*. Lees wrote that
Chomsky's book was 'one of the first serious attempts on the part of a linguist to
construct within the tradition of scientific theory construction a comprehensive
theory of language which may be understood in the same sense that a chemical,
biological theory is ordinarily understood by experts in those fields' (p. 377). Actually, the tone of the review as a whole made it clear that Lees regarded it as the

---

[1] Hamans (2014), making reference to the material in the Mouton archives, documents the process
of getting *Syntactic Structures* into print. It would seem that the revisions were actually fairly extensive,
or at least time-consuming.

[2] *Syntactic* Structures was released in February 1957 and Lees's review appeared in the July–
September issue of *Language*. Actually, Lees's review was not the first: In July of that year a short but
positive notice of the book written by the linguist Henk Schultink appeared in the Dutch newspaper
Nieuwe Rotterdamse Courant (see Noordegraff 2001; Hamans 2014).

only serious attempt, and a completely successful one at that. Let us look in the next few subsections at some crucial features of TGG presented there.

4.2.1.1 The key features of *Syntactic Structures*

The most important feature of *Syntactic Structures* is its conception of a grammar as a theory of a language, subject to the same constraints on construction and evaluation as any theory in the natural sciences. Prior to 1957, it was widely regarded, not just in linguistics, but throughout the humanities and social sciences, that a formal, yet nonempiricist, theory of a human attribute was impossible. Chomsky indicated that such a theory was possible. The central chapter of *Syntactic Structures*, 'On the Goals of Linguistic Theory' is devoted to demonstrating the parallels between linguistic theory, as he conceived it, and what uncontroversially would be taken to be scientific theories. Just as physics seeks to specify precisely the class of physical processes and biology the class of biological processes, it followed that a task of linguistics would be to provide 'a precise specification of the class of formalized grammars' (Chomsky 1962a: 534). Still, *Syntactic Structures* would not have attracted a huge amount of interest simply by presenting a novel theory of the nature of grammar. That is, the book was not merely an exercise in speculative philosophy of science. On the contrary, half of the monograph is devoted to the presentation and defense of a formal fragment of English grammar.

   Chomsky attacked the empiricist conception of linguistic theory held by the most influential post-Bloomfieldians, namely the condition that a grammatical description must be in principle mechanically extractable from the primary data. But such a condition, Chomsky argued, is not to be found in any science. In his view, the most linguistic theory can be expected to provide is an *evaluation* procedure for grammars, that is, a mechanical way of deciding between alternative grammars within a particular theory. And, as Chomsky pointed out, even an evaluation procedure is more than most sciences would hope to accomplish: 'There are few areas of science in which one would seriously consider the possibility of developing a general, practical, mechanical method for choosing among several theories, each compatible with the available data' (Chomsky 1957a: 53). Given the abandonment of the aim of literally 'discovering' a grammar, there need be no concern about a description that 'mixes levels' (see Chapter 1, § 1.2). Since a grammar would no longer result from a cookbook-like set of directions which tells the linguist to 'find the phonemes first', the rules and the inventory of phonemes, morphemes, etc. might be arrived at 'by intuition, guesswork, all sorts of partial methodological hints, reliance on past experience, etc.' (p. 56). If in the resultant description, syntactic information, say, entered into the statement of a phonological rule, there would be no cause for concern: The question of the interdependence of levels is one to be answered by empirical investigation rather than by methodological fiat.

4.2.1.2 Simplicity and the evaluation of grammars

To say that a theory provides an evaluation procedure for grammars obviously invites the question: By what criteria are grammars to be evaluated? Clearly, the nature of a successful linguistic description had to be made explicit. Chomsky termed the criteria of evaluation 'external conditions of adequacy' and in *Syntactic Structures* outlined four of them: 1. The sentences generated are acceptable to the native speaker; 2. Every case of a 'constructional homonymity' (the assignment of more than one structural description to a sentence) describes a real ambiguity; every case of ambiguity is represented by constructional homonymity; 3. Differential interpretations of superficially similar sentences are represented by different derivational histories. (His example involved the sentences *The picture was painted by a new technique* and *The picture was painted by a real artist*); 4. Sentences understood in similar ways are represented in similar ways at one level of description. But it is not sufficient that a grammatical analysis in isolation meet the external conditions of adequacy. In addition, it is necessary to posit 'a condition of generality' on grammars; 'we require that the grammar of a given language be constructed in accord with a specific theory of linguistic structure in which such terms as "phoneme" and "phrase" are defined independently of any particular language' (p. 50). The condition of generality (Chomsky used this term only once) corresponds to what were later called 'linguistic universals' and comprises those theoretical terms, notational conventions, etc. which interact in such a way as to allow the external conditions of adequacy to be met in the most linguistically revealing way. For example, since a grammar without transformational rules presumably could not meet the external conditions, the condition on generality demands the incorporation of such rules into the descriptive apparatus of the theory. But what of a case where there appeared to be more than one grammar, each meeting the external conditions? Here the evaluation procedure alluded to above would come into play. Chomsky hoped the condition of generality might be formulable so that given two alternative descriptions, the shorter one (as measured in terms of absolute length, number of symbols, or some such criterion) would always be the one of maximum generality as well.

4.2.1.3 Three models of linguistic description

Chomsky had two major goals in *Syntactic Structures*. First, he had the general goal of motivating a TGG that was subject to certain conditions of adequacy. But also, he had the more narrow goal of demonstrating that only a specific type of generative grammar had the ability to meet these conditions, namely a generative grammar embodying transformational as well as phrase structure rules. The former were inspired by, and are essentially generative reinterpretations of, the identically named rules proposed by his teacher Zellig Harris in his attempt to apply the methods of structural linguistics to the analysis of discourse (Harris 1957). Chomsky was in the peculiar position of having to argue against two generative grammatical models — finite state grammars and phrase structure grammars — which had very few public adherents. He had to do this because these models were the closest generative interpretations of the views of language current in the 1950s. Finite state grammars bore a close resemblance to (or were identical to, as in the case of Hockett 1955) the type of device promoted by communications theorists. The sorts of descriptions which phrase structure grammars provided were (for all practical purposes) identical to those which resulted from the post-Bloomfieldians' procedures. So Chomsky's demonstration of the inadequacy of these two models in Chapters 3, 4, and 5 of *Syntactic Structures* was directed to and was most convincing to those linguists who might have been won over to his general goal of constructing a formal nonempiricist linguistic theory, but still clung to the generative analogs of earlier views of language. Clearly, a linguist who rejected the need for generative rules, external conditions of adequacy, etc. would not have been terribly impressed by Chomsky's demonstration of the superiority of transformational grammar over phrase structure grammar. Chomsky contrasted the three models in terms of their 'weak generative capacity' and their 'strong generative capacity', to use terms which appeared a few years later. The former refers to their string-generating ability, the latter to their ability to assign structural descriptions to these strings. Since a grammar unable to generate all and only the sentences of a language is of no further empirical interest, the demonstration of the defect of a model in terms of weak generative capacity makes any discussion of its strong capacity unnecessary. Chomsky offered a proof that finite-state grammars could not even weakly generate the sentences of English. There was no need for Chomsky even to mention the more serious defects of finite-state grammars in terms of their strong generative capacity.

Chomsky did not question in *Syntactic Structures* that phrase structure grammars are capable of weakly generating the sentences of English. He rather argued that they can do so only in a cumbersome fashion and, furthermore, do not come close to assigning the correct structural descriptions to the sentences generated. His examples of the defects of phrase structure grammars were illustrated simultaneously with the demonstration that grammars containing the more powerful transformational rules can handle the same phenomena in an elegant and revealing manner. By far his most persuasive demonstration involved the English verbal auxiliary system. While Chomsky did not attempt to state the phrase structure rules which would be involved in generating all of the possible combinations of auxiliary verbs in English (and excluding the impossible ones), it was generally accepted at that time that such rules would have to be enormously complex. The *Syntactic Structures* analysis, however, treated the superficially discontinuous auxiliary morphemes *have... en* and *be... ing* as unit constituents generated by the phrase structure rules, and posited a simple transformational rule to permute the affixal and verbal elements into their surface positions, thus predicting the basic distribution of auxiliaries in simple declarative sentences. Moreover, Chomsky was able to show that the permutation rule, 'the Auxiliary Transformation' (later called 'Affix Hopping' by other linguists), interacts with rules forming simple negatives and simple yes–no questions to specify neatly the exact locations where 'supportive' *do* appears. The ingenuity of this analysis probably did more to win supporters for Chomsky than all of his metatheoretical statements about discovery and evaluation procedures and immediately led to some linguists' proposing transformational analyses of particular phenomena despite a lack of enthusiasm for the foundations of the theory itself (see, for example, Gleason 1961: 171–194 and the suspiciously Chomskyan analysis in Joos 1964: 53f.).

Chomsky's motivation of the Passive transformation was analogous to that of the Auxiliary transformation. He argued that the contextual restrictions holding between the passive morpheme, the passive *by*-phrase, and the transitive verb would be extraordinarily difficult to state by means of phrase structure rules. However, one transformational rule permuting the subject and the object and adding the morphemes that are characteristic of the passive construction (*be...en* and *by*) eliminates the need for any of these special restrictions. Chomsky's arguments for transformational rules in *Syntactic Structures* were all simplicity arguments. They all involved showing that a grammar with phrase structure rules alone required great complexity, a complexity that could be avoided only by the positing of a transformational rule. For example, Chomsky did not posit a transformational analysis of the auxiliary system because of the inability of phrase structure grammar to generate discontinuous morphemes as the unitary elements that they intuitively are. He based his analysis on formal simplicity alone, opting for a simple phrase structure rule and a simple transformational rule over a large number of cumbersome phrase structure rules. However, as he demonstrated, the generation of these morphemes as constituents turned out to be an important *by-product* of the analysis which was motivated on purely formal grounds. Likewise, Chomsky was unwilling to point to the undeniable semantic correspondences between declaratives and interrogatives, affirmatives and negatives, actives and passives, etc. as evidence for setting up transformations relating them. He felt that to use such evidence would have led merely to a stipulation of the correspondences, rather than to an explanation of them. Hence, the relevant transformations were motivated on the grounds of formal simplicity alone.

4.2.1.4 Grammar and meaning
Superficially, the relationship between syntax and semantics seems quite straightforward in *Syntactic Structures* and can be captured by the following quote: 'I think that we are forced to conclude that grammar is autonomous and independent of meaning [...]' (p. 17). The independence of grammar and meaning is stressed so many times in that book that many commentators have assumed that Chomsky simply took over the position of Harris and Bloch, an assumption often going hand-in-hand with the implication that this demonstrates that he had

not really broken completely from post-Bloomfieldian structuralism. But a careful reading of *Syntactic Structures* falsifies this conclusion. First of all, the independence of grammar in no way followed from his methodology, as it did for the post-Bloomfieldians. Chomsky was clear that the question of the relation of grammar and meaning is an empirical one. He gave example after example to illustrate his position: Speakers have intuitions that cannot be expressed in semantic terms; neither phonemic distinctness nor morpheme identity is wholly semantic; notions like 'subject' and 'object' defy strict semantic characterization; etc. In fact, Chomsky used the apparent non-paraphrase relationship between sentences like *Everyone in the room knows at least two languages* and *At least two languages are known by everyone in the room* as evidence that Passive (and transformations in general) cannot be defined strictly in terms of meaning. In other words, he was arguing that the assumption that syntax is semantically based is false, and any theory built on this assumption must therefore be fundamentally deficient. As he put it, 'Despite the undeniable interest and importance of semantic [...] studies of language, they appear to have no direct relevance to the problem of determining the set of grammatical utterances' (p. 17).

Second, an understanding of how Chomsky regarded the notion 'meaning' at that time helps put many of his comments in a different light. While his theory of meaning was fairly eclectic (in footnote 10 on page 103 he seemed to imply that much of meaning can be reduced to reference), he was then very much under the influence of the Oxford philosophers and their use theory of meaning. In fact, the words 'meaning' and 'use' are used almost interchangeably throughout *Syntactic Structures*: 'There is no aspect of linguistic study more subject to confusion and more in need of clear and careful formulation than that which deals with the points of connection betweensyntax and semantics. The real question that should be asked is "How are the syntactic devices available in a given language put to work in the actual use of this language?"' (p. 93). In other words, many of Chomsky's arguments in *Syntactic Structures* for the autonomy of syntax were in reality arguments for (what he would call a few years later) the competence-performance dichotomy. Many aspects of meaning, in his view at the time, were part of performance.

Third, he regarded as theoretically significant a whole set of systematic connections between syntax and semantics. For example, he pointed out that many of the traditional assertions about the semantic basis of syntax (which he argued to be empirically false) are very nearly true. Yet, he went on to say, there would be no possibility of providing an explanation of these facts if they had simply been assumed to be true. He noted other systematic connections, as in the following passage in which deep structure interpretation was foreshadowed (note again the 'performance' terminology): 'The general problem of analyzing the process of "understanding" is thus reduced, in a sense, to the problem of explaining how kernel sentences are understood, these being considered the basic "content elements" from which the usual, more complex sentences of real life are formed by transformational development' (p. 92). Likewise, later claims about the relationship of transformational rules and meaning were foreshadowed in statements like 'we find, however, that the transformations are, by and large, meaning-preserving [...]' (p. 123), a fact which would have never come to light if transformations 'had been investigated exclusively in terms of such notions as synonymity' (p. 101).

Finally and most importantly, Chomsky proposed that grammars be evaluated on the basis of their ability to lead to insights about the meanings of sentences:

> We can judge formal theories in terms of their ability to explain and clarify a variety of facts about the way in which sentences are used and understood. In other words, we should like the syntactic framework of the language that is isolated and exhibited by the grammar to be able to support semantic description, and we shall naturally rate more highly a theory of formal structure that leads to grammars that meet this requirement more fully. (p. 102)

4.2.2 What came before *Syntactic Structures*

Chomsky received all three of his degrees (BA, MA, and PhD) from the University of Pennsylvania, all in linguistics, and all under the direction of Zellig Harris. His undergraduate honors thesis, *Morphophonemics of Modern Hebrew* (*MMH*), completed in 1949, was a generative grammar of that language. However, since it is apparently the case that no copies are still extant, even in Chomsky's own possession (p. c. on numerous occasions), it seems reasonable to begin with his identically titled master's thesis. Even here things are a little complicated. The thesis was submitted and accepted in June 1951. Chomsky spent the next six months revising it, producing the new version that December (for extensive discussion of the similarities and differences between the two versions, see Daniels 2010). It was the revised version that was published much later (Chomsky 1979b [1951]) and will form the basis of the discussion to follow.

It was his teacher Harris's idea that he take on Modern Hebrew—both were fluent in that language:

> Harris suggested that I undertake a systematic structural grammar of some language. I chose Hebrew, which I knew fairly well. For a time I worked with an informant and applied methods of structural linguistics as I was then coming to understand them. The results, however, seemed to me rather dull and unsatisfying. Having no very clear idea as to how to proceed further, I abandoned these efforts and did what seemed natural; namely, I tried to construct a system of rules for generating the phonetic forms of sentences, that is, what is now called a generative grammar. I thought it might be possible to devise a system of recursive rules

to describe the form and structure of sentences, recasting the devices in Harris's methods for this purpose, and thus perhaps to achieve the kind of explanatory force that I recalled from historical grammar.

(Chomsky 1975b: 25)

The grammar produced in *MMH* focused, as might be expected, on morphophonemics, but all levels of grammar were conceived of as an integrated whole: 'The grammar consists of the following parts: 1. A syntactic statement giving permitted arrangements of morphemes in sentences; 2. A morphemic constituency statement giving permitted arrangements of morphophonemes in morphemes; 3. A series of morphological and morphophonemic statements transforming any grammatical sequence of morphemes into a sequence of phonemes; A phonetic statement (transforming phoneme sequences into phone sequences' (Chomsky 1979b [1951]: 3–4).

Chomsky, as Harris's student, still contemplated the idea of discovery procedures for establishing grammars:

Accordingly we might distinguish and consider separately two aspects of the linguistic analysis of a language, a process of 'discovery' consisting of the application of the mixture of formal and experimental procedures constituting linguistic method, and a process of 'description' consisting of the construction of a grammar describing the sentences which we know from step one to be grammatical, and framed in accordance with the criteria related to its special purposes.

(Chomsky 1979b [1951]: 1–2)

However, he explicitly by-passed them, assuming that discovery had been 'completed', and went on simply to present his generative grammar. Anticipating his discussion in *Syntactic Structures* six years later, he took the position that 'The grammar must be designed in such a way as to be the most efficient, economical, and elegant device generating just these sentences [of Modern Hebrew]' (p. 3).

Thanks to the impression he made upon the philosopher Nelson Goodman, with whom he took courses as an MA student at Pennsylvania, Chomsky won a prestigious Junior Fellowship in the Society of Fellows at Harvard, where he worked from 1951 to 1955. Ironically, his project was to improve the techniques of structural linguistics—he even published one paper with this goal in mind (Chomsky 1953). But little by little, his work in TGG became his central focus. Two individuals, the philosopher Yehoshua Bar-Hillel and the linguist Morris Halle, stand out above all others in their encouragement of Chomsky to pursue his ideas along these lines. It was Bar-Hillel who convinced him to put aside all hesitations and postulate (as his intuitions had already told him was correct) something very much like the reconstructed historical forms at the abstract morphophonemic level. And it was Halle, whom Chomsky met in the fall of 1951, who, as a result of their constant discussions, was the most decisive factor in causing him to abandon any hope of a procedural approach to linguistic analysis. Here is Chomsky's own account of his moment of truth:

> By 1953, I came to the same conclusion [as Halle]: if the discovery procedures did not work, it was not because I had failed to formulate them correctly but because the entire approach was wrong. In retrospect I cannot understand why it took me so long to reach this conclusion. I remember exactly the moment when I finally felt convinced. On board ship in mid-Atlantic, aided by a bout of seasickness, on a rickety tub that was listing noticeably, it had been sunk by the Germans and was now making its first voyage after having been salvaged. It suddenly seemed that there was a good reason the obvious reason why several years of intense effort devoted to improving discovery procedures had come to naught, while the work I had been doing during the same period on generative grammars and explanatory theory, in almost complete isolation, seemed to be consistently yielding interesting results.
>
> (Chomsky 1979a: 131)

With post-Bloomfieldian structural linguistics now permanently in his past, Chomsky began writing *The Logical Structure of Linguistic Theory* (*LSLT*), his exposition of the goals, assumptions, and methodology of TGG (one chapter of which earned him his PhD from Pennsylvania). This 900-page volume, which was completed in 1955, contains the initial proposals for the formalization and evaluation of grammars which would underlie all subsequent generative research. *LSLT* laid the foundations for TGG and even today is cited for its original insights about grammatical processes. Some of the formal mechanisms proposed in *LSLT* went into eclipse for decades, only to be resuscitated in recent years. Much of what appears in *Syntactic Structures* was anticipated in *LSLT*.

Chomsky and Halle teamed with Chomsky's fellow student at Penn Fred Lukoff in 1956 to publish the first generative phonological analysis 'On accent and juncture in English' (Chomsky et al. 1956). This paper, which proposed a retreatment of English suprasegmentals, hit the post-Bloomfieldians where they were weakest. In place of the four degrees of phonemic stress which previous treatments hypothesized, they were able to predict the full range of phonetic stress possibilities with only a simple phonemic accented-unaccented distinction. They achieved this economy by assuming a set of ordered rules sensitive to underlying junctures placed at certain morpheme boundaries. Since their analysis resulted in a non-biunique relation between phonemics and phonetics and violated the prohibition against mixing levels, it was incompatible with post-Bloomfieldian methodology. But, they argued, four important benefits resulted from abandoning these methodological constraints: The constituent organization imposed to state the stress rules most simply coincided with that which would be required for other levels of description; the binary phonemic feature of 'accent' made special suprasegmental phonemes unnecessary; the simplicity and symmetry of the rules proposed contrasted markedly with the inelegant earlier account; and the rules predicted how native speakers could assign stress patterns to new utterances in a consistent and uniform manner.

4.2.3 Generative phonology

Generative phonology, in essence, synthesized three contemporary trends in linguistics. First, it incorporated the unformalized insights about phonological (or, more correctly, morphophonological) processes which characterized the work of Edward Sapir and his students. Second, it drew from the post-Bloomfieldians the practice of explicit formalization of all rules. And, finally, it owed to the Prague School the overall explanatory goals of phonological theory, as well as some specific insights (e.g. distinctive features).

The first major work of generative phonology was Halle's *The Sound Pattern of Russian* (Halle 1959). While his specific rules for Russian would be modified many times, the book is remembered primarily for its argument against the structuralist theory of the phoneme. Halle took the following condition as essential to that theory:

> A phonological description must include instructions for inferring (deriving) the proper phonological representation of any speech event, without recourse to information not contained in the physical signal.[3]

(Halle 1959: 21)

Halle showed that this condition led to an uneconomical account of obstruent voicing in Russian, namely that the same generalization would have to be stated in both the mapping from morphophonemes to phonemes and from phonemes to speech. He concluded:

> Phonemic representations, therefore, constitute an additional level of representation made necessary only by the attempt to satisfy [the above stated] condition. If [this] condition can be dispensed with, then there is also no need for the 'phonemic' representation.

---

[3] A footnote here cites Hockett (1951), where it is claimed that '[f]or a notation to be phonemic, we require a bi-unique one-one relation rather than a one-many relation [between representation and utterance]' (Hockett 1951: 340). Hockett took the biuniqueness requirement (first formulated, I believe, in Harris 1944) quite seriously. Hockett's article discusses two papers by Bernard Bloch (Bloch 1946b, 1950). He wrote: 'What is deceptively simple in the earlier treatment turns out to be quite complicated in the later — but the more complicated treatment is also more accurate' (p. 341), by which he means that the earlier treatment violated the biuniqueness requirement, while the later one obeyed it.

All that is needed, then, are morphophonemic (soon to be called 'underlying phonological') representations and surface phonetic representations.

In Chomsky & Halle (1960) the analysis of English stress was simplified still further. By incorporating syntactic categorial information into the stress rules, they were able to dispense with underlying phonemic accent entirely and, at the same time, eliminate the phonemic /i/ required in the 1956 paper. That year also saw the publication of Stockwell (1960), the first attempt to incorporate pitch into a generative description.

The major theoretical discussion of generative phonology prior to Chomsky and Halle's *The Sound Pattern of English* (Chomsky & Halle 1968) was Halle's article 'Phonology in generative grammar' (Halle 1962). Halle gave the first clear statement of the economy gained by formulating phonological rules in terms of distinctive features rather than in terms of indivisible phonemes. He further argued (using an example based on Sanskrit vowel sandhi) that the ordering of rule statements would, at one and the same time, lead to both a minimization of feature specifications and an analysis which intuitively was the most insightful as well. While this was by no means the first example given of phonological rule ordering, it was the first concrete illustration of the theoretical interrelatedness of this concept with that of distinctive features and the simplicity criterion for evaluating alternative analyses.

Halle broke ground in three other important areas in this article. First, he explained how differences between dialects could be explained by hypothesizing that they contained the same set of rules applying in different orders. Second, he gave a broad overview of how generative phonology was suited to the description of language change. He suggested that rule addition characteristically takes place at the end of the grammar (or at the end of 'natural subdivisions' in it). Hence, it is no accident that the synchronic order of rules characteristically mirrors their relative chronology, a point first observed by Bloomfield in his study of Menomini (Bloomfield 1939a) (see § 4.3.3.3 below). He went on to give what he claimed was an example of a case (from the history of English) where two phonemes which had merged, later reappeared, the reemerging phonemes corresponding exactly to their historical antecedents. Since such a phenomenon would be inexplicable under an account of phonology that assumed biuniqueness, Halle's example pointed to the need for an abstract level of representation not simply extractable from the superficial phonetic data. Finally, Halle gave the first theoretical explanation of the diminished language learning ability of the adult, arguing that the wholesale restructuring of a grammar is beyond their capabilities. While few of Halle's specific theoretical claims stand unaltered today, except in the most general terms, the importance of 'Phonology in generative grammar' should not be underestimated. This article was the closest thing to a '*Syntactic Structures* of phonology', that is, the basic theoretical statement that would direct research in this area of linguistics for years.

4.2.4 From *Syntactic Structures* to *Aspects of the Theory of Syntax*

In the eight years between the publication of *Syntactic Structures* and Chomsky's next major work *Aspects of the Theory of Syntax* (Chomsky 1965), syntactic theory underwent a great number of changes.[4] The model of syntax proposed in the earlier book contained two types of rules: phrase-structure rules and transformations. The former expanded the initial symbol S(entence) to create an underlying constituent representation for the sentence. Lexical items as well as syntactic categories were introduced by these rules. Transformations performed two types of functions: They distorted underlying grammatical relations (as in the case of passives, which were essentially derived from actives); and they created complex sentences out of simple ones. For example, the sentence *John thinks that Bill will leave* was derived by an embedding transformation that (simplifying somewhat) combined *John thinks* and *Bill will leave*. *Aspects* introduced what came to be known as the 'standard theory' of generative syntax. In this model, the recursive function of the grammar was taken over by the phrase-structure rules; embedding transformations were thereby dispensed with. At the same time phrase-structure rules introducing lexical items were eliminated in favor of a separate lexicon, i.e. a list of the lexical items of the language, along with an algorithm for inserting these items into the derivation. The elimination of embedding transformations along with the creation of a lexicon allowed for the first time a distinct level of 'deep structure' to be defined. This level was of central importance to the standard theory, since here was also the locus of semantic interpretation. Cyclically applying transformational rules mapped deep structures onto surface structures.

Chomsky himself did not bring up the question of the psychological implications of TGG in either *LSLT* or *Syntactic Structures*. He wrote later that it would have been 'too audacious' for him to have done so (Chomsky 1975b: 35). Two pieces of evidence give credence to the idea that he did have such implications in mind around this time. First, Lees closed his review of *Syntactic Structures* with a frontal attack on inductivist learning theory, arguing that there could be no alternative but to conclude that the grammar the linguist constructed was 'in the head' of the speaker. But if that be the case, then how could these highly abstract principles possibly be learned inductively? 'It would seem', he wrote, 'that our notions of human learning are due for some considerable sophistication' (Lees 1957: 408). Since nobody has ever questioned the idea that Lees wrote his review in close consultation with Chomsky, one might fairly conclude that Chomsky too had come to the conclusion that grammars were both psychologically real and unattainable by prevalent conceptions of learning.

---

[4] See Newmeyer (1986b, chapter 3) for a much more detailed treatment of these changes.

Second, only a year after the publication of *Syntactic Structures*, Chomsky explicitly argued that the acquisition of grammar demanded the postulation of a complex innate mechanism designed for that particular purpose:

> [...] it seems to me that to account for the ability to learn a language, we must ascribe a rather complex 'built-in' structure to the organism. That is, the [language acquisition device] will have complex properties beyond the ability to match, generalize, abstract, and categorize items in the simple ways that are usually considered to be available to other organisms. In other words, the particular direction that language learning follows may turn out to be determined by genetically determined maturation of complex 'information-processing' abilities, to an extent that has not, in the past, been considered at all likely.
>
> (Chomsky 1958: 433)

Chomsky's review of B. F. Skinner's *Verbal Behavior* a year later (Chomsky 1959b) stressed that his theory of language is a psychological model of an aspect of human knowledge.[5] Chomsky's review represents, even after the passage of sixty years, the basic refutation of behaviorist psychology. The review took in turn each basic construct of behaviorism, and demonstrated that either it led to false predictions or was simply devoid of content. Chomsky went on to argue that this ability indicates that rather than being born 'blank slates', children have a genetic predisposition to structure the acquisition of linguistic knowledge in a highly specific way.[6]

By 1965, with the publication of *Aspects*, Chomsky had come to characterize TGG explicitly as a 'rationalist' theory, in the sense that it posits innate principles that determine the form of acquired knowledge. As part of the theory's conceptual apparatus, Chomsky reintroduced two terms long out of fashion in academic discussion: 'innate ideas' and 'mind'. For Chomsky, 'innate ideas' are simply those properties of the grammar that are inborn and constrain the acquisition of knowledge. He argued that, based on their abstractness, complexity, and limited amount of relevant information presented to the child, many grammatical constraints are 'prewired', so to speak, into the child, rather than acquired by anything we might reasonably call 'learning'. In other words, these constraints have to be regarded as 'innate ideas'.

---

[5] Just as Lees had volunteered his review of *Syntactic Structures*, Chomsky volunteered his review of *Verbal Behavior* (Chomsky to Bloch, February 3, 1958; BBA).

[6] Here is the reaction of the noted psychologist Jerome Bruner to Chomsky's review: 'Electric: Noam at his best, mercilessly out for the kill, daring, brilliant, on the side of the angels [...] in the same category as St. George slaying the dragon' (Bruner 1983: 159–160).

4.3 On the question of a 'Chomskyan revolution'

One of the most hotly debated topics in the historiography of linguistics is whether the field underwent a 'Chomskyan revolution' and, if so, when that revolution occurred.[7] I think that all can agree that whether there was a Chomskyan revolution in linguistics depends on two factors: what one's criteria are for a successful scientific revolution and, given those criteria, what particular features made (or did not make) Chomsky's work 'revolutionary'.[8] I attempt to sort all of that out in what follows. § 4.3.1 discusses scientific revolutions in general and how they might be identified. I argue that discussions about whether there was a Chomskyan revolution are bound to be futile; it is more interesting, I think, to discuss the 'originality' of a set of ideas than whether they were 'revolutionary' or not. § 4.3.2 address the originality of Chomsky's proposals for linguistics in the 1950s and early 1960s, concluding that in certain respects they were indeed quite original. And § 4.3.3 discusses what have been pointed to as antecedents to the main ideas of early TGG.

4.3.1 On scientific revolutions

In an article that I published almost forty years ago (Newmeyer 1986a), I argued at length that the field of linguistics had undergone a 'Chomskyan revolution', which was set in motion with the appearance of *Syntactic Structures*.[9] My argument was based on the criteria for scientific revolutions developed by the philosopher Larry Laudan in his book *Progress and its Problems* (Laudan 1977). Laudan rejected the popular idea (derived from, though not explicitly stated, in the work of Kuhn 1970) that scientific revolutions are characterized by 'uniformity of consent' in the relevant community. In such a view, we recognize a scientific paradigm by the fact

---

[7] For thorough treatments of the various positions on whether or not there was a Chomskyan revolution in linguistics (and, if so, when), see ten Hacken (2007) and Kertész (2017). It needs to be stressed that Chomsky himself has always denied that the field has undergone a 'Chomskyan revolution' (see especially Chomsky 1982: 42–43). In a lecture given thirty years later, he told the audience: 'My feeling about linguistics is that we're in a pre-Galilean stage. Maybe there will come a scientific revolution, but we are still struggling towards it' (Chomsky 2011a).

[8] In a critique of Koerner (2002c) and his earlier writing, John Joseph notes that '[i]f one restricts the definition of "revolution" to a break which severs *all* ties with the past, in which *all* elements are overturned, then it is true that neither structuralism or generativism would qualify. But probably neither would any historical movement or event. Discontinuity is always partial; the question is whether it is significant and, secondarily, sudden. Generativism qualifies as a "revolution" on both scores' (Joseph 1991: 218; see also Joseph 2010: 1–2).

[9] The reaction to this paper on the part of established historiographers of linguistics was in general quite hostile (see especially Koerner 1989 and Murray 1994). Koerner wrote to Archibald Hill: 'At the time of my writing my March 17th letter to you, I had not yet taken notice of Fritz Newmeyer's piece in the March issue of *Language*; I believe that we can only be disturbed that a paper of this [-niveau] could be published in our still most important journal, and so prominently too!' (Koerner to Hill, June 22, 1986; AHA).

that all but a few holdouts are involved in developing it. Laudan pointed out that such cannot be right:

> We speak of the Darwinian revolution in nineteenth-century biology, even though it almost certainly the case that only a small fraction of working biologists in the last half of the nineteenth century were Darwinians. We speak of a Newtonian revolution in early eighteenth century physics, even though most natural philosophers in the period were not Newtonians.
>
> (Laudan 1977: 137)

What criterion, then, uniquely characterizes a scientific revolution? According to Laudan:

> [A] scientific revolution occurs, not necessarily when all, or even a majority, of the scientific community accepts a new research tradition, but rather when a new research tradition comes along which generates enough interest (perhaps through a high initial rate of progress) that scientists in the relevant field feel, whatever their own research tradition commitments, that they have to come to terms with the budding research tradition. Newton created the stir he did because, once the *Principia* and the *Opticks* were published, almost every working physicist felt that he had to deal with the Newtonian view of the world. For many, this meant finding cogent arguments against the Newtonian system. But what was almost universally agreed was that Newton had developed a way of approaching natural phenomena which could not be ignored. Similarly, late nineteenth century biologists, whether fervent Darwinians or confirmed anti-evolutionists, found themselves having to debate the merits of Darwinism. To put the matter in a more general fashion, I am suggesting that *a scientific revolution occurs when a research tradition, hitherto unknown to, or ignored by, scientists in a given field, reaches a point of development where scientists in the field feel obliged to consider it seriously as a contender for the allegiance of themselves or their colleagues.*
>
> (Laudan 1977: 137–138; emphasis in original)

By Laudan's criteria, there can be no question that the field underwent a 'Chomskyan revolution', and one that began with publication of *Syntactic Structures*. As Dell Hymes noted the year before the publication of *Aspects*, 'it remains that transformational grammar has established itself as the reference point for discussion of linguistic theory. [...] It remains the case that it has been Chomsky who has effectively opened the American linguistic scene to its present free and fruitful discussion' (Hymes 1964a: 25). In other words, by 1964 it was Chomsky and his theory that formed the focal point for debates about how to carry out theoretical linguistics. There was a Chomskyan revolution in the Laudanian sense because anyone who hoped to win general acceptance for a new theory of language was obligated to show how the theory is better than Chomsky's.

The question that has gnawed on me for many years is whether we should accept at face value Laudan's characterization of what it takes for there to be a scientific revolution. My main problem is that it is purely *sociological*. It is true that the linguists of the world have felt, with few exceptions, that they have to address Chomsky's theories. But that doesn't make Chomsky's approach to linguistics either original or, needless to say, correct. All that one might conclude is that he has been the most clever linguist in getting his voice heard.

In searching for a more adequate way of ascertaining whether a particular theory merits the term 'revolutionary' I discovered that the great majority of philosophers of science offer essentially sociological definitions of what it takes for there to be a scientific revolution. Consider two examples. The approach of Nicholas Mullins is explicitly sociological, focusing on the importance of the *rhetoric* of revolution among the supporters of a particular theory and the strength and visibility of the social networks uniting them (see Mullins 1973, 1975). I. Bernard Cohen proposes four tests, all essentially sociological, for the correct attribution of a revolution (Cohen 1985). First, the scientists involved in the development must perceive themselves as revolutionaries, and relevant contemporaries must agree that a revolution is underway. Second, documentary histories must count it as a revolution. Third, later historians and philosophers must agree with this attribution and, fourth, so must later scientists working in that field or its successors. By including both reports from the time of the alleged revolution and later historiographical judgments, Cohen excludes people who claimed in their day to be revolutionaries but who had insufficient impact on the field to sustain the judgment of history.[10]

Probably the best known work in the history and philosophy of science is Thomas Kuhn's *The Structure of Scientific Revolutions* (Kuhn 1970). In fact, there is an important non-sociological component to Kuhn's approach, as it involves references to 'progress', 'successful problem solving', 'anomalies', and the like. It seems fair to write, however, that the crucial features argued for by Kuhn have not withstood scrutiny. In particular the idea that for every scientific field there is a relatively steady phase of 'normal science', characterized by 'paradigms' that are literally 'incommensurable' with respect to the paradigms that preceded and followed this phase, is generally regarded to have been refuted.

Given the difficulty of identifying revolutions in even the most established sciences, it seems to me that devoting any more space to arguing that linguistics has (or has not) seen a Chomskyan revolution is a useless exercise. In the next section

---

[10] Nickles (2017) points out that Cohen's approach would deny the existence of a Copernican revolution, since nobody paid any attention to Copernicus for a half century after he proposed heliocentric theory.

I attempt to make precise to what extent the 1950s work of Chomsky—and, in phonology, Halle—was *original*, that is, to what extent it proposed ways of thinking about language that had not been proposed at an earlier time.

4.3.2 The originality of transformational generative grammar

There is an enormous literature devoted to arguing that not only is transformational generative grammar not a revolutionary approach to language, but that it is not even an original one. This literature, by and large, has an interesting feature: The aspects of TGG that it claims to be non-revolutionary (or even unoriginal) were never claimed by advocates of the theory to be revolutionary (or original). There is, to be sure, a multiplicity of ways in which TGG can be compared with respect to earlier theories. Hence Rulon Wells's remark that 'Whether the change that actually took place — the advent of and eager reception of the approach called transformation theory — should be described as internal or external, as a revision and rehabilitation of Descriptive Linguistics, or as a displacement of it, is no simple one [...]' (Wells 1963: 48). Nevertheless, there are two features of the TGG proposed in the 1950s that strike me as truly original, as well as being of the utmost importance for the development of the field of linguistics.

The first was a central feature of Chomsky's MA thesis, delivered in 1951. This thesis proposed the first generative grammar of a natural language in which each sentence generated was provided with a full structural description. Generative grammars had been mooted earlier (both of artificial and natural languages), but only those that weakly generated the strings of the language. Providing these sentences with structures was a crucial development and one that was at the base of all subsequent work in TGG, whatever the framework. Furthermore, the idea that grammars are a set of structured strings made it imperative to provide an explanation of how such objects could be acquired and used, and thereby ushered in the cognitive revolution that was well underway less than a decade later.

The second dates from Halle's book *The Sound Pattern of Russian*, published in 1959. Here was the first argued refutation of the structuralist phoneme. The phoneme had been universally regarded as the greatest success story of structural linguistics of every variety. If Halle was correct (and more and more linguists would come to the conclusion that he was), then the major results of the preceding generation would have to be rethought. And, as history has shown, they were rethought. Even the more 'surfacey' approaches to phonology, such as Joan Bybee's 'natural generative phonology' (Hooper 1976) have not advocated a return to the structuralist phoneme. By the 1970s the structuralist phoneme was effectively dead, advocated only by those who had been trained in linguistics in previous generations.[11]

---

[11] But see Schane (1971) for a (partial and unsuccessful) attempt to resuscitate the phoneme.

In other words, both features were both original and instrumental in changing the direction of the field as it existed in the mid 1950s.

4.3.3 The roots of transformational generative grammar in earlier work

The following subsections examine the critical literature, in particular with respect to what extent it successfully refutes what I have pinpointed in § 4.3.2 as the genuinely original features of TGG. We examine the question of whether TGG was a 'structuralist' theory (§ 4.3.3.1), whether it was the first model to propose the idea of a generative grammar (§ 4.3.3.2), whether it was the first to propose derivations embodying ordered rules (§ 4.3.3.3), whether it was the first to incorporate transformational rules (§ 4.3.3.4), whether it was the first to insist that a grammatical description must project beyond a corpus (§ 4.3.3.5), and whether it was the first to suggest that there was an intimate connection between language and mid (§ 4.3.3.6). As we will see, all of these ideas were antecedent to TGG.

4.3.3.1 Structuralism

There were, needless to say, numerous respects in which early TGG retained crucial conceptions of its historical antecedents. Foremost among them is Saussure's great insight that at the heart of language lies a structured interrelationship of elements characterizable as an autonomous system. Such an insight is the essence of 'structuralism' and, since it is assumed throughout *Syntactic Structures* and Chomsky's subsequent work, one can, with good reason, refer to Chomsky as a 'structuralist'.[12] Some commentators have pointed to this fact in order to dismiss the idea that there could have been a Chomskyan revolution. Since structuralism was well established years before the publication of *Syntactic Structures*, by what criteria, such individuals ask, could it be correct to refer to a Chomskyan revolution? George Lakoff, for example, concluded from Chomsky's commitment to structural analysis that early TGG, rather than representing a revolutionary development, 'was a natural outgrowth of American structural linguistics' (Lakoff 1971: 267–268). The same point was made by Stephen Murray, who found 'the base of Chomsky's early work [...] in American structural linguistics, especially as developed by Zellig Harris' (Murray 1980: 76); by Dell Hymes and John Fought, who

---

[12] The 'structuralism' issue is confused by the fact that in the early 1960s, Chomsky and his followers began to reserve the label 'structuralist' for those synchronic approaches in the Saussurean tradition that do not share their views on theory construction. The result is that now within linguistics, when one speaks of a 'structuralist', it is normally understood that one is referring to a pre-Chomskyan or an anti-Chomskyan. Interestingly, commentators from outside the field have generally labelled Chomsky a 'structuralist', and we find his ideas discussed in most overviews of 20th century structuralism (see, for example, Lane 1970: 28–29 and De George & De George 1972: xx). However, it has been written in one synopsis of structuralism that 'the theoretical foundation that Chomsky laid with his notion of deep structure and human nature took its distance from structuralism in general [...]' (Dosse 1997 [1992]: 12).

regard *Syntactic Structures* as showing 'no evidence of basic revolutionary change' (Hymes & Fought 1981: 241); and, by Konrad Koerner, who feels that 'TGG is basically post-Saussurean structuralism, characterized by excessive concern with "langue" [...] to the detriment of "parole"' (Koerner 1983: 152).

Chomsky's 'structuralism', however, no more diminishes the importance of his approach than does Einstein's Newton-like search for physical laws undermine the importance of relativity theory. Saussure's victory was the victory of structuralism, just as Newton's victory was the victory of a lawful universe. As I wrote long ago: 'We would no more expect the next major turn in linguistics to be an anti-structuralist one than we would expect the next revolution in physics to return to divine intervention as an explanatory device' (Newmeyer 1986a: 5).[13] Chomsky's advance was an advance *within* structural linguistics—one which profoundly altered our conceptions of the nature of linguistic structure, and opened the way to an understanding of how its nature bears on the workings of the human mind. I am perfectly happy with the remark of Manfred Bierwisch, an early generativist, that TGG represents 'a new stage of structural linguistics' (Bierwisch 1966).

4.3.3.2 Generative grammars

I take the term 'generative grammar' to refer to a mathematical system that defines a set of strings by means of a procedure that constructs any member of the set without ever constructing a non-member.[14] Tomalin (2006), read together with a review of that book by Scholz & Pullum (2007), provides a good overview of the earlier twentieth-century background of generative grammars. The Scholz and Pullum review discusses the work of the mathematical logician Emil Post (see especially Post 1943, 1944, 1947) and concludes 'that it was Post who invented rewriting systems' (Scholz & Pullum 2007: 718).[15] The middle paper of the three coined the word 'generate' with respect to production systems, and the latter work by Post was the first to examine the question of generative power.

---

[13] Was I correct? Probably not. Since 1986 a number of non-structuralist theories of grammar have appeared, mainly under the rubric of 'usage-based' approaches and closely related 'connectionist' approaches. In my view, most of the models proposed covertly incorporate a structural core, but that discussion is for a later time.

[14] I would like to thank Geoffrey Pullum for his input on the material in this section.

[15] There are scattered references to Post in Chomsky's early work, but he did not cite the key 1943 and 1947 papers. According to Geoffrey Pullum:

> To sum up, although the citation record might make it look to a suspicious mind as if Chomsky has been deliberately steering his readers away from any possibility of discovering the papers that reveal Post's true relevance to the prehistory of generative grammar, basically the reverse is the case: Chomsky is the only linguist who ever even attempted to publicize Post in the 20th century. Other linguists, even mathematical linguists, did essentially nothing at all in that regard. The reason Chomsky never cited Post (1943) or Post (1947) is probably that he had not read them, and was not prepared to cite works he had not read (Pullum 2019).

There was other work in the foundations of logic and the philosophy of science, that influenced Chomsky, particularly the logical positivist variety that still held sway in the 1940s. I believe that Chomsky's thesis is the first place that points out that the procedures of American descriptivist linguists can be likened to the program of Rudolf Carnap's *Der Logische Aufbau der Welt* (Carnap 1928), which attempts to construct, by a series of definitions, the concepts of quality, sensation, and so on, directly from slices of experience.[16] Another influence is clearly Nelson Goodman, whose writings about elegance as a property of scientific statements Chomsky explicitly drew upon, even to the point of appealing to it as a justification for ordered rules in grammar (see Goodman 1943). And much of the formalism in the thesis (and accompanying terminology) is unmistakably drawn from Carnap's book *The Logical Syntax of Language* (Carnap 1937).

As noted above, Chomsky wrote his three theses under the direction of Zellig Harris. In fact, in a Preface to his *Methods in Structural Linguistics* dated January 1947, Harris notes that the teenage 'N. Chomsky has given much-needed assistance with the manuscript' (Harris 1951a: v). As Chomsky later remarked, 'That's how I learned linguistics, by proofreading Harris' book, which was fine for me, I really learned the field' (Sklar 1968: 215). So it is naturally worth asking to what extent Chomsky was indebted to Harris for the idea of generative grammars in general and working out the details in particular. As far as the former is concerned, Harris had a certain amount of mathematical training and was therefore undoubtedly aware of the work of Post, Carnap and the others cited in the preceding paragraphs. Six pages before the end of his *Methods* book, he mooted the possibility of a 'synthetic approach', which, loosely interpreted, amounts to a sort of generative grammar:

> The work of analysis leads right up to the statements which enable anyone to synthesize or predict utterances in the language. These statements form a deductive system with axiomatically defined initial elements and with theorems concerning the relations among them. The final theorems would indicate the structure of the utterances of the language in terms of the preceding parts of the system.
>
> (Harris 1951a: 372–373)

One might reasonably conclude that Harris's ideas here provided one of the inspirations for Chomsky in terms of formulating generative grammars of natural languages. But Harris's synthetic approach, not only clashes head on with the procedural approach developed in the bulk in the book, but is never developed to the slightest degree.

---

[16] Chomsky cites Carnap in the first version of his thesis, but not in the revised (and later published) version. I have no idea why Chomsky omitted the reference. In fact the revised version makes reference to only four published works: one each by Goodman, Greenberg, Harris, and Hockett.

It was essentially the idea suggested by Harris that Chomsky was to develop in his thesis. In an interesting sense Harris's *Methods* and Chomsky's thesis are inverses of each other. For Harris, the procedures are paramount, and the 'synthetic' approach is presented, on one page as a conceivable alternative to them, and on another as something that might be applied as a restatement of the grammar that results from the procedures—a novel form of 'structural restatement', if you will. Chomsky had not rejected a procedural approach in 1949 in toto—that would not happen until the 1950s. But his practice amounted to such a rejection, since he took as a point of departure a state of affairs in which the grammarian has already completed the procedures that have led to the identification of the grammatical elements of Hebrew.

Chomsky's essay bears the unmistakable stamp of Harris in another respect—in the confidence with which it assumes that syntax can be treated within the same overall system of principles as lower levels of grammar. Bloomfield himself had put forward a 'structuralist' view of syntax: we owe the idea of immediate constituent analysis to him (though there were antecedents). But Bloomfield felt that syntax was too 'complicated and hard to describe' (Bloomfield 1933: 201) to treat as one might phonology or morphology. Other American descriptivists had presented syntactic sketches before 1949 (see, for example, Pike 1943; Wells 1947b; Nida 1948a). But it is only with the work of Harris—and his student Chomsky—that we get the feeling of the possibility of a uniform package, in which the rules of phrase structure and those of allophonic detail each have their assigned place.

In any event, by 1951 Harris had never published a generative grammar of Hebrew, or even a fragment of one. Chomsky's thesis of that year was the first explicit generative grammar of a natural language—and one that provided a structural analysis of every sentence generated. And, I believe, it was the first to use the verb 'generate' in linguistics for the relation between a set of rules and a set of strings that the rules define as well-formed.

4.3.3.3 Morphophonemics, ordered rules, and derivations

The idea of describing morphophonemic generalizations in terms of 'process statements', where one level is more 'basic' than the other goes back to the earliest days of structural linguistics.[17] In 1930 Sapir described a set of alternations in Southern Paiute in terms of 'phonologic' representations converted to phonetic forms 'by the application of absolutely mechanical phonetic laws [i.e. rules — (FJN)] of spirantizing, alternating stresses, and unvoicing' (Sapir 1963 [1933]: 50–51, based

---

[17] To be accurate, it goes back to the work of the great Indian grammarian Pāṇini, who lived most likely in the fourth century BC. Bloomfield described Pāṇini's work in a 1929 review as 'one of the greatest monuments of human intelligence and (what concerns us more) an indispensable model for the description of languages' (Hockett 1970: 219). Also, I would like to thank Robert Ladd for his input on the material in this section. For more historical detail on the issues discussed here, see Anderson (2021: § 13.6-7).

on the more detailed discussion in Sapir 1930). Bloomfield's *Language* speaks of 'setting up' 'artificial underlying' or 'theoretical basic' forms (pp. 218–219), which undergo modification on their way to phonetics. Bloomfield was careful to caution the reader that:

> The terms 'before, after, first, then', and so on, in such statements, tell the *descriptive order*. The actual sequence of constituents, and their structural order (§13.3) are a part of the language, but the descriptive order of grammatical features is a fiction and results simply from our method of describing the forms; it goes without saying, for instance, that the speaker who says *knives*, does not first replace [f] with [v] and then add [-z], but merely utters a form (*knives*) which in certain features differs from a certain other form (namely, *knife*).
>
> (Bloomfield 1933: 213)

It was the interest of descriptive simplicity that led Bloomfield to posit underlying forms and regular rules:

> We have seen that when forms are partially similar, there may be a question as to which one we had better take as the underlying form, and that the structure of the language may decide this question for us, since, taking it one way, we get an unduly complicated description, and, taking it the other way, a relatively simple one. This same consideration often leads us to *set up* an artificial underlying form.
>
> (218; emphasis in original)

In an influential paper (reprinted in Joos's *Readings in Linguistics*), Swadesh & Voegelin (1939) propose underlying morphophonemic representations and a set of rules deriving the surface phonetics, in order to handle complex alternations in Tübatulabal. That year also saw the publication of Bloomfield's paper 'Menomini morphophonemics' (Bloomfield 1939a), which is certainly the most elaborate system of underlying forms and derivational rules published before the advent of generative phonology. For Bloomfield,

> The process of description leads us to set up each morphological element in a theoretical *basic* form, and then to state the deviations from this basic form which appear when the element is combined with other elements. If one starts with the basic forms and applies our statements [...] in the order in which we given them, one will finally arrive at the form of words as they are actually spoken. (pp. 105–106)

Thomas Bever, who wrote an entire MIT dissertation on Bloomfield's Menomini work, noted that '[Bloomfield's] rules attain a single chain of at least 12 critically ordered statements (or 11 ordering conditions)' (Bever 1967: 4).[18]

Process descriptions of morphophonemic alternations continued throughout the 1940s and into the 1950s. In Chapter 2, I discussed Jakobson's 'Russian conjugation' paper (Jakobson 1971c [1948]), which was explicitly based on Bloomfield's approach to morphophonemics. A year later, Rulon Wells published a paper in *Language* entitled 'Automatic alternations' (Wells 1949).

> In this paper, Wells introduces explicitly all of the reasoning that would character-ize the heart of generative phonology: (i) underlying forms (which he calls 'basic forms'), which may be abstract, (ii) rules that derive surface (phonemic) forms from the underlying forms by rules that dynamically modify a segment in the rule's focus when it occurs in a particular phonological environment, (iii) the crucial character of rule ordering in some cases and (iv) the necessity of intermediate forms in a derivation.
>
> (Goldsmith 2008: 38)

Even post-Bloomfieldian-oriented introductory textbooks and workbooks in the 1950s taught students about base forms and morphophonemic rules. So consider Henry A. Gleason's *Workbook in Descriptive Linguistics* (Gleason 1955b). One page (p. 31) presents data about the two different verb forms in Samoan. Gleason wrote:

> The best way to describe the structure is to set up a base form for each stem. If this is done correctly, all of the forms can be derived from this base form by an affix or a regular morphophonemic change. Determine the base forms that allow this, and write them in the space provided.
>
> (Gleason 1955b: 31)

Gleason then asked the students the following questions: 'From which set of forms can the base form be determined? What is the affix? What is the morphophonemic

---

[18] Bromberger & Halle (1989) imply strongly that Bloomfield's paper was actively suppressed by the community of post-Bloomfieldians. They write: 'The article was omitted —"inadvertently," accord-ing to Hockett 1970: 494), from Hockett's "Implications of Bloomfield's Algonquian studies," which was published in the issue of *Language* (24.1) dedicated to Bloomfield on the occasion of his sixtieth birthday in 1948 [=Hockett 1948b]. It is not referred to in Hockett (1954)'s influential "Two Models of Grammatical Description" (which echoes the passage quoted above from Bloomfield 1933 almost ver-batim); nor was it reprinted in Joos 1957b's *Readings in Linguistics*' (Bromberger & Halle 1989: 66–67). I am skeptical that the paper was suppressed. The scare quotes around 'inadvertently' imply a willful omission, for which I see no evidence. Bloomfield's paper is referred to both in Wells (1949) and Har-ris (1951a), which suggest familiarity with it among the post-Bloomfieldians. Hockett's 'Two models' paper contains surprisingly few references, though other process accounts are cited. However, he does cite Bloomfield's article in his introductory textbook (Hockett 1958). And while Joos did not publish Bloomfield (1939a), he did publish Swadesh & Voegelin (1939), which takes the same general approach. Encrevé (2000) mentions several more well-known post-Bloomfieldian articles that cite Bloomfield's Menomini paper.

change?', and 'If you were learning Samoan, what would these data suggest as the best form in which to learn the verb vocabulary?'

A few years later in the chapter on morphophonemic alternation in his introductory textbook, Hockett argued that purely on the basis of simplicity it would be useful to set up underlying forms and morphophonemic rules relating them to surface forms:

> Several times in the preceding survey we have made mention of 'base forms'. The recognition of one representation of a morpheme (or of a larger form, say a word) as a base form is sometimes merely a matter of descriptive convenience, but sometimes it has deeper significance. Thus in the case of *wife*: *wives*, we take /wájf/ as base form. The reason is obvious. [...] It would be much more complicated to work in the other direction, describing the conditions which call for /wájf/ and saying that, except under these conditions, the shape /wájv/ appears.
>
> (Hockett 1958: 281–282)

To be sure, not all linguists of the period were happy with such an approach to morphophonemics. The more empiricist of the post-Bloomfieldians were distressed by the somewhat massive appeal to unobservables that were part-and-parcel of such process-based treatments (for example, see the remarks on this question published by Martin Joos in his *Readings* and discussed in Chapter 3, § 3.4.2 of this book). As Gleason noted, 'One reason for the Bloomfieldian rejection of process description was the ease with which the statements could become teleological or anthropomorphic, or seem to. They disliked saying that morphemes changed or assimilated' (Gleason 1988: 48). Nevertheless, Charles Hockett in his paper 'Two models of grammatical description' (Hockett 1954) could contrast the more standard item-and-arrangement (IA) approach with the less practiced item-and-process (IP) approach and find them to be for the most part intertranslatable — and where they were not, neither came out obviously ahead of the other. On the other hand, Hockett wrote that he could not conceive of any meaning to 'ordering' but an historical one:

> If it be said that the English past-tense form *baked* is 'formed' from *bake* by a 'process' of 'suffixation', then no matter what disclaimer of historicity is made, it is impossible not to conclude that some kind of priority is being assigned to *bake*, as against either *baked* or the suffix. And if this priority is not historical, what is it?
>
> (Hockett 1954: 211)

Ironically, given the subsequent history of the field, Hockett noted that one objection to IP was that 'IA has been formalized, and IP has not' (Hockett 1954: 214).

From what I have written so far in this section, I have perhaps given the impression that generative phonology dates from the 1930s (if not before) and that therefore there was nothing original in the work of Halle and Chomsky. That would be an incorrect impression to come away with. The linguists referred to above did not think of themselves as doing phonology. What they were doing was morpho-phonemics (or morphophonology). None of this, in their minds, challenged the structuralist phoneme, because morphophonemic systems were independent of, and ran in parallel to, phonemic systems.[19] The originality of Halle's argument in *The Sound Pattern of Russian* derives from his *rejection* of the structuralist phoneme, and its replacement with a level — morphophonemics or systematic phonology—which would serve as input not just to morphophonemic rules, but to phonological ones as well. For the post-Bloomfieldians, underlying forms were analytic fictions; for generative phonology they were real. As D. Robert Ladd has pointed out:

> The real problem [for the post-Bloomfieldians] was the relation between the au-tonomous phoneme and abstract morphophonemic relations, and the reluctance to conclude that the autonomous phoneme might be the source of some of the issues. Ordered rules and derivations and underlying forms were not just 'in the air' — that was how you did morphophonemics, taught in Ling. 101. But the trou-ble was that nobody could agree on what morphophonemics was, or how it fitted with the surface phoneme, and since the surface phoneme was universally agreed to be a major scientific achievement, it was morphophonemics that kind of got marginalized theoretically.
>
> (p. c., January 4, 2021)

In effect, Halle concluded the phoneme (as it was understood by structuralists of all schools) was dead. As we see in § 4.4.2 below, the established structural linguists were horrified by Halle's conclusion.

4.3.3.4 Transformational rules

Konrad Koerner (1983), in an effort to downplay the interest and importance of Chomsky's early syntactic work, points out that Chomsky borrowed the notion of 'transformation' from his teacher Zellig Harris (p. 159). But Chomsky has *always* credited Zellig Harris for having originated them (e.g. Chomsky 1957a: 6). Such rules are simply one of any number of possible devices available to syntactic theory for the expression of formal generalizations. Not surprisingly, then, frameworks for syntactic analysis have appeared since 1957 which are wholly Chomskyan in their basic world-view, but which reject outright the necessity for transformational rules (cf. Koster 1978; Gazdar 1981).

---

[19] Thomas Bever writes of Bloomfield's 'explicit rejection of a taxonomic phonemic level' in the 'Menomini morphophonemics' article (Bever 1967: 5). In fact, there was no such rejection. Bloomfield was doing morphophonemics; he simply ignored the taxonomic phonemic level, which was irrelevant for the purposes of the article.

It has never been controversial, as far as I know, that Chomsky's theory of trans-formations is very different from Harris's. One of the most salient differences between the Harris and Chomsky theories is that grammatical transformations for Harris were essentially equivalence relations among sentences, whereas for Chom-sky they were rules of grammar. For example, Harris related (surface) active and passive sentences directly, while for Chomsky their relationship was mediated by a set of abstract transformational rules. As Robert Freidin noted: '[Chomskyan-style] mappings may iterate and thus cannot be simply relations between sen-tences. Furthermore, they rely crucially on constituent structure analysis, unlike Harrisian transformations' (Freidin 1994: 8).

4.3.3.5 Projecting beyond a corpus

Once grammarians started turning their attention to syntax, the problem of what would be encompassed in a grammatical description became acute. In fact, it had always been tacitly assumed that a grammatical description, at any level, would make predictions about elements not in a particular corpus. So for example, the statement that voiceless stops in English are aspirated word-initially was under-stood to apply to *all* voiceless stops, not just those in a particular word list, however long. Indeed, it was assumed that newly-coined words would follow the general-ization. No linguist in the 1930s or 1940s would have doubted that if a word like *tath* entered English, the initial /t/ would be aspirated. However, the open-ended nature of sentences (as opposed to phonemes and, to a lesser extent, morphemes) led to some discussion of whether and how one could project beyond a corpus. Rulon Wells raised this question in one of the first important syntactic studies:

> To demark what is grammatically impossible (ungrammatical) from what does not occur [in a corpus] merely for some stylistic or semantic reason is a difficult problem. We do not deal with it here because it is irrelevant to the theory of ICs [immediate constituents — (FJN)], which takes as its data all those utterances known to occur, and analyzes them.
>
> (Wells 1947b: 81)

Wells's position turned out not to be the predominant one. A year later Hockett reasserted the traditional view that a grammar of a language does not just give back the corpus:

> [T]he analysis of the linguistic scientist is to be of such a nature that the linguist can account also for utterances which are *not* in his corpus at a given time. That is, as a result of his examination he must be able to predict what *other* utterances the speakers of the language might produce [...]
>
> (Hockett 1948a: 269; emphasis in the original).

Some years later, Hockett repeated his assertion:

> The description must also be prescriptive, not of course in the Fidditch sense, but in the sense that by following the statements one must be able to generate any number of utterances in the language, above and beyond those observed in advance by the analyst—new utterances most, if not all, of which will pass the test of casual acceptance by a native speaker.
>
> (Hockett 1954: 232)

So why are these truisms worth calling attention to? The reason is that Koerner (2002b: 182) implied that they called into question the originality of Chomsky's thinking. But hardly anybody in the 1940s (or earlier or later) would have doubted that a grammar would necessarily project beyond a corpus. Such an idea was taken for granted, not just by Chomsky, but by the great bulk of American grammatical theorists.

4.3.3.6 Language and mind

As we have seen, by 1957 or 1958 Chomsky had come to conclude that the grammar was in some sense 'in the head' of the language learner/user. He was hardly the first to arrive at such a conclusion. A quarter century earlier, Edward Sapir (1963 [1933]) had argued that phonemic representation (as opposed to phonetic representation) was 'psychologically real', a term that I believe that he coined in this work. Roman Jakobson and other members of the Prague School saw the child as a 'little linguist', as is evidenced by his attempt to relate child language, aphasia, and linguistic universals (Jakobson 1968 [1941]). While Saussure and later European structuralists saw language as first and foremost a social phenomenon, social convention was what led speakers of the same language variety to share largely identical mental representations of their grammars.

By the mid 1930s, however, ascribing psychological reality to the phoneme and other linguistic constructs had fallen out of favor among American structuralists. Leonard Bloomfield in his book *Language* was adamant that it was unscientific to refer to mental processes at all. Consider his critique of Hermann Paul's *Principles of the History of Language* (Paul 1891):

> The other great weakness of Paul's *Principles* is his insistence upon 'psychological' interpretation. He accompanies his statements about language with a paraphrase in terms of mental processes which the speakers are supposed to have undergone. The only evidence for these mental processes is the linguistic process; they add nothing to the discussion, but only obscure it. [...] [Paul and the other Indo-Europeanists] resorted, whenever they dealt with fundamentals, to philosophical and psychological pseudo-explanations.
>
> (Bloomfield 1933: 17)

Throughout the book, Bloomfield contrasted mentalistic versus mechanistic explanations, opting in all cases for the latter. A committed positivist by this time, Bloomfield regarded any reference to 'mind' as inherently unscientific. *Language* was followed shortly by Twaddell (1935), which contrasted mental and physical interpretations of the phoneme. He ended up rejecting both, but the former with more virulence than the latter:

> All these definitions [by earlier linguists, all European] agree in the ascription of mental reality of the phoneme, and for me thus fail to meet the requirement of methodological feasibility, i.e. they identify an entity which is inaccessible to scientific methods within the frame of linguistic study. […] (1) we have no right to guess about the linguistic workings of an inaccessible mind and (2) we can secure no advantage from such guesses.
>
> (Twaddell 1935: 57)

Twaddell concluded that the phoneme was 'an abstractional fictitious unit' (p. 68). Such a position dominated post-Bloomfieldian linguistics for another two decades.

In a widely-cited passage in a 1948 paper, Charles Hockett made the following statements:

> The analytical process thus parallels what goes on in the nervous system of a language learner, particularly, perhaps, that of a child learning his first language. The child hears, and eventually produces, various utterances. Sooner or later, the child produces utterances he has not previously heard from someone else. […] [T]he linguist has to make his analysis overtly, in communicable form, in the shape of a set of statements which can be understood by any properly trained person, who in turn can predict utterances not yet observed with the same degree of accuracy as can the original analyst. The child's 'analysis' consists, on the other hand, of a mass of various synaptic potentials in his nervous system. The child in time comes to *behave* the language; the linguist must come to *state* it.
>
> (Hockett 1948a: 269–270; emphasis in original)

Many commentators (e.g. Koerner 2002b: 183) have concluded from this passage that Hockett had embraced mentalism a full decade before Chomsky had done so. That is not true. Hockett phrased the entire discussion in behavioristic stimulus-response terms. The child responds to a verbal stimulus in the following way: 'If I make such-and-such noises, those about me will react in a certain way' (p. 269). Hockett even ensured that the reader would avoid a mentalistic interpretation of his comments by stressing that 'We do not imply that any such "thought" passes through the "mind" of the child' (p. 269; the scare quotes around 'thought' and 'mind' are Hockett's).

If any American structuralists around 1950 (excluding those with Prague School orientations) had adopted a mentalistic approach to grammar before Chomsky, I am not aware of them. What made Chomsky's approach in the late 1950s so important in terms of the theory of language and mind was that it was syntax-centered. By focusing on syntax, Chomsky was able to lay the groundwork for an explanation of the most distinctive aspect of human language: its creativity. The importance of the centrality of syntax cannot be overstated. Phonological and morphological systems are for the most part closed and finite; whatever their complexity or intrinsic interest, their study does not lead automatically to an understanding of a speaker's capacity for linguistic novelty nor to an explanation of the infinitude of language. Yet earlier accounts had typically ignored syntax or excluded it from the theory of *langue* altogether. For Saussure, most syntagmatic relations were consigned to *parole*, as they were for the linguists of the Prague School, who treated them from the point of view of 'functional sentence perspective'. Zellig Harris, it is true, had begun in the late 1940s to undertake a formal analysis of intersentential syntactic relations (see Harris 1957 and much other work), but his empiricist commitment to developing mechanical procedures for grammatical analysis led him to overlook what the study of these relations implied for a theory of mind.

The fact that most of Chomsky's early work was syntax-centered lay at the foundation of the interdisciplinary research program that it initiated. Consider its effect on psychology. Psychologists had certainly taken an interest in pre-Chomskyan structural linguistics; for example, John B. Carroll had written: 'From linguistic theory we get the notion of a hierarchy of units [...]. It may be suggested that stretches of any kind of behavior may be organized in somewhat the same fashion' (Carroll 1953: 106). Yet the approach to language to which Carroll referred, by granting primary position to phonology or morphology, offered little to an understanding of language processing or more general aspects of verbal behavior. As a consequence, the results of structural linguistics were completely ignored in Skinner's *Verbal Behavior* (Skinner 1957) and given only limited attention in the major pre-Chomskyan survey of psycholinguistics, Osgood & Sebeok (1954). But shortly after Miller, Galanter, & Pribram (1960) had revealed to the community of psychologists the implications for the structure of human behavior latent in Chomsky's theory of syntax, the 'psycholinguistic revolution' (Greene 1972: 11) was well under way.

4.4 The mainstream reaction to early transformational generative grammar

We probe in this section how TGG was received by the mainstream American linguists of the 1950s and 1960s. § 4.4.1 outlines how *Syntactic Structures* and early generative work was regarded by this group of linguists. § 4.4.2 does the same for early generative phonology, and § 4.4.3 for Chomsky's *Aspects of the Theory of Syntax*.

4.4.1 The reaction to *Syntactic Structures* and other early syntactic studies

By and large, the reaction of the community of post-Bloomfieldians to *Syntactic Structures* was positive and fully comprehending of what made the work distinctive. Aside from Lees's piece discussed above, the major review of the book was published in *IJAL* (Voegelin 1958b). I must say that it is an odd piece of work: The space occupied by footnotes is larger than that occupied by main text, and the bulk of the latter is devoted to asking four unanswered questions: (1) Are transforms in syntax new?; (2) Will they start a Copernican revolution within linguistics?; (3) Is transform grammar incorporable in linguistic typology?; and (4) Is transform grammar elicitable? On the one hand, Voegelin did describe Chomsky as the 'most articulate developer' of Zellig Harris's model (p. 230). On the other hand, he recognized that a central feature of the book was its rejection of discovery procedures and concomitant abandonment of the prohibition against mixing levels. He wrote:

> And if transform grammar also persuades linguists to relegate phonemics to a preliminary stage of analysis (called 'discovery'), and to operate in final analysis (called 'description') exclusively with morphophonemics, it will have accomplished a Copernican revolution.
>
> (Voegelin 1958b: 229)

Other linguists in the following years recognized that Chomsky's arguments for the abandonment of positivist-dictated discovery procedures was the most original feature of *Syntactic Structures*. For example, Martin Joos wrote:

> [Generative grammar is] a heresy within the neo-Saussurean tradition rather than a competitor to it. What this movement most consequentially ignores [...] is the neo-Saussurean axiom [...] 'Text signals its own structure'. From this tacit assumption there follows automatically the most troublesome rule of neo-Bloomfieldian methodology: the rule demanding 'separation of levels' [...] But [the generativist] leaders are able to point out that *no other science has a parallel rule*.
>
> (Joos 1961: 17–18; emphasis added)

Charles Hockett, far from viewing generative grammar as a mere logical exten-
sion of his own and other work in the post-Bloomfieldian tradition, went so far as
to characterize the publication of *Syntactic Structures* as one of 'only four major
breakthroughs' in the history of modern linguistics (Hockett 1965: 185). Hockett
wrote:

> Between Sir William [Jones's] address and the present Thirty-Ninth Annual Meet-
> ing of the Linguistic Society of America there is a span of 178 years. Half of 178
> is 89, a prime number. If we add that to 1786 [the date of Jones's address] we
> reach the year 1875, in which appeared Karl Verner's 'Eine Ausnahme der ersten
> Lautverschiebung'. Thereafter, two successive steps of 41 years each [...] bring us
> to the posthumous publication of Ferdinand de Saussure's *Cours de linguistique
> générale* and then to Noam Chomsky's *Syntactic Structures*. I have allowed my-
> self this bit of numerology because I know none of you will take it seriously. But
> behind this persiflage there is a sober intent. Our fraternity has accomplished a
> great deal in the short span of 178 years; yet, in my opinion, there have been only
> four major breakthroughs. All else that we have done relates to these four in one
> way or another.
>
> (Hockett 1965: 185)

Hockett recognized that the major breakthrough of *Syntactic Structures* was its
abandonment of empiricist constraints on theory formation and evaluation—
which, as he noted, involved distinguishing discovery from evaluation procedures,
and practical description and formal theory, which required setting the formal
requirements that a theory must meet. Hockett referred the various components
of nonempiricist theory collectively as the 'accountability hypothesis' and wrote
(p. 196) 'that it is a breakthrough I am certain'.

Bernard Bloch, the editor of *Language* at the time, also recognized the importance of Chomsky's early work:

> I'm an admirer of Chomsky's from way back, and an admirer of Harris's of even
> longer standing; and I'm convinced that transformation theory (or whatever you
> want to call it) is a tremendously important advance in grammatical thinking.
> Though I don't know the ins and outs of it well enough to use it myself, or even
> to lecture on it, I expect great things of it.
>
> (Bloch to Lees, July 31, 1959; BBA)

Chomsky has not only contributed to the literature of structural linguistics, he
has fired the imagination of dozens of scholars throughout the country. It is interesting to note that young workers in the field, especially the most brilliant
among them, are particularly susceptible to his spell. One of the liveliest and

most promising developments in grammatical theory in recent years is Chomsky's transformation grammar. I call it Chomsky's even though Zellig Harris was
perhaps the original proponent. It is above all Chomsky who had developed the
theory and had given it its current vogue.

(Bloch to William Locke, October 26, 1960 in a
letter supporting Chomsky's promotion to Full Professor; BBA)

To be sure, Bloch does not specify what made TGG a 'tremendously important advance' or why the most brilliant young workers were attracted to it. But what could
he have had in mind besides Chomsky's showing how the syntactic properties of
language might be analyzed in an approach that rejected positivist constraints on
theory formation?[20]

It was really just in later years that historiographers and other commentators decided that *Syntactic Structures* was but a minor deviation from post-Bloomfieldian
business as usual (see § 4.3.3.1 for some representative quotes). That was not how
the leading figures of American linguistics in the late 1950s and early 1960s saw
the theory presented in *Syntactic Structures* and developed over the next few years.
Unfortunately, the question of the importance of Chomsky's ideas have become
entangled with whether or not they were 'revolutionary'. So it will be recalled that
Hymes and Fought saw in *Syntactic Structures* 'no evidence of basic revolutionary
change' (Hymes & Fought 1981: 241). But they do in fact recognize what was most
important about the book:

Chomsky's true argument with the Bloomfieldians was with regard to the kind
of evaluation procedure, the kind of formal justification of a linguistic analysis, or linguistic theory, that should be followed. To the criterion of theoretically
possible induction, he opposed the criterion of theoretically definable simplicity
(generality).

(Hymes & Fought 1981: 180)

But his 'true argument' was an argument about what linguistic theory was all about.
How could that not be considered important?

---

[20] Even Chomsky acknowledged that Bloch took positive steps to abet his career: 'I always found
him sympathetic, though I don't know how interested he was in the work I was doing. He requested a
copy of *LSLT* and also of *MMH* and also invited me several times to speak at the Yale Linguistics Club.
We had several discussions on these occasions. I recall them quite well, particularly, because interest
in the work I was doing on the part of professional linguistics was extremely rare' (Murray 1980: 78,
citing a p. c. from Chomsky on May 30, 1977). It was Bloch, of course, who published Lees's glowing
review of *Syntactic Structures* and Chomsky's devastating review of Skinner's *Verbal Behavior*.

4.4.2 The reaction to early generative phonology

The post-Bloomfieldian reaction to generative phonology was overwhelmingly negative. And it is easy to see why it would be — the phoneme (and with it, the level of grammar that it entailed) was widely seen as the greatest result ever of structural linguistics. As Archibald Hill put it plaintively, 'I could stay with the transformationalists pretty well, until they attacked my darling, the phoneme. I will never be a complete transformationalist because I am still a phonemicist' (Hill 1980: 75). The critiques ranged from mild, as in the case of Householder (1965), to virulent, as in the case of Hockett (1968: 3, where he wrote that 'Chomskyan-Hallean "phonology" [is] completely bankrupt') and Trager (1968: 78, where we find the assertion that 'it is worse than 'bankrupt' — it is 'a product of a fantastic never-never land'). What all of these critiques shared was dismay at the abandonment of the structuralist phoneme. If any leading post-Bloomfieldian wrote favorably about work such as Halle (1959, 1962), Chomsky (1964a), or Chomsky & Halle (1968), I am not aware of it.[21] Stephen Murray wrote correctly:

> What outraged neo-Bloomfieldians was not the theory of syntax, but the dismissal of phonemics. When Halle (1959), Chomsky & Halle (1968) and Postal (1964a, 1968) declared that classing sounds into phonemes was useless, they rejected the phonemic work of two preceding generations of linguists. The elevation of morphophonemics and the exclusion of phonemics was far more provocative than anything Chomsky could have said about syntax or behaviorism vs. mentalism. Phonemics was the central creation of 'scientific linguistics'. It could not be lightly tossed aside by those who devoted their career to phonemic analysis.
>
> (Murray 1994: 238)

4.4.3 The reaction to *Aspects of the Theory of Syntax*

There were surprisingly few published critiques of *Aspects* from the community of post-Bloomfieldians. Most were surely appalled at the overtly mentalist foundations of the theory present there and the abstractness of its treatment of syntactic phenomena. Charles Hockett left no doubt about his position, writing that 'Chomsky's outlook [...] is so radically different from Bloomfield's and from my own that there is, at present, no available frame of reference external to both within which they can be compared' (Hockett 1966b: 156) and referring later to 'the speculations of the neo-medieval philosopher Noam Chomsky' (Hockett 1967: 142–144). Robert Hall warned that Chomsky is 'threatening to negate all the

---

[21] I make an exception for Robert Stockwell and Sol Saporta, both of whom were quite young at the time (see Stockwell 1960 and Saporta 1965).

progress achieved over four centuries [and] dragging our understanding of language back down to a state of medieval ignorance and obscurantism' (Hall 1968: 128–129). But most, for whatever reason, simply ignored *Aspects*. As far as the treatment of syntax in that book is concerned, probably most would have agreed with the assessment of Sydney Lamb (not technically a post-Bloomfieldian) when he wrote:

> The remaining, major portion of *Aspects* is devoted largely to the new TG treatment of syntax, particularly to Chomsky's concept of deep structure. An unconscious self-parody, it is perhaps its own severest critic, in that it demonstrates very effectively the needless complexity forced upon the grammarian by mutation description and the level-mixing it entails. Indeed, this book may go down in linguistic history as the *reductio ad absurdum* of process description in synchronic linguistics. If it does, it will have made an unintended but very real contribution.
>
> (Lamb 1967: 415)

4.5 Chomsky in the spotlight: Examining some of his claims about his early days

It is a truism that people are not necessarily their own best biographers. Chomsky has made a number of published claims about aspects of his early days in linguistics (that is, from the late 1940s to the late 1950s) that have been challenged by historiographers. In this section, I review these claims and the challenges to them, providing best evaluation of them that I can muster. § 4.5.1 involves the publication history of *LSLT*; § 4.5.2 Chomsky's not citing Bloomfield's 'Menomini morphophonemics' paper; § 4.5.3 the extent to which Harris paid attention to what Chomsky was doing; and § 4.5.4 Chomsky's revision of *LSLT*.

4.5.1 'I have never heard of the alleged offers to publish *LSLT*'

In the Introduction to the printed version of *LSLT*, Chomsky wrote that in 1956 he 'submitted parts of the manuscript to the Technology Press of MIT for consideration of potential publication. It was rejected, with the not unreasonable observation that an unknown author taking a rather unconventional approach should submit articles based on this material to professional journals before planning to publish such a comprehensive and detailed manuscript as a book' (Chomsky 1975b: 3). There was no mention of submission to other publishers. Stephen Murray, however, claimed that 'One would be hard pressed to guess that *two* publishers were interested in publishing *LSLT* in 1957' (Murray 1980: 78;

emphasis in original). Murray's only (unhelpful) support for such a claim was information passed on to him by 'Informant 5'. Murray later wrote that Chomsky had written him that he had 'never heard of the alleged offers to publish *LSLT*' and that he 'didn't submit book proposals anywhere' (Murray 1999: 262). Murray counters that both North Holland and Mouton offered to publish *LSLT* in the late 1950s and early 1960s. To make his case, Murray cited on page 263 an aerogram from Chomsky to the Mouton editor Cornelis van Schooneveld, held at the CVSC, stating that 'I have a tentative agreement with North Holland to publish it', as well as correspondence from van Schooneveld stating that Mouton wanted to publish the manuscript.

In Newmeyer (2014: fn. 7) I repeated the material in the preceding paragraph, along with the stated wish that Murray might had scanned the letter from van Schooneveld, rather than just reprinting its contents. Shortly after the publication of my article I was contacted via email by Jan Paul Hinrichs, an archivist in charge of the CVSC in the Leiden University Library. Hinrichs told me that 'this letter exists and is held in the [library]. I have quoted from this letter in my forward to my book *The C. H. van Schooneveld Collection in Leiden University Library* [= Hinrichs 2001]' (p. c., May 27, 2014). On my first trip to Leiden after receiving Hinrichs' message I went to the library and scanned Chomsky's aerogram to van Schooneveld (Figure 4.1). What Murray wrote was true.

At my urging, Hinrichs wrote a letter to the journal *Language* reaffirming the existence of the aerogram and quoting it in its entirety (Hinrichs 2014: 561). Chomsky wrote in a reply to Hinrichs: 'I have no record or memory of that letter, but it looks authentic. It is true that I was revising the manuscript, but never finished doing so. Other projects intervened. The partially revised 1956 manuscript is what was published (in part) in 1975' (Chomsky 2014: 561).

Several years later, as part of a longer email exchange, I asked Chomsky how he could have forgotten by 1975 that he had received a letter from Mouton that they would be 'interested' in publishing *LSLT* and a 'tentative agreement' from North Holland to publish it. He told me that he forgotten about it because 'I never took seriously [any letter] from Mouton, who, at the time, was publishing anything because Dutch publishing was so cheap' (p. c., November 1, 2017). That comment echoed what Chomsky had written twenty years earlier:

> At the time Mouton was publishing just about anything, so they decided they'd publish it along with a thousand other worthless things that were coming out. That's the story of *Syntactic Structures*: course notes for undergraduate science students published by accident in Europe.
>
> (Chomsky 1975b: 162–163)

I leave it to the reader to decide if the above remarks from Chomsky jibe with the tone of the letter that he wrote to van Schooneveld. But one point needs stressing.

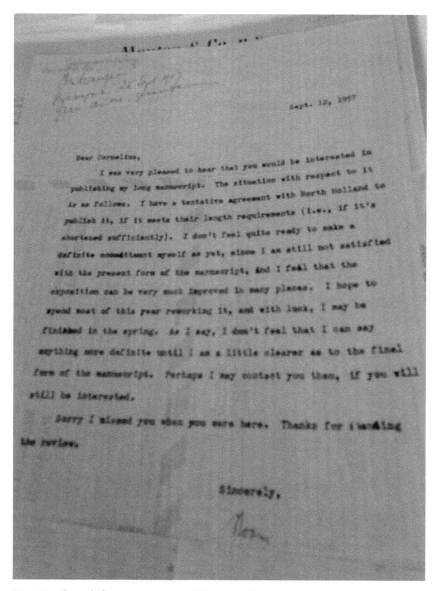

Fig. 4.1 Chomsky's aerogram to van Schooneveld

Mouton (but not so much North Holland) did indeed develop a reputation for publishing too much of too low quality. But in 1957 they were still riding high, having published the year before Jakobson and Halle's *Fundamentals of Language* (Jakobson & Halle 1956) as the first volume in their Janua Linguarum Series Minor. *Syntactic Structures* was the fourth book in the series. It is hard for me to believe that in 1957 an offer to publish with Mouton (or North Holland, for that matter) would have been a forgettable experience.

4.5.2 'My *MMH* was written, I regret to say, in ignorance of Bloomfield's study'

As discussed in § 4.3.3.3 above, one of the major works in morphophonemics in the context of American structuralism was Bloomfield's 'Menomini morphophonemics' paper (Bloomfield 1939a). While appeal to underlying forms and ordered rules were commonplace in morphophonemic analysis in those days, these constructs are probably more highly articulated in the Bloomfield paper than in any other publication by Bloomfield himself or his post-Bloomfieldian followers. Chomsky's MA thesis *The Morphophonemics of Modern Hebrew* (Chomsky 1951), in keeping with the spirit of the times, also makes use of these devices. Chomsky wrote later that 'My *MMH* was written, I regret to say, in ignorance of Bloomfield's study' (Chomsky 1975b: 47) and 'there is Bloomfield's 'Menomini morphophonemics,' (MM) published only a few years earlier [than my thesis], though I did not know about it at the time (Chomsky 1979b: 112). Historiographers of linguistics, in general, have howled in disbelief that Chomsky could not have been aware of MM as a student and have implied strongly that he covered up knowledge of the paper so as to make his own work seem more original:

> [...] I believe that the similarities between the strategy and techniques of Bloomfield's 'Menomini morphophonemics' and the architecture of early Chomskyan generative phonology are most plausibly explained by Chomsky's prior acquaintance with the Bloomfield paper, either directly or through summaries in Harris (1951a). I regard Chomsky's denial of any such influence by Bloomfield as another example of his solipsism [...]
>
> (Fought 1999: 316)

> Given Harris' manner of conducting himself as a mentor and Chomsky's enthusiasm for doing linguistics with him during the late 1940s and early 1950s — not to mention Chomsky's voracious reading habits, then as still today, one would be hard pressed to believe that when he was writing his BA honors paper in 1949, Chomsky was unaware of Bloomfield's proposals concerning rule ordering and morphophonemic analysis, whether or not he had read Bloomfield's *Language* and his 1939 Menomini article at the time or not.
>
> (Koerner 2003: 19)

Chomsky, as it will be recalled, was thanked in 1947 by his teacher Zellig Harris for help with the manuscript of the latter's *Methods in Structural Linguistics*

(Harris 1951a) and later wrote that he had learned linguistics by doing so. Chomsky's detractors (see especially Koerner 2003, 2004) have pointed out that there are several references to MM in Harris's book. If he had proof-read the book, they say, how could he have missed these references? Furthermore, they say, MM appeared in *Travaux du Cercle Linguistique de Prague*, one of the few journals of general linguistics in the world and one which was at the University of Pennsylvania library in the 1940s. Surely either desire to master the important literature of the field or a direct recommendation from Harris to read it would have steered Chomsky to MM. We know that Harris had a high opinion of MM from his six references to it in his earlier 'Morpheme alternants' paper (Harris 1942). So doesn't all of the evidence, then, point to Chomsky having read MM by the time he started to write *MMH*?

I agree with Daniels (2010) that the answer is 'Probably, no'. As far as the six references in the 'Morpheme alternants' papers are concerned, they do little more than mine data from Bloomfield's paper. Daniels goes on to note:

> Koerner (2004: 71) identifies three mentions of the article in Harris 1951a (231, 237, 336) but does note that the first two are, again, simply as a source of data and the third disposes of (one of Bloomfield's cases of) rule ordering by reanalyzing it in terms of morphophonemes. Thus this cannot be taken as pointing to a source for Chomsky's notion of rule ordering.
>
> (Daniels 2010: 177)

In short, I cannot think of any reason why Chomsky would have had an 'Aha moment' while proofing Harris's book. Underlying morphophonemes and derivations with rule ordering were widely posited in the late 1940s. There is nothing in Harris's book about Bloomfield's use of these constructs that would have overly attracted Chomsky's attention. The originality of *MMH*, again, derives not from rule ordering, but from the fact that a full structural description is posited for each sentence generated.

4.5.3 'It's next to inconceivable, for example, that Harris looked at my Ph. D. dissertation or *LSLT*'

Chomsky wrote the following in the Preface to *Syntactic Structures*:

> During the entire period of this research I have had the benefit of very frequent and lengthy discussions with Zellig S. Harris. So many of his ideas and suggestions are incorporated in the text below and in the research on which it is based that I will make no attempt to indicate them by special reference.
>
> (Chomsky 1957a: 6)

The Preface to his PhD dissertation contains similar wording: 'This study was carried out in close collaboration with Zellig Harris, to whom I am indebted for many of the fundamental underlying ideas.' Years later, in the Introduction to the revised edition of *LSLT*, Chomsky noted that 'While working on *LSLT* I discussed all aspects of this material frequently and in great detail with Zellig Harris, whose influence is obvious throughout' (Chomsky 1975b: 4).

Harris, for his part, wrote warmly about his interactions with Chomsky. To give an example, on February 7, 1991, Charles F. Hockett wrote the following to John Goldsmith:

> Quite apart from publications, a number of us (Bloch, Trager, Harris, Voegelin, Smith, Joos) were in active correspondence in the late 1940s and early 1950s. I have (or did have; some of them are lost) letters from Zellig Harris that mention a young student named Chomsky. One of them speaks enthusiastically of Chomsky's work on Hebrew morphophonemics, saying that Chomsky had found a way to put the ordering of morphophonemic rules on a logical basis.
>
> (Goldsmith 2008: 48–49)

In his 'Discourse analysis' paper, Harris wrote that it 'is a pleasure to acknowledge here the cooperation of three men who have collaborated with me in developing the method and in analyzing various texts: Fred Lukoff, Noam Chomsky, and A. F. Brown (Harris 1952: 1). And in another paper published a few years later, Harris asserted that 'My many conversations with Chomsky have sharpened the work presented here, in addition to being a great pleasure in themselves' (Harris 1957: 23). Harris also went on to praise Chomsky and his work on more than one occasion, as is fitting for an advisor. For example, Harris wrote the following to Bernard Bloch on December 19, 1950:

> A student of mine, A. N. Chomsky has been doing a great deal of work in formulation of linguistic procedures and has also done considerable work with Goodman and Martin. Last year I [gave] him the morphological and morphophonemic material which I had here. He added to it a great deal by means of informant work and turned out a rigorous detailed morphophonemic [analysis] which I am sending to you under separate cover. I thought you would be interested in it for its own sake. In addition I wonder whether you think there would be any point in publishing it and if so, in what form. (BBA)

A few years later, in another letter to Bloch, Harris wrote: 'It was just awfully nice of you to send me Bar-Hillel's paper. I discussed it with Chomsky [...]' (February 23, 1954; BBA).

However, further along in Chomsky's introduction to *LSLT*, there is a passage in which he seems almost to contradict what he had written earlier in the piece: 'I therefore assumed that whatever I was doing, it was not real scientific linguistics, but something else, obscure in status. This feeling was reinforced by the almost total lack of interest in *MMH* on the part of linguists whose work I respected' (a footnote here makes an exception for Henry Hoenigswald).[22] Chomsky even asserted later that 'Harris never looked at [the thesis] and no one in the field reacted to it' (quoted in Barsky 2007: 53 as a p. c. from Chomsky on March 31, 1995), flatly contradicting Hockett's letter to Goldsmith. I suppose in principle that Harris could have exhibited an 'almost total lack of interest in *MMH*,' which he 'never even looked at' and then a few years later enjoyed lengthy and productive discussions with Chomsky about *LSLT* and *Syntactic Structures*, though that seems implausible to me. But by the 1990s, Chomsky seemed to dismiss any possible interest by Harris in this later work as well, writing '[Zellig Harris] never paid the slightest attention to [it] and probably thought that [it] was crazy'[23] (Barsky 1997: 54). To that we can add the assertion by Chomsky that he is 'sure that Harris never looked at my 1949, 1951 work on generative grammar', and that 'it's next to inconceivable, for example, that Harris looked at my PhD dissertation or *LSLT*', and that he and Harris did not discuss this material during the 1950s (Goldsmith 2005: 720; p. c. from Chomsky).

I find Chomsky's change of tune about Harris's interest totally flabbergasting. For one thing, there is even more evidence that *MMH* was not all that ignored:

Chomsky was asked by Harry Hoijer to review for *IJAL* two major books on phonology, Hockett's *Manual* (Chomsky 1957b) and Jakobson and Halle's *Fundamentals* (Chomsky 1957c). Chomsky had not yet published anything on phonology; for some time he had been concentrating on syntax. That means that the significance, if not the details, of *MMH* was already widely recognized by 1955.

(Daniels 2010: 188)

[22] Note also: 'The only faculty member who looked at the thesis was Hoenigswald, out of a sense of responsibility. Harris had no interest in it' (Sperlich 2006: 38).
[23] The word 'it' appears twice in the Barsky quote in square brackets. Its antecedent is not one hundred percent clear. Chomsky is referring to work later than *MMH*, but how much later I am not sure.

Who but Harris would have advocated on behalf of Chomsky with Hoijer? And what would his advocacy have been based on besides admiration for *MMH*?

Chomsky's later claims about Harris's attention to his work dovetail with another assertion that he has made repeatedly over the years:

> I actually have no serious professional qualifications in any field that was identifiable 40 years ago — which is why I am teaching at MIT, a scientific university, where no one cared much about credentials. I'm largely self-taught (including linguistics), and my work happens to have ranged fairly widely.
>
> (Chomsky 1994: 300)

No serious professional qualifications? Imperfect credentials? Largely self-taught in linguistics? I cannot think of any word besides 'absurd' to describe such claims.[24] Chomsky was the leading student of one of America's leading structural linguists in one of the few departments of linguistics in the United States at the time. By his own admission, he was invited to speak at Yale while still a student. He published a full article in the *Journal of Symbolic Logic* at the age of 24 (Chomsky 1953) and one in *Language* at the age of 26 (Chomsky 1955a). He was indeed fortunate to land at MIT, where he did not have to deal with an entrenched post-Bloomfieldian presence. But he seems to have had other employment options. According to Dell Hymes, who was then a junior faculty member at Harvard, 'Noam entertained hopes of employment at Harvard, but being in Cambridge at MIT was not quite being marginal: it was still being in Cambridge! [...] He had many chances to move. Indiana [which had a well-established linguistics program — (FJN)] tried to get him about 1957-8' (Murray 1980: 82).

I have to agree with Randy Harris: 'Let's be clear what these accusations [against Zellig Harris] amount to. If true, they suggest stunning professional negligence on Harris's part; if false, they approach libel' (Harris 2018). I have no intention of speculating on what would have led Chomsky to assert that Harris never read the three theses, on the cover of which his signature appears. But I find this assertion quite distressing.

---

[24] For a similar assessment, see Goldsmith (1998). I certainly do not mean to imply that Chomsky was a *typical* linguistics student. How could he have been? He 'was, after all, a very aberrant young linguist. He was unmistakably competent, but he lacked many of the standard qualifications: He had not done fieldwork; he was not interested in work tied closely to language teaching; his working methods were unorthodox; his theoretical stance seemed a bit esoteric' (Gleason 1988: 59–60).

4.5.4 'In editing [*LSLT*] for publication now, I have made no attempt to bring it up to date or to introduce revisions in the light of subsequent work'

As we have seen, Chomsky chose not to revise *LSLT* for publication in the late 1950s and early 1960s. Given the high degree of interest in the work and the fact that dozens (possibly hundreds) of copies of the manuscript were in circulation, he decided to publish *LSLT* with a long historical introduction in 1975 (Chomsky 1975a). His description of the revised version is as follows:

> In editing [*LSLT*] for publication now, I have made no attempt to bring it up to date or to introduce revisions in the light of subsequent work. The editing has been limited to correction of some obvious minor errors, standardization of notation and terminology, a few clarifying comments, and deletion of a fair amount of material (major deletions are indicated in the text, in some cases, with a brief paraphrase of the omitted material).
>
> (Chomsky 1975b: 1)

I own a dittoed copy[25] of *LSLT* dated June 1955 that was made available to students and guests at MIT (I was the latter) in academic year 1968–1969. Soon after the appearance of the revised version, curiosity let me to compare the two versions page-by-page. I was unprepared for the discovery of how different they were. I never followed up on this discovery, as I had many other historical issues to occupy my time. However, my attention was recently called to an unpublished Columbia University dissertation by Thomas Ryckman (Ryckman 1986), who is now a philosopher at Stanford University. Ryckman also compared the two versions of *LSLT* and found 'literally hundreds of changes, totaling thousands of words, and primarily in Chapters I-V (= Chapters X and I-IV of the 1955 and 1956 versions) which deal with methodological and conceptual rather than technical issues. While many of these changes are rewordings or alterations that do not substantially change content, there is a perceptible difference of nuance between the 1955 and 1975 versions' (Ryckman 1986: 144). Some of these post facto changes were in the direction of making *LSLT* seem less operationalist and more realist than it actually was intended to be. Ryckman's comparison of the two versions goes on for pages; I now compare only a few of the differences between the two versions.

---

[25] For the younger readers: Dittoing was a primitive method of duplication of documents in use between the 1950s and 1970s. One master could produce a few dozen smudgy, purple-inked copies, reeking of chemicals. My copy of *LSLT* must have been produced at the end of the run, since some pages are barely readable.

In the 1955 version Chomsky wrote:[26]

Wells has pointed out recently that philosophers have, by and large, rejected as a general criterion of significance, the strong kind of reductionism that, we are suggesting as necessary for our particular purposes. He offers this in criticism of Bloomfield's program of avoiding mentalistic foundations for linguistic theory. It is true that many philosophers have given up a certain form of reductionism, of which Bloomfield's program (and our restatement of it) is an instance, as a *general* criterion for significance [...]However I do not believe that this is relevant to Bloomfield's antimentalism. The fact that a certain criterion of significance has been abandoned does not mean that the bars are down, and that 'ideas' and 'meanings' become proper terms for linguistics, any more than it means that ghosts are proper concepts for physics. If this rejection of an old criterion is not followed by construction of a new one, then it simply has no bearing on the selection of legitimate terms for a scientific theory. Where it is followed by some new sense of 'significance', then if this new sense is at all adequate, it seems to me that it will rule out mentalism for what were essentially Bloomfield's reasons, i.e., its obscurity and general uselessness in linguistic theory.

(Chomsky 1955b: I-19-20; emphasis in original)

Now compare this passage to the one that appeared twenty years later:

Wells has pointed out recently that philosophers have, by and large, rejected as a general criterion of significance, the strong kind of reductionism that, we are suggesting as appropriate for our particular purposes. He offers this in criticism of Bloomfield's program of avoiding mentalistic foundations for linguistic theory. It is true that many philosophers have given up, as a *general* requirement for significance the kind of reduction that our restatement of Bloomfield's program has as its goal [...]. However I do not believe that this is relevant to Bloomfield's antimentalism, or to the approach to linguistic theory that we have outlined. The fact that a certain general criterion of significance has been abandoned does not mean that the bars are down, and that 'ideas' and 'meanings' become proper terms for linguistics. If this rejection of an old criterion is not followed by construction of a new one, then it simply has no bearing on the selection of legitimate terms for a scientific theory. If it followed by a new analysis of 'significance', then if this is at all adequate, it seems to me that it will rule out mentalism for what were essentially Bloomfield's reasons, i.e., its obscurity and inherent untestability.

(Chomsky 1975a: 85-86; emphasis in original)

---

[26] Katz (1981: 33) also pointed to the original version of this quote in arguing that in 1955 Chomsky's position on mentalism was little difference from Bloomfield's. Katz (p. 41) also noted that the following

As can be seen, in the 1975 version of this passage, the word 'necessary' was replaced by 'appropriate' and the wording 'a certain form of reductionism, of which Bloomfield's program (and our restatement of it) is an instance, as a *general* criterion for significance' was replaced by 'as a general criterion for significance, the kind of reduction that our restatement of Bloomfield's program has as its goal. The sentence beginning 'However' in the original passage was extended as follows: 'However I do not believe that this is relevant to Bloomfield's antimentalism, or to the approach to linguistic theory that we have outlined'. And in the last sentence, 'general uselessness' was replaced by 'inherent untestability'.

Later in the chapter, Chomsky wrote in 1955:

> At present it seems to me proper to say that whereas we know of many grammatical notions that have no semantic basis, we know of none for which a significant and general semantic analysis is forthcoming. And at present at least, this justifies the tentative identification of grammar with distributional analysis.
>
> (Chomsky 1955b: 1-45)

In the 1975 version, the last sentence of the above quote was dropped and replaced by 'This justifies the tentative assertion that the theory of linguistic form does not have semantic foundations' (Chomsky 1975a: 97).

Ryckman writes:

> Similarly, many references to the 'operational' character of the primitive notions of linguistic theory have been deleted from the 1975 version (e.g., at I-20-21 corresponding to 1975: 86, at I-15 corresponding to 1975: 83, at X-714 corresponding to 1975: 61, at I-24 corresponding to 1975: 87) although, as can be seen in the above quotation, some remain. In addition, the 1975 version contains at least, one reference to 'universal grammar': 'The program of developing a general linguistic theory is reminiscent, in certain respects of much earlier attempts to develop a universal grammar' (108), whereas neither this term nor 'language universals' occurs in 1955.
>
> (Ryckman 1986: 144)

Ryckman provides several more pages of significant contrasts between the 1955 version and the 1975 version of *LSLT*. My only conclusion is that if one desires to know what Chomsky was thinking in 1955, it is recommended that one read the

quote from the 1955 version of *LSLT* was dropped in the 1975 version: '[…] I think that there is hope of developing that aspect of linguistic theory being studied here on the basis of a small number of operational primitives, and that introduction of dispositions (or mentalistic terms) is either irrelevant, or trivializes the theory' (Chomsky 1955b: I-20-21).

earlier version, which is available in print or microfilm at many university libraries around the world.[27]

4.6 Linguistics, MIT, Chomsky, and the military

When I took my first course in generative grammar in 1966, the main text was naturally Chomsky's *Aspects of the Theory of Syntax* (Chomsky 1965), which had been published the year before. The first page of text, preceding even the Preface, was the 'Acknowledgement', where I was shocked to find the following paragraph:

> The research reported in this document was made possible by support extended the Massachusetts Institute of Technology, Research Laboratory of Electronics, by the JOINT SERVICES ELECTRONICS PROGRAMS (U.S. Army, U.S. Navy, and U.S. Air Force) under Contract No. DA-36-039-AMC-03200(E); additional support was received from the U.S. Air Force (Electronic Systems Division under contract AF19(628)-2487), the National Science Foundation (Grant GP-2495), the National Institutes of Health (Grant MH-04737-04), and the National Aeronautics and Space Administration (Grant NsG-496).
>
> (Chomsky 1965: np)

Why on earth, I asked myself, would the US Air Force and NASA be interested in supporting a highly abstract treatment of syntactic structure? I found the acknowledgement particularly troubling since at the time I was a member of the radical group Students for a Democratic Society and Chomsky himself was becoming known for his from-the-left critique of American foreign policy. This section attempts to provide at least a partial answer to my question. § 4.6.1 continues the discussion in Chapter 1 concerning military interest in linguistics. § 4.6.2 looks at MIT and its relationship to defense funding. And § 4.6.3 zeroes in on Chomsky himself with respect to support from the military.

---

[27] Some of the changes that Chomsky made in the revised version strike me as simply bizarre. For example, there are two references to Bloomfield's 'Menomini morphophonemics' paper (see § 4.5.2) in the 1975 version that were not there in the 1955 version. Thank goodness they were not there, since according to Bromberger & Halle (1989: 67), Chomsky didn't know about the Bloomfield paper until Halle called his attention to it in the late 1950s. Stranger still are the gratuitous updatings of terminology that lead the revised version to be quite anachronistic. To give one example, in the first version, segments of a string are 'permuted' (Chomsky 1955b: VIII-392), while in the later version they are 'moved' (Chomsky 1975a: 322). Chomsky was not to use the term 'movement' until the early 1960s.

4.6.1 Linguistics and the military

In Chapter 1, § 1.5.4, we saw how crucial governmental (and, in particular, military) support was for the development of the field of linguistics in the United States during and immediately after the Second World War. In the 1950s, the lion's share of Defense Department and related funding went to the (then promising) area of machine translation (MT).[28] According to most sources, the idea of MT was first raised by Warren Weaver in a letter to Norbert Wiener in March 1947. This was apparently the first non-numerical application of computers ever proposed. Weaver followed up his letter with a memorandum to 20 or 30 individuals, elaborating his ideas. The response was enthusiastic; in the 1950s and early 1960s, MT research was undertaken with unbridled optimism. The American military was not long in seeing the promise of MT for its own interests. As of the mid-1960s, the military had injected over 20 million dollars into MT projects (Martin-Nielsen 2010: 142). For example, in 1956 the Air Force supported research on a Russian-English dictionary. That same year, the CIA began funding MT research at Georgetown University. In 1957 the Air Force funded MT groups at Ramo-Wooldridge and at the Rand Corporation. By 1960 not just the Air Force and the CIA, but also the American Army and Navy had become involved. Almost all of this research involved trained linguists or individuals like Yehoshua Bar-Hillel who had close ties to the linguistics community. But as the 1960s progressed, there was more and more disillusionment with the progress being made in MT. In 1963 the CIA withdrew funding of the Georgetown group and in 1966 a NSF-sponsored committee recommended that support for MT in the United States be discontinued. The committee report noted that 'there has been no machine translation of general scientific text, and none is in immediate prospect' (Pierce & Carroll 1966: 19). Linguists arrived at 'the firm conviction that machine translation had been a failure or, at best, very unlikely to be a useful technology' (Hutchins 1986: 9). Soon, interest in MT was 'something to keep quiet about; it was almost shameful' (p. 12). Decades were to pass before MT was to become an important project for linguists and those in related fields.

Defense Department funding was quite helpful to early generative grammar. Most grants went to 'think tanks' like the RAND Corporation, the MITRE Corporation (see § 4.6.2), and the System Development Corporation, which sought to use formal grammar to help develop MT and question-answering systems. Two large defense grants, however, went directly to generative research in university linguistics departments: one to MIT in the mid-1960s and the other, a few years later, to UCLA. In a 1971 interview, Colonel Edmund P. Gaines, director of systems design and development at the Air Force's Hanscom Field, gave these reasons for funding linguistics research projects:

[28] The material in this paragraph is derived from Hutchins (2000: 7–9).

The Air Force has an increasingly large investment in so-called 'command and control' computer systems. Such systems contain information about the status of our forces and are used in planning and executing military operations. For example, defense of the continental United States against air and missile attack is possible in part because of the use of such computer systems. And of course, such systems support our forces in Vietnam. [...] We sponsored linguistic research in order to learn how to build command and control systems that could understand English queries directly. Of course, studies like the UCLA study are but the first step toward achieving this goal. It does seem clear, however, that the successful operation of such systems will depend on insights gained from linguistic research. [...].

(p. c., March 1, 1971)

Colonel Gaines went on to express the Air Force's 'satisfaction' with UCLA's work. However, to the best of my knowledge, the UCLA study, formulated in the (non-Chomskyan) framework of case grammar (Fillmore 1968) and published as Stockwell, Schachter, & Partee (1973), never moved command and control systems forward by one inch.

In any event, direct military funding of basic linguistic research stopped after the Mansfield Amendment to a 1969 appropriations bill was passed. The amendment barred the Defense Department from using its funds 'to carry out any research project or study unless such project or study has a direct and apparent relationship to a specific military function'.

4.6.2 MIT and the military

In 1979 Chomsky told an interviewer:

In the intellectual milieu of Cambridge [i.e. at MIT and Harvard — (FJN)] there was a great impact of the remarkable technological developments associated with World War II. Computers, electronics, acoustics, mathematical theory of communication, cybernetics, all the technological approaches to human behavior enjoyed an extraordinary vogue. The human sciences were being reconstructed on the basis of these concepts. It was all connected.

(Chomsky 1979: 128)

MIT, given its role as an institution devoted (as its name implies) to technology, focused more on the scientific and technological aspects of these developments than did Harvard. Indeed, the rapid success of generative grammar was facilitated by the fact that it was able to draw on the vast resources of MIT, where Chomsky was hired in 1956, the year after he received his PhD. From the start, linguistics at MIT was affiliated with the Research Laboratory of Electronics (RLE), which played an important supportive role in the early years of the program. Originally part of the MIT Radiation Laboratory, where, incidentally, radar was developed during World War II, the RLE continued the work of the Radiation Laboratory after the war under a joint services contract (i.e., a contract under which each of the armed services contributed funds). While the specific makeup of the RLE changed over the years, throughout most of the 1960s it comprised three disciplines: General Physics, Plasma Dynamics, and Communication Sciences and Engineering (which included MIT's acoustics laboratory). When Morris Halle, who had a position with the laboratory, organized the linguistics PhD program in 1960, it seemed natural to classify linguistics, too, as a 'communication science'. Linguistics thus came under the purview of the RLE, eligible for funds from the Department of Defense, which paid the overhead, student support, and even a portion of faculty salaries.

Mention must now be made of the MITRE Corporation, a research and development organization with close ties to MIT and located in Bedford, Massachusetts.[29] An important role, if not the main role, of the MITRE Corporation was to find military applications for the latest scientific developments.[30] MITRE was jointly set up in 1958 by MIT and the US Air Force in order to develop air defense and 'command and control' technology for both nuclear and conventional warfare. In the 1960s MIT linguists, in particular ten or so students, were heavily involved at MITRE. It has been written that 'the MITRE English Preprocessor [...] system was intended to translate English sentences into instructions in a formal command and control language, but almost all of the research has gone into the development of the transformational grammar and a procedure for performing the syntactic analysis' (Newell 1968: 271). Chris Knight writes, citing a February 1964 article from MIT's official journal, the *Technology Review*:

Air Force Lieutenant Samuel Jay Keyser [later director of MIT's linguistics program — (FJN)] explains his thinking. Once a computer has been appropriately programmed in the light of Chomsky's insights, writes Keyser, it will be 'endowed with the ability to recognize instructions imparted to it in perfectly ordinary English, thereby eliminating a necessity for highly specialized languages that intervene between a man and a computer'. He continues:

In fact a great deal of work in doing just this has already been undertaken. Donald E. Walker of the MITRE Corporation, Associate Professor G. Hubert Matthews of

---

[29] I owe much of the information that follows to Knight (2017b).
[30] The MITRE Corporation still exists. According to its web page, 'We bring innovative ideas into existence in areas as varied as artificial intelligence, intuitive data science, quantum information science, health informatics, space security, policy and economic expertise, trustworthy autonomy, cyber threat sharing, and cyber resilience'. How much of this work has direct, or even indirect, military application I do not know. Undoubtedly a fair amount of it does.

MIT and J. Bruce Fraser [then a student at MIT and at one point a Project Mon-
itor for an Air Force contract supporting MIT linguistics — (FJN)] have placed a
significant portion of the grammar of English on a computer.

(Keyser 1964: 31)

A follow-up article by Keyser was published by the MITRE Corporation in 1965.
Here, Keyser discusses the limitations of the various artificial 'control languages'
then being used in the military's command and control systems. He refers both
to the SAGE air defense system and to the various computer control languages of
the US Air Force (473L), the Navy (NAVCOSSACT) and NORAD (425L) etc.

Keyser goes on to suggest an alternative in the form of an 'English control language' developed on the basis of Chomsky's linguistic insights. During the course
of his technical discussion, Keyser cites Chomsky's classic sample sentence, 'Colorless green ideas sleep furiously'. He then incorporates words such as 'aircraft',
'fighter', 'bomber', and 'missile', combining them in such sentences as:

The bomber the fighter attacked landed safely.
The bomber the fighter the radar spotted attacked landed safely. (Keyser
1965: 499)

(Knight 2017b)

It seems unlikely that the military ever made use of any of the technical papers that
the linguists at MITRE produced. Certainly the MIT students who worked there
did not feel that they were doing military work. Just the opposite, in fact. Barbara
Partee, who was one of the students, wrote that '[f]or a while, the Air Force was
convinced that supporting pure research in generative grammar was a national
priority, and we all tried to convince ourselves that taking Air Force money for such
purposes was consistent with our consciences, possibly even a benign subversion
of the military-industrial complex' (Partee 2005: fn. 8). By the end of the 1960s, the
Air Force had lost interest in generative grammar and the MITRE funding came
to an end.

4.6.3 Chomsky and the military

It is no more than a myth, albeit a longstanding one, that Chomsky tailored his
ideas about grammatical analysis to meet the needs of MT (Hall 1965; Herdan
1968; Maher 1980). Chomsky was a member of a MT research team at MIT in the
mid 1950s, but he left it in short order due to his lack of interest in its ongoing work.
Indeed, Victor Yngve, an MT pioneer, accused Chomsky of prioritizing his own
theory over approaches that were more computationally suitable to the task at hand

(see Yngve 2000: 56, 64–66).[31] Tired of what he saw as Chomsky's obstructionist attitude towards MT, Yngve left MIT for Chicago in 1965.

What about Chomsky's own feelings about the military support for research in generative grammar? In general, it has not troubled him. At one point in the 1960s he wrote the following in a letter published in the *New York Review of Books*:

> I have given a good bit of thought to [...] resigning from MIT, which is, more than any other university associated with the activities of the department of 'defense' [...]. As to MIT, I think that its involvement in the war effort is tragic and indefensible. One should, I feel, resist this subversion of the university in every possible way.
>
> (Chomsky 1967a: March 23, 1967)

But a few weeks later, he drastically modified his earlier statement, writing in another letter that 'This [earlier] statement is unfair and needs clarification. As far as I know, MIT as an institution has no involvement in the war effort. Individuals at MIT, as elsewhere, have a direct involvement, and that is what I had in mind' (Chomsky 1967b: April 20, 1967).

The second quote above pretty much condenses the position that he has taken since the 1960s. For example, along with Barbara Partee, he looked at military funding of his work as benign and resulting essentially from the Department of Defense's not paying a whole lot of attention to where it directed its money:

> Ever since the Second World War, the Defense Department has been a main channel for the support of the universities, because Congress and society as a whole have been unwilling to provide adequate public funds. Luckily, Congress doesn't look too closely at the Defense Department budget, and the Defense Department, which is a vast and complex organization, doesn't look too closely at the projects it supports — its right hand doesn't know what its left hand is doing. Until 1969, more than half the MIT budget came from the Defense Department, but this funding at MIT is a bookkeeping trick. Although I'm a full- time teacher, MIT paid only thirty to fifty percent of my salary. The rest came from other sources — most of it from the Defense Department. But I got the money through MIT.
>
> (quoted in Mehta 1971: 152)

Along the same lines, MIT-directed war research was balanced by the 'libertarian values' espoused by that institution:

> It's true that MIT is a major institution of war research. But it's also true that it embodies very important libertarian values [...]. Now these things coexist. It's not that simple, it's not just all bad or all good. And it's the particular balance in which they coexist that makes an institute that produces weapons of war willing

---

[31] Yngve had hired Chomsky on Harris's recommendation (Goldsmith 1998: 174).

to tolerate, in fact, in many ways even encourage, a person who is involved in civil
disobedience against the war.

(Chomsky 2011b [1971]: 144)

Anyone condemning him for working at MIT, Chomsky wrote, would have to condemn Karl Marx for studying at the British Museum, once 'the symbol of the most
vicious imperialism in the world' (Chomsky 2011b [1971]: 144) and accepting gifts
of money from Engels—whose family made its fortune in the cotton industry.

Critics of Chomsky from the left have delighted in calling attention to the military support of his early work. More than one has cited the acknowledgements like
that which opened § 4.6 to bolster their charge that the theory's foundations are
'reactionary' or 'idealistic' (Thompson 1969). The most extensive left-orientated
examination by far of Chomsky and his military funding is Chris Knight's book
Decoding Chomsky: Science and Revolutionary Politics (Knight 2017a). Knight
takes the startling position that Chomsky *intentionally* made his theory unintelli-
gible so that the military could make no use of it. Here is Knight's clearest statement
to that effect:

> His preferred choice was always to treat language as something so utterly abstract
> and other-worldly — so completely removed from any practical application —
> that no matter what insights he came up with, nothing could possibly be used to
> kill anyone.
>
> (Knight 2018b)

Knight is clear that he believes that Chomsky's theory has become increasingly
abstract and that purely practical and ethical motivations led him in that direction:

> Had Chomsky in his early years gone down that road, allowing his models to
> become more concrete and useable, it would have been the US military who ben-
> efited most. To his credit, Chomsky was never willing to do this. My argument is
> simple. As soon as an approach of his looked as if it might work, he began to feel
> anxious. His conscience was too strong and before long he would recoil back —
> always toward some further extreme of other-worldliness and abstraction.
>
> (Knight 2018a)

In fact, in Knight's view, universal grammar was Chomsky's escape mechanism
by which he made his theories irrelevant for any practical (including military)
purpose:

> From [the 1960s] on, as Chomsky's political positions became more publicly
> known, whenever he modified his linguistic theories he did so only in one di-
> rection: never toward greater realism, always toward what Adele Goldberg has

rightly described as 'ever-increasing layers of abstractness' (Goldberg 2006: 4). Instead of studying languages, Chomsky focused exclusively on something of his own making — Universal Grammar. Since this could not be precisely specified, Chomsky's approach had one great advantage. It soon became clear that nothing worked, or could possibly work. Once this realization sank in, Chomsky the activist was safe. Never again would the US military imagine they could use his work to develop systems of computerized command and control. Unfortunately, this same abstractness meant that his models had little apparent relevance to what the rest of us term 'language', offering few insights into how language might have evolved in the past or how it is continuously being created and re-created by speakers today.

(Knight 2017b)

And with respect to Chomsky's 'British Museum defense', Knight replies sarcastically that 'Chomsky here seems to be easing his political conscience by claiming that Karl Marx's institutional environment was actually *more* "oppressive" and indeed "vicious" than the Pentagon-sponsored electronics lab in which he worked. Somehow, he manages to draw a favorable comparison between himself as a full-time salaried employee in one of the most advanced weapons research laboratories in the world and an impoverished Marx, taking notes for revolutionary purposes in a public library — the reading room of the British Museum' (Knight 2017a: 112–113).

As one might expect, Chomsky dismisses the charge that aspects of his theory can be derived from the origin of the funds that support it:

Knight's crucial charge [...] is that military funding influenced my scientific work. There is a very simple way to verify the charge: determine whether (and if so how) the work changed from the time I was a graduate student at Harvard with no military funding, to my early years at MIT, when its funding was quite generally military, to subsequent years when I received no military funding at all. Answer: not in the slightest relevant way — which is doubtless why Knight evades this test. Exactly the same is true of the other researchers in the same programme. End of story. And an end to the slanderous charges against all of us.

(Chomsky 2017: 39, May 4, 2017)

Chomsky is right here. The idea that he has proposed highly abstract approaches to grammar to fend off potential military applications is implausible, to put it mildly. Knight is aware that 'from the beginning of his career at MIT' (Knight 2018b), Chomsky preferred a formal abstract approach to language. The beginning of Chomsky's career, however, was his production of *LSLT*, which appeared before military interest in his work. So how could his initial formal abstract treatment of language have been driven by a desire to develop a theory that could not be used to kill anyone? Knight goes on to write that his students at MITRE 'would tinker with his latest theory to make it more realistic' and that 'Chomsky went along with this for a while, but then resolved to retreat into pure abstraction.' I have no idea what Knight is talking about here. I am unaware of any MITRE-employed students tinkering with the theory to make it more 'realistic' or with Chomsky going along with their tinkering. In the late 1960s (after the MITRE period), Chomsky did indeed propose a variant to his theory that might be argued to be less abstract in a certain way than his earlier variants (the so-called 'lexicalist hypothesis'—Chomsky 1970), but he motivated it on purely linguistic-internal grounds. The relationship between this theoretical variant and the potential for military funding is obscure, to say the least. In fact, Chomsky's work has not had any military funding or the promise of any for over fifty years. It seems highly unlikely that the theoretical turns that Chomsky has taken in the 80% of his career since around 1970 have been influenced by the desire to keep his distance from the military. Also, while his theories have evolved considerably over the past 60 years, I see little overall change in terms of their abstractness. I disagree with Knight (and with Goldberg) that Chomsky's current minimalist program is more abstract that his previous approaches to syntax. In some ways, given its stripped down ontology, it seems even less abstract than the frameworks that he proposed from the 1970s to the 1990s.

Personally, I have never been that impressed by the critique of Chomsky for working at MIT. It's really just a matter of degree. The University of Washington, a public institution and the one where I spent my entire working career, has always been up to its ears in defense contracts. As recently as 2020, 'the U.S. Navy has awarded University of Washington's Applied Physics Laboratory a potential 10-year, $218.8M contract for research, development, test and evaluation support to Department of Defense programs' (from the Applied Physics Laboratory web page). I would guess that every American academic, excepting those who teach at small four-year colleges, rubs shoulders with colleagues who draw resources from the military.

By the 1980s less abstract versions of generative grammar were being developed, and some of them indeed seemed more amenable to practical applications (including military ones) than Chomsky's research at the time. Much of this work has taken place at Stanford and satellite organizations around that university. The most important of the resultant projects, the LinGO system, has never received any military funding primarily because the manager of that system, a devout Mennonite, refuses to accept it. Today, the military is a huge backer of work in natural language processing. However, most work in that area is based on 'deep learning' (that is, neural networks trained on very large corpora), making use of virtually no insights from linguistics. It might be pointed out that the neural network approach to cognition is anathema to Chomsky.

According to Knight, Chomsky insists 'that human language is purely individual, not a system of social communication' (Knight 2018b). That is a gross oversimplification of Chomsky's position. It is true that Chomsky has always focused on language as a cognitive faculty—he has as much right as anybody to follow his own interests. But he has never denigrated other orientations to the study of language, as he stressed in the following quote:

> Internalist biolinguistic inquiry does not, of course, question the legitimacy of other approaches to language, any more than internalist inquiry into bee communication invalidates the study of how the relevant internal organization of bees enters into their social structure. The investigations do not conflict; they are mutually supportive. In the case of humans, though not other organisms, the issues are subject to controversy, often impassioned, and needless.
>
> (Chomsky 2001: 34)

In fact, Chomsky has devoted dozens, if not hundreds, of pages to exposing the manipulative use of language, in particular by the leaders of the American political establishment and their apologists, and to showing that the term 'freedom of speech' is often used as a protective cover by those who would wish to deny it to others. In one book for example, he exposes the use of terms like 'aggression', 'doves', 'hawks', 'peace process', and 'terrorism' in American political discourse (Chomsky 1986). Surely, the fact that Chomsky sees no inconsistency between such work and his grammatical theorizing (to the point where both occur within the covers of the same volume) is prima facie evidence that he believes that the study of formal grammars and their properties complements, rather than challenges, the study of language in its communicative setting.

4.7 Summary

This chapter has touched on a variety of issues related to the TGG of the 1950s and the 1960s, beginning with discussion of the origins and early development of the theory. I go on to reopen the question of whether the field underwent a 'Chomskyan revolution' at that time, concluding that the question is hopelessly muddled. Instead, I discuss which aspects of early TGG were truly original and pinpoint two: the idea that a grammar provides a full structural description of the sentences generated and that the structuralist phoneme needs to be abandoned. In general, Chomsky's opponents (leading historiographers of linguistic among them) have failed to recognize these two features and have focused instead on aspects of the theory for which originality was never claimed. I go on to argue that Chomsky's remarks pertaining to own recollection of his 'early days' need to be taken with a grain of salt. The published record refutes some of his assertions that have received widespread attention. Finally, I take on the issue of defense spending on linguistics during this time period. I reject the claim that such funding had profound effects on the content of TGG, and point out that military funding is so pervasive at American universities that receiving such funding or interacting professionally with scholars who receive it is practically unavoidable.

5

The diffusion of generativist ideas

5.1 Introduction

Just as the preceding chapter treated the birth of and early reactions to TGG, the present one focuses on what the generativists themselves did to diffuse their ideas to the linguistic public. I argue that, despite certain opinions to the contrary, they did everything humanly possible to propagate their theory.

As we have seen, as early as 1964 a commentator had written: '[T]ransformational grammar has established itself as the reference point for discussion of linguistic theory. […] It remains the case that it has been Chomsky who has effectively opened the American linguistic scene to its present free and fruitful discussion' (Hymes 1964a: 25).[1]

A year later, there was talk of a 'Chomskyan revolution' in the field (Bach 1965a: 111–112; Levin 1965: 92; Thorne 1965: 74). How did the theory of transformational generative grammar succeed so rapidly, that is, in seven or eight years after the publication of *Syntactic Structures* (Chomsky 1957a)? The most important reason by far is that a wide spectrum of the linguistic community found the theory to be either correct or on the right track (for extensive discussion, see Newmeyer 1986b: ch. 2). The time was right for a radical shift in focus from the description of linguistic forms to a generative mechanism that provided structural analyses of these forms. Generative grammar provided new and powerful tools for linguistic analysis, which played a crucial role in attracting people to the enterprise. At the same time, the early generativists provided concrete and detailed accounts of longstanding problems for grammatical theory, such as the discontinuous nature of the English auxiliary morphemes, long-distance dependencies, the intricacies of Slavic

[1] Thanks to Thomas Bever, Greg Carlson, Robert Freidin, Jay Keyser, Barbara Partee, and David Perlmutter for reading the entire earlier version of this chapter and making some valuable suggestions. I also wish to thank the great number of colleagues who took the time to share their thoughts and memories with me about the old days: Stephen Anderson, Emmon Bach, Ray Cattell, Paul Chapin, Donna Christian, Noam Chomsky, Charles Fillmore, Lily Fillmore, Bruce Fraser, Donald Freeman, Lila Gleitman, Allene Grognet, Morris Halle, Florence Warshawsky Harris, James Harris, Randy Harris, Paul Kiparsky, Susumu Kuno, Robin Lakoff, Terence Langendoen, Jean-Claude Milner, Wayne O'Neil, Barbara Partee, David Pesetsky, Paul Postal, Peter Reich, Neil Smith, Donca Steriade, Rudolph Troike, Peter Trudgill, Anna Wierzbicka, and Arnold Zwicky. It goes without saying that none of these individuals is responsible for any assertions made in this chapter.

American Linguistics in Transition. Frederick J. Newmeyer, Oxford University Press.
© Frederick J. Newmeyer (2022). DOI: 10.1093/oso/9780192843760.003.0005

morphophonemics, and much more. These accounts demonstrated to a sizeable number of linguists that the foundations of the theory led directly to empirical results, and were not merely speculative philosophy.

Needless to say, a significant percentage of linguists rejected generative grammar in the 1950s and 1960s and it remains the case today that a significant percentage would not consider themselves to be advocates of the theory. But even among practitioners and sympathizers, there has long been a feeling that generative grammar succeeded *despite* the professional behavior of its early developers, and not in any way *because of* that behavior. To read some of the critical literature that has appeared over the past half-century, the early MIT linguists formed an elitist in-group, interested in talking only to each other by means of inaccessible 'underground' publications. Indeed, it has been argued that they went to such lengths to erect a barrier between themselves and the outside world of linguistics that the early period of generative grammar was no less than a 'decade of private knowledge', a term that first appears in Ney (1975).

The most comprehensive 'decade of private knowledge' assessment is a central feature of a University of Toronto dissertation written by Janet Nielsen (Nielsen 2010).[2] Nielsen is by no means anti-generative, writing that '[B]y bringing problematic data constructions, formalization, language creativity, and psychological validity to the forefront, Chomsky's program fundamentally changed the conception of explanation in syntax' (Nielsen 2010: 122). Nevertheless, she charges that '[F]rom 1957 to 1968 transformational grammar operated an underground culture: research was *deliberately* kept out of mainstream journals, and work was narrowly circulated in mimeograph form among a select group of insiders. Those with close connections to MIT, where the transformational school was centered, had privileged access to new research—and those outside found it difficult, and at times impossible, to access transformational work' (Nielsen 2010: 23; emphasis added). Nielson goes on to write that 'MIT transformationalists *shunned academic journals*, deliberately kept their work private, and maintained a tight network of communicants' (242–243; emphasis added). Indeed, '[a]ll the key figures in early transformational grammar, from Chomsky to Lees to Postal to McCawley, produced underground documents. This culture of private knowledge was, as we will see, a mechanism for group cohesion, a statement against mainstream publishing outlets, and a reflection of rapid research progress' (p. 252). She gives many examples which purport to demonstrate a culture of private knowledge, most of which are illustrated and addressed below.

The goal of this chapter is to reply to Nielsen's assessment and to those commentaries on which it is based. I argue that they are all either greatly exaggerated

---

[2] The cover page of my copy of Nielsen's thesis gives the name as 'Janet Nielsen' and the date as '2010'. She was later to publish under the name 'Janet Martin-Nielsen' (Martin-Nielsen 2010, 2011, 2012). In these publications, she refers to her thesis as 'Martin-Nielsen (2009)'. I cite the work here as 'Nielsen (2010)', since that appears to be the official bibliographical reference.

or flat out wrong. As we see in what follows, the early generativists had a knack for availing themselves of every possible means of spreading the word about the new theory.

One might wonder what purpose is served by examining in detail the actions of linguists from so long ago. If for no other reason, I would argue that it is never out of place to 'set the record straight'. If the claims by Nielsen and others went unanswered, they would set a baseline for future historiographers of linguistics. That would be unfortunate. Moreover, questions about the propagation of scientific ideas have always been of wide-ranging interest. There is still active discussion, for example, about the role of the Royal Society in the rapid success of Newtonian physics. Also, we are now at about the point where there is enough distance between then and now to allow an intelligent conversation about what went on and why a half-century ago. And finally, and more poignantly, the active participants in the early days of TGG are either no longer with us or are well past retirement age. In a certain number of years, it will no longer be possible to draw on the first-hand testimonials that help bring history to life.

The chapter is organized as follows. § 5.2 overviews the early days of the MIT linguistics program, followed by § 5.3, which calls attention to the existence of claims that members of this program resisted publication of their research results. § 5.4 reviews the publication record of prominent generativists from this period and demonstrates that they were profuse publishers. § 5.5 takes on what is often called the 'underground literature' put out by generative grammarians at that time and shows that most of it was quite readily available to any interested party. § 5.6 details the means other than publication that were employed at the time to help propagate the theory, while § 5.7 attempts to explain the origins of the idea that MIT linguists were possessors of an occult 'private knowledge'. § 5.8 is a brief conclusion.

5.2 The beginnings of generative grammar at MIT

It seems reasonable to begin with a brief sketch of the development of the linguistics program at MIT.[3] As discussed in Chapter 4, §4.6.2, the early history of the program was tightly interwoven with the Research Laboratory of Electronics (RLE) at that institution. In 1946, when the RLE was founded, one of its four major research groups was called 'Communications and Related Subjects'. At the RLE, William Locke, then Chairman of the Department of Modern Languages, directed a group doing research on the acoustics of speech. In 1951 Morris Halle, at the time a student of Roman Jakobson's at Harvard, was hired by the Department, where he taught Russian and German, and by the RLE, where he did phonetic research. 'It can be said that Morris Halle's official arrival marked the actual beginning of the

---

[3] What follows draws heavily on the discussion in Harris and Harris (1974).

linguistics group at MIT, not only because he was its first member but also because it is generally acknowledged that he has been its chief architect and builder as well' (Harris and Harris 1974: np).

The picture changed dramatically with the hiring of Noam Chomsky in 1955. Chomsky was to receive a PhD in linguistics from Pennsylvania and was completing four years as a Junior Fellow at Harvard. With Chomsky's hiring (again, both in Modern Languages and the RLE), research on syntactic theory was to become increasingly prominent. New appointments soon followed: Joseph Applegate and G. Hubert Matthews in 1956, Edward Klima in 1957, Jerry Fodor in 1959, and Jerrold J. Katz in 1961.[4] In 1960, Roman Jakobson, who had been a visiting professor at MIT in 1957, was appointed an Institute Professor in the Department of Modern Languages, while still retaining his affiliation with Harvard. In 1959 the first two PhD theses were completed under the direction of Chomsky and Halle, one by George Hughes on speech analysis and another by Robert B. Lees on English nominalizations. Given the inability of Modern Languages to award a doctorate, as well as the RLE connection, the degree-granting department was Electrical Engineering.

In 1961 a graduate program in linguistics was approved at MIT under the Department of Modern Languages, leading to the degree of Doctor of Philosophy in Linguistics. Seven students were admitted in the fall of that year and ten more in the fall of 1962. Thirteen received the PhD degree in 1965, one in 1966, and five in 1967. In terms of hiring, Paul Postal, a Yale PhD, joined the department in 1963 (and left after two years), Kenneth Hale, an Indiana PhD was hired in 1966, and Wayne O'Neil, a Wisconsin PhD, in 1968. The other hires in the 1960s were all graduates of the program: Paul Kiparsky, James Harris, and John R. Ross.

5.3 Accusations of 'private knowledge'

In a paper published in 1975, James Ney excoriated the early generative grammarians for what he saw as their practice of circulating their research findings only among themselves, resulting in the 1960s and early 1970s being what he called 'a decade of private knowledge':

> [I]t is the intent of this article [...] to examine the dissemination of information amongst the community of linguists and scholars interested in the study of language. From this, the attempt will be made to show that for linguists the period from the early 1960s to the early 1970s was indeed a decade of private knowledge [...].
>
> Ney 1975: 143)

---

[4] Applegate, Matthews, and Klima were in Modern Languages and Katz and Fodor in the Department of Humanities. All were at some point affiliated with the RLE.

If one was not part of the 'inner circle', then it appears that one was out of luck:

[T]he early grammars seemed to be circulated in unpublished form amongst a coterie of linguists which constituted the inner circle of the early transformational movement. These grammars and other studies were referred to in footnotes in the published journal articles but appeared to be generally unobtainable for scores of scholars interested in the study of language. During the latter part of the decade this problem was alleviated somewhat by the appearance of numerous linguistics journals and by the apparent ease with which many scholars were able to publish books and monographs in the area of linguistic studies. There are, however, still far too many reports to various government agencies and other such materials on the topic of general linguistic theory that are difficult for the average scholar to obtain. For both of these reasons,[5] the decade under consideration has been a decade of private knowledge for linguistics.

(Ney 1975: 143–144)

Ney's complaint echoed others that had been made more than a decade earlier. For example, the Dutch linguist E. M. Uhlenbeck had written that:

[n]ot all of Chomsky's 13 publications on syntax are generally available. To his thesis called 'The Logical Structure of Linguistic Theory' quoted by himself and by Lees several times, I had no access. His two contributions to the 3rd and 4th Conference on Problems in the Analysis of English held in Texas were also not accessible. The same goes for his article on 'Explanatory Models in Linguistics'.

(Uhlenbeck 1963: 3)

A few years later Fred Householder remarked that 'these young men, in the first instance, talk only or chiefly to each other; exchanging Xeroxes and dittoed copies for a long time before communicating their paradoxes to the outside world' (Householder 1971: xi), while P. H. Matthews in a review of one of the first compendia of generative literature remarked that 'of the eighty transfomationalist papers listed [in the references to Jacobs and Rosenbaum 1970] forty are available in microfilm or mimeograph at best, and upwards of fifteen are scarcely available at all ("Unpublished, untitled paper on [...] MIT", "Remarks delivered at [...]", and so on). Surely this is a discourtesy to all but a handful of readers' (Matthews 1972: 125). These implied charges of elitism were reinforced the observation by Robert Stockwell that 'if you weren't on the right mailing lists you could be seriously out-of-date in a few months' (Stockwell 1998: 238) and by Henry A. Gleason's recollection that 'an objection [to a generativist paper at an LSA meeting] would be answered by the simple assertion that the matter had been taken

---

[5] Ney also illustrated 'private knowledge' by the profuse use of personal introspective judgments of acceptability. The present chapter has nothing to say about that issue (but see Newmeyer 1983).

care of and warranted no further discussion. This would be supported by the citing of a paper in the underground press—a paper whose existence the objector
had no way of knowing about, and which he would for some years have no opportunity to see' (Gleason 1988: 65–66). Other commentators have made similar
remarks: 'Instead of submitting work to journal refereeing, Chomskians circulated mimeographed analyses' (Murray 1994: 245) and 'Though peer review was
freely available—and extraordinarily forbearing, given the ill-founded viciousness
of many attacks—generativists sidestepped regular publication channels in favor
of circulating mimeographed papers' (Nevin 2010: 161).

Finally, we have already looked at the key passages from Nielsen (2010) that
claim that early generativists 'shunned academic journals' and 'deliberately kept
their work private'. The next section demonstrates that such charges lack factual
foundation.

5.4 The early generative grammarians were committed to publication

Chomsky's coming out to the world of linguistics was via his book *Syntactic Structures*. This work was about as mainstream as any publication could possibly be,
given that at the time Mouton was an important publisher of linguistics work (see
Chapter 4, § 4.5.1). And if anything it was rushed to publication, based as it was
on his lecture notes for a class at MIT that he had taught the year before (Chomsky
1975b: 3). Let us examine the publication record between 1957 and 1969 of four
leading generative grammarians in that period, Noam Chomsky, Morris Halle,
Robert B. Lees, and Paul Postal.[6]

In that period, Chomsky published six books, which is more than the average
scholar writes in his or her lifetime. The publishers, aside from Mouton, were MIT
Press, Harper & Row, and Harcourt Brace & World. I would hardly describe any of
them as 'marginal'. As far as refereed journals are concerned, Chomsky published
in *International Journal of American Linguistics* (twice), *American Documentation*,
Language (three times), *Information and Control* (three times), *Proceedings of the
Aristotelian Society*, *Word* (twice), *Journal of Linguistics*, *College English* (twice),
Syntheses (twice), *The Listener*, *The Pedagogic Reporter*, and *Educational Review*.
Twenty-five articles appeared in collections. What is more, he published one article
in Hebrew, six in French, and three in Japanese, which would seem to indicate a
desire to reach past a narrow Anglophone audience.

Halle published two books between 1957 and 1969. His articles and reviews appeared in *Journal of the Acoustic Society of America* (four times), *Kratylos, Nuovo*

---

[6] I ignore non-linguistic publications, such as Postal's two anthropological contributions and
Chomsky's political writings.

Cimento, International Journal of Slavic Linguistics and Poetics, Word (twice), *Language* (twice), *Information and Control, Journal of Linguistics* (twice), *College English, International Social Science Journal, Slavic and East European Journal,* and *The Study of English.* He had nineteen articles in collections and he published in Russian and French, as well as in English.

Lees had two books in that period, plus an edited book in Turkish (he also published in Russian three times). He contributed to the following journals: *Mechanical Translation, Nuclear Science and Engineering, Anthropological Linguistics* (twice), *Language* (five times), *Word* (twice), *Language Learning, American Speech, Zeitschrift für Phonetik, Gengo Kenkyu, General Linguistics, Linguistics* (twice), *Foundations of Language, Indogermanische Forschungen, Journal of the Conference on College Composition and Communication, Türk Dili Araştırmaları Yilliği-Belletin,* and *International Journal of American Linguistics.* He also had two articles in collections.

Between 1957 and 1969 Postal had three books and published in the journals *International Journal of American Linguistics* (four times, one article being reprinted in a Czech journal), *Harvard Education Review, Foundations of Language* (twice), *Language, International Social Science Journal,* and *American Anthropologist.* Six papers appeared in collections and one in Russian.

The culture of publishing one's research results was effectively communicated to the students. The first three years that PhD's were awarded at MIT were 1965, 1966, and 1967. Those receiving the degree in those years were Thomas Bever, Paul Chapin, James Fidelholtz, James Foley, Bruce Fraser, Jeffrey Gruber, Barbara Hall (Partee), James Harris, Paul Kiparsky, Sige-Yuki Kuroda, Terence Langendoen, Philip Lieberman, Theodore Lightner, Stanley Petrick, James McCawley, Peter Rosenbaum, John R. Ross, Sanford Schane, and Arnold Zwicky. In the 1960s all of them with the exception of Chapin, Fidelholtz, and Lightner published either books, refereed journal articles, or in easily accessible anthologies, while Chapin and Lightner published in the year 1970.[7] In most cases, what they published was based on their dissertation or was a revised version of the dissertation itself.

If MIT linguists had been indifferent to publishing their research results, they would hardly have been the driving force behind the formation of a new journal in the late 1960s. Yet, department members played a crucial role in launching *Linguistic Inquiry*:

> [Morris Halle] felt, I think, that it was 'difficult' to get articles in generative grammar published, not because of any discrimination against generative grammar, but rather because there was a glut of potential articles and a paucity of journal outlets; mainly, just two, *Language* and *Word.* He suggested to Curly Bowen that the MIT Press start a journal in linguistics and when Curly, naturally enough,

---

[7] I exclude publications in working papers and technical reports (see below, § 5.5.2).

wondered who would edit it, he suggested me. I'm sure Noam was involved in these discussions, but I have no specific memory of that being the case. So you can see that the founding of *LI* fits in very nicely with the thesis that the generativists were not inclined to hide their lights under a bushel. I met with Curly and agreed to edit the journal for 5 years. That was 42 years ago, going on 43.

(Jay Keyser, p. c., January 1, 2013)

In sum, the evidence weighs heavily against the idea that the early generative grammarians 'shunned academic journals' and 'deliberately kept their work private'.

5.5   On the so-called 'underground literature'

Not everything written by a generative grammarian in the 1950s and 1960s appeared immediately (or with a short delay) in a mainstream journal or book. James McCawley popularized the idea that there was also a significant 'underground literature: the many papers that have been circulated in office-duplicator or in project reports but have not been given normal publication in journals or books' (McCawley 1976b: 1). These writings have been discussed at great length in Nielsen (2010), which devotes a chapter to discussing 'three subtypes of underground literature' (Nielsen 2010: 248) produced by generative grammarians between 1957 and 1968: 'manuscripts written in forms and styles appropriate for publication, but which were deliberately circulated privately and informally' (p. 248), the institutional or laboratory report, and 'manuscripts which were deliberately written in forms inappropriate for publication, and circulated privately' (p. 251).

In this section I discuss the literature in question, following Nielsen's categories. I argue that most of it was available to any interested linguist, thereby calling into question the appropriateness of the word 'underground'.

5.5.1   Polished manuscripts 'deliberately circulated privately'

Nielsen refers to four manuscripts 'deliberately circulated privately': Chomsky's *The Logical Structure of Linguistic Theory*; Lees's 'What are transformations?'; Postal's *Some Syntactic Rules in Mohawk*, and Ross's *Constraints on Variables in Syntax*. They are discussed in the following four subsections.

5.5.1.1   *The Logical Structure of Linguistic Theory*
Nielsen (2010) singles out Chomsky's manuscript *The Logical Structure of Linguistic Theory* (*LSLT*) as the most important non-publication in this category (see Chapter 4, § 4.2.2, 4.5.1). One can dispute whether *LSLT* was 'written in forms

and styles appropriate for publication', but one cannot dispute its importance. The question is why it was not published in 1955 or soon afterwards. The most direct reason is that it is unlikely that more than a small handful of linguists active at the time could have understood its formalism, a fact that surely deterred Chomsky from revising it rapidly for publication. Moreover as Chomsky noted, 'After I returned to MIT in the fall [of 1959], this [work on generative phonology] and other work took precedence, and I never did return to the revision of the remaining chapters (Chomsky 1975b: 4). In any event, the great bulk of *LSLT was in fact published at the time*, some key sections appearing in *Syntactic Structures* and others immediately thereafter in a series of articles published in the late 1950s and early 1960s: Chomsky and Miller 1958, 1963; Chomsky 1959a, 1961a, b, 1962a, b; 1963; and Chomsky and Schutzenberger 1963. It was really just the material dealing with phonology and (to a certain extent) morphology that were not published, and that because Chomsky had by the end of the 1950s drastically revised his notions of how these 'lower levels' of grammatical structure operated. One can fault Chomsky for not stressing sufficiently that if one wanted to know what was in *LSLT*, then all that one needed to do was to read his book and subsequent articles. But one cannot fault him for not making the material in *LSLT* available (this point was made in Bach 1965b: 281).

One wonders in fact how very difficult it was to obtain a copy of *LSLT* in those days. Fred Householder recalls that he simply borrowed one from another colleague:

> [...] Ed Stankiewicz lent me the first three chapters of the *Logical Theory of Linguistic Structure* [*sic*] by Chomsky. That book really got me excited. It was around this time that Zellig Harris gave his Presidential Address (on transformations) at the LSA meetings in Chicago.
>
> (Householder 1980: 199)

Harris was LSA president in 1955, the year that *LSLT* was completed. One might point out that Stankiewicz had no connection with MIT nor did he ever become a generative grammarian. And consider the following recollection by Gleason:

> In 1955 [Chomsky's] thesis was submitted. It was available at the Linguistic Institute that summer and was discussed. A few linguists found it very difficult; most found it quite impossible. A few thought some of the points were possibly interesting; most simply had no idea as to how it might relate to what they knew as linguistics.
>
> (Gleason 1988: 60)

In a footnote to this passage Gleason wrote: 'Or, perhaps, it was his *The Logical Structure of Linguistic Theory*; my memory is not quite clear. In any case it was something far more mathematical in its reasoning than anyone there had ever seen labeled as "linguistics"' (Gleason 1988: 60). Gleason was certainly correct in the footnote, since Chomsky's doctoral thesis (which was essentially a small proper subpart of *LSLT*), was never widely circulated, not even among linguists at MIT. At that institute, held at the University of Chicago, the teaching staff, aside from Gleason, consisted of Isidore Dyen (Yale University), William J. Gedney (American Council of Learned Societies), Charles F. Hockett (Cornell University), Fang-Kuei Li (University of Washington), Floyd G. Lounsbury (Yale University), Robert O. Swan (University of Pennsylvania), Donald E. Walker (Rice Institute), and twelve members of the Chicago faculty (*LSAB* 29, 1956: 17).[8] The courses given there were attended by 65 students. If even just a small percentage of these individuals availed themselves of a copy of *LSLT*, it would have been subsequently transported from coast to coast in the United States. Chomsky in 1975 wrote: 'I have not kept count, but there must be several hundred copies [of *LSLT* in circulation]' (Chomsky 1975b: 3).

5.5.1.2 Robert B. Lees's paper 'What are transformations?'

I had never heard of Lees's paper 'What are transformations?' (Lees 1976 [1960]) until it appeared in McCawley's anthology of 'underground' papers (McCawley 1976c; see § 5.5.3 below), and this despite my having been Lees's own PhD student in the 1960s. And in fact the paper had already been published in the Russian journal *Voprosy Jazykoznanija*. Even in the 1976 English translation all of the examples are drawn from Russian. It is a mystery to me why McCawley (and hence Nielsen) would consider this to be an 'underground' publication. It does little more than review the ABCs of generative grammar in a way that could have been found in several publications from the early 1960s.

5.5.1.3 Paul Postal's PhD thesis *Some Syntactic Rules in Mohawk*

Postal submitted his Yale University dissertation, entitled *Some Syntactic Rules in Mohawk* and written under the direction of Floyd Lounsbury, in 1962. However, it was not published until 1979 (Postal 1979 [1962]). To help us understand why it was not published immediately, let's first recall that junior scholars did not generally rush to publish their dissertations, as they do today. We tend to forget that there was a time, long ago, when a tenure-track post at a university was not limited to those who had published their dissertations, two or three papers based on it, and had begun to explore new avenues of research. So we can fault Postal only if his work was of such importance that to not publish it would have been detrimental to the field. Was it of great importance? It is historically noteworthy in its being one of the first generative dissertations and the very first, I think, to deal primarily

---

[8] There were actually three institutes that summer, one at Chicago, one at the University of Michigan, and one at Georgetown University. I assume that Gleason was referring to the Chicago institute, since he was on the teaching staff there.

with an Amerindian language. But if the number of citations to a work is a good guide to its importance, then Postal's thesis was not in the first rank. It was referred to in passing in Chomsky (1964a) and Chomsky (1965), but very rarely thereafter. For example, we find no reference to it in Ross (1967), nor in the first three major generative anthologies: Bach & Harms (1968); Reibel & Schane (1969); and Jacobs & Rosenbaum (1970).

As was the case with *LSLT*, everything of importance in Postal's thesis was published separately, in particular in Postal (1964a, b,c). Anybody who felt the desire to read the entire work could have done as I did and order a copy from University Microfilms.

5.5.1.4 John R. Ross's PhD thesis *Constraints on Variables in Syntax*

One cannot dispute the importance of Ross's 1967 MIT dissertation *Constraints on Variables in Syntax*. I know of no study that would allow me to confirm my intuition, but I am quite certain that it is the most cited PhD thesis ever produced in the field of linguistics. Yet it was not published by a mainstream publisher until 1985 and then under the revised title *Infinite Syntax!* (Ross 1985). But that does not mean that it was not easily obtainable. The following year the Indiana University Linguistic Club (see below, § 5.5.4) made it available to anybody in the world who might desire a copy and for a very moderate fee. Hence there is no sense in which Ross's thesis could be called an 'underground document'. Nielsen complains however that:

> [i]n John Robert Ross' *Constraints on Variables in Syntax*, for example, 32 documents in his 67-item bibliography — just under half of the items he references — are listed as 'unpublished paper', 'unpublished mimeograph', 'mimeographed', 'unpublished Ph.D. thesis', 'working paper', or are listed as appearing in technical project reports. He includes nine of his own works, none of which had been published: one unpublished paper, one unpublished mimeograph, his master's thesis, one unpublished ditto, two Harvard Computation Laboratory Reports, and three 'to appear' articles.
>
> (Nielsen 2010: 258)[9]

Was it really the case that almost half of Ross's citations would have been unavailable to the average working linguist of the period? Absolutely not. Here is my breakdown of his sixty-seven references: cited as published or in press—thirty; published in 1967–1969—four; published in 1970 or later—seven; never

---

[9] Dissertations (as compared to published volumes) have always been top-heavy with references to unpublished material. Consider a twenty-first century example, a highly-regarded Stanford PhD thesis on questions of lexical semantics (Koontz-Garboden 2007). The bibliography contains 6 references to unpublished manuscripts, 16 to unpublished theses, 6 to working papers, 4 to presentations, and 7 to talk handouts. The main difference between 1967 and 2007 is that in the latter year most of the references could be tracked down on the internet.

published—seven;[10] published by the Indiana University Linguistic Club before 1970—three; in technical reports or departmental working paper volumes (see below, § 5.5.2)—nine; a thesis (and therefore available from University Microfilms)— seven. By my count only fourteen references—the material published in 1970 or later or not published at all—would have been unavailable to the late 60s linguist who was willing to put forward a small amount of effort. And of course, then as now, one could generally receive a copy of a paper by writing the author for one.[11]

5.5.2 The institutional and laboratory reports

Nielsen's second category of 'underground literature' prevalent in the late 1950s and 1960s is the institutional, or laboratory, report. This includes, most prominently, the MIT Research Laboratory of Electronics *Quarterly Progress Reports* (§ 5.5.2.1) and the Harvard Computation Laboratory Reports' (§ 5.5.2.2) (Nielsen 2010: 250). Let us examine them and then turn to working papers (§ 5.5.2.3).

5.5.2.1 The RLE *Quarterly Progress Reports*
Several important linguistics papers were published in the 1960s in the RLE's *Quarterly Progress Reports* (QPRs), typically appearing in the same issue with papers on neurophysiology, communications biophysics, and cognitive information processing. The QPRs provided a rapid outlet for the dissemination of research results. Some articles were later published in mainstream journals, but others were not. The *QPR* papers were not in any sense 'underground publications'. Many university libraries subscribed to *QPRs* from their beginning in 1946 or started their collection in the next decade or two. In an informal survey, I found that 12 of the first 16 university library catalogs I looked at showed *QPRs* going back to the 1960s or earlier, namely Alberta, Arizona, UC Berkeley, UC Davis, the Claremont Colleges, Cornell, Notre Dame, Oregon, San Diego State, Stanford, Texas, and Washington State.

5.5.2.2 The Harvard Computation Laboratory Reports
Between 1965 and 1974 the Computation Laboratory of Harvard produced a series of red-covered reports to the National Science Foundation under the rubric of 'Mathematical Linguistics and Automatic Translation'. They were generally referred to in the linguistics community as 'NSF-26', 'NSF-28', and so on. The first in the linguistics series, NSF-16, was George Lakoff's landmark Indiana dissertation *On the Nature of Syntactic Irregularity* (Lakoff 1965). Most of the subsequent

---

[10] One of the never-published papers was a proper subpart of Ross's thesis itself. I have no idea why he cited it.
[11] One could reply to P. H. Mathews (see above, § 5.3) by providing a similar breakdown for the references in Jacobs & Rosenbaum (1970) as for those in Ross' thesis.

NSF reports were collections of papers written primarily by linguists at Harvard and MIT (Ross cites five of them in his thesis). They were available to anybody who asked for them. Susumu Kuno, who was the principal investigator of the NSF grant during most of this period, writes:

> In 1965, I started editing reports to NSF that contain papers on formal linguistics. NSF-16 (1965), which consisted of a dissertation by George Lakoff, who had joined my NSF project the previous year, was the first of such reports. My vague recollection is that the last volume of the series was NSF-31 (1974), *Adjectives and Adjective Complement Constructions in English* by Arlene Berman, but since my copy has been lost, I can't vouch for it. During 1965-1974, my vague recollection was that we had about 200 copies made of each report. We must have met any requests for copies as long as they were available, but I don't recall running out of copies, so around 200 copies per report must have been the extent of the circulation of the reports.
>
> (Susumu Kuno, p. c., October 3, 2012)

Two hundred copies does not sound like a lot, but one must consider the size of the field at the time. To put things into perspective, consider William Labov's *The Social Stratification of English in New York City* (Labov 1966), which was as important for variationist sociolinguistics as *Syntactic Structures* was for syntactic theory. According to Allene Grognet, who was the editor for the book at the Center for Applied Linguistics, the initial press run was '500 copies, or 1000 at the very most' (p. c., October 12, 2012).

5.5.2.3 Working papers

Two of Ross's citations were to departmental working papers, one from Ohio State University and one from the University of Pennsylvania. There was nothing 'underground' about them. Virtually every department of linguistics has put out a series of working papers at some point in its history. At first they tended to be free for the asking, then free with postage included, and then available only for a fee. Now, of course, they are mostly on line. In the 1960s a letter or telephone call to OSU or Penn would have resulted in a free copy for anybody interested.

Ross also referred to two working papers from the MITRE Corporation (see Chapter 4, § 4.6.1). Several MIT students in the early 1960s had summer research positions at MITRE. According to Bruce Fraser, who was one of those students:

> The MITRE paper Haj cites was available from MITRE as well as by contacting me directly. Same as if I worked at IBM today. I have heard it said that it was difficult to get MIT papers, but I've never believed it. We at MIT wanted to spread the word and looked for every opportunity to do so. Maybe people who have spread

this rumor had trouble understanding the linguistics and used this claim as a convenient excuse.

(Bruce Fraser, p. c., June 16, 2013)

5.5.3 The third type of 'underground literature' and McCawley's edited volume

Nielsen writes:

The third and final type of underground literature are manuscripts which were deliberately written in forms inappropriate for publication, and circulated privately. Witty, satirical, and often downright rude, this style of underground literature is associated most prominently with the generative semantics movement (circa 1968-1974). In the late 1960s, however, it straddled the border between regular transformational literature and generative semantics.

(Nielsen 2010: 251)

Oddly, Nielsen gives only two examples: Paul Postal's 'Linguistic anarchy notes' (Postal 1976 [1967]) and Jerry Morgan's 'Cryptic note II and WAGS III' (Morgan 1976 [1969]). She is certainly correct that they were 'inappropriate for publication', which perhaps goes a long way toward the explanation of why they were not at first published. But James McCawley did indeed publish them in his *Notes from the Linguistic Underground* (McCawley 1976c) and it is to this book that we now turn.

No publication by a generative grammarian has done more than McCawley's *Notes* to incorrectly convey the idea that a significant underground literature existed at the time. The book itself is a motley collection of 22 contributions, some of which actually had already been published, some that were put on the back burner by the author, given his or her belief that they were not particularly interesting, and some that never should have been written in the first place. The common thread is that McCawley had seen them and was intrigued by them, not that they had played an important role in the development of the theory. My somewhat blunt assessment can be confirmed by looking at the citation list in six important publications from the early to mid 1970s: three by interpretive semanticists (Chomsky 1972; Jackendoff 1972; Emonds 1976) and three by generative semanticists (Lakoff 1972 [1970]; Postal 1971; McCawley 1976a). Excluding McCawley (1976a), the remaining five works refer to only 3 out of the 22 papers in McCawley's *Notes* collection, namely to Harris (1976 [1965])[12]; Lakoff (1976 [1969]); and

---

[12] Florence Warshawsky Harris wrote the 1965 paper while a first-year graduate student at MIT. She did not complete the program, nor become a professional linguist. When I asked her why she did not

Karttunen (1976 [1969]). All three of these papers, whose interest is uncontestable, had been published by the Indiana University Linguistics Club before they appeared in *Notes*: in 1974, 1969, and 1971 respectively. McCawley himself refers only to 8 of the 22. We might be dealing with an 'underground' literature here, but not one which appears to have had any significant consequences for linguistic theorizing. Those who knew Jim McCawley well, and I count myself lucky to be in that category, recognized *Notes from the Linguistic Underground* as a reflection of his puckish anarchism, with his choice of contents to be taken with a grain of salt.

5.5.4 More informal publication outlets

By the mid to late 1960s it was clear to most MIT linguists that the time lag between finishing the draft of a paper and its appearance in print in a conventional journal was too long. To remedy this situation, in early 1967 a few members of the department set up the Program for the Exchange of Generative Studies (PEGS). The idea was to create a formal mechanism for the distribution of unpublished papers, in particular to help counteract the view that MIT linguists were myopic and inward-looking. Over the next year, as the number of participants grew, PEGS was taken over, at the request of its organizers, by the ERIC Clearinghouse for Linguistics at the Center for Applied Linguistics. Within the first three months of the takeover, 40,000 mimeographed copies were reproduced and mailed. However, '[f]aced with an expanding operation which it could not under the terms of its mandate handle for an extended period, the clearing-house turned over the PEGS program in 1969 to a newly established linguistic journal' (Roberts and Woyna 1972: 17).[13]

The slack was taken up by the Indiana University Linguistics Club (IULC), founded by the Indiana Department of Linguistics in 1968 'to support the activities of students in linguistics and related fields' (from the IULC web page). While the IULC did not then, nor does it have now, an explicit generative orientation, the vast majority of its publications have presupposed generative grammar. The following is a complete list of IULC authors in the 1960s: Adrian Akmajian, Noam Chomsky, Susan Fischer, Ray Jackendoff, Lauri Karttunen, Carol Kiparsky, Paul Kiparsky, Charles Kisseberth, Andreas Koutsoudas, George Lakoff, D. Terence Langendoen, Roger Lass, Byron Marshall, James McCawley, J. R. Ross, Gerald Sanders, Carlota Smith, Robert Wall, and Wolfgang Wölck. Typically, a paper submitted to the IULC could be available for distribution at a very reasonable fee within a few

publish the paper earlier, she replied: 'I just never thought about it. And nobody asked me until Jim McCawley did' (p. c., October 14, 2012).

[13] The question is: 'Which journal?' I had assumed that it was *Linguistic Inquiry*, but Jay Keyser has no recollection of the PEGS program being turned over to *LI* (p. c., January 1, 2013). No other journal fills the bill and neither Roberts nor Woyna are still here to tell us.

months. As such, it provided an ideal mechanism for generative linguists to diffuse their ideas quickly and to a wide audience.

5.5.5   A little historical perspective

There is a long history of complaints that some seemingly important piece of literature is unavailable. Consider an example from pre-generative days (this quote was given in Chapter 3, § 3.6 in a different context):

> In 1934, almost as an immediate response to Bloomfield's *Language* ([Bloomfield 1933]) Chao Yuen Ren had published a paper entitled 'The nonuniqueness of phonemic solutions of phonetic systems' in the *Bulletin of the Institute of History and Philology, Academia Sinica*, a journal that was not on the regular reading lists of many North American linguists ([Chao 1934]). For that matter, it was received in very few North American libraries. At a later time some linguists — particularly graduate students — began to worry a little about some of the claims commonly made on behalf of linguistics — often by their teachers. Chao's paper began to attract some interest. Still, it was hard to obtain and few actually read it. I remember hearing of it — not once but repeatedly — from people who had heard about it from someone who had allegedly read it. It was said that it had been duplicated and that copies were circulating; I never saw one. (It was before the days of cheap and easy photocopying, and before the days of a highly active underground press in linguistics.) [...] Then in 1957 Joos published *Readings in Linguistics* ([Joos 1957b]), and with this, Chao's paper became easily and generally available — bearing an imprimatur as a fundamental paper in the development of Bloomfieldianism.
>
> (Gleason 1988: 56)

The later Bloomfieldians were not immune to holding onto important manuscripts for years before publishing them. Randy Harris (1993: 271) notes that Zellig Harris's *Methods in Structural Linguistics* (Harris 1951a) 'made the rounds for several years before publication, and Nida's *Synopsis [of English Syntax* = Nida 1960 [1943]] was available only in thesis form until 1960 and cited personal contact with one linguist or another as the source for some idea'.

Throughout the 1960s, the principal rival to transformational generative grammar, at least in North America, was stratificational grammar. Getting enough published information on the theory to render an informed judgment about it was painfully difficult. Emmon Bach complained: 'Lamb has presented various facets of his system before in lectures but aside from a semi-official publication of a pedagogical manual there has been little in print on which to base as appraisal of his ideas' (Bach 1965b: 276–277). The situation was barely improved with the publication of Lamb's *Outline of Stratificational Grammar* the following year (Lamb 1966), after circulating in manuscript form for several years. This 100-page book was generally considered to be too sketchy and (at the same time) too impenetrable to serve as a counterfoil to Chomsky's *Syntactic Structures* or *Aspects of the Theory of Syntax*.[14]

Finally, it should be noted that the paper that most would regard as the foundational document of linguistic pragmatics, H. P. Grice's 'Logic and conversation' (Grice 1975), circulated informally for eight years before seeing publication.

5.5.6 Summary

At first reading, Robert Stockwell's remark that 'if you weren't on the right mailing lists you could be seriously out-of-date in a few months' (Stockwell 1998: 238) sounds quite damning. But we have to raise the question of what it took to get on a mailing list. Stockwell himself recalls that the only requirement was 'sending back comments and questions' and that the MIT linguists were 'unfailingly generous' in sharing their work (quoted in Nielsen 2010: 256–257). James Ney did write that the generativist 'underground' literature was 'generally unobtainable' (Ney 1975: 143), but he gives no indication of what he did to try to obtain it. I have never heard of a single case where a MIT-based linguist refused to send a copy of his or her work to anyone who asked for one, regardless of their theoretical orientation.

Paul Chapin, a 1967 MIT PhD., finds that:

> [t]he claim that MIT restricted distribution of working papers in those days, though, is laughable. The complaint at the time was the opposite, that people were being bombarded by a constant stream of papers from MIT faculty and students, more than they had the time or the interest to read.
>
> (Paul Chapin, p. c., October 1, 2012)

In sum, with a minimal amount of effort, any linguist in the world could have had access to the vast majority of the writings of the vast majority of generative grammarians.

---

[14] Peter Reich recalls (p. c., October 17, 2012) that 'most [stratificational grammar] people found that their papers were rejected by mainstream journals'. Be that as it may, at the time there were plenty of 'non-mainstream' journals and other publishing outlets that Lamb and others could have turned to. Leafing through the linguistics journals of the 1960s reveals literally hundreds of non-generative and anti-generative publications.

5.6 Further examples of MIT outreach

The rapid publication of their research results was the most important means by which the early generative grammarians diffused the new theory, but it was not the only means. Scholarly publications were supplemented by textbooks (§ 5.6.1), participation at the LSA and other professional meetings (§ 5.6.2), teaching at Linguistic Institutes (§ 5.6.3), and hosting at MIT interested visitors from around the world (§ 5.6.4). § 5.6.5 discusses the adoption of the theory by non-MIT linguists in 1960s as well as the impact of the first class of MIT PhD's finding employment at universities all over the United States.

5.6.1 Textbooks

The first textbook in generative grammar appeared even before the first class of MIT linguists received their PhD's, namely Emmon Bach's *An Introduction to Transformational Grammars* (Bach 1964). It was an instant success, all of its reviews with which I am familiar giving a glowing account (see Peng 1965; Hale 1965; Montgomery 1965; Chafe 1965). What is especially noteworthy from our point of view is that Bach had no affiliation, then or earlier, with the linguistics program at MIT. Nevertheless, he 'especially' thanks Noam Chomsky and Paul Postal 'for comments and suggestions' (Bach 1964: vi). Quite obviously, his being an outsider to MIT did not prevent faculty members there from taking a keen interest in his work. Despite that fact, Nielson could write:

> The market for linguistics textbooks in 1960s America was largely uniform, with one exception: at MIT only authors with close links to that institution were looked upon favorably. While Bach's book was widely used at universities across the country, it was 'officially ignored' at MIT — a result of its author having never been part of the MIT establishment.
>
> (Nielsen 2010: 215)

A footnote at this point states 'Bach, *Interview*'. However, its scope is not clear. Are the quotes around 'officially ignored' meant to imply that these were Bach's own words? Or were they Nielsen's scare quotes? In any event, I doubt that the failure to use Bach's textbook was a reflection of his not being an establishment figure. I was a guest at MIT a few years later (academic year 1968–1969) and I don't remember *any* class there using a textbook. As David Perlmutter recalls: 'The syntax courses had no basic curriculum; for the most part, each professor talked about what he was currently working on, with little regard for what the students knew or understood. In this, I think, they were basically copying Noam's teaching style, since that is what he did in his courses' (p. c., February 5, 2013). Morris

Halle (2011) states that the great 'innovation in teaching methods' at MIT was that 'teaching was mainly conversations between people who are interested in the [same] problems'. Graduate students all had their own offices. They were told that 'if you want to learn something, you'd better hang around the office and you might learn something that nobody is going to teach you in your class'.

That same year saw the publication of another textbook, Paul Roberts' *English Syntax: Alternate Edition* (Roberts 1964). Roberts' book was geared to the applied linguistics market as much as Bach's was to the market for books introducing theoretical linguistics. Roberts noted in the Acknowledgements:

> Professor Chomsky cooperated with me closely in the preparation of the text. He read the first two versions, and we discussed them at great length, after which considerable revisions were undertaken. Problems of terminology were solved by agreement between us.
>
> (Roberts 1964: vii)

Chomsky, whose passion for applied linguistics has never been thought to be excessive, even contributed an Introduction to the book (Chomsky 1964b).

5.6.2 LSA and other meetings

The outreach by MIT linguists is manifested in their participation at the summer and annual meetings of the LSA in the late 1950s and early 1960s. Chomsky was absent from the LSA program in those years, though the slack was taken up by others in the Department. At the winter meeting in Chicago at the end of 1957— just months after the publication of *Syntactic Structures*—Applegate, Halle, Lees, and Matthews gave talks. All four of them, along with Edward Klima, presented their work at LSA meetings in the following few years. But the most extraordinary fact is the number of MIT students who presented at the meetings. Such is in part a consequence of the fact that the PhD program had an informal requirement that in the course of their graduate studies students should submit an abstract to the LSA (James McCawley, p. c., July 1982). In 1963 and 1964 over half of the graduate students at MIT gave LSA talks: Thomas Bever, Bruce Fraser, Barbara Hall, Paul Kiparsky, Terence Langendoen, James McCawley, Stanley Petrick, Peter Rosenbaum, John R. Ross, Sanford Schane, and Arnold Zwicky. What is especially noteworthy about this fact is that prior to the early 1960s, it was primarily established figures in the field who presented at the LSA. The first group of students at MIT initiated a tradition of student presenters that continues to this day.[15]

---

[15] Archibald Hill wrote that before 1961, 'papers by students had been at least extremely rare, if not unknown' (Hill 1991: 101). However, Julia Falk has pointed out to me (p.c., October 19, 2013) that

202 THE DIFFUSION OF GENERATIVIST IDEAS

Chomsky, despite his absence from LSA meetings, accepted a number of speaking invitations at conferences and institutes. In 1958 he gave a Forum Lecture at the LSA Linguistic Institute at the University of Michigan, making him at 29 years of age perhaps the youngest scholar ever to be accorded that particular honor. Two of his conference papers are legendary: one at the Third Texas Conference on Problems of Linguistic Analysis in English in 1958 (published as Chomsky 1962b)[16] and the other as one of four plenary speakers at the Ninth International Congress of Linguists in 1962 (published as Chomsky 1964a and elsewhere). Commentators generally agree that these presentations and the resultant publications were instrumental in broadcasting TGG to the outside world of linguists. The efforts extended to non-linguists as well. To give just one example, in 1960 Chomsky and Halle were on the program of a symposium in New York entitled 'The Structure of Language and its Mathematical Aspects', which was sponsored by the American Mathematical Society. The publications Chomsky (1961a) and Halle (1961) resulted from this symposium.

Again, their zeal for presenting their work orally as well as in written form indicates that the first linguists at MIT were anything but inward looking.

5.6.3 Linguistic Institutes

Since 1928 the LSA has sponsored Linguistic Institutes, held during the summer at some university campus (see Chapter 1, § 1.5.3). They were held yearly in the 1960s. The teaching staff at each Institute is composed of local faculty members, supplemented by distinguished visitors from other institutions, all subject to the approval of the LSA's Executive Committee.[17] One does not 'volunteer' to teach at an Institute, so the absence of MIT faculty from the list of teachers during the first few years after 1957 should not be taken to imply a lack of willingness to teach. The University of Texas hosted the Institutes in 1960 and 1961. At the first, Lees, who

---

Hill exaggerates here. As she noted, the *LSAB* 21, 1948, reports that at the 1947 LSA summer meeting a resolution was passed commending the Summer Institute of Linguistics for 'its impressive series of publications' and for 'the papers presented by its students at this meeting' (p. 4).

[16] Chomsky cannot be blamed for the four-year publishing delay. In fact, Archibald Hill, who organized four yearly conferences in the 1950s, did not succeed in publishing the proceedings of the first and second conferences (1956 and 1957) until 1962 either. Chomsky was invited back to the fourth conference in 1959 to talk on generative phonology. 'The proceedings never reached publication, and the early Chomskyans for the most part believed that the conference organizers had suppressed them. Chomsky evidently tried unsuccessfully to get Hill to release his 1959 paper for Fodor and Katz's important anthology, *The Structure of Language* (1964), which only added fuel to the complaints' (Harris 1993: 272).

[17] In recent years the LSA executive committee has exerted fairly strict control over the Institutes, monitoring the content of the courses offered and the roster of visiting faculty members. Julia Falk has suggested to me (p.c., October 21, 2013) that in earlier decades the host institution was able to act more independently from the LSA in the running of the Institutes. This change, which was probably gradual, would be an interesting topic for further research.

was by then working at IBM, 'took part in in a seminar on current linguistic theory' (*LSAB* 34, 1961: 22). The first full course in generative grammar was offered at the 1961 Institute by Emmon Bach. Archibald Hill, who was both Secretary-Treasurer of the LSA and Director of the two Texas Institutes, recalled:

> Academically, these were the years in which the full impact of transformational analysis was for the first time felt by the linguistic community, and the Institute did its best to see that transformational analysts were fully heard. Indeed, the campus joke of those years was that linguists were divided into transformers, resistors, and transistors.
>
> (Hill 1964: 11)

Generative grammar has been represented in the course offerings at every succeeding Institute, except for the ones held in 1962 at the University of Washington and 1967 at the University of Michigan, and even at the latter one Morris Halle and Charles Fillmore delivered invited Forum Lectures.

5.6.4 Visitors to MIT

An important part of the attempt on the part of MIT linguists to spread the theory of generative grammar to as wide an audience as possible was to host a steady stream of visitors, partly for the exchange of ideas that such entailed and partly in the hope that they would return to their home institutions to implant knowledge of the new theory among their colleagues and students. Three foreign linguists were visiting professors at MIT in the 1960s: the Indo-Europeanist Jerzy Kuryłowicz from Krakow (during 1962–1963 and 1964–1965), the classicist and stylistics specialist Peter Colaclides from Athens (during 1964–1965), and the Sanskritist J. Frits Staal from Amsterdam (during 1966–1967). According to Paul Kiparsky:

> 'Outsiders' like Kuryłowicz, and some years later Frits Staal, were invited to teach courses. We were skeptical in some cases, but not hostile, and their ideas ultimately had an impact. Kuryłowicz was pushing markedness, and some us thought it was an important idea, and years later it was adopted in Ch. 9 of [*The Sound Pattern of English*]. Another year he lectured on IE accent and ablaut. Both his courses meant a lot to me, and he wrote them up into books that are considered classics. Staal's course on Panini changed my life.
>
> (Paul Kiparsky, p. c., December 2, 2012)

There were three different levels of 'visitorship' at MIT below the professorial level in the 1960s. The highest in terms of recognition had the title 'Visiting Scientist'.

It is easy to track down their names, though not always their external affiliations or linguistic interests, because they were listed above every linguistics article published in a *QPR*. Among those who arrived from abroad were M. J. Chayen and Neil Smith from Great Britain, Anna Wierzbicka from Poland, Jean-Claude Milner and Nicolas Ruwet from France, and Ray Cattell from Australia. Unfortunately no records survive of those who, like me in 1968–1969, had the title 'Guest of the Research Laboratory of Electronics' or of those who simply spent a few weeks or months at MIT attending classes and interacting with faculty and students, but without an official title. My estimate is that there were at least a dozen individuals each year in the second and third categories.

The recollections of the Visiting Scientists about their time spent at MIT in this period are almost entirely glowing. Neil Smith writes: 'MIT was a revelation. There was huge enthusiasm, appallingly hard work, and remarkable talent. I found myself again a neophyte, but being a post-doctoral "Visitor" I was spared the ignominy of having to turn in term papers proving my inadequacy. The worst embarrassment was discovering that the nice man I'd tried to explain "generative grammar" to at a welcoming reception was Paul Kiparsky. I had gone to MIT because of Chomsky, but when I arrived, he was away. Fortunately, Morris Halle took me under his wing, and in due course I became a phonologist. The riches on offer were remarkable: courses by Roman Jakobson on language and poetics […]' (Smith 2002: 266). Below are the personal reminiscences of three other Visiting Scientists from that period:

> My year as an NSF post-doc at MIT was the most important year of my professional life […] I didn't feel at all like an 'outsider' at MIT. The MIT people were the most thoroughly professional academic colleagues I ever encountered, before or since my time there. Neither the faculty nor the graduate students treated me with disdain for what I didn't know (which was plenty); rather, they were interested in and respected me for what I did know, and were very helpful in pointing me to sources where I could learn more about my weak areas.
>
> (Donald Freeman, p. c., October 22, 2012)

> I was very much welcomed by the students […]. I was 'correctly' received by the faculty. But I understood rapidly that Halle considered that I did not belong there. That said, he was right and he gave me a chance. I needed one or two months to understand how everything functioned […]. One could say that I succeeded, because I published two papers in the [*QPR*]. […] I had two meetings with Morris Halle about my phonology articles. At that point I understood that his reservations at the beginning had disappeared.
>
> (Jean-Claude Milner, p. c., October 19, 2012; my translation from the French)

It blew my mind to be sitting in lectures by Chomsky, Halle and others, and I still regard it as the most important year in my life, as far as intellectual development was concerned.

(Ray Cattell, p. c., March 20, 2013)

One Visiting Scientist, however, had an unpleasant experience. For Anna Wierzbicka, the memory of the year she spent at MIT (1966–1967) was 'painful' (p. c., October 26, 2012). What distinguished her from the others is that she arrived committed to an alternative theory of grammar based on Andrzej Boguslawski's conception of universal semantic primes (see Boguslawski 1970; Wierzbicka 1972; and much later work). She 'did not expect that linguists at MIT would be necessarily receptive to [this theory]'. At the beginning of the year she tried to convince John R. Ross and George Lakoff that deep structure was both semantic and universal. 'Both Haj and George listened to me politely but told me that Boguslawski and I were too radical and that they wouldn't want to go that far themselves.' Wierzbicka continued: 'You can imagine my shock when one day [they] announced [in their jointly-taught class] that they were abandoning Chomsky's position on the relationship between syntax and semantics, and rejecting a syntactic "deep structure" in favour of a deeper, universal, semantic deep structure. […] They didn't refer to our conversations at all.'

5.6.5 Generative grammarians outside of MIT

It seems implausible to me that success could have been achieved so rapidly without non-MIT linguists actively contributing to the theory. Certainly then, 'outsiders' had enough access to the relevant published (and unpublished) materials to enable them to write convincingly on the theory. By way of confirmation, in 1965 William Orr Dingwall published a book entitled *Transformational Generative Grammar: A Bibliography* with 962 entries (Dingwall 1965). Many of these entries were works that criticized TGG and some, it must be said, had no apparent relationship to TGG at all. However, subtracting these, there were still hundreds of generative publications extant in 1965. The vast majority of them were written by scholars who had no connection with MIT, thereby illustrating the success of MIT outreach.

The journal *Language* was, then as now, the most widely distributed linguistics journal in the world. Consider how many full articles were published in that journal between 1957 and 1969 which either presupposed or argued for a generative approach to the topic in question:

Vol. 36	Lees (1960a), Stockwell (1960)
Vol. 37	Smith (1961)
Vol. 38	Bach (1962)
Vol. 39	Lees and Klima (1963), Katz and Fodor (1963)
Vol. 40	Klima (1964), Zeps (1964), Smith (1964), Katz (1964), O' Neil (1964)
Vol. 41	Foley (1965), Saporta (1965), Gleitman (1965), Closs (1965), Langacker (1965), Fromkin (1965), Klein (1965)
Vol. 42	Langendoen (1966), Harms (1966), Schane (1966)
Vol. 43	Chomsky (1967c), Stanley (1967), Bach (1967), Foley (1967), Kiparsky (1967), Voyles (1967), Malone (1967), Doherty and Schwartz (1967), Gruber (1967)
Vol. 44	McKay (1968), Langacker (1968), Weinstock (1968), Hasegawa (1968), Kuroda (1968), Cressey (1968), Huntley (1968), Wang (1968), Voyles (1968), Schwartz (1968), Anshen and Schreiber (1968)
Vol 45	Contreras (1969), Dixon (1969), Rigsby and Silverstein (1969), Langacker (1969a, b), Lakoff (1969), Labov (1969), Fasold (1969), Huddleston (1969), Cairns (1969)

One is struck by the number of papers, especially in the later years, by linguists who had not been members of the MIT department or long-term visitors to it. Clearly, they were able to access the generative work that they needed well enough to pass review in a highly competitive journal.

And it was not just the journal *Language* in which generative-related articles appeared. The first volume of *Journal of Linguistics*, published in the United Kingdom and the organ of the Linguistics Association of Great Britain, appeared in 1965. Four of the six main articles dealt with generative grammar, either supporting it (Chomsky & Halle 1965; Thorne 1965); or criticizing it (Householder 1965; Matthews 1965). Thorne, Householder, and Matthews, none of whom had direct MIT connections, were able to inform themselves sufficiently about the ins and outs of the new theory.

It is uncontroversial, I think, that the most important journal article in generative syntax published between 1957 and 1965 was Charles Fillmore's 'The position of embedding transformations in a grammar' (Fillmore 1963). This article laid the basis for the transformational cycle and the successor mechanisms that are still assumed to be correct by the great majority of generative syntacticians (for discussion, see Freidin 1999).[18] Fillmore had never been to MIT. He remarked to me (p. c., some time in the 1980s) how 'nurturing' the MIT faculty had been to him

---

[18] The first proposal for a syntactic cycle appears in Chomsky, Halle, and Lukoff (1956), where it is applied to the handling of sentence stress. This paper had no influence on future syntactic theorizing, however.

in his research project, singling out Paul Postal, who is cited in the acknowledgements to that paper, as being especially helpful. A propos of this remark, Postal informed me in an email (overly modestly, I suspect):

> I can't actually remember reading and commenting on Chuck's work, but it would not surprise me if I did and I certainly know of nothing which suggests he is mistaken or making anything up.
>
> (Paul Postal, p. c., July 25, 2012)

As stressed in Newmeyer (1986b: 41–43), an important factor in the success of the theory is the happy fact that all of the first PhD's in linguistics for MIT found employment at major universities. The late 1960s saw the biggest expansion of the American university system in history, so there were sufficient funds to create departments of linguistics where none had existed before. 'It did not matter that Hockett and Hall were at Cornell, Trager and Smith at Buffalo, or Harris and Hiż at Pennsylvania. New departments could always be founded to serve as academic bases for generative grammar from the very beginning' (Newmeyer 1986b: 43). But Nielsen implies incorrectly that generative-oriented departments were founded mainly by MIT linguists or their students:

> In the 1960s, transformational theory was brought to the University of California at San Diego by Edward Klima, to the University of Chicago by James McCawley, to the University of Illinois by Robert Lees, to Indiana University by Andreas Koutsoudas, to the University of Massachusetts by Robert Binnick, to Ohio State University by Arnold Zwicky, to the University of Texas at Austin by Stanley Peters, to the University of Washington by Frederick Newmeyer, and, of course, to UCLA by Robert Stockwell. Many of these young transformationalist-oriented programs quickly built productive graduate programs, training large numbers of students in transformational theory.
>
> (Nielsen 2010: 281–282)

Most of these statements are incorrect. Leonard Newmark and David Reibel, both early enthusiasts of generative grammar, were already at San Diego when the first MIT linguists, Sanford Schane and Sige-Yuki Kuroda (not Edward Klima) were hired in 1965. The theory was hardly 'brought' to Indiana by Andreas Koutsoudas, since he was already on the faculty when he adopted it. The same can be said about Fred Householder, a long-time Indiana faculty member, who was quite enthusiastic about generative grammar for a while and even directed George Lakoff's 1965 PhD dissertation. The Massachusetts department was founded by Donald Freeman, who had had a post-doc at MIT (see above) and was the one who hired Binnick and several other generativists. Charles Fillmore at Ohio State had independently adopted generative grammar in the early 1960s before he hired Terence

Langendoen from MIT in 1965 (Arnold Zwicky did not arrive there until 1969). Emmon Bach and Robert Harms, neither MIT-trained linguists, had established a generative presence at Texas well before Peters joined the faculty. When I was hired at Washington in 1969, Sol Saporta and Heles Contreras, neither of whom had ever been to MIT, had created a generative-oriented department there. Finally, Stockwell (along with Paul Schachter and Victoria Fromkin) turned the UCLA program into a largely generative one before the hiring of its first MIT PhD, Barbara Partee, in 1965. The fact that they had had no affiliation with MIT shows how simple it was to master the theory without direct MIT guidance. None of Nielsen's mistakes taken individually are particularly significant or even historiographically very interesting. But they need to be addressed because their cumulative effect is to reinforce the idea that there was once a 'decade of private knowledge'.

5.7 Some explanations for the spread of the 'private knowledge' idea

When I suggested to some 1960s-era MIT linguists that they were often perceived as members of an inward-looking clique, the reaction was incredulity. Here are two typical comments:

> So it is kind of vague in my mind who a putative clique of MIT people dismissive of outsiders might have included. It is true there was a lot of circulating of those horrible purple papers,[19] and no doubt the circle to whom they were sent was not huge. But that was probably due essentially to the physical difficulties of producing and mailing them more than any desire to keep them exclusive. [...] So in sum, while I am obviously terribly vague on details, the idea that MIT people formed a sort of closed clique strikes me as entirely wrong. If that had been the case, the doctrines would hardly have so successfully spread and influenced people. What is no doubt true is that lots of linguists external to the MIT world which developed resented the increasing influence it had and the way its ideas were spread by young people like me and others in sometimes offensive and ill-considered ways.
> (Paul Postal, p. c., July 25, 2012)

> [The idea that we] tried to keep [our ideas limited to a small circle] strikes me as flat wrong. We were as hungry for recognition as anyone; if we could have blogged this stuff, we would have. It's just that these things were, most of them, rough drafts (many expanded into, or incorporated into, regular publications).
> (Arnold Zwicky, p. c., October 6, 2012)

---

[19] On the purple papers, see Chapter 4, fn. 25.

And yet, the perception persists of an off-putting MIT isolationism. Why would that be? There are three principal reasons, I believe. First, the rapid pace of change in the field meant that not everybody outside of MIT could access the most recent work as rapidly as those on the inside could (§ 5.7.1). Second, the public behavior of some early generativists was extremely aggressive at times and when not aggressive, it could be very insular (§ 5.7.2). Third and closely related, the self-identity of the students at MIT in the 1960s was very much wrapped up in the idea that they, and they alone, represented the future of linguistics (§ 5.7.3).

5.7.1 The consequences of a rapidly evolving discipline

The 1960s, and in particular the earlier part of that decade, was a time when the theory was evolving at an extremely rapid pace. As Thomas Bever observed, 'during this period virtually *every* grad student paper introduced something novel into the field; we were all busy working out this brand new paradigm and everyone could make almost immediate contributions. That made the period intoxicating for the students, but frustrating for people who were not right there on the spot' (p. c., October 31, 2012). Naturally, generative linguists cited each others' unpublished work. It would have been unethical not to cite some paper, whether published or not, for an original idea. So given the higher percentage of 'original ideas' then than there are now, the absolute percentage of references to unpublished work might well have been higher fifty years ago than it is today. That certainly could have helped to fuel the idea of 'private knowledge'. But there is no reason to think that the time lag between the completion of a paper and its formal publication was any longer then than it is now. It's just that the rapid tempo of theoretical change at the time made it more inevitable that work not yet sent off to press would be cited.

5.7.2 Aggressive and insular public behavior

In the last sentence of his quote in § 5.7, Paul Postal puts his finger on one of the reasons that the early generativists were often seen as members of a inward-looking clique. In a nutshell, more than a few were badly-behaved in public. Well before 1960, Lees's behavior at meetings led him to be seen as the hatchet man of generative grammar:[20]

A very direct man, [Lees] employed a style calculated to shock and enrage which he now describes (with characteristic bluntness) as 'getting up at meetings and

[20] To call Lees's personality 'abrasive' does not do it sufficient justice. Morris Halle told me that Lees had the same style when addressing administrators at MIT. 'If a day went by for Lees without his insulting somebody in a position of power, then he would consider that day a failure' (Morris Halle, p. c., December 17, 1978).

calling people *stupid*'. These tactics made him a legend among the transformationalists, but they did not endear him to the other side; Householder cautiously
begins a review of Lees's *Grammar of English Nominalizations* with the remark
that Lees 'is noted as a redoubtable scholarly feuder and cutter-down to size'
(Householder 1962: 326), probably the mildest terms used by his opponents.

(Harris 1993: 72)

By the early 1960s Paul Postal had eclipsed Lees in his degree of rhetorical
vituperativeness:

> Postal was even less loved by the Bloomfieldians. Like Lees, he is warm and genial
> in personal settings, and quite tolerant of opposing viewpoints. But his reputation
> for intellectual savagery is well-deserved, rooted firmly in his public demeanor at
> conferences, especially in the early years. The stories are legion, most of which fol-
> low the same scenario. Postal sits through some anonymous, relatively innocuous,
> descriptive paper cataloguing the phonemic system of a little-known language.
> He stands up, begins with a blast like 'this paper has absolutely nothing to do
> with the study of human languages', and proceeds to offer a barrage of argu-
> ments detailing its worthlessness — often making upwards of a dozen distinct
> counter-arguments against both the specific data used and the framework it is
> couched in.

(Harris 1993: 72)

And consider the following:

> An example of rare disapproval of excessively vehement discussion followed the
> Joos paper [at the 1963 annual LSA meeting], which was a sketch, with a handout,
> of p. 76 of *The English Verb: Form and Meanings* (Joos 1964). An over-enthusiastic
> devotee of the latest type of grammatical theory [Paul Postal] attacked the paper
> as essentially ignorant; both the audience and the presiding officer disapproved,
> and it was ruled that the discussant's remarks were off the record. In consequence,
> his name does not appear at its proper place, p. 24, in *Bulletin* 37.

(Hill 1991: 122)

The style that advocates of the new theory often assumed in public was not limited
only to those linguists trained at MIT. It even reproduced itself on the otherwise
laid-back West Coast. As Victoria Fromkin recalls:

> [T]he early years following the publication of *Syntactic Structures* were exciting
> ones; the 'revolution' had begun. The weekly linguistics seminars at the Rand
> Corporation in Santa Monica more resembled the storming of the Winter palace
> than scholarly discussions.

(Fromkin 1991: 79)

One assumes that she was referring to herself and Robert Stockwell as being the two principal stormers. Neither had ever been known to mince words.

Even when the behavior of the generativists at public meetings was not openly aggressive, and it was not aggressive more often than it was, it was sometimes reflective of an in-group mentality that was quite off-putting to more than one participant. Comments like 'If you had read Paul's (or George's or Dave's, or who-sever) paper on such-and-such, then your analysis would have been better' were not uncommon. Needless to say, the presenter would not be likely to know which Paul (or George or Dave) was being referred to, much less the content of his paper. Or just as bad, 'a current MIT grad student would start [his or her conference paper] with something more or less equivalent to, "I presuppose the version of [the theory] presented in Chomsky's lectures this semester"' (Barbara Partee, p. c., October 31, 2012). Good luck if you were not at the lectures. And recall Henry A. Gleason's remark (§ 5.3) that 'an objection [to a generativist paper at an LSA meeting] would be answered by the simple assertion that the matter had been taken care of and warranted no further discussion. This would be supported by the citing of a paper in the underground press—a paper whose existence the objector had no way of knowing about, and which he would for some years have no opportunity to see' (Gleason 1988: 65–66).

It is not at all clear to me whether the progress of the theory was advanced or retarded by the rhetorical style of some of its advocates. It was certainly off-putting to many, but at the same time, especially for students, it created a mystique around members of the MIT group that quite a few young people (like myself at the time) found very engaging. One thing is clear: It helped to set the early generative grammarians apart as a distinct group with a distinct agenda, and thereby contributed to the idea that they were possessors of 'private knowledge' denied to the linguistic public at large.

5.7.3 MIT student mentality

The first students in the MIT linguistics program in the early 1960s were a breed apart. They had to be. It took courage, prescience, and a spirit of adventure for a high-achieving college senior to seek out as a mentor a relatively unknown junior scholar based in an institution known almost exclusively for science and engineering.[21] As David Perlmutter, a 1968 MIT PhD, has written: 'The graduate program in linguistics, begun in 1961, tended to attract students with an iconoclastic bent at a time when students who wanted to play it safe saw the upstart program at MIT as a risky bet. They went to Cornell to study with Hockett, to

---

[21] Morris Halle (2011) tells a story, perhaps apocryphal, of the reaction of MIT President Howard Johnson when told that MIT had just been named as having the best doctoral program in linguistics in the United States. Johnson replied: 'We have a linguistics program?'

Yale to study with Bloch, to Berkeley to study Amerindian linguistics, or to other programs that promised a more secure career (Perlmutter 2010: xix). Not surprisingly, then, many MIT students felt imbued with a sense of destiny and of their own importance. It would be up to them, and them alone, to remake the field of linguistics by diffusing TGG to the rest of the world.[22] In Barbara Partee's words: 'We all felt like pioneers in an exciting new venture' (Partee 2005: 4). Such a feeling was marvelous, needless to say, in creating an esprit de corps and the self-confidence necessary to propagate the theory. Another positive effect was that it extended to the hearty welcoming of visitors from outside MIT, at least those who arrived there for instruction in the local brand of linguistics (see above, § 5.6.4). Anybody who was officially part of the MIT coterie was automatically regarded as a colleague. But on the negative side, it led MIT students (though, interestingly, not MIT faculty) to be skeptical that anybody could have truly mastered the theory who had not spent hours and hours probing its intricacy within the walls of MIT's Building 20. Emmon Bach felt this condescending attitude very keenly:

> Early encounters with various MIT students [...] invariably had this sort of 'where did you come from' and 'how did you find out' cast about them. I availed myself of Fillmore's rejoinder: 'Well, I can read!' The last comment of this sort was from my colleague Joan [Bresnan] at UMass much later, when she paid me the supreme compliment of telling me she had thought I had an MIT degree for the longest time! I think Barbara [Partee] went off to UCLA with a certain missionary fervor about her.
>
> (Emmon Bach, p. c., July 25, 2012)

Robin Lakoff, who was a PhD student at Harvard in the early and mid 1960s, recalls the behavior of members of the audience at MIT when unsympathetic visitors from the outside world came to speak:[23]

> I remember well the times that non-transformationalists would speak at MIT, in those early years when the field still saw itself as fighting for survival in a hostile world. Rather than attempting to charm, conciliate, find points of connection, the circle at MIT regularly went for blood, Points were made by obvious public demolition; the question or counterexample that brought the offender to his knees [was] repeated for weeks or months afterwards with relish.
>
> (Lakoff 1989: 967–968)

---

[22] And to a significant degree they succeeded. As of this writing, seven MIT linguistics PhD's from the 1960s (and four more from the 1970s) have been elected President of the Linguistic Society of America.

[23] Lakoff goes on to write: 'But by 1964, certainly, the battle was won. No more opponents came riding into Cambridge eager to joust with the champion' (Lakoff 1989: 968).

When I first read this passage, I assumed that Lakoff was referring primarily to MIT students since, aside from Paul Postal, the core linguistics faculty members were generally polite (albeit forceful) in professional interactions. It was typically the students who 'went for blood'. Lakoff confirmed my assumption:

> Most of the hostility towards non-generative visiting speakers was done by grad students (and postdocs), who vied with one another to be both theoretically and personally obnoxious to anyone not of the MIT community who came to give a talk. [...] The students aren't really to blame. They were encouraged by their teachers and the 'bad guys' perspective,[24] and MIT was generally both a closed-in and a highly competitive place.
>
> (Robin Lakoff, p. c., October 26, 2012)

Barbara Partee, an MIT PhD student in the early 1960s, confirms Lakoff's assessment of student behavior in that period:[25]

> This note is to back up Robin Lakoff's impression. I was kind of shocked when I saw what happened when the faculty invited non-generative visiting speakers — I have vivid memories of [one MIT faculty member] making audible comments and snickering to whoever was sitting next to him or behind him, in ways the speaker must have been able to see and hear. That was the model we were exposed to. I didn't like it — that wasn't the way I had been brought up. I readily learned about being critical, but I hope I didn't learn to be rude. I remember when Sydney Lamb came and gave a talk about his theory of Stratificational Grammar. I had read one of his articles in preparation, I think, and thought (naively) that I could offer him some counter-arguments that would lead him to abandon that theory. So I made an appointment to talk with him and gave him my arguments. I don't remember much about the conversation (but he didn't abandon his theory). What

[24] The class at MIT covering non-generative approaches was universally known as 'The Bad Guys Course'. Chomsky wrote to me: 'In the early '60s, I was working on topics in history of linguistics/philosophy that are discussed in *Current Issues, Aspects, Cartesian Linguistics, Language and Mind*. And as usual taught a course on what I was working on. It became pretty clear that students weren't interested, so I handed it over to junior faculty to run it as they and the students liked. They changed it to a course on contemporary critique of generative grammar, which, as you know, was widespread and quite passionate, and other approaches; and it soon came to be called by them the 'bad guys' course. I didn't like that. Morris didn't either. But it was their baby, and we didn't interfere.' (p. c., October 28, 2012)

[25] By the end of that decade, if not before, the older establishment figures in the field were giving as much as they were taking. James Harris, a 1967 MIT PhD, recalls: 'At a talk at Cornell (in the late '60s, I think), I was treated to the most viciously nasty unprovoked attack, by a mature looking guy, I've ever witnessed. I didn't know who this jerk was, and I responded in kind (to applause from the audience). Turned out that the assailant was Charles Hockett' (p. c., November 9, 2012). Harris goes on: 'In Berkeley at around the same time, Henry Lee Smith (of Trager-Smith English phonology fame) confided to me that he didn't know "what the hell those MIT guys think they're doing, but it certainly isn't phonology." Smith was sure of this because he and Trager were among the wise men who had "founded modern phonology" (his words). So much for the kindness of strangers (neither of whom was a visiting speaker at MIT).'

I do remember is my classmates teasing me mercilessly for several days thereafter as a 'Lamb-lover' just because I had made an appointment to talk to him.

(Barbara Partee, p. c., October 28, 2012)

For Paul Kiparsky, however, 'there was no habitual hostile treatment of people from outside of MIT who came to give talks'. Rather, 'people were just excited about engaging different ideas. For example, when Gilbert Harman's 'Generative Grammars without Transformation Rules: A Defense of Phrase Structure' came out in *Language* 1963, an emergency meeting of the department was called almost immediately and we went through the whole thing in detail until we concluded to our great relief that it was a 'notational variant' of transformational grammar (whether rightly so, I can't tell)' (p. c., December 3, 2012). Kiparsky also disputes Lakoff's assertion that MIT was in any way 'closed-in':

As for 'closed-in', to me it felt the exact opposite. Actually it was the most wide open place I've been at before or since. Building 20 housed exciting research such as Jerry Lettvin's, who was very accessible and a hoot to talk to. A number of us sat in on Putnam's courses, as well as psychology courses (Lukas Teuber, Davis Howes, who ran an aphasia project with Geschwind, Eric Lenneberg at Harvard). I went to lots of Indo-European courses at Harvard and interacted with their students. I was very much encouraged to do so by Morris Halle. [...] As I recall, some students attended math courses, those of Hartley Rogers, among others.

(Paul Kiparsky, p. c., December 2, 2012)

Thomas Bever, a classmate of both Partee and Kiparsky, did agree that MIT students could be confrontational at times. However, for him their behavior was purely defensive:

As to hostility to 'outsiders'. It is of course Robbie's prerogative to express how she felt about treatment of 'outsiders'. But I think that for many of us it was not the 'outsider-ness' that was at issue. During the period 1961-1965 there was a serious intellectual conflict between MITniks and the Linguistics Establishment. Many senior linguists (Hockett, Joos, Gibson, Lehmann, etc.) suddenly found themselves surrounded by a lot of young self-assured critics, with out-of-the-blue arguments that their basic assumptions were wrong and 'unscientific'. LSA meetings involved real strategic pre-planning, discussing ahead who would criticize whom at each meeting. We all felt the presence of a mission. And for our part, we all felt somewhat beleaguered by conservative inertia in the field.

(Thomas Bever, p. c., October 28, 2012)

MIT students, either because they wanted to or because they felt that they had to, erected a rhetorical wall between themselves and much of the surrounding community of linguists. One can easily see how such attitudes and behavior contributed to the view that the early generativists shared among themselves some degree of 'private knowledge'.

5.8 Conclusion

This chapter has taken on aspects of the early days of the theory of generative grammar, that is the late 1950s and the 1960s. We have seen how MIT faculty and students went about diffusing their ideas to a broader audience. They used every means at their disposal at the time: publishing books, journal articles, anthology chapters, and technical reports; aiding the writing of textbooks; giving conference talks; teaching at LSA Institutes; and hosting numerous visitors to MIT. All of these measures contributed to the rapid success of the theory. To read some of the critical literature, however, the early MIT linguists formed an elitist in-group, talking only to each other by means of inaccessible 'underground' publications and thereby erecting a barrier between themselves and the outside world of linguistics. We have seen that their tactics for reaching out to the linguistics community as a whole overshadowed any elitist behavior. And in particular, there was no significant 'underground' literature to obstruct the acceptance of the new theory.

6

The European reception of early transformational generative grammar

6.1 Introduction

The previous chapter opened with a selection of quotes from 1965 attesting to the idea that the field had undergone a 'Chomskyan revolution'.[1] However, all but one of these quotes was by an American (the exception was James Thorne from the United Kingdom). The success of Chomsky's ideas in the United States leads inevitably the question of the reaction to TGG in other countries. This topic was introduced briefly in Chapter 2, § 2.6, where it was pointed out that several important European structuralists reacted quite negatively to the new theory. The present chapter addresses further the European reception of TGG, particularly in the 1970s and 1980s. However, two factors lead unfortunately to a fairly superficial treatment: space limitations and the fact that there is no overarching generalization. Each European country needs to be examined separately.

§ 6.2 offers some general remarks about the introduction of TGG into Europe and § 6.3 reviews the reception of the theory in each European country. § 6.4 is a brief conclusion.

6.2 TGG in Europe: Some general remarks

TGG was slow getting off the ground in Europe. With a few exceptions to be discussed below, very few European countries had active centers of generative grammar before the 1970s or later. It is still the case that some European countries have no more than a small handful of generativists. Indeed, the first collection of generative papers written and edited by European generativists did not appear until 1973 (Kiefer & Ruwet 1973), with contributions from the Netherlands, the United Kingdom, Poland, East Germany, West Germany, France, Hungary,

---

[1] I would like to thank Hans Basbøll, Camiel Hamans, and Pieter Seuren for their comments on the entire pre-final version of this chapter. Others who provided input to me are acknowledged in the appropriate section. I bear sole responsibility for errors of fact and interpretation.

American Linguistics in Transition. Frederick J. Newmeyer, Oxford University Press.
© Frederick J. Newmeyer (2022). DOI: 10.1093/oso/9780192843760.003.0006

the USSR, Sweden, and Romania. In his chapter, Manfred Bierwisch noted that there was nothing particularly distinctive about TGG, as practiced in Europe, remarking:

> Although since the early sixties an increasing number of linguists in Europe have been attracted by the theory of generative grammar, they do not form in any serious sense a particular trend or school of anything of this kind that could be contrasted to corresponding research that could be done elsewhere in the world. Hence the heading *Generative Grammar in Western Europe* does not specify a coherent and self-contained topic.
>
> (Bierwisch 1973: 69)

As we will see, in later years European generative work came to be seen as, perhaps not distinctive, but as comparable or perhaps superior to such work as practiced in the United States.

The most important event regarding TGG in Europe took place towards the end of the period that is focused upon in this chapter. I am referring to the founding of Generative Linguistics in the Old World (GLOW) in 1977, with the goal of furthering the study of generative grammar by organizing an annual spring conference and periodical summer schools, and by publishing a newsletter that discusses current intellectual (and organizational) issues in the field. The 1977 and 1978 meetings were held in Amsterdam, followed in yearly succession by Pisa, Nijmegen, Göttingen, Paris, and York. The success of GLOW needs to be tempered by the realization that the world of European TGG has been a small one. In the words of Henk van Riemsdijk, one of the three principal founders of GLOW (along with Jan Koster and Jean-Roger Vergnaud):[2]

> Looking back to the initial stages of GLOW, 20 years ago, I had something like an idea that that was the start and we would slowly conquer some power basis in Europe, not to become the only game in Europe, but at least one of the major ones. I think many generativists, especially young ones, tend to be quite mistaken about the extent to which that has been successful. The reason is that we have made some progress, we have centers where we attract students. These students get a good training, they go to conferences, the whole world in which they move is a generative world. But they often don't realize that it is an extremely small world.
>
> (van Riemsdijk 1998: 18)

While I have no statistics to back up my intuition, I believe that the International Cognitive Linguistics Association, when it meets in Europe, outdraws GLOW by

---

[2] Joseph Emonds informs me that the GLOW organizational meeting was presided over by these three linguists in a café overlooking the Luxembourg Gardens in Paris, with Emonds and others as participants (p. c., March 7, 2021).

a factor of two to one, and that more linguists in Europe consider themselves 'functionalists' than consider themselves 'generativists'. At the same time, however, it must be said that the influence of TGG seems to have greatly exceeded the number of scholars actually working in that approach. In the 1980s 'there were many more references to 'standard TGG' than to other (e.g. 'functional') alternative paradigms; in reality, the knowledge of and interest in, functional schools outside one's own was much smaller than the knowledge of TGG; this I take as evidence that TGG was felt to be such a strong paradigm in Europe that other paradigms should use it for comparison, even when they declared themselves anti-TGG' (Hans Basbøll, p. c., January 13, 2021).

6.3 TGG in Europe: A country-by-country breakdown

In this section I overview the early days of TGG in all of the European countries that existed at the time.[3] I divide them into Western Europe (§ 6.3.1), Nordic Europe (§ 6.3.2), Eastern Europe (§ 6.3.3), and Southern Europe (§ 6.3.4). I will be the first to acknowledge that these divisions are to a certain extent arbitrary. For example, I assign Denmark to Nordic Europe and Greece to Southern Europe. But geographically speaking, the former could as easily be in Western Europe, and the latter could as easily be in Eastern Europe. My categories are to a certain extent reflective of the Cold War that raged in the 1960s and 1970s. If I were overviewing the current situation, there would be a category entitled 'Central Europe', a term that practically disappeared from English between 1945 and 1989.

6.3.1 Western Europe

This section reviews the advent of TGG in the United Kingdom, Ireland, the Netherlands, Belgium, Luxembourg, France, Switzerland, Germany, and Austria.

The United Kingdom.[4] The United Kingdom is TGG's biggest European success story. By the end of the 1970s most British departments had generative orientations. A summary statement by Peter Matthews indicates the ease of acceptance of TGG in that country:

> If you are asking in effect if I, or others that I knew of, found it difficult as followers of Chomsky either to get a job or to teach the subject as we wished, the answer basically is no, not at all.
>
> (p. c., March 12, 2018)

---

[3] I omit the 'micro-states' Andorra, Monaco, the Vatican City, San Marino, and Liechtenstein. As far as I know, no generative grammar was being done in these places between the 1950s and the 1980s.
[4] I would like to thank P. H. Matthews and Pieter Seuren for their input to this section.

As a matter of fact, TGG had a presence in the UK even in the 1950s. Matthews has written:

> W. S. Allen's advice was that I should get a copy of Chomsky's *Syntactic Structures* (1957), published two years earlier. [...] It was an eye-opener
>
> (Matthews 2002: 201).

> In America [in 1963–1964] I had come to know John Lyons and Jimmy Thorne, both near contemporaries, and, on returning to this country, two of us at least believed we were a triumvirate whose mission was to open colleagues' minds to new, especially to Chomsky's early, ideas. (p. 205)

Allen had the distinction of reading *Syntactic Structures* before it was even published. He recalls:

> In 1956 I saw a pre-print of Noam Chomsky's first major work, his *Syntactic Structures*, published in 1957. It seemed to me that this, with its transformational-generative approach, might provide a solution to Lyons's problem [of how to relate sentences occurring in different grammatical structures which one intuitively felt to belong together] — and so it proved to be. He successfully adapted and refined Chomsky's basic ideas to his own ends, his dissertation was duly completed in 1961 and was published in a revised form by the Philological Society in 1963 [= his book *Structural Semantics* (Lyons 1963)].
>
> (Allen 2002: 21)

A glowing review of *Syntactic Structures* was the first publication by John Lyons, where he found the book 'most interesting' (Lyons 1958: 109) and 'very convincingly argued' (p. 111). In the same volume as the abovementioned papers by Matthews and Allen, Lyons wrote:

> I read *Syntactic Structures* in the early summer of 1957. This proved to be a turning point in my career. [Chomsky's work] helped me resolve the theoretical and methodological problems I was having with my research. At a later stage of my career, I developed a broader interest in generative grammar.
>
> (Lyons 2002: 174)

Other British linguists, however, were more guarded in their assessment of early TGG, or were downright hostile. Consider the reactions of Joseph Cremona, Geoffrey Leech, and N. E. Collinge:

> When I came into contact with Noam Chomsky's *Syntactic Structures*, two or three years after its publication in 1957 (an old pupil, Peter Matthews, was the

first to draw attention to the work), and digested it together with the author's subsequent ideas in the course of the 1960s, I could see that the direction being taken would be exciting and productive, but came to the conclusion that to take on transformational grammar at this stage of my life would in practice mean having to abandon virtually all my other linguistic interests.

(Cremona 2002: 88)

Although MIT taught me a great deal, particularly about the habit of rigorous thought and application of theory, the MIT approach to linguistics was too constraining for my taste.

(Leech 2002: 159)

Sadly, the advent of the first version of Chomskyism had already [in 1962–1963] begun to impose a constricting religiosity upon at least the American scholarly world.

(Collinge 2002: 70)

Nevertheless, despite the resistance to TGG from some of the older generation of British linguists, the theory was successful in capturing the interest of those entering the field in the 1960s and 1970s.

The Dutch linguist Pieter Seuren was another early contributor to TGG in the UK, introducing many students to generative grammar, some of whom later went on to become prominent (though not necessarily in later years as generativists):

Fortunately, I was selected as a writer of a Dutch language course for English students at Cambridge University in 1966. There, the head of the new linguistics department, John Trim, immediately saw that I was not a language-course writer but a theoretical linguist. So he made sure that I was appointed to a lectureship in linguistics in his department. I also became a fellow of Darwin College. At Cambridge, we had an exceptionally good crop of students, including Bernard Comrie, John Hawkins, Nigel Vincent, Robin Cooper, Andy Radford and quite a few other now well-known linguists. I once made a count and came to eleven linguistics professors who went through our department as students between 1966 and 1970. For those days, this was extraordinary. All these students were, as I said, steeped in the TGG of the late 1960s — although I myself was already veering towards generative semantics (becoming a good friend of Jim McCawley). The students largely abandoned TGG and went their own way, but for Andy Radford, who remained a staunch Chomskyan.[5]

(p. c., July 13, 2018)

---

[5] While Hawkins, Vincent, and Cooper are not 'staunch Chomskyans' in the literal sense, their work complements Chomskyan conceptions, rather than opposes them. Comrie, on the other hand, became quite anti-generative.

Thanks in large part to Seuren's efforts, Cambridge was an important place of generative studies by 1970. However, he had much less success at Oxford, where he was a fellow of Magdalen College between 1971 and 1974. Oxford was then (and is now to a considerable extent) steeped in philological and philosophical approaches to language, as opposed to purely grammatical ones.

The UK, of course, had been a leading center of structural linguistics before 1957. One of the world's most prominent linguists between the 1930s and the 1950s was J. R. Firth, whose work on prosody anticipated generative approaches to that topic decades later. But Firth left no enduring *organizational* legacy with a vested interest in developing his ideas. His leading student, Michael Halliday went off in his own direction to found the school of systemic-functional linguistics. Halliday was quite opposed to TGG from the beginning, but he left University College London (and the UK) in 1971. After his departure, the department there rapidly developed a generative orientation.

Ireland.[6] In Ireland the long tradition of Celtic studies has always dominated academic work on language. Also, compared to many other countries, Irish scholars were involved early on with the sociology of language and with language planning theory, due to the interest in the revitalization of Irish. The same could be said for applied linguistics, given the desire to spread knowledge of that language. In the late 1970s, the Irish Association for Applied Linguistics (IRAAL) was organized, representing the only linguistic society in the country.

The main instigator of generative studies in Ireland was Conn Ó Cléirigh, who was the Professor and Chair of Linguistics in University College Dublin (UCD). Jeffrey Kallen told me (p. c., February 21, 2021) that sometime in the early 1980s, Ó Cléirigh and he were involved in a public forum sponsored by IRAAL, where he put the case that Ireland needed to do much more in linguistic theory—that there was only one small linguistics department (the one in UCD), which turned out few graduates and very few PhD's. Kallen concluded that it was therefore time to start building programs. Ó Cléirigh's opposite view was interesting, in that he advanced the suggestion that Ireland, being a small country, couldn't really compete with large linguistics departments, and that it really would be better if advanced linguistics students went abroad for their PhD's and then came back home.

Despite Ó Cléirigh's views on building linguistics programs in Ireland, he was nevertheless an enthusiastic advocate of generative grammar, even though he himself did not publish in the framework. In preparation for his opportunity to develop a degree program in linguistics, he spent the academic year 1964–1965 at UCLA and took courses with Robert Stockwell and Barbara Partee among others. James McCloskey reports (p. c., February 21, 2021) that when he studied with Ó Cléirigh in the very early 1970s the latter already knew Richard Montague's name and why his work might be important. In the course of that year in Los Angeles, he saw very

[6] I would like to thank Jeffrey Kallen and James McCloskey for their input to this section.

clearly the link between von Humboldt's work (which he was already enthralled by) and the emerging generative paradigm—for which he had come to UCLA. Because he had earned all of the stamps of approval of a traditional induction into the world of Celtic Studies and Indo-European, Ó Cléirigh was given a free hand in designing the undergraduate curriculum for the new BA program and what he did was to design it so that the first year was devoted to American structuralism (Pike, Hockett, Bloomfield, Sapir, and so on) and to Indo-European historical linguistics, while the second year was devoted to generative grammar (syntax and phonology) and more advanced historical linguistics.

Thanks to the efforts initiated by Ó Cléirigh, in due course, Ireland became, while not one of the major centers of generative research in Europe, at least a place where, at several universities, one could study the approach under some leading generative grammarians.

The Netherlands.[7] Another generative success story is the Netherlands. As one summary article put it: 'Every university [in the Netherlands] has generative research today. The most important locales are Groningen, Utrecht, and Tilburg'[8] (Haider, Prinzhorn, & van Riemsdijk 1987).

The first review of *Syntactic Structures* appeared in the Netherlands even before the review by Robert B. Lees in *Language*. As noted in Chapter 4, fn. 2, in July of that year a notice of the book written by Henk Schultink appeared (see Noordegraff 2001; Hamans 2014). Schultink had worked in the framework of glossematics in Copenhagen. After returning to the Netherlands, he became a fervent generative grammarian, recommending the approach to many of his colleagues. Another early Dutch review of *Syntactic Structures* described it as an 'epoch-making little book' (van Holk 1962: 216), though it was full of specific criticisms.

As we saw in Chapter 2, § 3.4, the European attack on Chomsky was led by two Dutch linguists associated with the journal *Lingua*, Anton Reichling and E. M. Uhlenbeck. But again, as in the United Kingdom, resistance to TGG from the older linguists did not prevent the younger from adopting the theory. Indeed, according to Everaert & Reuland (2011), the opposition to TGG by Reichling and Uhlenbeck only served to draw attention to the new theory.

The first generative dissertation in the Netherlands was written in 1966 by Albert Kraak and which was the focus of an intergenerational source of conflict:[9]

[7] I would like to thank Henk van Riemsdijk and Pieter Seuren for their input to this section.
[8] In the original German: 'Zur Zeit gibt es an jeder Universität generative Forschung. Schwerpunkte gibt es in Groningen, Utrecht und Tilburg.'
[9] Kraak had 'the bad luck that [Edward] Klima had independently developed similar ideas, so that he could only apply Klima's ideas to Dutch data rather than contribute to the development of generative theory. In this respect, Seuren's dissertation of 1968 [Seuren 1969] had the same problem as Kraak; he developed independently a number of ideas which were also being developed at MIT by George Lakoff and John Robert Ross' (Verkuyl 1990: 7).

The events surrounding Kraak's defense highly contributed to the politicization of this clash of paradigms. Its subject was a generative analysis of negative sentences. The intended thesis supervisor was the Professor of Dutch Linguistics ([Wytze] Hellinga), but he declared himself unwilling to continue the supervision. This responsibility was then taken over by the philosopher J. F. Staal, who held one of the philosophy chairs in Amsterdam. Staal was well acquainted with Chomsky's work, and convinced of its importance (e.g. Staal 1962).

(Everaert & Reuland 2011: 2)

Everaert and Reuland go on to note, however, the situation began to change quite profoundly, with greater and greater acceptance of generative grammar (see below for an explanation of this circumstance).

Interestingly, Pieter Seuren had played a crucial role in the development of TGG in the Netherlands before he departed for the UK. As early as 1958 there was group led by Seuren and Rudolf de Rijk that was studying *Syntactic Structures* (Hamans 2015). Seuren recalls:

I had set up an unofficial working party for the study of TGG on March 1st, 1958, the day after I took my MA-exam, by ringing up my good friend Rudolf de Rijk, who at the time studied foundations of mathematics with Evert Beth together with linguistics, and who later became a very well-known specialist in Basque, and my friend and colleague [Albert] Remmert Kraak. Our little group was quickly extended with Wim Klooster and Henk Verkuyl and, as from 1962, with tens of others, among whom Jan Koster, Henk van Riemsdijk and practically all the other Dutch generativists of that generation. In the early 1960s, we were about forty people, and our official head was Frits Staal, who had become a philosophy professor at Amsterdam University in 1962 and had immediately given our still unofficial group official university status. This group was the origin of the entire contingent of present-day Dutch generativists. The TGG we studied was, of course, still of the 'orthodox' kind, as generative semantics had not come about yet. I myself became a 'generative semanticist' after an intensive study of Katz & Postal's 1964 *Integrated Theory of Linguistic Descriptions*, which we read and discussed in the working party.

(p. c., July 13, 2018)

1975 was a crucial year for the development of generative grammar in the Netherlands (van Riemsdijk 1987: 482–483). In that year two foreign linguists were hired to complement the native Dutch scholars who were developing Dutch generativism on their own: Ivonne Bordelois at the University of Utrecht and Marina Nespor at the University of Amsterdam. Also that year appeared two important works: Jan Koster's article on Dutch as an SOV language (Koster 1975) and Arnold Evers's dissertation on verb raising in Dutch and German (Evers 1975). A year later, Henk van Riemsdijk, Jean-Yves Pollock (from Paris), and others organized a conference called 'Green Ideas Blown Up'. The success of this meeting led directly to the founding of GLOW (see § 6.2).

According to van Riemsdijk, there were several reasons for the success of TGG in the Netherlands:

> First, opposition to generative grammar was relatively minimal in Holland be-
> cause the protagonists of the 'old guard' were not close, each pursuing his own
> 'theory'. [P. C.] Paardekooper was a true syntactician, his grammar of Dutch,
> though in a very idiosyncratic pseudoformalism, contains lots of important in-
> sights. Reichling was more a philosopher and semanticist than anything else.
> Uhlenbeck was mostly into exotic languages, in particular Javanese. [P. A.] Ver-
> burg was a bit like Reichling but also on his own, and [Albert W.] De Groot was
> largely a structuralist grammarian. They were not so much fighting as ignoring
> each other. There was no Dutch Linguistic Society to speak of, let alone an attempt
> at creating a 'school' as opposed to the Prague, Copenhagen and Paris Circles.
>
> Second, The Dutch intelligentsia, at that time, tended to be quite liberal. [...]
> Most typically, Simon Dik was Reichling's star student and naturally became his
> successor at an early age. When, in 1970, I came to Holland from Paris, he was
> happy to have me in his department, become his PhD student, give me a job, etc.
> All this in spite of the fact that he was an anti-generativist while he knew full well
> that I was a Chomskyan. [Later] Simon Dik did want to get rid of me. But the way
> he did it was to support me very strongly in getting a full professorship, which
> was successful in 1981.
>
> (p. c., February 20, 2018)

Van Riemsdijk in a 1990 paper added a few more reasons: The student upheavals of the 1960s led to more democracy, Holland's small size has made it international, open to new ideas, and the country has a long tradition of scientific publishing (van Riemsdijk 1990).

Henk Verkuyl gives a complementary explanation for the success of generative grammar in the Netherlands:

> There are countries in which generative grammar came, saw and lost, as in France,
> Spain, and some other European countries. My main thesis is that generative
> grammar has been successful in the Netherlands due to a conjunction of three
> factors: (a) there was an internationally recognized strong philosophical-logical
> tradition which helped it through its first stage; (b) the linguistic establishment of
> the fifties and sixties was rather weak and quite incoherently organized into local
> schools; (c) at the peak of the generative success the universities needed a lot of
> people so that a lot of places could be filled by young generativists.
>
> (Verkuyl 1990: 2–3)

Belgium.[10] Generative grammar has had an active presence in Belgium since the 1960s, though it has never dominated linguistic theorizing as it has in the Netherlands. Indeed, cognitive and functional linguistics have long had a stronger presence in Belgium than generative grammar. The most important figure in bringing TGG to Belgium was Wim de Geest; Yvan Putseys and René Dirven were also quite influential (the latter later became an important figure in cognitive linguistics). Other linguists who played a role in the early days were were Dries de Bleecker of the University of Leuven, Roger van de Velde of the University of Gent, André Hantson of the Facultés Universitaires Notre Dame de la Paix, and Liliane Tasmowski-De Ryck of the University of Antwerp (p.c. Wim de Geest, via Dany Jaspers, January 13, 2021).

According to Jaspers,

> In the early sixties, de Geest spent a month in Cambridge for a summer course at Selwyn College, in the same group as Barbara Lewandowska [a Polish linguist — (FJN)]. Wim went there to take English language courses, but also learned about generative grammar and realized that it represented a novel approach *compared* to the traditional, historical-comparative and structuralist paradigms. De Geest concluded that he wanted to write a dissertation in generative grammar and realized that the only option was to seek contact in the Netherlands, where TGG had already found fertile ground somewhat earlier. The Dutch linguist Remmert Kraak, who had studied for a year at MIT and returned to Amsterdam, became Wim's supervisor.
>
> (p. c., Dany Jaspers, January 13, 2021)

In fact, Dutch linguists have long played an important role in bolstering the position of generative grammar in Belgium: Henk van Riemsdijk, Jan Koster, Pieter Seuren, and Teun Hoekstra stand out as worthy of mention.

De Geest defended his Nijmegen dissertation in 1972, with a work on bare infinitival complements entitled *Complementaire constructies bij verba sentiendi in het Nederlands*. The preface to this work sketches the history of TGG in Belgium up to that point, stressing the importance of the courses offered by Kraak between 1965 and 1967 at the *Postuniversitair Centrum* in Hasselt in the province of Limburg. Those courses were set up by the then governor of Limburg, Louis Roppe, who was doing what he could to make the expansion of the university system of those days include a full university in Hasselt. The governor came in contact with Flip Droste, a Dutch-born linguist whose PhD was from Nijmegen in 1956, but who moved to Leuven, Belgium in 1968 and was instrumental in early TGG in that country. De Geest also published a paper on the state of the art of TGG in Belgium (De Geest 1967). Thanks to funding in 1967 and 1968 from the Dutch

---

[10] I would like to thank Dany Jaspers for his input to this section.

Ministry of Education and Science (Ministerie van Onderwijs en Wetenschappen), De Geest could regularly visit the Instituut voor Neerlandistiek at the University of Amsterdam, where his closest contact (and host during his stays in the Netherlands), especially during the time his supervisor Kraak was at MIT, was Wim Klooster.

In 1972 de Geest became a professor of Dutch and General Linguistics at Universitaire Faculteiten Sint-Aloysius (UFSAL) in Brussels, and together with his colleague Yvan Putseys, a professor of English Linguistics there, published and organized seminars in generative grammar at UFSAL starting in the 1980s. The first one, in April 1982, was a symposium organized by Annie Zaenen, a Belgian based in the United States, on 'Non-Transformational Generative Grammar'. Later seminars featured talks by Joseph Aoun, Diana Archangeli, Carmen Dobrovie-Sorin, and many other generative grammarians.

Generative phonology was well established in Belgium before generative syntax (Haider, Prinzhorn, & van Riemsdijk 1987: 474). For example Didier Goyvaerts's co-edited book on *The Sound Pattern of English* (Goyvaerts & Pullum 1975) was very important, as was Paul Verluyten's dissertation on French prosody (Verluyten 1982). As far as more recent work in syntax is concerned, in addition to Dany Jaspers, the following syntacticians have international reputations in that subfield: Liliane Haegeman (at Ghent University), Johan Rooryck (at Leiden University), and Guido Vanden Wyngaerd (at the Center for Research in Syntax, Semantics, and Phonology, in Brussels). Jaspers served as president of GLOW in 2013–2014, when he directed the 2014 meeting in Brussels.

Luxembourg. There was no generative linguistics carried out in Luxembourg during the 1960s and 1970s for the simple reason that there was no university in the country at that time. People generally studied in France, Germany, or Belgium. Today the focus of linguists in Luxembourg appears to be bilingualism, language planning, and related areas, rather than grammatical theory.

France.[11] The situation in France could not be more different from that in the UK and the Netherlands. After a promising start, generative grammar went into retreat in France.

Today there are scattered centres of generative grammar (mostly in Paris[12]), but the theory as a whole cannot be said to be widely influential or being developed with reference to French or any regional languages or dialects.

According to Camiel Hamans, 'the first French linguist who occupied himself with Chomsky's work was [...] Maurice Gross' (Hamans 2015: 2). His interest dates from at least 1961, when on a UNESCO grant to Harvard, he came in contact with

---

[11] I would like to thank Joseph Emonds and Pierre Pica for their input to this section.

[12] Haider, Prinzhorn, & van Riemsdijk (1987: 476) wrote that Paris is the European city with the greatest number of generative grammarians. I doubt that such is true today. Utrecht, Barcelona, Potsdam (Berlin), and Tromsø, among others, almost certainly have more.

the mathematician and Chomsky's collaborator Marcel-Paul Schützenberger. Two early French generativists have written:[13]

[As far as Maurice Gross is concerned], it is via the scientific study of automatic translation that he little-by-little established connections with linguists. That led Gross to work one winter [in 1961] at MIT with Chomsky, the famous place and famous person on the East Coast, but practically unknown in Europe. A methodological person, he was also extremely seductive, knowing how to charm people with three well-chosen examples and a smile; it took several years before discovering that his computer scientist self harbored a linguist. He spent another winter [1964] in Philadelphia with Harris. This time he accomplished the metamorphosis that made a 'new style' linguist out of him.

(Chevalier & Encrevé 2006: 259)

Back in France, Gross worked in Schützenberger's CNRS laboratory (the CNRS is the main French scientific research body). He became a professor in 1969 at Université Paris VIII (Vincennes) and later at Université Paris VI (Jussieu) and helped to build a strong linguistic program at both places. He was the teacher of François Dell, who was to establish the study of generative phonology in France. 'It was Gross who directed Dell's attention to *Syntactic Structures* and advised him to go to MIT, where he arrived in 1967, just before the 1968 student revolt in Paris, and where he stayed to write his PhD under Halle's supervision' (Hamans 2015: 3). Dell's 1970 PhD thesis was entitled *Les règles phonologiques tardives et la morphologie derivationalle du français*. A few years later he published the first introduction to generative phonology in French (Dell 1973).

Another important figure in the early days of generative grammar in France is the Belgian Nicolas Ruwet. Hamans (2015) describes his adoption of generative grammar as 'a conversion tale' (p. 4). To illustrate, in 1963, Ruwet attended a seminar directed by the psychoanalyst Jacques Lacan:

While on a trip together with Lacan's daughter and other friends in a house that Lacan had rented in Saint-Tropez, Ruwet discovered Chomsky entirely by accident. 'I was alone in the room that Lacan used as a study and there was a little blue book, published by Mouton, lying on his desk. It was Chomsky's *Syntactic*

---

[13] In the original French: '[À propos de Maurice Gross], c'est par la traduction automatique à la recherche de scientifiques qui s'établit peu à peu le lien avec les linguistes; elle avait conduit Gross à travailler un hiver [en 1961] au MIT avec Chomsky, lieu et personnage célèbres sur la côte est, presque inconnus en Europe. Méthodique, il était lui aussi extrêmement séduisant, sachant charmer avec trois exemples significatifs et un sourire; il mit plusieurs années avant de découvrir que l'informaticien recouvrait en lui un linguiste; un autre passé aux États-Unis [en 1964], chez Harris à Philadelphie, cette fois, accomplit la métamorphose et fit de lui un maître en linguistique *new style*'.

Structures. I ordered it right away at the end of the vacation and found it very interesting but I did not understand a thing. There were still too many pieces missing'.

(Dosse 1997 [1992]: 4)

A year later:[14]

In 1964, a friend lent him a book by Paul Postal that had just appeared, *Constituent Structure: A Study of Contemporary Models of Syntactic Description*. He read this study on the train between Liège and Paris; that's when in his own words he had a 'road to Damascus' experience. By the time of his arrival in Paris, he knew that he would be a generativist.

(Aroui & Zribi-Hertz 2002: 109)

Ruwet's book *Introduction à la grammaire générative* (Ruwet 1966) was instrumental in introducing many French students to TGG. Along with translations of Chomsky's *Syntactic Structures* and *Aspects of the Theory of Syntax*, it was everywhere in the windows of the Latin Quarter bookstores at the start of the seventies.

A third important TGG pioneer in France was Jean-Claude Milner, who had been a student of philosophy, with his ideas shaped by Lacan and Louis Althusser. He spent a year as a Fulbright Visiting Scientist at MIT in 1966–1967, lodging with Roman Jakobson (as did Nicolas Ruwet in the following year) and even contributed articles on phonology to the *QPR* (see Chapter 5, § 5.6.4). Milner later translated Chomsky's *Aspects of the Theory of Syntax* into French. He became Director of the Laboratory of Formal Linguistics at the Université Paris VII (Diderot) and was instrumental in building a generative program there.[15]

Henk van Riemsdijk, who was in France in the late 1960s, helped to attract interest in TGG during his stay there. And work in that theory really took off with the arrival of Richard Kayne from MIT at Vincennes in 1969. Kayne's charisma, articulateness, and strong rapport with Chomsky acted as a lightning rod for attracting a group of young generativists.[16] Lectures given by the MIT-trained Joseph Emonds in 1970 and again in 1976 also played an important role. New faculty and many

---

[14] In the original French: 'En 1964, un ami lui prête un livre de P. Postal, qui vient de paraître: *Constituent Structure. A study of Contemporary Models of Syntactic Description*. Il lit cet essai dans le train Liège-Paris; et c'est alors, selon ses propres termes, 'le chemin de Damas': en arrivant à Paris, il sait qu'il sera générativiste.'

[15] Milner, taking the original statement of purpose of *Linguistic Inquiry* at its word, managed to publish, over objections, that journal's only article in French (Milner 1978).

[16] Chomsky and other American generativists have always credited Kayne for being the driving force in the development of TGG in France (see Barsky 2007: 62). However, Hamans (2015) feels that Chomsky exaggerates Kayne's importance. I would say that the first wave of French generativism had little to do with Kayne, but by the mid 1970s Kayne was the center of what many called the Chomskyan 'cult' of followers who fought against the anti-Chomsky backlash.

students (French and international) migrated in France in the 1970s (mostly to several Parisian universities). Some of the most important publications in French generative syntax date from that period. French generative grammar was in its heyday in the late 1970s, where important young contributors were Alain Rouveret, Jean-Roger Vergnaud, Jean-Yves Pollock, Mitsou Ronat, and the American Jacqueline Guéron.

Several factors, however, reversed the generativist gains in France, starting in the late 1970s and early 1980s. Perhaps the most damaging were the (separate) 'defections' of Gross, Milner, and Ruwet. Gross, as a student of Zellig Harris, as well as of Chomsky, was never comfortable with the increasingly abstract direction that generative syntax took in the 1960s. He severed all ties with Chomsky and his approach in the late 1970s, publishing an article entitled 'On the failure of generative grammar' (Gross 1979). Milner, like many French intellectuals, was highly influenced by Marxism and French phenomenology, and was never comfortable with the explicitly biological 'language organ' approach of Chomsky's, as it developed in the late 1960s and in the 1970s. Milner explicitly challenged and responded to the GLOW Manifesto, the biologically realist statement drafted by Jan Koster, Henk van Riemsdijk, and Jean-Roger Vergnaud for the first *GLOW Newsletter* in 1978.[17] He pinpointed the following as the key points of the Manifesto:

(A) Linguistic theory must be interpreted in 'realistic' terms; i.e. there is a reality of the language faculty and languages, which linguistic theory aims to express adequately.

(B) The reality of the language faculty and languages has essential psychological substance.

(C) A psychological reality is a specifiable state of a mental organ.

Milner went on to express his skepticism at all three propositions. As Pica & Rooryck (1994) observe (I think correctly), the French, in general, favor 'external' theories, not 'internal' ones. Perhaps for this reason, generative phonology has fared better in France than generative syntax. Before his retirement, the phonologist Dell occupied an important position in the CNRS and a number of other generative phonologists have made their mark in France, some trained internally, like Bernard Laks, and some externally, like G. N. Clements.

Pica & Rooryck (1994) give several other reasons why the early promise of TGG in France was not fulfilled. First, the comprehensive grammar of French, a main goal in the 1970s, was never completed. Second, French publishers, other than *Le Seuil*, have always been reluctant to publish in generative grammar. Third, many French generativists never learned to navigate the waters of the French

---

[17] For the Manifesto, see https://glowlinguistics.org/about/history/manifesto/, and for Milner's reply, see https://glowlinguistics.org/milners-reply/.

educational system.[18] And fourth, the existence of a stronger anti-Americanism than in most European countries led to suspicion of an American-originated theory. As example of the growing difficulty faced by French generativists, in the late 1970s Gilles Fauconnier and Pierre Encrevé attempted to create a new linguistic society in Paris that would be welcoming to generative grammarians. Their efforts were in vain (Chevalier & Encrevé 2006: 53).

In a personal communication (March 1, 2018) Pierre Pica elaborated on the remarks that he and Rooryck had made in print over a decade earlier:

> In my opinion, the French situation is due to many factors, the most important of which are the following two: The influence of Marxism was strong in France and the idea that language could be reduced to a biological faculty was totally misunderstood (say, by Jean-Claude Milner). Secondly, European structuralism was also strong, partly because of its association with Marxism through the dialectic. The problem was that at least in France most people interpreted *Syntactic Structures* as a prelude to [mathematically-oriented] work by Maurice Gross and by Chomsky and Schützenberger. When they realized it was going in another direction, they did not like it at all. Nicolas Ruwet's case is a variant of the same thing. A cultivated man as he was, he was not very interested by the subtleties of the linguistic data (see his book *Syntax and Human Experience* [Ruwet 1991]).

> There is a third factor that no one speaks about: the rigidity and old-fashioned style of French institutions, where students did not have scholarships, office hours and the like. It was just impossible for a normal student to work in these conditions, so generative grammar could only develop in more sophisticated circles like an École Normale or an École Polytechnique. The reason I mention all this, is that although the situation has changed, the main factors are still there. Formal semantics is accepted because it is formal (not associated to the mentalist issue), but very few people do real syntax. When they do syntax, they are really doing psycholinguistics. A huge part of linguistics is absorbed by neuroscience (again away from the mentalist vs. nonmentalist issue). Note that France has a huge sector of linguistics dedicated to the study of languages across the planet, most of it mainly descriptive/functional linguistics. This sector remains opposed to more theoretical studies.

Switzerland.[19] As far as I know, there was no generative grammar in Switzerland until the early 1970s. Its beginnings in Switzerland are linked to the creation of

---

[18] Joseph Emonds, however, feels that Pica and Rooryck exaggerate here, writing 'Milner and Gross did very well. Ruwet was Belgian. Encrevé ended up in the Ministry. The Kayne cult, which includes Pica, Vergnaud (resident in the US), and Guéron (an American) never learned' (p. c., March 7, 2021).

[19] I would like to thank Jacques Moeschler for his input to this section.

a chair in general linguistics at the University of Neuchâtel in 1971. While other chairs in general linguistics were created at the end of the 1960s in French-speaking Switzerland (at Lausanne and Geneva), they were occupied by linguists trained by André Martinet (in functional linguistics). Around that time, the appointment of a lecturer at the University of Neuchâtel of a young linguist trained there, Eddy Roulet, made it possible to introduce generative grammar at that institution, with courses ranging from phonology to syntax to semantics. Interestingly, Roulet was self-taught in generative grammar, which he learned by reading the microfilms of the manuscript of Chomsky's *LSLT* (Jacques Moeschler, p. c., January 5, 2012). The various translations of Chomsky's works into French (see above) enabled students in French-speaking Switzerland to read early work in generative grammar. Roulet's teaching made it possible to train four doctoral students in ten years, all of whom obtained teaching positions in the universities of French-speaking Switzerland: Anne-Claude Berthoud (in 1983, Lausanne), Christian Rubattel (in 1984, Neuchâtel), Éric Wehrli & Jacques Moeschler (in 1987 and in 1997, Geneva). In addition, the creation of a chair of French linguistics in 1977 at the University of Geneva, occupied by Roulet, introduced the teaching of generative grammar of French.

It was only 1983, with the creation of a chair in English linguistics at the University of Geneva, that generative grammar really took root in Switzerland. That year Liliane Haegeman was appointed to a professorial position, followed a year later by Luigi Rizzi and Adriana Belletti in general and Italian linguistics. However, syntactic theory never developed in other Swiss universities, due to the tradition that departments (and their chairs) be oriented to older-style studies of French and German. While there are generative grammarians in German-speaking Switzerland, those linguists trained in modern frameworks are much more likely to work in typology, functional linguistics, and cognitive linguistics than in generative grammar.

Germany.[20] Germany was divided until 1989 and so was the reception of TGG. Nowhere in Germany was there a strong structuralist tradition. That fact both impeded and facilitated TGG in Germany. 'Impeded' since it was not taken for granted that there was a structuralist core to grammar. 'Facilitated' since there was no dominant structuralist approach to oppose TGG. Indeed, according to Vater (1971: 7), the first German structuralist publication did not appear until well after the war, namely Glinz (1952).

TGG had more initial success in the East than in the West. Wolfgang Steinitz and Manfred Bierwisch were instrumental in the Arbeitsgruppe Strukturelle Grammatik in East Berlin, where much work in TGG took place in the 1960s. Steinitz

---

[20] I would like to thank Manfred Bierwisch and Dieter Wunderlich for their input to this section. For more detail on many of the topics treated here, see Everaert & Reuland (2011, § 2.4), and Hamans (2015).

was a Finno-Ugric specialist who was fired from his position at Friedrich Wilhelm University in Berlin in 1933 on account of his being a Jewish communist. He took refuge in the Soviet Union at that time, lived in Sweden between 1938 and 1946, and returned to Berlin that year to take a position at the Humboldt University in East Berlin, the renamed Friedrich Wilhelm University. Bierwisch had studied at the Karl Marx University in Leipzig in the early 1950s, but was arrested in 1952 for illegal possession of the West German magazine *Der Monat*. He served ten months of an eighteen month sentence and, surprisingly, was able to land a job in 1956 at the German Academy of Sciences.

At the invitation of Steinitz and Bierwisch, American generativists gave lectures in East Berlin in 1961 and at Magdeburg in 1964. The following is Manfred Bierwisch's personal recollection of events:

> The Arbeitsgruppe Grammatik at the East Berlin Academy of Sciences, which I had joined in 1958, was one of the first places in East and West Germany where the importance of *Syntactic Structures* was recognized right away. I still remember being impressed by the booklet (and by Bob Lees' programmatic review of it in *Language* [Lees 1957]) in the late fifties. The ASG (= Arbeitsgruppe Strukturelle Grammatik, as it was called later on, indicating its largely quite suspect structuralist orientation) had been initiated by Wolfgang Steinitz in the mid-fifties and the connection between Jakobson and Steinitz, who used to be the vice-president of the Academy, was sort of situational background, which originated in pre-war times and had nothing to do with generative grammar. As a matter of fact, I wrote a dissertation that was very much influenced by Jakobson and Hjelmslev. The fascination with TGG came only with *Syntactic Structures* and Lees' *Grammar of English Nominalizations* [Lees 1960c]. Contact by mail with Chomsky brought us extensive comments on our first (still very tentative) attempts in the new framework.
>
> Second, in 1961, right after the Berlin Wall, we had a small conference in East Berlin, which Bob Lees attended (and in fact dominated), bringing the top news from MIT. This was instrumental for my *Grammatik des deutschen Verbs* [Bierwisch 1963], which was, I believe, the first attempt to apply principles of TGG to German (simultaneously with an early study of Emmon Bach in *Language* [Bach 1962]). These attempts, by the way, established the view of German as a verb-final language. Connections with Hungarian colleagues (Kiefer, Szépe) were helpful in further developments, which led to the dominating role of TGG at the second symposium 'Zeichen und System der Sprache' in Magdeburg (which, by the way, had a predecessor 1959 in Erfurt, which was still completely pre-generative, where Jakobson, however, at least mentioned Chomsky). In 1962 we started the series *Studia Grammatica*, which was intended as a forum for TGG.

Third, the conference in Magdeburg 1964 was attended a.o. by Ed Klima, Haj Ross, Bruce Fraser, and I believe Paul Kiparsky. Chomsky, who was strongly invited to give a key address, did not participate, but had authorized Bruce Fraser to present central chapters from *Aspects of the Theory of Syntax*, which was by then in preparation. In a way, Magdeburg was the initial occasion for the 'standard theory' to start its successful career in Germany.

Fourth, after a couple of years of successful work in Generative Grammar in various place, especially the linguistics department at the University of Leipzig, and of course at the ASG, a fairly strange ideological campaign against GG in general and Chomsky's 'biologism' in particular was launched by the Communist Party in the GDR in 1968, which caused a lot of trouble, and did almost, but not quite, end research in TGG at the East German Academy. But that was long after *Syntactic Structures* and *Aspects*, a German translation of which, produced in the ASG, had appeared simultaneously with Suhrkamp and the GDR-Academy publishing house.

(p. c., February 17, 2018)

Unfortunately, Steinitz died young and Bierwisch, being at a research institute, was not able to set up a program (Hamans 2015). After the Communist Party's intervention, described by Bierwisch, generative grammar stagnated in the East until reunification.

In West Germany in the late 1960s, TGG was attractive to a group of advanced graduate students (Dieter Wunderlich, p. c., February 15, 2018). Shortly later, they organized yearly meetings called Lingustisches Kolloquium, which attracted students from Denmark and the Netherlands (and more European countries in later years):

This brings us back to the very beginning of the Colloquium in 1966, when the Colloquium started in Hamburg-Harburg as a meeting of students, candidates for a doctor's degree, and young university assistants. They had heard about 'a new way of doing linguistics over there in America and were more and more dissatisfied with the way it was done in Western Germany, where linguistics was essentially a sub-discipline of philology. The new American way called itself 'generative grammar', and it was the aim of the first conveners to make themselves acquainted with what was then called 'modern linguistics' as a whole and generative grammar in particular. This is why the newly born institution bore the name 'Linguistisches Kolloquium über generative Grammatik' [until 1970].

(Kürschner 2009)

Despite this promising start, in West Germany and later in Germany as a whole, TGG has never had more than a small foothold. According to Haider, Prinzhorn, & van Riemsdijk (1987: 474), part of the problem is that quite a few German syntacticians were attracted to the model of generative semantics (see Newmeyer 1986b: chapter 4) in the late 1960s and early 1970s. After the collapse of this model, the linguists involved were drawn to work in semantics and pragmatics, as opposed to syntax.

Everaert & Reuland (2011) attribute the slow progress of generative grammar in part to the nature of the German university system:

> What one can observe at the end of the sixties is a situation in Germany that is comparable in volume to the situation in the Netherlands, but, crucially, not in the proportion of the total volume of linguistic research. Just like in the Netherlands, the end of the sixties resulted in a confrontation between the younger generation and the established faculty (Boeder et al. 1998). This revolt included a revolt against the traditional philological conception of linguistics, in some universities. However, unlike in the Netherlands, the students' revolt of the sixties did not deeply affect the power structure in the German universities. As it is often remarked, in the Netherlands the professors kept their robes, but lost their power, in Germany it was the other way round. Another difference resides in the requirements for an academic career. The Dutch system has the doctorate as the main precondition. The German system has two degrees, the doctorate and the *Habilitation*. This entails that it takes longer before the qualifications for a senior faculty position are met. It is our impression that the two factors together contributed to a relative slow-down in development.
>
> (Everaert & Reuland 2011: 7)

In the course of his assessment of the first twenty years of GLOW, Henk van Riemsdijk wrote:

> Take a country like Germany. It is not a poor country, they've got a lot of universities. But if you want to pinpoint the centers of generative grammar, depending on your generosity, you end up with maybe half a dozen. [...] But, take Germany again, it is people in discourse analysis and pragmatics and so on that are in power.
>
> (van Riemsdijk 1998: 18)

Van Riemsdijk could have also mentioned formal semantics, which has many practitioners in Germany. There are actually quite a few German generativists, but they tend to be scattered around the country.

Austria.[21] In Austria, generative grammar got off the ground in 1973, when Wolfgang Dressler at the University of Vienna organized a 'Generative Woche' at the beginning of the winter semester 1973–1974. Dressler had been an instructor at UCLA in 1970 and a visiting professor at Ohio State University in 1971–1972.

---

[21] I would like to thank Hubert Haider for his input to this section.

At the Woche, he lectured on generative phonology, Thomas Perry on generative semantics, and Lyle Jenkins on generative syntax. Dressler had hired Jenkins
and Perry as assistant professors at that time in the newly founded Department
of General Linguistics. Hubert Haider, who was to become the leading generative
syntactician in Austria, was one of the first students. Gaberell Drachman was another important figure. His PhD was from the University of Chicago and he too
taught at Ohio State in the early 1970s. He was hired at the University of Salzburg
in 1973, where he built a generative-oriented program. Drachman was at first a
phonologist and then a syntactician working primarily on Greek (he had lived in
Greece between 1955 and 1962; see § 6.3.4).

In 1974 the yearly forum for generative grammar, Generative Grammatik des
Südens (GGS), was organized by the German Marga Reis and her Czech assistant Jindrich Toman, who is now a professor at the University of Michigan. GGS
became the main forum for generativists in southern Germany and Austria. It
usually convenes once per semester in one of the southern universities of the ger-
manosphere (whence 'des Südens'), with generativists taking part who are mainly
from Konstanz, Passau, Regensburg, Tübingen, and Vienna. GGS still exists as an
annual conference but has lost its original round-table character since turning into
a mid-size conference. In 1979 the LSA-directed Linguistic Institute was held at
Salzburg, marking the first time that an Institute was held outside of the United
States.

6.3.2 Nordic Europe

One of the first public appearances of generative grammar in the Nordic countries might have been at the First International Conference of Nordic and General
Linguistics, organized by Hreinn Benediktsson, and which took place in Reyk-
javik in 1969. This conference was held every three years. 'The development of
generative grammar is reflected in the later meetings and proceedings of these conferences, although generativists have sometimes either boycotted the conference
or held separate parallel sections and produced a separate publication' (Hovdhaugen et al. 2000: 397).[22] However, the most important vehicle for introducing TGG
into mainland Scandinavia were the three Scandinavian Summer Schools in 1969,
1970, and 1971, the first two held in Stockholm and the third near Copenhagen.
About thirty participated in the two intensive weeks of each school, mostly students, but also some established linguists. There were three teachers each year,
one in phonology, one in syntax, and one in semantics: In 1969 there was Paul

---

[22] It is a mystery to me why generativists would have boycotted the conference, given that they seem
to have been welcomed as participants.

Kiparsky, John R. Ross, and James McCawley; in 1970 John R. Ross (now lecturing in phonology, in particular English stress), David Perlmutter and Paul Postal; and in 1971 Stephen Anderson, Dave Perlmutter (again) and Charles Fillmore. Hans Basbøll remembers these summer schools

> as quite extraordinary, and they had a huge influence on Scandinavian linguistics. They also resulted in important Scandinavian networks, since many of the participants came to occupy key professorships (e.g. in Norway, Thorstein Fretheim; in Sweden, Per Linell, Östen Dahl, and Jens Allwood; in Finland, Fred Karlsson and Auli Hakulinen (Kalevi Wiik was already a professor); and in Denmark, Jørgen Rischel, Torben Vestergaard, and myself.[23]

(p. c., January 13, 2021)

'These summer schools were influential for two reasons. First, they offered top-level international teaching and ample opportunity to talk to the teachers. Secondly, they brought together young Nordic linguists, many of whom are now professors in the various Nordic countries. In a real sense, an influential 'invisible college' (cf. Solla Price 1963) was born in those days, i.e. a network of people knowing each other well and in positions to affect future development' (Hovdhaugen et al. 2000: 307).

Many of the participants in these summer schools were active in creating new activities for the younger generations of Scandinavian linguists, including Scandinavian Conferences of Linguistics (organized by Östen Dahl in 1974), The Nordic Association of Linguists (founded in 1976), and the *Nordic Journal of Linguistics* (founded in 1978). These activities, which are still ongoing, have not been restricted to TGG, even though the central founding members were well acquainted with that approach. Many went on to develop their scientific careers within other frameworks, in particular functional or cognitive ones.

According to Hovdhaugen et al., 2000 saw what might have been the first generative-oriented dissertations in the Nordic countries. That by Ulf Teleman (1969) was a generative description of definite and indefinite modifiers in Swedish, and that by Östen Dahl (1969) argued that the so-called syntactic standard theory

---

[23] Stephen Anderson recalls that Frans Gregersen was also one of the auditors (p. c., April 18, 2021). Anderson continues:

> Following that summer school, I spent most of 1972-3 in Copenhagen, with the aid of a Harvard sabbatical and an ACLS grant, plus a lot of help from Eli Fischer-Jørgensen. In the fall, I gave a series of lectures on phonology at the Copenhagen Institut for Lingvistik. In the spring, I was contacted by Östen Dahl (I think) in Göteborg. They had obtained funding for Einar Haugen to visit, but Einar was unable to take it up, for health reasons. I was asked to fill in for him (six weeks at a Full Professor's salary), and so gave a series of lectures on phonology there. Besides Östen, I also came to know Lars-Gunnar Andersson, and discussed with him where he might go in the US to get more training (he went to UMass, I think).

had to be enriched with a layer of topic-comment structure. Dahl united Prague School inspiration with generative syntax, largely using examples drawn from Russian.

The remainder of this section discusses early generative grammar in Denmark, Sweden, Norway, Finland, and Iceland.

Denmark.[24] Denmark is an example of a country where a preexisting structuralist tradition acted as an impediment to the development of TGG. The theory of Louis Hjelmslev was a formal implementation of basic Saussurean constructs and which attracted quite a bit of interest around the world, including in the United States (see, for example, Haugen 1951). This theory, glossematics, which Hjelmslev developed along with Hans Uldall, dominated Danish linguistics for decades (see Hjelmslev 1961 [1953]). At the same time, Denmark was one of the relatively few places in the 1950s with active ongoing work in syntax. Paul Diderichsen proposed a syntactic model, most appropriate for languages like Danish, with fixed word order that made use of ordered slots into which different sentence constituents could be inserted. This work along with that of Hjelmslev and Uldall, combined to make the acceptance of TGG a bit problematic. It has been noted that 'Danish linguists already had a formal linguistic theory. As pointed out by Herslund (1996), the Danes probably did not feel the need for another theory, and especially not a theory of syntax, since they also had Diderichsen's theory of syntactic fields. There were also those who were simply tired of the intense theoretical discussions of glossematic theory, and as a consequence were generally skeptical towards all-encompassing linguistic theories, especially those with a formalistic flavor' (Hovdhaugen et al. 2000: 314). Niels Davidsen-Nielsen, who wrote the first Danish generative-oriented paper in 1968 (Davidsen-Nielsen 1968), recalls:

> As a whole there was great disagreement between linguists in Denmark about the new type of grammar from America. One important reason for that was undoubtedly that many of them continued clinging on to Glossematics and being loyal to Louis Hjelmslev.
>
> (p. c., February 15, 2018)

Hans Basbøll concurs, writing:

> I think the Chomskyan revolution (nightmare according to Martinet) was less strong in Denmark than in the other Scandinavian countries, due to the strong position of Glossematics in [the Copenhagen Linguistic Circle (CLC)] and Denmark more generally, at the time. I remember Henning Spang-Hanssen (well known for works within and around Glossematics, Professor of Mathematical and Applied Linguistics), gave a talk in CLC on 'Quid novi ex Chomsky?'. He discussed *Syntactic Structures* in his lectures in the sixties, I recall. I remember

---

[24] I would like to thank Niels Davidsen-Nielsen and Hans Basbøll for their input to this section.

there were a number of young linguists in the sixties who were interested in TG, but typically, they knew structural linguistics well. In Sweden, there was not a strong structuralist tradition—despite Malmberg—but mainly a more traditional philological tradition.

(p. c., February 15, 2018)

Nevertheless, a number of Danes in the 1970s and 1980s contributed to generative grammar, and in particular to generative phonology. The 1974 dissertation on West Greenlandic phonology by Jørgen Rischel (Rischel 1974), which was to a large extent generative, was one of the first studies in that framework on a polysynthetic language. Hans Basbøll took on syllabication in Danish, French, and Italian, as well as the status of the Danish stød (Basbøll 1985). Michael Herslund has noted that this work has earned Basbøll an international reputation (Herslund 1996). However, both Rischel and Basbøll came to distance themselves from mainstream generative phonology to a certain degree.

Sweden.[25] Generative grammar has had a presence in Sweden since the 1960s, though an earlier homegrown structuralist tradition dominated by Bertil Malmberg (see Malmberg 1963) combined with a certain amount of resistance from influential Swedish linguists, such as Björn Collinder (see Collinder 1970), prevented TGG from dominating the linguistics scene. The theory came to Sweden via the University of Gothenburg. Alvar Ellegård, who was professor of English there, presented Chomsky's ideas in the biggest Swedish daily newspaper, *Dagens Nyheter,* in 1965 or 1966. He also started to teach the generative syntax of English and around 1967 and invited Paul Kiparsky to teach generative phonology and some syntax at Gothenburg. The next year James McCawley was invited and taught syntax and generative semantics. Around that time Ellegård was able to initiate 'general linguistics' as a subsection of the English department, where some generative work was initiated. In the Slavic department of the same university, Östen Dahl adopted Chomskyan linguistics (see above). Ellegård then asked Dahl to start up a linguistics program in Gothenburg. At some point in the early 1970s, linguistics became its own department.

Between around 1969 and 1972, generative semantics was the most practiced approach in Gothenburg. That changed to Montague grammar around 1972 or 1973. Jens Allwood notes (p. c., February 16, 2021) that Dahl, Lars-Gunnar Andersson and himself attended the LSA summer institute at SUNY-Buffalo in 1971 and became acquainted with the extensive breadth of linguistics (e.g. sociolinguistics, psycholinguistics, neurolinguistics, anthropological linguistics, semantics, speech act theory, child language, and more). Their acquaintance with these areas led to establishing all these as special courses in the linguistics departments that had

---

[25] I would like to thank Jens Allwood, Östen Dahl, and Elisabet Engdahl for their input to this section.

been started in Lund, Stockholm, and Umeå around 1970. Uppsala followed a little later, starting with phonetics. Peter af Trampe at Stockholm and Åke Viberg
at Uppsala published the first Swedish introduction to transformational grammar
in 1972 (Trampe & Viberg 1972). There were also summer schools in Sweden in
1969–1970, mainly teaching phonology and syntax. John R. Ross, Paul Postal, and
(Allwood thinks) Ferenc Kiefer taught at these summer schools and many of the
people who later became faculty of the new linguistics departments in Sweden
met there, including Per Linell, Jan Anward, Östen Dahl, Stig Eliasson (a Harvard
PhD), Sven Öhman, Bengt Sigurd, Eva Ejerhed, Lars-Gunnar Andersson, and Jens
Allwood. As in Denmark, Swedish linguists contributed to generative phonology.
An 'important Nordic contribution to phonology which had an impact on the
development of phonological theory was Per Linell's critical analysis of generative phonology (Linell 1974, 1979), which was published in a recognized series by
a leading international publishing house. Linell criticized the abstractness of the
underlying forms of orthodox generative phonology and suggested more concrete
representations and less complex rule systems. Stig Eliasson made numerous contributions to the study of phonology in various languages, including Swedish. An
early contribution to the field was Bengt Sigurd's work from 1966 which examined
the relations between historical changes in Old Norse and ordered phonological
rules. Claes-Christian Elert also applied generative phonology in his descriptions
of Swedish' (Hovdhaugen et al. 2000: 317). Ferenc Kiefer's *Swedish Morphology*
(Kiefer 1970) was one of the first publications to argue for a separate morphological component in generative grammar, while Dahl published on indefinites (Dahl
1970) and generics (Dahl 1975) in international publications.

In later years, the major work in Chomskyan linguistics was to take place departments of Swedish and Nordic languages in Sweden, most notably in Lund under
Christer Platzack. Platzack was the first generative syntactician to be appointed to
a professorship in Scandinavian languages.

Norway.[26] Norway, with no home-grown structuralist tradition, has come
to rival the UK and the Netherlands in the amount of generativist research
carried out.

> In Norway, the new trends in linguistics from MIT were received with great in-
> terest by most linguists. In the early 1960s, both Knut Bergsland and Carl Hj.
> Borgstrøm gave courses and seminars in transformational grammar, and Jacob
> Mey, who was lecturer of general linguistics in Oslo 1961-1968, did much to
> introduce the new perspectives in linguistics to both students and established
> linguists. Generative grammar was also greeted with interest in most of the
> other linguistics departments, but interest was limited in the departments of
> Scandinavian languages in Norway.
>
> (Hovdhaugen et al. 2000: 314)

---

[26] I would like to thank Knut Tarald Taraldsen for his input to this section.

Tarald Taraldsen confirms the assertion in the final sentence, informing me that 'Nordic departments in Norway maintained a fairly hostile attitude to generative linguistics, just as they had remained skeptical of structuralism' (p. c., March 10, 2021).

The introduction to TGG by the Norwegian linguist Even Hovdhaugen (Hovdhaugen 1969) was the first published in a Nordic country and one of the first in the world. The book was updated two years later. Two young linguists, Thorstein Fretheim (at Oslo, later Trondheim) and Lars Hellan (at Trondheim), were actively carrying out research based on generative theories by the early 1970s. In 1977, Fretheim edited a collection of papers by Hovdhaugen, Hellan, Jan Engh, and himself (Fretheim 1977). Both Fretheim and Hellan also lectured extensively on generative topics and inspired interest in generative grammar among their students. Per-Kristian Halvorsen and Knut Tarald Taraldsen were attracted to generative grammar as a result of attending Fretheim's seminars in 1972 and subsequently produced doctoral dissertations within a generative framework.

By the mid-1980s a majority of universities in Norway had either generative-oriented programs or places where one could study the theory. Aside from Trondhein, the universities at Bergen and Tromsø have been especially important. At Bergen one faculty member was Helge Dyvik, a graduate student in the late 1970s, then a professor in the linguistics department from the early 1980s. He wrote his dissertation on issues of philosophy of science as they related to generative theory. (He soon turned to LFG and computational linguistics.) Kirsti Koch Christensen was also at Bergen. She became a professor of linguistics specializing in Japanese and East Asian linguistics, did research within the mainstream Chomskyan paradigm, and subsequently became the Rector of the University. In the 1980s the University of Bergen also recruited two generativist post-docs from Trondheim, Torbjørn Nordgård and Lars Johnsen. Per-Kristian Halvorsen, who had a PhD from the University of Texas, was an adjunct professor there in the early 1980s, while being employed at Xerox. The Tromsø department was founded by Taraldsen, who even filled in one year for Chomsky at MIT. The Center for the Advanced Study in Theoretical Linguistics (CASTL), based in Tromsø, since its founding in 2002 has become a destination for generative grammarians from all over the world. It is one of the largest centers devoted to linguistic research anywhere, and has served as the administrative host of the Nordic Center of Excellence in Microcomparative Syntax (NORMS) and the Eastern European School in Generative Grammar (EGG).

Finland.[27] Finland, like Sweden, has long had a generative presence without that approach being in any sense dominant. Fred Karlsson mentions that the Swede Sven Öhman, professor of phonetics at Uppsala from 1969, told him that he first heard of Chomsky around 1960 at one of the summer sessions of the Nordiska

---

[27] I would like to thank Fred Karlsson for his input to this section.

Sommaruniversitetet from the Finn Paavo Siro (Fred Karlsson, p. c., February 21, 2021). Siro was professor of Finnish 1965–1975 at Tampere University in Finland. In the early 1940s (in the middle of the Second World War) he published a few papers in *Virittäjä*, Finland's only major linguistic journal, where he tried to apply symbolic logic to the description of Finnish. These papers were heavily criticized by Paavo Ravila, at the time professor of Finno-Ugric studies at the University of Turku, the leading linguist in Finland from around 1940 to 1965. According to Karlsson, Siro's early interest in syntactic formalization was probably the reason that he was attracted by the work of the early Chomsky. In the summer of 1967 Siro and Kalevi Wiik, professor of phonetics at the University of Turku from 1968, jointly taught a course on transformational grammar at the Summer University session at Tampere. Karlsson went on to note that he attended that course, his first in generative grammar, which had about fifteen students. The main course topic was a description of the (controversial) verb phrase in Finnish.

In 1963 Paavo Ravila published a (critical) overview of *Syntactic Structures*-style TGG in *Virittäjä* (Ravila 1963). As far as Karlsson is aware, this was the first time the theory was mentioned in written form in a public linguistic forum in Finland. The paper was read in session at the December 1962 meeting of the Finno-Ugrian Society, founded in 1883, so quite a few scholars in Finno-Ugrian and Finnic studies must have heard about it then.

The first professorship of general linguistics was established at the University of Helsinki in the fall semester of 1966 with Wiik as acting incumbent. The first generative course in Helsinki was taught by him that semester and the first major generative publication was Wiik (1967), an abstract *SPE*-style description of Finnish morphophonology. In the early 1970s a number of younger linguists started applying generative ideas, in alphabetical order Auli Hakulinen, Orvokki Heinämäki, Fred Karlsson, and Matti Leiwo. According to Karlsson, their work was mostly met by skepticism and criticism, first and foremost, by Terho Itkonen.

Iceland.[28] The best sources for early generative grammar in Iceland are Thráinsson (1996) and Hovdhaugen et al. (2000: 314–320). What follows draws heavily from the latter. As in Norway, TGG was not faced with an entrenched structuralist ascendancy, and hence was able to make rapid gains. Actually, very little generative work was done in that country before the late 1970s, though an introductory text in generative syntax was published earlier in that decade (Gunnarsson 1973). The Icelander who pioneered generative studies, both in phonology and in syntax, was Höskuldur Thráinsson. His autosegmental account of preaspiration in Icelandic (Thráinsson 1978) was the first major generative phonological study by an Icelandic linguist and his Harvard dissertation on Icelandic complementation (Thráinsson 1979) the first major syntactic study. By the mid 1980s, generative grammar was flourishing in Iceland.

---

[28] I would like to thank Höskuldur Thráinsson for his input to this section.

Icelandic generative studies benefited from the relative large number of America-based linguists who worked on that language very early on, including Stephen R. Anderson (Anderson 1969), Avery Andrews (Andrews 1973), Gregory Iverson (Iverson 1978), Joan Maling (Maling 1990 [1980]), and Annie Zaenen (Zaenen 1980). If I am not mistaken, all have spent time in Iceland, working with local linguists, and were involved in helping to build programs there.

6.3.3   Eastern Europe

The following subsections treat the arrival of generative grammar in the self-described 'communist' countries, with the exception of East Germany, whose situation was discussed in § 6.3.1. They are treated in the following order: The Soviet Union, Czechoslovakia, Poland, Hungary, Yugoslavia, Romania, Bulgaria, Albania, Estonia, Latvia, and Lithuania.

The Soviet Union. Structural approaches to language of any variety were impeded in the Soviet Union for a long time by the official adherence to the ideas of Nikolaj Jakovlevič Marr, ideas that can only be described as 'crackpot' (see Rubenstein 1951; Newmeyer 1986c: 114–118). In a nutshell, Marr argued that economic revolutions (in the Marxist sense) produced linguistic revolutions, i. e. that there were feudal languages, capitalist languages, socialist languages, and so on. Therefore, all varieties of structuralism were outlawed until 1950. As late as 1949 the Presidium of the USSR Academy of Sciences endorsed his theories, labeling comparative and structural linguistics 'bourgeois', 'reactionary', 'racist', and 'justifying an imperialist foreign policy'. The disaffected linguists who had (forbidden) contacts with their colleagues in other countries sought aid in the highest quarter of the land—they went to Stalin. And Stalin intervened for them personally, on their behalf. On May 9, 1950 the newspaper *Pravda* launched an 'open discussion' on linguistic matters. The upshot was that Stalin denounced Marr's theories. What he did was no less that to assert the autonomy of grammar; formal approaches were now acceptable.

Structural linguistics started making headway in the Soviet Union only in the very late 1950s, largely in response to the needs of machine translation. And that was the gateway by which TGG was accepted (for a short time) there. In many parts of Europe, TGG was rejected because it was too formal. But in the Soviet Union, TGG initially attracted interest because of its being highly formalized.

> For some Soviet, and later Russian, researchers the postulate of highly accurate, fully automated translation, came to be the focus of theoretical NLP development. These ideas were based on the assumptions of Hjelmslev and Chomsky that natural language, like the artificial languages of mathematics and logic, is a kind of calculus.
>
> (Piotrovskij 2000: 235)

In an article published in *Word* in 1962, the leading Soviet linguist N. D. Andreyev made many positive remarks about TGG, given his belief that it could advance mathematical linguistics (Andreyev 1962). That same year, *Syntactic Structures* was published as a chapter of a book, where, again, its applicability to computational tasks was emphasized (Alpatov 2014: 164), and the works of other generativists were presented, including those by Katz, McCawley, and Fillmore (Venkova 2019). Along the same lines, consider the following quote from Milka Ivić, in her historiography of the field[29]:

> Generative grammar, although it arose in the U.S.A., has been enthusiastically received in the Soviet Union, primarily because of its possible applications in machine translation.
>
> (Ivić 1965)

But by the 1970s the psychological and philosophical implications of Chomsky's ideas led TGG to be disfavored by the academic establishment. From around 1972 on, almost all writing about Chomsky was highly critical (Alpatov 2014: 165). The two leading Soviet generativists were forced to emigrate to North America, Sebastian Shaumyan in 1975 and Igor Mel'čuk a year later.[30] Mel'čuk has written:

> My life changed in 1976. After twenty years at the Institute of Linguistics I was fired for political reasons. Believing that the Soviet authorities were serious when they signed the Helsinki agreement in August 1975, I had written a letter to the *New York Times* [...] protesting the treatment of the dissident physicist, Academician Andrej Sakharov. [...] I wrote to the Americans believing they might help. It worked, there were bombardments of protest letters and protests in New York, he was released for operation and survived. For me, however, it was the end of my career. I was fired (25 March 1976) and could not get a job anywhere in the Soviet Union. I became a 'social parasite' [...].
>
> (Mel'čuk 2000: 222)

---

[29] Around the same time, the historiographer of linguistics Maurice Leroy made a parallel observation:

> [...] N. Chomsky, in particular, has undertaken a far-reaching analysis of grammatical structure by working out a formalization of linguistic levels according to the methods of formal logic. Studies such as these have proved especially valuable for the practical purposes of language teaching. They are also at the basis of applied linguistics, one of whose most spectacular achievements, brought about by the collaboration of linguists with mathematicians and technicians, is undoubtedly the development of machine translation. Work on these lines has gone ahead particularly in Russia and the English-speaking countries [...]
> (Leroy 1967 [1963]: 81)

[30] As noted in Everaert & Reuland (2011), however, neither Shaumyan nor Mel'čuk had any commitment to the psychological aspects of the theory.

According to Haider, Prinzhorn, & van Riemsdijk (1987: 481), there was only one generative grammarian left in the Soviet Union at that time, a scholar based in Kaliningrad.

Czechoslovakia. Czechoslovakia (later the Czech Republic and Slovakia) provides another example of how the existence of a strong structuralist tradition impeded the development of TGG. Perhaps the most flourishing school of structural linguistics in the interwar years was developed by scholars associated with the Linguistic Circle of Prague. As noted in Chapter 2, § 2.7, it was the Praguean linguists who developed the theory of functional sentence perspective (FSP), an approach that looks at the utterance from the point of view of the information conveyed by it (Mathesius 1983 [1927]).[31] The key construct in FSP came to be 'communicative dynamism' (CD), the idea that the new information content in a sentence increases as the sentence progresses (Firbas 1965). This work was the forerunner both to current day functional linguistics and modern studies of information structure, many of which are carried out within the generative paradigm (Newmeyer 2001).

Though the school was partly crippled by the Stalinist regime after the war, the general feeling was that the Czechs did not 'need' a new theory emanating from the other side of the ocean. As in the Soviet Union, it was the mathematical and computational implications of the theory that attracted the most interest, rather than the cognitive implications (Everaert & Reuland 2011: 5). Nevertheless, the two leading Prague School linguists of the late twentieth century, Petr Sgall and Eva Hajičová, attempted to unify PS conceptions with work that was being done in generative grammar at the time. Sgall, Hajičová, & Benesová (1973) pulled together the articles of the individual authors over the previous few years and proposed to integrate FSP into a generative semantic model of grammar whose semantic representations were case grammar trees. This work, called 'functional generative description' (FGD), incorporates the notion of CD, but in a more precise sense than that of Firbas. The authors derive the amount of CD of a grammatical element from its role in semantic interpretation, based on its degree of 'communicative importance'. However, given that the element with the greatest amount of communicative importance tends to be sentence-final, the idea of a gradual rise in CD is maintained. FGD is updated and treated in greater detail in Sgall, Hajičová, & Panevová (1986).

The PS alternative to 'mainstream' generative grammar has been to attempt an integrated formal model of structure, meaning, and use, in which each compo-

---

[31] The Pragueans, like many European linguists at the time, considered themselves both 'structuralists' and 'functionalists'.

nent retains some degree of autonomy. How the PS linguists place themselves with respect to other trends can be appreciated from the following colorful metaphor:

> The former, Chomskyan, Montaguian, and other trends — if viewed from a Praguian perspective under which the whole 'building' of communication within a linguistic community rests on its 'basement' consisting in the common language — construct this basement without realizing that it is a basement rather than a whole house. […] On the other hand the pragmatically oriented trends […] would like to erect the building without any basement, arguing that those concentrating on the basement can never build the house. […] For those who are willing to divide the labor, since they realize that language is a complex instrument of human communication and that a systematic description of the instrument should be integrated into that of the activity, the Praguian approach offers useful starting points.
>
> (Sgall 1987: 174)

I do not think that this approach has triggered a great deal of interest outside of the borders of the former Czechoslovakia. I have found very few references to current Praguean work either in the functionalist literature or in the generative literature. Today, it must be acknowledged, the Czech Republic and Slovakia are not leading centers of linguistics of any variety. Henk van Riemsdijk has offered the opinion that

> the Prague school hasn't led to any significant insights for 30 years now. So that it makes no sense and you can see that the younger generation would actually like to do other things, like generative grammar, or formal semantics. They would love to be part of an international enterprise, which they don't get to be because their superiors tend to be rather fierce and control the jobs. So they have to do Prague school. So what you see is that the younger generation give talks in which they sort of disguise what they really want to do under a lot of Prague school terminology.
>
> (van Riemsdijk 1998: 19)

Poland.[32] Poland was the first country in what was then the Eastern Bloc to open the door to TGG. The news about generative grammar was brought to Poland from America by two prominent linguists, Jacek Fisiak and Kazimierz Polański. Both Fisiak and Polański spent a research year in the United States, Fisiak at UCLA in 1963–1964, and Polański at Yale in 1969–1970. Poland, unlike the Soviet Union and Czechoslovakia, was relatively liberal, allowing travel to, and contacts with, the West. TGG was never banned for ideological reasons there. According to Jerzy

---

[32] I would like to thank Jerzy Rubach, Przemyslaw Pawelec, and Ewa Jaworska for their input to this section.

Rubach, 'Fisiak had superb managerial skills and sufficient political influence to shield budding generativists from being accused of spreading the wrong theories on the communist soil. I remember linguists from Czechoslovakia and Bulgaria who pretended that they came to Poland on a tourist visit since they were afraid to tell the truth at their home universities' (p. c., January 26, 2021).

Rubach went on to write: 'Fisiak was quick to turn words into actions and in 1971 he started a series of English–Polish Contrastive Conferences that were organized twice a year (in May and in December). The conferences were always held in small towns that were tourist resorts. All participants stayed in the same building together, went to the same meetings together, had meals together, drank vodka together (quite a bit of it), sang songs together, and danced together. (Fisiak himself was an excellent dancer.) In sum, the atmosphere was more than fit to fruitfully discuss research in generative linguistics. I know this first hand because I attended almost all of these conferences.'

The first Contrastive Conference was held in Karpacz in 1971 and then every year for some twenty years. The conferences were attended by young linguists from all linguistics departments in Polish Institutes of English Studies.[33] The list of participants was drawn up by Fisiak himself and people who did not make sufficient progress were dropped from the list. About half of the participants came from abroad: from both Western and Eastern Europe and the United States. Fisiak understood that young generativists needed a publication venue in order to grow and he started a journal-type series entitled *Papers and Studies in Contrastive Linguistics*, which came out once or twice a year.

Neither Fisiak or Polański were generative grammarians per se, though the latter worked a bit in syntax. Aside from Polański, the foundations of generative syntax in Poland were laid down by Barbara Lewandowska-Tomaszczyk, Tomasz P. Krzeszowski, and Aleksander Szwedek, and of generative phonology by Roman Laskowski, Edmund Gussmann, and Jerzy Rubach. Gussmann learned of generative phonology when he had a fellowship to Iceland between 1968 and 1970. In 1973, Rubach went to Stanford for a year of graduate studies funded by the Department of State and a Polish-American foundation in Chicago. In 1978 Gussmann received a Fulbright fellowship, which he spent at MIT. Rubach followed him in 1979, also on a Fulbright and also at MIT.

By the late 1970s generative linguistics became the dominant paradigm for all linguists in all Institutes of English Studies in Poland.

---

[33] I am informed by Przemyslaw Pawelec (p. c., January 28, 2021) that in the Polish system, till this day, linguistics is taught as part of a particular language institute: Institute of English Studies, Institute of French Studies, Institute of German Studies, and so forth, which themselves are part of the Faculty of Philology. Generative grammar quickly became the dominant paradigm in the English Institutes, but not in Polish, French, and so on. This situation has led to a certain amount of inter-institute friction, as those in Polish have often resented work done in that language at an Institute of English, for example.

Hungary.[34] According to Szabolcsi (1985), before the 1960s most work by Hungarian linguists was historical-comparative oriented, particularly pertaining to the Finno-Ugric family. In 1964 several Hungarian linguists, among them Ferenc Kiefer, Zsigmond Telegdi, and György Szépe received Ford scholarships to the United States, where they studied generative linguistics. They started teaching it when they returned back in Hungary. Kiefer was especially important in this respect:

> We Hungarian linguists also have reasons beyond his scholarly work to be thankful to Ferenc Kiefer. Nobody has done more for the substantive and institutional modernization of linguistics in Hungary and for its integration into the international academic world than he did. The early 1960s, when his career started, was a period of complete isolation for Hungarian linguistics, mainly due to the inaccessibility of international linguistic journals and foreign books, and the impossibility of international scholarly relations and trips to the West. Hungarian linguists continued the pre-structuralist descriptive and historical linguistic tradition – partly in defense from the ideologically-politically determined turnarounds (Marrism and anti-Marrism) of Soviet linguistics. Despite these circumstances, Ferenc Kiefer and a few members of his generation came to know about the generative linguistic revolution, and in a brief period of thawing around 1964, they had a chance to study generative linguistics with Ford-scholarships at the best universities of the USA [Kiefer was at MIT and UCLA — (FJN)]. When they returned to Hungary, they started disseminating what they had learned there. They taught generative linguistics at Eötvös Loránd University, and also organized informal study circles for linguists from other universities.
>
> (É Kiss 2020: 395–396)

In 1973 Kiefer coedited with Nicolas Ruwet a volume entitled *Generative Grammar in Europe* (Kiefer & Ruwet 1973; see above, § 6.2, and for discussion Hamans 2015: 11).

In the mid-1970s, however, progress in generative grammar stalled for two reasons. First, as in West Germany, those young Hungarian linguists who had been attracted to generative semantics abandoned generative grammar entirely with the collapse of that model, and ended up doing typology and formal semantics (Haider, Prinzhorn, & van Riemsdijk 1987: 481). Second, as in the Soviet Union and Czechoslovakia, the idea of an innate universal grammar was deemed contrary to Marxism. Also, according to Szabolcsi, there was a widespread feeling among established linguists there that generative syntax was not well adapted to accounting for the structure of Hungarian. Therefore, generative theory remained peripheral

---

[34] I would like to thank Katalin É Kiss for her input to this section.

at the Hungarian universities for quite some time. The center for generative linguistic research was, and has been ever since, the Research Institute for Linguistics of the Hungarian Academy of Sciences.

GLOW did a lot to support Hungarian linguists interested in generative theory, providing invitations, fellowships, manuscripts, and publication possibilities. The first GLOW meeting in Hungary was organized in Budapest in 1987 at the Research Institute for Linguistics. The first generative papers by Hungarian linguists in international linguistic journals appeared in 1981 (Szabolcsi 1981 and É Kiss 1981).

Yugoslavia.[35] TGG had a presence in Yugoslavia beginning in the late 1960s, thanks to the publications of Ranko Bugarski (Bugarski 1969a, b, 1972). In 1971 Bugarski introduced Chomsky's *Syntactic Structures* in his syntax class at the University of Belgrade, though he never taught generative syntax extensively. In 1972, Olga Mišeska Tomić, who had received her PhD from the University of Washington, Seattle, started teaching generative grammar at the University of Skopje. She spent several years at that university, and then at the University of Novi Sad—a city which became the stronghold of generative grammar in the former Yugoslavia. In the 1980s, Milena Milojević Sheppard started teaching generative grammar at the University of Ljubljana. And at the University of Zagreb, Višnja Josipović, who had graduated from MIT, taught generative phonology for some time in the late 1980s, while at the University of Sarajevo, Nedžad Leko started teaching generative grammar much later.

The pioneers of generative linguistics in Yugoslavia were overwhelmingly professors of English. Aside from those mentioned in the preceding paragraph, attention should be called to Vladimir Ivir and Radoslav Katičić in Zagreb, Gordana Opačić in Niš, and Midhat Riđanović in Sarajevo. Most of these individuals supervised theses with generative orientations.

Bugarski's 1972 book is a selection of Chomsky's writings (translated by Bugarski himself), including several articles, excerpts of lectures, blocks of text from *Syntactic Structures* and *Aspects of the Theory of Syntax* and most of *Language and Mind*). The book was well received and got favorable reviews in different parts of Yugoslavia and even abroad (including one by Eric Hamp, then review editor of *IJAL*). Chomsky himself wrote to express his satisfaction, explaining that he had consulted Wayles Browne as an expert in both the subject matter and the language of the volume, and Roman Jakobson—to whom I had sent a copy at Chomsky's suggestion) replied with a thank-you postcard referring to my "excellent translation" of Chomsky's work' (Ranko Bugarski, p. c., March 3, 2021).

Unlike in other officially communist countries, state ideology never prevented the adoption and spread of generativist work:

---

[35] I would like to thank Ranko Bugarski and Olga Mišeska Tomić for their input to this section.

Generative grammar was never criticized in Yugoslavia for being 'un-Marxist'. Yugoslavia was a far more liberal society than the Eastern Bloc countries. Also, GG — or linguistic theory in general — never really caught the public eye to the extent that even the ideologically alert politicians might start wondering. I never heard of anyone having problems of that kind.

(Ranko Bugarski, p. c., March 3, 2021)

There are centers of generative research in most of the successor nations to Yugoslavia. I can attest from personal experience to the existence of active groups in Slovenia and Serbia.

Romania.[36] The development of generative grammar in Romania was always sensitive to the political climate. After the Declaration of Independence of the Romanian Communist Party of April 1964 (which displeased Moscow), there followed almost a decade of increasing cultural freedom for Romanians, which primarily meant access to western books and publications. As a result, TGG flourished in this period.

Early TGG in Romania took advantage of the strong Romanian structuralist tradition, headed by Alexandru Rosetti. Rosetti had been working in the structuralist paradigm since the thirties and was also the director of one of the two linguistic institutes of the Romanian Academy. Rosetti became an active promoter and even a contributor to TGG (e.g. Rosetti 1971). For the Romanians, TGG was regarded simply as a variant of structuralism, rather than as a new theory replacing structuralism. For example, in Maria Manoliu Manea's survey of structuralist approaches to language (Manoliu Manea 1973), TGG was presented as a second stage of American descriptivism. Alexandra Cornilescu informs me that Manoliu Manea

found a clever way of introducing Chomsky's original ideas on language. She noticed that, unlike some American structuralists, who ignored the development of European thought, Chomsky turned to it and, with hindsight, found predecessors in the European rationalist tradition. Creativity, universal grammar, language acquisition were briefly discussed by Maria Manoliu in a section called 'Cartesianism and generative grammar' (1973: 59). Thus the author managed both to briefly acquaint the reader with Chomsky's ideas and to avoid an extended discussion of Chomsky's mentalist-rationalist theory, largely incompatible with the Marxist views of language as a social phenomenon, based on communication. The same strategy was adopted by other linguists, too.

(p. c. March 15, 2021)

---

[36] I would like to thank Alexandra Cornilescu and Sanda Golopenția Eretescu for their input to this section.

As a result of the relative cultural freedom of the late sixties and early seventies, a number of young Romanian scholars, such as Emanuel Vasiliu, Maria Manoliu Manea, Aurel Trofin, Sanda Golopenția Eretescu, and others were able to spend time in the United States, in universities where they taught Romanian or had research grants. There was also an international project that encouraged the development of TGG in Romania, namely the Romanian-English Contrastive Analysis Project (1968–1976), which involved the Center for Applied Linguistics on the American side and the University of Bucharest and the Institute for Phonetics and Dialectology on the Romanian side. The project was aimed at producing a contrastive grammar of the two languages, with a view to improving the teaching of English in Romania. The project meant the acquisition of a large number of books, a number of nine-months grants for doing research in the US, as well as visits from American linguists, including Eric Hamp, William Nemser, and Charles Fillmore.

Golopenția Eretescu (1978) traces the origins of TGG in Romania to a survey article published sixteen years earlier (Vasiliu 1962). The 1960s saw a number of publications by Vasiliu and Golopentia Eretscu (Golopenția Eretescu 1967, Vasiliu & Golopentia Eretescu 1969, among others). In 1969 Chomsky's *Aspects of the Theory of Syntax* was translated into Romanian by Paul Schveiger and James Augerot—that and the German translation were the first ever written. Two more early generative books deserve mention: *Le groupe nominal et la nominalization en français modern* by Mariana Tuțescu (Tuțescu 1972) and Manoliu Manea's book *Tipologie și Istorie: Elemente de Sintaxă Comparată Romanică [Typology and History: Elements of Comparative Romance Syntax]* (Manoliu Manea 1977).

TGG was also an institutional success story at this time, being taught in some of the major universities of the country, including Bucharest, Cluj, and Iasi. Generally it was taught in English departments, but also in French departments, and at the University of Bucharest in the Romanian Department. Incidentally, two linguists with international reputations, Donka Farkas at UC Santa Cruz and Carmen Dobrovie-Sorin at Paris VII, were in the same class on English generative syntax at the University of Bucharest in the fall of 1973.

Unfortunately, however, generative grammar in Romania fell into decline by the late 1970s. According to Diego Pescarini:

In Romania the publication of Chomsky's works practically stopped for political reasons. To limit the influence of foreign countries and organizations, Ceaușescu inaugurated autarchic policies that increased the country's isolation. [...] With the new policy of the authoritarian state, scientific exchanges, projects and international collaborations were suspended.

(Pescarini in press: ms, p. 6)

Alexandra Cornilescu has confirmed Pescarini's dark assessment:

> In the early seventies, there were signs that the more liberal political climate was changing. For people like myself, 1974 was the turning point, which marked a progressive isolation from the West and increased nationalism and megalomania on the political scene. Contacts with the West were drastically reduced, few if any American linguists came to Bucharest and most Romanian linguists could not travel either. Even worse, distinguished linguists like Maria Manoliu Manea and Sanda Golopentia left the country.
>
> The visible impact of 1974 was a drastic reduction of the subscriptions to linguistic journals (e.g. *Linguistic Inquiry*, *Linguistics and Philosophy*, *NLLT* a.o. were no longer available). Gradually, books from the west were no longer bought either. Incidentally and funnily, *Lectures on Government and Binding* was not acquired by any Romanian library, probably because it was thought to be a political book and it is still not available in the Central Library of the University, while *Knowledge of Language*, with a less threatening title, was bought in 1988.
>
> Without books, journals and contacts, it became materially impossible to survive as a generative linguist. As an example, I came to read *LGB* in 1983, borrowing it from Eugene Fong, a Fulbright lecturer who had come to teach English and learn Romanian, but who happened to be a generative linguist. Needless to say, reading the book was a shock, since I had never heard of 'binding', 'control', 'Case-filter', etc. before, and most of *LGB*'s bibliography was not available in Bucharest.
>
> (p. c., April 4, 2021)

There are generative grammarians in Romania today, though the theory can hardly be said to be predominant.

Bulgaria. This section is based on Venkova (2019), a fascinating article that documents the ways in which Bulgarian linguists before 1989 managed to circumvent the Communist authorities' efforts to suppress work in TGG. Here, as elsewhere in Eastern Europe, 'TGG was criticized on philosophical grounds for not following dialectical materialism' (p. 52). 'Despite the censorship, TGG gained popularity in Bulgaria of that time [i.e. in the 1960s and 1970s—(FJN)] and generative methodology was applied in the study of Bulgarian language as well. What is specific about such works is that they followed particular evasive techniques, "attenuating" the American origin of generativism, so that it could be acceptable for the censorship pressure' (p. 53). One tactic was to refer to TGG almost exclusively via Soviet sources, that is, to translations of generative work into Russian and to the publications of Soviet commentators on TGG. For example, the first generative grammar of Bulgarian, Penchev (1984), introduced TGG with a quote from the Russian work Zholj (1980) and cited Soviet linguists, rather than Chomsky. Along the same lines, in the 1960s and 1970s, Bulgarian generativists often published their work in Russian, which 'led to a specific evasive style of describing and referring to the original American model' (Venkova 2019: 54).

Another strategy used by Bulgarian linguists to throw off the censors was to employ a very indirect translation of technical terms. So 'transformational-generative grammar' became 'engineering linguistics', 'mathematization of linguistics', 'machine translation', or 'computational linguistics'. And several Bulgarian linguists used terms like 'transformation' and 'deep structure' as if they themselves had coined them, without any indication of their provenance.

So in summary, there was a fair amount of TGG done in Bulgaria between the 1960s and the 1980s, but because of the peculiarities of the situation there, such work was cut off from generative studies in the rest of the world.

Albania. According to Mosko (2014), no generative work was done in Albania until the twenty-first century.

Estonia. Estonia was part of the USSR in the time period under consideration. Nevertheless, developments in academia took place somewhat independently there with respect to the Soviet mainstream. As far as the arrival of TGG in that country is concerned, it has been written:

> 1965 witnessed the 'formal' birth of the Generative Grammar Group (GGG) at the University of Tartu ('formal' meaning that its activities were approved by the university administration; without such approval its own publications etc. would have been impossible). The research group was founded by Huno Rätsep, then Associate Professor of Estonian, now professor emeritus and member of the Estonian Academy of Sciences. Since the early 1960's, Rätsep had taught the general theme 'new directions in linguistics', including different schools of structural linguistics. Now generative grammar became the central topic (but not the only one). Thus, we can say that general (theoretical) linguistics in Estonia was imported from America (USA), as it happened also in Finland (Karlsson 1997: 91). Most of the 'first generation' theoretically-oriented professors and researchers in linguistics emerged from the GGG.
>
> (Õim, Pajusalu, & Tragel 2006: 88)

Õim, et al. do not trace the subsequent developments of generative grammar in Estonia. However, they do note that 'at present at least 90 per cent of Estonian theoretical linguistic research belongs to the functional (including cognitive) type. When, how, and why this change occurred is difficult to explain in a few words' (pp. 88–89).

Latvia. An article published in a Latvian journal of the humanities and social sciences notes the following:

> Syntactic theories based on generative grammar frameworks seem to be hardly used in Latvia, if at all. Absence of this tradition in Latvia stems from the fact that

Russian linguistic schools during the Soviet era were anti-generativist, and thus the approach was virtually inaccessible to the Soviet-ruled linguistic minority.

(Apse 2007: 77)

Lithuania.[37] Generative grammar has never been widely practiced in Lithuania. The first work in TGG was a 1971 doctoral dissertation written in English by Laimutis Valeika, entitled *Nominal Constructions in Lithuanian and their Counterparts in English.* Another dissertation followed in 1973 by Emma Geniušienė on the passive voice in Lithuanian. 'Similar to most other Soviet dissertations, this work is a detailed fact and data-oriented description. However, in this instance the description appeals to transformational rules' (Artūras Ratkus, p. c., March 2, 2021). According to Geniušienė:

> The people in the linguistic circles in Vilnius were certainly familiar with the theory of generative grammar, as literature was available. I myself was the proud owner of a copy of the first edition of N. Chomsky's *Syntactic Structures.* I vaguely recall private discussions of the theory with Prof. V. Ambrazas [1930–2018], a leading grammarian and very erudite, and some other people. But I do not recall any contributions to or application of the theory. As to the authorities, they were surely unaware of its existence and there were no public discussions.
>
> (p. c., March 8, 2021)

Geniušienė went on to inform me that she looked up the entry on generative grammar in *Lietuvių kalbos enciklopedija* [*Encyclopaedia of Lithuanian*], edited by Ambrazas in 1999 and was surprised to find the following statement: 'Some people applied the principles of generative grammar to the analysis of Lithuanian' (p. 213). It must certainly be true, Geniušienė wrote, since the entry was most likely written by Prof. Ambrazas himself, who knew best.

6.3.4 Southern Europe

In this section we examine the origins and early development of generative grammar in Italy, Spain, Portugal, Greece, Cyprus, and Malta.

Italy.[38] TGG first came to the attention of Italian linguists as early as the 1950s, with the publication of a review of *Syntactic Structures* by Giuseppe Francescato (Francescato 1958). The reviewer was not unsympathetic, but felt that Chomsky's approach was at one and the same time too limited and too complex. However,

---

[37] I would like to thank Emma Geniušienė, Artūras Ratkus, and Miguel Villanueva Svensson for their input to this section.
[38] I would like to thank Giorgio Graffi and Annarita Puglielli for their input to this section.

little or no generative work was carried out in Italy for quite some time afterwards. Annarita Puglielli recalls:

I believe that the first time *Syntactic Structures* was introduced in an Italian University was in 1960/61 when a seminar was held by Prof. S. Sacks from Berkeley University for students at the Università la Sapienza in Roma. I was studying at that time and 'happened' to register for that seminar that was optional and not part of any official course. There was a special program financed by the Ford Foundation that brought for some years American linguists in our Faculty with the aim of improving the linguistic knowledge of language teachers. The only linguistics taught at the time in Italian universities was historical linguistics and there were few places where structural linguistics (Saussure etc.) was talked about. I doubt that *Syntactic Structures* had been introduced in university courses before 1969 when I started to teach Linguistics in Rome. In 1967 the Società di Linguistica Italiana was started and in 1969 the first congress on generative grammar and its application to the description of Italian was organized. The spread of the theory found and still finds strong resistance in the Italian academic world, but over the years several linguists adopted this theoretical approach with very good results and contributed to its diffusion and development.

(p. c., February 21, 2018)

Puglielli's last sentence appears to be a bit of a modesty-based understatement to me. Far more than 'several' Italian linguists have been involved in the diffusion and development of generative theory. Giorgio Graffi attributes the relative success of Italian generative grammar to the absence of a prior structuralist tradition:

If therefore, in other countries [...] structuralism presented an obstacle which generative grammar was to overcome, in Italy in the 1960s, the at first timid and later tumultuous manifestation of an interest in structural linguistics undoubtedly prepared the way for generative grammar, even if in a non-definitive manner, because it aroused interest in linguistic theory. In reality, one cannot speak of a genuine structuralist period in Italy because so little work was carried out, and the work which was done in the sphere of this paradigm was almost exclusively phonological, according to the framework of the Prague School [...]. In effect, research in generative grammar began to be conducted already in the 1960s in Italy, even if in a largely 'clandestine' manner. Such research most likely had its start in the Faculty of Magistero ('Education') at the University of Rome, where, at the time, no institutionalized teaching of linguistics was offered, either under the traditional name of 'Glottologia' or under the name (which was by this time considered almost revolutionary) of 'Linguistica generale', but where courses (for reasons largely due to chance) were held in which themes of generative grammar were dealt with, at least in part.

(Graffi 1990: 149).

According to Haider, Prinzhorn, & van Riemsdijk (1987: 477), the first generative research groups were formed in the early 1970s, around the time that Chomsky's major works were translated into Italian. One group was established at the Consiglio Nazionale della Ricerche in Rome and the other at the University of Padua. By the middle of the decade, the Scoula Normale Superiore in Pisa had become the center of generative activity under the leadership of Luigi Rizzi and Adriana Belletti. Their efforts led to Chomsky's spending a research semester there in 1979. Here the government-binding theory (Chomsky 1981) was born as a result of a series of GLOW lectures by him, as well as associated workshops. Finally, attention should be called to the *Rivista di Grammatica Generativa*, founded in 1976 by Francesco Antinucci and Guglielmo Cinque. The Rivista was one of the first European journals devoted exclusively to generative grammar. It has featured articles by Noam Chomsky, Richard Kayne, Larry Hyman, Henk van Riemsdijk, and many other internationally prominent generativists.

I think that it is fair to say that no country more than Italy has produced as many notable generative grammarians with as few programs and resources devoted to that theory. In the words of Giorgio Graffi:

> I hope I won't be accused of chauvinism (an attitude which I consider to be among the most detestable in the world) if I assert that the prestige of Italian generative linguistics is remarkable, not only on a European level, but on a world-wide level as well; as they say, 'the facts speak for themselves': the current president of GLOW is Italian, the European editors of *Linguistic Inquiry* are Italian, many books by Italian authors are present in the major international collections of literature on generative grammar.
>
> (Graffi 1990: 147)

More than thirty years later generative grammar is still thriving in Italy at several universities.

Spain.[39]Demonte, García-Billido, & Mascaró (1982) point to the 'slow development' of TGG in Spain and of the 'isolation' of Spanish generativists. Generative work began to attract attention with the translation by Carlos Otero of Chomsky's *Aspects of the Theory of Syntax* in 1970 and his *Syntactic Structures* in 1974 (with a preface by Chomsky). 'Needless to say, the university professors of philology ignored both books. Only some time later things began to change because some of their students became interested in generative grammar' (Carlos Otero, p. c., February 21, 2018). Interestingly, Everaert and Reuland note that

> cultural and linguistic oppression might have had a positive effect on the development of generative grammar in Catalonia. Demonte et al. claim that in the late

---

[39] I would like to thank Violeta Demonte, Carlos Otero, and María Luisa Rivero for their input to this section.

sixties and early seventies students at the University of Barcelona got interested in generative grammar and that Gabriel Ferrater (mainly known as a poet; he died in 1972) played an important role in its development. Although he did not have a university degree 'he was accepted by the academic system and began teaching courses in both Catalan universities, more or less at the same time that most of the new group of generative grammarians were absorbed by the recently [1968] created Universidad Autonoma' (Demonte, García-Billido, & Mascaró. 1982: 12).

(Everaert & Reuland 2011: 10)

María Luisa Rivero and Violeta Demonte provided me with information on the early reception of the theory in Spain (p. c., March 1, 2018):

In the late sixties, generative grammar begun to be discussed, among topics in philosophy, literature, and linguistics, in an informal gathering (Spanish *tertulia*) called Círculo Lingüístico de Madrid. The participants were Agustín García Calvo, a well-known classicist and poet, Carlos Piera, a linguist and now well-known poet who was a student at the time and went on to get a PhD in linguistics at UCLA, Rafael Sánchez Ferlosio, a very famous and much honored literary author (whose best known novel is *El Jarama*) and grammarian, and Victor Sánchez de Zavala, an engineer, philosopher, and linguist who would go on to play a crucial role in all activities concerning generative grammar in Spain in later years.

In 1967, very prominent Spanish intellectuals with a leftist orientation created a Centro de Enseñanza e Investigación (CEISA) (Center of Teaching and Research) to modernize academic life in Spain, during the very dark period of the Franco regime. Within a Sciences and Humanities course offered by this center from February 1967 to May 1967, Carlos Otero Pelegrín spoke on 'Lingüística transformacional'. Víctor Sánchez de Zavala participated in the activities of this center, and so did Ernesto García Camarero, a mathematician who would be the vice-chair and later the chair of the Centro de Cálculo of the University of Madrid beginning in 1968, a site of many activities on generative grammar in the following years. The Centro published a regular Bulletin that included articles on generative grammar. The Seminario de Lingüística Matemática, which would become a continuous and active forum for generative grammar, began at the end of 1968 at the Centro de Cálculo of the University of Madrid (later Universidad Complutense). This seminar ended in the summer of 1971.

Despite the above, TGG was never able to achieve a strong organizational presence in Spain. As elsewhere, there have always been outstanding generative grammarians in Spain, but they tend to be isolated and scattered across the country.

Portugal.[40] Until the 1970s, language studies at Portuguese universities were mainly philological in nature. Structuralism never got a real foothold in Portugal. There were thus no strong theoretical barriers to TGG, which explains its relatively easy path in Lisbon and, to some extent, in Porto (but not in Coimbra, which had a very closed philological tradition). In fact, the institutionalization of TGG at the Romance Philology Department of the Faculdade de Letras da Universidade de Lisboa (RP/FLUL) would have been considerably more difficult without the support of the (arguably) most important Portuguese philologist at the time, Luís Filipe Lindley Cintra, then a 'Catedrático' Professor at RP/FLUL. His moral and administrative assistance in the early 1970s both in the formation of Grupo de Estudos de Linguística Teórica (GELT) and in the creation of linguistics courses with a TGG perspective at RP/FLUL was invaluable.

In 1968, Maria Helena Mateus (who held a teaching position at the Romance Philology Department of RP/FLUL) and José António Meireles (then a student at RP/FLUL) started meeting informally in Lisbon to discuss TGG, until then practically unknown in Portugal. They were joined at the end of 1969 by Eduardo Raposo, also a student at RP/FLUL. In 1970, Meireles, Raposo, and Isabel Faria (also a student at RP/FLUL) formed a group dedicated to the study of TGG, namely, GELT, which had an office at the Centro de Estudos Filológicos (later renamed Centro de Linguística da Universidade de Lisboa). GELT organized collective discussions of topics in Portuguese syntax as well as readings of works in TGG such as *Syntactic Structures*, *Aspects of the Theory of Syntax* and Nicolas Ruwet's *Introduction à la grammaire générative*—a book which was instrumental in the TGG training of GELT members. Later, other students from RP/FLUL joined GELT, among whom were Inês Duarte, Ana Brito, Gabriela Matos, Fátima Oliveira, Amália Andrade, and Manuela Âmbar. It is also worth mentioning the attendance by GELT members at the Linguistic Institutes of the Linguistic Society of America (1972, 1974, and 1978), as well as at the Fourth International Summer School in Pisa in 1977, which facilitated the inclusion of the Portuguese linguists in the international TGG network and produced contacts with linguists such as John R. Ross, David Perlmutter, Paul Postal, Luigi Rizzi, and Guglielmo Cinque, among others.

In the early 1970s, the first 'licenciatura' dissertations in generative syntax appeared: Meireles in 1972 (on complementation in Portuguese), Raposo in 1973 (on the inflected infinitive), and Faria also in 1973 (on the subjunctive mood). In 1972, Meireles was given a teaching position at RP/FLUL, followed by Faria and Raposo in 1973. Together with Mateus (who taught phonology), they started teaching syntax and semantics within a TGG framework. Later on, Duarte, Brito, and Oliveira were hired by the Faculty of Letters of Porto, where they were instrumental (together with Óscar Lopes, a Professor of Literature with strong interests

---

[40] I would like to thank a colleague who prefers to remain anonymous for their input to this section.

in both linguistics and logic) in introducing TGG there. From this point on, TGG was on its way to becoming a central framework in the linguistics curricula in both Lisbon and Porto (and was arguably the dominant framework at RP/FLUL). This was facilitated by the publication in 1975 of an annotated translation of *Aspects* by Meireles and Raposo, and by Raposo's book *Introdução à Gramática Generativa: Sintaxe do Português* (Raposo 1978), in the sense that both works helped make TGG available to students with little or no knowledge of English.

Greece.[41] According to Dimitra Theophanopoulou-Kontou (p. c., February 28, 2021), TGG was viewed at first indifferently by Greek philologists, professors, intellectuals, prominent persons in Greek society, and even some linguists, because in that period all the above were involved in a long language quarrel, known as '*glossiko zetema*' which divided the country for more than twenty years. The quarrel was about which of the two styles of Greek, the literary or the colloquial, ought to prevail as a unified common Modern Greek. The quarrel ended in 1976 with the prevalence of the colloquial form, enriched with lexical elements from the literary language.

Linguistics in Greece in the 1960s was nowhere an independent field of study. Rather it was part of departments of philology, themselves part of schools of philosophy. As such, TGG did not meet with a very welcome response from those directing these departments. According to Theophanopoulou-Kontou, things began to change somewhat at Athens University in the late 1960s as a result of lectures by Gaberell Drachman (see § 6.3.1) and Angeliki Malikouti-Drachman, organized by Georgios Kourmoulis, the rector of the university and onetime Minister of Education. The enthusiasm generated by these lectures led to Greek students attending the LSA Linguistic Institute, held at Ohio State University in 1970. At around the same time Georgios Babiniotis, interestingly himself a onetime rector of the university and Minister of Education, became a professor at Athens University and established linguistics there as a separate discipline. At Athens and elsewhere, more and more students adopted generative grammar. The situation was abetted by exchange programs (involving both students and faculty) with Salzburg University and Reading University in England, where the Greek Eirene Philippaki-Warburton was located.

Following the pattern of many European countries, there are a number of generative linguists in Greece today, but they tend to be scattered around the country.

Cyprus.[42] Brian Newton wrote an important early phonological study of Cypriot Greek (Newton 1972). However, there was no generative grammar practiced in Cyprus itself until much later. The reason for this is that the University of

[41] I would like to thank Dimitra Theophanopoulou-Kontou for her input to this section.
[42] I would like to thank Kleanthes Grohmann and Phoevos Panagiotidis for their input to this section.

Cyprus was not founded until 1989. Today there is an active center of generative research at that university, which dates from the late 1990s. According to Phoevos Panagiotidis:

> I believe that the first linguist to have taught and worked in a tenure-track position in Cyprus must have been Amalia Arvaniti in the late 90s, a phonologist at the University of Cyprus, followed in 2001 by Stavroula Tsiplakou (also in UCy) and in 2002 by me at Cyprus College (now European University Cyprus). Of course, Anna Roussou and others had already served as a visitor in UCy already.
>
> My understanding is that generative linguistics in Cyprus begins with Kleanthes Grohmann in 2004. He put the island on the map with at least four moves:
>
> 1. He co-organized the 2006 Cyprus Syntaxfest with me, 'the most important event in generative linguistics for 2006', according to Larson. This was made up from two conferences: Edges in Syntax (organized by me in Cyprus College) and InterPhases (by KKG in UCy). We attracted a number of speakers (Chomsky, Kayne, Larson, and many many more), whereas no fewer than three edited volumes were churned out of the many papers presented (not proceedings).
> 2. He continued organizing conferences. By now generative linguists are the default linguists in Cyprus, partly thanks to his tireless work involving organizing conferences, bringing over Chomsky to receive an honorary doctorate in 2006, public talks, and much more.
> 3. He attracted funding, mostly within the frame of his Cyprus Acquisition Team (CAT), producing a steady flow of research work on the acquisition of Cypriot Greek.
> 4. He founded the journal *Biolinguistics*. (p. c., March 4, 2021)

Malta.[43] Unlike Cyprus, Malta has a university whose roots date back to the sixteenth century. However, in the 1960s and 1970s there were courses at the time introducing generative grammar, but no program devoted to it or even individuals who were primarily generativists. Ray Fabri notes:

> I was myself a student reading for a BA in English in the early 70s (1972 - 75) [in Malta]. Our lecturers then were all British, and I remember our linguistics lecturer (Eddie Williams, now prof. I believe at Bangor University, UK) introducing us to transformational grammar, which some of us hated (I did!!) because we couldn't quite understand what it was all about, but also because we were more into literature than linguistics at the time. I myself 'converted' to being a great

---

[43] I would like to thank Ray Fabri for his input to this section.

'fan' (also making linguistics my career) later on, after a short career as an English teacher (both locally and abroad in Germany). Indeed, even when I came back to Malta in 1996, after a long stay in Germany, none of my Maltese colleagues locally were working within a strictly generative framework.

(p. c., March 7, 2021)

6.4 Concluding remarks

Let me conclude by pointing to an interesting paradox: The achievements of European generative grammarians are vastly out of proportion to the number of practitioners, as compared to the United States. In an interview that I conducted in 1978, Chomsky made the following startling statement:

> When I think of who around the world truly understands what I am trying to accomplish, I would have to say that all but a few are Europeans.
>
> (Noam Chomsky, p. c., December 13, 1978)

Along the same lines, a few years later Chomsky wrote: 'There is far more material that I read with interest than was ever true in the past. Most of it comes from Europe, in fact, [...]' (Chomsky 1982: 69). And more recently, the Dutch linguist Hans Bennis made a comparable observation:

> If you were to make a list of the 50 most important contributors to generative grammar today, about 40 would be Europeans.
>
> (Hans Bennis, p. c., 2002)

How might one explain the paradox? Perhaps it is the case that most European generative grammarians, being in the minority, have to work harder and therefore have produced more results. Perhaps their physical distance from MIT has worked to European generativists' advantage, given that it has left them more 'on their own'. Or perhaps the European scholarly tradition has played a role. The explanation of this paradox (if it has one) is for future research.

7

The contested LSA presidential election of 1970

7.1 Introduction

Whether there was a successful 'Chomskyan revolution' or not, post-Bloomfieldian structuralists continued to play an important role in the LSA for years after the publication of *Syntactic Structures* in 1957. One of their number, namely Martin Joos (see Chapter 3), was nominated for the LSA presidency in 1970. The ensuing brouhaha around his nomination is important enough to merit a full chapter of this book, as it sheds considerable light on the state of the field in the transitional period from structuralism to TGG.

Every year the LSA Nominating Committee puts forward an 'official' slate of candidates. One nominee is for the office of Vice-President. If elected, he or she serves in that office for one year and as President the following.[1] Any ten members, separately and in writing, can challenge the official candidate and nominate somebody else. In the ninety-seven-year history of the LSA, the official candidate for President has been challenged only once.[2] In 1970, Dwight Bolinger opposed the official candidate Martin Joos and defeated him easily. We have seen both of these individuals—in particular, Joos—earlier in the book. This chapter discusses and analyzes the election, which somewhat obliquely is related to the transition from post-Bloomfieldian structuralism to generative grammar. We see that it was mainly personal and generational factors, rather than intellectual ones, that underlay Bolinger's successful challenge. As it turns out, virtually nothing has been published to date on the 1970 election. Fortunately, there is a wealth of material in various archives in the United States which contain letters and other documents relevant to the election, and of which I make copious use.

The chapter is organized as follows. § 7.2 introduces the two presidential candidates, Martin Joos and Dwight Bolinger. § 7.3 outlines the prelude to the election,

---

[1] The practice of the Vice-President acceding automatically to the presidency the following year was instituted in 1969. Before then the President and the Vice-President were elected separately.

[2] To be fully accurate, Bolinger's challenge was the only one that came to a vote of the membership. In 2005, Ivan Sag collected ten signatures in opposition to Stephen Anderson's nomination and sent them to the LSA secretariat. However, he withdrew his challenge before the vote deadline.

American Linguistics in Transition. Frederick J. Newmeyer, Oxford University Press.
© Frederick J. Newmeyer (2022). DOI: 10.1093/oso/9780192843760.003.0007

while §7.4 reviews the internal debate among LSA members over the two candidates. § 7.5 discusses the election results and § 7.6 contains brief concluding remarks.

7.2 The antagonists: Martin Joos and Dwight Bolinger

In this section we review the pre-1970 careers of the two electoral opponents, Martin Joos (§ 7.2.1) and Dwight Bolinger (§ 7.2.2). However, since Joos's career path and personality are treated in some detail in Chapter 3, especially § 3.2.3, the remarks here will be rather perfunctory.

7.2.1 Martin Joos

In 1970 Martin Joos was the official candidate for the 1971 vice-presidency, that is, he was chosen for this role by the Nominating Committee of the LSA. Under normal circumstances, this nomination would have led automatically to his ascending to the presidency in 1972. At the time of his nomination, Joos was a professor in the Department of Linguistics at the University of Toronto, having stepped down as Director of the Linguistics Centre there the year before. Between 1946 and 1966 he was a professor (and sometime chair) in the Department of Germanic Languages at the University of Wisconsin. As discussed earlier, Joos was a prominent post-Bloomfieldian linguist, and one who identified with the more extremely positivist of the linguists in that group. Even at the relatively young age of sixty-three (the time of the election), Joos was perceived by many as mentally unstable and as manifesting increasingly erratic behavior. In the words of Roger Shuy:

> Joos was a good scholar who was aloof, self-important, and gave the impression that he was above the rest of us. I didn't think he'd represent our field well to outsiders. I remember him carrying his own book around with him and reading aloud out of it at times when this seemed totally inappropriate.
>
> (Roger Shuy, p. c., November 9, 2015)

Joos's cothinkers on most issues included Bernard Bloch, Zellig Harris, George Trager, and Charles Hockett. All four had served as LSA President, in 1953, 1955, 1960, and 1964 respectively. Joos had been Vice-President in 1952, but that was before that office automatically led to the presidency the following year (see fn. 1). There was a widespread feeling among the older LSA members, as we see below, that it was Joos's turn to be President.

It is worth concluding this section by reminding the reader that Joos was quite a bit more accepting of generative grammar than were many of his contemporaries.

To repeat the quote presented in Chapter 4, § 4.4.1, he hit the nail on the head with his characterization of the principal difference between post-Bloomfieldian linguistics and generative grammar:

> [Generative grammar is] a heresy within the neo-Saussurean tradition rather than a competitor to it. What this movement most consequentially ignores [...] is the neo-Saussurean axiom [...] 'Text signals its own structure'. From this tacit assumption there follows automatically the most troublesome rule of neo-Bloomfieldian methodology: the rule demanding 'separation of levels' [...]. But [the generativist] leaders are able to point out that *no other science has a parallel rule*.
>
> (Joos 1961: 17–18; emphasis added)

And he was later, as we have seen in Chapter 3, § 3.5.2, to make the following remarkably even-tempered assertion:

> Now when anybody holds that the existence of two kinds of linguistics — taxonomic and, for example, generative-transformational — strictly implies the inferiority or even nullity of one of them, that opinion can only be pernicious no matter which of the two is denigrated. Both extreme views will fade out in due course, especially as each side reads more of what has been published by the other.
>
> (Joos 1966: vi)

7.2.2 Dwight Bolinger

In 1970 Dwight Bolinger was a professor in the Department of Romance Languages and Literatures at Harvard, where he had been teaching since 1963. His posts before then were in Spanish at the University of Southern California between 1944 and 1960 and the University of Colorado between 1960 and 1963. By 1970 he had been the author of a number of books on widely-differing topics, including *What is Freedom? For the Individual – for Society?*(Bolinger 1941a), *The Symbolism of Music* (Bolinger 1941b), *Intensive Spanish* (Bolinger 1948), *Spanish Review Grammar* (Bolinger 1956), *Interrogative Structures of American English* (Bolinger 1957), *Modern Spanish,* (Bolinger 1960a), *Generality, Gradience, and the All-or-none* (Bolinger 1961), *Forms of English: Accent, Morpheme, Order* (Bolinger 1965b), and the introductory text *Aspects of Language* (Bolinger 1968). But Bolinger is known primarily for his dozens of published articles, many of which were later anthologized, on the subtleties of meaning (in its broadest sense), on gradient judgments, on intonation contours, and on the limitations of formal approaches, whether structuralist or generative. Bolinger had the remarkable ability to characterize the (intuitively) correct discourse context for any English sentence. It has been written that he had 'the greatest feel for linguistic data of any living grammarian' (Newmeyer 1983: 113) and that he was 'one of the most distinguished semanticists of the age, with an uncanny ear for the nuances of words' (Nunberg 1992).

Bolinger never took the structuralist position that sees the grammar of a language as an integrated whole. That is, his writings provided detailed studies of the meanings and uses of a wide variety of English grammatical constructions, without there ever being a hint that each individual study might ultimately be a piece of a holistic 'Grammar of English'. His anti-structuralism put him in opposition both to the post-Bloomfieldian orthodoxy of the 1940s and 1950s and to the generative approach that followed it. Bolinger's 'unintegrated' view of linguistic structure was reflected in his writing style, which was airy and charming, but which made it difficult for the reader to grasp the empirical claims and their consequences for a theory of language. To illustrate this point, Bernard Bloch, the editor of *Language* in 1951, rejected a submission from Bolinger that year on the following grounds:[3]

Dear Mr. Bolinger,

It sounds hypocritical or even downright dishonest to say that I thoroughly enjoyed reading your paper on Linear Modification; and yet it's perfectly true. You write so well […], your style is so smooth and yet so witty, and your examples are so carefully chosen, that it always gives me genuine pleasure to read your stuff. […] And yet—and yet. Maybe that's precisely what's wrong with your articles—or rather, precisely what I find necessary to object to; that they are clever causeries, belletristic essays about (around and about) a linguistic subject, rather than the tightly argued, technically oriented articles they might be. […]

Sincerely yours,
B. Bloch

Bolinger was one of the earliest and most persistent critics of generative grammar. In an article in the journal *Word* (Bolinger 1960b), he did grant that 'transformational analysis […] is scarcely more than a proposal, albeit a tremendously fertile one' (p. 375). However, in the course of his reply to a mostly negative review of Bolinger (1957) by Robert B. Lees (Lees 1960b), he went on to put forward the question:

---

[3] A carbon copy of this letter can be found in the BBA. It was also reprinted in Bolinger (1991: 24–25).

Does this mean that [generative] models of the kind proposed by Lees are of no use? Not at all. It is the sort of 'crude analysis' that may well be adequate for purposes of M[achine] T[ranslation] even if it is patently inadequate for purposes of a linguistic description. [...] Where the transformational model applies to completely grammaticized phenomena, it qualifies as a linguistic analysis. Where it is applied to imperfectly grammaticized or ungrammaticized phenomena [the kind of phenomena that Bolinger considered the norm for language—(FJN)], it is a form of linguistic engineering.

(Bolinger 1960b: 389)

As a Harvard professor throughout most of the 1960s and therefore down the street from MIT in its heyday, Bolinger was well aware of what was emanating from the latter institution. However, as his obituary noted:

But Bolinger was antiformalist. The theories Chomsky proposed were anathema to him, even though he admired Chomsky personally, indeed quite extravagantly — especially with respect to the wide range of liberal political views on which they were in complete accord. He joined in the linguistic fun around Cambridge by thinking up counterexamples.

(Stockwell 1993: 108)

In short, Bolinger was a functionalist *avant l'heure*. Talmy Givón, one of the leading proponents of the functionalist orientation, was to acknowledge 'Dwight Bolinger, for teaching that language could only be understood in the context of communication' (Givón 1979: xiv).

As far as personality is concerned, Bolinger could not have been any more different from Joos. Put simply, he was:

Much loved by a large number of his peers. During the memorial services at the cemetery, numerous speakers commented warmly on what an incredibly responsible and helpful correspondent he was: when people wrote to him they got an answer, usually by return mail, and often the kind of answer that they found immediately helpful.

(Stockwell 1993: 99)

Bolinger served on the LSA Executive Committee in 1965 and 1966, shortly after he arrived at Harvard. But geography prevented him from being an active member of the Society before then. In the days before affordable air travel, he remarked regretfully: 'I spent the first two-thirds of my years of employment in parts of the country that made trips to annual meetings too difficult and expensive for me to enjoy many of them' (Bolinger 1991: 21).

7.3 The prelude to the 1970 election

In this section, we examine the LSA as it stood in 1970 (§ 7.3.1), the tasks and composition of its Nominating Committee (§ 7.3.2), and the challenge to Joos's nomination mounted by Dwight Bolinger (§ 7.3.3).

7.3.1 The LSA in early 1970

The 1960s were a decade of great expansion for the LSA. *LSAB* 34, 1961: 12 lists a total membership of 1777 in 1960. By 1969, the membership was 4673 (*LSAB* 43, 1970: 10), that is, close to a tripling in size. The field itself was much changed as well, of course. In 1960 the theory of transformational generative grammar was but three years old and the first class of graduate students at MIT would not arrive for another year. LSA activities reflected this change to a certain degree. Let us compare the first number of the journal *Language* in 1960 (vol. 36, no. 1) with first number in 1970 (vol. 46, no. 1), the latter being the most recent to have appeared before the Nominating Committee was to present its slate. In the 1960 issue, there are two articles on mainstream historical linguistics, one in the framework of post-Bloomfieldian linguistics, and one in tagmemics. Ten years later, of the nine articles, two were analyses within generative phonology and two within generative semantics (which had recently appeared as a challenge to Chomsky's approach to generative syntax). One might also compare the 1959 Annual Meeting of the LSA with the 1969 meeting. In 1959, twenty-eight papers were presented, only one of which (by Robert B. Lees) adopted TGG. At the meeting a decade later, seventy-eight papers were presented, at times in three parallel sessions, and of which perhaps a third were generative.

The generative ascendency was not reflected, however, in the administrative structure of the Society. In 1970, the President, Charles Ferguson was a sociolinguist, the Vice-President, Eric Hamp a historical linguist, the Secretary-Treasurer, Thomas Sebeok a Prague-School-influenced semiotician, and the Editor, William Bright, a sociolinguist. The Executive Committee was composed of Henry Lee Smith, Sol Saporta, Ernst Pulgram, Carleton Hodge, William Labov, and Carroll Reed. Of these, only Saporta was even marginally a generativist (he was primarily known for his structuralist analyses of Spanish). In fact, only three generative grammarians had been members of the Executive Committee in the 1960s: Morris Halle from 1963 to 1965, Robert Stockwell from 1965 to 1967, and Noam Chomsky from 1966 to 1968.

Despite the remarkable growth of the LSA in the 1960s, the Society operated throughout most of that decade without a single full-time employee or space of its own. Business was handled in the house of Secretary-Treasurer Archibald Hill in Austin, Texas. Something needed to be done. In 1966, Thomas Sebeok, Chairman of the Society's Long-Range Planning Committee, set out 'to prepare—for the Executive Committee's consideration and approval—a comprehensive proposal for raising foundation support, including items having to do with this redistribution in the functions of the secretariat and of the treasury, as well as with future Linguistic Institutes, with particular attention to financial support (both summer study aids and advanced graduate fellowships) for students, for a possible expansion of the Society's publication program, and perhaps for other, as yet not fully anticipated, projects of vital interest to the Society' (*LSAB* 40, 1967: 25). The following year Sebeok and his committee drafted a formal proposal to the Ford Foundation for a grant running from 1968 through 1972 'for support for the Society's Linguistic Institutes and publication programs, and for secretarial, fiscal, and other services to be set up in a Washington office of the Secretary-Treasurer' (*LSAB* 41, 1968: 23). The application was successful. The following year Sebeok reported:

> The Committee on Long Range Planning is pleased to announce that The Ford Foundation has, this May, approved a grant of $300,000 to the Society over a five-year period strengthening the Society's secretariat functions and operating Summer Linguistic Institutes. This grant will make it possible for the Society to improve its present services to the Membership and to construct a framework for providing additional services in the future.
>
> (*LSAB* 42, 1969: 26)

Part-and-parcel of the grant was the establishment of a national office in Washington, DC in space rented from the Center for Applied Linguistics, along with salaried administrative and supporting staff.

The grant, then, would be up for renegotiation in 1972, the year that the Vice-President elected in 1970 (for 1971) would take office as President. It was on the minds of many in the LSA leadership that this individual should ideally possess the skills and personal traits that would allow him or her to engineer a trouble-free grant renewal.

7.3.2 The 1970 Nominating Committee

In 1970 the LSA Constitution contained the following provisions for nominations and elections:

> 6. There shall be a Nominating Committee consisting of three members, one of them being elected each year to serve for three years. The member whose term is about to expire shall act as chairman. 7. The Nominating Committee shall nominate one person each for the position of Vice President and each vacant position on the Executive Committee and on the Nominating Committee. A mail ballot shall be submitted to the members not less than three months in advance of the annual meeting. The ballot shall allow for additional nominations, and if two months before the annual meeting ten or more members have separately and in writing nominated any additional persons for any position a special run-off election shall be held by mail. A quorum shall consist of those replies which have been received by the Secretary within two months of the mailing of ballots.
>
> (*LSAB* 47, 1970: 23)

The one curious feature of this process, which was changed the following year, was the fact that the Nominating Committee nominated its own replacement members, leading to a self-perpetuating group of nominators. In any event, in 1970 the committee was composed of Herbert Paper, Chairman; Emmon Bach; and W. Nelson Francis. Let us look at each in turn.

Paper was both a professor in the Near Eastern Languages and Linguistics Department at the University of Michigan and Chairman of that university's Department of Linguistics. Paper was a prominent Yiddishist, and was among the first to teach university-level Yiddish courses in the United States. He also specialized in a number of languages of (what was then called) the Near East, in particular Hebrew and Elamite. His major publication before 1970 was his co-authored book *The Writing System of Modern Persian* (Paper & Jazayery 1955). As his interests were mainly philological, he was not an active participant in the debates about grammatical analysis that were raging in the 1960s.

Bach was Professor of Germanic Languages and Linguistics at the University of Texas. He was one of two linguists in the early 1960s who became prominent generative syntacticians without having had any institutional affiliation with MIT (the other was Charles Fillmore). His popular *An Introduction to Transformational Grammars* (Bach 1964) was the first textbook in generative syntax and his coedited book *Universals in Linguistic Theory* (Bach & Harms 1968) was perhaps the most important anthology of generativist writings in that decade.

Francis was Professor of Linguistics and English at Brown University. His specialty was the history and grammar of English, to the study of which he had contributed several books before 1970 (Francis 1958, 1963; Francis & Kučera 1967). Francis was also one of the first corpus linguists, and by 1970 had begun, with Henry Kučera, to compile a text collection called 'The Brown University Standard Corpus of Present-Day American English'. The writings of Francis clearly show a debt to the prominent post-Bloomfieldian linguists (in particular Bloch and Trager), but he did not, as far as I know, take part in the debates over theory and methodology.

The question, then, is why Paper, Bach, and Francis would have nominated Martin Joos for the presidency. None were strictly speaking his co-thinkers (though Francis was in shooting range) and Joos's views must have been anathema to Bach. The only answer to this question that makes any sense to me is that the three of them shared in the general consensus that it was Joos's turn.

On April 28, 1970 Paper wrote the following letter to Sebeok (who was now Secretary-Treasurer[4]):

Dear Tom:

Here at long last and after much discussion in the Nominating Committee is the slate of nominees for next year's LSA officers:

President	Eric Hamp (as per the constitution)[5]
Vice-Pres:	Martin Joos
Exec. Comm.	John Ross, Ilse Lehiste
Nominating Comm.	Leonard Newmark
Editor:	William Bright
Sec-Treas:	Thomas A. Sebeok

If you have any questions, please call me on the phone. It would be easier than writing letters, as we all know.

Best wishes.

As ever,

Herbert H. Paper (Paper to Sebeok, 28 April, 1970; LSAA)

---

[4] A year later, Bach was Chair of the Nominating Committee. Sebeok wrote to him: 'I should like to pass on for your consideration that there has been a great deal of pressure recently to have more women serving on the Executive Committee; (as you may have heard, there was a considerable fuss about this at the Buffalo Open Meeting, and I must say that some of the sentiments expressed seemed just and appropriate to me)' (Sebeok to Bach, August 25, 1971; LSAA). From that point forward, there were always at least two women on the committee. But Sebeok's sentiments were not always what one might call 'progressive'. Later in the decade, Victoria Fromkin, who was now Secretary-Treasurer, wrote to prominent members, asking 'What special methods might we take to attract more linguists who are members of ethnic minority groups?' (Fromkin to various members, June 18, 1976; TSA). Sebeok replied: '[…] the intellectual structure of linguistics is, in my judgment, not generally attractive to the kind of people that I think you mean when you speak of "ethnic minority groups"' (Sebeok to Fromkin, June 30, 1976; TSA).

[5] What Paper means here is that Hamp's nomination was a mere formality, as he was already Vice-President.

Sebeok must have contacted Joos right away to inform him of his nomination, since the former received a reply from the latter in a very short time. Joos wrote to Sebeok: 'Yes, I will serve as Vice President of the Society for 1971 if elected, with the routine that follows according to the Constitution as it stands from time to time' (Joos to Sebeok, May 10, 1970; LSAA).

7.3.3 Bolinger challenges Joos

As far as I am aware, only one publication has ever even mentioned the 1970 election, much less analyzed it. In his reminiscences about his career trajectory, Bolinger wrote:

> This brings me to the last episode, which is the 1972 presidency of the Society. The constitution provided for a write-in ballot, but I think it had never been used before in the case of a presidential candidate. The choice of the Nominating Committee was Martin Joos. This was perfectly natural, given the tradition of seeing the office of president as a recognition of scholarship and of service in the Society. The members of the Committee felt that this was an honor long overdue to Martin Joos, and that was true. *But there were objections, especially from a good many of the younger members of the Society* who felt that someone outspokenly identified with the Old Guard was not the right choice, and *two of them approached me to ask if I would be willing to have my name put in as an alternative.* I consented, I guess because I could think of myself as having a neutral enough shade to be acceptable to both sides, as long as it appeared that there was going to be a contest one way or another.
>
> (Bolinger 1991: 30–31; emphasis added)

The two 'younger members' who approached Bolinger were William Labov (who was 43 years old at the time) and Bruce Fraser, who was born in 1938. Labov, a professor at Columbia University, was even by 1970 considered the world's leading sociolinguist. An industrial chemist until 1961, his 1963 MA thesis on language and language change on the island of Martha's Vineyard ushered in a new way of looking at structured variation in language. His subsequent 1964 PhD dissertation (Labov 1966) on the social stratification of language in New York City and the publications that followed it demonstrated that much of the everyday variability in speech is systematic, showing both social and linguistic regularities. While neither Bolinger nor Labov were generative grammarians, there was little in common between the former's informal treatment to meaning and use and the latter's rigorously quantitative approach to variation. Labov's major 1970s work, *Sociolinguistic Patterns* (Labov 1972), does not contain a single reference to Bolinger; the latter's most important book of the decade, *Meaning and Form* (Bolinger 1977), refers to a few of Labov's empirical observations, but there is no mention of his theoretical stance.

Bruce Fraser was in the first graduating class at MIT in 1965, writing a dissertation under Chomsky entitled *An Examination of the Verb-Particle Construction in English* (published later as Fraser 1976). However, by 1970 Fraser had all but given up work in generative syntax, focusing instead on pragmatics and discourse analysis. At the time, he was Director of the Language Research Foundation (LRF) in Cambridge, Massachusetts, which 'was founded with the mission of promoting collaborative research on language acquisition by linguists at local institutions, such as MIT and Harvard'.[6] Fraser and Bolinger were well acquainted; indeed, the latter participated in LRF activities at the time. Bolinger's book *The Phrasal Verb in English* (Bolinger 1971) both acknowledged Fraser's dissertation on the topic and cited it several times.

Bruce Fraser recalls:

> My recollections, pretty hazy, were that Bill and I talked several times at how outraged we were that Joos was the nominee and talked about who we might get to replace him. We landed on Dwight. I don't remember if Bill talked to him, or I did (I had an office very close to his), or if someone else did, but he agreed, and we pushed his candidacy.
>
> (p. c., November 9, 2015)

I believe that Bolinger was being more than a little evasive in writing that the primary objection to Joos was that he was 'outspokenly identified with the Old Guard'. I assume that Bolinger had in mind the post-Bloomfieldian 'Old Guard'. He could not have been talking about age per se, since he and Joos were born the same year. But even so, two central 'Old Guard' members were elected LSA President in later years (Rulon Wells in 1976 and Fred Householder in 1981), as were two structuralists with Prague School ties (Thomas Sebeok in 1975 and Robert Austerlitz in 1990).[7] No, the opposition to Joos was based to a large extent on his erratic personality. As Roger Shuy put it (see § 7.2.1), 'I didn't think he'd represent our field well to outsiders'. Recollections by others tend to support my interpretation:

> The story I heard about that election was that Joos was losing it at the time, a bit gaga; and the LSA was in a dicey financial state and needed someone at the helm with full mental capacities. So they got Bolinger to run against Joos.
>
> (Sarah Thomason, p. c., November 9, 2015)

---

[6] In the 1980s LRF was succeeded by the organisation LEX America (see https://www.lexlrf.org/our-mission.html).

[7] Stanley Newman, a Sapirean structuralist, was nominated for the 1984 presidency, but he passed away before the election. His candidacy was replaced by Henry Kahane, a historical linguist.

My understanding at the time was that a group of 'variationist'-minded colleagues connected in one or another way to Philadelphia and to the Center for Applied Linguistics in Washington, DC conjured up all sorts of negatives and disasters looming for the whole profession were Martin made LSA President. To be sure, Martin became increasingly loopy as he aged [...].

(Michael Silverstein, p. c., December 19, 2015)

Perhaps this is what Bolinger was hinting at, but there was in fact more than Joos's personality behind the movement to oppose him. For most young linguists, Joos was a symbol of how linguistics used to be done. The young linguists around 1970 fell roughly into two groups. On the one hand there were generative grammarians, who were brought up with the idea that Joos was the arch-bogeyman, given his often-repeated empiricist dogmatic stance (see Chapter 3). My feeling is that the vast majority of linguists with this orientation (practically all of whom were young) supported Bolinger, either not knowing or not caring that he was even more anti-generative than Joos. And on the other hand, there were, as Silverstein put it, 'variationist-minded colleagues', who were mostly quite young as well, and saw in Joos's rigid structuralism the antithesis of what they were trying to achieve intellectually.[8]

As noted in § 7.3.2, Labov and Fraser had to be in possession of ten signatures nominating Bolinger no less than two months before the Annual Meeting. Since the meeting was to begin on December 28, that gave them a deadline of October 28. They had no trouble at all meeting it. Interestingly, Bolinger played an active role in the process of signature-gathering, as the following letter indicates:

Dear Bill (if I'm not presuming):

On the question of other possible signers I suggest Anna Hatcher at Indiana, Robert Di Pietro at Georgetown, Milt Cowan or Bob Hall at Cornell, Phil Lieberman at Connecticut, Bob Politzer at Stanford (if Greenberg is not available), Sol Saporta at Washington and Ernst Pulgram at Michigan. [...] I've not mentioned anybody here [i. e., at Harvard — (FJN)] because that might look like a put up job.

I can come up with some more if you need them. For instance, if a name from outside the USA would be good to have, Randolph Quirk at University College London or Angus McIntosh at Edinburgh or Hans Marchand at Tübingen would probably be willing.

Sincerely,

Dwight Bolinger (Bolinger to Labov, 21 October 1970; DBA)

---

[8] An anonymous referee suggests that variationists might have felt a kind of intellectual kinship with Bolinger's perspective, given that for both a fine-grained analysis requires considering the broader context of the utterance. That is certainly possible, though there is little if any textual evidence supporting Bolinger's influence on Labovian-style variationist work.

Evidently Bolinger did not know Labov well enough at the time to be secure in using a first-name address. I find it very interesting that most of Bolinger's suggestions were of individuals who were not only 'Old Guard' in some sense, but in two cases inveterate post-Bloomfieldians. Cowan, let us recall, had been LSA Secretary-Treasurer between 1941 and 1950, that is during the heyday of this approach, while Hall was a close co-thinker. Hatcher, Politzer, Greenberg, Pulgram, Quirk, McIntosh, and Marchand were hardly 'younger members of the Society'. Bolinger at the time did not have a 'generation gap' in mind.

We do not know the names of the signers of the nomination letters, but we do know that Labov and Fraser met the October 28 deadline by submitting forty-six letters, thirty-six more than was necessary. On October 24, Bolinger wrote to Sebeok: 'This is just to say that I am honored to accept the nomination for vice president of LSA' (DBA). Labov explained to Bolinger why all of the ballots for him were anonymous:

Dear Dwight,

As you have already seen, the ballots that were sent out on October 29th didn't list any sponsors or signatures. That was the policy that Tom Sebeok had to make because he got some early nominations along with requests that the names NOT be made public.

I think this came about because so many of the older and LSA-loyal type people are personally involved with Joos. They don't want to hurt him, yet they don't want to hurt the association either. When they heard indirectly that there was a movement afoot to nominate you, they felt they had to do something to support it, but not at the cost of telling Joos publicly that he was rejected.

[...]

Originally, I thought that a follow-up letter with forty or fifty signatures supporting you would be a good idea. But now I think it wouldn't be, and Bruce agrees with me on this. First because the general reaction against the nomination of Joos and in favor of your nomination was broader and more spontaneous than I had even expected. Secondly, because there was a first welling up of hurt feelings among some older members ("We can't do this to Martin"). [...] It's unfortunate if Joos should suffer the indignity of being the first presidential candidate rejected, and many think it would be better to have several nominations to begin with. [...]

Sincerely,

Bill Labov (Labov to Bolinger, 1 November 1970; DBA)

Apparently discussions between Labov and Bolinger raised the issue about whether the latter should 'campaign' for the presidency, because on November 7 Bolinger wrote 'I agree absolutely with the idea that campaigning should be avoided. One criticism that I heard locally was directed at "politicizing" the association, and we would be inviting more such if we did more than leave matters to the untutored choice of the members' (DBA).

7.4 The internal debate over the contested election

The opposition to Bolinger's nomination among many older members was quite fierce. Murray Fowler, Joos's one-time colleague at the University of Wisconsin, was perhaps the first to rise to his defense, writing to Sebeok that:

> To insult him in at this time [just before his retirement — (FJN)] is an act which I find nearly, but not quite, inconceivable. [...] To treat him as it is apparently proposed to treat him is an inhumane act to which I will never be a party. [...] Lest I seem to be protesting without proposing a solution, I offer a very simple one — that Dwight Bolinger be persuaded that he should not lend his name to any campaign such as this. [...] If it is not stopped, I shall have to consider whether the Linguistic Society of America is a society to which I should wish to continue to belong.
>
> (Fowler to Sebeok, October 28, 1970; LSAA)

Fowler went on to compare the attempt to defeat Joos with the 'coup' against Joshua Whatmough that led to his removal as President of the Ninth International Congress of Linguists in 1962 and his replacement by Einar Haugen:[9]

> I should think the proposal to disregard the action of the Nominating Committee to be inconceivable in these circumstances were I not perfectly aware of a remarkably similar incident in the removal of Joshua Whatmough, my teacher, from the Presidency of the International Congress. Whatever reasons those who were responsible for Whatmough's supersession may have found to justify their action to their own several consciences — and I heard them all, I feel sure, at the time — it was a cruel and inhumane thing to do. Only those who knew Joshua Whatmough well can ever understand how cruel it was.

Sebeok's reply to Fowler, dated November 4, did little more than to review the LSA constitution and its procedure for elections and to 'hope that you will not, for a moment, consider resigning from the Society' (LSAA). Fowler did indeed resign from the LSA on November 9, expressing the opinion that the instigators 'have exceeded their rights as members of the human community' (LSAA). He was never to rejoin.

---

[9] Konrad Koerner (1989: 116) would like to know '[w]hat happened to Joshua Whatmough [...], who 'was chief figure in securing the invitation for the 9th International Congress to meet in the United States, and who was instrumental in obtaining two substantial grants for support for that congress' (as Eric P. Hamp reports in *Language* 42.622, 1966)'. The only account that I am aware of was published in Hall (1975: 191–193). Hall writes that Whatmough was removed because 'he began to behave in a highly irrational way' (p. 192). To cite one of the many examples, 'He was overbearing and dictatorial in his treatment of the committees which he had named, and inflicted needless humiliations on at least two of the men whom he himself has placed on the committees (Uriel Weinreich and Morris Halle)' (p. 192).

The most concerted effort to encourage Bolinger to pull out was a letter drafted by Winfred Lehmann and Archibald Hill and sent out to a large number of LSA members (we have no record of precisely who):

Dear Fellow LSA Members:

[…] We find ourselves alarmed at the recent move to set up a second candidate for Vice-President with automatic advancement to the Presidency. The reasons for our alarm are –

1) We feel that the presidency of the LSA is an honorary position given in recognition of service to the society and contribution to our science. To refuse this honor, after official nomination, to a member adjudged fitting by the committee to whom choice is delegated, is an unprecedented and bitter reproof, which would be open to the interpretation of being a rejection of the candidate's scholarship, personality, or both.
2) We feel that the difficulty in raising funds, which has been rumored to be the reason for [finding an alternative to Joos], is something which could more properly be handled by delegation of the fund-raising function to someone suited to it, than by any action which could be interpreted as defining fund-raising as a principal qualification of our President.
3) Negatively, we state emphatically that our objection to this movement has nothing to do with the character and status of the proposed second candidate, who will certainly reach the Presidency in years to come. For the present year, however, we urge the second candidate to withdraw his name, since we are convinced that withdrawal would be for the good of the society, and be an important and statesmanlike act of generosity.

Sincerely yours,
Winfred Lehmann and Archibald Hill (29 October 1970; LSAA)

The letter was endorsed by at least the following linguists: Harry Hoijer, Yuen Ren Chao, Albert Marckwardt, Samuel Martin, W. Freeman Twaddell, George Trager, Carl Voegelin, William Gedney, Rulon Wells, Warren Cowgill, Robert Stockwell, Theo Vennemann, and George Lane.

Stockwell and Vennemann were both generative grammarians at the time, a fact which illustrates that 'ideological' differences were not at the root of the campaign to elect Bolinger instead of Joos. In fact, Stockwell was in the *vanguard* of LSA members urging Bolinger to withdraw. In a memorandum to his colleagues at UCLA he identified the Ford Foundation grant renewal process as the reason that there was doubt in Joos's competence as a possible President:[10]

---

[10] Stockwell headed his memo 'CONFIDENTIAL', but it began with the following words: 'This memorandum is confidential with respect to only two individuals, namely the two concerned: Martin Joos

[...] However, a number of members of the society, for whom I have the highest respect and with whom I take issue on this matter with the greatest reluctance, have concluded that Martin Joos is a poor choice for the office because it is during 1972 that the current grant which supports the Washington office will be renegotiated. Though most of the negotiations will be carried out by Thomas A. Sebeok, these members assume that Joos will be involved, and they are not confident of his ability to represent the society. They are therefore nominating Dwight Bolinger to run against Joos in this election.

(Stockwell to his colleagues in UCLA Linguistics, 20 October 1970; LSAA)

For Stockwell, 'any such consideration as grant negotiations is a morally improper basis to reject, in his late years, a venerable, long respected, and extremely dedicated colleague. It would, I quietly add, be equally wrong to reject Dwight Bolinger if he were the original candidate.'

Sebeok's view was that using the excuse of renegotiating the grant was a red herring:

[...] What surprises me is the reason you give for preference of some members for Bolinger, as against Joos: that the issue is the negotiation of a renewal of the Ford grant, when the present five-year grant expires. [...] What I believe is that the identity of the Vice-President or President will not matter to the Ford Foundation one way of the others. Our case will have to be resolved on its merits alone, and will neither stand nor fall on the question of whether Joos or Bolinger is in office in any particular year. [...]

(Sebeok to Stockwell, October 30, 1970; LSAA)

Stockwell's quick reply to Sebeok revealed his true feelings about Joos's nomination:

[...] I believe [...] that the nominating committee did a stupid thing, but once they did it we should live with it, as we have lived with several other stupid nominations they have made in the past,[11] rather than hurt the old man. For me it's a simple humane issue, nothing else. Anyway, we're stuck with it now, and a lot of people are going to be damned unhappy if Dwight wins, even though he is obviously the more deserving.

(Stockwell to Sebeok, November 6, 1970; LSAA)

---

and Dwight Bolinger. I would appreciate your not passing it on to them, for reasons that will become obvious. I don't care who else sees it'. Did Stockwell sincerely believe that a widely-distributed letter would not fall into the hands of the two principal figures discussed in it?

[11] What historiographer would not want to know what the other stupid nominations were?

In that same letter Stockwell mentioned getting phone calls from several people ('ringleaders' he called them) asking him to support Bolinger. In fact, there was a huge phone-calling campaign. The young linguists in my department, including myself, all received calls from Bruce Fraser urging us to vote for Bolinger in the election.[12]

The months of November and early December saw a feverish back and forth between him and (mostly older) members of the society.

Dear Prof. Bolinger:

Monday, to my dismay, I received a ballot from the secretariat of the Linguistic Society of America announcing your nomination as an additional candidate for the office of Vice President through 1971. I have great admiration for your contributions to our field [...]. However, Martin Joos has been a member of the society even years longer; he is on the verge of retirement; and it is an evil comment on our society that in thirty-four years of distinguished membership he has never held one of the offices which it is such an honor to hold. [...]. Some people are annoyed by Joos's personality, and some (especially younger ones) regard his sort of linguistics as utterly passé. Neither attitude is justification for not having honored him long ago. [...] I am going to return my ballot, casting my vote for Joos. It is my hope that the majority will do the same, leaving you for a later term. I wish I could persuade you to withdraw your candidacy, even at this late date.

(Charles Hockett to Bolinger, November 4, 1970; DBA)

Bolinger replied to Hockett on November 7, beginning his letter by expressing distress that Hockett had addressed him as 'Prof. Bolinger'. Bolinger went on to tell Hockett that '[i]t is only right that, feeling as you do, you should vote for Martin, or even campaign for him'.

Not all letters to Bolinger were as negative as Hockett's. That written by William Moulton was quite measured in tone:

Dear Dwight,

LSA troubles! Bill Labov telephoned me some weeks ago and asked me to be one of the ten (or more) signers to nominate you. Out of sheer sentimental friendship for Martin Joos I declined. Now I have a letter from Arch Hill and Win Lehmann, asking me to sign a letter putting pressure on you to withdraw. I have also declined to sign this, though for quite different reasons: I consider it highly improper, and obviously against the spirit of the LSA constitution. If ten or more

---

[12] As for me, I was predisposed not to vote for Joos, given the (to me) theoretically backward positions that he took in his *Readings in Linguistics*. I am not sure that I had ever heard of Dwight Bolinger in 1970. I doubt that his work was on many departmental reading lists, whether structuralist or generativist. I suspect that I was not alone at the time in taking an 'anybody but Joos' stance.

members want you to run, and you agree, the constitution says that you are also a properly nominated candidate. [...] Anyway, best wishes to you and God save us all!

Yours,
Bill [Moulton]

(Moulton to Bolinger, November 3, 1970; DBA)

In an undated reply to Moulton, though probably written in early November, Bolinger mentioned that he had 'learned of the letter [from Hill and Lehmann] from Karl Teeter, though I have not seen it yet—I have however received one individual such request, not, I'm happy to say, presented in unfriendly terms' (DBA).

And in fact, some of the older linguists were quite supportive of Bolinger's challenge. Consider the following lively message from Yakov Malkiel:

> There is considerable, even enthusiastic, approval of your candidacy for the Vice-Presidency of the LSA along the West Coast among the "independent voters". You certainly can count on MY vote! And I hope you not follow any pressure brought to bear on you (and designed to make you withdraw from the race) to influence your judgment. We need a sound Vice-President in 1971 and an equally sound President in 1972 — rather than a living corpse or a mummy! [...]
>
> (Malkiel to Bolinger, November 3, 1970; DBA)

Bolinger thanked Malkiel in a letter dated November 7, but wondered aloud 'whether I was quite sane when I said yes' (DBA).

Bolinger's reply to the several people who asked him to withdraw his candidature was that it would be against the spirit of the LSA constitution for him to opt out of the election. For example:

> [...] The best reply I can make is the same as I gave to one other member of the Society who takes the same stand as you. It was that the position I find myself in is one I incurred but did not invite, and if I thought that my withdrawal might be the simple solution that you sense it to be I would not hesitate. [...] The members who thought that they had a recourse in the Society's constitution would feel that they had been cheated, and there is too much of that kind of frustration going on around these days. [...]
>
> (Bolinger to Lehmann, November 26, 1970; DBA)

I find Bolinger's message to Lehmann to be somewhat odd. The LSA Constitution *allows* a challenge, but it doesn't *require* one. And it certainly does not require a potential challenger to stay in the race if they would rather not do so. Lehmann's reply to Bolinger was quite conciliatory:

[…] But I suppose that if [Joos] doesn't make it, he'll survive. Most of us would be hard pressed to name the past presidents of the Society and now that there's a pay-for-your-own bar [at LSA meetings], [the President] doesn't even have a big pow-wow in his apartment after his address. […]

(Lehmann to Bolinger, December 8, 1970; DBA)

In my first interpretation it seemed like Lehmann was implying that people got so drunk at the cash bar that they forgot who was President the year before. However, perhaps Lehmann was simply suggesting that memories of previous presidencies fade and there was no longer a social gathering over which the president presided. The implication is that the presidency is less important than one might think.

Let us turn now to the election itself.

7.5 The election results and their aftermath

According to *LSA Bulletin* 48, Feb. 1971, ballots had been mailed to 4141 personal members and 1308 votes were cast. It was announced at the December meeting that Bolinger had defeated Joos. However, the actual number of votes for each candidate was never released. In a letter the following spring to LSA member Margaret Damsen, Sebeok explained why:

> Whether or not to publish the actual figures was the subject of a good deal of agonized discussion among the officers and members of the Executive Committee, and it was finally decided not to publish them because of the lopsided nature of the numbers, which would have, it was felt, embarrassed the losing candidate. Since this was the first time the Society was ever confronted with a situation of this sort in its entire history,[13] there was no precedent to guide us, and we had to steer between the point of view that you express (and with which, incidentally, I am personally sympathetic), and personal delicacy. Incidentally, the Constitution does not require that figures of this sort be disclosed.

(Sebeok to Damsen, April 26, 1971; LSAA)

Nevertheless, we have two memos, both undated, from Sebeok to Diana Riehl, the Administrative Assistant of the LSA. The first, which appears to be from mid-November, reports 197 votes for Joos and 376 for Bolinger. The second, most likely from mid-December, reports 400 for Joos and 818 for Bolinger (both

---

[13] That is not strictly speaking correct. There had been two earlier nomination challenges, though not for the presidency. In 1940 George Lane challenged the official nominee J Milton Cowan for the post of Secretary-Treasurer. It was reported in *LSAB* 17: 31, from 1941, that Cowan received 42 votes and Lane 18 (see Chapter 1, § 1.5.5). In 1958 James Sledd challenged one of the official candidates for Executive Committee, William Austin. Sledd defeated Austin, though the distribution of votes was not reported (see *LSAB* 35: 20, from 1959).

LSAA). Given that 1308 votes were cast, the final tally was probably something like 419 votes for Joos and 889 for Bolinger.

We have only scanty evidence about the personal reactions of Joos to his defeat and Bolinger to his victory. On the one hand, Joos seemed to accept the outcome with good grace. At the conclusion of the winter meeting Bolinger wrote to Joos:

> Dear Martin,
>
> This is just to say that I appreciate your friendliness and your sportsmanship in these last few days, and welcomed the chance to exchange a view or two and know you a bit better — which if I have fallen short of it in the past was my fault.
>
> Sincerely,
> Dwight Bolinger
>
> (Bolinger to Joos, December 31, 1970; MJA)

On the other hand, Joos was very wary about LSA involvements after the election. In reply to a call for participation in LSA activities sent out by past Secretary-Treasurers Archibald Hill and J Milton Cowan, Joos replied:

> Well, then, I want you to do exactly one thing — for me: Please do what you can to make sure that I never again appear to be in line for any position such as, or to any significant degree analogous to, those which the present LSA Constitution envisages as within the purview of the Nominating Committee. [...]
>
> (Joos to Hill and Cowan, August 3, 1971; MJA)

A few years later, Adam Makkai and others were in the process of setting up the organization Linguistic Association of Canada and the United States (LACUS), hoping to attract (in Makkai's words) a 'long list of genuine linguists who are fed up with the LSA and the MITnik establishment'.[14] To Makkai, Joos was an ideal candidate for membership. However, Joos gave a long list of reasons why he would not participate, one of which was '[...] Sixth, any possibility that Bolinger will be there will keep me far away. [...]' (Joos to Makkai, July 2, 1974; MJA).

Joos's mental and physical health declined in the 1970s; he passed away at the age of 69 in 1978. William Samarin considered 'it unfortunate to have known Joos only at the end of his life, when his eccentricities seemed to overshadow his magisterial intellect' (Samarin 1998: 212). Bolinger, on the other hand, went from honor

---

[14] 'MITnik' is a derogatory term for a generative grammarian, not much (if ever) used since the 1970s.

to honor, including that of being elected the first President of LACUS in 1975–1976 and winning the Orwell Award for his book *Language: The Loaded Weapon* (Bolinger 1980). He died in 1992.[15]

7.6 Concluding remarks

In a drama unprecedented in LSA history, the official candidate for the office of President was challenged and defeated. Dwight Bolinger allowed his name to be put in opposition to Martin Joos's and received close to seventy percent of the votes. Two factors played major roles in this drama. On the one hand:

> [The movement to oppose Joos] was all about Martin Joos's personality. Although it seemed to be apparent that his turn had come, so that it would be insulting to him if anyone else were nominated, there were enough people around who disliked Joos and perhaps supposed that (somehow, because of his personality) it would be harmful for the well-being of LSA if he were president, that an informal search for an alternative was undertaken. Dwight Bolinger was a highly respected linguist who was a non-participant in LSA politics and governance, but someone who, it was agreed, would make a good president and who deserved to be honored. It was just a way of avoiding a Joos presidency. Joos had made it known (to at least a few people, including me) that he had a kidney problem and wasn't going to be around much longer, and that his turn to be president had come and that they had better give it to him soon, before his imminent incapacitation and/or death.
>
> (Sydney Lamb, p. c., November 9, 2019)

But there was more to the opposition to Joos than his unpleasant personality. It appears to be the case that most of the younger members of the LSA—sociolinguists and generative grammarians alike—voted overwhelmingly for Bolinger. I would say that for them Joos represented the post-Bloomfieldian establishment, which showed little interest in either linguistic variation or fleshing out the formal properties of universal grammar respectively. The fact that Bolinger himself was neither social variationist nor generativist was irrelevant.

[15] Margaret Thomas (p. c., July 1, 2021) raises the question of whether Bolinger's presidency was instrumental to the success of the renewal of the Ford Foundation grant. I doubt it: By all accounts it was Sebeok who saw the grant application through from beginning to end.

8

Charles Hockett's attempt to resign from the LSA in 1982

8.1 Introduction

The present chapter, like the preceding one, documents an episode in the history of American linguistics related to the transition from post-Bloomfieldian structuralism to TGG. Charles Hockett was throughout the 1940s and early 1950s the most prominent linguist of the post-Bloomfieldian school that dominated grammatical theory in the United States. His initial reaction to the appearance of generative grammar was mixed, in that he saw both plusses and minuses in the new theory. However, by the mid-1960s, Hockett had become virulently opposed to the direction that Chomsky and his co-thinkers were taking. Indeed, many of his publications in the last thirty-some-odd years of his life were devoted to some extent to combatting generative grammar. Hockett saw the LSA, of which he had been President in 1964, as complicit in the generative ascendancy. Indeed, he saw the LSA as being under the control of generative linguists. For that reason, in 1982 he made an unsuccessful attempt to resign from the LSA. The bulk of this chapter is devoted to the presentation and discussion of the series of letters between Hockett and other prominent LSA members surrounding his resignation attempt. Almost all of this material is drawn from the LSA Archive at the University of Missouri.

The interest of this chapter for the historiography of linguistics is in part its documentation of what was in all probability the closure of the Bloomfieldian era, that is, it chronicles the last stand of a central post-Bloomfieldian linguist in the face of the changing direction of the field. But I would go on to say that its importance lies not so much in Hockett's resignation attempt per se, but on the light that it shines on the personal and professional interactions of leading LSA members in the early 1980s.

The chapter is organized as follows. § 8.2 presents a sketch of the life and work of Charles Hockett and § 8.3 is devoted to the 1982 fund drive organized by the LSA to raise $300,000 in support of its activities. § 8.4 reprints, with discussion, Hockett's letter of resignation from the LSA and the reaction to it among leading LSA members. § 8.5 calls attention to the disconnect between Hockett's perception of the field and reality, and § 8.6 contains brief concluding remarks.

American Linguistics in Transition. Frederick J. Newmeyer, Oxford University Press.
© Frederick J. Newmeyer (2022). DOI: 10.1093/oso/9780192843760.003.0008

8.2 Charles Hockett

Let us begin with a view of Hockett's ideas and career trajectory. Here and elsewhere in the chapter, I have made the decision to repeat verbatim some passages that appeared earlier in this book (and will appear later), in particular in Chapter 1, § 1.2; Chapter 3, § 3.4.1; Chapter 4, §§ 4.3.3.3, 4.3.3.5, 4.4.1, 4.4.2; and Chapter 9, § 9.3.2. While such a practice is generally frowned upon for valid stylistic reasons, it seems necessary here in order to avoid a disjointed presentation.

Hockett 'was regarded by many of his peers as the preeminent figure in American linguistics' (Golla 2001:6) and was 'probably *the* general theorist of his generation' (Koerner 1989: 128; emphasis in original). From the early 1940s until well into the 1950s he set the tone for American descriptive linguistics. As one measure of his importance, Martin Joos's edited volume *Readings in Linguistics: The Development of Descriptive Linguistics in America Since 1925* (Joos 1957b; see Chapter 3 for discussion) contained seven of Hockett's publications. The runner up, Zellig Harris, had only four. Falk (2003) contains a figure called 'Linguists included on lists of leading American descriptivists' (p. 132), drawn from six sources from 1942 to 1999. Three names appear in all six sources: Bernard Bloch, Hockett, and George Trager; Zellig Harris appears on five lists, all but the 1942 source.[1] As a major spokesperson for the positivist tendency that reigned supreme in the United States, most of his analytical and methodological papers until the late 1950s were involved in fleshing out how one might construct the grammar of a language using a set of purely form-based (i.e. non-semantic) procedures, in which the intuitions of the native speaker in principle played no role.

In some publications Hockett did in fact appear to break free from empiricist constraints on theory-formation, writing for example that '[T]he analytical process thus parallels what goes on in the nervous system of a language learner [...] The child hears, and eventually produces, various utterances. Sooner or later, the child produces utterances he has not previously heard from someone else' (Hockett 1948a: 270). Analogously, he wrote a few years later that '[A] model must be productive: when applied to a given language, the results must make possible the creation of an indefinite number of valid new utterances' (Hockett 1954: 232). As pointed out in Chapter 4, § 4.3.3.5, some commentators (e.g. Koerner 1989: 127–128) have cited these passages as a means to diminish Chomsky's originality by pointing to what a strong degree Hockett 'was ahead of his time' (Koerner 1989: 128), and by implication was the originator of generative grammar. Such a view cannot be maintained. First of all, Chomsky's 1949 undergraduate thesis (Chomsky 1949) and his 1951 master's thesis (later published as Chomsky 1979b [1951]),

---

[1] An anonymous referee, however, suggests that 'Hockett may have gained the position as "most prominent" later by his continued and vociferous resistance to the rise of generative linguistics, but that was (in my opinion) because other main figures had lost interest in resistance by the late 1960s (or, as in Bloch's case, because they had died by then)'.

which propose a generative account of Hebrew, formulate rule systems that assign a full structural description to every linguistic expression generated. There is not a hint of anything comparable in either of Hockett's publications. And there is no reason to believe that these two papers represented for Hockett a break from operationalism. His late 1950s textbook *A Course in Modern Linguistics* (Hockett 1958) referred to 'the step-by-step procedures' (p. 102) for the linguist to follow, designed to end up with a taxonomic display of the grammatical elements of the language. For Hockett in 1958, as fifteen years earlier, 'Linguistics is a classificatory science' (Hockett 1942: 3).

Hockett received his PhD from Yale University in 1939 with a dissertation written under Edward Sapir on the Algonquian language Potawatomi. He then spent two years with Bloomfield at the University of Chicago doing post-doctoral work. His contribution to the war effort was the production of language teaching materials, particularly focusing on Chinese. In 1946, Hockett was hired by Cornell University, where he remained until 1986. He finished his career as an Adjunct Professor at Rice University.

Hockett is perhaps best remembered today for his starting a dialogue on what he termed the 'design features' of language, that is, those properties that all human languages share, but which, in their totality, are absent from every known type of animal communication (see especially Hockett 1960). These include properties such as 'arbitrariness' (there being no necessary connection between the sounds used and the message being sent); 'displacement' (the possibility of being able to communicate about things that are not present); and 'duality of patterning' (the combination of speech sounds to make meaningful words, which can be recombined to make sentences). Many if not most general discussions of human language evolution refer to Hockett's features.

Hockett is also noteworthy for being one of the pioneers of information theory:

> Hockett had a remarkable gift for mathematics and mathematical and formal systems. In 1953, he produced a review of Shannon and Weaver's work on communication theory (Hockett 1953's review of Shannon & Weaver 1948), and the information-theoretical approach became, as he put it, part of his standard intellectual equipment (Hockett 1977: 19). One result was the inclusion in the *Manual of Phonology* [Hockett 1955] of an introductory section presenting a finite-state Markovian view of speech communication and grammar, essentially of the kind that Chomsky famously critiqued in *Syntactic Structures* (Chomsky 1957a). Hockett himself quite soon rejected that approach as not fitting the nature of human language, while retaining the view that information science had important contributions to make to linguistics.
>
> (Gair 2003: 603)

Gregory Radick has provided a complementary sketch of Hockett's information-theoretic studies:

> Hockett later recalled, 'There had to be implications for linguistics and anthropology [in the work of Shannon and Weaver], and I set out to discover what they were' (Hockett 1977: 18). His self-education in the abstract, probability-saturated analysis of message encoding, transmission, and decoding along telephonic lines (literal and figurative), and in associated concepts such as noise, channel capacity, and information, took an important step forward in the summer of 1951, when he participated in an intensive summer school on communications theory at MIT. In 1952 he made a linguistically directed contribution in his own right, with a short paper in *Philosophy of Science* [Hockett 1952b] on the quantification of 'semantic noise' (arising, he explained, from 'a discrepancy between the codes used by transmitter and receiver').
>
> (Radick 2016: 67)

More specifically, it is worth calling attention to Hockett (1955) and Hockett (1966c), where the notion of 'functional load' (Martinet 1955) is quantified. The functional load of an element of a grammar, informally stated, is the work required to distinguish it from other elements. By applying algebraic grammar and matroid lattice theory, Hockett was able to derive the measures of entropy used by Shannon in information theory. He concluded: 'The method can be used to measure the work of phonemes, allophones, or components, and should therefore be useful regardless of the outcome of present disputes in the field of phonology. Subjective impressions suggest that there is a balance point in speech between the force of least effort, making for lowest redundancy, and the practical need to be understood, pressing for lower entropy' (Hockett 1966c: 1).

As implied above, Hockett was also one of the pioneers of mathematical linguistics, being the first, I believe, to propose a finite-state grammar as an potential model of human language syntax. Here his legacy is less celebrated, to a large extent as a result of a devastating review of Hockett (1966b) (which was published separately as Hockett 1966a) by James McCawley. McCawley offered the opinion that 'Hockett's "Language, mathematics, and linguistics" (155–304) does not justice to any of the three topics mentioned in its title. The mathematics is amateurish; the linguistics is a procession of straw men, whom Hockett does even bother to knock down but leaves tottering on their straw legs; and language is largely ignored' (McCawley 1968: 571). I have found few references to Hockett's 1960s proposals in current work in mathematical linguistics.[2]

---

[2] A contemporary mathematical linguist has put it bluntly: 'About Hockett's influence on current work, I'd be inclined to say that the short story is that (perhaps in part because of McCawley) there is no such influence. No mathematical linguists felt like following up any of Hockett's odd modifications of generative grammar, or adopting his wacky terminology ("harp" for a set of strings was one). The recent upsurge in applied statistics does not connect at all with Hockett's odd little effort in the introduction to *A Manual of Phonology*, which I find incredibly feeble (his sample grammar generates an extremely

286 HOCKETT'S ATTEMPT TO RESIGN FROM LSA, 1982

As far as Hockett's reaction to generative grammar is concerned, his initial assessment was in fact quite positive.[3] Indeed, he described *Syntactic Structures* as 'our fourth major breakthrough' in the history of linguistics (Hockett 1965: 196) and recognized that its most important feature was its stressing the need to 'distinguish between any sort of discovery procedure on the one hand and, on the other, any sort of characterization of a language' (p. 197). Yet, just a year later, Hockett would write: 'Chomsky's outlook—not merely on language but also on mathematics, perhaps on everything—is so radically different from Bloomfield's and from my own that there is, at present, no available frame of reference external to both within which they can be compared' (Hockett 1966b: 156). What could have caused him to change his mind so quickly? In fact, he tells us. The first chapter of Chomsky newly-published book *Aspects of the Theory of Syntax* (Chomsky 1965), with its unabashedly rationalist foundations, so dismayed Hockett that he broke any intellectual ties that he might have forged with generative grammar. He flirted with stratificational grammar a bit in that same publication (Hockett 1966b: § 6.5), but soon abandoned the idea that language could even be considered a well-defined system (Hockett 1968). Roman Jakobson hit the nail on the head when he said: 'It is very difficult for me to know what Hockett's position on any question is […]. He changes his mind every day' (quoted in Mehta 1971: 235).

Bernard Bloch might have been characterized as 'the truest Bloomfieldian of them all' (Stark 1972: 387), but it was Hockett who did the most to preserve Leonard Bloomfield's legacy. It was Hockett whom Bloomfield chose to be his literary executor and it was Hockett who edited the anthology of Bloomfield's work (Hockett 1970), an abridged edition of which appeared as Hockett (1987c).[4] In his editor's introduction to the volume, Hockett noted regretfully that 'Bloomfield's voice of wisdom has been stilled for two decades. The mantle of leadership which he wore so gracefully […] has fallen to the ground, for none of us has the wisdom or power to bear it. […] We can still know, if we will but heed, his reaction to the pettishness, the prima-donnaism, and the neglect of already accumulated experiences, and the antiscientific bias that have all too often characterized our discussions' (Hockett 1987b: vii). The unabridged edition contained a contribution by William Mouton on Bloomfield as a Germanist (Moulton 1970). Hockett was quite distressed by some wording by Moulton in the latter's draft version of his contribution:

Now, in your last paragraph, it is the passage beginning after the semicolon in line eight from the bottom and running practically to the end that bothers me. A reference to 'new directions' made in the latter half of the seventh decade of

small finite language, and he gave no indication of understanding that he would need some possibility of looping back in his finite state machine)' (Geoffrey Pullum, p. c., April 5, 2021).
  [3] For discussion of Hockett's early views on Chomsky's theorizing, see Falk (2003) and Radick (2016).
  [4] Hockett turned over all of the royalties from the abridged edition to the LACUS Foundation (for a description of LACUS see Chapter 7, § 7.5 and Chapter 9, § 9.1). I interpret this gesture as an act of defiance against what he saw as the generativist dominance of the field.

the twentieth century will be interpreted by almost every reader—at least, every reader on this side of the Atlantic—as a reference to Chomsky's views. [...] Whether you so intend or not, many a reader will interpret your passage as saying that you believe that if Bloomfield were still alive he would be a supporter of those particular new views. [...] [Your wording] should not be understood, or misunderstood, as an underscoring of an opinion that Bloomfield today would be a Chomskyite.

(Hockett to Moulton, January 6, 1969; CHA)

Moulton's final version modified the wording that Hockett found objectionable.

From the mid-1960s to the early 1980s, Hockett, in published work and in interviews, found many opportunities to excoriate Chomsky and his ideas. His book-length critique of generative grammar, *The State of the Art*, found 'Chomskyan-Hallean "phonology"[...] completely bankrupt' (Hockett 1968: 3). A few years later he informed an interviewer that generative grammar was a 'theory spawned by a generation of vipers' (Mehta 1971: 175), whose studies 'are as worthless as horoscopes' (p. 218). But by the mid-1980s until his death, Hockett pretty much ignored work in the Chomskyan tradition. His 1987 book *Refurbishing our Foundations* (Hockett 1987a) presented an informal hearer-based account of the processing of linguistic input, devoting a chapter to each level of linguistic structure. The dozen or so references to generative work in the book were fairly neutral. He even expressed the balanced opinion that '[...] many of the issues to which linguists in the Chomskyan tradition devote their attention are, it seems to me, no more than artefacts of their frame of reference. (But let us remember that there is nothing new about that. The Decade of the Phoneme was characterized by irrelevant questions about phonology, and the Decade of the Morpheme by equally impertinent morphological queries. Progress in linguistics seems to be made mainly by painfully discovering which issues are real, which ones spurious.)' (Hockett 1987a: 84).

There is a general consensus that Hockett died a very bitter man. And it is easy to understand why he would be bitter. As noted by the historiographer Randy Harris, 'Hockett has reason to complain—not least because he was the Bloomfieldian-most-likely, [...] pretty much swept aside in the prime of his career' (Harris 1993: 53).

Hockett joined the LSA in 1939 and became a life member in 1952. However, compared to many of his contemporaries, he was not particularly active in the day-to-day affairs of the Society. He served on only one standing committee: From 1952 to 1954 he was a member of the Committee on Publications (which was renamed the '*Language* Editorial Board' in 1971). However, given his stature in the field, he was elected LSA President in 1964 without opposition. Like many of his generation, he felt that the LSA had come under the control of Chomskyan linguists and wrote to Martin Joos on June 26, 1972: 'For about two years I have been tempted to resign my membership in the LSA, not to save money (since I am a life member) but just to avoid cluttering my shelves with absolute junk' (MJA). As we see below, a decade later he attempted to make good on his temptation.

8.3 The LSA's Fund for the Future of Linguistics

In 1981 the LSA found itself dangerously short of available funds. The non-renewable Ford Foundation grant for support of Linguistic Institute fellowships was due to expire in 1983 and the Society, which had been renting office space from the Center for Applied Linguistics for some years (see Chapter 7: § 7.3.1), felt that it was time to acquire its own premesis. The *LSA Bulletin* no. 90 of March 1981 reported that 'The Executive Committee received preliminary plans for a 1982 fund raising campaign aimed at increasing the Society's endowment. […] The fund drive will be headed by a Committee of LSA Presidents and will incorporate a wide range of fund-raising activities' (p. 6). Eugene Nida, a Past President of the LSA and former Finance Committee Chair, was appointed to head the drive and to solicit the endorsement of all of the other past presidents for the display of their names on the letterhead of (what was soon to be called) the Fund for the Future of Linguistics (FFL). The initial goal was to raise $150,000 (*LSAB* 94, 1982: 1), which was soon raised to $300,000 (*LSAB* 97, 1982: 14). Secretary-Treasurer Victoria Fromkin sent the following letter dated August 1982 to LSA members:

Dear Colleague:

We need your help to insure the future of linguistics. In the past, with generous membership and foundation support, LSA has been able to enhance the quality of linguistic scholarship. Changing foundation priorities now force us to look to ourselves to insure the support and encouragement of young and seasoned scholars. We are therefore launching the Fund for the Future of Linguistics, aiming to raise $300,000.00 by September 1985. Your regular dues will continue to fund LANGUAGE, the LSA BULLETIN, and the Annual Meeting, but we need these additional funds for Linguistic Institutes, student fellowships, other publications, conferences, symposia, and similar special activities. Please note that LSA is applying for a National Endowment for the Humanities Challenge Grant. If awarded, contributions to the Fund for the Future of Linguistics will be matched by $1.00 in Federal funds for each $3.00 contributed. Please contribute as much as you possibly can. Become a life member for only $1,000.00. Insure the future of linguistics.

Sincerely yours,
Victoria A. Fromkin (LSAA)

At the top left of the page were the names of past presidents of the LSA in a list entitled 'COMMITTEE OF PRESIDENTS'. All were listed with three exceptions: Zellig Harris, George Trager and—Charles Hockett. Why did these three (implicitly) fail to support the FFL? William Moulton, one of the past presidents, had a hypothesis:

> These three exceptions are fascinating: [Hockett, Harris, and Trager] are without doubt the most "difficult" of all living presidents. (The late Bernard Bloch once said of Trager: George Trager is so difficult that he would even be fired from George Trager University.) Yet now I believe I understand. As I recall, all of us past Presidents were asked whether we would be willing to serve on the Committee of Presidents. Presumably the most "difficult" past Presidents all said no: Harris 1955, Trager 1960, Hockett 1964. Come to think of it, they are all so "difficult" that they probably did not even answer!
>
> (Moulton to John Hammer, LSA Associate Secretary,
> December 1, 1982; LSAA)[5]

As we see in the following section, it was more than Hockett's 'difficulty' that kept him from endorsing the FFL.

In any event, thanks to the National Endowment for the Humanities approving the challenge grant (*LSAB* 99, 1983: 1) and to matching grants from a wide variety of American corporations, that sum was attained by 1985 (*LSAB* 109, 1985: 12). The *LSAB* 112, 1986, reported that 'through February 28, 1986 we raised $362,295.65, and contributions are still coming' (p. 7). In other words, the FFL was a great success.

8.4 Hockett takes action

Several factors culminating in the autumn of 1982 spurred Hockett to make good on his long-expressed desire to resign from the LSA. The most important, given that it was the first mentioned, was the establishment of the FFL, of whose existence he had surely been aware for months:

Dear Victoria,

I have read your letter of 9 November about the Fund for the Future of Linguistics. The problem of my proper comportment as a former president of the LSA has

---

[5] An anonymous referee would appreciate more detail on the 'difficulty' of the three named linguists. A full account would require a chapter with a length of the present one, though a few remarks might prove interesting. Harris's 'difficulty' stemmed from his general uncollegiality: he was famous for not replying to correspondence and for shunning collaborative work (p. c., Noam Chomsky, December 12, 1978). Trager was the bane of university administrators and of his own colleagues, leading him to drift from job to job throughout his career. Hockett was considered 'difficult' because of his intellectual intransigence. By way of example, J Milton Cowan recalls a very young Hockett admonishing his mentor Leonard Bloomfield by telling him, 'The trouble with you Mr. Bloomfield, is that you don't believe in the phonemic principle' (Cowan 1991: 70).

disturbed me for some time. I have finally been forced to the unhappy conclusion that my only appropriate action is to resign from the Society. This is my official letter of resignation.

You are entitled to an explanation, as is Bill Bright [the editor of *Language*] and as are my fellow former presidents. They will therefore receive copies of this communication.

[...] If the Society were today what is was at the beginning, I would joyfully work through it to insure the future of our branch of science. But even when I was president, two decades ago, things were changing, and now they have altered beyond recognition. [letter continued below]

The 'crowning blow' triggering his resignation was an editorial decision by Bright:

For me the crowning blow was the rejection by the editor a few weeks ago of a careful and calm critique by Konrad Koerner, the best historian of linguistics we have, of some 1984-style rewriting of recent linguistic history. That act of the editor and his advisors put adherence to the party line above the search for truth, and I will have none of it. [letter continued below]

The paper submitted by Koerner was entitled 'The Chomskyan "revolution" and its historiography: A few critical remarks'. In large part it was a vigorous critique of the account of the development of TGG published in Newmeyer (1980). Bright sent the paper to three referees, myself and two others suggested by Koerner himself: Hockett and Dell Hymes. I recommended rejection, Hymes was negative but ambivalent, and Hockett recommended acceptance enthusiastically. Bright rejected the paper (for more on the editorial decision, see Bright's reply below).[6]

Finally, Hockett pointed to inability of his best students from the 1970s to find employment in the field, obliquely blaming this circumstance on the idea that Chomskyan linguists now controlled the job market:[7]

---

[6] Koerner published a revised version of paper successfully the following year in a different journal (Koerner 1983). He published it two more times after that, each revised from the time before (Koerner 1989 and Koerner 2002b).

[7] See Chapter 9 of this volume for evidence that generative grammarians were not particularly favored in hiring decisions in the 1970s and 1980s. A propos of Hockett's 'three best students', D. Robert Ladd, a 1978 Cornell PhD who maintained a correspondence with Hockett well into the 1980s, has the following to say: 'Doing a little triangulating between the preface to *Refurbishing our Foundations* and what I know independently and/or can infer from drawing a blank on Google, it turns out I can make an educated guess about who the three students in question are. If I'm right, I can tell you that one of them did in fact have an academic career in linguistics, but at the price of leaving the US (I'm not talking about myself!). The other two apparently set out for alternative careers; in one case the Google trail goes cold in the early 1980s, but the other one seems to have ended up as a lawyer. I can't speculate about the one whose trail goes cold, but the other two I'm thinking of were thoughtful solid scholars who were decidedly not trendy and worked on non-trendy topics. Obviously, it wasn't just non-generative scholars who got squeezed out of careers due to bad luck, bad timing, lack of trendiness, lack of charisma, and so on, but I think that in a different time and place both of the two I'm thinking of would have had decent academic careers (and as I said, one of them did, just not in the US). If I'm wrong about those being the three, there's at least one other person who doesn't appear in the preface to *Refurbishing* that he might have been referring to, who also had an academic career, in the US, but not exactly in linguistics' (p. c., May 26, 2020).

[...] I find it extremely disheartening that my three best students, all trained during the 1970s [...] have had to turn to other activities to make a living. The academic positions they should be holding were already filled or controlled by third- and fourth-raters ignorant of our long tradition, individuals who could not reach up to tie the shoestrings of our giant predecessors to say nothing of climbing onto their shoulders, but who hewed to the party line and could neither tolerate nor understand brilliance shining from a different source. These top-quality students of mine were perhaps my most crucial contribution to the Future of Linguistics. It is not my responsibility if, for totally extraneous reasons, their contribution will never bear fruit. [...]

Perhaps you can see from the foregoing that, from my point of view, the invitation in your letter is, in effect, a request that I lend moral and financial support to policies and practices directly antithetical to my own scientific and ethical principles. [...] Even my continued membership in the Society would constitute a degree of endorsement I would consider improper; hence my resignation.

With great regret,
Charles F. Hockett

(Hockett to Fromkin, November 15, 1982, with cc's to past
LSA presidents; LSAA)

Both Bright and Fromkin were quick to respond to Hockett's letter. Bright's reply was sent first:

Dear Chas,

A copy of your letter to Vicki Fromkin, dated 15 November, 1982, has just reached me. I hope somebody argues you out of your lamentable decision, but I won't attempt that. I only want to make these few points:

(1) For lack of space, I have to reject over 80% of the papers submitted to <u>Language</u>, including many which are unquestionably valuable and worthy for publication. Against this background, I don't think significance can be attached to the rejection of any specific paper.

(2) As regards Koerner's paper, I got three reports from referees (two of them suggested by Koerner) before making a decision: one positive, one negative, and one in-between. I rejected the paper after consideration of all three reports and of the manuscript itself. I rejected it not because I adhere to any "party line", but because I thought a lot of it was only an echo of material that has previously been published by Hymes, by Murray in Koerner's journal, and by Koerner himself—and that a lot more was simply inaccurate in terms of my own experience of American linguistics since the 1950s.

(3) Your letter seems to associate me not only with "adherence to the party line", but also with "the partisan <u>suppression</u> of disagreement". Well, I guess I knew when I

took on this job that I was going to get shot at from several directions; but things seem to be getting worse. I've recently been learning that various linguists at MIT and U. Mass are unwilling to write or review for Language—and some of them are unwilling to join the LSA—because they see the journal and the society as irrelevant or even hostile to their interests.

I've gotten accustomed to all this, but I still don't like it. [...] The Executive Committee which re-nominated me this year included Dell Hymes as President, plus other renegades from the 'party line' such as Fred Householder, Ives Goddard, Herb Penzl, and Paul Friedrich. In the most recent (Sept.) issue of Language you can find not only two papers in 'mainline' generative phonology, but also a long article on 'formal syntax' which sharply challenges Chomsky; articles on intonation, on typology, and on sociolinguistics which reflect no 'party line' that I can see; and a very favorable review of a book by you. My point is that I still see both the LSA and Language as very open to diversity and to frank disagreement.

I've taken this much trouble to write to you because YOUR work has played such an important role in my development as a linguist. I sincerely hope that you'll decide to remain in the LSA.

Sincerely,
William Bright
Editor, Language

                              (Bright to Hockett, November 24, 1982; LSAA)

Fromkin was even more upset than Bright by Hockett's decision:

Dear Charles,

Your letter of November 15, 1982, made me more unhappy than any single event since my election as Secretary-Treasurer of the LSA. I think I once mentioned to you that your textbook was my introduction to linguistics, in my first course taught by Harry Hoijer. That book and that course changed my life [...]. I cannot of course argue with your perception of the present situation in our field, although I do not see it as you do. In fact, I see more 'eclecticism' today than when I entered the discipline, and greater breadth of subject matter, and more competition of theories. The leadership of the Society as represented by its officers and executive committee members during my tenure as Secretary-Treasurer would, I think, support this view.

I have read Bill Bright's letter to you since he kindly sent me a copy. It seems to me he has stated the case for Language much better than I could. I would, however, suggest that Bill, as editor of the journal, has been meticulous in his struggle to publish what is good no matter what the theoretical background of the writer. [...]

When I first read your letter I was going to simply write to you to say I was sorry you had reached a decision to resign from the Society. [...] whatever its weaknesses, it cannot be strengthened if the critics among us leave us to continue without them.

Sincerely,
Victoria A. Fromkin (Fromkin to Hockett, 30 November 1982; LSAA)

Dell Hymes, who was the current LSA President, weighed in with a letter to Bright that questioned the well-foundedness of Hockett's decision:

Dear Bill,

I am very sorry to learn that the paper by Koerner has become the focus of a flap. John Hammer told me on the phone Wednesday that Hockett has resigned from the LSA, using the paper as the reason. [...] Certainly it cannot be that Koerner or his paper is sole cause, but rather that there are attitudes and misperceptions ready to be ignited.

While I would ordinarily be loath to make public a private judgment, especially in a case in which I have other relationships with the person, I think that the interests of the Society and my responsibility to it dictate that it should be known that you received advice from me about the paper. As you know, I waffled a bit in my opinion, but came down on the side of not thinking the paper to have sufficient merit, as a paper in the history of linguistics, to command publication in Language. No one could want more that I myself to see history of linguistics presented in Language. I did not think it a strong example of the genre. [...] Not well organized, not well written, rather loose and disjointed; and not with all that much novel or significant to say.[8]

[Consider the present LSA leadership]—Vicki as Secretary-Treasurer, Gene Nida as head of the fund drive, a troike of presidents, past, present and elect that consists of Fred Householder, myself and Art Abramson [none a generative grammarian—(FJN)]. If anyone has a right to complain, it might be the followers of Noam. [...] Certainly the controversy a year ago over a review felt unfair to Noam, or at least in bad taste, shows that the shoe is sometimes on the other foot.[9] [...]

All best,
Dell

(Hymes to Bright, November 26, 1982; LSAA)

[8] Koerner (2002b) included a footnote on the rejection of his submission by Language. In his take on the situation, Dell Hymes's principal complaint was that he 'had not sufficiently considered his [i.e. Hymes's] work on the subject' (p. 196).

[9] Hymes is referring to a review of Smith & Wilson (1979) by Robert Binnick. Criticizing the book's failing to cite Chomsky's predecessors, Binnick noted that 'even Stalin's sycophants admitted the existence of Lenin' (Binnick 1981: 183).

294 HOCKETT'S ATTEMPT TO RESIGN FROM LSA, 1982

Fromkin received a number of letters from prominent LSA members taking a stand on Hockett's resignation letter, some critical of the letter and some supportive. William Moulton's fell into the former category:

Dear Vicki,

I have just received a copy of Chas Hockett's letter of 15 Nov 82 to you, in which — in high dudgeon — he nobly resigns from the LSA. [...] I have known Chas for over forty years, cherish him as a friend, and have the profoundest admiration for him as a linguist. Especially in regard to matters of (for him) HIGH PRINCIPLE, he has had his easy periods and his difficult periods. [...] Fortunately for me, during 1947–1960 (when we colleagues at Cornell) he was in his easy period. Before that he was certainly difficult, and after that he apparently became difficult — and apparently still is.

In a way, I sympathize with Chas. Linguistics in the USA is now in a curious period. [...] [W]hen I give talks here and there about phonology, I am in effect laughed at because I do not hew to the party line of generative phonology. But this does not bother me: this, too, shall pass. When I was a young linguist, people were laughed at if they did not hew to the party line of structuralism. I didn't; and I remember once being laughed at by the late and beloved Bernard Bloch.

O tempora, o mores! Quo usque tandem? All is transitory. Linguistic schools and party lines come and go. Let us only hope that, in the long run, we shall make PROGRESS (whatever that may be). [...] Chas is on my list of people to call in connection with the Fund for the Future of Linguistics. And just as I started to type this paragraph, I received a call from the CAL [Center for Applied Linguistics] suggesting that I not call Chas. Incredible! Of course, I shall not do so. [...][10]

Fervently yours,
William G. Moulton

(Moulton to Fromkin, November 17, 1982; LSAA)

On the other hand, James Copeland, who would welcome Hockett at Rice University a few years later, expressed nothing but sympathy for Hockett's action:

Dear Professor Fromkin:

[...] Our new department has a great interest in the future of linguistics and also has ample funds to support worthy causes. At the same time, we find among ourselves considerable resonance for the views expressed in Hockett's letter, as well as

---

[10] Moulton ended up phoning J Milton Cowan ('Will contribute'), Henry M. Hoenigswald ('Will contribute'), Henry Allen Gleason ('Will NOT contribute'), Paul Garvin ('his wife, Madeline Mathiot, felt sure that Paul would contribute'), D. Terence Langendoen ('he had ALREADY contributed'), Ernst Pulgram ('Will contribute'), James Sledd ('Will contribute'), Rudolph Troike (Will contribute') and Ralph Ward ('temporarily unreachable') (Moulton to Nida, November 30, 1982; LSAA).

great respect for Hockett himself. We too have some doubt about whether the LSA broadly represents the field of linguistics as it once did. Some of our department members have already expressed their dissatisfaction with the LSA by allowing their membership to lapse, without writing letters as Chas did. [...]

With all best wishes,
James E. Copeland
Acting Chairman

(Copeland to Fromkin, November 22, 1982; LSAA)

Fromkin passed Copeland's letter on to Hymes, who replied to him on November 30, writing 'especially to assure you that the circumstances are not as they appear to have been represented to Chas Hockett. I myself was a reader this summer of the Koerner manuscript and could not really recommend it for publication. It did not seem to me of sufficient quality'. Hymes went on to repeat from his letter to Bright of November 26 the composition of the LSA Executive Committee and concluded that 'One might argue that there is a prejudice <u>against</u> adherents of Chomsky's work in the offices of the Society' (LSAA).

Of all of the back-and-forth letters the autumn of 1982, the one of greatest historical interest was sent by Kenneth Pike to Hockett. Pike bitterly recalled his own snubbing in the past by some of the major figures in post-Bloomfieldian structuralism:

Dear Chas,

Thanks for your letter about LSA which I received a few days ago—and have been pondering carefully. [...] If I read you correctly, and I may not, your assertion is that times have changed radically, and that in the former generation all points of view found ready access to <u>Language</u>. This is false. Bloch, for example, rejected my <u>Intonation of American English</u>, even though in my presence Bloomfield urged him to publish it. Bloch rejected my <u>Tone Languages</u>. He also rejected my "Grammatical Prerequisites"—one item which was of some interest to the transformational grammarians. [...] [I]n the last generation you were on the "inside" of the climate, and did not feel the freeze. Nor was it just one person—one editor—involved. Martin Joos in his preliminary letter suggesting persons whose materials should be enclosed in his "readings" to describe "the development of descriptive linguistics in America since 1925" listed a couple of my articles. Every one was rejected from the published version—because, he told me, people in the discipline objected. Yet in that very volume you have <u>seven</u> of your articles reprinted. This historical perspective is indeed hard on you—but it ought not be allowed to blind you. [...]

Let me urge you to reconsider your resignation. We need to support the Society. In my view, there has been a great deal of broadening of perspective in the last ten years. Let's have some part in encouraging that.

Cordially yours,
Kenneth L. Pike

(Pike to Hockett, November 30, 1982; LSAA)

One assumes that Hockett did not attend the 1982 LSA meeting, which was held in San Diego between December 37 and December 30. In an aerogramme dated January 7, 1983, Hockett told his former student Robert Ladd that 'I have resigned my membership in the LSA because of its dreadful domination by TG fanatics'. What he must have not known at that moment was that LSA Associate Secretary John Hammer had just sent him the following letter:

Dear Professor Hockett,

[...] Your decision to resign from the LSA unfortunately presents certain admin- istrative problems. [...] You have been a Life Member since 1952 [...] The LSA Constitution provides no mechanism for one to terminate one's life membership.

(Hammer to Hockett, January 4, 1983; LSAA).

And, indeed, every LSA membership register from then on listed Hockett as a member. What is more, Hockett published four items in *Language* after his res- ignation attempt: two obituaries (Hockett 1993b, 1995), a book review (Hockett 1997), and a book notice (Hockett 1993a).[11]

8.5 Hockett's perception of the field and reality

Nobody would have disputed the idea that in 1982 generative grammar was the most visible approach to linguistics in the United States (if not in the world) and that Noam Chomsky was the best-known linguist. We have seen ample documen- tary evidence, both in his publications and personal letters, that Hockett was quite disturbed by this fact. If I may quote an anonymous referee, 'I think Hockett saw himself as the crown prince in line to inherit the throne; when Chomsky and his first spectacular cluster of students and other early adherents burst on the scene, Hockett lost his chance of glory. Generative grammar was visibly on the rise. Hock- ett and a few of his equally embittered contemporaries had that part right'. But what

---

[11] Eugene Nida wrote: 'I have a feeling that a good deal of [Hockett's] antagonism to the Linguistic Society of America will fade, either because of time lag or because people understood something of Chas' personality' (Nida to Moulton, December 21, 1982; LSAA). Perhaps Nida was right.

Hockett had wrong was the idea that by the 1980s generative grammar institutionally dominated the American field of linguistics. The entire following chapter of this book is devoted to documenting the disconnect between the visibility of generative grammar and its organizational success. While I am sure that Hockett felt genuine distress, given his belief that the field had 'altered beyond recognition', if he had dug a little deeper, he would have discovered a field that was most certainly not dominated organizationally by one single approach to the study of language.

8.6 Concluding remarks

This chapter has documented an episode in the history of American linguistics. In 1982 Charles Hockett, perhaps the most prominent American linguist of the preceding generation, attempted to resign from the Linguistic Society of America on the grounds that the organization had fallen into the hands of generative grammarians. The interest of this episode derives, not from the simple fact of Hockett's resignation attempt, but rather from the light it sheds on the personal and professional interrelationships between the leading linguists of the time. Examining personal correspondence between such figures as Victoria Fromkin, William Bright, Dell Hymes, Kenneth Pike, and others brings into clear focus the dynamics at the center of the LSA, as well as highlighting the generational shift that was ongoing in the American linguistics scene.

9

The generativist non-dominance of the field in the 1970s and 1980s

9.1 Introduction

As we have seen in earlier chapters, by 1970 (and perhaps earlier) generative grammar had become the most visible approach to linguistic theory in the world. That
is, it was the principal theory either to be practised or to be opposed. Analogously,
Noam Chomsky had become the world's most visible theorist. This chapter focuses
on whether generativists held the major positions of power in American linguistics in the 1970s and 1980s (i.e. two or three decades after the appearance of the
approach) and whether they received a disproportionate share of grant and other
funding. My—perhaps surprising—conclusion is that they did not. In other words,
in contrast with their post-Bloomfieldian predecessors, visibility did not engender
organizational dominance.[1] This chapter is devoted to a documentation and an
explanation of this fact.

In general, historiographers of linguistics have taken a position contrary to
mine. Consider Stephen O. Murray and E. F. K. Koerner. Murray, whose professional specialty was the informal groupings and networks within the field of
linguistics (see Murray 1983, 1994), wrote that 'Chomsky did not make a revolution with [*Syntactic Structures*]' (Murray 1980: 81); rather he and his associates
engineered a 'palace coup in 1962' (p. 82). Koerner, the editor of the journal *Historiographia Linguistica* and author of hundreds of historiographically-oriented
books and articles, concurs, making reference to '"organizational linguistics"
(which is largely controlled by people associated with Chomsky's views) [...]'
(Koerner 1989: 135). Among historiographers of linguistics, ideas like these have
become part of the accepted canon. At the Fourteenth International Conference
on the History of the Language Sciences, held in Paris in August 2017, several
presenters mentioned in passing (without feeling the need to document their statements) the idea of a generative-dominated field of linguistics, where Chomsky and

---

[1] A few decades earlier in 1946, when post-Bloomfieldian linguistics was dominant, all eight of the
members of the LSA Executive Committee were either structuralists or their close allies (see Chapter 1,
§ 1.4.1).

American Linguistics in Transition. Frederick J. Newmeyer, Oxford University Press.
© Frederick J. Newmeyer (2022). DOI: 10.1093/oso/9780192843760.003.0009

his supporters set the standard for hiring and publication, often ruthlessly abusing their power. Consider a few more quotes along these lines from those who have published in the history of linguistics.

> An increasing number of linguists have realized that this allegedly linguistic revolution was a social coup d'état. (Anttila 1975: 171)

> [...] the paralyzing vibrations emanating from the banks of the Charles River [i.e. from MIT—(FJN)] [represent] totalitarian enslavement. (Makkai 1975: xi)

> [...] as all admit, transformationalists have succeeded in capturing the organs of power. (Gray 1976: 49)

> The greatest 'power' in the TG paradigm is not in its theory [...], but rather in its hegemony over academic linguistics. (Maher 1980: 4) [...] *Language*, the organ of the Linguistic Society of America (LSA), is a TG-dominated journal [...] (p. 30)

At least two of the above individuals took steps to attempt to counter what they saw as generativist hegemony in the field. In 1974 Makkai was the primary founder of the organization Linguistic Association of Canada and the United States (LACUS), hoping to attract (in Makkai's words) a 'long list of genuine linguists who are fed up with the LSA and the MITnik establishment' (see Chapter 7, § 7.5). LACUS exists to this day. The following year Konrad Koerner initiated the John Benjamins-edited series Current Issues in Linguistic Theory (CILT). The back cover of every volume contains a veiled reference to the power wielded by generative grammarians in the field:

> Since the spectrum of possibilities in linguistic theory construction is much broader and more variegated than students of linguistics have perhaps been led to believe, the [...] series has been established in order to provide a forum for the presentation and discussion of linguistic opinions of scholars who do not necessarily accept the prevailing mode of thought in linguistic science.

At this writing, 351 books have been published in the CILT series.

The idea that generative grammarians wielded absolute power in the field was not generally shared by practitioners of that approach in the seventies and eighties. I was elected Secretary-Treasurer of the LSA at the end of this period, in 1989. When I took office, I was shocked by the number of leading generativists who were not members. Over the next few years, I made it a point to contact them personally to encourage them to join (or, in many cases, to rejoin). The reply to my email by James Higginbotham was typical.

> Why should I join the LSA? If you look at who the officers are, what gets presented at meetings, and what's published in *Language*, I don't see much connection with what we are trying to accomplish at MIT.
>
> (p. c., February 17, 1992)

Other generative grammarians have recently offered me the same reasons for not wishing to be LSA members at that time (in the case of Prince and Emonds) or why they felt alienated from the Society (in the case of Dresher).

> I did receive the impression early on [i.e. in the 1970s —(FJN)] that the LSA represented overall a kind of inertial view of the field, in which innovative theoretical linguistics was nowhere near as central as I took it to be. I also didn't associate the LSA with new initiatives that would liven things up.
>
> (Alan Prince, p. c., December 3, 2019)

> In the 70s, I didn't want to spend the money [on LSA membership] and the LSA was not generative, at least in general. I never saw how going to the LSA or paying dues led to better linguistics by me or anyone else.
>
> (Joseph Emonds, p. c., December 4, 2019)

> When I started in linguistics (generative linguistics, in the seventies, a bit after the author), I considered the LSA to be something of a dinosaur, and I did not consider *Language* to be the most important journal, at least for my papers.
>
> (B. Elan Dresher, p. c., September 3, 2020)

Before proceeding, I wish to dismiss without further comment Stephen Murray's implication that generative grammar was institutionally dominant as early as 1962. The only thing of interest for our purposes that happened that year was the holding of the Ninth International Congress of Linguists in Cambridge, Massachusetts with Morris Halle and William Locke, who was chair of the Modern Languages Department at MIT, on the Local Arrangements Committee. After Zellig Harris turned down his invitation to present one of the five plenary talks, Halle and Locke were able to have him replaced by Chomsky. As noted in Newmeyer (1986b: 42–43), this stroke of luck was instrumental in presenting Chomsky to the world as the face of American linguistics.[2] But there is no justification for the idea that the adding of Chomsky to the program represented a 'palace coup'. What was the

---

[2] There has been more than a half-century of speculation about why Harris pulled out and how he came to be replaced by Chomsky. Here is what Bruce Nevin, one of Harris's advisees, has to say: 'As to the Congress, [Harris's colleague] Naomi Sager has told me that he had another commitment and that he supported Noam taking his place as a way of furthering his career; just as he (together with Goodman) had earlier sponsored him to the Harvard fellowship, to Bloch, in protection from the draft, and in many other matters. Zellig had been Noam's protector and mentor from an early age [...]' (p. c., 3 March 2020).

'palace'? Presumably the headquarters of the LSA. In that year the LSA secretariat was squeezed into the back room of Secretary-Treasurer Archibald Hill's house in Austin, Texas. Perhaps Murray was imagining some even more metaphorical palace. If so, I am at a loss to explain what he might have had in mind. Institutionally, generative grammar amounted to next to nothing in 1962 and for several years thereafter. At the time of the International Congress, the graduate program at MIT was only a year old and I doubt that there were more than a dozen generative grammarians in the entire world.

No, if generative grammarians ever took control of the organs of power in the field, it would have to have been in later decades. The remainder of this chapter attempts an exhaustive investigation of institutional linguistics in the United States from 1970 to 1989—the period in which claims of generativist dominance were the most widespread in academic publications. As we will see, generativists, for the most part, far from being comfortably ensconced in their 'palace', found themselves outside of its walls. At the same time, it is important to stress that generativists were not an oppressed minority either. They did occupy some important posts in the LSA, did have papers published in *Language*, and did receive some important grants. However, they remained institutional minoritarians throughout this period.

Let us begin to try to unravel the brute facts about generative predominance or not in the field in these two decades. Such is not an easy task. By what standards should we describe someone as a 'generative grammarian' or a publication or presentation as 'generative'? Many subfields of linguistics, such as formal semantics, pragmatics, phonetics, and even sociolinguistics, have been influenced to one degree or another by generative grammar. Yet one would be loath to describe, say, Kai von Fintel, Laurence Horn, Patricia Keating, and John Rickford as 'generative grammarians' on the basis of some of their work being compatible with basic generative notions or even on the basis of its assuming certain features of that model. Then there are linguists who work in formal frameworks which are 'Chomskyan' only in the broadest sense of the term. Where do they fit in? And finally, any facile characterization of a person as a generative grammarian or not has to face the fact that people's positions change over time. The institution from which one received one's PhD or the theory adopted in one's earliest work is in general not a good indicator of one's theoretical stance in later years.[3] An interesting fact is that a solid majority of Chomsky's syntax students from the 1960s were, a decade or two later, developing frameworks of grammatical analysis that their teacher opposed. At the same time, three of Chomsky's closest co-thinkers in the 1980s, David Lightfoot, Sandra Chung, and Robert Freidin, had received their degrees from Michigan,

---

[3] To give an extreme example, Emmon Bach, one of the leading formal linguists of the last half of the twentieth century, wrote his 1959 University of Chicago dissertation on the German romantic poet Friedrich Hölderlin.

Harvard, and Indiana respectively, none of which were major centers of generative grammar. Or take George Lakoff and Ronald Langacker. In 1968 they were clearly generative grammarians and in 1988 they clearly were not. When did they make their transitions from one to the other? Based on the published record, that is not an easy question to answer. Given that there is a frequent disparity between one's institutional training and one's later theoretical stance and general interests, I focus in all cases on one's outlook at the relevant period under discussion. So, for example, in Appendix A I classify Bruce Fraser as a 'pragmaticist and discourse analyst' in 1976–1978 because that represents the work that he was doing at the time. The fact that he was one of Chomsky's first syntax students is of no relevance for me.[4]

Throughout this chapter I describe someone as a 'generativist' if they fulfill one of two criteria: either if their work at the relevant time period contributes to generative syntax, phonology, or morphology; or if the conclusion of their work (say, in neurolinguistics, psycholinguistics, or wherever) is that the results presented therein demonstrate that basic generative principles are correct. By 'basic generative principles' I mean the idea that humans possess a cognitive faculty dedicated to language (called 'competence' or 'I-language') embodied by discrete, complex, and abstract rules and principles. I must stress that simple agreement alone (in print or via personal communication) with the basic tenets of generative grammar will not for me qualify someone ipso facto as being a 'generativist'. Furthermore, I distinguish two types of generative grammarians, as far as syntax is concerned: 'MIT-style' and 'non-MIT-style'. An 'MIT-style generative grammarian' works in the current framework under development by Chomsky, which for our time period would be publications such as Chomsky (1971, 1973, 1981, 1986). A 'non-MIT-style generative grammarian' is a formal linguist whose work lies in the tradition initiated in Chomsky (1957a) and Chomsky (1965), but who rejects his later frameworks. Examples from the earlier period would be generative semanticists (Lakoff 1971), case grammarians (Fillmore 1968), and relational grammarians (Perlmutter 1983); examples from the later period would be those who work in models like lexical-functional grammar (Bresnan 1978) and generalized phrase structure grammar (Gazdar, Klein, Pullum, & Sag 1985).

My criteria for published articles and for grant proposals are essentially the same. I consider a journal article, say, to be 'generativist' if it contributes to generative syntax, phonology, or morphology, or if its conclusion is that the results presented therein demonstrate that basic generative principles are correct.

---

[4] Historiographers, in general, focus on the origins of the individual under discussion rather than on their orientation at the relevant time period. So Koerner (1989: 136), in trying to make an argument for Chomskyan organizational dominance in the field, notes that Elizabeth Traugott, 'an early associate of the TGG school', was LSA President in 1987. But by 1987 Traugott had become one of the intellectual leaders of the functionalist alternative to generative grammar.

The chapter is organized as follows. § 9.2 reviews generative predominance (or not) in LSA elected offices, § 9.3 in the pages of *Language*, § 9.4 at LSA meetings, § 9.5 at LSA Institutes, § 9.6 in grant awards, and § 9.7 in departmental composition. § 9.8 is a general discussion followed by a conclusion. Several appendices provide detailed supporting evidence for the claims made earlier in the chapter.

9.2 Generativist predominance (or not) in LSA elected offices

For every elected LSA office, the Nominating Committee presents an official slate to the membership. By default the Committee generally proposes only one candidate for each vacant office, though any ten members can, via a written petition, nominate a second candidate, thereby leading to a contested election. In 1970, for example, Martin Joos, the official candidate for the 1972 presidency, was challenged and defeated by Dwight Bolinger (see Chapter 7 for discussion). We examine below the leanings of the LSA Presidents (§ 9.2.1), Secretary-Treasurers (§ 9.2.2), Editors of *Language* (§ 9.2.3), members of the Executive Committee (Appendix A, p. 324), and of the Nominating Committee (Appendix B, p. 326).

9.2.1 The Presidents of the LSA

The following list presents the Presidents of the LSA between 1970 and 1989, along with a short description of their professional-intellectual orientation at the time of their presidency.

1970   Charles A. Ferguson, a sociolinguist
1971   Eric P. Hamp, a historical linguist
1972   Dwight L. Bolinger, a descriptive linguist and critic of generative grammar
1973   Winfred P. Lehmann, a historical linguist
1974   Morris Halle, a generative phonologist
1975   Thomas Sebeok, a Prague-school-oriented structuralist and semiotician
1976   Rulon S. Wells, a post-Bloomfieldian structuralist
1977   Joseph H. Greenberg, a historical linguist, Africanist, and typologist
1978   Peter Ladefoged, a phonetician
1979   William Labov, a sociolinguist
1980   Ilse Lehiste, a phonetician
1981   Fred W. Householder, a post-Bloomfieldian structuralist
1982   Dell H. Hymes, an anthropological linguist
1983   Arthur S. Abramson, a phonetician

1984   Henry R. Kahane, a historical linguist
1985   Victoria A. Fromkin, a neurolinguist and phonetician and a strong
        advocate of generative grammar
1986   Barbara H. Partee, a formal semanticist
1987   Elizabeth C. Traugott, a functionalist linguist known for her work on
        grammaticalization
1988   Calvert Watkins, a historical linguist
1989   William Bright, a sociolinguist

If it is the LSA President who is supposed to sit upon the palace throne, one can only conclude from this list that generativists had conspicuously less elegant seating arrangements in the 1970s and 1980s. Only one President was a generative grammarian and only one other a fulsome advocate of the theory. Indeed, there was only one other linguist whose work could even be considered 'formal'. One might object, however, that, given that the presidency of the LSA is essentially honorary and that Presidents are often chosen for their accomplishments in the distant past, it would be more appropriate to examine the individuals who have occupied the positions of Secretary-Treasurer and Editor of *Language*. These two posts involve day-to-day responsibilities and a certain amount of influence (if not power). The next two subsections examine the holders of these offices.

9.2.2 The Secretary-Treasurers of the LSA

The Secretary-Treasurer is nominated by the Executive Committee and elected on a yearly ballot by the membership. He or she is, in effect, the liaison between the membership and the full-time paid staff in Washington, DC. This office is extremely demanding in terms of time obligations, as it involves daily contact with the staff that often lasted an hour or more by telephone in the days before email. Here is the list of Secretary-Treasurers during our time period.

1952–1968   Archibald A. Hill, a post-Bloomfieldian structuralist
1968–1974   Thomas Sebeok, a Prague-school-oriented structuralist and
             semiotician
1974–1979   Arthur S. Abramson, a phonetician
1979–1984   Victoria Fromkin, a neurolinguist and phonetician and a strong
             advocate of generative grammar
1984–1989   D. Terence Langendoen, an MIT PhD whose dissertation was on
             the London School of Linguistics and who in the 1980s published
             in a dozen different subfields, from computational linguistics to
             discourse analysis
1989–1994   Frederick J. Newmeyer, at the time an MIT-style syntactician, and
             who had published two books on the history of linguistics

Here one could make a better case for generative dominance. The last three of the six holders of the position had strong generative orientations (though in Langendoen's case it was anything but MIT-style).[5]

9.2.3 The Editors of *Language*

The Editor of *Language* is nominated by the Executive Committee and elected by the membership.[6] He or she has the final say on what appears in the journal, relying on the advice of an appointed Editorial Board (see Appendix C-1, p. 328). There were only two editors in the 1970s and 1980s.

1966–1987   William Bright, a sociolinguist
1988–1994   Sarah G. Thomason, a historical linguist

Neither Editor was in any sense a generative grammarian. It would be hard to imagine why either of them would be 'naturally' biased in favor of generative-oriented submissions.[7]

  For the sake of completeness, I include the names and orientations of the occupants of the two other elected LSA offices: the members of the Executive Committee (Appendix A, p. 324) and of the Nominating Committee (Appendix B, p. 326)). As far as the former is concerned, even counting mere sympathizers, generativists failed to make up a majority of Executive Committee members in the 1970s and 1980s. There are as many functionalist linguists as formal syntacticians (of any type) and only two generative phonologists. And as far as the latter is concerned, here again, one would be hard pressed to read into the list a bias toward generative grammar. There are pro-generativists, anti-generativists, and non-generativists in roughly equal number.

9.3 Generative predominance (or not) in the pages of *Language*

Before turning to the analysis presented below, the reader might wish to turn to Appendix C-1 (p. 328), where are listed the Associate Editors of *Language* in the 1970s and 1980s, and to Appendix C-2 (p. 329), which presents the author, article title, and subject matter of the full articles published in *Language* in 1970, 1980, and 1989.[8]

---

[5] For what it's worth, the Secretary-Treasurer immediately after me was Elizabeth Traugott, a functionalist linguist known for her work on grammaticalization, and the current holder of that office (in 2021) is Lenore Grenoble, a specialist in language contact and language policy.
[6] For a history of the journal *Language* and other LSA publications, see Dawson & Joseph (2014).
[7] Bright would certainly not be. In the context of a hiring decision at his home institution of UCLA in the late 1970s, he argued that his department 'put too much emphasis on syntactic/semantic theory' and that they should hire a sociolinguist instead of a formal semanticist (Bright 1980: 129).
[8] One should bear in mind that in the 1970s and 1980s there was a time lag of about nine months to two years or more between the submission of a paper to *Language* and its appearance in published

As can be seen, roughly half of the Editorial Board members between 1970 and 1989 were generative grammarians. By that criterion, it would be a bit far-fetched to identify *Language* as 'a TG-dominated journal' at the time. For me, the most striking fact is the small number of MIT-style syntacticians (only four). Three times that number were formal syntacticians working primarily in non-Chomskyan frameworks.

As far as the articles published in *Language* in 1970 are concerned, it would be difficult to conclude that the journal was under the yoke of Chomsky and his MIT-based colleagues in 1970. There was only one published article (or perhaps two) that adopted his current framework. At the same time, there were eight or so articles in frameworks that he had spent several year combatting—generative semantics in particular. The historiographical article by Aarsleff is one of the most anti-Chomskyan pieces ever published anywhere. And as we can see, *Language* became considerably *less* generative in the decade from 1970 to 1980. Being generous, possibly a quarter of the papers have a generative orientation.

Looking at 1989, we see a rise in the number of generative-oriented articles compared to nine years earlier. Perhaps slightly over half adopted this way of looking at language, which is hardly enough to characterize the journal as under the thrall of Chomsky and his co-thinkers. Indeed, what I find most interesting is that only three articles addressed problems from the point of view of the government-binding theory (Chomsky 1981, 1986), even though that approach (arguably Chomsky's most successful in terms of attracting interest from the linguistic community as a whole) was in its heyday in the late 1980s.[9]

Both editors in our time period were explicitly committed to the journal's representing a wide range of subfields and particular approaches:

> Basically, I believe *Language* should be aimed at the broadest possible linguistic audience. On the one hand, this means a preference for articles which are significant for general linguistics, as opposed to articles of more specialized appeal. On the other hand, it means I like to see that all the major interests within linguistics are fairly represented in the journal: synchronic and diachronic studies, phonology and syntax, pure and hyphenated linguistics.
>
> (Bright, 'Editor's Report', *LSAB 64*, 1975: 11)

> The actual policy is this: articles written in any theoretical framework are appropriate for *Language*. [...] Relevance is defined with respect to languages and

---

form. Hence the contents of *Language* might not have reflected current trends to the extent that papers presented at LSA meetings did (see below § 9.4).

[9] If I may be permitted a totally personal comment, I worked in generative semantics until that framework collapsed in the early 1970s. I had pretty much given up on syntax entirely until Chomsky's *Lectures on Government and Binding* appeared in 1981. I was hooked! My colleague for many years at the University of Washington, Heles Contreras, followed a very similar trajectory.

analytic issues, not to schools of linguistics. In practice, this means that a Relational Grammarian does not have the right to decide that a Tagmemic analysis of a given topic can safely be ignored; a functionalist does not have the right to disregard a competing account of a particular phenomenon simply because it is laden with formalism; a GB proponent does not have the right to reinvent the wheel simply because the earlier invention was couched in an LFG framework; and the converse of each of these examples (and whatever others you can think of) also holds.

(Thomason, 'Editor's Department', *Language* 65, 1989: 919)

Indeed, Bright remarked that he 'was chosen as Editor in 1966 partly because he was not seen as a partisan of any of the theoretical 'camps' prominent at the time'. He added that 'if it is true that I was named because I was in fact a mugwump—defined as a bird that sits on a fence with its mug on one side and its wump on the other—then I am glad to accept the label, and am content to avoid extremes on either side' (Bright, 'Editor's Report', *LSAB* 119, 1989: 9).

As the 1970 article by Aarsleff indicates, Bright had no hesitation in publishing material critical of Chomsky. Far from it. The 1970s and 1980s saw an article entitled 'On the failure of generative grammar' (Gross 1979) and a single issue (vol. 58, no. 1, March 1982) contains an article by Ronald Langacker presenting an alternative conception of grammar from Chomsky's (Langacker 1982), a review article by Harold Schiffman that derides generative grammar for its hypothesizing the 'ideal speaker/hearer' and categorial rules (Schiffman 1982), and a laudatory review by Jeri Jaeger and Robert Van Valin of a book (Prideaux, Derwing, & Baker 1980) that concludes that Chomsky's approach is disconfirmed by psycholinguistic experimentation.

That said, both Bright and Thomason recognized the fact that going by sheer numbers alone, generative grammar (of whatever variety) was the most worked in approach to grammatical analysis and that the journal could not be insensitive to that fact:

> It is clear that the overwhelming majority of papers submitted, and of those published, take for granted certain principles of generative grammar. But it appears equally clear to me that 'schools' of linguistics are much less clearly definable than they were a few years ago; and many of the papers which I have been most happy to accept seem to me quite unclassifiable as to 'school'. My only conscious policy in these matters, then, is that all types of papers are welcome which shed new light on language.
>
> (Bright, 'Editor's Report', *LSAB* 64, 1975: 11)

The theoretical, and specifically generative, focus of *Language* in recent years reflects the development of the field itself: the various offshoots of early transformational grammar have had an enormous influence on the field. Most contemporary theoretically-oriented research, including large amounts of description-with-theory, is couched in generative terms. So the author of a phonological, morphological, or syntactic article directed to a wide audience of general linguists will almost inevitably have to take note of relevant generative research.

(Thomason, 'Editor's Department', Language 65, 1989: 445)

Bright implicitly, and Thomason explicitly, were referring, as Thomason put it, to 'theoretically-oriented research, including large amounts of description-with-theory'. It is hard to imagine that Bright meant that the totality of papers published in *Language* '[took] for granted certain principles of generative grammar', since most did not deal in any way with questions of grammatical analysis. Thomason later remarked: 'As in 1988, the largest category of submissions in 1989 was syntax (51 mss.). Phonology and historical linguistics were represented by 21 submissions each [...]' (Thomason, 'Editor's Department', *Language* 66, 1990: 214). Since the vast majority of syntax submissions in 1989 would have been generative-oriented, it is not surprising that the percentage of generative papers published would have been as high as it was.

It appears that whatever one's interests were in linguistics, one believed that the journal best represented interests opposed to yours. As a dramatic illustration of my point, I quote part of a message from Sarah Thomason, who was editor of *Language* from 1988 to 1994:

> I may have told you about the memorable week when I got two letters from disgruntled authors whose papers I'd rejected. One said that obviously I would reject her paper since I was clearly biased against anything generative; the other said that obviously I would reject their paper since I only published generative articles. I resisted, with some difficulty, the urge to send each letter to the other letter-writer. It's interesting how perception can blind a person to facts.

(p. c., November 25, 2019)

To summarize, the journal *Language* was not in any way dominated by followers of Chomsky, nor even by generative grammarians of any variety.

9.4 Generative predominance (or not) at LSA meetings

Every year in the winter (between Christmas and New Year's Day in the 1970s and 1980s) the LSA holds its annual meeting, with a full program of refereed-abstract talks, usually supplemented by invited plenary lectures, symposia, and colloquia (the latter two generally refereed). In those summers when there was a Linguistic Institute (see § 9.5), another program of talks was held. The presentations are decided by the Program Committee, which is appointed by the Executive Committee. Appendix D (p. 333) lists the Program Committee members between 1970 and 1989. On this list generative grammarians are so much in the minority that no further comment is needed.

Let us turn now to the annual meeting programs in 1970, 1980, and 1989. At the 1970 annual meeting in Washington, there were 65 talks in two parallel sessions. None of the sub-sessions had a named theme. By my count, the talks broke down as follows: historical linguistics (9), generative phonology (9), generative syntax (not including generative semantics) (9), non-generative language acquisition (4), pure description (4), non-generative phonology (3), semantics (3), generative semantics (3), pragmatics and discourse analysis (3), other (18). In the 'other' category were talks in various frameworks: tagmemics, Prague school linguistics, Columbia school linguistics, and the framework under development by Wallace Chafe. There were two symposia, neither organized by generative grammarians: one by Charles Ferguson entitled 'Language and intelligence' and one by Rulon Wells entitled 'Semantics and transformational grammar'. Both symposia included presentations by generative grammarians, though they were in the minority.

At the 1980 meeting in San Antonio, there were 240 talks, with at times six parallel sessions, each sub-session having a named theme. Below are the named sub-sessions, followed by my estimation of whether the talks in them were generative-oriented or not.

American Indian linguistics (mostly non-generative)
Applied & psycholinguistics (mostly non-generative)
Discourse analysis (non-generative)
Discourse communication (non-generative)
Historical linguistics (2) (non-generative)
Language acquisition (mixed generative and non-generative)
Language acquisition/syntax (mixed generative and non-generative)
Morphology (mostly generative)
Phonetics/historical linguistics (mixed generative and non-generative)
Phonetics/phonology (non-generative)
Phonology (mostly generative)
Phonology/morphology (mixed generative and non-generative)
Phonology/historical linguistics (mixed generative and non-generative)
Semantics (3) (mixed generative and non-generative)
Sociolinguistics (3) (non-generative)
Sociolinguistics/discourse analysis (non-generative)
Syntax (5) (mostly generative)
Syntax/semantics (non-generative)
Varia (non-generative)

There were four special sessions: 'Language contact' (non-generative), 'Junction grammar' (unclassifiable, given the information that I have), 'The object of linguistic inquiry' (mixed generative and non-generative) and 'Nahuatl' (non-generative). Finally, there was one (non-generative) colloquium, organized by Anuradha Saksena and entitled 'A semantic typology of causatives'. This was not a generative-dominated LSA meeting.

The 1989 meeting in Washington comprised 219 talks in 34 sessions, as follows:

American sign language (mixed generative and non-generative)
Celtic syntax (generative)
Conditions on phonological rules and representations (generative)
Computational linguistics (non-generative)
Discourse analysis (3) (non-generative)
Experimental phonology and phonetics (mostly non-generative)
Historical linguistics (non-generative)
Language and the law (non-generative)
Language contact (non-generative)
Morphology (mixed generative and non-generative)
Neurolinguistics (non-generative)
Phonetics (non-generative)
Phonology: feature theory (mixed generative and non-generative)
Phonology: underspecification (generative)
Pragmatics (non-generative)
Prosodic phonology: extraprosodicity (generative)
Prosodic phonology: stress (generative)
Prosodic phonology: syllables (generative)
Prosodic phonology: tone (generative)
Psycholinguistics (generative)
Semantics (3) (mostly non-generative)
Sociolinguistics (non-generative)
Syntax (6) (mostly generative)
Template morphology (generative)
Typology (non-generative)
Second and first language acquisition (mixed generative and non-generative)

There was a NSF Graduate Fellow Lecture by Barbara H. Partee, a formal semanticist, entitled 'Quantification and some questions for semantic typology'.

As was the case with the composition of the articles in *Language*, the percentage of generative-oriented talks at LSA meetings rose between 1980 and 1989. But even in the latter year, one could hardly speak of 'generative-dominated meeting'.

There was a certain amount of pressure, it would seem, to place a lid on the number of papers on generative syntax. D. Terence Langendoen, who was chair of the Program Committee in 1972, reported:

> It also appears that the Committee is somewhat harder on papers dealing with syntax and semantics than with other areas in linguistics, and that it deals more critically with papers on English than with papers that are on other languages or that do not concern themselves primarily with a single language. The particular bias against abstracts on English syntax undoubtedly reflects the somewhat conscious efforts of the Committee to 'balance' the program.
>
> (*LSAB 52*, 1972: 33)

9.5 Generative predominance (or not) at LSA summer Institutes

The Linguistic Institutes were held yearly in the 1970s and 1980, except for 1981, 1984, and 1988. The teaching staff at each Institute, again, is composed of local faculty members, supplemented by distinguished visitors from other institutions, all subject to the (normally pro forma) approval of the LSA's Executive Committee. Of the seventeen Institutes in our period, seven were held at a university whose linguistics faculty was at the time predominantly generative-oriented: Ohio State (1970), Massachusetts (1974), Illinois (1978), UCLA (1983), CUNY (1986), Stanford (1987), and Arizona (1989). That fact in and of itself means very little, since it has always been painfully difficult to find *any* host, whatever the orientation of their faculty, to take on the work and expense of running an Institute. However, the important fact for us that all of the generative-oriented departments invited prominent non-generative linguists to offer courses. The following is only a partial list.

1970   Robert Austerlitz, Madison Beeler, Mary Haas, Kostas Kazazis
1974   Raimo Anttila, Michael Arbib, Susumu Kuno
1978   Bernard Comrie, Charles Ferguson, Joshua Fishman, Peter Trudgill
1983   John Haiman, John Hawkins, Paul Hopper, Steven Krashen, Charles Li
1986   Jay Jasanoff, William Labov, Brian MacWhinney, Shana Poplack, David Sankoff
1987   William Croft, Penelope Eckert, Paul Hopper, Stephen Levinson, Ellen Prince
1989   Leanne Hinton, Claire Kramsch, Margaret Langdon, Michael Silverstein, Elizabeth Traugott

In other words, at any Institute in the 1970s and 1980s there were opportunities to study models of grammar different from those advocated and practiced by generative grammarians.

9.6 Generative predominance (or not) in obtaining grants

If generative grammarians held organizational power in the field of linguistics, then one assumes that it would have been they, and not their rivals, who would have been most successful in obtaining monetary grants. However, the evidence does not support that idea. Quite the contrary, in fact. The percentage of grants attributed to generative grammarians in the 1970s and 1980s was exceedingly small. I support this assertion to pointing to grants awarded by the National Science Foundation (§ 9.6.1), the American Council of Learned Societies (§ 9.6.2), the Guggenheim Foundation (§ 9.6.3), the National Endowment for the Humanities (§ 9.6.4), the Fulbright-Hayes Program (§ 9.6.5), the National Institute of Mental Health (§ 9.6.6), and the Ford Foundation (§ 9.6.7).

9.6.1 National Science Foundation grants

Of all granting agencies, the National Science Foundation (NSF) was probably the most generous in its support of linguistics in the 1970s and 1980s. The NSF is a United States government agency that supports fundamental research and education in all the nonmedical fields of science and engineering. The Linguistics Program per se at NSF was not initiated until 1976, though many grants were awarded before then under their Division of Social Sciences. Paul Chapin was Program Director for Linguistics from that year on. Chapin, in fact, had a PhD in Linguistics, awarded by MIT, and which focused on English syntax. At the time that Chapin's appointment was announced, there were grumblings that he would be biased toward generative work. In fact, that did not happen. As his 2015 obituary pointed out:

> As a 1967 Ph.D. graduate from MIT, Paul could have expressed a particular professional bias for generative grammar while at NSF. [...] Since NSF is the primary source of government support for the field, the NSF program director has a supremely important influence: Paul used this influence with a great sense of critical judgment but with an equal sense of impartiality in a field rife with academic conflicts. The 25 year period of his stewardship of the program witnessed some of the most extreme disagreements within the language sciences, pitting rationalists against associationists, structuralists against functionalists, nativists against empiricists: They all were struggling for NSF support during a time of increasingly limited resources. Paul stood above these arguments, and insisted on supporting any affordable proposal that had promise for important

results, both theoretical and empirical, whatever the philosophical stripe of the investigators. He could see past the intellectual commercials accompanying a project into its value in propelling the field forward. Without him, research support could easily have fallen into one camp or another with an ultimate loss for everyone.

(Thomas Bever, Merrill Garrett, and Cecile McKee: https://www.linguisticsociety.org/news/2015/07/02/memoriam-paul-chapin)

I was able to track down the names of only a few of Chapin's appointed panel members during the 1970s and 1980s.[10]

1976	William O. Dingwall, Victoria Fromkin, Ives Goddard, Roger Shuy, Carlota Smith, Arnold Zwicky
1978	Victoria Fromkin, Eric Hamp, Harlan Lane, Barbara Partee, Roger Shuy, Carlota Smith
1983	Susumu Kuno, Melissa Bowerman, Michael Krauss, Peter McNeilage, Brian MacWhinney, Gillian Sankoff
1988	Bernard Comrie, Lila Gleitman, Pauline Jacobson, Chin-Woo Kim, John Rickford, Michael Tanenhaus

Aside from Arnold Zwicky and Pauline Jacobson (who is more of a semanticist), I do not see a single generative syntactician or phonologist in these lists. There are generative-leaning psycholinguists, but otherwise the panelists are primarily phoneticians, sociolinguists, semanticists, and non-generative-oriented psycholinguists.

Koerner (1989: 136) has claimed that 'of the millions of dollars distributed by the [NSF's] Linguistics Program, MIT and its branch plants [I assume that Koerner is referring sarcastically here to universities with generative-oriented programs—(FJN)] have received—and I am referring to the later 1960s and early 1970s especially—a considerable, and at times rather disproportionate amount (as may be gathered from the NSFs annual reports)'. Koerner did not provide either copies of these reports or of the information contained in them. There is a good reason that he did not do so, namely because they show the precise opposite of what he claimed. Here are the figures for 1966 through 1972 (to view the full list, see Appendix E-1, p. 335).

---

[10] Joan Maling, the current Program Director for Linguistics, informed me: 'NSF used to provide some information about panelists, by Division, I believe, and not by individual programs. I do, of course, have such a list, but at the moment we are not allowed to give out that information. If anything, NSF policy is headed in the direction of more privacy rather than transparency. Individual panelists may reveal that they've served on a panel, but are not allowed to reveal the identity of their co-panelists. Sorry I can't be more helpful' (p. c., December 3, 2019).

1966   17 grants, of which one was for generative research (Kenneth Hale, 'A grammatical study of Walbiri')

1967   35 grants, of which one was for generative research (P. Gough, 'Transformational Grammar and comprehension')

1968   26 grants, of which two were for generative research (P. Gough, 'Transformational Grammar and comprehension' [continued]; S. Jay Keyser, Investigations into Universal Grammar')

1969   32 grants, of which two were for generative research (Paul Newman, 'Transformational studies of Chadic languages in Africa; Emmon Bach and P. Stanley Peters, 'Theory of Transformational Grammar')

1970   35 grants, of which five were for generative research (Edward Klima, 'La Jolla conference on linguistic theory and the structure of English'; George Lakoff, 'Generative Semantics'; A. Stroll and Edward Klima, 'Theoretical investigations of translation, descriptions and deep structure'; Charles Cairns, 'Theory of phonological and phonetic universals', Winfred Lehmann, 'Theoretical investigations of diachronic syntax' [possibly generative])

1971   50 grants, of which four were for generative research (S. Jay Keyser, 'Phonology and syntax of English'; J. R. Ross 'Theory of generative semantics'; Paul Schachter and George Bedell, 'Theories of Transformational Generative syntax; Ronald Langacker, 'Doctoral dissertation research in linguistics' [possibly generative])

1972   47 grants, of which four were for generative research (George Lakoff, 'Generative Semantics [continued]'; Charles Cairns, 'Theory of phonological and phonetic universals' [continued]; P. Stanley Peters, 'Theoretical investigations of Transformational Grammar'; Susumu Kuno, 'Research in formal linguistics' [possibly generative])

The major grant recipient by far in this period was Zellig Harris, who was awarded three grants totalling $760,600.

From 1976 to the present, all NSF grants under their linguistics program can be searched for under the URL https://nsf.gov/awardsearch/advancedSearch.jsp.[11] The search reveals the following results for 1980, 1985, and 1989:

---

[11] Grant data are available online from before that year, though the NSF web page warns us that 'Data prior to 1976 may be less complete'. Koerner (2002b: 194) writes that he consulted the NSF annual report from 1974 and '[f]rom it I could gather that the major scholars of the day (like Charles Ferguson of Stanford for the Phonological Archive) received a grant of $30,000 or $40,000, none other than Morris Halle of MIT received an amount of many times that much, $120,000 or more, for a project entitled "The study of language"'. In fact, the web page lists no grant at all for Halle. However, it does list two for Ferguson, both with Joseph Greenberg as co-principal investigator, totaling $418,500. That same year, William Labov received a grant for $198,000. Of the five other grants listed for 1974, one was for generative-oriented research: Peter Culicover and Kenneth Wexler were awarded $68,800 for a project entitled 'Acquisition constraints on a theory of language structure'.

1980   42 grants, of which five were for generative research and six more which appeared to be clearly generative-influenced.
1985   43 grants, of which nine were for generative research and five more which appeared to be clearly generative-influenced.
1989   35 grants, of which seven were for generative research and three more which appeared to be clearly generative-influenced.

9.6.2 American Council of Learned Society grants

Over the last century, the institution that has provided the most direct financial support to the field of linguistics is the American Council of Learned Societies (ACLS; for discussion, see Chapter 3, § 3.2.2). The ACLS provided me with a spreadsheet listing its grants in linguistics since 1936. But something is wrong. It lists 61 grants between 1936 and 1961, 59 between 2001 and 2018, but only three between 1961 and 2001. ACLS personnel have been either unable or unwilling to explain to me this obvious error. These three are all within our time period: In 1971 Carleton Hodge of Indiana University received a Grant-in-Aid, in 1982 Robert S. Bower of Fu Jen Catholic University received a Mellon Fellowship (administered by ACLS), and 1989 Jean Ann of the University of Arizona received a China Studies Program Dissertation Fellowship. Hodge was certainly not a generative grammarian; I know nothing about the other two awardees.

Fortunately, the *LSA Bulletins* in the 1970s and 1980s noted some (but not all) of the ACLS grant recipients, often omitting their affiliation and project name. They are listed in Appendix E-2 (p. 346). I see some prominent (and not so prominent) generative grammarians in these lists, but they are well in the minority. I would hazard a guess that between ten and fifteen percent of those awarded ACLS grants in our period were generativists.

9.6.3 Guggenheim Foundation grants

The John Simon Guggenheim Foundation is a nonprofit that offers grants 'to further the development of scholars and artists by assisting them to engage in research in any field of knowledge and creation in any of the arts, under the freest possible conditions' (from their web page). Approximately 175 fellowships are awarded each year. Between 1970 and 1989, a total of 68 were awarded in the field of linguistics. They can be found at https://www.gf.org/fellows/all-fellows/?fellowpage=4. Of the 68, I recognized twelve as being generative grammarians: Stephen R. Anderson, Ivonne Bordelois, Joan Bresnan, Matthew Chen, Noam Chomsky, Joseph Emonds, C.-T. James Huang, Larry Hyman, S.-Y. Kuroda, David Perlmutter, John Robert Ross, and Arnold Zwicky, and two more as formal semanticists with close ties to generative grammar: Robin Cooper and P. Stanley Peters. Even allowing for the possibility that I missed a few whose names were unfamiliar to me and whose grant details I was unable to track down, generativists received well under half of the Guggenheims in the 1970s and 1980s.

9.6.4 National Endowment for the Humanities grants

The National Endowment for the Humanities is an independent federal agency of the U.S. government, established by the National Foundation on the Arts and the Humanities Act of 1965, dedicated to supporting research, education, preservation, and public programs in the humanities. Its grants in linguistics over the years can be found at https://securegrants.neh.gov/publicquery/main. aspx. Let us examine more closely their grants in 1970, 1980, and 1989 (listed in Appendix E-3, p. 350). In 1970, there were 11 awards, two for generative research (Demers and Capek). In 1980, there were 30 awards, one for clearly generative research (Wasow) and two for possible generative research (Heath, Stanley). In 1989, there were 23 awards, four for generative research (Broselow, Speas, Everett, Lobeck).

9.6.5 Fulbright-Hayes (and other Fulbright-related) awards

The Fulbright-Hays Program—a Fulbright Program funded by a Congressional appropriation to the United States Department of Education—awards grants to individual American teachers and administrators, pre-doctoral students, and postdoctoral faculty, as well as to American institutions and organizations. Fulbright funding in particular supports research and training efforts overseas that focus on non-Western foreign languages and area studies. I have not located a web page that lists all of their grants in linguistics, but the *LSA Bulletins* announced most or all of their awardees (listed in Appendix E-4, p. 353). I certainly see prominent generativists named here for the 1970s and 1980s (E. Wayles Browne, Richard Kayne, John R. Ross, and John Whitman). I also see just as many prominent non-generativists (Adam Makkai, Robert Kirsner, Norman McQuown, and Dennis Preston). The vast majority of the awardees appear to be graduate students, whose fields of research are impossible to determine.

9.6.6 National Institute of Mental Health grants

The National Institute of Mental Health (NIMH) is a component part of the National Institute of Health, which, in turn, is an agency of the United States

Department of Health and Human Services, which is the primary agency of the United States government responsible for biomedical and health-related research. The mission of NIMH is 'to transform the understanding and treatment of mental illnesses through basic and clinical research, paving the way for prevention, recovery, and cure' (from its web page). Surprisingly, given this statement, the NIMH funds what can only be described as basic linguistic research. One *LSA Bulletin* (no. 64, March 1975) lists the awardees in linguistics from 1973 (see Appendix E-5, p. 356). Morris Halle received an award, but so did Charles Ferguson, John Gumperz, Charles Osgood, David Premack, and Joel Sherzer.

9.6.7 Ford Foundation grants

The Ford Foundation has as its mission to 'reduce poverty and injustice, strengthen democratic values, promote international cooperation, and advance human achievement' (from its web page). No generative grammarian has ever received a Ford Foundation grant, as the foundation objects to the fact that generativists 'have isolated [the field] from the world of nonlinguistic events and concentrated on abstract and formal theories about the nature and structure of language' (Fox & Skolnick 1975: 6). Most of their linguistics support appears to have been in applied linguistics and sociolinguistics, though a complete list is unobtainable. The Ford Foundation was instrumental in providing initial funding the Center for Applied Linguistics in 1959, and in 1979 (according to *LSAB* 81, 1979) sponsored a conference on 'English in non-native contexts'.

9.7 Generative predominance (or not) in departmental composition

In this section I outline the number and ranking of PhD programs in linguistics in 1987 (§ 9.7.1), followed by job announcements in an *LSA Bulletin* from that year (§ 9.7.2).

9.7.1 PhD programs in linguistics in 1987

1987 was the only year in our time period where I was able to locate both an LSA-produced *Directory of Programs in Linguistics in the United States and Canada* and a National Research Council-sponsored ranking of the twenty best PhD programs in the field. In that year, there were 51 PhD programs in linguistics in the United States. At the vast majority of them, one could study with non-generativists. Indeed, for about a quarter of them there were no generativists at all listed in the

Directory.[12] But what about those departments that were rated in the top tier? They were ranked as follows: 1: MIT; 2: UCLA; 3: Texas; 4: Chicago; 5–6: Pennsylvania, UC Berkeley; 7–8: Massachusetts, UC San Diego; 9: Stanford; 10–11: Ohio State, Illinois; 12: Harvard; 13–16: CUNY, Hawaii, Yale; 17: Washington; 18–20: Arizona, Cornell, Connecticut. Every one of these departments with the possible exception of Yale had at least one generative grammarian on its faculty, though in the case of UC Berkeley it was only generative phonology that was represented. At almost all of them with a strong generative presence, it was possible to study with a well-known non-generative grammarian: Raimo Anttila, Pamela Munro, and John Du Bois at UCLA; Joel Sherzer and Anthony Woodbury at Texas; Ellen Prince, Gillian Sankoff, and John Fought at Pennsylvania; George Lakoff, John Ohala, and Eve Sweetser at UC Berkeley; Jeffrey Elman and Ronald Langacker at UC San Diego; Elizabeth Traugott at Stanford; Susumu Kuno at Harvard; Richard Otheguy at CUNY; Stanley Starosta at Hawaii; and Joseph Grimes and Linda Waugh at Cornell. Furthermore, the historiographers who asserted MIT or generative dominance of the field in our time period never seemed to distinguish between MIT-style and non-MIT-style generative syntax. But it is worth pointing out that over half of the generative syntacticians in the top-rated departments were working in frameworks that Chomsky opposed, in some case virulently. Some examples are Edward Keenan and Paul Schachter at UCLA; C. L. Baker at Texas; James McCawley and Jerrold Sadock at Chicago; Charles Fillmore at UC Berkeley; Emmon Bach at Massachusetts; David Perlmutter at UC San Diego; Joan Bresnan, Ivan Sag, and Thomas Wasow at Stanford; Michael Geis and Arnold Zwicky at Ohio State; Georgia Green and Jerry Morgan at Illinois; D. Terence Langendoen at CUNY; Michael Brame and Joseph Emonds at Washington; and Carol Rosen at Cornell.

In sum, there might be weak evidence for generative dominance in the leading departments in 1987, but there is none at all for 'Chomskyan' dominance, where the term is applied narrowly.

9.7.2 Job postings in 1987

Before 1983, jobs in linguistics were advertised mainly by letters and small posters mailed to individual departments. From the late 1990s on, the internet (and in particular the blog Linguist List) took on this function. But starting in October 1983, it was the LSA, via its *Bulletin*, which was the major source of job announcements. Let us look at those jobs advertised by American colleges and universities in *LSAB* 117 from October 1987.

---

[12] In what follows, I exclude both emeritus faculty and those listed under the heading 'Linguists in Other Departments'. If the latter were included, then the percentage of generativists would be much lower than what I report here.

Brown University, in computational cognitive science
Brown University, in psycholinguistics
Brown University, in linguistic theory with a specialty in semantics
Cornell University, two positions in which two of the following three specializations would be desirable: sociolinguistics, Spanish and/or Portuguese linguistics, and Germanic linguistics
George Mason University, in second language acquisition or other branch of applied linguistics
Hamilton College, in general linguistics
Harvard University, in theoretical linguistics with a specialization in syntactic theory
Indiana University, in second language acquisition and other areas of applied linguistics
Johns Hopkins University, in cognitive science (linguistics)
Michigan State University, in Japanese
Michigan State University, in sociolinguistics
Purdue University, in English linguistics with a specialty in syntax
Rutgers University at Camden, in historical linguistics or sociolinguistics
SUNY Albany, as director of the linguistics program and with theoretical interests
SUNY Albany, in French with a special interest in sociolinguistics
Texas A&M University, in sociolinguistics
University of California, Berkeley, in phonological theory
University of California, Irvine, two positions, both involving German
University of California, San Diego, in cognitive or functional linguistics
University of California, San Diego, in syntactic theory
University of California, San Diego, in language and communication
University of Colorado, in discourse
University of Delaware, in theoretical syntax
University of Delaware for a full professorship, subfield unspecified
University of Illinois, in English as an international language and related areas
University of Iowa, for two positions in syntax
University of Michigan, in theoretical linguistics
University of Michigan, in literacy and discourse
University of New Mexico, in Navajo and Native American linguistics
University of Oklahoma, in English as a second language
University of Pittsburgh, specialization open, but with the ability to teach phonology and morphology
University of Pittsburgh, in applied linguistics
University of Pittsburgh, in syntax with an interest in computational linguistics
University of Rochester, in syntactic theory
Wright State University, in TESOL

I do not see any evidence here for a Chomskyan domination of the job market. It is very likely that advertisers for positions in 'syntactic theory' or 'theoretical syntax' had generative grammarians in mind, but there were only four such positions posted. These were well outnumbered by ads for sociolinguists or applied linguists.

9.8 Discussion

As we have seen, the visibility and intellectual success of generative grammar in the 1970s and 1980s was not matched by the ability of its advocates to dominate the field's organs of power or to secure a major share of grant funding. Let us consider some possible reasons why this was the case. I begin with grant awards. Why did generative grammarians do rather poorly in these two decades in the grant-receiving department? No full answer to this question is possible without knowing what percentage of grant applicants were generativists and what their acceptance and rejection rate was. Such information is unfortunately unobtainable. But I would hazard the guess that for each grant-awarding program, the percentage of generative *applicants* was disproportionately small. Generative grammarians are as likely to hold international conferences, to hire language consultants, and to travel to distant lands to do fieldwork as any other group of linguists. That costs money. But beyond that, generative research is more often than not cheap (dare I say it?) armchair linguistics, at least as far as purely grammatical investigations are concerned. No pricey laboratory equipment is needed, nor specialized software packages. Generative grammarians rarely need to fund research assistants to aid experimental work or to run subjects. In other words, I see no evidence that generativists were singled out for discrimination in the two decades under discussion by virtue of their theoretical orientation. They in all likelihood were not as grant-oriented to begin with as their colleagues in other subfields.

The explanation for the relatively small amount of generativist work—and especially MIT-style syntax—in the pages of *Language* is more complex. The two most important generative-oriented journals were founded in our time period: *Linguistic Inquiry* in 1970 and *Natural Language and Linguistic Theory* in 1983. It is my impression that for grammatical theorists to publish in these two journals has always conferred vastly more prestige than to publish in *Language*. For whatever reason, most generativists have valued sharing their latest ideas with their immediate peers more than sharing them with the field as a whole, thereby leading to the downplaying of the importance of *Language*. It is true that other subfield-oriented journals began operation in this period: *Language and Society* (in 1972), *Cognition* (in 1972), and *Linguistics and Philosophy* (in 1977), to give three examples. But sociolinguists, say, seem more outward-looking than generative syntacticians and are therefore more inclined to submit their work to *Language*.

Also, it appears that generative grammarians are much more critical of *each other's* work than are practitioners of other subfields. In 1982 or 1983 I asked

Editor William Bright why generative syntax—and especially MIT-style generative syntax—was so poorly represented in the pages of *Language*. He told me to
blame the referees. Referee reports from generative syntacticians tended (at least in
that time period) to be much more likely to recommend rejection than those from
specialists in other domains. With only a bit of exaggeration, generative syntactician referees tend to look for the worst in each submission, while sociolinguists
and applied linguist referees tend to supportively accentuate the submission's positive aspects. Since an editor is forced to follow the recommendations he or she
receives, a smaller percentage of generative papers end up in published form than
those from other subfields.

Another reason for the relatively small amount of generative work in the pages
of *Language* derives from both the immaturity and the internal diversity of the field
of linguistics. The former is reflected in the literally dozens of different approaches
to grammar that have appeared over the past half century, with some high percentage of these being introduced in the 1970s and 1980s. Now nobody would say
that there should be 'affirmative action for theories', where each and every one de-
serves equal representation in journal pages. But at the same time it seems that
editors of broad spectrum journals like *Language* feel that it is only proper to cut
new ideas some slack, given that agreed upon details of what a grammatical theory
should be are fairly minimal. Note that it was *Language* that published a glowing
review (Lees 1957) of a book (*Syntactic Structures*) by an unknown author, namely
Noam Chomsky. And *Language* also, some years later, published one of the first
papers in American functional linguistics (Haiman 1980) and in cognitive linguistics (Langacker 1982). The lack of generativist dominance in the pages of *Language*
also stems in part from diversity of interests that come under the heading 'linguistics'. The names of the organized sessions at LSA meetings (see § 9.4) give one
a feel for this diversity. Broad subareas like discourse analysis, sociolinguistics,
experimental phonetics, pragmatics, lexical semantics, and so on have as much
right to be covered in *Language* as does generative grammar (or, for that matter, other approaches to grammatical analysis). The space available for the latter is
correspondingly limited.

It is a very interesting question why generativists—and in particular those doing
MIT-style syntax—have been so poorly represented in LSA offices. To answer this
question, we need to look at Chomsky's attitude to the field. He at first seemed
quite positively disposed to the LSA. He became a life member in 1957 and actually
served on the LSA Executive Committee in 1966, 1967, and 1968.[13] Around that
time he published an article in the volume of *Language* dedicated to the memory of
Bernard Bloch (Chomsky 1967c). But that was the last piece he has ever published
in the journal. Chomsky was asked to serve as LSA President every year in the

---

[13] Though Chomsky appeared at only two of the six meetings during his tenure of office. He was
proxied for by Henry Kučera once, by Robert B. Lees twice, and once did not send a proxy.

1970s and early 1980s. After a dozen or so refusals, he ceased being asked. His alienation from the field at this point was so great that he could write:

> As I look back over my own relation to the field, at every point it has been completely isolated, or almost completely isolated. I do not see that the situation is very different now [...]. But I cannot think of any time when the kind of work that I was doing was of any interest to any more than a very tiny fraction of people in the field.
>
> (Chomsky 1982: 42–43)

My feeling is that Chomsky actually believes what he writes here. Indeed such a belief is part of what sustains him. Unfortunately, Chomsky's view of his relation to the field has rubbed off on many of his most ardent supporters and have kept them from participating in LSA activities or even in some cases from joining. Norbert Hornstein, a close associate of Chomsky's, edits a popular blog dealing with a wide range of linguistic themes, focusing on the foundations of linguistic theory. He expressed outrage that the journal *Language* would organize a discussion around Vyvyan Evans' cognitive linguistics manifesto *The Language Myth* and he went on to write:

> Generativists have always considered *Language* the place you publish when you can't get your stuff into *LI* or *NLLT*, or *Lingua* or [...]. It is far down the list of desirable publishing venues. [...] Maybe it's time for Generativists to either leave the LSA or the LSA should consider replacing the editors [of *Language*].
>
> (Hornstein 2015)

The ellipsis after '*Lingua* or' is Hornstein's, not mine.

I think that the bitterest pill for Chomsky to swallow has been the fact that his earliest students, almost without exception, resisted his 1970s change of direction in generative syntax. As he put it:

> It seems to me what is different now [from twenty or so years earlier] is that a good deal of the field from which I feel isolated happens to be comprised of former students, or their students, whereas previously it was just other linguists.
>
> (Chomsky 1982: 42).

What Chomsky writes here is nothing less than the truth. Few, if any, American linguists have had as many PhD students as Chomsky, and few, if any, have had as many of their students cease to follow them after receiving their degrees. I do not think that it is a coincidence that the bulk of Chomsky's students who would become LSA officers and active committee members were not (or perhaps one should write 'no longer') MIT-style syntacticians. What we find are individuals

like Joan Bresnan, Janet Fodor, Ray Jackendoff, D. Terence Langendoen, Joan Maling, Barbara Partee, David Perlmutter, John R. Ross, Arnold Zwicky, and others,
all of whom were developing models of grammar markedly different from Chomsky's. Rejecting Chomsky (or at least rejecting his current orientation) seemed to
go hand-in-hand with accepting the LSA. For Chomsky, and for a sizeable number of his closest co-thinkers, the LSA and its journal were simply not part of their
professional identity.

To conclude, the attention garnered by generative grammar in the 1970s and
1980s was not matched by a corresponding success on the part of its advocates in
being able to dominate the field in any organizational way. When we look at LSA
offices, publications in *Language*, presentations at LSA meetings, grant awards, and
so on, we find that these individuals, far from occupying the metaphorical 'palace
of linguistics', found themselves, for the most part, outside of its walls.[14]

---

[14] In a recent article in a working papers volume (Newmeyer 2018) and in a blog posting (Newmeyer
2020), I investigate the current degree of generative domination of the LSA and its journal. To make a
long story short, nothing has changed since the 1980s.

The members of the LSA Executive Committee in the 1970s and 1980s

The Executive Committee in the 1970s and 1980s met twice a year, normally in either the spring or concurrently with the summer Linguistic Institute (if there was one) and on the day preceding the Annual Meeting in December. The Committee has the final say on where summer institutes will be held (see § 9.5), the format of LSA meetings, on what propositions will be brought before the membership, and virtually every other matter regarding LSA activities. Each year the Nominating Committee presented to the Executive Committee a candidate (or, later, two competing candidates) to fill the vacant position on the latter committee. The following is a list of Executive Committee members in the 1970s and 1980s.[1]

1968–1970	Sol Saporta, at the time a strong supporter of generative grammar; Ernst Pulgram, a historical linguist
1969–1971	Carlton Hodge, a specialist in Afroasiatic languages; Henry Lee Smith, a post-Bloomfieldian structuralist
1970–1972	William Labov, a sociolinguist; Carroll Reed, a dialectologist
1971–1973	J. R. Ross, a non-MIT-style syntactician; Ilse Lehiste, a phonetician
1972–1974	Charles Fillmore, a non-MIT-style syntactician; D. Terence Langendoen, a polymath with a generative orientation
1973–1975	William Gedney, a specialist in Southeast Asian languages; Maria Tsiapera, a historical linguist and historiographer of linguistics
1974–1976	Victoria Fromkin, a neurolinguist and phonetician and a strong advocate of generative grammar; Calvert Watkins, a historical linguist
1975–1977	Robin Lakoff, a sociolinguist, pragmaticist, and discourse analyst; Kostas Kazazis, a specialist in Balkan languages
1976–1978	Robins Burling, a specialist in language acquisition and Tibeto-Burman languages; Bruce Fraser, a pragmaticist and discourse analyst
1977–1979	Susumo Kuno, a functionalist linguist; Margaret Langdon, a specialist in Amerindian languages

[1] An anonymous referee has asked me, for the sake of general interest, to provide the names and specializations of the defeated candidates. Unfortunately, that is not possible. Starting around 1980 the names of the candidates were no longer published in the *LSA Bulletins*. Instead, each member was sent a special mail ballot to fill in and return. Perhaps sample ballots are preserved in the LSA Archive at the University of Missouri, but I don't recall seeing them there.

1978–1980	Eve Clark, a language acquisition specialist; James McCawley, a non-MIT-style syntactician
1979–1981	John Gumperz, an anthropological linguist; Robert Longacre, a discourse analyst
1980–1982	Carlota Smith, a semanticist and Navajo specialist; Ives Goddard, a specialist in Amerindian languages
1981–1983	Osamu Fujimora, a phonetician; Herbert Penzl, a Germanicist
1982–1984	Paul Friedrich, an anthropological linguist; Elizabeth Traugott, a functionalist linguist
1983–1985	Warren Cowgill, a historical linguist; Lila Gleitman, a psycholinguist, very favorable to generative grammar
1984–1986	Joseph Grimes, a discourse analyst, computational linguist, and specialist in Amerindian languages; Elizabeth Selkirk, a generative phonologist
1985–1987	Robert Austerlitz, a specialist in languages spoken in the circumpolar regions; Sandra Thompson, a functionalist linguist
1986–1988	Kenneth Hale, an MIT-style syntactician; Arnold Zwicky, a non-MIT-style syntactician
1987–1989	Alton Becker, a functionalist linguist; Wallace Chafe, a functionalist linguist
1988–1990	Ann Farmer, an MIT-style syntactician; John Goldsmith, a generative phonologist[2]
1989–1991	Joan Bybee, a functionalist linguist; Robert D. King, a historical linguist and Germanicist with a generativist orientation

[2] Goldsmith challenged and defeated the official nominee, David Lightfoot, an MIT-style syntactician.

APPENDIX B

The members of the LSA Nominating Committee in the 1970s and 1980s

As noted in Chapter 7, § 7.3.2, The Nominating Committee was, at first, strangely self-perpetuating, as the committee itself selected a candidate to fill an empty slot on that very committee. In 1972 the LSA Constitution was amended so that the Nominating Committee was charged to nominate three individuals for the vacant position instead of only one. By 1978 candidates for the Nominating Committee were chosen by the Executive Committee, which selected six candidates for the two vacant positions, to be voted on by the membership. And in 1989 the Nominating Committee was no more elective: The President with the approval of the Executive Committee proposed its members, who then proposed two candidates for each vacant position on the Executive Committee. Below are the members of the Nominating Committee in our time period:[1]

1968–1970   Herbert Paper, a specialist in Yiddish and the languages of the Middle East
1969–1971   W. Nelson Francis, a specialist in English grammar and language history and an early corpus linguist
1970–1972   Emmon Bach, a non-MIT-style syntactician
1971–1973   Leonard Newmark, a language teaching specialist
1972–1974   Edward Stankiewicz, a Slavicist structural linguist
1973–1975   Carlota Smith, a semanticist and Navajo specialist[2]
1974–1976   James McCawley, a non-MIT-style syntactician
1975–1977   Paul Friedrich, an anthropological linguist
1976–1978   Elizabeth Traugott, a functionalist linguist
1977–1979   Wallace Chafe, a functionalist linguist
1978–1980   Barbara Partee, a formal semanticist
1979–1981   Sandra Thompson, a functionalist linguist; Arnold Zwicky, a non-MIT-style syntactician
1980–1982   Robert Austerlitz, a specialist in languages spoken in the circumpolar regions; Dwight Bolinger, a descriptive linguist and critic of generative grammar
1981–1983   Morris Halle, a generative phonologist; Frances Ingemann, a phonetician

[1] The Nominating Committee was considered so important that the names of its members were printed on the inside cover of *Language* between 1940 and 2002.
[2] Smith challenged and defeated the official nominee, Robert Harms, a generative phonologist.

1982–1984	Kenneth Hale, an MIT-style syntactician; Eric Hamp, a historical linguist
1983–1985	Charles Fillmore, a non-MIT-style syntactician; Gillian Sankoff, a sociolinguist
1984–1986	Ilse Lehiste, a phonetician; Deborah Tannen, a sociolinguist
1985–1987	Paul Kiparsky, a generative phonologist; Donna Jo Napoli, a polymath with a generative orientation
1986–1988	Paul Hopper, a functionalist linguist; Sally McConnell-Ginet, a semanticist known for her work on language and gender
1987–1989	Peter Ladefoged, a phonetician; Frederick Newmeyer, an MIT-style syntactician
1988–1990	Bernard Comrie, a functionalist linguist; Ellen Prince, a discourse analyst
1989	Scott Delancey, a functionalist linguist
1989–1991	Deborah Schiffrin, a discourse analyst; Michael Silverstein, an anthropological linguist

APPENDIX C

Associate Editors of and example articles in *Language* in the 1970s and 1980s

Appendix C1: The Associate Editors of *Language* in the 1970s and 1980s

Neither William Bright nor Sarah Thomason, the two Editors of *Language* during our time period, were generativists. However, one might speculate that their appointed Associate Editors (called 'Members of the Committee on Publications' until 1971) were inveterate supporters of that approach, thereby giving credence to Maher's accusation in 1980 that *Language* was 'a TG-dominated journal'. Here is a list of the Associate Editors between 1970 and 1989.

1966–1975	Warren Cowgill, a historical linguist
1966–1973	Barbara H. Partee, a formal semanticist
1968–1970	Raven McDavid, a dialectologist
1968–1972	William S.-Y. Wang, a historical linguist and Chinese specialist
1969–1972	James McCawley, a non-MIT-style syntactician
1970–1973	Paul Schachter, a non-MIT-style syntactician
1971–1977	Ronald Langacker, a non-MIT-style syntactician
1973–1976	Robert D. King, a historical linguist and Germanicist with a generativist orientation
1973–1979	Arnold Zwicky, a non-MIT-style syntactician
1974–1979	Robert Stockwell, a phonologist, historical linguist, and vocal advocate of generative grammar; Sandra Thompson, a functionalist linguist
1975	Robin Lakoff, a sociolinguist, pragmaticist, and discourse analyst
1976–1979	Raimo Anttila, a historical linguist and virulent opponent of generative grammar
1977–1980	Stephen Anderson, a generative phonologist; Michael Kac, a non-MIT-style-syntactician; D. Terence Langendoen, a polymath with a generative orientation; Ronald Macaulay, a sociolinguist; Sanford Schane, a generative phonologist
1978	Victoria Fromkin, a neurolinguist and phonetician and a strong advocate of generative grammar
1978–1980	James Hoard, a generative phonologist; Pamela Munro, a specialist in Amerindian languages
1979–1980	Lila Gleitman, a psycholinguist with a strong generative orientation

1980–1982	Bernard Comrie; a typologist; Jorge Hankamer, a non-MIT-style-syntactician; Johanna Nichols, a typologist; María-Luisa Rivero, a generative syntactician, working in various frameworks
1981	P. Stanley Peters, a semanticist and non-MIT-style-syntactician
1981–1983	Mary Clayton, a (mostly) generative phonologist; Larry Hyman, a generative phonologist, Donna Jo Napoli, a polymath with a generative orientation; Joel Sherzer, an anthropological linguist
1981–1984	Edith Moravcsik, a typologist; Frederick Newmeyer, an MIT-style syntactician; Eve Clark, a language acquisition specialist
1982–1983	David Dowty, a formal semanticist
1983–1985	Sandra Chung, an MIT-style syntactician; John Haiman, a functionalist linguist; Geoffrey Pullum, a non-MIT-style-syntactician; Sarah Thomason, a historical linguist
1984–1987	William Frawley, a semanticist and language and literacy specialist; Jane Hill, an anthropological linguist; Ellen Kaisse, a generative phonologist; David Lightfoot, an MIT-style syntactician; John McCarthy, a generative phonologist
1985–1987	C. L. Baker, a non-MIT-style-syntactician; Scott Delancey, a functionalist linguist; Lise Menn, a neurolinguist
1986–1987	Barbara Abbott, a formal semanticist; Judith Aissen, a non-MIT-style syntactician; Paul Hopper, a functionalist linguist; Ray Jackendoff, a non-MIT-style syntactician
1988	Robin Cooper, a formal semanticist; Sheila Embleton, a historical linguist and sociolinguist; Kenneth Hale, an MIT-style syntactician; Paul Newman, an Africanist
1988–1989	Alice Harris, a historical linguist; Brian Joseph, a historical linguist; James McCawley, a non-MIT-style syntactician; Anthony Woodbury, a specialist in Amerindian languages; Annie Zaenen, a non-MIT-style syntactician; Nancy Dorian, a sociolinguist; Melissa Bowerman, a psycholinguist; George N. Clements, a generative phonologist
1989	Niko Besnier, a field linguist; Patricia Keating, a phonetician; Richard Oehrle, a non-MIT-style-syntactician; Peter Sells, a non-MIT-style syntactician

Appendix C2: The articles in *Language* in 1970, 1980, and 1989

Language, Volume 46, 1970

Number 1

George Cardona: The Indo-Iranian construction mana (mama) krtam (historical linguistics)

B. A. van Nooten: The vocalic declensions in Panini's grammar (historical linguistics)

Östen Dahl: Some notes on indefinites (generative semantics)

Haim Blanc: Dual and pseudo-dual in the Arabic dialects (historical linguistics)

Larry M. Hyman: How concrete is phonology? (generative phonology)

Sarah C. Gudschinsky and Harold & Frances Popovich: Native reaction and phonetic similarity in Maxakalí phonology (descriptive linguistics)

Mario Saltarelli: Spanish plural formation: apocope or epenthesis? (generative phonology)

William E. Rutherford: Some observations concerning subordinate clauses in English (generative semantics)

Number 2

Archibald A. Hill: Laymen, lexicographers, and linguists (lexicography)

Jane J. Robinson: Dependency structures and transformational rules (formal non-MIT-style syntax)

James D. McCawley: English as a VSO language (generative semantics)

Randolph Quirk: Aspect and variant inflection in English verbs (descriptivism)

Philip Lieberman, Masayuki Sawashima, Katherine S. Harris, and Thomas Gay: The articulatory implementation of the breath-group and prominence (phonetics)

Joseph L. Malone: In defense of non-uniqueness of phonological representations (anti-generative phonology)

Mantaro J. Hashimoto: Internal evidence for Ancient Chinese palatal endings (historical linguistics)

Paul G. Chapin: Samoan pronominalization (case grammar)

Paul Friedrich: Shape in grammar (semantic typology)

Joseph E. Grimes and Naomi Glock: A Saramaccan narrative pattern (discourse analysis/generative semantics)

Arlene I. Moskowitz: The two-year-old stage in the acquisition of English phonology (child language acquisition)

Number 3

Ralph W. Fasold: Two models of socially significant linguistic variation (sociolinguistics)

David Sankoff: On the rate of replacement of word-meaning relationships (historical linguistics)

Hans Aarsleff: The history of linguistics and Professor Chomsky (history of linguistics)

Geoffrey Sampson: On the need for a phonological base (nonstandard generative phonology)

George Lakoff: Global rules (generative semantics)

Maria-Luisa Rivero: A surface structure constraint on negation (in the general area of MIT-style syntax)

Number 4

Robert E. Longacre: Sentence structure as a statement calculus (non-generative syntax)

Talmy Givon: Notes on the semantic structure of English adjectives (generative semantics)

Robin Lakoff: Tense and its relation to participants (generative/descriptive semantics)

Ray C. Dougherty: A grammar of coordinate conjoined structures (MIT-style syntax)

Robert Hetzron: Nonverbal sentences and degrees of definiteness in Hungarian (semantics)

James W. Harris: A note on Spanish plural formation (generative phonology)

Language, Volume 56, 1980

Number 1

Jerrold J. Katz: Chomsky on meaning (critique of Chomsky's approach to semantics)

Alice Davison: Peculiar passives (typology, semantics)

Michael Shapiro: Russian conjugation: Theory and hermeneutic (a Jakobsonian analysis)

Grover Hudson: Automatic alternations in non-transformational phonology (critique of generative phonology)

Fausto Cercignani: Early 'umlaut' phenomena in the Germanic languages (historical linguistics)

Andres M. Kristol: Color systems in southern Italy: A case of regression (historical linguistics, typology)

Number 2

Paul J. Hopper and Sandra A. Thompson: Transitivity in grammar and discourse (functionalist linguistics)

Jerrold M. Sadock: Noun incorporation in Greenlandic: A case of syntactic word formation (formal, but non-Chomskyan morphology)

Leanne Hinton: When sounds go wild: Phonological change and syntactic re-analysis in Havasupai (variable rule analysis)

Brian Joseph: Linguistic universals and syntactic change (historical linguistics with some generative assumptions)

Shana Poplack: Deletion and disambiguation in Puerto Rican Spanish (variable rule analysis)

Lois Bloom, Karin Lifter and Jeremie Hafitz: Semantics of verbs and the development of verb inflection in child language (child language acquisition)

Number 3

Peter Ladefoged: What are linguistic sounds made of? (phonetics)

William Pagliuca and Richard Mowrey: On certain evidence for the feature [Grave] (anti-generative phonology)

John Haiman: The iconicity of grammar: Isomorphism and motivation (functionalist linguistics)

Keith Allan: Nouns and countability (semantics)

Deborah L. Nanni: On the surface syntax of constructions with easy-type adjectives (generative syntax, not particularly MIT-style)

Georgia M. Green: Some wherefores of English inversions (discourse analysis)

Janet Pierrehumbert: The Finnish possessive suffixes (generative morphology)

Sandra Chung and William J. Seiter: The history of raising and relativization in Polynesian (generative syntax/historical linguistics)

Number 4

Peter Cole, Wayne Harbert, Gabriella Hermon and S. N. Sridhar: The acquisition of subjecthood (generative approach to acquisition)

Mark Aronoff: Contextuals (the semantics of conversation)

Ruth A. Berman: The case of an (S)VO language: Subjectless constructions in Modern Hebrew (non-generative)

Alan Timberlake: Reference conditions on Russian reflexivization (non-generative)

Igor A. Mel'čuk: Animacy in Russian cardinal numerals and adjectives as an inflectional category

Anuradha Saksena: The affected agent (non-generative)

Language, Volume 65, 1989

Number 1

Eve V. Clark & Kathie L. Carpenter: The notion of source in language acquisition (nongenerative language acquisition)

Elizabeth Closs Traugott: On the rise of epistemic meanings in English: An example of subjectification in semantic change (functionalist approach to grammaticalization)

Katherine Demuth: Maturation and the acquisition of the Sesotho passive (language acquisition, critical of a generative analysis)

Kenneth N. Stevens & Samuel Jay Keyser: Primary features and their enhancement in consonants (phonetics)

Number 2

J. Gropen, S. Pinker, M. Hollander, R. Goldberg, & R. Wilson: The learnability and acquisition of the dative alternation in English (child language acquisition)

R. Armin Mester & Junko Ito: Feature predictability and underspecification: Palatal prosody in Japanese mimetics (generative phonology)

Sara Thomas Rosen: Two types of noun incorporation: A lexical analysis (generative morphology)

Donka F. Farkas & Jerrold M. Sadock: Preverb climbing in Hungarian (non-MIT-style syntax)

Daniel L. Everett: Clitic doubling, reflexives, and word order alternations in Yagua (MIT-style syntax)

Number 3

D. H. Whalen & Patrice S. Beddor: Connections between nasality and vowel duration and height: Elucidation of the Eastern Algonquian intrusive nasal (phonetics)

Douglas Biber & Edward Finegan: Drift and the evolution of English style: A history of three genres (stylistic analysis)

Judith L. Aissen: Agreement controllers and Tzotzil comitatives (non-MIT-style analysis)

Susan Steele: Subject values (analysis of agreement, bringing in concepts from different formal frameworks)

Number 4

Anne Zribi-Hertz: Anaphor binding and narrative point of view: English reflexive pronouns in sentence and discourse (MIT-style syntax)

Peter Coopmans: Where stylistic and syntactic processes meet: Locative inversion in English (MIT-style syntax)

Geraldine Legendre: Inversion with certain French experiencer verbs (non-MIT-style syntax)

Calvert Watkins: New parameters in historical linguistics, philology, and culture history (historical linguistics)

The members of the LSA Program Committee in the 1970s and the 1980s

The following lists members of the Program Committee, omitting those ex officio members who were on the committee by virtue of their affiliation with a local institution.

1969–1970	Bernard Spolsky, a sociolinguist and applied linguist; Robert Longacre, a discourse analyst
1969–1971	Theodore Walters, an applied linguist
1970–1971	Warren Cowgill, a historical linguist; D. Terence Langendoen, a polymath with a generative orientation
1971–1972	William Orr Dingwall, a neurolinguist; Roger Shuy, a sociolinguist
1971–1973	Paul Friedrich, an anthropological linguist; Arnold Zwicky, a non-MIT-style syntactician
1972–1974	Arthur Abramson, a phonetician; Paul Kiparsky, a generative phonologist
1973–1975	Eve Clark, a language acquisition specialist; Oswald Werner, and anthropological linguist
1974–1976	John Fought, an ethnolinguist; Harry Whitaker, a neurolinguist
1975–1977	Janet Fodor, a generative-oriented psycholinguist; Ernst Pulgram, a historical linguist
1976–1978	Michael Silverstein, an anthropological linguist
1977–1978	Sally McLendon, an anthropological linguist
1977–1979	Richard Smaby, a mathematical and computational linguist; Bernard Spolsky, a sociolinguist and applied linguist
1978–1980	Stephen Anderson, a generative phonologist; Henry Hoenigswald, a historical linguist
1979–1981	Jean Berko Gleason, a language acquisition specialist; William Merrifield, an anthropological linguist
1980–1982	Joan Bresnan, a non-MIT-style syntactician; Jacqueline Schachter, an applied linguist
1981–1983	Joan Bybee, a functionalist linguist; George Cardona, a historical linguist
1982–1984	Joseph Grimes, a discourse analyst, computational linguist, and specialist in Amerindian languages; Ivan Sag, a non-MIT-style syntactician
1983–1985	Lily Wong Fillmore, an applied linguist; Stanley Peters, a semanticist and non-MIT-style syntactician
1984–1986	Lyle Campbell, a historical linguist; Ladislav Zgusta, a historical linguist
1985–1987	Paula Menyuk, a language acquisition specialist; David Michaels, a phonetician and generative phonologist

1986–1988	Sandra Chung, an MIT-style syntactician; John McCarthy, a generative phonologist
1987–1989	Byron Bender, a specialist in Micronesian languages; Deborah Tannen, a sociolinguist
1988–1990	David Dowty, a semanticist; Donca Steriade, a generative phonologist
1989–1991	Jay Jasanoff, a historical linguist; Lise Menn, a neurolinguist

Grant recipients in American linguistics in the 1970s and 1980s

Appendix E1: National Science Foundation, Division of Social Sciences, Grants in support of linguistics research awarded during fiscal years 1966 through 1972

NATIONAL SCIENCE FOUNDATION

DIVISION OF SOCIAL SCIENCES

GRANTS IN SUPPORT OF LINGUISTICS RESEARCH AWARDED DURING

FISCAL YEARS 1966 THROUGH 1972

NATIONAL SCIENCE FOUNDATION

DIVISION OF SOCIAL SCIENCES

Grants in Support of Linguistics Research Awarded During Fiscal Years 1966 Through 1972*

Grant No.	Investigator & Institution	Title	Amount	Duration (Months)
FY 1966				
GS-935	H. M. Hoenigswald/ U Pennsylvania	Conference on Indo-European and the Indo-Europeans	$ 4,900	12
GS-949	H. J. Landar/ Los Angeles State College	Taxonomic Bibliography of North American Indian Languages	45,400	24
GS-953	L. A. Jakobovits/ U Illinois	Repetition in Behavior	17,200	24
GS-979	A. C. Satterthwaite/ Washington St. U	Sentence for Sentence Translation: Arabic-English	25,600	12
GS-997	E. P. Hamp/ Newberry Library	Conference on Linguistic Bibliography and Computer Technology	5,300	12
GS-1027	A. Rapoport/ U Michigan	Psycholinguistic Models	37,300	12
GS-1029	F. W. Wicker/ Tufts U	Scaling the Intrinsic Meanings of Speech Sounds	5,000	24

* N. B. - Does not include support awarded through the Foundation's Office of Science Information Service or its Divisions of Education.

Grant No.	Institution	Title	Amount	Duration (Months)
GS-1127	K. L. Hale/ U Arizona	A Grammatical Study of Walbiri	$19,600	12
GS-1137	K. L. Pike/ U Michigan	Doctoral Dissertation Research in Linguistics	2,000	12
GS-1139	W. R. Miller/ U Utah	Development of Shoshoni-Panamint Dialects	24,300	24
GS-1147	P. Ladefoged/ U California (LA)	Speech Communication Research Facility	58,000	12
GS-1149	C. A. Callaghan/ Ohio St. U	Analysis of Miwok Languages	11,100	24
GS-1153	J. Bruner/ Harvard U	Language and Cognition	110,900	24
GS-1175	F. Lounsbury/ Yale U	Mayan Linguistics	47,300	24
GS-1182	E. Stankiewicz/ U Chicago	Accentual Patterns of the Slavic Languages	56,800	24
GS-1219	R. H. Fifield/ U Michigan	XXVII International Congress of Orientalists	5,000	18
GS-1241	E. Sibley/ Soc. Sci. Research Council	Sociolinguistics	76,900	24

Grant No.	Investigator & Institution	Title	Amount	Duration (Months)
FY 1967				
GS-934 Amend. #1	J. E. Grimes R. Andree/ U Oklahoma	Linguistic Information Retrieval for Analysis of Aboriginal Languages	$ 11,400	
GS-1283	W. J. Samarin/ Hartford Seminary	Correlates of Expressive Language in African Ideophones	2,300	12
GS-1288	M. McCaskey/ Georgetown U	Doctoral Dissertation Research in Linguistics	2,600	6
GS-1297	N. H. Zide/ U Chicago	A Comparative Munda Phonology	128,200	30
GS-1308	H. Kucera/ Brown U	Doctoral Dissertation Research in Linguistics	3,400	12
GS-1318	F. Ingemann/ U Kansas	Analysis of the Ipili-Payiala Language of New Guinea	15,400	9
GS-1321	S. Lamb/ Yale U	Linguistic Automation	123,000	24
GS-1325	J. Pierce/ Portland St. U	Indigenous Languages of Oregon	14,800	27
GS-1332	N. McQuown/ U Chicago	Mayan Linguistics	47,800	24
GS-1357	M. D. Kinkade/ U Kansas	Linguistics of the Pacific Northwest	43,700	21
GS-1372	P. Gough/ Indiana U	Transformational Grammar and Comprehension	42,900	24

- 3 -

Grant No.	Investigator & Institution	Title	Amount	Duration (Months)
GS-1400	H. M. Hoenigswald/ U Pennsylvania	Doctoral Dissertation Research in Linguistics	$ 1,700	12
GS-1410	S. Elbert/ U Hawaii	Puluwat Linguistics	24,200	12
GS-1426	P. Ladefoged V. Fromkin/ U California (LA)	Linguistic Phonetics	49,100	24
GS-1430	W. Wang/ U California (B)	Phonological Research on Chinese Dialects	81,900	24
GS-1443	N. McQuown/ U Chicago	Decipherment of Maya Hieroglyphic Writing	84,600	24
GS-1449	Z. Harris/ U Pennsylvania	Linguistic Transformations Project	448,700	24
GS-1463	R. Oswalt/ U California (B)	Pomo Language Project	6,800	6
GS-1468	I. Dyen/ Yale U	Genetic Classification of Languages-Austronesian	76,900	24
GS-1522	T. Sebeok/ Center for Applied Linguistics	Preparation of Oceanic Linguistics	37,800	24
GS-1535	F. Lounsbury/ Yale U	Doctoral Dissertation Research in Linguistics	8,400	16
GS-1548	J. Ullian/ Washington U	Automata and Context Free Languages	10,700	12
GS-1578	W. Wang/ U California (B)	Phonology Research Facility	41,800	12

- 4 -

Grant No.	Investigator & Institution	Title	Amount	Duration (Months)
GS-1579	C. Frake/ Stanford U	Linguistic Analysis of Creole Languages	$ 49,700	24
GS-1603	W. Elmendorf/ U Wisconsin	Yukian Linguistic Family	4,800	12
GS-1605	J. E. Grimes R. Andree/ U Oklahoma	Computer Support of Linguistic Field Research	115,200	24
GS-1621	J. Berry/ Northwestern U	Phonetics Laboratory for Linguistic and Sociolinguistic Research	25,500	12
GS-1624	G. O'Grady/ U Hawaii	A Comparative Study in Australian Linguistics	32,500	18
GS-1629	R. Howren/ U Iowa	Dogrib, A Northern Athapaskan Language	11,600	12
GS-1645	D. Stuart/ Georgetown U	Doctoral Dissertation Research in Linguistics	4,100	6
GS-1654	A. Schutz/ U Hawaii	Linguistic Study of Nguna	11,500	12
GS-1687	A. Juilland/ Stanford U	Frequency-Based Studies of Language Structure	152,300	24
GS-1718	H. Josselson/ Wayne State U	Computer-Aided Linguistic Analysis of Russian Lexicon	165,000	24
GS-1748	E. Haugen/ Harvard U	Scandinavian Languages	92,300	24
C-516	P. Garvin/ Bunker-Ramo Corp.	Computer-Based Research on Linguistic Universals	133,146	24

- 5 -

Grant No.	Investigator & Institution	Title	Amount	Duration (Months)
FY 1968				
GS-1769	H. C. Conklin/ Yale U	Doctoral Dissertation Research in Linguistics	$ 5,750	18
GS-1831	V. Carroll/ U Hawaii	Nukuoro Linguistics	34,400	24
GS-1864	S. B. Brent/ Wayne State U	Conceptualization and Linguistic Expression of Relationships	49,600	24
GS-1869	S. Lieberson/ U Washington	Demographic Analysis of Linguistic Pluralism	14,100	12
GS-1880	C. A. Ferguson J. H. Greenberg/ Stanford U	Development of Parameters for Archiving Cross-Linguistic Data	133,900	24
GS-1889	L. C. Thompson/ U Hawaii	Analysis of Linguistic Relationships	91,400	24
GS-1892	P. B. Gough/ U Texas	Transformational Grammar and Comprehension	24,300	12
GS-1909	D. Taylor/ George Wash. U	Linguistic Investigation of the Coastal Arawak of Guiana	16,300	12
GS-1919	E. Sibley/ Soc. Sci. Research Council	Sociolinguistics	66,900	18
GS-1934	S. Kuno/ Harvard U	Computational Linguistics	106,400	24
GS-1941	C. Day/ U Rochester	Lexical Structure in Jacaltec	19,100	18

- 6 -

Grant No.	Investigator & Institution	Title	Amount	Duration (Months)
GS-1965	G. J. Suci/ Cornell U	Assessing the Comprehension Process in Language	$ 23,900	29
GS-1987	W. Labov/ Columbia U	A Quantitative Study of Sound Changes in Progress	49,300	24
GS-1994	H. J. Landar/ Calif. St. College (Los Angeles)	Taxonomic Bibliography of American Indian Languages North of Mexico	29,300	24
GS-2001	H. Rubenstein/ Lehigh U	Program of Linguistic Research	132,800	24
GS-2005	S. J. Keyser/ Brandeis U	Investigations Into Universal Grammar	43,900	24
GS-2012X	C. E. Osgood L. A. Jakobovitz/ U Illinois (Urbana)	Comparative Psycholinguistics	134,200	24
GS-2017	W. R. Miller/ U Utah	Language Variation in American Indian Speech Communities	18,900	12
GS-2022	I. Dyen/ Yale U	Doctoral Dissertation Research in Linguistics	4,700	15
GS-2040	M. G. Owen/ U Washington	Semantic Structure of Maya	27,300	24
GS-2051	B. Biggs/ U Hawaii	Comparative Polynesian Linguistics	7,100	7
GS-2059	G. Jochnowitz/ Queens College	Synchronic and Diachronic Analyses of Judeo-Italian Dialects	4,570	12

- 7 -

Grant No.	Investigator & Institution	Title	Amount	Duration (Months)
GS-2108	P. F. MacNeilage W. Wang/ U California (B)	Program of Speech Research	$116,900	24
GS-2118	D. M. Topping/ U Hawaii	Chamorro Linguistics	9,600	12
GS-2160	F. C. C. Peng/ U Hawaii	A Synchronic Study of the Ainu Language	10,200	12
GS-2210	G. H. Harman/ Princeton U	Investigation of Phrase Structure Grammar	9,600	12
FY 1969				
GS-1443X Amend. #1	N. A. McQuown/ U Chicago	Decipherment of Maya Hieroglyphic Writing	58,800	24
GS-1522 Amend. #1	T. A. Sebeok/ Center for Applied Linguistics	Preparation of Oceanic Linguistics	7,675	22
GS-2251	R. Howren/ U Iowa	A Northern Athapaskan American Indian Language	11,400	12
GS-2269	M. E. Krauss/ U Alaska	Alaska Native Languages Project	24,000	12
GS-2271	J. Friedman/ U Michigan	Computer Aids to Linguistic Research	57,000	24
GS-2279	P. Newman/ Yale U	Transformational Studies of Chadic Languages of Africa	54,100	28
GS-2301	W. A. Woods/ Harvard U	Theory and Computational Techniques for Semantic Interpretation of Natural Language	52,400	24

- 8 -

Grant No.	Investigator & Institution	Title	Amount	Duration (Months)
GS-2302	S. M. Lamb/ Yale U	Linguistic Automation	$ 58,900	12
GS-2327	D. S. Worth/ U California (LA)	Computer-Aided Analysis of Russian Derivational Morphology	62,300	24
GS-2329	C. A. Ferguson/ Stanford U	Aspects of the Acquisition of English Phonology	75,800	24
GS-2337	P. J. Jensen/ U Florida	Doctoral Dissertation Research in Linguistics	1,700	12
GS-2351	N. A. McQuown/ U Chicago	Doctoral Dissertation Research in Linguistics	2,200	12
GS-2360	C. D. Chretien/ U California (B)	Typological Study of Languages	17,000	9
GS-2376	C. A. Callaghan/ Ohio State U	Analysis of Miwok Languages	13,800	18
GS-2386	W. Wang/ U California (B)	Phonological Research on Chinese Dialects	127,100	24
GS-2397	E. Stankiewicz/ U Chicago	Accentual Patterns of the Slavic Languages	31,900	12
GS-2398	I. Dyen/ Yale U	Genetic Classification of Languages - Austronesian	60,600	24
GS-2417	W. R. Miller/ U Utah	Research on Language Acquisition	4,800	15
GS-2438	G. Cardona/ U Pennsylvania	Contributions of Indian Grammarians to Linguistics	25,600	15

- 9 -

Grant No.	Investigator & Institution	Title	Amount	Duration (Months)
GS-2462	N. Sager/ New York U	Computer-Based Investigation of Linguistic Structure	$ 57,900	24
GS-2468	E. W. Bach F. S. Peters/ U Texas	Theory of Transformational Grammar	81,200	24
GS-2470	N. A. McQuown/ U Chicago	Doctoral Dissertation Research in Linguistics	2,100	12
GS-2498	G. L. Trager/ Southern Methodist U	Doctoral Dissertation Research in Linguistics	3,800	15
GS-2500	P. G. Chapin/ U California (SD)	Research in Computational Linguistics	34,000	24
GS-2504	T. A. Sebeok/ Center for Applied Linguistics	Preparation of Linguistics in North America	36,400	24
GS-2509	Z. S. Harris/ U Pennsylvania	Theory and Computation of Linguistic Transformations	246,900	24
GS-2515	D. Davidson/ Princeton U	Interdisciplinary Conference on the Semantics of Natural Language	4,300	12
GS-2550	S. Lamb/ Yale U	Doctoral Dissertation Research in Linguistics	2,300	18
GS-2561	J. E. Hoard D. Kinkade/ U Kansas	Linguistics of the Pacific Northwest	82,300	24
GS-2595	S. Klein/ U Wisconsin	Research in Automatic Linguistic Analysis	44,600	24

- 10 -

Grant No.	Investigator & Institution	Title	Amount	Duration (Months)
GS-2615	B. Dreben W. V. Quine/ Harvard U	Philosophy and History of Logic and Language	$ 53,600	24
GS-2643	A. J. Schutz/ U Hawaii	Linguistic Study of Nguna	14,400	12

FY 1970

Grant No.	Investigator & Institution	Title	Amount	Duration (Months)
GS-1522 Amend. #2	T. A. Sebeok/ Center for Applied Linguistics	Preparation of _Oceanic Linguistics_	2,027	39
GS-2685	H. P. McKaughan/ U Hawaii	Grammatical Analysis of the Jeh Language of South Vietnam	20,100	12
GS-2722	G. L. Trager/ Southern Methodist U	Doctoral Dissertation Research in Linguistics	2,600	12
GS-2741 Amend. #1	P. N. Ladefoged/ U California (LA)	Computerized Research on Speech	94,600	24
GS-2757	D. H. Davidson/ Ctr for Adv Study in the Behav Sci	Foundations of Linguistics	21,800	12
GS-2766	M. H. Langdon/ U California (SD)	Conference on Hokan Languages	6,900	12
GS-2799	D. H. Hymes/ U Pennsylvania	Doctoral Dissertation Research in Linguistics	1,600	12
GS-2841	G. M. Schramm/ U Michigan	Doctoral Dissertation Research in Linguistics	2,450	12

- 11 -

Grant No.	Investigator & Institution	Title	Amount	Duration (Months)
GS-2845	E. S. Klima/ U California (SD)	La Jolla Conference on Linguistic Theory and the Structure of English	$ 9,000	12
GS-2858	S. Kuno/ Harvard U	Research in Mathematical Linguistics	75,200	24
GS-2859	V. Fromkin P. N. Ladefoged/ U California (LA)	Linguistic Phonetics	60,500	24
GS-2860	G. D. McNeill/ U Chicago	Speech Rate in Child Language	48,100	24
GS-2867	J. G. Fought/ U Pennsylvania	Cholan Linguistics	42,700	24
GS-2881	L. C. Thompson/ U Hawaii	Doctoral Dissertation Research in Linguistics	2,200	12
GS-2885	C. Watkins/ Harvard U	Research on Indo-European Noun Morphology	27,900	24
GS-2887	W. Labov/ U Pennsylvania	Doctoral Dissertation Research in Linguistics	4,000	18
GS-2909	D. H. Hymes/ U Pennsylvania	Doctoral Dissertation Research in Linguistics	1,850	12
GS-2917	H. B. Gerard/ U California (LA)	Speech Parapraxes and the Development of Language	166,300	24
GS-2930	P. Kay/ U California (B)	Doctoral Dissertation Research in Linguistics	850	12
GS-2939	G. Lakoff/ U Michigan	Generative Semantics	58,800	24

- 12 -

Grant No.	Investigator & Institution	Title	Amount	Duration (Months)
GS-2941	C. A. Ferguson J. H. Greenberg/ Stanford U	Archival Research on Language Universals	$195,100	24
GS-2946	M. B. Emeneau U California (B)	Doctoral Dissertation Research in Linguistics	2,650	3
GS-2961	I. Dyen/ Yale U	Doctoral Dissertation Research in Linguistics	3,400	12
GS-2979	M. Black/ Cornell U	Foundations of Theoretical Linguistics	37,700	14
GS-2982	A. Stroll E. S. Klima/ U California (SD)	Theoretical Investigations of Translation, Descriptions and Deep Structures	58,200	24
GS-2987	E. Hamp/ U Chicago	Conference on Eskimo Linguistics	12,000	12
GS-2988	L. C. Thompson/ U Hawaii	Linguistic Relationships	128,900	24
GS-3017	H. P. McKaughan/ U Hawaii	Maranao Linguistic Studies	28,200	24
GS-3022	M. G. Owen/ U Washington	Syntactic and Semantic Studies of Yucatec	38,100	24
GS-3031	W. Goodenough/ U Pennsylvania	Doctoral Dissertation Research in Linguistics	5,500	24
GS-3034	G. J. Parker/ U Hawaii	Linguistic Study of the Huaylas-Conchucos Dialect of Quechua	6,900	12

- 13 -

Grant No.	Investigator & Institution	Title	Amount	Duration (Months)
GS-3044	C. E. Cairns/ U Texas	Theory of Phonological and Phonetic Universals	$ 25,800	24
GS-3056	J. M. Crawford/ U Georgia	Southeastern Indian Languages Project	9,300	12
GS-3081	W. P. Lehmann/ U Texas	Theoretical Investigation of Diachronic Syntax	24,400	12
GS-3118	S. McLendon/ CUNY	Doctoral Dissertation Research in Linguistics	6,000	12
FY 1971				
GS-2012X1	C. E. Osgood L. A. Jakobovitz/ U Illinois	Comparative Psycholinguistics	53,300	12
GS-2595 Amend. #1	S. Klein/ U Wisconsin	Research in Automatic Linguistic Analysis	6,900	24
GS-3001 Amend. #1	E. G. Mishler/ Harvard U	Social Context Effects on Language and Communication	1,300	24
GS-3124	L. R. Stark/ U Wisconsin	Mosetano Linguistics	17,000	36
GS-3133	C. A. Ferguson/ Stanford U	Doctoral Dissertation Research in Linguistics	3,450	12
GS-3161	W. Cowgill/ Yale U	Doctoral Dissertation Research in Linguistics	2,900	12
GS-3178	J. H. Greenberg/ Stanford U	Genetic Classification of South and Central American Languages	23,400	9

- 14 -

Grant No.	Investigator & Institution	Title	Amount	Duration (Months)
GS-3179	S. J. Keyser/ Brandeis U	Phonology and Syntax of English	$ 74,800	24
GS-3180	J. E. Grimes/ Cornell U	Cross Language Study of Discourse Structures	59,200	24
GS-3192	N. A. McQuown/ U Chicago	Doctoral Dissertation Research in Linguistics	3,700	24
GS-3202	J. R. Ross/ Language Research Foundation	Theory of Generative Semantics	28,400	12
GS-3204	P. Schachter B. Bedell/ U California (LA)	Theories of Transformational-Generative Syntax	64,800	24
GS-3206	G. W. Grace/ U Hawaii	Doctoral Dissertation Research in Linguistics	2,800	20
GS-3208	J. K. E. Hitchcock/ SUNY (Buffalo)	Doctoral Dissertation Research in Linguistics	3,250	12
GS-3211	M. Herzog/ Columbia U	Doctoral Dissertation Research in Linguistics	1,400	12
GS-3212	N. C. Bodman/ Cornell U	Doctoral Dissertation Research in Linguistics	4,050	12
GS-3218	P. F. MacNeilage/ U Texas	Program of Speech Research	59,800	24
GS-3221	E. C. Polome/ U Texas	Doctoral Dissertation Research in Linguistics	7,900	12

- 15 -

Grant No.	Investigator & Institution	Title	Amount	Duration (Months)
GS-3232	M. D. Loflin B. J. Biddle D. G. Hays/ U Missouri	The Analysis of Discourse in Social Interaction	$ 33,200	12
GS-3245	C. A. Ferguson/ Stanford U	Doctoral Dissertation Research in Linguistics	4,050	12
GS-3257	D. S. Worth/ U California (LA)	Computer-Aided Analysis of Russian Derivational Morphology	150,800	24
GS-3279	V. H. Yngve/ U Chicago	Complex Information Processing in Human and Artificial Systems	35,000	24
GS-3282	H. H. Josselson/ Wayne State U	Computer-Aided Linguistic Analysis of Russian Lexicon	75,000	24
GS-3285	D. J. Foss P. B. Gough/ U Texas	Psycholinguistic Studies of Comprehension	40,000	24
GS-3287	W. Labov/ U Pennsylvania	A Quantitative Study of Sound Changes in Progress	48,400	24
GS-27231	H. Rubenstein/ Lehigh U	Program of Linguistic Research	50,800	12
GS-27294	S. M. Ervin-Tripp/ U California (B)	Doctoral Dissertation Research in Linguistics	2,200	12
GS-27324	H. Pitkin/ Columbia U	Lexicon and Reconstruction of an American Indian Family of Languages in Northern California	20,100	12
GS-27373	J. M. Cowan/ Cornell U	Doctoral Dissertation Research in Linguistics	1,500	8

- 16 -

Grant No.	Investigator & Institution	Title	Amount	Duration (Months)
GS-27421	L. G. Hutchinson/ U Minnesota	Doctoral Dissertation Research in Linguistics	$ 1,400	12
GS-27534	D. Jenness/ Soc. Sci. Research Council	Sociolinguistic Research	38,200	24
GS-27732	R. Langacker/ U California (SD)	Doctoral Dissertation Research in Linguistics	1,950	12
GS-27925	N. Sager/ New York U	Computer-Based Investigation of Linguistic Structure	53,200	24
GS-28212	C. O. Frake/ Stanford U	Creole Languages and Linguistic Theory	31,300	12
GS-28344	D. I. Slobin/ U California (B)	Doctoral Dissertation Research in Linguistics	3,100	12
GS-28354	F. S. Cooper A. M. Liberman/ Haskins Labs, Inc.	A Digital Playback for Research on Natural Speech	136,400	24
GS-28548	G. W. Grace/ U Hawaii	New Caledonian Linguistics	9,900	12
GS-28589	D. G. Hays/ SUNY (Buffalo)	Conference on Developmental Psycholinguistics	20,100	12
GJ-28599	S. Y. Sedelow/ U Kansas	A Center for Computational Research on Language	12,000	12
GS-28645	W. V. Quine/ Harvard U	Philosophy and History of Logic and Language	28,000	12

- 17 -

Grant No.	Investigator & Institution	Title	Amount	Duration (Months)
GS-28659	Z. S. Harris/ U Pennsylvania	Theory and Computation of Linguistic Transformations	$ 65,000	12
GS-28812X	J. M. Crawford/ U Georgia	Southeastern Indian Language Project	27,800	12
GS-28817	M. E. Krauss/ U Alaska	St. Lawrence Island Eskimo Phonology	25,600	12
GS-28818	R. Ferrell/ Washington St. U	A Dictionary of the Paiwan Language in Taiwan	5,500	12
GS-28908	A. E. Bell/ U Colorado	Diachronic Processes of Word Combination	4,800	12
GS-28968	E. Haugen/ Harvard U	History and Structure of the Scandinavian Languages	49,400	12
GS-29071	T. A. Sebeok/ Center for Applied Linguistics	Current Trends in the Historiography of Linguistics	42,600	24
GS-29192	H. C. Fleming/ Boston U	The Ethnography and Linguistics of the Dime Tribe	40,600	24
GS-29244	J. P. Wang/ Michigan State U	Doctoral Dissertation Research in Linguistics	2,150	12
GS-30107	I. Dyen/ Yale U	Doctoral Dissertation Research in Linguistics	2,950	12

FY 1972

Grant No.	Investigator & Institution	Title	Amount	Duration (Months)
GS-1605 Amend. #1	J. Morrison R. Andree J. Sweeney/ U Oklahoma	Collaborative Research in Development of Linguistic Field-Data Archive	127,100	24

- 18 -

Grant No.	Investigator & Institution	Title	Amount	Duration (Months)
GS-2012X2	C. E. Osgood/ U Illinois	Comparative Psycholinguistics	$ 54,200	12
GS-2059 Amend. #1	G. Jochnowitz/ Queens C	Synchronic and Diachronic Analyses of Judeo-Italian Dialects	1,530	18
GS-2386 Amend. #1	W. Wang J. Ohala/ U California (B)	Program of Research on the Processes of Phonological Change	250,500	24
GS-2561 Amend. #1	M. D. Kinkade/ U Kansas	Linguistics of the Pacific Northwest	54,200	24
GS-2939 Amend. #1	G. Lakoff/ U Michigan	Generative Semantics	49,100	24
GS-2941 Amend. #1	C. A. Ferguson J. H. Greenberg/ Carnegie-Mellon U	Archival Research on Language Universals	20,700	9
GS-3057 Amend. #1	J. Halm R. Howren/ U Iowa	Linguistic and Cultural Variation Among Athapaskan Indians	77,100	24
GS-3081 Amend. #1	W. P. Lehmann/ U Texas	Theoretical Investigation of Diachronic Syntax	37,300	12
GS-3180 Amend. #1	J. E. Grimes/ Cornell U	Cross Language Study of Discourse Structures	44,600	24
GS-28354 Amend. #1	F. S. Cooper A. M. Liberman/ Haskins Labs, Inc.	A Digital Playback for Research on Natural Speech	53,500	24
GS-28548 Amend. #1	G. W. Grace/ U Hawaii	New Caledonian Linguistics	20,900	24

- 19 -

Grant No.	Investigator & Institution	Title	Amount	Duration (Months)
GS-28659 Amend. #1	A. K. Joshi Z. S. Harris/ U Pennsylvania	An Algorithm for a Transformational Analysis of English Sentences	$ 24,900	12
GS-28812X1	J. M. Crawford/ U Georgia	Southeastern Indian Language Project	28,900	12
GS-30040	E. V. Clark/ Stanford U	The Acquisition of Semantic Distinctions in Children's Speech	55,100	24
GS-30047	C. E. Cairns/ Queens C	Theory of Phonological and Phonetic Universals	7,000	12
GS-30137	H. Pitkin/ Columbia U	Doctoral Dissertation Research in Linguistics	4,000	24
GS-30138	C. F. Voegelin/ Indiana U	Doctoral Dissertation Research in Linguistics	1,350	12
GS-30421 Amend. #1	C. Day/ U Rochester	Jacaltec Dictionary	23,800	19
GS-30546	J. J. Gumperz/ U California (B)	Communicative Competence of Bilinguals	77,900	24
GS-30962	C. A. Ferguson/ Stanford U	Comparative Research on the Acquisition of Phonology	163,500	24
GS-31225	A. K. Romney/ U California (B)	Doctoral Dissertation Research in Linguistics	2,900	12
GS-31281	E. Stankiewicz/ Yale U	The Accent Patterns of the Slavic Languages	8,300	12
GS-31295	J. E. Grimes/ Cornell U	Collaborative Research in Development of a Linguistic Field-Data Archive	28,600	24

- 20 -

Grant No.	Investigator & Institution	Title	Amount	Duration (Months)
GS-31309	J. Friedman/ U Michigan	Computer Aids to Linguistic Research	$ 77,700	24
GS-31349	W. C. Stokoe, Jr./ Gallaudet C	Semantics and Grammar in American Sign Language	73,700	24
GS-31403	H. Pitkin/ Columbia U	Doctoral Dissertation Research in Linguistics	5,200	12
GS-31687	D. I. Slobin/ U California (B)	Doctoral Dissertation Research in Linguistics	6,000	12
GS-31494	I. Lehiste/ Ohio State U	Linguistic Units and Boundaries	24,300	12
GS-31636	C. Garvey/ Johns Hopkins U	Discourse Analysis of Two-Person Problem-Solving Communication	33,800	18
GS-31912	T. S. Smith/ U California (SD)	Equipment for Research in Experimental Linguistics	57,200	12
GS-31968	J. H. Greenberg/ Stanford U	Genetic Classification of South and Central American Languages	37,900	24
GS-32144	S. Peters/ U Texas	Theoretical Investigation of Transformational Grammar	47,700	24
GS-32153	S. McLendon/ Hunter C (CUNY)	A Dictionary of Eastern Pomo	15,600	12
GS-32154	H. Pitkin/ Columbia U	A Dictionary of Yuki, A Language of Northern California	11,100	12
GS-32399	A. E. Roberts/ Center for Applied Linguistics	Conference on Research Trends in Computational Linguistics	17,000	6

- 21 -

Appendix E2: ACLS grantees mentioned in an *LSA Bulletin* between 1970 and 1989

NOTE: The names, affiliations, and proposals are listed below as they appear in the *Bulletin*. I omit travel grants.

Bulletin 43, April 1970, p. 30:
Received ACLS grants or fellowships for linguistics research: Erwin Esper, William O. Hendricks, Alfred Hudson, Kostas Kazazis, Anthony Salys.

Bulletin 57, June 1973, p. 25:
Three LSA members received fellowships for linguistic studies: Arthur Abramson, Sydney Lamb, Albert Schutz.

Bulletin 62, October 1974, p. 25:
The American Council of Learned Societies recently awarded 101 grants in aid for post-doctoral research in the humanities and related social sciences. Among the recipients were Ray Cordell Dougherty, Associate Professor of Linguistics, New York University: Pierce and Lovejoy on the History of Linguistic Methodology; Charles O. Frake, Professor of Anthropology, Stanford University: Language and Ethnic Identity; Andreas Koutsoudas, Professor of Linguistics, Indiana University: The Applications and Ordering of Grammatical Rules: Counter-feeding Order; La Raw Maran, Assistant Professor of Linguistics, Indiana University: A Linguistic Study of Jinghpaw-Kachin; Raoul S. Smith, Associate Professor of

Linguistics, Northwestern University: Late l8th and Early 19th Century Manuscripts Written in Phonetic Transcription by Jonathan Fisher; Edward F. Tuttle, Assistant Professor of Italian, University of California, Los Angeles: Consonantal Weakening in Italo-Romance.

Bulletin 65, June 1975, pp. 13–14:
ACLS FELLOWSHIPS Ninety-four post-doctoral fellowships were awarded by the American Council of Learned Societies to scholars for periods of six months to one year. The following list includes the title of the research and university affiliation of individuals who received fellowships in linguistics and related areas. Connie C. Eble, Asst Prof English, U North Carolina: Late Old English Inflectional System. John M. Fyler, Asst Prof English, Tufts U: Ovidian Structure in Chaucer's Poetry. Richard E. Grandy, Assoc Prof Philosophy, U North Carolina: Study in Syntactic and Semantic Theories in Linguistics. Robert A. Macdonald, Prof Spanish, U Richmond: Linguistic Analysis of the Especulo of Alfonso X of Castile. Wilhelm F. H. Nicolaisen, Prof English, SUNY, Binghamton: A Concise Dictionary of Scottish Place Names. James T. Siegel, Assoc Prof Anthropology, Cornell U: Narrative and Language in a Traditional Society (Atjeh). Leslie L. Threatte, Jr., Asst Prof Classics, U Cal, Berkeley: The Grammar of Attic Inscriptions. Elizabeth C. Traugott, Assoc Prof Linguistics, Stanford U: The Space of Linguistic Time.

Ardath M. Clark received an ACLS grant-in- aid for research in philology and diachronic linguistics with particular references to Middle English phonology, syntax, metrics, lexicology and dialectology. The title of the project is: 'Troilus and Criseyde: Editing a Critical Authoritative Text'.

Bulletin 66, October 1975, pp. 17–18:
ACLS FELLOWSHIPS, STUDY FELLOWSHIPS AND GRANTS-IN-AID During 1974-75, the American Council of Learned Societies, in national competitions, awarded 78 fellowships, 13 study fellowships and 133 grants-in-aid for post-doctoral research in the humanities and related social sciences. The following list includes the title of the research and university affiliation of individuals who received these awards in linguistics and related areas: Fellowships Elizabeth Traugott (Stanford Univ) The Space of Linguistic Time Craig B. Williamson (Swathmore Coll) Anthropological Approaches to Old English Poetry.

Study Fellowships Glendon E. Bryce (Princeton Theological Seminary) Study in Theory and Application of Structuralist Methodologies Richard E. Grandy (Univ North Carolina) Study in Syntactic and Semantic Theories in Linguistics.

Grants-in-aid Edith A. Folb (Univ Cal, Irvine) Language and the Black Woman Eugene Green (Boston Univ) Linguistic and Social Properties of Massachusetts Place-names. Karl H. Menges (Columbia Univ) The Grammar of the Tungus Languages.

Bulletin 69, June 1976, pp. 9–10:
ACLS GRANTS & FELLOWSHIPS The American Council of Learned Societies (ACLS) awarded a large number of grants under its various programs during fiscal year 1975. Of these, 13 were in support of study and research in linguistics and related fields. The recipients were: Apostolos N. Athanassakis, University of California, Santa Barbara: A philological commentary on Iliad I; Weldon South Coblin, Jr., University of Iowa: Chinese phonology of the Eastern Han period; Jarmila Emmerova, Charles University, Prague: Research at Emory University on contemporary American language and culture; Edith A. Folb, University of California, Irvine: Language and the black woman; Eugene Green, Boston University: Linguistic and social properties of Massachusetts place-names; Eleanor H. Jorden, Cornell: A sociolinguistic study in Japan of attitudes toward language and their

effect on inter-cultural communication; Young Key Kim-Renaud, University of Hawaii: Research on vowel harmony in the Korean language; Bogusław Lawendowski, University of Warsaw: Research at Indiana University on a linguistic analysis of emotive forms of communication in American English; Karl H. Menges, Columbia University: The grammar of Tungus languages; Harold F. Schiffman, University of Washington: Incipient bilingualism among Sri Lanka's Indian Moors; Dan I. Slobin, University of California, Berkeley, and Dogan Cuceloglu, Hacettepe University: Research in the US and Turkey on language reform, person perception, and values in Turkey; D. Rodney Watson, University of Manchester: Research at SUNY Buffalo on minority group study with special reference to language use in interpersonal relations; George M. Williams, Jr., SUNY Buffalo: East German theories of the relation between the social use of language and linguistic structure.

In addition, ACLS has awarded ninety-seven fellowships for periods of 6 months to one year. The fellows are associated with 64 colleges and universities in the United States and Canada. The following list includes the title of the research and university affiliation of individuals who received fellowships in linguistics and related areas: Roger S. Bagnali, Columbia University: Study of Demotic Egyptian language and documents; Robert A. Frei din, Purdue University: Constraints on transformational grammar; Carol Kates, Ithaca College: A phenomenological description of linguistic meaning; Anson Rainey, Tel-Aviv University: A grammar of the West Semitized el-Amarna Tablets.

Bulletin 70, October 1976, p. 15:
ACLS GRANTS AND FELLOWSHIPS The American Council of Learned Societies recently announced that during 1975-76 several grants and fellowships were awarded to individual scholars for research in linguistics and related areas. The list of recipients, grouped according to the ACLS grant and/or fellowship program making the award, includes the academic affiliation and research project of the awardee. Grants for Research on Chinese Civilization: Jerry Norman, University of Washington: A comparative historical study of the Min Dialects; Lien-sheng Yang, Harvard University: A study of colloquial and semi-colloquial Chinese in T'ang, Sung, and Yřian times. Research Fellowships for Recent Recipients of the PhD: Judith L. Aissen, Harvard University: The syntax of causative constructions; William J. Ashby, University of California, Santa Barbara: A sociolinguistic study of Parisian French; Christian J.W. Kloesel, Texas Tech University: Speculative grammar from Duns Scotus to Charles Peirce; Joan M. Maling, Brandeis University: Studies in diachronic and comparative syntax; Masayoshi Shibatani, University of Southern California: Interactions between syntax and logic. Grants-in-Aid: Stephen R. Anderson, University of California, Los Angeles: Syntax and morphology in the Nootka language; Morton W. Bloomfield, Harvard University: Oral poetry of the Xhosa and Zulu peoples of South Africa; Ronald E. Buckalew, Pennsylvania State University: An edition of AElfric's Grammar and Glossary; James M. Crawford, University of Georgia: Mobilian trade language; Richard C. Steiner, Yeshiva University: Glottalized ejectives in proto-Semi tic. Grants for Research in East European Studies: Antonin Dostál, Brown University: The beginning of Christianity among the Slavs: A textual investigation of the Euchologium Sinaiticum. Grants for Study of East European Languages: Albanian: Victor A. Friedman, University of North Carolina. Czech: Nancy B. Fowler, University of Michigan; Olga Peters, Yale University. Hungarian: Elizabeth M. La Cava, Indiana University. Macedonian: Alexander L. Albin, University of California, Los Angeles. Romanian: Thomas D. Cravens, University of Arizona; Ella Fry, University of Florida. Serbo-Croatian: Naomi Berkowitz, University of Washington. Slovenian: William R. Schmalstieg, Pennsylvania State University.

Bulletin 74, October 1977, p. 17:
ACLS GRANTS AND FELLOWSHIPS The American Council of Learned Societies (ACLS) recently announced the recipients of awards under the East European Study, Grants- in-Aid, Grants for Research on Chinese Civilization and Grants-in-Aid for Recent Recipients of the PhD programs. The following list includes the title of the research project and the university affiliation of the individuals who received grants in linguistics and related areas: Janet Byron (Cleveland SU) The Use of Two Standard Dialects among the Albanians of Yugoslavia; Andrew R. Durkin (Indiana U) The Life and Works of Sergej Aksakov; Margaret Egan (Wesleyan U & Yale U) The Old Provencal <u>vidas</u> in the Medieval Commentary Tradition; Irene R. Fairley (Northeastern U) Visual Stylistics; Natalie K. Moyle (U Virginia) Turkish Dime Novels, The Transition from Folklore to Literature; Peter Steiner (U Michigan) A Comparative Study of Russian Formalism and Prague Structuralism; Shou-hsin Teng (U Massachusetts) Syntactic Structures of Amoy; Charles D. Van Tiiyl (Bacone C) Tibetan Language Materials; Stephen Wallace (U Houston) Jakartan Patterns of <u>I and Thou</u>; Joseph M. Williams (U Chicago) Linguistic Evidence of Social Mobility in Early Modern English.

   In addition, the ACLS has awarded fellowships under the Recent Recipients of the PhD and Post-Doctoral Research Programs for research and study in the humanities and related social sciences. Those receiving fellowships in support of study and research in linguistics and related fields include: Ann Banfield (UC-Berkeley) Study of the Philosophy of Language; Elisabeth O. Selkirk (U Massachusetts) The Syllable in Phonological Representation; Robert M. Vago (Queens C-CUNY) The Description of Vowel Harmony.

Bulletin 97, October 1982, p. 17:
The American Council of Learned Societies has awarded Grants-In-Aid to 97 scholars including: Thomas T. Field, U MD, Baltimore and Arthur K. Spears, U CA, Santa Cruz. The American Council of Learned Societies announced that 75 post-doctoral fellowships had been awarded in a recent competition. Awardees included: Stephen Anderson, UCLA and Jane Grimshaw, Brandeis U.

Bulletin 101, October 1983, p. 13:
Donka F. Farkas of Pennsylvania S U was awarded a postdoctoral research grant in the 1983 ACLS East European Studies Grant Program.

Bulletin 105, October 1984, p. 16:
The American Council of Learned Societies has recently awarded 35 fellowships to recent recipients of the PhD for research in the humanities and social sciences including one grant to DANIEL E. EVERETT (S U Campinas, Brazil) to study 'Comparative Syntax and Government Binding Theory.' CLAUDIA ROSS (Purdue U) has been awarded a grant from the American Council of Learned Societies program in Chinese studies for a research project entitled "The Verb Phrase in Mandarin Chinese."

Bulletin 109, October 1985, p. 19:
The American Council of Learned Societies has awarded fellowships and grants to scholars under seven programs of support for research in the humanities and related social sciences. Linguists who have received these awards include: William H. Baxter, U MI: A handbook of old Chinese phonology; W. South Coblin, U IA: A study of the old Tibetan inscriptions; David A. Frick, U CA-Berkeley: Polish sacred philology in the Reformation and Counter-Reformation; Victor A. Friedman, U NC-Chapel Hill: A comparative grammar of Balkan verbal categories; Paul W. Kroll, U CO: Revelations in verse and songs of transcendence in medieval Taoism; Theodore Huters, U MN: The influence of Qing dynasty theories of

writing on the development of modern Chinese literature; Matthew W. Stolper, U Chicago: Xenophon's Belesys, the Kasr Archive, and Archaemenid Babylonia.

Bulletin 113, October 1986, p. 16:
American Council of Learned Societies and the Social Science Research Council: Susan Gal, Rutgers U, has been awarded a research grant to work on a comparative study of bilingualism in East Europe.

Bulletin 117, October 1987, p. 19:
American Council of Learned Societies: The following were among 94 scholars who received grants-in-aid for postdoctoral research: Guy Bailey (TX A&M): "The Roots of Black English; "and John Goldsmith (U Chicago):"A Generation of Linguists." The grants were funded by the John D. and Catherine T. MacArthur Foundation. Jaklin Kornfilt (Syracuse U) received a fellowship funded by the Carnegie Corporation and NEH to do research on Turkish syntax and syntactic theory.

Bulletin 121, October 1988, p. 19:
American Council of Learned Societies: The following received awards to pursue re- search: Janet Bing (Old Dominion U), sound system of Gborbo; Sara Kimbal, Hittite phonology; David W. Lightfoot (U MD-College Park), syntactic change; Hy V. Luong (Johns Hopkins U), language, political ideology, and history in modern Vietnam: 1867-1987; and Carol Scotton (U SC), lexical code borrowing and code switching in Kenya and Zimbabwe.

Bulletin 125, October 1989, p. 16:
American Council of Learned Societies: Frances Karttunen (U TX-Austin) was one of 87 recipients of grants-in-aid for post- doctoral research in the humanities and related social sciences. following people recently received fellowships for the academic year 1989-90: Dennis E. Baron (U IL-Urbana); Charles L. Briggs (Vassar C); Ellen I. Broselow (SUNY Stony Brook); Mary S. Erbaugh; Robert D. Hoberman (SUNY-Stony Brook); and Ronald K. Macaulay (Pitzer C). Linguists who received summer stipends include: Lawrence K. Carpenter (U N FL); Paul D Deane (U Cntrl FL); Daniel L. Everett (U Pittsburgh); Edward L. Greenstein (Jewish Theological Sem of America); Janine Scancarelli (U KY); and Margaret J. Speas (U WI-Madison). Division of Research Programs grants were awarded to: Lloyd A. Kasten (U WI-Madison); Charles N. Li (U CA-Santa Barbara); Albert L. Lloyd (U PA); Leonard D. Newmark (U CA-San Diego); David S. Rood (U CO-Boulder); and Ladislav Zgusta (U IL- Urbana). Other grants were awarded to Allan R. Taylor (U CO-Boulder) to support a conference on the Greenberg classification of the native languages of the Americas and related problems in prehistory research and to Gene Searchinger to produce four one-hour films on the nature of language and the discipline of linguistics.

Appendix E3: National Endowment for the Humanities Grants in Linguistics: 1970, 1980, and 1989

1970 (11 awards)

Demetrius J. Georgacas, University of North Dakota, 'Modern Greek-English Dictionary'
Richard A. Demers, University of Arizona, 'Generative Phonology and Sound Change'
Nathan Suskind, CUNY Research Foundation, 'Great Dictionary of the Yiddish Language'

James L. Funkhauser, St. Louis Community College at Forest Park, 'Translating Negro Dialect into Standard Dialect'

Fred W. Hanes, Indiana State University, Terre Haute, 'Cordell Gift of Rare Books'

Stanley M. Tsuzaki, University of Hawaii, Honolulu, 'Survey of Pidgin and Creole Languages: Bibliography'

R. L. Cowser, Jr, Wharton County Junior College, (title not available)

Michael J. Capek, MIT, 'A Comparative Syntax of Verbs in Shakespeare and Modern English'

Karen Brockman, Miami University, Oxford, 'American Indian Languages, Especially Mesquakie and Algonkian'

Marron C. Fort, Villanova University, (title not available)

Russell A. Fraser, University of Michigan, 'Early Modern English Dictionary'

1980 (30 awards)

Jeffrey Heath, University of Michigan, 'Linguistic Theory And The Writing of Grammars'

Thomas A. Sebeok, Indiana University, 'The Effects of Nonverbal Cuing In Face-to-Face Interaction'

Michael Shapiro, Brown University, 'Language as Semiotic'

Franklin C. Southworth, Society for South India Studies, 'Linguistic Archaeology of The South Asian Subcontinent'

Thomas A. Wasow, Stanford University, 'Thematic Relations and Exceptions in the Theory of Grammar'

Saralyn R. Daly, Unaffiliated Independent Scholar, 'Description of Middle English Dialects'

Marion L. Huffines, Bucknell University, 'Investigation of the English of the Pennsylvania Germans'

Dennis L. Jarrett, Northern New Mexico Community College, 'A Linguistic Analysis of the Reading of a Literary Text'

Tena L. Jeremiah, Unknown institution, 'An Ethnographic Study of the Communication of Urban Adolescent Black Women'

Muriel R. Schulz, Unknown institution, 'The Importance of Reading for Writers'

Raven I. McDavid, University of Chicago, 'American Dialects: Regional and Social'

Brian D. Joseph, Ohio State University, The Loss of the Infinitive in the Balkan Languages

Deborah F. Tannen, Georgetown University, 'A Comparison of Spoken and Written Narratives in English and Greek'

Edith A. Folb, San Francisco State University Foundation Inc., 'An Historical and Textual Analysis of Black Teenage Vocabulary Use'

Julia P. Stanley, Unknown institution, 'Identification of Syntactic Target Structures'

Arlene C. Malinowski, Unknown institution, 'Selected Linguistic Features of Contemporary Judeo-Spanish in Turkey'

Nancy C. Dorian, Unknown institution, 'Oral History of the East Sutherland (Scotland) Fisherfolk'

Marcia L. Hurlow, Unknown institution, 'Linguistics and the Remedial Writer'

Ann W. Lewin, National Children's Museum, 'Planning for Communications Exhibit'

Marianne Shapiro, Unknown institution, 'Translation of Three Old Provencal Grammars'

Zygmunt Frajzyngier, University of Colorado, 'Structure of the Simple Sentence in Proto-Chadic'

T. Givon, Southern Ute Indian Tribe, 'Ute Traditional Narrative and Word-order Change'

John V. Van Cleve, Gallaudet University, 'Planning and Assessment Study of Encyclopedia of the Deaf and Deafness'
Marianne Mithun, SUNY Research Foundation, 'Cayuga Indian Grammar'
Peter M. Boyd-Bowman, SUNY Research Foundation, 'The Lexico Hispanoamericano del siglo XIX: Linguistic Analysis of Spanish American Documents'
Herbert A. Strauss, Research Foundation for Jewish Immigration, 'International Biographical Dictionary of Central European Emigres, 1933-45'
Jay L. Robinson, University of Michigan, 'Middle English Dictionary'
Lee A. Pederson, Emory University, 'Linguistic Atlas of the Gulf States'
Michael Silverstein, University of Chicago, 'Lexicography in New World Context'
Garland D. Bills, University of New Mexico, 'Symposium on Athapaskan Comparative Linguistics and Language Planning'
1989 (23 awards)
Benjamin H. Orr, Secondary School, 'Native Americans Language and Literature'
Ronald K. Macaulay, Pitzer College, 'A Linguistic Study of Urban Scottish Dialects'
Ellen Broselow, SUNY Research Foundation, 'The Sound Structure of the Major Arabic Dialects'
Charles L. Briggs, Vassar College, 'Gender and Power in Native South American Discourse'
Mary S. Erbaugh, Unaffiliated Independent Scholar, 'Language and Social Change in Modern China'
Fernando Penalosa, Unaffiliated Independent Scholar, 'Comparative Study of Mayan Folk Tales'
Ronald P. Schaefer, Southern Illinois University, 'English Translation of Emai Narratives'
Aaron Bar-Adon, University of Texas, 'The Saga of the Revival of Hebrew: The Second Phase (1904-18)'
Lawrence K. Carpenter, University of North Florida, 'Creation Cycle Myths in Lowland Ecuadorian Quichua: Form, Content, and Change'
Margaret Speas, University of Wisconsin, 'Phrase Structure and Transformational Theory: A Study in Linguistics'
Daniel L. Everett, University of Pittsburgh, 'Sound Systems of the Amazonian Languages'
Anne C. Lobeck, University of Alabama, Birmingham, 'Concepts of Proper Government in Linguistic Theory'
Paul D. Deane, University of Central Florida, 'Cognitive Explanations for Syntactic Constraints'
Charles K. Williams, University of Montana, 'The Comparative Method in Historical Syntax: The Chaldic Language Family of West Africa as a Case Study'
Janine Scancarelli, University of Kentucky, 'Cherokee Texts: Recording, Transcribing, and Analyzing to Produce a Linguistics Data Base'
Charles N. Li, University of California, Santa Barbara, 'A Functional Reference Grammar of Hmong–Phase II'
Ladislav Zgusta, University of Illinois, 'The MANUAL OF LEXICOGRAPHY: A New Version'
Leonard Newmark University of California, San Diego, 'Albanian-English Dictionary'
David S. Rood, University of Colorado, Boulder, 'Comparative Siouan Dictionary'
Lee A. Pederson, Emory University, 'Completion of the Linguistic Atlas of the Gulf States'
J. Kathryn Josserand, Unaffiliated Independent Scholar, 'A Handbook of Classic Maya Inscriptions (Western Lowlands)'

Gerard Diffloth, Cornell University, 'A Khmer (Cambodian) Etymological Lexicon'
Allan R. Taylor, University of Colorado, 'Language and Prehistory in the Americas: A
Conference on the Greenberg Classification'

Appendix E4: Fulbright-Hays (and other Fulbright) grants mentioned in an *LSA Bulletin* between 1970 and 1989 [with presentation, punctuation, etc. as printed in the *Bulletin*]

Bulletin 70, October 1976, p. 15:
1976-77 FULBRIGHT-HAYS AWARDS The following members of the Society have been
selected American Fulbright- Hays Scholars for 1976-77 in linguistics and English as a foreign language: Michele Anciaux, University of Washington; Gerald Berent, University of
North Carolina; James T. Critz, University of Washington; Ray C. Dougherty, New York
University; James W. Gair, Cornell University; Beverly Hartford, Indiana University; Einar
I. Haugen, Harvard University; Vera M. Henzl, Stanford University; John V. Hinds, Uni-
versity of Hawaii; Henry M. Hoenigswald, University of Pennsylvania; Gloria Jameson,
California Polytechnic State University; D. Terrence Langendoen, City University of New
York; Carlos Maeztu, University of San Carlos, Guatemala; Howard P. McKaughan, Uni-
versity of Hawaii; Blair Rudes, State University of New York, Buffalo; Susan A. Savage,
Georgetown University; Margaret G. Sheil, State University of New York, Oneonta; Patri-
cia Stanley, Washington State University; James Tollefson, Stanford University; Anthony J.
Vitale, Cornell University.

Bulletin 74, October 1977 pp. 17–18:
1977-78 FULBRIGHT-HAYS AWARDS The Board of Foreign Scholarships has announced
482 awards to American scholars for work in 81 countries in a variety of disciplines for the
program year 1977-78, and affiliation arrangements on U.S. campuses have been made for
a comparable number of scholars from abroad. Those receiving awards in Linguistics and
TEFL include: Liga Abolins, Indiana U; Adrian Akmajian, U Arizona; Judith E. Boss, Ne-
braska U; Teddi G. Bynum, Pählavi U; Nancy J. Cochrane, U Texas; David N. Cohen, USC;
Gilbert D. Couts, American U; James T. Critz, U Washington; Kathleen L. Dahir, Georgia
Southern C; James E. Devlin, SUNY-Oneonta; Nadine Dutcher, World Bank; James L. Fi-
delholtz, U Maryland; Catherine A. Fisher, U Illinois-Chicago Circle; William R. Gaines,
Indiana U; George Galamba, San Francisco State C; Philip C. Hauptman, U Ottawa; Fred-
erick G. Hensey, U Texas; Margaret Hunter, Millard School District, Delta, Utah; Richard
S. Kayne, U Paris VIII; Edna L. Koenig, U Texas; Carl E. Lindeman, U Riyadh; Carlos A.
Maeztu, U San Carlos; Derry L. Malsch, U Oregon; James I. McClintock, Michigan SU;
Richard L. McLain, SUNY-Binghamton; Michael P. Menager, Albany Unified School Dis-
trict, California; Deborah J. Mickens, Seattle, WA; Carl R. Mills, U Cincinnati; James R.
Nattinger, Portland State U; Emily R. Nutku, U Maryland; Theodore Olsson, U Pacific;
Richard M. Payne, U Tunis; Elizabeth Riddle, U Illinois- Urbana; Mary K. Rippberger,
North Valley, CA; Blair Rudes, SUNY-Buffalo; James D. Rumford, Department of Educa-
tion, State of Hawaii; Philip A.S. Sedlak, USC; Margaret G. Shell, SUNY-Oneonta; Patricia
Stanley, Washington SU; Richard Wanderer, Flushing, NY; Sandra Wenner, USC; Richard
Wiest, American Library, Bucharest, Romania; Dick L. Williams, Lewis & Clark C; Leslie
N. Wilson, Florida SU; Arnold M. Zwicky, Ohio State U.

Bulletin 78, October 1978 pp. 16–17
1978-79 FULBRIGHT-HAYS AWARDS The Board of Foreign Scholarships and the U.S. International Communication Agency have announced 500 awards to American scholars for university teaching, advanced research or consultation in 90 countries for the program year 1978-79. Those receiving awards in linguistics and TEFL include: LIGA ABOLINS, Indiana U; DIANA E. BARTLEY, U Wisconsin, Milwaukee; M. LIONEL BENDER, Southern Illinois U; ELEANOR C. BOONE, Peace Corps Project, School for International Training, Brattleboro, VT; STEVEN W. BOSWELL, Washington DC; ARTHUR J. BRONSTEIN, CUNY Herbert H. Lehman C; E. WAYLES BROWNE, Cornell U; TEDDI G. BYNUM, Pahlavi U; CATHLEEN D. CAKE, U Pittsburgh; MARY B. CLEMENS, McKinley Community School for Adults; KATHLEEN L. DAHIR, Georgia Southern C; JOEL S. DIAMOND, McKinley High School Annex; NAN ELSASSER, U New Mexico; ROBERT H. ERICKSON, U Illinois; JAMES L. FIDELHOLTZ, U Maryland; CATHERINE A. FISHER, U Illinois; ALAN GARFINKEL, Purdue U; MARILYN C. GLENN, SUNY Buffalo; FRANK R. HUGUS, U Mass Amherst; MARGARET O. HUNTER, Millard School District, Delta, UT; ROBERT B. KAPLAN, U Southern California; ALAN S. KAYE, California SU Fullerton; CARL KIRSCHNER, Rutgers U; EDNA L. KOENIG, U Texas Austin; D. ROBERT LADD, JR., Cornell U; MARY MARTIN LANE, Indiana U; ANATOLE LYOVIN, U Hawaii; CARLOS A. MAEZTU, U de San Carlos, Guatemala; DIANA M. MEYERS, Kuwait U; DEBORAH J. MICKENS, Ohio U; GINO P. MUZZATI, Inst National d'Electricite et Electronique, Algeria; HARRY M. NEFF, Damavand C, Iran; GEOFFREY B. NUNBERG, CUNY Brooklyn C; EMILY R. NUTKU, U Maryland; ELIZABETH M. RIDDLE, U Illinois; ANDREW D. ROGERS, Austin, TX; JAMES D. RUMFORD, Hawaii State Dept of Education; JILL SAGARIN, Arizona SU; MARIANNE R. SANTI LLO, SUNY Buffalo; JUNE SCHLEUTER, Lafayette C; PHILIP A.S. SEDLAK, U Southern California; LOUISA R. STARK, U Wisconsin; ROSE MARIE TOSCANO, U Rochester; RICHARD M. WEIST, SUNY Fredonia; RICHARD C. WIEST; JOHN M. WOOD, National Bureau of Standards

Bulletin 94, March 1982, p. 8:
Fulbright awards for 1981-82 have been made to the following scholars in the field of linguistics: Irene T. Brosnahan (Ill State U), Matthew Y, Chen (U Calif-San Diego), David Chisholm (U Arizona), William H. Cook (W Carolina U), Michael Detlefsen (U Minn), Michael Flynn (Hampshire C), Eugene A. Fong (U Houston), Eugene Green (Boston U), James E. Iannucci (St. Joseph's U), John B. Jensen (Fla Inti U), Katherine J. Johnson (Oscar Rose Comm C), Linda N. Levine (Mt Kisco, NY), Anatole Lyovin (U Hawaii), Norman A. McQuown (U Chicago), Rodney F. Moag (U Mich), Kenneth E. Naylor (Ohio State U), Dinh-Hoa Nguyen (So Ill U), Dennis M. O'Toole (Educ Testing Serv), Sandra Pinkerton (U Minn), Joel Rotenberg (MIT), Ann Louise Sen (U Rochester), Royal J. Skousen (Brigham Young U), Riley B. Smith (Bloorasburg State C), Anthony J. Vitale (SUNY), Erhard F.K. Voeltz (Honolulu, Hawaii), James C. Woodward (Gallaudet C), and Louis V. Zuck (U Mich). Fulbright-Hayes awards for 1981-82 have been made to the following graduate students in the field of linguistics: Daisy Addy (U Wash), James Fife (Calif Sch Professional Psych-San Diego), Robert Hasenfratz (Okla State U), Theodore Johnson (U Wash), Laura Keller (at large, No Dakota), Timothy Parker (U Calif-Berkeley), and Randall Preshun (Stanford U).

Bulletin 100, June 1983, p. 7
Fulbright awards for 1982-83 have been made to the following scholars in the field of linguistics: James L. Armagost (Kansas S U), Faith Beane (U Chicago), John G. Bordie (U TX, Austin), Robert T. Botne (Northwestern U), Gregory N. Carlson (Wayne S U), William H. Cook (W Carolina U), Mary E. Faraci (Florida Atlantic U), James E. Iannucci (St. Joseph's

C), Karen M. Jensen (Georgetown U), Katherine J. Johnson (Oscar Rose Junior C), Avis T. Jones (Resource Consultants, Inc.), Thomas Magner (PA S U), Roy C. Major (WA S U), Kevin M. McCarthy (U FL), Michael I. Miller (VA Commonwealth U), Carl R Mills (U Cincinnati), Jan L. Perkowski (U VA), Dennis R. Preston (SUNY at Fredonia), John R. Ross (Massachusetts Institute of Technology), Carol M. Scotton (Michigan S U), Stanislav Segert (UCLA), and Richard G. Werner (CO S U).

Bulletin 103, March 1984, p. 12
FULBRIGHT-HAYS AWARDS. The following is a list of graduate students of linguistics who have received Fulbright-Hays Awards for 1983- 84, with their U.S. institutions and the countries in which they will study: Nina Ardery, IN U, Bloomington: W Germany; Victoria Bergvall, Harvard U: Kenya; Catherine Bodin, U NC, Chapel Hill: France; Kathie Carpenter, Stanford U: Thailand; George T. Childs, U CA, Berkeley: Liberia; Katherine Cooper, IN U, Bloomington: W Germany; Andrea Dunn, U IL, Urbana-Champaign: Tanzania; David Lund, St Olaf C: W Germany; Ruth Lunt, U Pittsburgh: W Germany; Catherine Neill, Georgetown U: Thailand; Joel Nevis, no institutional affiliation, OH: Finland; Michael L. O' Dell, IN U, Bloomington: Finland; Gregory Trauth, U IL, Urbana-Champaign: W Germany; John Whitman, Harvard U: S Korea. o
   FULBRIGHT AWARDS. The following scholars in the field of linguistics have been awarded Fulbrights for 1983-84: Farrell Ackerman, U CA, Berkeley: Hungary; Andrew S. Allen, U TN, Knoxville: Romania; Faith Whitney Beane, U Chicago: Bulgaria; Simon Be las co, U SC: France; Joel Bradshaw, U Hawaii: Romania; William H. Cook, Western Carolina U: Poland; James E. Copeland, Rice U: W Germany; Mary E. Faraci, FL Atlantic U: Romania; Morris Halle, MIT: France; Randall J. Hendrick, U NC, Chapel Hill: England & France; Robert K. Herbert, SUNY, Binghamton: Poland; Taco J. Homburg, U MI: Netherlands; Katherine J. Johnson, Oscar Rose Jr C: Poland; Avis T. Jones, McLean, VA: Gabon; Johanna E. Katchen, PA S U: Yugoslavia; Robert S. Kirsner, UCLA: Netherlands; Anthony S. Kroch, U PA: Brazil; Pamela Martin, Teachers C, Columbia U: Yugoslavia; Kevin M. McCarthy, U FL: Saudi Arabia; Michael I. Miller, VA Commonwealth U: Poland; Dennis M. Muchisky, U NM: Poland; Mark S. Patkowski, Hofstra U: Rwanda; Jan L. Perkowski, U VA: Romania; Ernest A. Scatton, SUNY, Albany: Bulgaria; Jacquelyn E. Schachter, USC: Israel; Richard W. Schmidt, U HI: Brazil; Robert M. Vago, Queens C, CUNY: Israel.

Bulletin 107, March 1985, p. 13
Fulbright-Hays Awards. The following is a list of graduate students of linguistics who have received Fulbright-Hays awards for 1984-85, with their US institutions and the countries in which they will study: David Bogdan (U FL), Poland; Julie Cionco (NM S U), West Germany; Robert M. DeSilva (U MI), Finland; Karen Gallob (U CO-Boulder), Mauritius; Amanda Hirsch (Oberlin C), Austria; Merelyn Mims (U Cincinnati), Cameroon; Lori A. Schwabenbauer (La Salle U), Fiji; Eva L. Szalay (VA Poly tech Inst & S U), West Germany; John Whitman (Harvard U), South Korea; Jessica S. Williams (U PA), Singapore.
   Fulbright Awards. The following linguists have been awarded Fulbrights for 1984-85: Farrell Ackerman (U CA-Berkeley), Hungary; Faith W. Beane (U Chicago), Bulgaria; Helen C. Beresovsky (U PA), Norway; George N. Clements (Cornell U), Kenya; William J. Greenberg (UCLA), Poland; Beverly S. Hartford (IN U), Nepal; Robert K. Herbert (SUNY-Binghamton), Poland; Thomas N. Huckin (U MI), Brazil; Grover M. Hudson (MI S U), Ethiopia; John P. Hutchison (Boston U), Niger; M. Karen Jogan (Albright C), Peru; Theodore C. Johnson (Walla Walla C), Poland; Avis T. Jones, Gabon; Frances E. Karttunen (U TX-Austin), Finland; Anthony S. Kroch (U PA), Brazil; Mehdi Marashi (U UT), USSR; Pamela Martin (Teachers C of Columbia U), Yugoslavia; John J. Ohala (U CA- Berkeley),

Denmark; Sandra Pinkerton (U MN), Brazil; James A. Reeds (U MO-Kansas City), Poland; Roger B. Speegle (TX Wesleyan C), West Bank; Erhard F. Voeltz, Burundi; Margaret K. Woodworth (U GA), Poland; Martha S. Wright (U MA-Amherst), Netherland

Bulletin 109, October 1985, p. 19
The following are this year's Fulbright scholars, with their home institutions and the countries where they are teaching or doing research: H.G. Bartelt, Yavapai C: West Germany; Katherine A. Demuth, U CA- Berkeley: Mozambique; Richard M. Frankel, Wayne SU: Sweden; William J. Frawley, U DE: Poland; Daryl K. Gibb, Automated Language Processing Systems (Provo, UT): Finland; Robert J. Jarvella, U Umea (Sweden): Poland; Theodore C. Johnson, U WA: Poland; John M. Lipski, U Houston: Philippines; Adam Makkai, U IL-Chicago: Singapore; Muriel R. Schulz, CSU-Fullerton: Austria; Susan C. Shepherd, Free U of Berlin: Poland; William A. Smalley, Bethel C (MN): Thailand; Erhard F.K. Voeltz, independent scholar, Minneapolis: Burundi.

Bulletin 111, March 1986, p. 14
Fulbright Awards: The following linguists have been awarded Fulbrights for 1985-86: H.G. Bartelt, Yavapai C: West Germany; Katherine A. Demuth, U CA-Berkeley: Mozambique; Richard M. Frankel, Wayne SU: Sweden; William J. Frawley, U DE: Poland; Daryl K. Gibb, Automated Language Processing Systems, Provo, UT: Finland; Robert J. Jarvella, U Umea (Sweden): Poland; Theodore C. Johnson, U WA: Poland; John M. Lipski, U Houston: Philippines; Adam Makkai, U IL-Chicago: Singapore; Muriel R. Schulz, CSU-Fullerton: Austria; Susan C. Shepherd, Free U-Berlin: Poland; William A. Smalley, Bethel C: Thailand; Erhard F.K, Voeltz, independent scholar, Minneapolis, MN: Burundi.

Fulbright-Hayes Awards: The following is a list of graduate students of linguistics who have received Fulbright-Hayes awards for 1985-86, with their US institutions and the countries in which they will study: Steven Diamond, U CA-Berkeley: Taiwan; Nicholas G. Faraclas, U CA- Berkeley: Papua New Guinea; Mark R. Hale, Harvard U: West Germany; Michael Inman, Colgate U: Sri Lanka; Marshall Lewis, no institutional affiliation, Indiana: Togo; Jay Nash, U IL-Urbana-Champaign: Zaire; Ann L. Sittig, U NE-Lincoln: Peru; John Te Velde, U WA: West Germany; Samuel Walters, U TX-Austin: Tunisia.

Bulletin 115, March 1987, p. 12

Fulbright Awards: The following linguists have been awarded Fulbrights for 1986-87: John Algeo, U GA: United Kingdom; A. L. Becker, U MI: Malaysia; Charles M. Carlton, U Rochester: Brazil; J R. Cowan, U IL-Urbana: West Germany; Dorothy Disterheft, U SC: Ireland; Hans H. Hock, U IL-Urbana: India; Judith N. Levi, Northwestern U: India; Joan M. Maling, Brandeis U: Ireland; David F. Marshall, U ND: China; William W. Megenney, U CA-Riverside: Venezuela; Rocky V. Miranda, U MN: India; Susan C. Shepherd, Free U Berlin: Poland..

Appendix E5: National Institute of Mental Health grants in 1973

From *LSA Bulletin* 64, March 1975, p. 43
The Division of Extramural Research Programs of the National Institute of Mental Health (NIMH) awarded 1,329 research grants in fiscal 1973. Eighteen of these were for research in linguistics and related areas, for a total of $97,663. The following list includes the investigator, institution, title, and amount for each such linguistic research grant:

Christopher W. Alexander, U California, Berkeley. Environmental Pattern Language, $56,768.

James E. Deese, U Virginia. Psycholinguistic Investigations, $20,283.

Charles A. Ferguson, Stanford U. Processes of Cultural, Lexical Change, $4,228.

James J. Fox, Harvard U. Formal Systems of Dyadic Languages, $28,863.

Catherine J. Garvey, Johns Hopkins U. Varieties and Functions of Early Social Speech, $24,257.

Henry G. Gleitman, U Pennsylvania. The Acquisition of Linguistic Structure, $10,359.

John J. Gumperz, U California, Berkeley. Language-Behavior Research Laboratory, $80,494.

Morris Halle, Massachusetts Institute of Technology.The Study of Language, $274,626.

Zellig S. Harris, U Pennsylvania. Objective and Subjective Components of Grammar, $75, 873.

James J. Jenkins, U Minnesota. Studies of Speech Perception and Recognition, $24,779.

Sally McLendon, Hunter C. Cultural Patterning of Information in Discourse, $33,913.

Claudia I. Mitchell-Kernan, Harvard U.The Acquisition of Sociolinguistic Skills by Children, $50,127.

Douglas L. Nelson, U South Florida.Words as Sets of Features Coding Phonological Cues, $20,961.

Charles E. Osgood, U Illinois. Studies on Comparative Psycholinguistics, $81,332.

David Premack, U California, Santa Barbara. Language and Infra-human Primates, $48,605.

Joel F. Sherzer, U Texas, Austin. Ethnographic Patterns of Speech, $5,295.

Edward E. Smith, Stanford U. Visual and Semantic Processing of Letters and Words, $29,876.

Robert L. Williams, Institute of Black Studies. Conference on Language Development in the Black Child, $11,996.

Afterword

I can't think of any other book that I've written where I learned so much in the process of its preparation. With any luck, a lot of my newfound knowledge has been communicated effectively to you the reader. Let me give one example of an important fact that I had been unaware of a few years ago. I had always known that the early generative grammarians had, despite a lot of conventional wisdom to the contrary, used every means at their disposal to broadcast the ins and outs of their theory. What I was unprepared to discover was how their antecedents in American structuralism went even farther in that regard and how much more that they had to do. Generative grammarians, for our part, launched a critique of an approach that at least accepted the idea that a structural core was at the heart of language and that it required an explicitly formulated model to explicate its properties. Sapir, Bloomfield, and their students could take nothing like that for granted. From the Institutes that they organized, to their war work, to their relentless campaigning for an autonomous field of linguistics, I found their championing of the particular worldview that they shared to be nothing less than inspirational.

Before undertaking this volume, my knowledge of European models of structural linguists was fairly minimal and even more minimal was how advocates of these models regarded and interacted with their American contemporaries. It wasn't easy for either side, as broader philosophical differences and a startlingly different terminology generally stood in the way of mutual understanding, much less mutual appreciation. I was heartened to see how these differences started to break down as time went on. And speaking of Europe, I can't begin to say how much I learned about the reception of generative grammar in each nation of the old continent. About forty colleagues in thirty-one countries were kind enough to supply me with information and personal reminiscences about the reaction to the new theory in their respective countries. If I had included all of the material in all of their email messages to me, the book would have been about a hundred pages longer.

Finally, the greatest pleasure that I had in preparing this book was in rummaging through the archives left by the prominent linguists of the 1940s through the 1970s. The letters that they left to their scholarly descendants range from instructional to self-damaging to hilarious. How many of them considered the possibility that they would appear in print in the somewhat distant future? And did any of them know that their generation would be the last to bequeath to posterity their most intimate thoughts about the field and their colleagues? Even those of us who save our emails today (does anybody print them out anymore?) have little confidence that they will still be on some server fifty years from now. In any event, the material in these archives provided me (and again, hopefully you the reader) with a picture of the field and its practitioners that one could never hope to extract from the published record.

References

Akmajian, Adrian, Richard A. Demers, Ann K. Farmer, and Robert M. Harnish (1997). *Linguistics: An Introduction to Language and Communication, 4th Edition*. Cambridge, MA: MIT Press.

Allen, W. Sidney (2002). 'Personal History', in Keith Brown and Vivien Law (eds.), *Linguistics in Britain: Personal Histories*. Oxford: Blackwell, 14–27.

Alpatov, Vladimir (2014). 'Soviet Linguistics and World Linguistics', in Vadim Kasevich, Yuri Kleiner, and Patrick Sériot (eds.), *History of Linguistics 2011*. Amsterdam: John Benjamins, 159–167.

Anderson, Stephen R. (1969). *West-Scandinavian Vowel Systems and the Ordering of Phonological Rules*, Unpublished PhD dissertation, MIT.

Anderson, Stephen R. (1985). *Phonology in the Twentieth Century*. Chicago: University of Chicago Press.

Anderson, Stephen R. (2021). *Phonology in the Twentieth Century: Second Edition*. Chicago: University of Chicago Press.

Andresen, Julie T. (1990). *Linguistics in America 1769–1924: A Critical History*. London: Routledge.

Andrews, Avery (1973). 'Agreement and Deletion', *Chicago Linguistic Society* 9: 22–33.

Andreyev, N. D. (1962). 'Models as a Tool in the Development of Linguistic Theory', *Word* 18: 186–197.

Anshen, Frank, and Peter A. Schreiber (1968). 'A Focus Transformation of Modern Standard Arabic', *Language* 44: 792–797.

Anttila, Raimo (1975). 'Revelation as Linguistic Revolution', in Adam Makkai and Valerie Makkai (eds.), *The First LACUS Forum*. Columbia, SC: Hornbeam Press, 171–176.

Apse, Linda (2007). 'Who Is Afraid of Generative Syntax?', *Humanities and Social Sciences. Latvia* 4 (53): 77–89.

Aronoff, Mark, and Carol Padden (2011). 'Sign Language Verb Agreement and the Ontology of Morphosyntactic Categories', *Theoretical Linguistics* 37: 143–152.

Aroui, Jean-Louis, and Anne Zribi-Hertz (2002). 'In Memoriam Nicolas Ruwet 1933–2001', *Le français modern* 70: 109–111.

Aurora, Simone (2017). 'From Structure to Machine: Deleuze and Guattari's Philosophy of Linguistics', *Deleuze Studies* 11: 405–428.

Bach, Emmon (1962). 'The Order of Elements in a Transformational Grammar of German', *Language* 38: 263–269.

Bach, Emmon (1964). *An Introduction to Transformational Grammars*. New York: Holt, Rinehart and Winston.

Bach, Emmon (1965a). 'Structural Linguistics and the Philosophy of Science', *Diogenes* 51: 111–28.

Bach, Emmon (1965b). 'Review of C. I. J. M. Stuart (ed.), *Report of the Fifteenth Annual (First International) Round Table Meeting on Linguistics and Language Sciences*', *Word* 21: 273–285.

Bach, Emmon (1967). '*Have* and *Be* in English Syntax', *Language* 43: 462–485.

Bach, Emmon (1995). 'The Politics of Universal Grammar', Paper presented at Linguistic Society of America Annual Meeting, New Orleans.

Bach, Emmon, and Robert Harms (eds.) (1968). *Universals in Linguistic Theory*. New York: Holt, Rinehart, and Winston.

Bally, Charles (1935). *Le langage et la vie* [Language and Life], second edition. Zurich: Max Niehans.

Bally, Charles (1965 [1932]). *Linguistique générale et linguistique française*. Bern: Francke.

Barsky, Robert F. (1997). *Noam Chomsky: A Life of Dissent*. Cambridge, MA: MIT Press.

Barsky, Robert F. (2007). *The Chomsky Effect: A Radical Works Beyond the Ivory Tower*. Cambridge, MA: MIT Press.

Basbøll, Hans (1985). 'Stød in Modern Danish', *Folia Linguistica* 19: 1–50.

Basset, Samuel E. (1938). *The Poetry of Homer*. Berkeley: University of California Press.

Bazell, C. E. (1949). 'Syntactic Relations and Linguistic Typology', *Cahiers Ferdinand de Saussure* 8: 5–20.

Bender, Harold H. (1921). *A Lithuanian Etymological Index*. Princeton: Princeton University Press.

Benítez-Burraco, Antonio, and Victor Longa (2010). 'Evo-Devo—Of Course, but Which One? Some Comments on Chomsky's Analogies between the Biolinguistic Approach and Evo-Devo', *Biolinguistics* 4: 308–323.

Berreby, David (1994). 'The Linguistics Wars', *The Sciences* 34: 44–50.

Bever, Thomas G. (1967). *Leonard Bloomfield and the Phonology of the Menomini Language*. Unpublished PhD dissertation, MIT.

Biberauer, Theresa (ed.) (2008). *The Limits of Syntactic Variation*. Amsterdam: John Benjamins.

Bierwisch, Manfred (1963). *Grammatik Des Deutschen Verbs* (= *Studia Grammatica, Vol. 2*). Berlin: Studia Grammatica.

Bierwisch, Manfred (1966). 'Strukturalismus: Geschichte, Probleme und Methoden', *Kursbuch* 5: 77–152.

Bierwisch, Manfred (1973). 'Generative Grammar and European Linguistics', in Ferenc Kiefer and Nicolas Ruwet (eds.), *Generative Grammar in Europe*. Dordrecht: Reidel, 69–111.

Binnick, Robert (1981). 'Review of Neil Smith and Deirdre Wilson, *Modern Linguistics*', *Language* 57: 182–183.

Bloch, Bernard (1941). 'Phonemic Overlapping', *American Speech*: 278–284, reprinted in 1957 in M. Joos (ed.), *Readings in Linguistics*. Washington: American Council of Learned Societies, 93–96.

Bloch, Bernard (1946a). 'Notes', *Language* 22: 267.

Bloch, Bernard (1946b). 'Studies in Colloquial Japanese: II. Syntax', *Language* 22: 200-48, reprinted in 1957 in M. Joos (ed.), *Readings in Linguistics*. Washington: American Council of Learned Societies, 154–185.

Bloch, Bernard (1947a). 'English Verb Inflection', *Language* 23: 399–418, reprinted in 1957 in M. Joos (ed.), *Readings in Linguistics*. Washington: American Council of Learned Societies, 243–254.

Bloch, Bernard (1947b). 'Notes', *Language* 23: 313.

Bloch, Bernard (1948). 'A Set of Postulates for Phonemic Analysis', *Language* 24: 3–46.

Bloch, Bernard (1950). 'Studies in Colloquial Japanese IV: Phonemics', *Language* 26: 86–125, reprinted in 1957 in M. Joos (ed.), *Readings in Linguistics*. Washington: American Council of Learned Societies, 329–348.

Bloch, Bernard, and Eleanor H. Jorden (1945). *Spoken Japanese, Vol. 1, Units 1–12*. New York: Holt.

Bloch, Bernard, and Eleanor H. Jorden (1946). *Spoken Japanese, Vol. 2, Units 13–30*. New York: Holt.

Bloch, Bernard, and George L.Trager (1942). *Outline of Linguistic Analysis*. Baltimore: Waverly Press.

Bloomfield, Leonard (1911). 'The Indo-European Palatals in Sanskrit', *American Journal of Philology* 32: 36–57.

Bloomfield, Leonard (1914). *Introduction to the Study of Language*. New York: Henry Holt & Co. (New ed., with an introduction by Joseph F. Kess, Amsterdam: John Benjamins, 1983).

Bloomfield, Leonard (1917). *Tagálog Texts with Grammatical Analysis*. Urbana: University of Illinois Press.

Bloomfield, Leonard (1922). 'Review of Edward Sapir, *Language*', *Classical Weekly* 15: 142–143.

Bloomfield, Leonard (1924a). 'Review of Ferdinand de Saussure, *Cours de linguistique générale*', *Modern Language Journal* 8: 317–319.

Bloomfield, Leonard (1924b). 'The Menomini Language', *Proceedings of the Twenty-First International Congress of Americanists* 1: 336–343.

Bloomfield, Leonard (1925a). 'On the Sound System of Central Algonquin', *Language* 1: 130–156.

Bloomfield, Leonard (1925b). 'Notes on the Fox Language', *International Journal of American Linguistics* 3: 219–232.

Bloomfield, Leonard (1925c). 'Why a Linguistic Society?', *Language* 1: 1–5.

Bloomfield, Leonard (1926). 'A Set of Postulates for the Science of Language', *Language* 2: 153-64, reprinted in 1957 in M.Joos (ed.), *Readings in Linguistics*. Washington: American Council of Learned Societies, 26–31.

Bloomfield, Leonard (1933). *Language*. New York: Holt.

Bloomfield, Leonard (1939a). 'Menomini Morphophonemics', *Travaux du Cercle Linguistique de Prague* 8: 105–115.

Bloomfield, Leonard (1939b). *Linguistic Aspects of Science*. Chicago: University of Chicago Press.

Bloomfield, Leonard (1946). 'Twenty-One Years of the Linguistic Society', *Language* 22: 1–3.

Bloomfield, Leonard (1972). 'The Original Preface to *Linguistic Structures of Native America*', *International Journal of American Linguistics* 38: 265–266.

Boas, Franz (1889). 'On Alternating Sounds', *American Anthropologist (old series)*2: 47–53.

Boas, Franz (1911). *Handbook of American Indian Languages*. Washington: Georgetown University Press.

Boas, Franz (1917). 'Introductory', *International Journal of American Linguistics*1: 1–8.

Boas, Franz (1938). *The Mind of Primitive Man*. New York: Macmillan.

Bobaljik, Jonathan (2015). 'Suppletion: Some Theoretical Implications', *Annual Review of Linguistics*1: 1–18.

Boeder, Winfried, Christoph Schroeder, Karl Heinz Wagner, and Wolfgang Wildgen (eds.) (1998). *Sprache in Raum und Zeit: In Memoriam Johannes Bechert*. Tübingen: Narr.

Boguslawski, Andrzej (1970). 'On Semantic Primitives and Meaningfulness', in A. J. Greimas (ed.), *Sign, Language, Culture*. The Hague: Mouton, 143–152.

Bolinger, Dwight (1941a). *What Is Freedom? For the Individual – for Society?*. Norman, Oklahoma: Cooperative Books.

Bolinger, Dwight (1941b). *The Symbolism of Music*. Yellow Springs, Ohio: Antioch Press.

Bolinger, Dwight (1948). *Intensive Spanish*. Philadelphia: Russell Press.

Bolinger, Dwight (1956). *Spanish Review Grammar*. New York: Holt.

Bolinger, Dwight (1957). *Interrogative Structures of American English*. University, Alabama: University of Alabama Press.

Bolinger, Dwight (1960a). *Modern Spanish*. New York: Harcourt, Brace & World.

Bolinger, Dwight (1960b). 'Linguistic Science and Linguistic Engineering', *Word* 16: 374–391.

Bolinger, Dwight (1961). *Generality, Gradience, and the All-or-None*, Janua Linguarum, 14. The Hague: Mouton.

Bolinger, Dwight (1965a). 'Pitch Accent and Sentence Rhythm', in Dwight Bolinger (ed.), *Forms of English: Accent, Morpheme, Order*. Cambridge, MA: Harvard University Press, 139–180.

Bolinger, Dwight (ed.) (1965b). *Forms of English: Accent, Morpheme, Order*. Cambridge, MA: Harvard University Press.

Bolinger, Dwight (1965c [1952]). 'Linear Modification', in Dwight Bolinger (ed.), *Forms of English: Accent, Morpheme, Order*. Cambridge, MA: Harvard University Press, 279–307.

Bolinger, Dwight (1968). *Aspects of Language*. New York: Harcourt, Brace & World.

Bolinger, Dwight (1971). *The Phrasal Verb in English*. Cambridge, MA: Harvard University Press.

Bolinger, Dwight (1977). *Meaning and Form*, English Language Series, 11. London: Longman.

Bolinger, Dwight (1980). *Language: The Loaded Weapon*. New York: Routledge.

Bolinger, Dwight (1986). *Intonation and Its Parts: Melody in Spoken English*. Stanford, CA: Stanford University Press.

Bolinger, Dwight (1989). *Intonation and Its Uses: Melody in Grammar and Discourse*. Stanford, CA: Stanford University Press.

Bolinger, Dwight (1991). 'First Person, Not Singular', in E. F. K. Koerner (ed.), *First Person Singular II*. Amsterdam: John Benjamins, 19–45.

Bolling, George M. (1929). 'Linguistics and Philology', *Language* 5: 27–32.

Bolling, George M. (1944). *The Athetized Lines of the Iliad*. Baltimore: Linguistic Society of America.

Bolling, George M. (1949). 'Οφρα in the Homeric Poems', *Language* 25: 379–387.

Borsley, Robert D. (1991). *Syntactic Theory: A Unified Approach*. London: Edward Arnold.

Botha, Rudolf (1992). *Challenging Chomsky: The Generative Garden Game*. Oxford: Blackwell.

Brax, Ralph S. (1981). *The First Student Movement: Student Activism in the United States During the 1930s*. Port Washington, NY: Kennikat.

Bresnan, Joan W. (1978). 'A Realistic Transformational Grammar', in Morris Halle, Joan Bresnan, and George Miller (eds.), *Linguistic Theory and Psychological Reality*. Cambridge, MA: MIT Press, 1–59.

Bright, William O. (1980). 'American Linguistics: A Western View', in Boyd Davis and Raymond O'Cain (eds.), *First Person Singular: Papers from the Conference on an Oral Archive for the History of American Linguistics*. Amsterdam: John Benjamins, 123–130.

Bromberger, Sylvain, and Morris Halle (1989). 'Why Phonology Is Different', *Linguistic Inquiry* 20: 51–70.

Bruner, Jerome (1983). *In Search of Mind*. New York: Harper and Row.

Buck, Carl D. (1927). 'A New Darius Inscription', *Language* 3: 1–5.

Bugarski, Ranko (1969a). 'Pojmovno-Terminološki Osvrt na Generativnu Gramatiku [A Conceptual and Terminological Look at Generative Grammmar]', *Delo* 7: 869–876.

Bugarski, Ranko (1969b). 'Generativni Model Jezika [the Generative Model of Language]', *Književne novine* August 5, 1969.

Bugarski, Ranko (1972). *Noam Čomski, Gramatika i Um [Grammar and Mind]*. Beograd: Nolit. Second, enlarged edition 1979.

Bybee, Joan L. (2009). 'Language Universals and Usage-Based Theory', in Morten H. Christiansen, Christopher Collins, and Shimon Edelman (eds.), *Language Universals*. Oxford: Oxford University Press, 17–39.

Cairns, Charles E. (1969). 'Markedness, Neutralization, and Universal Redundancy Rules', *Language* 45: 863–885.

Cantineau, Jean (1952). 'Les oppositions significatives', *Cahiers Ferdinand de Saussure* 10: 11–40.

Carlson, Gregory, Brian Joseph, and Sarah G. Thomason (2012). 'Introduction: The Best of *Language*'. https://www.linguisticsociety.org/resource/introduction-best-language, last accessed April 9, 2021.

Carnap, Rudolf (1928). *Der Logische Aufbau Der Welt*. Berlin-Schlachtensee: Weltkreis-Verlag.

Carnap, Rudolf (1937). *The Logical Syntax of Language*. New York: Harcourt, Brace.

Carroll, John B. (1953). *The Study of Language*. Cambridge, MA: Harvard University Press.

Chafe, Wallace L. (1965). 'Review of E. Bach, *An Introduction to Transformational Grammars*', *American Anthropologist* 67: 150–151.

Chafe, Wallace L. (1970). *Meaning and the Structure of Language*. Chicago: University of Chicago Press.

Chao, Yuen-Ren (1934). 'The Nonuniqueness of Phonemic Solutions of Phonetic Systems', *Bulletin of the Institute of History and Philology, Academia Sinica* 4, part 4: 363–397, reprinted in 1957 in M. Joos (ed.), *Readings in Linguistics*. Washington: American Council of Learned Societies, 38–54.

Chevalier, Jean-Claude, and Pierre Encrevé (2006). *Combats pour la linguistique, de Martinet à Kristeva: Essai de dramaturgie épistémologique*. Paris: ENS Éditions.

Chomsky, Noam (1949). *Morphophonemics of Modern Hebrew*, Unpublished BA thesis, University of Pennsylvania.

Chomsky, Noam (1951). *Morphophonemics of Modern Hebrew*, MA thesis, University of Pennsylvania.

Chomsky, Noam (1953). 'Systems of Syntactic Analysis', *Journal of Symbolic Logic* 18: 242–256.

Chomsky, Noam (1955a). 'Logical Syntax and Semantics: Their Linguistic Relevance', *Language* 31: 36–45.

Chomsky, Noam (1955b). *The Logical Structure of Linguistic Theory*. Cambridge, MA: Unpublished ms, a revised version of which appeared in 1975, published by University of Chicago Press.

Chomsky, Noam (1957a). *Syntactic Structures*. The Hague: Mouton.

Chomsky, Noam (1957b). 'Review of C. Hockett, *Manual of Phonology*', *IJAL* 23: 223–234.

Chomsky, Noam (1957c). 'Review of J. Jakobson and M. Halle, *Fundamentals of Language*', *International Journal of American Linguistics* 23: 234–242.

Chomsky, Noam (1958). 'Linguistics, Logic, Psychology, and Computers', in John W. Carr III (ed.), *Computer Programming and Artificial Intelligence: An Intensive Course*. Ann Arbor, Mich.: University of Michigan College of Engineering, 429–454.

Chomsky, Noam (1959a). 'On Certain Formal Properties of Grammars', *Information and Control* 2: 137–167, reprinted in 1965 in R.Luce, R. Bush, and E. Galanter (eds.) *Readings in Mathematical* Psychology, *vol. 2.* New York: Wiley and Sons, 122–155.

Chomsky, Noam (1959b). 'Review of B. F. Skinner, *Verbal Behavior*', *Language* 35: 26–57.

Chomsky, Noam (1961a). 'On the Notion "Rule of Grammar"', in Roman Jakobson (ed.), *Proceedings of Symposia in Applied* Mathematics *12: Structure of Language and Its Mathematical Aspects.* Providence, RI: American Mathematical Society, 6–24, reprinted in 1964 in J. Fodor and J. Katz (eds.), *The Structure of Language: Readings in the Philosophy of Language.* New York: Prentice-Hall, 119–136.

Chomsky, Noam (1961b). 'Some Methodological Remarks on Generative Grammar', *Word* 17: 219–239.

Chomsky, Noam (1962a). 'Explanatory Models in Linguistics', in E. Nagel, P. Suppes, and A. Tarski (eds.), *Logic, Methodology, and Philosophy of Science.* Stanford, CA: Stanford University Press, 528–550.

Chomsky, Noam (1962b). 'A Transformational Approach to Syntax', in Archibald Hill (ed.), *Proceedings of the Third Texas Conference on Problems of Linguistic Analysis in English.* Austin: University of Texas Press, 124–158, reprinted in 1964 in J. Fodor and J. Katz (eds.), *The Structure of Language: Readings in the Philosophy of Language.* Englewood Cliffs, NJ: Prentice-Hall, 211–243.

Chomsky, Noam (1963). 'Formal Properties of Grammars', in R. Duncan Luce, Robert R. Bush, and Eugene Galanter (eds.), *Readings in Mathematical Psychology, Volume II.* New York: John Wiley & Sons, 323–418.

Chomsky, Noam (1964a). *Current Issues in Linguistic Theory.* The Hague: Mouton.

Chomsky, Noam (1964b). 'Introduction', *English Syntax, by Paul Roberts.* New York: Harcourt, Brace and World, ix–xv.

Chomsky, Noam (1964c). 'The Logical Basis of Linguistic Theory', in Horace G. Lunt (ed.), *Proceedings of the Ninth International Congress of Linguists.* The Hague: Mouton, 914–977.

Chomsky, Noam (1965). *Aspects of the Theory of Syntax.* Cambridge, MA: MIT Press.

Chomsky, Noam (1967a). 'Letter', *New York Review of Books* March 23, 1967.

Chomsky, Noam (1967b). 'Letter', *New York Review of Books* April 20, 1967.

Chomsky, Noam (1967c). 'Some General Properties of Phonological Rules', *Language* 43: 102–128.

Chomsky, Noam (1970). 'Remarks on Nominalization', in Roderick Jacobs and Peter Rosenbaum (eds.), *Readings in English Transformational Grammar.* Waltham, MA: Ginn, 184–221, reprinted in 1972 in N. Chomsky, *Studies on Semantics in Generative Grammar.* The Hague: Mouton, 11–61.

Chomsky, Noam (1971). 'Deep Structure, Surface Structure, and Semantic Interpretation', in Danny Steinberg and Leon Jakobovits (eds.), *Semantics: An Interdisciplinary Reader in Philosophy, Linguistics, and Psychology.* Cambridge: Cambridge University Press, 183–216, reprinted in 1972 in N. Chomsky (ed.), *Studies on Semantics in Generative Grammar.* The Hague: Mouton, 62–119.

Chomsky, Noam (ed.) (1972). *Studies on Semantics in Generative Grammar.* The Hague: Mouton.

Chomsky, Noam (1973). 'Conditions on Transformations', in Steven Anderson and Paul Kiparsky (eds.), *A Festschrift for Morris Halle.* New York: Holt Rinehart & Winston, 232–286.

Chomsky, Noam (1975a). *The Logical Structure of Linguistic Theory [Revised Version of 1955 Manuscript with a New Introduction].* Chicago: University of Chicago Press.

Chomsky, Noam (1975b). 'Introduction', *The Logical Structure of Linguistic Theory*. Chicago: University of Chicago Press, 1–53.

Chomsky, Noam (1979a). *Language and Responsibility: Based on Conversations with Mitsou Ronat*. New York: Pantheon.

Chomsky, Noam (1979b [1951]). *Morphophonemics of Modern Hebrew*. New York: Garland.

Chomsky, Noam (1981). *Lectures on Government and Binding*. Dordrecht: Foris.

Chomsky, Noam (1982). *The Generative Enterprise: A Discussion with Riny Huybregts and Henk Van Riemsdijk*. Dordrecht: Foris.

Chomsky, Noam (1986). *Knowledge of Language: Its Nature, Origin, and Use*. New York: Praeger.

Chomsky, Noam (1994). 'On Linguistics and Politics [Interview with Günther Grewendorf]', *Protosociology* 6: 293–303.

Chomsky, Noam (2001). 'Derivation by Phase', in Michael Kenstowicz (ed.), *Ken Hale: A Life in Language*. Cambridge, MA: MIT Press, 1–52.

Chomsky, Noam (2007a). 'Of Minds and Language', *Biolinguistics* 1: 9–27.

Chomsky, Noam (2007b). 'Biolinguistic Explorations', *International Journal of Philosophical Studies* 15: 1–21.

Chomsky, Noam (2008). 'On Phases', in Robert Freidin, Carlos P. Otero, and Maria-Luisa Zubizarreta (eds.), *Foundational Issues in Linguistic Theory: Essays in Honor of Jean-Roger Vergnaud*. Cambridge, MA: MIT Press, 133–166.

Chomsky, Noam (2011a). 'Lecture 4', Paper presented at Fifty Years of Linguistics at MIT, Cambridge, MA.

Chomsky, Noam (2011b [1971]). *Human Nature: Justice Versus Power: The Chomsky-Foucault Debate*. London: Souvenir Press.

Chomsky, Noam (2014). 'Letter', *Language* 90: 561.

Chomsky, Noam (2017). 'Letter', *London Review of Books* 39: May 4, 2017.

Chomsky, Noam, Morris Halle, and Fred Lukoff (1956). 'On Accent and Juncture in English', in Morris Halle, Horace G. Lunt, and H. MacLean (eds.), *For Roman Jakobson: Essays on the Occasion of His Sixtieth Birthday*. The Hague: Mouton, 65–80.

Chomsky, Noam, and George Miller (1958). 'Finite State Languages', *Information and Control* 1: 91–112, reprinted 1965 in R. Luce, R. Bush, and E. Galanter (eds.), *Readings in Mathematical Psychology 2*. New York: Wiley and Sons, 156–171.

Chomsky, Noam, and George Miller (1963). 'Introduction to the Formal Analysis of Natural Languages', in Philip Luce, R. Bush, and E. Galanter (eds.), *Handbook of Mathematical Psychology, Volume 2*. New York: Wiley, 269–322.

Chomsky, Noam, and M. P. Schutzenberger (1963). 'The Algebraic Theory of Context-Free Languages', in P. Braffort and D. Hirshberg (eds.), *Computer Programming and Formal Systems: Studies in Logic*. Amsterdam: North-Holland, 118–161.

Chomsky, Noam, and Morris Halle (1960). 'The Morphophonemics of English', *MIT Quarterly Progress Report* 58: 275–281.

Chomsky, Noam, and Morris Halle (1965). 'Some Controversial Questions in Phonological Theory', *Journal of Linguistics* 1: 97–138.

Chomsky, Noam, and Morris Halle (1968). *The Sound Pattern of English*. New York: Harper and Row.

Cinque, Guilliermo, and Luigi Rizzi (2010). 'The Cartography of Syntactic Structures', in Bernd Heine and Heiko Narrog (eds.), *The Oxford Handbook of Linguistic Analysis*. Oxford: Oxford University Press, 51–65.

Closs, Elizabeth (1965). 'Diachronic Syntax and Generative Grammar', *Language* 41: 402–415.

Cohen, I. B. (1985). *Revolution in Science*, Harvard University Press: Cambridge, MA.

Cole, Peter, and Gabi Hermon (2015). 'Grammar of Binding in the Languages of the World: Innate or Learned?', *Cognition* 141: 138–160.

Collinder, Björn (1970). *Noam Chomsky und die generative Grammatik: Eine kritische Betrachtung*, Acta Universitatis Upsaliensis Ns .2:1. Uppsala: Almqvist & Wiksell.

Collinge, N. E. (2002). 'Personal History', in Keith Brown and Vivien Law (eds.), *Linguistics in Britain: Personal Histories*. Oxford: Blackwell, 67–77.

Collitz, Hermann (1925). 'The Scope and Aims of Linguistic Science [Abstract]', *Language* 1: 14–16.

Collitz, Hermann (1926). 'A Century of Grimm's Law', *Language* 2: 174–183.

Comrie, Bernard (2001). 'Theories of Universal Grammar in the Late 20th Century', in Sylvain Auroux, E. F. K. Koerner, Hans-Josef Niederehe, and Kees Versteegh (eds.), *History of the Language Sciences: An International Handbook on the Evolution of the Study of Language from the Beginnings to the Present, Vol. 2*. Berlin: De Gruyter, 1461–1467.

Contreras, Heles (1969). 'Simplicity, Descriptive Adequacy, and Binary Features', *Language* 45: 1–8.

Cook, Vivian J. (2011). 'Linguistic Relativity and Language Teaching', in Vivian J. Cook and Bene Bassetti (eds.), *Language and Bilingual Cognition*. Abingdon: Routledge.

Cornyn, William S. (1948). 'On the Classification of Russian Verbs', *Language* 24: 64–75.

Cowan, J Milton (1948). 'An Experimental Study of Pause in English Grammar', *American Speech* 23: 89–99.

Cowan, J Milton (1975). 'Peace and War', *LSA Bulletin* 64: 28–34.

Cowan, J Milton (1987). 'The Whimsical Bloomfield', *Historiographia Linguistica* 14: 23–37, reprinted in 1987 in Robert A. Hall, Jr. (ed.), *Leonard Bloomfield: Essays on his Life and Work*. Amsterdam & Philadelphia: John Benjamins, 23–37.

Cowan, J Milton (1991). 'American Linguistics at Peace and War', in E. F. K. Koerner (ed.), *First Person Singular II*. Amsterdam: John Benjamins, 67–82. [Revision of J. M. Cowan, 'Peace and War'. 1975. *LSA Bulletin* 64, 1975, 28–34.]

Cremona, Joseph (2002). 'Personal History', in Keith Brown and Vivien Law (eds.), *Linguistics in Britain: Personal Histories*. Oxford: Blackwell, 78–90.

Cressey, William W. (1968). 'Relative Adverbs in Spanish: A Transformational Analysis', *Language* 44: 487–500.

Croft, William (2000). 'Parts of Speech as Language Universals and as Language-Particular Categories', in Petra M. Vogel and Bernard Comrie (eds.), *Approaches to the Typology of Word Classes*. Berlin: Mouton de Gruyter, 65–102.

Croft, William (2003). *Typology and Universals: Second Edition*. Cambridge: Cambridge University Press.

Croft, William (2017). 'Typology and Universals', in Mark Aronoff and Janie Rees-Miller (eds.), *The Blackwell Handbook of Linguistics, 2nd Edition*. Oxford: Basil Blackwell, 39–55.

Dahl, Östen (1969). *Topic and Comment: A Study in Russian and General Transformational Grammar*. Göteborg: Elandres Boktryckeri.

Dahl, Östen (1970). 'Some Notes on Indefinites', *Language* 46: 33–41.

Dahl, Östen (1975). 'On Generics', in Edward L. Keenan (ed.), *Formal Semantics of Natural Language*. London: Cambridge University Press, 99–111.

Daneš, František (1957). Intonace a věta ve spisovuě cestiné [Sentence Intonation on Present-Day Standard Czech]. Prague: Ceskoslovenské akademie ved.

Daneš, František (1960). 'Sentence Intonation from a Functional Point of View', *Word* 16: 34–54.

Daneš, František (1964). 'A Three-Level Approach to Syntax', *Travaux linguistiques de Prague*1: 225–240.

Daniels, Peter T. (2010). 'Chomsky 1951a and Chomsky 1951b', in Douglas A. Kibbee (ed.), *Chomskyan (R)evolutions*. Amsterdam: John Benjamins.

Darnell, Regna D. (1990). *Edward Sapir: Linguiust, Anthropologist, Humanist*, University of California Press: Berkeley.

Davidsen-Nielsen, Niels (1968). 'Transformationsgrammatik', *Meddelelser fra Gymnasieskolernes Engelslkaerforening*.

Dawson, Hope C., and Brian D. Joseph (2014). 'On the History of LSA Publications: Stability and Change'. https://www.linguisticsociety.org/sites/default/files/LSA-90%20Publications.pdf., last accessed April 10, 2021.

De Geest, Wim (1967). 'De huidige Stand van de Transformationeel-Generatieve Taalbeschrijving van het Nederlands', in F. G. Droste and Wim de Geest (eds.), *Linguistiek*. Hasselt: Limburgse Akademische Bibliotheek, 35–81.

De George, Richard, and Fernande De George (eds.) (1972). *The Structuralists: From Marx to Lévi-Strauss*. Garden City, NY: Doubleday.

Dell, François (1973). *Les règles et les sons: Introduction à la phonologie générative*. Paris: Hermann.

Demonte, Violeta, Paloma García-Billido, and Joan Mascaró (1982). 'Generative Grammar in Spain', *GLOW Newsletter* 9: 11–14.

Dik, Simon (1968). *Coordination: Its Implications for the Theory of General Linguistics*. Amsterdam: North-Holland.

Diller, Karl (1971). *Generative Grammar, Structural Linguistics, and Language Teaching*. Rowley, MA: Newbury House.

Diller, Karl (1978). *The Language Teaching Controversy*. Rowley, MA: Newbury House.

Dingwall, William O. (1965). *Transformational Generative Grammar: A Bibliography*. Washington: Center for Applied Linguistics.

Dixon, R. M. W. (1969). 'Relative Clauses and Possessive Phrases in Two Australian Languages', *Language* 45: 35–44.

Dixon, R. M. W. (2007). 'Roman Jakobson and the Two-Dollar Bills', *Historiographia Linguistica* 34: 435–440.

Doherty, Paul C., and Arthur Schwartz (1967). 'The Syntax of the Compared Adjective in English', *Language* 43: 903–936.

Dosse, François (1997 [1992]). *History of Structuralism. The Sign Sets, 1967–Present*. Minneapolis: University of Minnesota Press.

É Kiss, Katalin (1981). 'Structural Relations in Hungarian, a "Free" Word Order Language', *Linguistic Inquiry* 12: 185–213.

É Kiss, Katalin (2020). 'Remembering Ferenc Kiefer', *Acta Linguistica Academica* 67: 395–396.

Emonds, Joseph E. (1976). *A Transformational Approach to English Syntax*. New York: Academic Press.

Encrevé, Pierre (2000). 'The Old and the New: Some Remarks on Phonology and Its History', *Folia Linguistica* 34: 56–84.

Eramian, Gregory M. (1988). 'Edward Sapir and the Prague School', *Historiographia Linguistica* 15: 377–399.

Everaert, Martin, and Eric Reuland (2011). 'Generative Grammar in Europe: Some Historical Impressions', in Bernd Kortmann and Johan van der Auwera (eds.), *The Languages and Linguistics of Europe: A Comprehensive Guide*. Berlin: de Gruyter Mouton, 867–886.

Evers, Arnold (1975). *The Transformational Cycle in Dutch and German*, Unpublished PhD dissertation, University of Utrecht.

Faculté des Lettres de l'Université de Genève (ed.), (1939). *Mélanges de linguistique offerts à Charles Bally*. Geneva: Georg et Cie.

Falk, Julia S. (1995). 'Words without Grammar: Linguists and the International Auxiliary Language Movement in the United States', *Language and Communication* 15: 241–259.

Falk, Julia S. (1998). 'The American Shift from Historical to Non-Historical Linguistics: E. H. Sturtevant and the First Linguistic Institutes', *Language and Communication* 18: 171–180.

Falk, Julia S. (1999). *Women, Language, and Linguistics: Three American Stories from the First Half of the Twentieth Century*. London: Routledge.

Falk, Julia S. (2003). 'Turn to the History of Linguistics: Noam Chomsky and Charles Hockett in the 1960s', *Historiographia Linguistica* 30: 129–185.

Falk, Julia S. (2004). 'Saussure and American Linguistics', in Carol Sanders (ed.), *The Cambridge Companion to Saussure*. Cambridge: Cambridge University Press, 107–123.

Falk, Julia S. (2014). 'The LSA Linguistic Institutes', Paper presented at Annual Meeting of the Linguistic Society of America, Minneapolis.

Falk, Julia S. (2017). 'From William Dwight Whitney to Leonard Bloomfield: Hanns Oertel's Lectures'. Unpublished ms, Michigan State University.

Falk, Julia S., and John E. Joseph (1994). 'The Saleski Family and the Founding of the LSA Linguistic Institutes', *Historiographia Linguistica* 21: 137–156.

Fasold, Ralph (1969). 'Tense and the Form *Be* in Black English', *Language* 45: 763–776.

Ferguson, Charles A. (1978). 'Historical Background of Universals Research', in J. H. Greenberg (ed.), *Universals of Human Language. Vol. 1: Method and Theory*. Stanford, CA: Stanford University Press, 7–32.

Field, H. F. (1927). 'Review of E. Lerch, *Historische Französische* Syntax', *Modern Philology* 24: 366–72.

Fillmore, Charles J. (1963). 'The Position of Embedding Transformations in a Grammar', *Word* 19: 208–31.

Fillmore, Charles J. (1968). 'The Case for Case', in Emmon Bach and Robert Harms (eds.), *Universals in Linguistic Theory*. New York: Holt, Rinehart and Winston, 1–90.

Firbas, Jan (1964). 'On Defining the Theme in Functional Sentence Analysis', *Travaux Linguistique de Prague* 1: 267–280.

Firbas, Jan (1965). 'A Note on Transition Proper in Functional Sentence Perspective', *Philologia Pragensia* 8: 170–176.

Firbas, Jan (1966). 'Non-Thematic Subjects in Contemporary English', *Travaux Linguistique de Prague* 2: 229–236.

Firth, J. R. (ed.) (1957). *Papers in Linguistics 1934–1951*. Oxford: Oxford University Press.

Fischer-Jørgensen, Eli (1949). 'Kenneth L. Pike's Analysis of American English Intonation', *Lingua* 2: 3–13.

Flom, George T. (1923). *The Language of the Konungs Skuggsja*. Urbana, IL: University of Illimois Press.

Foley, James (1965). 'Prothesis in the Latin Verb *Sum*', *Language* 41: 59–64.

Foley, James (1967). 'Spanish Plural Formation', *Language* 43: 486–493.

Fought, John (1995). 'American Structuralism', in E. F. K. Koerner and R. E. Asher (eds.), *Concise History of the Language Sciences: From the Sumerians to the Cognitivists*. Cambridge: Pergamon, 295–306.

Fought, John (1999). 'Leonard Bloomfield's Linguistic Legacy: Later Uses of Some Technical Features', *Historiographia Linguistica* 26: 313–332.

Fox, Melvin J., and Betty P. Skolnick (1975). *Language in Education: Problems and Prospects in Research and Teaching*. New York: The Ford Foundation.

Francescato, Giuseppe (1958). 'Review of Noam Chomsky, *Syntactic Structures*', *Archivo Glottologico Italiano* 43: 66–69.

Francis, W. Nelson (1958). *The Structure of American English*. New York: Ronald Press.

Francis, W. Nelson (1963). *The History of English*. New York: W. W. Norton.

Francis, W. Nelson, and Henry Kučera (1967). *Compositional Analysis of Present-Day American English*. Providence: Brown University Press.

Fraser, Bruce (1976). *The Verb-Particle Combination in English*. New York: Academic Press.

Frei, Henri (1929). *La grammaire des fautes*. Paris: Geuthner.

Freidin, Robert (1994). 'Conceptual Shifts in the Theory of Grammar, 1951–1992', in Carlos Otero (ed.), *Noam Chomsky: Critical Assessments*. New York: Routledge.

Freidin, Robert (1999). 'Cyclicity and Minimalism', in Samuel David Epstein and Norbert Hornstein (eds.), *Working Minimalism*. Cambridge, MA: MIT Press, 95–126.

Freidin, Robert (2020). '*Syntactic Structures*: A Radical Appreciation', *LingBuzz* 005422.

Fretheim, Thorstein (ed.) (1977). *Sentrale Problemer i Norsk Syntaks*. Oslo: Universitetsforlaget.

Friebert, Stuart (2019). 'Martin Joos'. *The Font — A Literary Journal for Language Teachers*. http://thefontjournal.com/martin-joos/, last accessed April 9, 2021.

Fromkin, Victoria A. (1965). 'On System-Structure Phonology', *Language* 41: 601–609.

Fromkin, Victoria A. (1991). 'Language and Brain: Redefining the Goals and Methodology of Linguistics', in Asa Kasher (ed.), *The Chomskyan Turn: Generative, Linguistics, Philosophy, Mathematics, and Psychology*. Oxford: Blackwell, 78–103.

Fromkin, Victoria A., and Robert Rodman (1983). *An Introduction to Language:Third Edition*. New York: Holt, Rinehart and Winston.

Gair, James W. (2003). 'Obituary of Charles F. Hockett', *Language* 79: 600–14.

Gass, Susan, and Josh Ard (1980). 'L2 Data: Their Relevance for Language Universals', *TESOL Quarterly* 14: 443–452.

Gazdar, Gerald (1981). 'Phrase Structure Grammar', in Pauline Jacobson and Geoffrey K. Pullum (eds.), *The Nature of Syntactic Representation*. Dordrecht: Reidel, 131–186.

Gazdar, Gerald, Ewan Klein, Geoffrey Pullum, and Ivan Sag (1985). *Generalized Phrase Structure Grammar*. Cambridge, MA: Harvard University Press.

Givón, Talmy (1979). *On Understanding Grammar*. New York: Academic Press.

Gleason, Henry A. (1955a). *An Introduction to Descriptive Linguistics*. New York: Holt, Rinehart, and Winston.

Gleason, Henry A. (1955b). *Workbook in Descriptive Linguistics*. New York: Holt.

Gleason, Henry A. (1961). *An Introduction to Descriptive Linguistics: Second Edition*. New York: Holt, Rinehart, and Winston.

Gleason, Henry A. (1988). 'Theories in Conflict: North American Linguistics in the Fifties and Sixties'. Unpublished ms, University of Toronto.

Gleitman, Lila (1965). 'Coordinating Conjunctions in English', *Language* 41: 260–293.

Glinz, Hans (1952). *Das innere Form des Deutschen*. Berlin: Francke Verlag.

Godel, Robert (1966). 'F. De Saussure's Theory of Language', in Thomas A. Sebeok (ed.), *Current Trends in Linguistics, Volume 3: Theoretical Foundations*. The Hague: Mouton, 479–493.

Godel, Robert (ed.), (1969). *A Geneva School Reader in Linguistics*. Bloomington: Indiana University Press.

Goetze, Albrecht (1938). *The Hittite Ritual of Tunnawi*. New Haven, CT: American Oriental Society.

Goldberg, Adele E. (2006). *Constructions at Work: The Nature of Generalization in Language*. Oxford: Oxford University Press.

Goldsmith, John A. (1998). 'Review of R. Barsky, *Noam Chomsky: A Life of Dissent*', *Journal of the History of the Behavioral Sciences* 34: 173–180.

Goldsmith, John A. (2005). 'Review of B. Nevin, *The Legacy of Zellig Harris*', *Language* 81: 719–736.

Goldsmith, John A. (2008). 'Generative Phonology in the Late 1940s', *Phonology* 25: 37–59.

Goldsmith, John A., and Bernard Laks (2019). *Battle in the Mind Fields*. Chicago: University of Chicago Press.

Golla, Victor (2001). 'Charles Hockett (1916–2000) [Obituary]', *SSILA Newsletter* 19: 6–7.

Golopenția Eretescu, Sanda (1967). 'Vowel Alternations in Transformational Grammar', *Phonologie der Gegenwart* 4: 134–140.

Golopenția Eretescu, Sanda (1978). 'Transformational Romanian Grammar', in Alexandru Rosetti (ed.), *Current Trends in Romanian Linguistics*. Bucharest: Editura Academiei Republicii Socialiste România, 163–201.

Gonda, Jan (1948). 'The Comparative Method as Applied to Indonesian Languages', *Lingua* 1: 86–101.

Goodman, Nelson (1943). 'On the Simplicity of Ideas', *Journal of Symbolic Logic* 8: 107–121.

Goyvaerts, Didier, and Geoffrey K. Pullum (eds.) (1975). *Essays on the Sound Pattern of English*. Ghent: Story-Scientia.

Graffi, Giorgio (1990). 'Generative Grammar in Italy', in Joan Mascaró and Marina Nespor (eds.), *Grammar in Progress*, Dordrecht: Foris, 147–152.

Graves, Mortimer (1950). *A Neglected Facet of the National Security Problem*. Washington: American Council of Learned Societies.

Graves, Mortimer (1951). 'Comments in the Session Entitled "Meeting the Government's Need in Languages"', in John De Francis (ed.), *Report on the Second Annual Round Table Meeting on Linguistics and Language Teaching*. Washington: Georgetown University Press, 1.

Graves, Mortimer, and J Milton Cowan (1942). 'Excerpt of Report of the First Year's Operation of the Intensive Language Program of the American Council of Learned Societies', *Hispania* 25: 490.

Gray, Bennison (1976). 'Counter-Revolution in the Hierarchy', *Forum Linguisticum* 1: 38–50.

Gray, Louis H. (1931). 'Review of L. Hjelmslev, *Principes de grammaire générale*', *American Journal of Philology* 52: 77–81.

Gray, Louis H. (1939). *Foundations of Language*, Macmillan: New York.

Greenberg, Joseph H. (1963). 'Some Universals of Grammar with Special Reference to the Order of Meaningful Elements', in Joseph Greenberg (ed.), *Universals of Language*. Cambridge, MA: MIT Press, 73–113.

Greenberg, Joseph H. (1973). 'Linguistics as a Pilot Science', in Eric Hamp (ed.), *Themes in Linguistics: The 1970s*. The Hague: Mouton, 45–60.

Greenberg, Joseph H. (1975). 'Research on Language Universals', *Annual Review of Anthropology* 4: 75–94.

Greenberg, Joseph H. (1994). 'The Influence of *Word* and the Linguistic Circle of New York on My Intellectual Development', *Word* 45: 19–25.

Greene, Judith (1972). *Psycholinguistics: Chomsky and Psychology*. Harmondsworth: Penguin.

Grice, H. P. (1975). 'Logic and Conversation', in Peter Cole and Jerry Morgan (eds.), *Syntax and Semantics, Vol. 3: Speech Acts: Syntax and Semantics, Volume 3*. New York: Academic Press, 41–58.

Gross, Maurice (1979). 'On the Failure of Generative Grammar', *Language* 55: 859–885.

Gruber, Jeffrey S. (1967). 'Look and See', *Language* 43: 937–947.

Gunnarsson, Jón (1973). *Málmyndunarfraethi*. Rekjavik: Ithunn.

Haas, Mary R. (1943). 'The Linguist as a Teacher of Languages', *Language* 19: 203–208.

Haas, Mary R. (1946). 'Techniques of Intensifying in Thai', *Word* 2: 127–30.

Hahn, E. Adelaide (1953). *Subjunctive and Optative: Their Origin as Futures*. Lancaster, PA: Lancaster Press.

Haider, Hubert, Martin Prinzhorn, and Henk van Riemsdijk (1987). 'Syntax Report — Generative Grammatik in Europa: Report on Generative Grammar in Europe', *Folia Linguistica* 21: 471–487.

Haiman, John (1980). 'The Iconicity of Grammar: Isomorphism and Motivation', *Language* 56: 515–540.

Hakuta, Kenji (1986). *Mirror of Language: The Debate on Bilingualism*. New York: Basic Books.

Hale, Kenneth L. (1965). 'Review of E. Bach, *An Introduction to Transformational Grammars*', *International Journal of American Linguistics* 31: 265–270.

Hall, Robert A. (1946). 'The State of Linguistics: Crisis or Reaction?', *Italica* 23: 30–34.

Hall, Robert A. (1951–1952). 'American Linguistics, 1925–1950', *Archivum Linguisticum* 3–4: 101–125, 1–16.

Hall, Robert A. (1965). 'Fact and Fiction in Grammatical Analysis', *Foundations of Language* 1: 337–345.

Hall, Robert A. (1968). *Essay on Language*. New York: Chilton Books.

Hall, Robert A. (1969). 'Some Recent Developments in American Linguistics', *Neuphilologische Mitteilungen* 70: 192–227.

Hall, Robert A. (1975). *Stormy Petrel in Linguistics*. Ithaca, NY: Spoken Language Services.

Hall, Robert A. (1980). *Was Morris Swadesh a Martyr?* Ithaca, NY: Linguistica.

Hall, Robert A. (1987). 'Review of C. Hockett, *The State of the Art*', in Robert A. Hall (ed.), *Linguistics and Pseudo-Linguistics*. Amsterdam: John Benjamins, 58–79.

Hall, Robert A. (1990a). 'A Further Note on the Joos Notes', *Historiographia Linguistica* 17: 231–233.

Hall, Robert A. (1990b). *A Life for Language: A Biographical Memoir of Leonard Bloomfield*. Amsterdam: John Benjamins.

Hall, Robert A. (1991). '165 Broadway', *Historiographia Linguistica* 18: 153–166.

Halle, Morris (1959). *The Sound Pattern of Russian*. The Hague: Mouton.

Halle, Morris (1961). 'On the Role of Simplicity in Linguistic Descriptions', in Roman Jakobson (ed.), *Proceedings of Symposia in Applied Mathematics 12: Structure of Language and Its Mathematical Aspects*. Providence, RI: American Mathematical Society, 89–94.

Halle, Morris (1962). 'Phonology in Generative Grammar', *Word* 18: 54–72.

Halle, Morris (1988). 'The Bloomfield–Jakobson Correspondence, 1944–1946', *Language* 64: 737–754.

Halle, Morris (2011). 'Lecture 10', Paper presented at Fifty Years of Linguistics at MIT, Cambridge, MA.

Halliday, M. A. K. (1961). 'Categories of the Theory of Grammar', *Word* 17: 241–292.

Hamans, Camiel (2014). 'The Coming About of *Syntactic Structures*', *Beiträge zur Geschichte der Sprachwissenschaft* 24: 133–156.

Hamans, Camiel (2015). 'How Generative Grammar Landed in Europe', in Gerda Haßler (ed.), *Metasprachliche Reflexion und Diskontinuität — Wendepunkte, Krisenzeiten, Umbrüche*. Münster: Nodus Publikationen.

Hamp, Eric (1961). 'General Linguistics — the United States in the Fifties', in Christine Mohrmann, Alf Sommerfelt, and Joshua Whatmough (eds.), *Trends in European and American Linguistics, 1930–1960*. Utrecht: Spectrum, 165–195.

Hamp, Eric (1966). 'Preface', in Eric Hamp, Fred W. Householder, and Robert Austerlitz (eds.), *Readings in Linguistics II*. Chicago: University of Chicago Press, v–vii.

Hamp, Eric (1995a). 'Foreword', in Eric Hamp, Martin Joos, Fred W. Householder, and Robert Austerlitz (eds.), *Readings in Linguistics I and II: Abridged Edition*. Chicago: University of Chicago Press, v–viii.

Hamp, Eric (1995b). 'Preface to Volume 2 of *Readings in Linguistics*', in Eric Hamp, Martin Joos, Fred W. Householder, and Robert Austerlitz (eds.), *Readings in Linguistics I and II: Abridged Edition*. Chicago: University of Chicago Press, xi–xii.

Hamp, Eric, Fred W. Householder, and Robert Austerlitz (eds.) (1966). *Readings in Linguistics II*. Chicago: University of Chicago Press.

Hamp, Eric, Martin Joos, Fred W. Householder, and Robert Austerlitz (eds.) (1995). *Readings in Linguistics I and II: Abridged Edition*. Chicago: University of Chicago Press.

Hanley, Miles L. (1951). *Word Index to James Joyce's Ulysses*. Madison: University of Wisconsin Press.

Harms, Robert T. (1966). 'The Measurement of Phonological Economy', *Language* 42: 602–611.

Harris, Florence W. (1976 [1965]). 'Reflexivization', in James D. McCawley (ed.), *Syntax and Semantics, Volume 7: Notes from the Linguistic Underground*. New York: Academic Press, 63–83.

Harris, Florence W., and James Harris (1974). 'The Development of the Linguistics Program at the Massachusetts Institute of Technology'. Unpublished ms, MIT. Available at http://ling50.mit.edu/harris-development. Last accessed April 10, 2021.

Harris, Randy A. (1993). *The Linguistics Wars*. Oxford: Oxford University Press (second edition 2021).

Harris, Randy A. (2018). 'The History of a Science: Unreliable Narrators and How Science Moves On', Open Democracy, n.p.

Harris, Zellig S. (1941). 'Review of N. Trubetzkoy, *Grundzüge der Phonologie*', *Language* 17: 345–349.

Harris, Zellig S. (1942). 'Morpheme Alternants in Linguistic Analysis', *Language* 18: 169–180, reprinted in 1957 in M. Joos (ed.), *Readings in Linguistics*. Washington: American Council of Learned Societies, 109–115.

Harris, Zellig S. (1944). 'Simultaneous Components in Phonology', *Language* 20: 181–205, reprinted in 1957 in M. Joos (ed.), *Readings in Linguistics*. Washington: American Council of Learned Societies, 124–138.

Harris, Zellig S. (1951a). *Methods in Structural Linguistics*. Chicago: University of Chicago Press.

Harris, Zellig S. (1951b). 'Review of D. G. Mandelbaum (ed.), *Selected Writings of Edward Sapir in Language, Culture and Personality*', *Language* 27: 288–333.

Harris, Zellig S. (1952). 'Discourse Analysis', *Language* 28: 1–30.

Harris, Zellig S. (1957). 'Co-Occurrence and Transformation in Linguistic Structure', *Language* 33: 283–340.

Harris, Zellig S. (1973). 'Review of Charles Hockett (ed.), *A Leonard Bloomfield Anthology*', *International Journal of American Linguistics* 39: 252–255.

Harris, Zellig S., and Donald C. Swanson (1940). 'Review of Louis H. Gray, *Foundations of Language*', *Language* 16: 216–231.

Hasegawa, Kinsuke (1968). 'The Passive Construction in English', *Language* 44: 230–243.

Haugen, Einar (1949). 'Problems of Bilingualism', *Lingua* 2: 271–290.

Haugen, Einar (1951). 'Directions in Modern Linguistics', *Language* 27: 211–222, reprinted in 1957 in M. Joos (ed.), *Readings in Linguistics*. Washington: American Council of Learned Societies, 357–363.

Haugen, Einar (1979). 'Introduction', in Henry M. Hoenigswald (ed.), *The European Background of American Linguistics: Papers of the Third Golden Anniversary Symposium of the Linguistic Society of America*. Dordrecht: Foris, 1–3.

Haugen, Einar (1980). 'On the Making of a Linguist', in Boyd Davis and Raymond O'Cain (eds.), *First Person Singular: Papers from the Conference on an Oral Archive for the History of American Linguistics*. Amsterdam: John Benjamins, 131–143.

Herdan, Gustav (1968). 'Götzendammerung at MIT', *Zeitschrift für Phonetik* 21: 223–231.

Herslund, Michael (1996). 'Generative Linguistics in Denmark', in Carol Henriksen, Even Hovdhaugen, Fred Karlsson, and Bengt Sigurd (eds.), *Studies in the Development of Linguistics in Denmark, Finland, Iceland, Norway, and Sweden*. Oslo: Novus.

Hill, Archibald A. (1936). 'Phonetic and Phonemic Change', *Language* 12: 15–22, reprinted in 1957 in M. Joos (ed.), *Readings in Linguistics*. Washington: American Council of Learned Societies, 81–84.

Hill, Archibald A. (ed.) (1962). *Proceedings of the Second Texas Conference on Problems of Linguistic Analysis in English*. Austin: University of Texas Press.

Hill, Archibald A. (1964). 'History of the Linguistic Institute', *ACLS Newsletter* 15, 1–12.

Hill, Archibald A. (1966). *The Promises and Limitations of the Newest Type of Grammatical Analysis*. Cincinnati: University of Cincinnati Press.

Hill, Archibald A. (1978). 'The Middle Years', *LSA Bulletin* 64: 34–39.

Hill, Archibald A. (1979). 'Obituary: Martin Joos', *Language* 55: 665–669.

Hill, Archibald A. (1980). 'How Many Revolutions Can a Linguist Live Through?', in Boyd Davis and Raymond O'Cain (eds.), *First Person Singular: Papers from the Conference on an Oral Archive for the History of American Linguistics*. Amsterdam: John Benjamins, 69–76.

Hill, Archibald A. (1991). 'The Linguistic Society of America and North American Linguistics, 1950–1968', *Historiographia Linguistica* 18: 49–152.

Hinrichs, Jan Paul (2001). *The C. H. Van Schooneveld Collection in Leiden University Library*. Leiden: Leiden University Library.

Hinrichs, Jan Paul (2014). 'Regarding the Letter from Chomsky', *Language* 90: 561.

Hjelmslev, Louis (1928). *Principes de grammaire générale*. Copenhagen: Bianco Luno.

Hjelmslev, Louis (1961 [1953]). *Prolegomena to a Theory of Language*. Baltimore: Indiana University Publications in Anthropology and Linguistics.

Hock, Hans H., and Brian D. Joseph (1996). *Language History, Language Change, and Language Relationship: An Introduction to Historical and Comparative Linguistics*. Berlin: Mouton de Gruyter.

Hockett, Charles F. (1942). 'A System of Descriptive Phonology', *Language* 18: 3–21, reprinted in 1957 in M. Joos (ed.), *Readings in Linguistics*. Washington: American Council of Learned Societies, 97–108.

Hockett, Charles F. (1948a). 'A Note on "Structure"', *International Journal of American Linguistics* 14: 269–271, reprinted in 1957 in M. Joos (ed.), *Readings in Linguistics*. Washington: American Council of Learned Societies, 279–280.

Hockett, Charles F. (1948b). 'Implications of Bloomfield's Algonquian Studies', *Language* 24: 117–131, reprinted in 1957 in M. Joos (ed.), *Readings in Linguistics*. Washington: American Council of Learned Societies, 281–289.

Hockett, Charles F. (1951). 'Review of A. Martinet, *Phonology as Functional Phonetics*', *Language* 27: 333–342.

Hockett, Charles F. (1952a). 'A Formal Statement of Morpheme Analysis', *Studies in Linguistics* 10: 27–39.

Hockett, Charles F. (1952b). 'An Approach to the Quantification of Semantic Noise', *Philosophy of Science* 19: 257–260.

Hockett, Charles F. (1952c). 'Review of *Travaux du Cercle Linguistique de Copenhague, V: Recherches structurales*', *International Journal of American Linguistics* 18: 86–99.

Hockett, Charles F. (1953). 'Review of C. Shannon and W. Weaver, *The Mathematical Theory of Communiction*', *Language* 29: 69–93.

Hockett, Charles F. (1954). 'Two Models of Grammatical Description', *Word* 10: 210–234, reprinted in 1957 in M. Joos (ed.), *Readings in Linguistics*. Washington: American Council of Learned Societies, 386–399.

Hockett, Charles F. (1955). *Manual of Phonology*. Baltimore: Waverly Press.

Hockett, Charles F. (1958). *A Course in Modern Linguistics*. New York: Macmillan.

Hockett, Charles F. (1960). 'The Origin of Speech', *Scientific American* 203: 88–96.

Hockett, Charles F. (1965). 'Sound Change', *Language* 41: 185–204.

Hockett, Charles F. (1966a). *Language, Mathematics, and Linguistics*. The Hague: Mouton. [Also published in slightly revised form in Thomas Sebeok (ed.), *Current Trends in Linguistics, Vol. 3: Theoretical Foundations*. The Hague: Mouton, 1966, 155–304.]

Hockett, Charles F. (1966b). 'Language, Mathematics, and Linguistics', in Thomas Sebeok (ed.), *Current Trends in Linguistics, Vol. 3: Theoretical Foundations*. The Hague: Mouton, 155–304.

Hockett, Charles F. (1966c). *The Quantification of Functional Load: A Linguistic Problem*. Santa Monica, CA: The RAND Corporation.

Hockett, Charles F. (1967). 'Review of Eric Lenneberg, *The Biological Foundations of Language*', *Scientific American* 217: 141–144.

Hockett, Charles F. (1968). *The State of the Art*. Mouton: The Hague.

Hockett, Charles F. (ed.) (1970). *A Leonard Bloomfield Anthology*. Bloomington: Indiana University Press.

Hockett, Charles F. (1977). *The View from Language*. Athens, GA: University of Georgia Press.

Hockett, Charles F. (1980). 'Preserving the Heritage', in Boyd Davis and Raymond O'Cain (eds.), *First Person Singular: Papers from the Conference on an Oral Archive for the History of American Linguistics*. Amsterdam: John Benjamins, 99–107.

Hockett, Charles F. (1987a). *Refurbishing Our Foundations*. Amsterdam: John Benjamins.

Hockett, Charles F. (1987b). 'Editor's Preface', in Charles F. Hockett (ed.), *A Leonard Bloomfield Anthology: Abridged Edition*. Chicago: University of Chicago Press, vii–viii.

Hockett, Charles F. (1987c). 'Letters from Bloomfield to Michelson and Sapir', in Robert A. Hall and E. F. K. Koerner (eds.), *Leonard Bloomfield: Essays of His Life and Work.* Amsterdam: John Benjamins, 39–60.

Hockett, Charles F. (1993a). 'Book Notice on G. Cannon, *The Life and Mind of Oriental Jones*', *Language* 69: 196.

Hockett, Charles F. (1993b). 'George Leonard Trager [Obituary]', *Language* 69: 778–788.

Hockett, Charles F. (1995). 'J Milton Cowan [Obituary]', *Language* 71: 341–348.

Hockett, Charles F. (1997). 'Review of P. Daniels and W. Bright (eds.), *The World's Writing Systems*', *Language* 73: 379–385.

Hoenigswald, Henry M. (1964). 'Obituary of George M. Bolling', *Language* 40: 329–336.

Holmes, Urban T. (1931). 'Germanic Influences on Old French Syntax', *Language* 7: 194–199.

Holmes, Urban T. (1940). 'Review of *Mélanges de linguistique offerts à Charles Bally*', *Language* 16: 237–240.

Hooper, Joan B. (1976). *An Introduction to Natural Generative Phonology.* New York: Academic Press.

Hornstein, Norbert (2015), 'Does the LSA and Its Flagship Journal "*Language*" have any Regard for Generative Grammar?'. WebLog: Faculty of Language, <Online: http://facultyoflanguage.blogspot.com>, August 17, 2015. Last accessed April 12, 2021.

Householder, Fred W. (1947). 'A Descriptive Analysis of Latin Declensions', *Word* 3: 48–58.

Householder, Fred W. (1952). 'Review of Daniel Jones, *The Phoneme: Its Nature and Use*', *International Journal of American Linguistics* 18: 99–105.

Householder, Fred W. (1962). 'Review of R. B. Lees, *Grammar of English Nominalizations*', *Word* 18: 326–353.

Householder, Fred W. (1965). 'On Some Recent Claims in Phonological Theory', *Journal of Linguistics* 1: 13–34.

Householder, Fred W. (1971). *Linguistic Speculations.* Cambridge: Cambridge University Press.

Householder, Fred W. (1980). 'A Sketch of How I Came to Be in Linguistics', in Boyd Davis and Raymond O'Cain (eds.), *First Person Singular: Papers from the Conference on an Oral Archive for the History of American Linguistics.* Amsterdam: John Benjamins, 193–199.

Hovdhaugen, Even (1969). *Transformasjonell Generativ Grammatikk: En Innføring.* Oslo: Universitetsforlaget.

Hovdhaugen, Even, Fred Karlsson, Carol Henriksen, and Bengt Sigurd (2000). *The History of Linguistics in the Nordic Countries.* Helsinki: Societas Scientiarum Fennica.

Huck, Geoffrey J., and John A. Goldsmith (1994). *Ideology and Linguistic Theory: Noam Chomsky and the Deep Structure Debates.* London: Routledge.

Huddleston, Rodney (1969). 'Some Observations on Tense and Deixis in English', *Language* 45: 777–806.

Huntley, D. G. (1968). 'Two Cases of Analogical Feature Substitution in Slavic', *Language* 44: 501–506.

Hutchins, W. John (1986). *Machine Translation: Past, Present, and Future.* Chichester, UK: Ellis Horwood.

Hutchins, W. John (2000). 'The First Decades of Machine Translation: Overview, Chronology, Sources', in W. John Hutchins (ed.), *Early Years in Machine Translation: Memories and Biographies of Pioneers.* Amsterdam: John Benjamins, 1–15.

Hymes, Dell H. (1958). 'Review of M. Joos (ed.), *Readings in Linguistics*', *American Anthropologist* 60: 416–418.

Hymes, Dell H. (1964a). 'Directions in (Ethno-)Linguistic Theory', in A. K. Romney and R. G. D'Andrade (eds.), *Transcultural Studies in Cognition (American Anthropologist 66:3, Part 2)*. Washington: American Anthropological Association, 6–56.

Hymes, Dell H. (ed.) (1964b). *Language in Culture and Society: A Reader in Linguistics and Anthropology*. New York: Harper and Row.

Hymes, Dell H. (1980). 'Review of R. A. Hall, Jr., *Stormy Petrel in Linguistics*', *Language* 56: 648–652.

Hymes, Dell H., and John Fought (1975). 'American Structuralism', in Thomas A. Sebeok (ed.), *Current Trends in Linguistics, Vol. 13: Historiography of Linguistics*. The Hague: Mouton, 903–1176.

Hymes, Dell H., and John Fought (1981). *American Structuralism*. The Hague: Mouton.

Iverson, Gregory K. (1978). 'Synchronic Umlaut in Old Icelandic', *Nordic Journal of Linguistics* 1: 121–139.

Ivič, Milka (1965). *Trends in Linguistics*. The Hague: Mouton.

Jackendoff, Ray (1972). *Semantic Interpretation in Generative Grammar*. Cambridge, MA: MIT Press.

Jacobs, Roderick A., and Peter S. Rosenbaum (eds.) (1970). *Readings in English Transformational Grammar*. Waltham, MA: Ginn.

Jakobson, Roman (1941). *Kindersprache, Aphasie und allgemeine Lautgesetze*. Uppsala: Almqvist & Wiksell.

Jakobson, Roman (1944). 'Franz Boas' Approach to Language', *International Journal of American Linguistics* 10: 188–195.

Jakobson, Roman (1959). 'Boas' View of Grammatical Meaning', in W. Goldschmidt (ed.), *The Anthropology of Franz Boas: Essay on the Centennial of His Birth* (American Anthropological Association, *Memoir 89*), 2: *Word and Language*. Menasha, Wisconsin: Mouton, 139–145, reprinted 1971 in R. Jakobson (ed), *Selected Writings: Vol. 2, Word and Language*. The Hague: Mouton, 71, 489–496.

Jakobson, Roman (1968 [1941]). *Child Language, Aphasia, and Phonological Universals*, 72. The Hague: Mouton.

Jakobson, Roman (1971a [1957]). 'Typological Studies and Their Contribution to Historical Comparative Linguistics', in Roman Jakobson (ed.), *Selected Writings, Vol. 1: Phonological Studies*. The Hague: Mouton, 523–532.

Jakobson, Roman (1971b [1957]). 'Notes on Gilyak', in Roman Jakobson (ed.), *Selected Writings, Volume 2: Word and Language*. The Hague: Mouton, 72–97.

Jakobson, Roman (1971c [1948]). 'Russian Conjugation', in R. Jakobson (ed.), *Selected Writings*, 2: Word and Language. The Hague: Mouton, 119–129.

Jakobson, Roman (1971d [1963]). 'Efforts toward a Means-End Model of Language in Interwar Continental Linguistics', in Roman Jakobson (ed.), *Selected Writings, Volume 2: Word and Language*. The Hague: Mouton, 522–526.

Jakobson, Roman (1971e [1949]). 'The Phonemic and Grammatical Aspects of Language in Their Interrelations', in Roman Jakobson (ed.), *Selected Writings, Volume 2: Word and Language*. The Hague: Mouton, 103–114.

Jakobson, Roman (1973). *Main Trends in the Science of Language*. London: Allen & Unwin.

Jakobson, Roman (ed.) (1975). *N. S. Trubetzkoy's Letters and Notes*. Mouton: The Hague.

Jakobson, Roman (1979). 'The Twentieth Century in European and American Linguistics: Movements and Continuity', in Henry M. Hoenigswald (ed.), *The European Background of American Linguistics: Papers of the Third Golden Anniversary Symposium of the Linguistic Society of America*. Dordrecht: Foris, 161–173.

Jakobson, Roman, and Morris Halle (1956). *Fundamentals of Language*. The Hague: Mouton.

Keyser, S. Jay (1965). 'Linguistic Theory and System Design', in Joseph Spiegel and Donald Walker (eds.), *Information System Sciences*. Washington: Spartan Books, 495–515.

Jespersen, Otto (1925). *Mankind, Nation and Individual from a Linguistic Point of View*. Oslo: H Aschehoug.

Jespersen, Otto (1928). *An International Language*. London: Allen & Unwin.

Jones, Daniel (1950). *The Phoneme: Its Nature and Use*. Cambridge: W. Heffer & Sons.

Joos, Martin (1948). *Acoustic Phonetics [= Language Monograph 23, Supplement to Language 24: 2]*. Baltimore: Waverly Press.

Joos, Martin (1950). 'Description of Language Design', *Journal of the Acoustic Society of America* 22: 701–708, reprinted in 1957 in M. Joos (ed.), *Readings in Linguistics*. Washington: American Council of Learned Societies, 372–378.

Joos, Martin (1957a). 'Preface', in Martin Joos (ed.), *Readings in Linguistics: The Development of Descriptive Linguistics in America since 1925*. New York: American Council of Learned Societies, v–vii.

Joos, Martin (ed.), (1957b). *Readings in Linguistics: The Development of Descriptive Linguistics in America since 1925*. New York: American Council of Learned Societies.

Joos, Martin (1958). 'Preface', in Martin Joos (ed.), *Readings in Linguistics, Second Edition*. New York: American Council of Learned Societies, v–vii.

Joos, Martin (1961). 'Linguistic Prospects in the United States', in C. Mohrmann, A. Sommerfelt, and J. Whatmough (eds.), *Trends in European and American Linguistics, 1930–1960*. Utrecht: Spectrum, 11–20.

Joos, Martin (1962). *The Five Clocks*. Bloomington: Indiana University Research Center in Anthropology.

Joos, Martin (1964). *The English Verb: Form and Meanings*. Madison: University of Wisconsin Press.

Joos, Martin (1966a). 'Preface', in Martin Joos (ed.), *Readings in Linguistics I: The Development of Descriptive Linguistics in America 1925–56, Fourth Edition*. Chicago: University of Chicago Press.

Joos, Martin (ed.) (1966b). *Readings in Linguistics I: The Development of Descriptive Linguistics in America 1925–56, Fourth Edition*. Chicago: University of Chicago Press.

Joos, Martin (1967). 'Bernard Bloch [Obituary]', *Language* 43: 3–19.

Joos, Martin (1972). 'Semantic Axiom Number One', *Language* 48: 257–265.

Joos, Martin (1986). *Notes on the Development of the Linguistic Society of America 1924 to 1950*. Ithaca: Privately printed by J. M. Cowan and C. Hockett.

Joos, Martin, and F. R. Whitesell (1951). *Middle High German Courtly Reader*. Madison: University of Wisconsin Press.

Joseph, John E. (1991). 'Review of E. F. K. Koerner, *Practicing Linguistic Historiography*', *Word* 42: 216–219.

Joseph, John E. (2010). 'Chomsky's Atavistic Revolution (with a Little Help from His Enemies)', in Douglas A. Kibbee (ed.), *Chomskyan (R)evolutions*. Amsterdam: John Benjamins, 1–18.

Joseph, John E. (2012). *Saussure*. Oxford: Oxford University Press.

Joseph, John E. (2019). 'Linguistics', in Mark Bever (ed.), *Modernism and the Social Sciences: Anglo-American Exchanges, c. 1918-1980*. Berkeley: University of California Press, 182–201.

Joseph, John E., and Frederick J. Newmeyer (2012). '"All Languages Are Equally Complex": The Rise and Fall of a Consensus', *Historiographia Linguistica* 39: 341–368.

Karlsson, Fred (1997). *Yleinen Kielitiede*. Helsinki: Yliopistopaino.

Karttunen, Lauri (1976 [1969]). 'Discourse Referents', in James D. McCawley (ed.), *Syntax and Semantics, Volume 7: Notes from the Linguistic Underground*. New York: Academic Press, 363–385. (Distributed by the Indiana University Linguistics Club in 1971.)

Katz, Jerrold J. (1964). 'Mentalism in Linguistics', *Language* 40: 124–137.

Katz, Jerrold J. (1981). *Language and Other Abstract Objects*. Totowa, NJ: Rowman and Littlefield.

Katz, Jerrold J., and Jerry A. Fodor (1963). 'The Structure of a Semantic Theory', *Language* 39: 170–210.

Keniston, Hayward (1930). 'The Subjunctive in Lazarillo De Tormes ', *Language* 6: 41–63.

Kent, Roland G. (1923). *Language and Philology: Our Debt to Greece and Rome*. London: G. Harrap & Co.

Kent, Roland G. (1933). 'Another Inscription of Xerxes ', *Language* 9: 229–231.

Kenyon, John S., and Thomas A. Knott (1944). *A Pronouncing Dictionary of American English*. Springfield, MA: Merriam-Webster.

Kertész, András (2017). *The Historiography of Generative Linguistics*. Tübingen: Narr.

Keyser, S. Jay (1964). 'Communication in a Lily Pond', *Technology Review* 66: 31–33.

Kiefer, Ferenc (1970). *Swedish Morphology*, Stockholm. Skriptor.

Kiefer, Ferenc, and Nicolas Ruwet (eds.) (1973). *Generative Grammar in Europe*. Dordrecht: Reidel.

Kilbury, James (1976). *The Development of Morphophonemic Theory*. Amsterdam: John Benjamins.

Kiparsky, Paul (1967). 'Sonorant Clusters in Greek', *Language* 43: 619–635.

Klein, Sheldon (1965). 'Control of Style with a Generative Grammar', *Language* 41: 619–631.

Klima, Edward S. (1964). 'Relatedness between Grammatical Systems', *Language* 40: 1–20.

Knight, Chris (2017a). *Decoding Chomsky: Science and Revolutionary Politics*. New Haven: Yale University Press.

Knight, Chris (2017b). 'The MITRE Corporation's Project to Use Chomsky's Linguistics for Their Weapons Systems', *Science and Revolution* (Chris Knight's blog on Noam Chomsky).

Knight, Chris (2018a). 'Why Chomsky Felt "Guilty Most of the Time": War Research and Linguistics at MIT', *OpenDemocracy*.

Knight, Chris (2018b). 'Chomsky's Choice: How the Linguist's Early Military Work Led to a Life of Campaigning against the Military', *OpenDemocracy*.

Koerner, E. F. K. (1983). 'The "Chomskyan Revolution" and Its Historiography: A Few Critical Remarks', *Language and Communication* 3: 147–169.

Koerner, E. F. K. (1984). 'Introduction', in E. F. K.Koerner (ed.), *Edward Sapir: Appraisals of His Life and Work*. Amsterdam: John Benjamins, xi–xxvii.

Koerner, E. F. K. (1989). 'The Chomskyan "Revolution" and Its Historiography: Observations of a Bystander", in E. F. K. Koerner (ed.), *Practicing Linguistic Historiography: Selected Essays*. Amsterdam: John Benjamins, 101–146.

Koerner, E. F. K. (2002a). 'American Structuralist Linguistics and the "Problem of Meaning"', in E. F. K. Koerner (ed.), *Toward a History of American Linguistics*. London: Routledge, 75–104.

Koerner, E. F. K. (2002b). 'The Chomskyan Revolution and Its Historiography', in E. F. K. Koerner (ed.), *Toward a History of American Linguistics*. London: Routledge, 151–209.

Koerner, E. F. K. (2002c). *Toward a History of American Linguistics*, Routledge Studies in the History of Linguistics, 5. London: Routledge.

Koerner, E. F. K. (2003). 'Remarks on the Origins of Morphophonemics in American Structuralist Linguistics', *Language and Communication* 23: 1–43.

Koerner, E. F. K. (2004). 'On "Influence" in Linguistic Historiography: Morphophonemics in American Structuralism', in E. F. K. Koerner (ed.), *Essays in the History of Linguistics*. Amsterdam: John Benjamins, 65–100.

Koontz-Garboden, Andrew (2007). *States, Changes of State, and the Monotonicity Hypothesis*, Unpublished PhD dissertation, Stanford University.

Koster, Jan (1975). 'Dutch as an SOV Language', *Linguistic Analysis* 1: 111–136.

Koster, Jan (1978). *Locality Principles in Syntax*. Dordrecht: Foris.

Kroeber, A. L. (1984). 'Reflections on Edward Sapir, Scholar and Man', in E. F. K. Koerner (ed.), *Edward Sapir: Appraisals of His Life and Work*. Amsterdam: John Benjamins, 131–139.

Kuhn, Thomas S. (1970). *The Structure of Scientific Revolutions, 2nd Edn*. Chicago: University of Chicago Press.

Kuno, Susumu (1972). 'Functional Sentence Perspective: A Case Study from Japanese and English', *Linguistic Inquiry* 3: 269–320.

Kurath, Hans (1939). *Linguistic Atlas of New England*. New York: AMS Press.

Kuroda, Sige-Yuki (1968). 'English Relativization and Certain Related Problems', *Language* 44: 244–266.

Kürschner, Wilfried (2009). 'Establishing the Linguistics Colloquium (1966–1975)'. <http://www.linguistisches-kolloquium.de/40_years_website.pdf>, last accessed April 10, 2021.

Labov, William (1966). *The Social Stratification of English in New York City*. Washington: Center for Applied Linguistics.

Labov, William (1969). 'Contraction, Deletion, and Inherent Variability of the English Copula', *Language* 45: 716–62.

Labov, William (1972). *Sociolinguistic Patterns*. Philadelphia: University of Pennsylvania Press.

Ladd, D. Robert (2020). 'Mid-Century American Phonology: The Post-Bloomfieldians', in B. Elan Dresher and Harry Van der Hulst (eds.), *Oxford Handbook of the History of Phonology*. Oxford: Oxford University Press.

Lakoff, George (1965). *On the Nature of Syntactic Irregularity*. PhD dissertation Indiana University, published in 1965 as *Report NSF-16* to the National Science Foundation and in 1970 under the title '*Irregularity in Syntax*' (New York: Holt*)*.

Lakoff, George (1971). 'On Generative Semantics', in Danny Steinberg and Leon Jakobovits (eds.), *Semantics: An Interdisciplinary Reader in Philosophy, Linguistics, and Psychology*. New York: Cambridge University Press, 232–296.

Lakoff, George (1972 [1970]). 'Linguistics and Natural Logic', in Donald Davidson and Gilbert Harmon (eds.), *The Semantics of Natural Language*. Dordrecht: Reidel, 545–665.

Lakoff, George (1976 [1969]). 'Pronouns and Reference', in James D. McCawley (ed.), *Syntax and Semantics, Volume 7: Notes from the Linguistic Underground*. New York: Academic Press, 275–335. (Circulated by the Indiana University Linguistics Club in 1969.)

Lakoff, Robin T. (1969). 'Some Reasons Why There Can't Be Any *Some-Any* Rule', *Language* 45: 608–615.

Lakoff, Robin T. (1989). 'The Way We Were: Or, the Real Actual Truth About Generative Semantics: A Memoir', *Journal of Pragmatics* 13: 939–988.

Lamb, Sydney M. (1966). *Outline of Stratificational Grammar*. Washington: Georgetown University Press.

Lamb, Sydney M. (1967). 'Reviews of N. Chomsky, *Current Issues in Linguistic Theory* and *Aspects of the Theory of Syntax*', *American Anthropologist* 69: 411–415.

Lane, George S. (1955). 'Obituary of Carl Darling Buck', *Language* 31: 181–189.

Lane, Michael (1970). *Introduction to Structuralism*. New York: Basic Books.

Langacker, Ronald W. (1965). 'French Interrogatives: A Transformational Description', *Language* 41: 587–600.

Langacker, Ronald W. (1968). 'Observations on French Possessives', *Language* 44: 51–75.

Langacker, Ronald W. (1969a). 'Mirror Image Rules II: Lexicon and Phonology', *Language* 45: 844–862.

Langacker, Ronald W. (1969b). 'Mirror Image Rules I: Syntax', *Language* 45: 575–598.

Langacker, Ronald W. (1982). 'Space Grammar, Analyzability, and the English Passive', *Language* 58: 22–80.

Langendoen, D. Terence (1966). 'A Restriction on Grassmann's Law in Greek', *Language* 42: 7–9.

Laudan, Larry (1977). *Progress and Its Problems: Toward a Theory of Scientific Growth*. Berkeley and Los Angeles: University of California Press.

Leech, Geoffrey (2002). 'Personal History', in Keith Brown and Vivien Law (eds.), *Linguistics in Britain: Personal Histories*. Oxford: Blackwell, 155–169.

Lees, Robert B. (1957). 'Review of Noam Chomsky, *Syntactic Structures*', *Language* 33: 375–408.

Lees, Robert B. (1960a). 'A Multiply Ambiguous Adjectival Construction in English', *Language* 36: 207–221.

Lees, Robert B. (1960b). 'Review of Dwight Bolinger, *Interrogative Structures of American English*', *Word* 16: 119–125.

Lees, Robert B. (1960c). *The Grammar of English Nominalizations*. The Hague: Mouton.

Lees, Robert B. (1976 [1960]). 'What Are Transformations?', in James D. McCawley (ed.), *Syntax and Semantics, Volume 7: Notes from the Linguistic Underground*. New York: Academic Press, 27–41.

Lees, Robert B., and Edward Klima (1963). 'Rules for English Pronominalization', *Language* 39: 17–28.

Lehmann, Christian (2004). 'Documentation of Grammar', *Lectures on Endangered Languages* 4: 61–74.

Lehmann, Christian (2010). 'Roots, Stems and Word Classes', in Umberto Ansaldo, Jan Don, and Roland Pfau (eds.), *Parts of Speech: Empirical and Theoretical Advances*. Amsterdam: John Benjamins, 43–64.

Lepschy, Giulio C. (1972). *A Survey of Structural Linguistics*. London: Faber and Faber.

Leroy, Maurice (1967 [1963]). *Main Trends in Modern Linguistics*. Berkeley: University of California Press.

Lesnin, I. M., Luba Petrova, and Leonard Bloomfield (1945). *Spoken Russian, Basic Course*. Madison: Published for the United States Armed Forces Institute by the Linguistic Society of America.

Levin, Samuel R. (1965). '*Langue* and *Parole* in American Linguistics', *Foundations of Language* 1: 83–94.

Lévi-Strauss, Claude (1953). 'Social Structure', in Sol Tax et al. (ed.), *An Appraisal of Anthropology Today*. Chicago: University of Chicago Press.

Lightner, Theodore (1968). 'Review of M. Joos (ed.), *Readings in Linguistics, 4th Edition*', *General Linguistics* 8: 44–61.

Lindblom, Bjorn (1990). 'Models of Phonetic Variation and Selection', *Phonetic Experimental Research, Institute of Linguistics, University of Stockholm* 11: 65–100.

Linell, Per (1974). *Problems of Psychological Reality in Generative Grammar: A Critical Assessment*. Uppsala: University of Uppsala.

Linell, Per (1979). *Psychological Reality in Phonology*. Cambridge: Cambridge University Press.

Lounsbury, Floyd G. (1959). 'Language', *Biennial Review of Anthropology* 1: 185–209.

Lyons, John (1958). 'Review of Noam Chomsky, *Syntactic Structures*', *Litera: Studies in Language and Literature (Istanbul)* 5: 109–115.

Lyons, John (1963). *Structural Semantics: An Analysis of Part of the Vocabulary of Plato*. Oxford: Blackwell.

Lyons, John (2002). 'Personal History', in Keith Brown and Vivien Law (eds.), *Linguistics in Britain: Personal Histories*. Oxford: Blackwell, 170–199.

MacQueen, John (1957). 'Review of M. Joos (ed.), *Readings in Linguistics*', *Quarterly Journal of Speech* 43: 324.

Maher, J. Peter (1980). 'The Transformational-Generative Paradigm: A Silver Anniversary Polemic', *Forum Linguisticum* 5: 1–35.

Makkai, Adam (1975). 'Why LACUS?', in Adam Makkai and Valerie B. Makkai (eds.), *The First LACUS Forum*. Columbia, SC: Hornbeam Press, ix–xii.

Maling, Joan (1990 [1980]). 'Inversion in Embedded Clauses in Modern Icelandic', in Maling, Joan and Annie Zaenen (eds.), *Modern Icelandic Syntax*. San Diego: Academic Press, 71–91.

Malkiel, Yakov (1966). 'Bernard Bloch [Obituary]', *Romance Philology* 16: 648.

Malkiel, Yakov (1979). 'Aspirations, Organization, Achievement', in Henry M. Hoenigswald (ed.), *The European Background of American Linguistics: Papers of the Third Golden Anniversary Symposium of the Linguistic Society of America*. Dordrecht: Foris, 107–119.

Malkiel, Yakov (1980). 'Autobiographic Sketch: Early Years in America', in Boyd Davis and Raymond O'Cain (eds.), *First Person Singular: Papers from the Conference on an Oral Archive for the History of American Linguistics*. Amsterdam: John Benjamins, 77–95.

Malmberg, Bertil (1963). *Structural Linguistics and Human Communication*. Heidelberg: Springer.

Malmberg, Bertil (1964 [1959]). *New Trends in Linguistics: An Orientation*, University of Lund: Institute of Phonetics.

Malone, Joseph L. (1967). 'A Transformational Re-Examination of English Questions', *Language* 43: 686–702.

Manoliu Manea, Maria (1973). *Structuralismul Lingvistic [Linguistic Structuralism]*. Bucharest: Editura didacticas i pedagogica.

Manoliu Manea, Maria (1977). *Tipologie si Istorie: Elemente se Sintaxă Comparată Romanică [Typology and History: Elements of Comparative Romance Syntax]*. Bucharest: Editura Universitatii din Bucuresti.

Marckwardt, Albert H. (1959). 'Linguistics and the NDEA', *Language Learning* 9: i–iv.

Marti, Berthe M. (1936). 'Proskynesis and Adorare', *Language* 12: 272–82.

Martinet, André (1949). *Phonology as Functional Phonetics*. London: Oxford University Press.

Martinet, André (1953). 'Structural Linguistics', in A. L. Kroeber (ed.), *Anthropology Today: An Encyclopedic Inventory*. Chicago: University of Chicago Press, 574–586.

Martinet, André (1955). *Économie des changements phonétiques*. Bern: A. Francke.

Martinet, André (1962). *A Functional View of Language*. Oxford: Oxford University Press.

Martinet, André (1974). 'Interview', in Herman Parrett (ed.), *Discussing Language*. The Hague: Mouton, 221–247.

Martinet, André (1993) 'Mémoires d'un linguiste: Vivre les langues'. Paris: Quai Voltaire.

Martinet, André (1994). 'A Early History of *Word* Volumes 1 to 25', *Word* 25: 27–37.

Martin-Nielsen, Janet (2010). 'This War for Men's Minds': The Birth of Human Science in the Cold War', *History of the Human Sciences* 23: 131–155.

Martin-Nielsen, Janet (2011). 'A Forgotten Social Science? Creating a Place for Linguistics in the Historical Dialogue', *Journal of the History of the Behavioral Sciences* 47: 147–172.

Martin-Nielsen, Janet (2012). '"It Was All Connected": Computers and Linguistics in Early Cold War America', in Mark Solovey and HamiltonCravens (eds.), *Cold War Social Science: Knowledge Production, Liberal Democracy, and Human Nature*. New York: Palgrave Macmillan, 63–78.

Mathesius, Vilém (1926). 'Linguistická Charaktistika a Její Místo V Moderním Jazykopytu [Linguistic Characterology and Its Place in Modern Linguistics]', *ČMF* [Journal for Modern Philology] 13: 35–40.

Mathesius, Vilém (1983 [1927]). 'Functional Linguistics', in Josef Vachek (ed.), *Praguiana: Some Basic and Less-Known Aspects of the Prague Linguistics School*. Amsterdam: John Benjamins, 121–142.

Matthews, Peter H. (1965). 'Problems of Selection in Transformational Grammar', *Journal of Linguistics* 1: 35–47.

Matthews, Peter H. (1972). 'Review of R. Jacobs and P. Rosenbaum (eds.), *Readings in English Transformational Grammar*', *Journal of Linguistics* 8: 125–136.

Matthews, Peter H. (1993). *Grammatical Theory in the United States from Bloomfield to Chomsky*. Cambridge: Cambridge University Press.

Matthews, Peter H. (2002). 'Personal History', in Keith Brown and Vivien Law (eds.), *Linguistics in Britain: Personal Histories*. Oxford: Blackwell, 200–212.

McCawley, James D. (1968). 'Review of Thomas Sebeok (ed.), *Current Trends in Linguistics, Vol. 3, Theoretical Foundations*', *Language* 44: 556–593.

McCawley, James D. (1974). '(Interview Conducted by Herman Parret)', in Herman Parret (ed.), *Discussing Language: Dialogues with Wallace L. Chafe, Noam Chomsky, Algirdas J. Greimas [and Others]*. The Hague: Mouton, 249–277.

McCawley, James D. (1976a). *Grammar and Meaning*. New York: Academic Press.

McCawley, James D. (1976b). 'Introduction', in James D. McCawley (ed.), *Syntax and Semantics, Volume 7: Notes from the Linguistic Underground*. New York: Academic Press, 1–19.

McCawley, James D. (ed.), (1976c). *Syntax and Semantics, Volume 7: Notes from the Linguistic Underground*. New York: Academic Press.

McCawley, James D. (1977). 'Jakobsonian Ideas in Generative Grammar', in Daniel Armstrong and C. H. Van Schooneveld (eds.), *Roman Jakobson: Echoes of His Scholarship*. Lisse: Peter de Ridder Press, 269–284.

McDavid, Raven I. (1954). 'Review of Harry R. Warfel, *Who Killed Grammar?*', *Studies in Linguistics* 12: 30–32.

McDavid, Raven I. (1980). 'Linguistics, through the Kitchen Door', in Boyd Davis and Raymond O'Cain (eds.), *First Person Singular: Papers from the Conference on an Oral Archive for the History of American Linguistics*, 1–20. Amsterdam: John Benjamins.

McKay, John C. (1968). 'Some Generative Rules for German Time Adverbials', *Language* 44: 25–50.

McQuown, Norman A. (1952). 'Review of Z. Harris, *Methods in Structural Linguistics*', *Language* 28: 495–504.

Mehta, Ved (1971). *John Is Easy to Please*. New York: Farrar, Straus & Giroux.

Meillet, Antoine (1953 [1903]). *Introduction à l'étude comparative des langues indo-européennes*. Paris.

Meillet, Antoine, and Marcel Cohen (1924). *Les langues du monde*. Paris: E. Champion.

Mel'čuk, Igor A. (2000). 'Machine Translation and Formal Linguistics in the USSR', in W. John Hutchins (ed.), *Early Years in Machine Translation: Memoires and Biographies of Pioneers*. Amsterdam: John Benjamins, 205–226.

Mencken, H. L. (1948). *The American Language: An Inquiry into the Development of English in the United States; Supplement II*. New York: Knopf.

Messing, Gordon M. (1951). 'Structuralism and Literary Tradition', *Language* 27: 1–12.

Mildenberger, Kenneth W. (1960). 'The National Defense Education Act and Linguistics', in Bernard Choseed (ed.), *Report of the Eleventh Annual Round Table Meeting on Linguistics and Language Studies*. Washington: Georgetown University Press, 157–168.

Miller, George A., Eugene Galanter, and Karl Pribram (1960). *Plans and the Structure of Behavior*. New York: Holt, Rinehart, and Winston.

Milner, Jean-Claude (1978). 'Cyclicité successive, comparatives, et cross-over en français (première partie)', *Linguistic Inquiry* 9: 673–693.

Mohrmann, Christine, Alf Sommerfelt, and Joshua Whatmough (eds.) (1961). *Trends in European and American Linguistics, 1930–1960*. Utrecht: Spectrum.

Montgomery, Christine (1965). 'Review of E. Bach, *An Introduction to Transformational Grammars*', *Language* 41: 632–640.

Moore, Terence, and Christine Carling (1982). *Language Understanding: Towards a Post-Chomskyan Linguistics*. New York: St. Martin's Press.

Morgan, Jerry L. (1976 [1969]). 'Cryptic Note II and Wags III ', in James D. McCawley (ed.), *Syntax and Semantics, Volume 7: Notes from the Linguistic Underground*. New York: Academic Press, 337–345.

Mosko, Eljana (2014). 'Generative Grammar in Albanian Linguistics', *Mediterranean Journal of Social Science* 5: 2387–2390.

Moulton, William G. (1961). 'Linguistics and Language Teaching in the United States 1940–1960', in Christine Mohrmann, Alf Sommerfelt, and Joshua Whatmough (eds.), *Trends in European and American Linguistics, 1930–1960*. Utrecht: Spectrum, 82–109.

Moulton, William G. (1970). 'Leonard Bloomfield as a Germanist', in Charles F. Hockett (ed.), *A Leonard Bloomfield Anthology*. Bloomington, IN: Indiana University Press, 512–523.

Muller, Henri F. (1945). 'Word', *Word* 1: 3–4.

Mullins, Nicholas C. (1973). *Theories and Theory Groups in American Sociology*. New York: Harper and Roe.

Mullins, Nicholas C. (1975). 'A Sociological Theory of Scientific Revolutions', in Karen D. Knorr, Hermann Strasser, and Hans Heorg Zilian (eds.), *Determinants and Controls of Scientific Development*. Dordrecht: Reidel.

Murray, Stephen O. (1980). 'Gatekeepers and the 'Chomskyan Revolution", *Journal of the History of the Behavioral Sciences* 16: 73–88.

Murray, Stephen O. (1983). *Group Formation in Social Science*. Edmonton: Linguistic Research, Inc.

Murray, Stephen O. (1989). 'Recent Studies of American Linguistics', *Historiographia Linguistica* 16: 149–171.

Murray, Stephen O. (1994). *Theory Groups and the Study of Language in North America: A Social History*. Amsterdam: John Benjamins.

Murray, Stephen O. (1997). 'A 1978 Interview with Mary R. Haas', *Anthropological Linguistics* 39: 695–722.

Murray, Stephen O. (1999). 'How *The Logical Structure of Linguistic Theory* Didn't Get Published During the 1950s or 1960s', in Sheila Embleton, John E. Joseph, and Hans-Josef

Niederehe (eds.), *The Emergence of the Modern Language Sciences: Studies on the Transition from Historical-Comparative to Structural Linguistics in Honour of E. F. K. Koerner, Volume 1*. Amsterdam: John Benjamins, 261–266.

Nevin, Bruce (2010). 'Noam and Zellig', in Douglas A. Kibbee (ed.), *Chomskyan (R)evolutions*. Amsterdam: John Benjamins, 103–168.

Newell, Allen (1968). 'The Trip Towards Flexibility', in George Bugliarello (ed.), *Bio-Engineering: An American View*. San Francisco: San Francisco Press, 269–285.

Newman, Stanley S. (1946). 'On the Stress System of English', *Word* 2: 171–187.

Newman, Stanley S. (1982). 'Toward a History of American Linguistics. [Review Article of B. Davis and R. O'Cain (eds.), First Person Singular]', *Historiographia Linguistica* 9: 135–143.

Newmeyer, Frederick J. (1980). *Linguistic Theory in America: The First Quarter Century of Transformational Generative Grammar*. New York: Academic Press.

Newmeyer, Frederick J. (1983). *Grammatical Theory: Its Limits and Its Possibilities*. Chicago: University of Chicago Press.

Newmeyer, Frederick J. (1986a). 'Has There Been a "Chomskyan Revolution" in Linguistics?', *Language* 62: 1–19, reprinted in 1996 in F. Newmeyer, *Generative Linguistics: A Historical Perspective*. London: Routledge, 23–38.

Newmeyer, Frederick J. (1986b). *Linguistic Theory in America: Second Edition*. New York: Academic Press.

Newmeyer, Frederick J. (1986c). *The Politics of Linguistics*. Chicago: University of Chicago Press.

Newmeyer, Frederick J. (2001). 'The Prague School and North American Functionalist Approaches to Syntax', *Journal of Linguistics* 37: 101–126.

Newmeyer, Frederick J. (2005). *Possible and Probable Languages: A Generative Perspective on Linguistic Typology*. Oxford: Oxford University Press.

Newmeyer, Frederick J. (2014). 'Getting the Word Out: The Early Generativists' Multi-Pronged Efforts to Diffuse Their Ideas', *Language* 90: 241–268.

Newmeyer, Frederick J. (2018). 'Is the LSA a Generativist-Dominated Organisation?', in Lisa Matthewson, Erin Guntly, Marianne Huijsmans, and Michael Rochemont (eds), *Wa7 Xweysás I Nqwal'úttensa I Ucwalmícwa: He Loves the People's Languages: Essays in Honour of Henry Davis*. Vancouver: University of British Columbia Working Papers in Linguistics, 3–12.

Newmeyer, Frederick J. (2020), 'Has the LSA Been a Generativist Dominated Organization?'. WebLog: History and Philosophy of the Language Sciences, <https://hiphilangsci.net/2020/01/22/lsa-generativist-dominated-organisation.>, Last accessed April 12, 2021.

Newton, Brian E. (1972). *Cypriot Greek: Its Phonology and Inflections*. The Hague: Mouton.

Ney, James W. (1975). 'The Decade of Private Knowledge: Linguistics from the Early 60s to the Early 70s', *Historiographia Linguistica* 2: 143–56.

Nickles, Thomas (2017) 'Scientific Revolutions', *Stanford Encyclopedia of Philosophy*. <https://plato.stanford.edu/entries/scientific-revolutions/>, last accessed April 12, 2021.

Nida, Eugene A. (1945). 'Linguistics and Ethnology in Translation Problems', *Word* 1: 194–208.

Nida, Eugene A. (1948a). 'The Analysis of Grammatical Constituents', *Language* 24: 168–177.

Nida, Eugene A. (1948b). 'The Identification of Morphemes', *Language* 24: 414–441, reprinted in 1957 in M. Joos (ed.), *Readings in Linguistics*. Washington: American Council of Learned Societies, 255–271.

Nida, Eugene A. (1960[1943]). *A Synopsis of English Syntax*. Norman, OK: The Summer Institute of Linguistics.

Nielsen, Janet (2010). *Private Knowledge, Public Tensions: Theory Commitment in Postwar American Linguistics*, Unpublished PhD dissertation, University of Toronto.

Noordegraff, Jan (2001). 'On the Publication Date of *Syntactic Structures*', *Historiographia Linguistica* 28: 225–228.

Nunberg, Geoffrey (1992), 'Hayakawa and Bolinger'. <https://linguistlist.org/issues/3/3-255.html>, last accessed April 13, 2021.

O' Neil, Wayne A. (1964). 'Faroese Vowel Morphophonemics', *Language* 40: 366–371.

O'Grady, William, Michael Dobrovolsky, and Mark Aronoff (1989). *Contemporary Linguistics: An Introduction*. New York: St. Martin's Press.

Õim, Haldur, Renate Pajusalu, and Ilona Tragel (2006). 'A Short History of General Linguistics in Estonia: Slightly Biased Towards Fred Karlsson', in Mickael Suominen (ed.), *A Man of Measure: Festschrift in Honour of Fred Karlsson on His 60th Birthday*. Helsinki: Linguistic Association of Finland.

Osgood, Charles, and Thomas A. Sebeok (eds.) (1954). *Psycholinguistics*. Baltimore: Indiana University Press.

Paper, Herbert H., and Mohammad H. Jazayery (1955). *The Writing System of Modern Persian*. Washington: American Council of Learned Societies.

Parker, William R. (1954). *The National Interest and Foreign Languages*. Washington: United States Government Printing Office.

Partee, Barbara (1971). 'On the Requirement that Transformations Preserve Meaning', in Charles J. Fillmore and D. TerenceLangendoen (eds.), *Studies in Linguistic Semantics*. New York: Holt, Rinehart, and Winston, 1–21.

Partee, Barbara H. (2005). 'Reflections of a Formal Semanticist as of Feb 2005'. Unpublished ms, University of Massachusetts.

Paul, Hermann (1891). *Principles of the History of Language (Translation of Second Edition)*. London: Longmans, Green, and Co.

Pei, Mario (1967). 'Review of M. Joos, *Readings in Linguistics, Volume I* (4th Edition) and E. Hamp, F. Householder, and R. Austerlitz, *Readings in Linguistics, Volume II*', *Modern Language Journal* 51: 312–314.

Penchev, Jordan [Пенчев, Йордан.] (1984). *Construction of the Bulgarian Sentence [Строеж На Българското Изречение]*. Sofia: Science and Art.

Peng, Fred C. C. (1965). 'Review of E. Bach, *An Introduction to Transformational Grammars*', *Lingua* 13: 291–304.

Perlmutter, David M. (ed.) (1983). *Studies in Relational Grammar, Vol. 1*. Chicago: University of Chicago Press.

Perlmutter, David M. (2010). 'My Path in Linguistics', in Donna B. Gerdts, John C. Moore, and Maria Polinksy (eds.), *Hypothesis A-Hypothesis B: Linguistic Explorations in Honor of David M. Perlmutter*. Cambridge, MA: MIT Press, xvii–xxxvii.

Pescarini, Diego (in press). 'The Reception of Generativism in Romance Linguistics', in Mark Aronoff (ed.), *Oxford Research Encyclopedia of Linguistics*. Oxford: Oxford University Press.

Pica, Pierre, and Johan Rooryck (1994). 'On the Development and Current Status of Generative Grammar in France: A Personal Point of View', in Carlos P. Otero (ed.), *Noam Chomsky: Critical Assessments*. New York: Routledge, 1–22.

Pierce, John R., and John B. Carroll (1966). *Language and Machines: Computers in Translation and Linguistics* (A report by the Automatic Language Processing Advisory Committee, Division of Behavioral Sciences, National Academy of Sciences, National Research Council). Washington, DC: National Research Council.

Pike, Kenneth L. (1943). 'Taxemes and Immediate Constituents', *Language* 19: 65–82.

Pike, Kenneth L. (1947a). *Phonemics: A Technique for Reducing Languages to Writing*. Ann Arbor, MI: University of Michigan Press.

Pike, Kenneth L. (1947b). 'Grammatical Prerequisites to Phonemic Analysis', *Word* 3: 155–172.

Pike, Kenneth L. (1954). *Language in Relation to a Unified Theory of the Structure of Human Behavior*. Glendale, CA: Summer Institue of Linguistics.

Pike, Kenneth L. (1958). 'Discussion', *Proceedings of the Eighth International Congress of Linguists*. Oslo: Oslo University Press.

Pike, Kenneth L. (1994). 'A Limited Perspective on *Word* Seen in a Transitional Moment between Paradigms', *Word* 45: 39–43.

Pinker, Steven (1994). *The Language Instinct: How the Mind Creates Language*. New York: Morrow.

Piotrovskij, Raimund G. (2000). 'MT in the Former USSR and in the Newly Independent States (NIS): Pre-History', in W. John Hutchins (ed.), *Early Years in Machine Translation: Memoires and Biographies of Pioneers*. Amsterdam: John Benjamins, 233–242.

Pittman, Richard S. (1948). 'Nuclear Structures in Linguistics', *Language* 24: 287–292, reprinted in 1957 in M. Joos (ed.), *Readings in Linguistics*. Washington: American Council of Learned Societies, 275–278.

ten Hacken, Pius (2007). *Chomskyan Linguistics and Its Competitors*. London: Oakville: Equinox.

Post, Emil L. (1943). 'Formal Reductions of the General Combinatorial Decision Problem', *American Journal of Mathematics* 65: 197–215.

Post, Emil L. (1944). 'Recursively Enumerable Sets of Positive Integers and Their Decision Problems', *Bulletin of the American Mathematical Society* 50: 284–316.

Post, Emil L. (1947). 'Recursive Unsolvability of a Problem of Thue', *Journal of Symbolic Logic* 12: 1–11.

Postal, Paul M. (1964a). *Constituent Structure: A Study of Contemporary Models of Syntactic Description*. Bloomington, IN: Indiana University Research Center in Anthropology, Folklore, and Linguistics.

Postal, Paul M. (1964b). 'Limitations of Phrase Structure Grammars', in Jerry A. Fodor and Jerrold J. Katz (eds.), *The Structure of Language: Readings in the Philosophy of Language*. Englewood Cliffs, NJ: Prentice-Hall, 137–151.

Postal, Paul M. (1964c). 'Mohawk Prefix Generation', in Horace G. Lunt (ed.), *Proceedings of the Ninth International Congress of Linguists*. The Hague: Mouton, 346–357.

Postal, Paul M. (1968). *Aspects of Phonological Theory*. New York: Harper and Row.

Postal, Paul M. (1971). *Cross-over Phenomena*. New York: Holt, Rinehart, and Winston.

Postal, Paul M. (1976 [1967]). 'Linguistic Anarchy Notes', in James D. McCawley (ed.), *Syntax and Semantics*, 1. New York: Academic Press, 201–226.

Postal, Paul M. (1979 [1962]). *Some Syntactic Rules of Mohawk*. New York: Garland.

Prideaux, Gary D., Bruce Derwing, and William Baker (eds.) (1980). *Experimental Linguistics*. Ghent: Story-Scientia.

Pullum, Geoffrey K. (2010). 'Creation Myths of Generative Grammar and the Mathematics Underlying *Syntactic Structures*', in Christian Ebert, Gerhard Jäger, and Jens Michaelis (eds.), *The Mathematics of Language*. Berlin: Springer Verlag, 238–254.

Pullum, Geoffrey K. (2011). 'On the Mathematical Foundations of *Syntactic Structures*', *Journal of Logic, Language and Information* 20: 277–296.

Pullum, Geoffrey K. (2017). 'Theory, Data, and the Epistemology of Syntax', in Marek Konopka and Angelika Wöllstein (eds.), *Grammatische Variation. Empirische Zugänge und theoretische Modellierung*. Berlin: De Gruyter, 283–298.

Pullum, Geoffrey K. (2019). 'Chronicling the Prehistory of Generative Grammar: Problems of Origination and Attribution', Paper presented at The Henry Sweet Society for the History of Linguistic Ideas, Edinburgh.

Radick, Gregory (2016). 'The Unmaking of a Modern Synthesis: Noam Chomsky, Charles Hockett, and the Politics of Behaviourism, 1955–1965', *Isis* 107: 49–73.

Ravila, Paavo (1963). 'Transformaatioteoria', *Virittäjä* 67: 1–16.

Read, Allen W. (1991). 'My Personal Journey through Lingistics', in E. F. K. Koerner (ed.), *First Person Singular II*. Amsterdam: John Benjamins, 273–288.

Reibel, David, and Sanford Schane (eds.) (1969). *Modern Studies in English*. Englewood Cliffs, NJ: Prentice-Hall.

Reichling, Anton (1961). 'Principles and Methods of Syntax: Cryptanalytical Formalism', *Lingua* 10: 1–17.

Rigsby, Bruce, and Michael Silverstein (1969). 'Nez Perce Vowels and Proto-Sahaptian Vowel Harmony', *Language* 45: 45–59.

Rischel, Jørgen (1974). *Topics in West Greenlandic Phonology*. Copenhagen: Akademisk Forlag.

Ritchie, William C., and Tej K. Bhatia (eds.) (1996). *Handbook of Second Language Acquisition*. New York: Academic Press.

Roberts, A. Hood, and Adam G. Woyna (1972). *Experiment in Fast Dissemination of Research in Selected Fields in Linguistics*. Arlington, VA: Center for Applied Linguistics.

Roberts, Paul (1964). *English Syntax: Alternate Edition*. New York: Harcourt, Brace and World.

Rosetti, Alexandru (1971). 'Remarques sur la grammaire générative transformationelle', *Revue Roumaine de Linguistique* 16: 1–4.

Ross, John R. (1967). *Constraints on Variables in Syntax*. PhD dissertation, MIT. Published in 1985 as *Infinite Syntax!*.

Ross, John R. (1985). *Infinite Syntax!* Norwood, NJ: Ablex.

Rubenstein, Herbert (1951). 'The Recent Conflict in Soviet Linguistics', *Language* 27: 281–287.

Rusiecki, Jan (1976). 'The Development of Contrastive Linguistics', *Interlanguage Studies Bulletin* 1: 12–44.

Ruwet, Nicolas (1966). *Introduction à la grammaire générative*. Paris: Plon.

Ruwet, Nicolas (1991). *Syntax and Human Experience*. Chicago: University of Chicago Press.

Ryckman, Thomas A. (1986). *Grammar and Information: An Investigation in Linguistic Metatheory*, Unpublished PhD dissertation, Columbia University.

Saleski, R. E. (1930). 'Review of Henri Frei, *La grammaire des fautes*', *Language* 6: 91–93.

Samarin, William J. (1998). 'C'est passionant d'être passioné', in E. F. K. Koerner (ed.), *First Person Singular III: Autobiographies by North American Scholars in the Language Sciences*. Amsterdam: John Benjamins, 187–226.

Sampson, Geoffrey (1975). *The Form of Language*. London: Weidenfeld and Nicolson.

Sampson, Geoffrey (1979). 'A Non-Nativist Account of Language Universals', *Linguistics and Philosophy* 3: 99–104.

Sampson, Geoffrey (1980). *Schools of Linguistics*. Stanford, CA: Stanford University Press.

Sampson, Geoffrey (1997). *Educating Eve: The Language Instinct Debate.* London: Continuum.

Sapir, Edward (1917). 'Linguistic Publications of the Bureau of American Ethnology: A General Review', *International Journal of American Linguistics* 1: 76–81.

Sapir, Edward (1921). *Language.* New York: Harcourt, Brace, and World.

Sapir, Edward (1925a). 'Sound Patterns in Language', *Language* 1: 37–51, reprinted in 1957 in M. Joos (ed.), *Readings in Linguistics.* Washington: American Council of Learned Societies, 19–25.

Sapir, Edward (1925b). 'Review of A. Meillet and M. Cohen, *Les langues du monde*', *Modern Language Notes* 40: 373–378.

Sapir, Edward (1926). 'Review of Otto Jespersen, *Mankind, Nation and Individual from a Linguistic Point of View*', *American Review of Sociology* 32: 488–499, reprinted in 2008 in *The Collected Works of Edward Sapir I.* Berlin: Mouton de Gruyter, 203.

Sapir, Edward (1929). 'The Status of Linguistics as a Science', *Language* 5: 207–214.

Sapir, Edward (1930). 'The Southern Paiute Language', *Proceedings of the American Academy of Arts and Sciences* 65: 1–536.

Sapir, Edward (1949 [1931]). 'The Concept of Phonetic Law as Tested in Primitive Languages by Leonard Bloomfield', in Stuart A. Rice (ed.), *Methods in Social Sciences:A Case Book.* Chicago: University of Chicago Press, reprinted in David G. Mandelbaum (ed.), *Selected Writings of Edward Sapir.* Berkeley: University of Chicago Press, 73–82.

Sapir, Edward (1963 [1933]). 'The Psychological Reality of Phonemes', in David G. Mandelbaum (ed.), *Selected Writings of Edward Sapir.* Berkeley: University of California Press, 46–60.

Sapir, Edward, and MorrisSwadesh (1946). 'American Indian Grammatical Categories', *Word* 2: 103–112.

Saporta, Sol (1965). 'Ordered Rules, Dialect Differences, and Historical Processes', *Language* 41: 218–224.

Saussure, Ferdinand de (1916). *Cours de linguistique générale.* Paris: Payot.

Saussure, Ferdinand de (1966 [1916]). *Course in General Linguistics.* New York: McGraw-Hill. [Translation of *Cours de linguistique générale.* Paris: Payot, 1916].

Schane, Sanford A. (1966). 'The Morphophonemics of the French Verb', *Language* 43: 746–758.

Schane, Sanford A. (1971). 'The Phoneme Revisited', *Language* 47: 503–521.

Schiffman, Harold F. (1982). 'Review of Murray B. Emeneau, *Language and Linguistic Area*', *Language* 58: 185–193.

Scholz, Barbara C., and Geoffrey K.Pullum (2007). 'Tracking the Origins of Transformational Generative Grammar (Review Article of M. Tomalin, *Linguistics and the Formal Sciences)*', *Journal of Linguistics* 43: 701–723.

Schwartz, Arthur (1968). 'Derivative Functions in Syntax', *Language* 44: 747–783.

Sebeok, Thomas (1945). 'Progressive Vowel Assimilation in Finish', *Cahiers Ferdinand de Saussure* 5: 38–40.

Sebeok, Thomas A, (1977). 'Roman Jakobson's Teaching in America', in Cornelis H. van Schooneveld (ed.), *Roman Jakobson: Echoes of his Scholarship.* Lisse: Peter de Ridder Press, 411–420.

Sebeok, Thomas A. (1946). *Finnish and Hungarian Case Systems, Their Form and Function.* Stockholm: Acta Instituti Hungarici Universitatis Holmiensis.

Senn, Alfred (1937). 'The Art of Linguistics', *Modern Language Journal* 21: 501–506.

Seuren, Pieter (1969). *Operators and Nucleus: A Contribution to the Theory of Grammar.* Cambridge: Cambridge University Press.

Sgall, Petr (1987). 'Prague Functionalism and Topic vs. Focus', in R. Dirven and V. Fried, *Functionalism in Linguistics*. Amsterdam: John Benjamins, 169–189.

Sgall, Petr, Eva Hajičová, and Eva Benesová (1973). *Topic, Focus, and Generative Semantics*. Kronberg: Scriptor.

Sgall, Petr, Eva Hajičová, and Jarmila Panevová (1986). *The Meaning of the Sentence in its Semantic and Pragmatic Aspects*. Dordrecht, Reidel.

Shannon, Claude, and Warren Weaver (1948). *A Mathematical Theory of Communication*. Urbana, IL: University of Illinois Press.

Shapiro, Michael (1974). 'Morphophonemics as Semiotic', *Acta Linguistica Hafniensia* 15: 29–49.

Skinner, B. F. (1957). *Verbal Behavior*. New York: Appleton-Century-Crofts.

Sklar, Robert (1968). 'Chomsky's Revolution in Linguistics', *The Nation* September 9: 213–217.

Smith, Carlota S. (1961). 'A Class of Complex Modifiers in English', *Language* 37: 342–365.

Smith, Carlota S. (1964). 'Determiners and Relative Clauses in a Generative Grammar of English', *Language* 40: 37–52.

Smith, Neil (1989). *The Twitter Machine: Reflections on Language*. Oxford: Blackwell.

Smith, Neil (1999). *Chomsky: Ideas and Ideals*. Cambridge: Cambridge University Press.

Smith, Neil (2002). 'Personal History', in Keith Brown and Vivien Law (eds.), *Linguistics in Britain: Personal Histories*. Oxford: Blackwell, 262–273.

Smith, Neil, and Deirdre Wilson (1979). *Modern Linguistics: The Results of Chomsky's Revolution*. Bloomington: Indiana University Press.

Smith, W. B. S. (1950). 'Review of Robert Hall, *Descriptive Italian Grammar*', *Studies in Linguistics* 8: 5–11.

Sperlich, Wolfgang (2006). *Noam Chomsky*. London: Reaction Books.

Spitzer, Leo (1946). 'The State of Linguistics: Crisis or Reaction?', *Modern Language Notes* 71: 497–502.

Staal, J. F. (1962). 'A Method of Linguistic Description: The Order of Consonants According to Panini', *Language* 38: 1–10.

Stankiewicz, Edward (1966). 'Slavic Morphophonemics in Its Typological and Diachronic Aspect', in Thomas A. Sebeok (ed.), *Current Trends in Linguistics, Vol. 3: Theoretical Foundations*. The Hague: Mouton, 495–520.

Stanley, Richard (1967). 'Redundancy Rules in Phonology', *Language*: 43.

Stark, Bruce R. (1972). 'The Bloomfieldian Model', *Lingua* 30: 385–421.

Stockwell, Robert P. (1960). 'The Place of Intonation in a Generative Grammar of English', *Language* 36: 300–367.

Stockwell, Robert P. (1993). 'Obituary: Dwight L. Bolinger', *Language* 69: 99–112.

Stockwell, Robert P. (1998). 'From English Philology to Linguistics and Back Again', in E. F. K. Koerner (ed.), *First Person Singular III: Autobiographies by North American Scholars in the Language Sciences*. Amsterdam: John Benjamins, 227–245.

Stockwell, Robert P., Paul Schachter, and Barbara Partee (1973). *The Major Syntactic Structures of English*. New York: Holt, Rinehart and Winston.

Sturtevant, Edgar H. (1917). *Linguistic Change: An Introduction to the Historical Study of Language*. Chicago: University of Chicago Press.

Sturtevant, Edgar H. (1925). 'The Organization of the LSA', *Classical Weekly* 18: 127–128.

Sturtevant, Edgar H. (1947). *An Introduction to Linguistic Science*. New Haven, CT: Yale University Press.

Sturtevant, Edgar H., and Roland Kent (1928). 'Linguistic Science and Classical Philology', *Classical Weekly* 22: 9–13.

Swadesh, Morris (1934). 'The Phonemic Principle', *Language* 10: 117–129, reprinted in 1957 in M. Joos (ed.), *Readings in Linguistics*. Washington: American Council of Learned Societies, 32–37.

Swadesh, Morris (1948). 'On Linguistic Mechanisms', *Science and Society* 12: 254–259.

Swadesh, Morris, and C. F. Voegelin (1939). 'A Problem in Phonological Alternation', *Language* 15: 1–10, reprinted in 1957 in M. Joos (ed.), *Readings in Linguistics*. Washington: American Council of Learned Societies, 88–92.

Swiggers, Pierre (1991). 'Roman Jakobson's Struggle in Wartime America', *Orbis* 36: 281–285.

Swiggers, Pierre (1994). '"The Study of the Linguistic Sciences is at Present Greatly Neglected in this Country": The Linguistic Society of America in the Making', *Orbis* 37: 299–304.

Szabolcsi, Anna (1981). 'Compositionality in Focus', *Folia Linguistica Societatis Linguisticae Europaeae* 15: 141–162.

Szabolcsi, Anna (1985). 'Generative Grammar in Hungary', *GLOW Newsletter* 15: 15–18.

Teeter, Karl V. (1963). 'Lexicostatistics and Genetic Relationship', *Language* 39: 638–648.

Teeter, Karl V. (1964). 'Descriptive Linguistics in America: Triviality vs. Irrelevance', *Word* 20: 197–206.

Teleman, Ulf (1969). *Studies in a Generative Grammar of Modern Swedish*, Unpublished PhD dissertation, Lund University.

Testenoire, Pierre-Yves (2019). 'Jakobson & Co.: La Linguistique À L'école Libre Des Hautes Études', *Les Dossiers de HEL [electronic supplement to Histoire Epistémologie Langage]* Paris: Société d'Histoire et d'Epistémologie des Sciences du Langage.

Thomas, Margaret (2002). 'Roger Bacon and Martin Joos: Generative Linguistics' Reading of the Past', *Historiographia Linguistica* 29: 339–378.

Thompson, J. S. (1969). 'The Reactionary Idealistic Foundations of Noam Chomsky's Linguistics', *Literature and Ideology* 4: 1–20.

Thorne, James P. (1965). 'Review of Paul Postal, *Constituent Structure*', *Journal of Linguistics* 1: 73–76.

Thráinsson, Höskuldur (1978). 'On the Phonology of Icelandic Preaspiration', *Nordic Journal of Linguistics* 1: 3–54.

Thráinsson, Höskuldur (1979). *On Complementation in Icelandic*, Unpublished PhD dissertation, Harvard University.

Thráinsson, Höskuldur (1996). 'Linguistics in Iceland in the 20th Century', in Carol Henriksen, Even Hovdhaugen, Fred Karlsson, and Bengt Sigurd (eds.), *Studies in the Development of Linguistics in Denmark, Finland, Iceland, Norway, and Sweden*. Oslo: Novus, 324–364.

Togeby, Knud (1965 [1951]). *Structure immanente de la langue française*. Paris: Librarie Larousse.

Tomalin, Marcus (2006). *Linguistics and the Formal Sciences: The Origins of Generative Grammar*. Cambridge: Cambridge University Press.

Trager, George L. (1934). 'The Phonemes of Russian', *Language* 10: 334–344.

Trager, George L. (1941). 'Review of Louis Hjelmslev, *La catégorie des cas*', *Language* 17: 172–174.

Trager, George L. (1946). 'Changes of Emphasis in Linguistics: A Comment', *Studies in Philology* 48: 461–464.

Trager, George L. (1948). 'Review of Lingua, Volume 1', *IJAL* 14: 207–209.

Trager, George L. (1950a). 'Brief Reviews', *Studies in Linguistics* 8: 99–100.

Trager, George L. (1950b). 'Review of K. Pike, *Phonemics: A Technique for Reducing Languages to Writing*', *Language* 26: 152–158.

Trager, George L. (1955). 'Language', *Encyclopaedia Britannica* 13: 695–702.

Trager, George L. (1958). 'Review of M. Joos (ed.), *Readings in Linguistics*', *Studies in Linguistics* 13: 34–36.

Trager, George L. (1968). 'Review of Charles Hockett, *The State of the Art*', *Studies in Linguistics* 20: 77–84.

Trager, George L., and Henry Lee Smith (1951). *An Outline of English Structure*. Norman, Oklahoma: Battenburg Press.

Trager, George L., and Joshua Whatmough (1966). 'Language', *Encyclopædia Britannica* 13: 697–704.

Trampe, Peter af, and Åke Viberg (1972). *Allmän Språketori och Grammatik: En Introduktion*. Lund: Gleerup.

Turner, James (2014). *Philology: The Forgotten Origins of the Modern Humanities*. Princeton: Princeton University Press.

Tuțescu, Mariana (1972). *Le groupe nominale et la nominalisation en français moderne*. Bucharest: Societatea Romana de Lingvistica Romanică.

Twaddell, W. Freeman (1935). 'On Defining the Phoneme', *Language* 11: 5–62, reprinted in 1957 in M. Joos (ed.), *Readings in Linguistics*. Washington: American Council of Learned Societies, 55–80.

Uhlenbeck, C. C. (1927). 'Review of P. W. Schmidt, *Die Sprachfamilien und Sprachkreise der Erde*', *International Journal of American Linguistics* 4: 229–233.

Uhlenbeck, E. M. (1949). 'The Structure of the Javanese Morpheme', *Lingua* 2: 239–270.

Uhlenbeck, E. M. (1959). 'Review of M. Joos (ed.), *Readings in Linguistics*', *Lingua* 8: 327–329.

Uhlenbeck, E. M. (1963). 'An Appraisal of Transformation Theory', *Lingua* 12: 1–18.

Uhlenbeck, E. M. (1975). *Critical Comments on Transformational Generative Grammar, 1962-1972*. The Hague: Smits.

Uhlenbeck, E. M. (1979). 'Linguistics in America 1924–1974: A Detached View', in Henry M. Hoenigswald (ed.), *The European Background of American Linguistics: Papers of the Third Golden Anniversary Symposium of the Linguistic Society of America*. Dordrecht: Foris, 121–145.

Vachek, Josef (ed.) (1964). *A Prague School Reader in Linguistics*. Bloomington: Indiana University Press.

Van Holk, A. G. F. (1962). 'On Transformations (Review of Noam Chomsky, *Syntactic Structures*)', *Synthese* 14: 216–223.

van Riemsdijk, Henk (1987). 'GLOW: The First Years', *Folia Linguistica* 21: 482–487.

van Riemsdijk, Henk (1990). 'Generative Syntax in the Netherlands', in Flor Aarts and Theo van Els (eds.), *Contemporary Dutch Linguistics*. Washington: Georgetown University Press, 140–151.

van Riemsdijk, Henk (1998). 'GLOW 1978–1998', *Glot International* 3: 18–19.

Van Valin, Robert D. (2007). 'Some Thoughts on the Reason for the Lesser Status of Typology in the USA as Opposed to Europe', *Linguistic Typology* 11: 253–57.

Vasiliu, Emanuel (1962). 'Lingvističeskie Urovni I Transformacionnye Struktury', *RL* 7: 251–256.

Vasiliu, Emanuel, and Sanda Golopentia Eretescu (1969). *Sintaxa Transformațională a Limbii Române [the Transformational Syntax of Romanian)*. Bucharest: EA.

Vater, Heinz (1971). 'Linguistics in West Germany', *Language Sciences* 16: 6–24.

Venkova, Tzvetomira (2019). 'Introducing American Generative Grammar to Bulgaria: The Art of Bypassing Censorship', in Unknown (ed.), *Beyond the Borders*. Sofia: Publishing House of Bulgarian Academy of Sciences, 51–58.

Verkuyl, Henk (1990). 'The Contribution of the Dutch to the Development of Linguistics', in Flor Aarts and Theovan Els (eds.), *Contemporary Dutch Linguistics*. Washington: Georgetown University Press, 1–22.

Verluyten, Paul (1982). *Recherches sur la prosodie et la métrique du français*, Unpublished PhD dissertation, University of Antwerp.

Voegelin, C. F. (1935). 'Shawnee Phonemes', *Language* 11: 23–37.

Voegelin, C. F. (1954). 'The ACLS Language Program', *International Journal of American Linguistics* 20: 70–74.

Voegelin, C. F. (1958a). Review of Martin Joos (ed.), *Readings in Linguistics*', *International Journal of American Linguistics* 24: 86.

Voegelin, C. F. (1958b). 'Review of Noam Chomsky, *Syntactic Structures*', *International Journal of American Linguistics* 24: 229–231.

Voegelin, C. F., and Zellig S. Harris (1952). 'Training in Anthropological Linguistics', *American Anthropologist* 54: 322–327.

Voegelin, C. F., and F. M. Voegelin (1963). 'On the History of Structuralizing in 20th Century America', *Anthropological Linguistics* 5: 12–35.

Voyles, Joseph B. (1967). 'Simplicity, Ordered Rules, and the First Sound Shift', *Language* 44: 720–746.

Voyles, Joseph B. (1968). 'Gothic and Germanic', *Language* 43: 636–660.

Wang, William S.-Y. (1968). 'Vowel Features, Paired Variables, and the English Vowel Shift', *Language* 44: 695–708.

Wardhaugh, Ronald (1970). 'The Contrastive Analysis Hypothesis', *TESOL Quarterly* 4: 123–30.

Weinstock, John (1968). 'Grimm's Law in Distinctive Features', *Language* 44: 224–229.

Wells, Rulon S. (1947a). 'De Saussure's System of Linguistics', *Word* 3: 1–31, reprinted in 1957 in M. Joos (ed.), *Readings in Linguistics*. Washington: American Council of Learned Societies, 1–18.

Wells, Rulon S. (1947b). 'Immediate Constituents', *Language* 23: 81–117, reprinted in 1957 in M. Joos (ed.), *Readings in Linguistics*. Washington: American Council of Learned Societies, 186–207.

Wells, Rulon S. (1949). 'Automatic Alternations', *Language* 25: 99–116.

Wells, Rulon S. (1954). 'Archiving and Language Typology', *International Journal of American Linguistics* 20: 101–107.

Wells, Rulon S. (1963). 'Some Neglected Opportunutues in Descriptive Linguistics', *Anthropological Linguistics* 5: 38–49.

Whitehall, Harold (1944). 'Some Languages Are Better Than Others. Review of F. Bodmer, *The Loom of Language*', *Kenyon Review* 6: 672–676.

Whitehall, Harold (1951). *Structural Essentials of English*. New York: Harcourt, Brace and Co.

Whitney, William D. (1867). *Language and the Study of Language: Twelve Lectures on the Principles of Linguistic Science*. London: N. Trübner.

Whitney, William D. (1875). *The Life and Growth of Language: An Outline of Linguistic Science*. New York: D. Appleton.

Whorf, Benjamin L. (1952). *Collected Papers on Metalinguistics*. Washington: Foreign Service Institute.

Whorf, Benjamin L. (1956). *Language, Thought and Reality: Selected Writings of Benjamin Lee Whorf.* Cambridge, MA: MIT Press.

Wierzbicka, Anna (1972). *Semantic Primitives.* Frankfurt: Athenäum.

Wierzbicka, Anna (2012). 'Understanding Others Requires Shared Concepts', *Pragmatics and Cognition* 20: 356–379.

Wiik, Kalevi (1967). *Suomen Kielen Morfofonemiikkaa.* Turku: Turun yliopiston fonetiikan laitoksen julkaisuja.

Wyld, Henry C. (1934). 'Studies in the Diction of *Layamon's Brut*', *Language* 13: 29–59.

Yallop, C. L. (1978). 'The Problem of Linguistic Universals', *Philosophia Reformata* 43: 61–72.

Yngve, Victor (2000). 'Early Research at MIT: In Search of an Adequate Theory', in W. J. Hutchins (ed.), *Early Years in Machine Translation: Memories and Biographies of Pioneers.* Amsterdam: John Benjamins.

Zaenen, Annie (1980). *Extraction Rules in Icelandic*, Unpublished PhD dissertation, Harvard University.

Zeps, Valdis J. (1964). 'Optional Rules in the Formation of the Old Church Slavonic Aorist', *Language* 40: 33–36.

Zholj, Konstantin [Жоль, Константин] (1980). 'Cognitive Functions of Analogy and Their Significance in the History of Philosophical Doctrines About Categories [Познавательные Функции Аналогии И Их Значение В Истории Философских Учений О Категориях]', in M. V. Popovich (ed.), *Logical and Epistemological Studies of the Categorical Structure of Thinking [Логико-Гносеологические Исследования Категориальной Структуры Мышления].* Kiev: Naukova Dumka, 310–336.

Zipf, George K. (1938). 'Review of A. Reichling, *Het Woord, een Studie Omtrent de Grondslag van Taal en Taalgerbruik*', *Modern Language Journal* 23: 232–233.

Index of Names

Index of Subjects

412 INDEX OF SUBJECTS

taxonomic approach 102, 106, 152, 263

transformational generative grammar (TGG) x, 1, 64, 75–77, 106–107, 112, 122, 124, 127–140, 144–148, 156–161, 176, 183–192, 196–214, 216–260, 262–264, 266–267, 270, 272, 282–283, 285–287, 290, 293, 296–329
  antecedents of basic concepts 145–156
  diffusion of theory in the community 183–215
  European reception 75–76, 216–260
  originality of 144–145
  overview of early work 127–134
  textbooks 200–201

Travaux du Cercle Linguistique de Prague 20, 64, 165

two-dollar bill conspiracy 59–60

'underground' literature 113, 184–185, 188, 190–199, 211

underlying forms or representations 4, 62, 75, 136, 138–139, 149–152, 164–165, 239

United Kingdom, generative grammar in 218–221

universals of language 5, 22, 54, 56, 75, 78, 125, 130, 154, 171, 178, 205, 247, 249

women in linguistics 8, 19, 37, 269

Word (journal) 69–71, 76, 115, 188–189

working papers 189, 193–196, 199

World War II and linguistics 6, 21, 32–34, 39, 41, 55, 58–59, 63, 67–69, 83–86, 284 *see also* military interest in linguistics

Yale Linguistics Club 159

Yale School 63, 65, 116 *see also* American structuralism

Yugoslavia, generative grammar in 248–249